Pittsburgh Series in Bibliography

RALPH WALDO EMERSON

Ralph Waldo Emerson

A DESCRIPTIVE BIBLIOGRAPHY

Joel Myerson

UNIVERSITY OF
PITTSBURGH PRESS
1982

The preparation of this volume was made possible (in part) by a grant from the Research Materials Program of the National Endowment for the Humanities, an independent Federal agency.

Published by the University of Pittsburgh Press, Pittsburgh, Pa. 15260
Feffer and Simons, Inc., London
Manufactured in the Unites States of America

Library of Congress Cataloging in Publication Data

Myerson, Joel.
  Ralph Waldo Emerson, a descriptive bibliography.

  (Pittsburgh series in bibliography)
  Includes index.
  1. Emerson, Ralph Waldo, 1803–1882—Bibliography.
2. Emerson, Ralph Waldo, 1803–1882–Bibliography—
First editions. I. Title. II. Series
Z8265.M94 [PS1631]   016.814'3   81-11502
ISBN 0-8229-3452-3   AACR2

for Greta

Contents

Acknowledgments

THIS bibliography is part of my ongoing study of American Transcendentalism. In compiling it I have incurred many debts of gratitude. Unhappily, I can only thank in a general way the many librarians who answered my questions about copies of Emerson's works at their institutions. I wish to express my appreciation to the following institutions and their staffs for help in using their collections during my visits to them: American Antiquarian Society, Andover-Harvard Theological Library, Boston Athenæum, Boston Public Library, The British Library, Brown University, Cambridge University, Columbia University, Concord Free Public Library, Duke University, Edinburgh University, Harvard University (Houghton and Widener libraries), Houghton Mifflin Company, Indiana University (Lilly Library), Library of Congress, Massachusetts Historical Society, Middlebury College, National Library of Scotland, New York Public Library (Berg Collection), Oxford University (Bodleian Library), Princeton University, Stanford University, Tulane University, University of California at Berkeley, University of North Carolina at Chapel Hill, University of South Carolina, University of Texas (Humanities Research Center), University of Vermont, University of Virginia (Clifton Waller Barrett Library of American Literature), Williams College (Chapin Library), and Yale University (Beinecke Library). Harriet Oglesby of the University of South Carolina library was especially helpful in obtaining books for me on loan.

Many people have helped me in this project and I would especially like to thank the following: Phyllis Andrews, Thomas Blanding, William H. Bond, Raymond R. Borst, Ronald Bosco, Robert Buckeye, William R. Cagle, Yvonne Chester, C. E. Frazer Clark, Jr., Rosemary Cullen, Rodney G. Dennis, Edward L. Doctoroff, Stephen Donadio, Ellen Dunlap, Walter Harding, Harrison M. Hayford, David W. Hill, Carolyn Jakeman, Glen M. Johnson, J. Harold Kittleson, Paul Kosiak, Erika C. D. Lindemann, Kenneth Lohf, Jerome Loving, Kevin MacDonnell, Charles W. Mann, J. Chesley Mathews, George Monteiro, Samuel Morrill, Marcia Moss, Ralph H. Orth, Richard Peters, Alan Seaburg, Marte Shaw, Joseph Slater, Virginia Smythe, Ernest Starr, Lola Szladits, William B. Todd, Louis L. Tucker, Keven P. Van Anglen, Robert L. Volz, Douglas Wilson, Elizabeth Witherell, and Richard Ziegfeld. Richard Taylor has photographed the materials in my collection with his usual excellence. I am grateful to Jeanne Drennan for her skillful copyediting of this book.

The bibliographical groundwork for the study of many nineteenth-century American authors was laid by Jacob Blanck in his *Bibliography of American Literature*. Like other scholars, I have been greatly aided by this work.

Matthew J. Bruccoli has been generous with his assistance, and this bibliography is much the better for it.

Eleanor M. Tilton graciously allowed me access to the materials she has assembled for her forthcoming supplementary edition of Emerson's letters, and has patiently answered many questions. I am also grateful to her for making available to me the working papers of Ralph L. Rusk, from whose work, like all students of Emerson, I have greatly profited.

A grant from the National Endowment for the Humanities, Division of Research Programs, greatly facilitated the research and preparation of this book. I am particularly grateful to George Farr for assistance.

The University of South Carolina has provided material support for the preparation of this book. I am grateful to William H. Nolte and George L. Geckle, chairmen of the department of English, for their help. I also wish to thank the following research assistants: Susan Cunha-Cheesman, Susan Naramore Maher, Paul Sagona, and especially Caroline Bokinsky, Robert E. Burkholder, and Stephen Garrison.

I am grateful to the following for permission to quote from manuscripts in their possession: Edinburgh University, Harvard University (Houghton Library), Isabelle Stuart Gardner Museum, Massachusetts Historical Society, New York Public Library, University of California at Los Angeles, and University of Virginia. I am equally grateful to the following libraries for permission to reproduce photographs of materials in their possession: American Antiquarian Society, Boston Athenæum, Boston Public Library, Cambridge University, Case-Western Reserve University, Columbia University, Concord Free Public Library, Duke University, Harvard University (Houghton Library and the Harry Elkins Widener Collection), Indiana University (Lilly Library), Library of Congress, Massachusetts Historical Society, Middlebury College, New York Public Library, Pennsylvania State University, and University of Virginia. The photographs of A 20.2 are by Barry Donahue.

Greta has patiently endured the steady encroachment of Emerson on our bookshelves and our time. More than anyone, she has helped me in finishing this book, and my debt to her for love, friendship, and support can but inadequately be recognized in dedicating this book to her.

Introduction

THIS descriptive bibliography of the works of Ralph Waldo Emerson is limited to writings by Emerson. Writings about Emerson are not listed, except in cases where they include something by Emerson published for the first time.

FORMAT

Section A lists chronlogically all books, pamphlets, and broadsides wholly or substantially by Emerson, including all printings of all editions in English and other languages through 1882, the year of Emerson's death, and all editions and reprintings in English through 1980.

The numbering system for Section A indicates the edition and printing for each entry. Thus, for *Nature, A3.1.a* indicates that this is the third title published by Emerson (*A3*), and that the entry describes the first edition (*1*), first printing (*a*). For multi-volume works, the number of the volume is often added to the numbering system; thus, for the first volume of *Journals, A52.I.1.a* indicates that this is the fifty-second title published by Emerson (*A52*), and that the entry describes the first volume (*I*), first edition (*1*), first printing (*a*). Issues are indicated by inferior numbers—thus $A21.1.a_2$ is the second issue of the first printing of *Nature; Addresses, and Lectures.* States are discussed in the text.

Each entry begins with a facsimile of the title page (with its dimensions given) and, where relevant, the copyright page, then pagination information and a collation of the gatherings. A description of the contents is followed, when needed, by a listing of the contents. A number sign (#) following a title indicates its first appearance in print; a dagger (†) indicates its first collected appearance; a section sign (§) indicates that it is attributed to Emerson. Information on typography and paper includes the dimensions of the printed text, type of paper, number of lines per page, and running heads. Thus 5″ × 3″ indicates the height and width of the area containing the text on a page; 5″ (4½″) × 3″ indicates the height (first from the top of the running head to the bottom of the last line of text, and second from the top of the first line of text to the bottom of the last line of text) and width of the printed area. When relevant, information on sheet bulk is given. All paper is white unless otherwise indicated. Binding information includes cloth types, descriptions of stampings, and notes on flyleaves, endpapers, page trimming, and page-edge gilding or staining. All wrappers are paper unless otherwise indicated. Dust jackets, when present, are fully described and usually reproduced.[1] Information on publication is drawn from Emerson's journals, letters, and unpublished manuscripts; publishers' records; copyright information (from both published and manuscript records of the Copyright Office); and contemporary book trade announcements. Locations are provided to identify the libraries holding copies of each title described.[2] Notes deal with information not discussed elsewhere in the entry.

Section B lists chronologically all collected editions of Emerson's writings through 1980, including those published, advertised, or sold as "Emerson's Writings" by Fields, Osgood and its successors (James R. Osgood; Houghton, Osgood; Houghton, Mifflin). Also, other contemporary editions which cumulate Emerson's works to date and posthumous editions which include the bulk of Emerson's published writings are listed. All works printed from the same plates are grouped together. Plate groups follow the order of the first apperance of the first work in each group unless otherwise indicated. A "Pedigree of Primary Collected Works" is provided at the beginning of the section. Printing information for individual volumes within a collected edition is usually given under the entry for that title in Section A. Thus all Houghton, Osgood and Houghton, Mifflin reprintings from the "Little Classic Edition" plates are, unless otherwise indicated, volumes in the "Little Classic Edition" of Emerson's writings; all Houghton, Mifflin reprintings from the *Riverside Edition* plates are, unless otherwise indicated, volumes in the *Riverside Edition,* trade printing, of Emerson's writings; and all Routledge reprintings from the *Riverside Edition* plates are, unless otherwise indicated, volumes in the *Riverside Edition (Copyright)* of Emerson's writings.

Section C lists chronologically all miscellaneous collections of Emerson's writings through 1980. Foreign-language editions published through 1882, the year of Emerson's death, are also listed. Included are anthologies, birthday books, and topical studies. Binding is assumed to be cloth or boards unless otherwise indicated. Locations are given for the copies examined.

Section D lists chronologically all titles in which material by Emerson appears for the first time in a book or pamphlet. Entries within a year are arranged alphabetically. Included are prose, poetry, and letters. All items are signed unless otherwise indicated. Previously published materials are so identified. The first printings only of these titles are described, but English editions and selected reprintings are also noted. Binding is assumed to be cloth or boards unless otherwise indicated. Locations are given for the copies examined.

Section E lists chronologically all first American and English publications in newspapers and magazines of material by Emerson through 1980. No attempt has been made to list contemporary accounts of Emerson's lectures. All items are signed unless otherwise indicated. When applicable, information on first book publication and first appearance in a book by Emerson is given.

---

1. Exceptions are partial dust jackets, unprinted glassine dust jackets, and dust jackets for the second or subsequent volumes in a series, such as *Early Lectures*.

2. Unfortunately, a number of copies examined by Blanck and listed in the *BAL* have since been lost or rebound, and thus are not listed in this book.

Section F lists chronologically all books edited by Emerson. Binding is assumed to be cloth or boards unless otherwise indicated. Locations are given for the copies examined.

Section G lists chronologically reprinted prose, poetry, and letters by Emerson in books and pamphlets through 1882, the year of his death. Entries within a single year are arranged alphabetically. All items are signed unless otherwise indicated. Binding is assumed to be cloth or boards unless otherwise indicated. Locations are given for the copies examined.

Section H lists chronologically material attributed to Emerson.

Section I lists chronologically references to possible publications by Emerson which have not been dealt with elsewhere in the bibliography.

An *appendix* lists principal works about Emerson.

TERMS AND METHODS

Edition. All copies of a book printed from a single setting of type—including all reprintings from standing type, from plates, or by photo-offset processes.

Printing. All copies of a book printed at one time (without removing the type or plates from the press).

State. States occur only within single printings and are created by an alteration not affecting the conditions of publication or sale to *some* copies of a given printing (by stop-press correction or cancellation of leaves). There must be two or more states.

Issue. Issues occur only within single printings and are created by an alteration affecting the conditions of publication or sale to *some* copies of a given printing (usually a title leaf alteration). There cannot be a first issue without a second.

Edition, printing, state, and *issue* have here been restricted to the sheets of the book.[3]

Publishers' advertisements are described but the reader should be aware that they generally exist in three forms. First, they may be integral with the first or last gatherings of the book. In such cases, variants between the advertisements can be used to determine the printing history of the book, since the advertisements were printed in the same press run as the rest of the work (see *The Conduct of Life* [A 26], for example). Second, in a few cases, advertisements may be imprinted on the endpapers of a book. While useful in determining when a copy may have been bound, these advertisements do not bear on a book's printing history. Likewise, the third form, inserted catalogues of publishers' advertisements, may indicate only binding and not printing histories. It can be stated unequivocally that the date on the inserted advertisements in a book has no bearing on the priority of a printing.

---

3. An argument could be made for extending the definition of *issue* in nineteenth-century books to include bindings as well. For example, the sheets of the first English printing by Fraser of *Essays* were bound up in G. W. Nickisson casings after the latter succeeded to Fraser's business. Likewise, copies of Emerson's books with mixed sheets and casings from Ticknor and Fields and its successors are common. In such cases it is difficult to avoid regarding the different bindings as *issues* because they do represent a deliberate attempt to alter the conditions of publication.

Dust jackets for Section A entries have been described in detail because they are part of the original publication effort and sometimes provide information about how the book was marketed. There is, of course, no certainty that a jacket now on a book was always on it.

For binding-cloth designations I have used the method proposed by G. Thomas Tanselle;[4] most of these cloth grains are illustrated in Jacob Blanck, ed., *Bibliography of American Literature* (New Haven: Yale University Press, 1955–).

Color specifications are based on the *ISCC-NBS Color Name Charts Illustrated with Centroid Colors* (National Bureau of Standards). Centroid numbers have not been assigned; instead, the general color designations have been used.[5]

The spines of bindings or dust jackets are printed horizontally unless otherwise indicated. The reader is to assume that vertically printed spines read from top to bottom unless otherwise indicated.

In the descriptions of title pages, bindings, and dust jackets, the color of the lettering is always black unless otherwise indicated.

Pagination for reprintings of Section A entries and for miscellaneous collections indicates the number of the last printed page in the book, exclusive of publishers' advertisements. Some items were reprinted from the plates of larger collections without a change in the pagination sequence. For these items, beginning and ending page numbers are reported. Thus *17–54 pp.* indicates that the first page in this 38-page book is *17* and the last is *54;* a note provides information on the plates used for the reprinting of the separate publication.

The term *royalty* cannot be applied to all of Emerson's works. For his earlier works, Emerson paid for composing and printing costs in return for a larger share of the profits than he would have received had he allowed the publisher to take all the financial risks. In such cases the usual author-publisher relationship was reversed: rather than be paid a share of the profits by the publisher, the author gave the publisher a commission for selling the books for which he had paid the costs of production. Therefore, the term *publisher's commission* is used whenever both the work's price and financial arrangements are known; the term *author's share* is used when only the financial arrangements are known.

Full bibliographical descriptions are provided for the first nineteenth-century American and English editions of works in Section A. Surprisingly, there are no English editions of Section A works published in the twentieth century. Condensed bibliographical descriptions are provided in the few cases where

---

4. G. Thomas Tanselle, "The Specifications of Binding Cloth," *The Library,* 21 (September 1966), 246–47. The reader should also consult Tanselle's excellent "The Bibliographical Description of Patterns," *Studies in Bibliography,* 23 (1970), 72–102, which reproduces all of the cloth grains illustrated in the *BAL* plus additional ones.

5. See G. Thomas Tanselle, "A System of Color Identification for Bibliographical Description," *Studies in Bibliography,* 20 (1967), 203–34, for a discussion of how this system can be fully employed. I feel, however, that the use of exact Centroid designations creates a false sense of precision, especially for nineteenth-century books. Oxidation, fading, wear, and nonuniform dyeing practices make precise color identification difficult, if not impossible. In any case, color identification by the Centroid system is inexact.

the first English edition of a nineteenth-century Section A entry appeared after 1900.

A number of miscellaneous collections of Emerson's writings have a publisher's imprint listing numerous geographical locations, usually cities in which the publisher had offices. In such cases, one to three cities are listed but four or more are described with a *[&c.]* following the first city listed.

A number of Emerson's works were published with cover titles. Those cover titles which are integral with the first (or only) gathering are designated a *cover title*. Where the cover title is printed on the front wrapper, the term *pamphlet* is added.

Copyright on Emerson's works prior to 1871 was registered with the clerk of the District Court of Massachusetts in two stages: first, the book's title was given and entered into the copyright books, then a copy of the published work was deposited. Both these dates are given when available.

Publication information for books published by Ticknor and Fields and its successors is drawn from a number of sources, the most important being publishers' records, including the *Costbooks,* at the Houghton Library and Houghton Mifflin Company, and Emerson's manuscript Account Books. Partial mansucript records of Emerson's accounts with James Munroe are available. No records with Phillips, Sampson survive, but information is available in Emerson's Account Books and in his correspondence following the dissolution of the firm in 1859. I have also used the Routledge Archives.

This bibliography also makes use of deposit and inscribed copies to help determine publication dates. Dates given for copies at BC, BE, BL, BO, and DLC are the dates written or stamped on the copies deposited for copyright at those institutions. Dates given for copies in other collections indicate either the date the copy was received into the collection or a date inscribed by a contemporary owner of the book. In all cases, these dates list either the month and year, or the day, month, and year; a parenthetical year-only date after a location indicates the year of publication (usually as determined from title page or copyright page information) of a later reprinting of a work at that institution.

Many of Emerson's works were sold in series. This is particularly true of the collected editions. When the series is identified in the work (such as on the title page or binding, or in a works half title), it is italicized. When the series is unidentified but can be ascertained from publishers' records or contemporary book trade announcements, it is placed within quotation marks.

All attributions of material appearing in the *Dial* are taken from my studies of the *Dial*.[6]

Dates of Emerson's letters, when not given in the printed source, are ascribed on the authority of the editions of Emerson's letters prepared by Ralph L. Rusk and Eleanor M. Tilton.

This bibliography is based upon evidence gathered from my personal inspection and collation of multiple copies of Emerson's works. For first English

---

6. See especially "An Annotated List of Contributions to the Boston *Dial*," *Studies in Bibliography*, 26 (1973), 133–66. Material in the *Dial* attributed to Emerson but which cannot be identified as his with certainty is included in Section H.

and American editions, only libraries holding copies that are bibliographically intact (not rebound or repaired) are listed. Exceptions are rebound copies containing non-bibliographical information, such as dated owners' inscriptions, which is mentioned in notes. The symbols used for American libraries are those employed by the National Union Catalog; those for Canadian libraries are the same as those listed in *Symbols of Canadian Libraries*, 7th ed. (Ottawa: National Library of Canada, 1977), which are here preceded by *Ca;* those for British libraries are the same as those listed in the *British Union-Catalogue of Periodicals*, which are here preceded by *B*. The following is an additional symbol:

JM Collection of Joel Myerson

The following abbreviations are used to refer to editions of Emerson's letters and journals:

CEC *The Correspondence of Emerson and Carlyle,* ed. Joseph Slater. New York: Columbia University Press, 1964.

JMN *The Journals and Miscellaneous Notebooks of Ralph Waldo Emerson,* ed. William H. Gilman et al. 14 vols. to date. Cambridge, Mass.: The Belknap Press of Harvard University Press, 1960–.

L   *The Letters of Ralph Waldo Emerson,* ed. Ralph L. Rusk. 6 vols. New York: Columbia University Press, 1939.

This bibliography is not an attempt to indicate the scarcity of Emerson's works and should not be taken as such. If there is only one location listed, it means that, of all the libraries I visited and corresponded with, only one had or reported having a copy with all the examined points intact; it does not mean that there is only one copy of that work in existence. For recent editions I have not listed as many locations as for earlier ones, where I have tried to be as comprehensive as possible.

A bibliography is more than just a listing of books; it is also a detailed study of an author's literary career. Readers of this book will find information on Emerson's literary reputation, as measured by sales of his books; Emerson's income from his books, or, to use William Charvat's phrase, his successful contribution to the profession of authorship in America; the popularity of individual works (especially poems and essays) by Emerson, as measured by separate publications and reprintings of them; the popularity of Emerson's writings in England and other foreign countries, as seen in the numerous editions and reprintings of his works abroad; and the textual history of Emerson's works. Students of American literary and publishing history will find this book rich in information on late nineteenth-century reprint firms, Anglo-American publishing relations, nineteenth-century anthologies, and private presses.

A bibliography is outdated the day it goes to the printer. Addenda and corrigenda are earnestly solicited.

The University of South Carolina
5 December 1980

A. Separate Publications

All books, pamphlets, and broadsides wholly or substantially by Emerson, including all printings of all editions in English through 1980, and all foreign-language editions through 1882, the year of Emerson's death, arranged chronologically.

A 1 [LETTER TO THE SECOND CHURCH AND SOCIETY]

A 1.1
Presumed first edition, only printing [1832]

LETTER

FROM THE

REV. R. W. EMERSON,

TO THE

SECOND CHURCH AND SOCIETY.

BOSTON:
PRINTED BY I. R. BUTTS.

A 1.1: Cover title, 7″ × 4⁷/₁₆″

[1–3] 4–8

[a]⁴

Contents: p. 1: title page; p. 2: blank; pp. 3–8: text.

Typography and paper: $4^{5}/_{16}'' \times 2^{1}/_{2}''$; wove paper; 26 lines per page. No running heads.

Binding: Cover title. All edges trimmed.

Publication: According to the "Standing Committee Records" of the Second Church and Society, it was "*Voted* that Three Hundred copies . . . be printed & distributed to the Proprietors, & Worshipers" (MHi). Charles Emerson wrote that this was "printed (not published)" (27, 29 December 1832, *L*, I, 361).

Locations: MBAt, MH, MWA.

Note: A bound copy (in a late binding) is at MWiW-C.

A 1.2
Presumed second edition, only printing [1832]

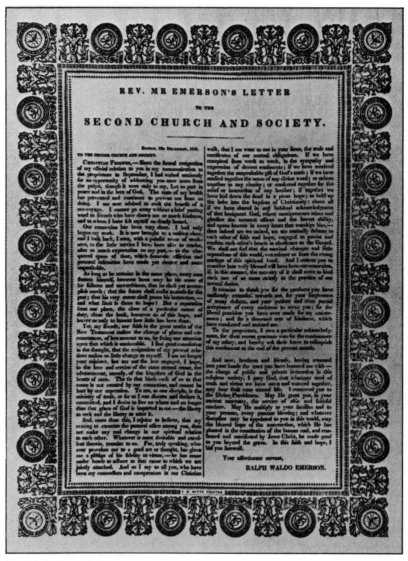

A 1.2: Broadside, 18¹/₈″ × 12″

Broadside, printed on recto only.

Typography and paper: ornamental border, 13⅝″ × 9⅜″; text, 9⅝″ × 6⅜″; satin; double columns: 56 lines in first column, 53 lines in second column. No running head.

Location: MH.

Note one: Another copy, trimmed and framed, is at MBAt.

Note two: Order of editions is arbitrary, but presumably the printing of 300 copies for members of the church would have come first. Both printings are from the same type, which was redistributed for the second printing.

A 2 [CONCORD CENTENNIAL DISCOURSE]

A 2.1
First edition, only printing (1835)

C. E. Norton from R.W.E.
[illegible]

A

HISTORICAL DISCOURSE,

DELIVERED BEFORE THE CITIZENS OF CONCORD,

12TH SEPTEMBER, 1835.

ON THE

SECOND CENTENNIAL ANNIVERSARY

OF THE INCORPORATION OF THE TOWN.

BY RALPH WALDO EMERSON.

PUBLISHED BY REQUEST.

CONCORD:
G. F. BEMIS, PRINTER.
1835.

A 2.1: $9^3/_4$″ × $6^7/_{16}$″

Two states have been noted: see collation below.

[1–3] 4–43 [44–45] 46–52

1st state: [1]⁴ 2⁴ [3]⁴ 4–6⁴ 7²

2nd state: [1]⁴ 2–6⁴ 7²

Contents: p. 1: title page; p. 2: blank; pp. 3–43: text; p. 44: blank; pp. 45–52: appendix.

Typography and paper: $5^7/_8$″ × $3^3/_8$″; wove paper; 34 lines per page. No running heads.

Binding: Light blue wrappers: front recto: 'MR. EMERSON'S | CENTENNIAL DIS-COURSE, | DELIVERED BEFORE THE CITIZENS OF CONCORD, | 12TH SEPTEMBER, 1835.'; front verso, back recto and verso: blank. Untrimmed.

Publication: On 7 November 1835, Charles Emerson wrote William Emerson that he had sent him a copy of the pamphlet (*L*, I, 453). Inscribed copy: MWA (from Emerson, 11 February 1836; lacks wrappers).

Printing: I. R. Butts, Boston.

Locations: 1st state: JM, MH, MHi, NN, TxU, ViU; 2nd state: MH, NNC.

Note one: Order of states is arbitrary, but presumably the state with the correct signing would come second.

Note two: A bound copy has been noted with the following comment, dated 1860, in Charles Eliot Norton's hand: "This discourse has become very rare, most of the copies having been destroyed, many years ago, in a fire at the office of the Town Clerk in Concord" (ViU).

OTHER EDITIONS

A 2.2
Second edition, only printing [ca. 1875]

A | HISTORICAL DISCOURSE, | DELIVERED BEFORE THE CITIZENS OF CONCORD, 12TH SEPTEMBER, 1835, | ON THE | SECOND CENTENNIAL ANNIVERSARY OF THE | INCORPORATION OF THE TOWN. | BY | RALPH WALDO EMERSON. | [rule] | REPUB-LISHED BY REQUEST. | [rule] | BOSTON: | FOR SALE BY W. B. CLARKE, | 162 WASHINGTON STREET.

48 pp. Cloth over flexible boards or wrappers. Inscribed copy: JM (cloth; from Edith Emerson Forbes, 18 April 1875). *Locations:* JM (both).

A 2.3
Concord. [Boston: Beacon, 1883].

4 pp. Head title. Also includes "Concord Hymn." *Old South Leaflets.* Also *Old South Leaflets, First Series,* 1883, no. 3. *Locations:* MH, WHi.

A 2.4
The Town Meeting. [Boston: Beacon, 1883].

8 pp. Head title. *Old South Leaflets.* Also *Old South Leaflets, First Series,* 1883, no. 4. *Locations:* MH, WHi.

No 6

MR. EMERSON'S

CENTENNIAL DISCOURSE,

DELIVERED BEFORE THE CITIZENS OF CONCORD,

12th SEPTEMBER, 1835.

Wrapper for A 2.1

A 3 NATURE

A 3.1.a
First American edition, first printing (1836)

NATURE.

"Nature is but an image or imitation of wisdom, the last thing
of the soul; nature being a thing which doth only do, but not
know."

PLOTINUS.

BOSTON:

JAMES MUNROE AND COMPANY.

M DCCC XXXVI.

A 3.1.a: $7^3/8'' \times 4^5/8''$

Entered, according to the Act of Congress, in the year 1836,
By JAMES MUNROE & Co.
in the Clerk's Office of the District Court of the District of
Massachusetts.

Cambridge Press:
Metcalf, Torry, & Ballou.

Two states have been noted:

1st state: page "94" misnumbered "92."

2d state: page "94" correctly numbered.

1st state: [1–5] 6–8 [9] 10–14 [15] 16–18 [19] 20–31 [32] 33–45 [46] 47–58 [59] 60–75 [76] 77–81 [82] 83–93 92 95 [96]

2d state: [1–5] . . . 83–95 [96]

$[a]^4 1-7^6 8^2$

Contents: p. 1: title page; p. 2: copyright page; p. 3: contents; p. 4: blank; pp. 5–8: "Introduction"; pp. 9–14: "Chapter I" ["Nature"]; pp. 15–18: "Commodity"; pp. 19–31: "Beauty"; pp. 32–45: "Language"; pp. 46–58: "Discipline"; pp. 59–75: "Idealism"; pp. 76–81: "Spirit"; pp. 82–95: "Prospects"; p. 96: blank.

Typography and paper: $4^5/_8''$ ($4^3/_8''$) × $2^{11}/_{16}''$; wove paper; 23 lines per page. Running heads: rectos: p. 7: 'INTRODUCTION.'; pp. 11–13: 'NATURE.'; pp. 17, 21–57, 61–95: titles of chapters; versos: pp. 6–8: 'INTRODUCTION.'; pp. 10–14: 'NATURE.'; pp. 16–30, 34–44, 48–74, 78–80, 84–94: titles of chapters.

Binding: Various cloth colors and types listed below, priority undetermined. Front cover: goldstamped 'NATURE' in center; variations in blindstamping listed below, priority undetermined; back cover: variations in blindstamping listed below, priority undetermined; spine: blank. Flyleaves in most copies. White endpapers. All edges trimmed.

Cloth 1: Dark brown C cloth (sand); light brown S cloth (diagonal fine rib) embossed with fernlike branches

Cloth 2: Blue, dark blue, dark brown, light brown, green, or purple CM cloth (patterned sand) embossed with corallike branches

Cloth 3: Brown H cloth (fine diaper)

Cloth 4: Dark brown S cloth (diagonal fine rib) embossed with oak leaves and acorns

Cloth 5: Dark blue T cloth (rib) embossed with ferns and dots

Cloth 6: Black or brown T cloth (rib)

Cloth 7: Blue, brown, dark brown, green, purple-red, or reddish brown V cloth (smooth) embossed with a diapering of small rosettes and tiny tuliplike florets

Cloth 8: Black, blue, or brown V cloth (smooth) embossed with an overall fine wormlike maze

Cloth 9: Light brown S cloth (diagonal fine rib) embossed with an overall pattern of small units resembling lightning bolts and tiny arrowheads

Bindings for A 3.1.a: Cloth 1, Stamping B; Cloth 2, Stamping E

Bindings for A 3.1.a: Cloth 4, Stamping B; Cloth 5, Stamping A

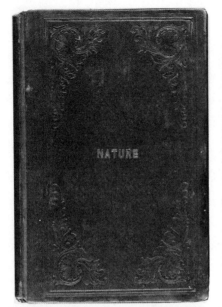

Bindings for A 3.1.a: Cloth 6, Stamping C; Cloth 6, Stamping D

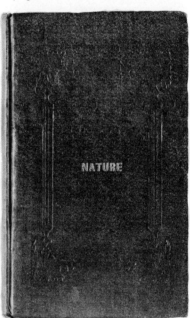

Bindings for A 3.1.a: Cloth 7, Stamping B; Cloth 8, Stamping A

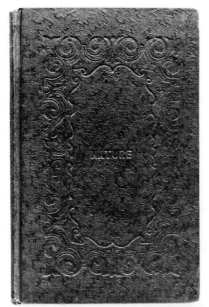

Bindings for A 3.1.a: Cloth 9, Stamping B; Cloth 10, Stamping E

Bindings for A 3.1.a: Cloth 11, Stamping A; Cloth 12, Stamping E

Bindings for A 3.1.a: Cloth 13, Stamping B; Cloth 15, Stamping B

Cloth 10: Medium brown P cloth (pebble) with large diamond-shaped panels, each containing a star

Cloth 11: Black coarse EC (weave) cloth

Cloth 12: Black T cloth (rib) embossed with a pattern of circles

Cloth 13: Brown P cloth (pebble) embossed with a snakelike maze

Cloth 14: Brown horizontal T cloth (rib)

Cloth 15: Medium brown P cloth (pebble)

Stamping A: Rectangular frame of fasceslike units with stylized leafy ornaments in each corner

Stamping B: Rectangular frame of rococo curved rules, swirls, stylized leaves, and other ornaments

Stamping C: Triple-rule rectangular frame with 2½″ stylized leafy ornament in each corner

Stamping D: Triple-rule rectangular frame with 1¾″ stylized leafy ornament in each corner

Stamping E: Covers are unstamped

Publication: Advertised as "This day published and received" in *Boston Daily Advertiser,* 9 September 1836, p. 3; as "This day published" in *Christian Register,* 10 September 1836, p. 14. Deposited for copyright: title, 8 September 1836; book, 23 November 1836. Deposit copy: now at OKentU (28 November 1836). Emerson wrote his brother William on 23 October 1836 that 500 copies had been sold "a fortnight since"

(*L*, II, 42). The entire printing may have been 1,500 copies. Emerson's accounts with James Munroe and Company (dating from January 1837) show that copies were bound on 6 February 1838, 1 January 1839, 5 December 1840, and 29 April 1842. According to the accounts, 23 copies were still in stock on 17 January 1844. Price, unknown. Author's share, 33^1/3¢ per copy.

Locations: 1st state: BE (2E), CtY (5A), InU (5A, 7B), JM (7B), MB (2E), MCo (8B), MH (7B), MHi (8B), NN (2A), NNC (7B), NjP (7B, 8B), PSt (5A), TxU (5A), ViU (2A, 7B, 10E), VtMiM (10E); 2nd state: BL (6D), CSt (2B), CtY (2A, 3E, 6D, 11A, 12B, 12E, 13B, 14A), DLC (7B, 11A), InU (7B), JM (2B, 2E, 3A, 6D, 9B, 15B), MB (7B), MCo (7B), MH (1B, 7B, 8A, 9A, 11B), MWA (7B), NN (2A, 3E, 4B, 6C), NNC (3E, 6C), OKentU (7B).

Note one: For miscellaneous bibliographical information, see the 1940 reprinting edited by Kenneth Walter Cameron (A 3.1.b).

Note two: Order of states is arbitrary, but presumably the state with the correct pagination would come second.

LATER PRINTINGS

A 3.1.b
New York: Scholars' Facsimiles & Reprints, 1940.

Facsimile reprinting. Edited with introduction, index-concordance, and bibliographical appendices by Kenneth Walter Cameron. Price, $3.50. *Location:* DLC (5 December 1940).

A 3.1.c
San Francisco: Chandler, [1968].

Facsimile reprinting. Wrappers. Edited with an introduction by Warner Berthoff. *Chandler Facsimile Editions in American Literature*. Price, $1.95. *Location:* JM.

A 3.2
Second American edition, only printing (1849)

NATURE.

BY

R. W. EMERSON.

A subtle chain of countless rings
The next unto the farthest brings ;
The eye reads omens where it goes,
And speaks all languages the rose ;
And, striving to be man, the worm
Mounts through all the spires of form.

NEW EDITION.

———◆———

BOSTON & CAMBRIDGE:
JAMES MUNROE & COMPANY.
M DCCC XLIX.

A 3.2: $7^{1}/_{8}''$ × $4^{7}/_{16}''$

Entered according to Act of Congress, in the year 1849,

By JAMES MUNROE AND COMPANY,

in the Clerk's Office of the District Court of the District of Massachusetts.

BOSTON :

THURSTON, TORRY AND COMPANY,

31 Devonshire Street.

[i–vi] [1] 2–3 [4–5] 6–8 [9–10] 11–12 [13] 14–22 [23] 24–33 [34] 35–44 [45] 46–58 [59] 60–63 [64] 65–74

[a]^4 ($-$a₄)1–4^8 5^4 6^1

Contents: p. i: 'NATURE.'; p. ii: blank; p. iii: title page; p. iv: copyright page; p. v: contents; p. vi: blank; pp. 1–3: 'INTRODUCTION.'; p. 4: blank; pp. 5–9: 'NATURE.'; pp. 10–12: 'COMMODITY.'; pp. 13–22: 'BEAUTY.'; pp. 23–33: 'LANGUAGE.'; pp. 34–44: 'DISCIPLINE.'; pp. 45–58: 'IDEALISM.'; pp. 59–63: 'SPIRIT.'; pp. 64–74: 'PROSPECTS.'.

Typography and paper: 5¼" (5") × 3"; wove paper; 28 lines per page. Running heads: rectos: pp. 3, 7–11, 15–21, 25–43, 47–57, 61–73: chapter titles; versos: pp. 2, 6–8, 12–32, 36–62, 66–74: chapter titles.

Binding: Black, dark brown, light brown, or dark grayish purple T cloth (rib). Front and back covers: variations in stamping listed below, priority undetermined; spine: blindstamped bands with goldstamped '[bottom to top] NATURE'. Flyleaves. Light yellow or yellow endpapers. All edges trimmed.

   Stamping A: Blindstamped frame of parallel double-rules with a floret in each boxed corner

   Stamping B: Blindstamped double-rule frame surrounding frame of florets with floral design inside corners

Publication: Emerson records in his journal that 250 copies were printed on 7 December 1849 (*JMN,* XI, 156). Emerson paid printing costs. Deposited for copyright: title, 22 August 1849; book, 22 February 1850. A manuscript record in Emerson's hand shows that five copies were still in stock in July 1853 (MH). Price, unknown. Author's share, 33¢ per copy.

Locations: CtY (B), DLC (B), JM (A, B), MWA (B).

Note one: Printed from the plates of *Nature; Addresses, and Lectures* (A 21.1).

Note two: The conjugate leaves of the front and back flyleaves are pasted under the pastedown endpapers.

Note three: Copies, all in binding B, have been noted with an 8-page Munroe catalogue, dated September 1849, inserted at the back: DLC, JM, MWA.

Note four: For a list of textual changes between the first and second editions, see *Nature, Addresses, and Lectures* (A 21.14.a).

A 3.3.a–b
First German edition (1868)

Die Natur. Ein Essay von Ralph Waldo Emerson. Hannover: Carl Meyer, 1868.

60 pp. Translated by Adolph Holtermann. Reprinted 1873. *Not seen.*

A 3.4
Boston: James R. Osgood, 1876.

93 pp. *Vest-Pocket Series,* no. 18. 2,000 copies printed 8 November 1876. Listed in *Publishers' Weekly,* 10 (2 December 1876), 942. Copyright, 20 November 1876. Price, 50¢. *Location:* JM.

A 3.5
New York: John B. Alden; Chicago: Alden Book Co., 1886.

7–54 pp. Wrappers. *The Elzevir Library,* vol. 5, no. 208, 25 May 1886. Price, 5¢. *Location:* CtW.

Note: From the plates of *Nature and Other Addresses* (C 16).

A 3.6
Nature and Compensation. Boston, New York, Chicago: Houghton, Mifflin, 1899.

114 pp. Wrappers. *Riverside Literature Series,* no. 131, 1 February 1899. Listed in *Publishers' Weekly,* 55 (22 April 1899), 673. Price, 15¢. Numerous reprintings. *Locations:* DLC (28 April 1899), JM.

A 3.7
New York: Maynard, Merrill, 1901.

77 pp. Wrappers. Edited by J. W. Abernethy. *Maynard's English Classics Series,* no. 227, n.s. no. 115, 1 May 1901. Price, 10¢. *Location:* DLC (14 March 1901).

A 3.8
[East Aurora, N.Y.: Roycrofters, 1905].

91 pp. Various bindings at various prices. Completed May 1905. Also advertised 100 copies on Japan vellum. *Location:* JM.

A 3.9
New York: Duffield, 1909.

53 pp. Advertised as included in "Rubric Series" for 60¢. Copyright, 9 October 1909. *Location:* JM.

A 3.10
Nature Essays. London and Edinburgh: T. N. Foulis, [1910].

115 pp. Limp leather. *The Holyrood Books,* no. 7. Printed September 1910. *Location:* BL (5 November 1910).

Note: Contains *Nature* and "The Method of Nature."

A 3.11
Second German edition [1929]

[Munich: Bremer Press, 1929].

86 pp. Boxed. Titles and initials designed by Anna Simons. 250 copies numbered i–ccl for Random House (the American distributor) and 280 copies numbered 1–280 for subscribers of the Bremer Press. Price, $25.00. *Location:* JM (inscribed by the printer, 1 October 1929).

A 3.12
Nature and The American Scholar. Tokyo: Kōbunsha, 1930.

88 pp. Advertised as "revised edition." *Not seen.*

A 3.13.a
New York: Liberal Arts Press, 1948.

45 pp. Wrappers. Edited with an introduction by Joseph L. Blau. *The Little Library of Liberal Arts*, no. 2. Price, 35¢. *Location:* JM.

A 3.13.b
Indianapolis and New York: Bobbs-Merrill, [n.d.].

Wrappers. *The Library of Liberal Arts*, no. 2. Numerous reprintings. *Location:* JM.

A 3.14.a
Emerson's Nature—*Origin, Growth, Meaning.* New York and Toronto: Dodd, Mead, 1969.

182 pp. Dust jacket. Edited by Merton M. Sealts, Jr., and Alfred R. Ferguson. Includes text of *Nature*. Price, $4.95. *Locations:* DLC (19 May 1969), JM.

A 3.14.b
Carbondale and Edwardsville: Southern Illinois University Press; London and Amsterdam: Feffer & Simons, 1979.

225 pp. Cloth (with dust jacket) or wrappers. *Second edition, enlarged. Locations:* DLC (7 August 1979), JM (both).

A 4 [CONCORD HYMN]

A 4.1
First edition, only printing [1837]

ORIGINAL HYMN.

By the rude bridge that arched the flood,
  Their flag to April's breeze unfurled,
Here, once, the embattled farmers stood,
  And fired the shot heard round the world.

The foe, long since, in silence slept;
  Alike, the conqueror silent sleeps;
And Time the ruinèd bridge has swept
  Down the dark stream which seaward creeps.

On this green bank, by this soft stream,
  We place with joy a votive stone,
That memory may their deed redeem,
  When, like our sires, our sons are gone.

O Thou who made those heroes dare
  To die, or leave their children free,—
Bid Time and Nature gently spare
  The shaft we raise to them and Thee.

A 4.1: Broadside, 6″ × 4³/₄″

Broadside, printed on recto

Typography and paper: ornamental border, 4⅝″ × 3⅝″; text, 3¹³/₁₆″ × 2¹¹/₁₆″; wove paper; 17 lines. No running head.

Publication: William Emerson wrote his mother on 27 June 1837 that his brother "has written a hymn . . . when it is printed will send you a copy" (*L*, II, 85). John Shepard Keyes, who sung in the choir at the occasion on 4 July 1837, recalled that "This hymn was printed on slips of paper about six inches square and plentifully supplied to the audience" (*Memoirs of Members of the Social Circle in Concord. Fifth Series* [Cambridge: University Press, 1940], p. 77).

Locations: MB, MH, MWiW-C.

A 4.2
[N.p.: n.p., n.d.].

Broadside, printed on recto. Size: 8″ × 4⅜″. *Location:* MWA.

A 4.3
["Concord Hymn" and "Fourth of July Ode"]. [N.p.: n.p., n.d.].

Anonymous. Broadside, laid paper, printed on recto. Size: 10½″ × 5″. *Location:* MH.

A 5 [AMERICAN SCHOLAR ADDRESS]

A 5.1
First American edition, only printing (1837)

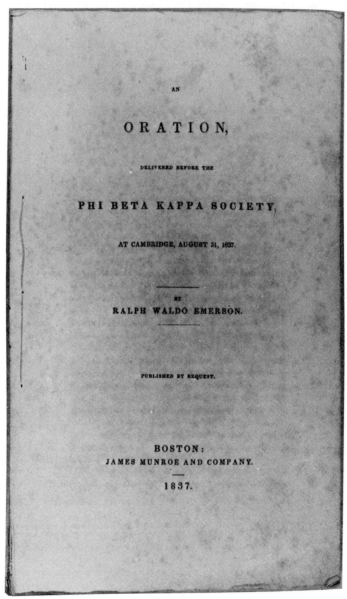

AN

ORATION,

DELIVERED BEFORE THE

PHI BETA KAPPA SOCIETY,

AT CAMBRIDGE, AUGUST 31, 1837.

———

BY

RALPH WALDO EMERSON.

———

PUBLISHED BY REQUEST.

BOSTON:
JAMES MUNROE AND COMPANY.
———
1837.

A 5.1: $9^{3}/_{4}'' \times 5^{7}/_{8}''$

[1–3] 4–26 [27–28]

[1]⁴ 2–3⁴ [4]²

Contents: p. 1: title page; p. 2: blank; pp. 3–26: text; pp. 27–28: blank.

Typography and paper: 6³/₁₆″ × 3¹/₂″; wove paper; 31 lines per page. No running heads.

Binding: Light tan or light orange brown paper wrappers; front recto: same as the title page within a double-rule frame with an ornament in each boxed corner; front verso, back recto and verso: blank. All edges trimmed.

Publication: On 13 September 1837, Emerson wrote Carlyle that the Address "is now being printed" (*CEC,* p. 169). Advertised as "In press—and will be published in a few days," in *Christian Register,* 16 September 1837, p. 149. Advertised as "Published this morning" (advertisement apparently dated 23 September) in *Christian Register,* 7 October 1837, p. 160. On 23 September 1837, James Munroe and Company wrote Emerson that 500 copies had been received from the binder that evening (MH). On 24 October 1837, Emerson entered in his journal that all 500 copies had sold in one month (*JMN,* V, 411). Price, 20¢. Publisher's commission, 5¢.

Printing: "Press of James Loring" (p. 26).

Locations: CSt, CtY, InU, MH, NN, RPB, TxU.

AN

ORATION,

DELIVERED BEFORE THE

PHI BETA KAPPA SOCIETY,

AT CAMBRIDGE, AUGUST 31, 1837,

BY

RALPH WALDO EMERSON.

PUBLISHED BY REQUEST.

BOSTON:
JAMES MUNROE AND COMPANY.
1837.

Wrapper for A 5.1

A 5.2
Second edition, only printing (1838)

Title page substitutes 'PUBLISHED BY REQUEST.' with 'SECOND EDITION.', and '1837' with '1838'.

[1–3] 4–32

[1]⁴ 2–4⁴

Contents: p. 1: title page; p. 2: printer's imprint; pp. 3–32: text.

Typography and paper: Page size: $9^3/8'' \times 5^5/8''$; text size: $6^3/8'' \times 3^7/8''$; wove paper; 32 lines per page. No running heads.

Binding: Light yellow-gray or light brown wrappers; front recto: same as the title page within a triple-rule frame; front verso, back recto and verso: blank. All edges trimmed.

Publication: On 26 January 1838, Emerson entered into his journal: "Today I send the Oration to press again" (*JMN,* V, 448). On 9 February 1838, Emerson wrote Carlyle that a "new edition is now printing" (*CEC,* p. 177). 515 copies printed 23 February 1838. Announced in the *Boston Evening Mercantile Journal,* 24 February 1838, p. 3. 190 copies were still in stock on 17 January 1844. Price, 20¢. Publisher's commission, 5¢.

Printing: Folsom, Wells, and Thurston, Cambridge (p. 2).

Locations: DLC, JM, MCo, MHi, RPB, TxU, ViU.

Note: A partial (pp. 1–24) set of pages has been noted: JM.

A 5.3.a
First English edition, first printing [1843]

MAN THINKING.

AN

ORATION.

BY RALPH WALDO EMERSON.

The words of such a man, what words he finds good to speak, are worth attending to.
                                                                    CARLYLE.

.LONDON:

C. E. MUDIE,

26, UPPER KING STREET, BLOOMSBURY SQUARE.

Price Fourpence.

A 5.3.a: Cover title, 8″ × 5″

[1–3] 4–24

[A]^{12}

Contents: p. 1: title page; p. 2: printer's imprint; pp. 3–24: text.

Typography and paper: 6^{1}/$_{8}$″ × 3^{1}/$_{2}$″; wove paper; 36 lines per page. No running heads.

Binding: Cover title. All edges trimmed.

Publication: Advertised as "just published,"*Athenæum,* no. 845 (6 January 1844), 21, and no. 862 (4 May 1844), 413. Inscribed copy: JM (29 December 1843).

Printing: "RICHARD KINDER, PRINTER, GREEN ARBOUR COURT, OLD BAILEY" (p. [2]).

Locations: BE, CSt, CtY, JM.

Note: Unquestionably a piracy, as is the second printing.

A 5.3.b
First English edition, second printing (1844)

The same as the first printing, except the cover title reads 'SQUARE. | 1844. | [rule]'.

Locations: BE, BL, BO, NNC.

LATER EDITIONS

A 5.4.a
New York: Maynard, Merrill, 1893.

51 pp. Wrappers. *Maynard's English Classics Series,* no. 123. Listed in *Critic,* 23 (2 December 1893), 369; in *Publishers' Weekly,* 44 (9 December 1893), 960. Price, 12¢. *Not seen.*

A 5.4.b
New York: Maynard, Merrill, 1902.

Maynard's English Classics Series, no. 123, n.s. no. 127, 1 April 1902. Price, 12¢. *Location:* KU.

A 5.5
New York: Laurentian Press, 1901.

59 pp., printed on one side of leaf only. Listed in *Publishers' Weekly,* 60 (20 July 1901), 72. Limited "to 510 copies, of which 25, numbered 1 to 25, are printed on Japan Vellum; 140, numbered 26–165, on Brown's hand-made paper; and 345, numbered 166 to 510, on Ruisdael hand-made paper." Prices: vellum, $10.00; Brown's paper, $7.50; Ruisdael paper, $5.00. *Locations:* NcD (Brown's), JM (vellum).

A 5.6
Ithaca, N.Y.: Cornell University Press, 1955.

24 pp. Woodcuts by Elfriede Abbe. 275 numbered copies, signed by the artist. Copyright, 11 October 1955. Price, $10.00. *Location:* JM.

A 5.7
"The American Scholar" Today. New York: Dodd, Mead, 1970.

93 pp. Wrappers. Edited by C. David Mead. Price, $2.50. *Location:* JM.

A 5.8
The Theory of Books is Noble. Philadelphia: Pickering, [n.d.].

Broadside, printed on recto only. Selection. *Location:* PPT.

A6 [PROSPECTUS FOR CARLYLE'S *FRENCH REVOLUTION*]

A6
First edition, only printing [1837]

BOSTON, OCT. 31, 1837.

SIR,—I have engaged Messrs. C. C. LITTLE and JAMES BROWN, to publish an American edition of THE HISTORY OF THE FRENCH REVOLUTION, by THOMAS CARLYLE. In addition to the wish of presenting to the public a work of great intrinsic value, I have the hope of securing a private benefit to the author, to whom all the profits arising from it will be transmitted. With this view, the publishers have made with me a liberal contract, by which they relinquish to the author all profit on the sale of such copies as shall be subscribed for. May I ask your aid in procuring, and transmitting to them, at 112 Washington street, the names of any subscribers.

R. W. EMERSON.

TERMS.

The Work will be published in two volumes, large 12mo. of from 450 to 500 pages each. It will be printed on a new type and good paper, and strongly done up in cloth, and delivered to subscribers at $2 50 a copy.

A6: 9¹⁵/₁₆″ × 7¹⁵/₁₆″

[1−4]

[a]^2

Contents: p. 1: text; pp. 2−4: blank.

Typography and paper: 2$^7/_{16}$″ × 5$^3/_{16}$″; pale blue wove paper; 13 lines. No running head.

Binding: Single sheet folded once; unbound.

Publication: On 29 December 1837, Emerson wrote his brother William that he had sent ten copies of the Prospectus to him (*L*, II, 104).

Location: MH.

A 7 [DIVINITY SCHOOL ADDRESS]

A 7.1
First American edition, only printing (1838)

AN

ADDRESS

DELIVERED

BEFORE THE SENIOR CLASS

IN

DIVINITY COLLEGE, CAMBRIDGE,

SUNDAY EVENING, 15 JULY, 1838.

By RALPH WALDO EMERSON.

BOSTON:
JAMES MUNROE AND COMPANY.
1838.

A 7.1: $9^3/_{16}'' \times 5^{11}/_{16}''$

[1–3] 4–31 [32]

[1]⁴ 2–4⁴

Contents: p. 1: title page; p. 2: printer's imprint; pp. 3–31: text; p. 32: blank.

Typography and paper: 6¹/₈″ × 3⁵/₈″; wove paper; 29 lines per page. No running heads.

Binding: Light blue wrappers; front recto: same as the title page within a triple-rule frame; front verso, back recto and verso: blank. All edges trimmed.

Publication: Although W. D. Wilson, one of the students who had invited Emerson to deliver the Address, wrote on 20 July 1838 that they had "concluded to print it merely" in an edition of 300 copies for private distribution, Emerson preferred commercial publication (MH). 1,000 copies were bound on 4 August 1838. On 21 [i.e., 20] August 1838, James Munroe and Company wrote Emerson that "we shall publish tomorrow," adding that the printer had forgotten to have "the copyright entered upon the back" (MH). Advertised as "Just published," in *Christian Register*, 25 August 1838, p. 135. On 15 March 1839, Emerson wrote Carlyle that "the whole thousand copies were bought up" (*CEC*, p. 217). Actually, four copies still were in stock on 1 July 1839; the printing was sold out by 1 January 1840. Inscribed copy: TxU (24 August 1838). Price, 20¢. Publisher's commission, 5¢.

Printing: "CAMBRIDGE PRESS: | METCALF, TORRY, AND BALLOU" (p. [2]).

Locations: InU, JM, MCo, MH, MH-AH, MHi, MWA, NN, NNC, RPB, TxU, ViU.

AN

ADDRESS

DELIVERED

BEFORE THE SENIOR CLASS

IN

DIVINITY COLLEGE, CAMBRIDGE,

SUNDAY EVENING, 15 JULY, 1838.

By RALPH WALDO EMERSON

BOSTON:

JAMES MUNROE AND COMPANY.

1838.

Wrapper for A 7.1

A 7.2
First Danish edition (1856)

Tale holdt til de ældre thelogiske Studerende ved Universtetet I Cambridge I Massachusetts. Kjøbenhavn: J. Lund, 1856.

32 pp. Translated by E. M. Thorson. *Not seen.*

OTHER EDITIONS

A 7.3.a
An Address. Chicago: Unity Publishing Committee, [1884].

11. pp. Head title. *Unity Mission* series, no. 8. Numerous reprintings; the latest reprint noted is dated 1888 and indicates that 6,000 copies had been printed. *Locations:* DLC, MB (1888).

A 7.3.b
An Address. Chicago: Colgrove, 1884.

Unity Church-Door Pulpit, series 1, no. 1, 8 April 1884. Price, 10¢. *Location:* CSt.

A 7.3.c
Chicago: Charles H. Kerr, 1889.

Unity Mission series, vol. 1, no. 8, January 1889. *Location:* MB.

A 7.4
First English edition, only printing (1903)

London: Philip Green, 1903.

88 pp. Introduction by W. C. Gannett and poem ("The Living God") by John W. Chadwick. Price, 1s. *Locations:* BE (10 June 1903), BL (10 June 1903), JM.

A 7.5.a–dd
Boston: American Unitarian Association, [1907].

22 pp. Wrappers or cover title. Published November 1907. *Memorable Sermons,* no. 9; later advertised as included in "Unitarian Tracts Series," no. C; also printed out of series. Numerous reprintings; the latest reprint noted is the 30th printing of June 1958. *Locations:* MH-AH (1907, 1958).

A 7.6.a–b
Boston: American Unitarian Association, 1938.

35 pp. Self-wrappers. Notes by Earl Morse Wilbur. *Centenary Edition.* Reprinted in 1941. *Locations:* JM, IaU (1941).

A 7.7
New York: [First Congregational Church], 1948.

24 pp. Wrappers. *Location:* NN.

A 8 [LITERARY ETHICS]

A 8.1
First edition, only printing (1838)

AN

ORATION,

DELIVERED BEFORE THE

LITERARY SOCIETIES

OF

DARTMOUTH COLLEGE,

JULY 24, 1838.

BY

RALPH WALDO EMERSON

PUBLISHED BY REQUEST

BOSTON:

CHARLES C. LITTLE AND JAMES BROWN.

1838

A 8.1: 9³/₁₆″ × 5³/₄″

[1–3] 4–30 [31–32]

[1]⁴ 2–4⁴

Contents: p. 1: title page; p. 2: printer's imprint; pp. 3–30: text; pp. 31–32: blank.

Typography and paper: 6³/₈″ × 3¹/₂″; wove paper; 32 lines per page. No running heads.

Binding: Light blue wrappers; front recto: same as the title page within a triple-rule frame; front verso, back recto and verso: blank. All edges trimmed.

Publication: On 14 August 1838, Emerson wrote Little and Brown that he had sent the first part of the manuscript the previous week and the second part the previous day, but he had not yet received proof (Collection of George T. Goodspeed). On 21 August 1838, he wrote to say that he had received some proof and was sending along the rest of his manuscript (PHi), and he entered in his journal that the oration was "printing" (*JMN*, VII, 52). On 1 September 1838, Emerson wrote Mary Moody Emerson that it "will be out in a day or two," but the next day he wrote both George Bush and his brother William that it was still not out (*L*, II, 153, 155, 157). Advertised for sale in *Christian Register*, 8 September 1838, p. 143. Listed in "New Publications," in *North American Review*, 47 (October 1838), 510. On 13 September 1838, Emerson sent his brother William copies of the oration (*L*, II, 160). Inscribed copy: MH (1 October 1838). 1,000 copies were printed. 26 copies were in stock on 1 January 1843, and the printing was sold out by 1 January 1844. Price, unknown. Royalty, unknown.

Printing: "CAMBRIDGE: | FOLSOM, WELLS, AND THURSTON, | PRINTERS TO THE UNIVERSITY" (p. [2]).

Locations: CtY, InU, MH, MH-AH, MHi, NN, NcD, NjP, RPB, TxU, ViU.

AN

ORATION,

DELIVERED BEFORE THE

LITERARY SOCIETIES

OF

DARTMOUTH COLLEGE,

JULY 24, 1838.

BY

RALPH WALDO EMERSON.

PUBLISHED BY REQUEST.

BOSTON:
CHARLES C. LITTLE AND JAMES BROWN.

1838.

Wrapper for A 8.1

A 8.2

New York: John B. Alden; Chicago: Alden Book Co., 1886.

[79]–101 pp. Wrappers. *The Elzevir Library,* vol. 5, no. 211, 15 June 1886. Price, 3¢. *Location:* CtW.

Note: From the plates of *Nature and Other Addresses* (C 16).

A 8.3

New York: Thomas Y. Crowell, [1905?].

34 pp. Advertised in various bindings at various prices. Also *Verona Edition;* advertised as included in "Laurel Series." *Location:* JM (both).

A 8.4

Emerson at Dartmouth. A Reprint of His Oration: Literary Ethics. Hanover, N.H.: Westholm, 1956.

40 pp. Unprinted glassine dust jacket. Introduction by Herbert Faulkner West. Limited to 300 numbered copies. Copyright, 23 April 1956. *Location:* JM.

A 9 [PROSPECTUS FOR CARLYLE'S *ESSAYS*]

A 9
First edition, only printing [1838]

PROSPECTUS.

THE subscriber has been induced by the repeated request of many individuals, added to the interest with which Mr. Carlyle's recent History has been received, to collect his Miscellaneous Writings. These papers are widely scattered in journals and magazines from the year 1827 to the present time; and most of them in journals not reprinted in this country. It is thought that a large proportion of these miscellanies would be more acceptable to the general reader than either of the works that have been already printed here. I propose to print the series of his critical and miscellaneous articles in chronological order, according to a list furnished by the author himself. At present, only two volumes will be published, with the intention, however, of completing the series, at a future time, in one or two volumes more. The profits of the sale will be transmitted to the author. As the publishers, James Munroe & Co., relinquish to him all profit on such copies as are subscribed for, I ask of his friends to send so many names as they can procure of purchasers of the work, to JAMES MUNROE & CO., 134 Washington Street, Boston, or to me.

R. W. EMERSON.

Concord, Mass., April 2, 1838.

TERMS.—The two volumes now in press will consist of 450 pages each, 12mo; — the type, paper, and binding to correspond with the first American Edition of SARTOR RESARTUS. Price — *two dollars and fifty cents.*

NAMES.	RESIDENCE.	NUMBER OF COPIES.

A 9: 9⅝" × 7¹³/₁₆"

[1–4]

[a]^2

Contents: p. 1: text; pp. 2–4: blank.

Typography and paper: 4$^1/_2$″ × 5$^7/_8$″; wove paper; 19 lines. No running head.

Binding: Single sheet folded once; unbound.

Publication: Emerson notes in his manuscript, "Circular of Carlyle's Miscellanies sent to," that 33 people were to receive a copy of the Prospectus (MH).

Location: MH.

A 10 ESSAYS [FIRST SERIES]

A 10.1.a
First American edition, first printing (1841)

ESSAYS:

BY

R. W. EMERSON.

BOSTON:

JAMES MUNROE AND COMPANY.

MDCCCXLI.

A 10.1.a: $7^3/_{16}''$ × $4^7/_{16}''$

Entered according to Act of Congress, in the year 1841, by
JAMES MUNROE & Co., in the Clerk's Office of the District
Court of the District of Massachusetts.

BOSTON:
PRINTED BY FREEMAN AND BOLLES,
WASHINGTON STREET.

[i–viii] [1–3] 4–33 [34–37] 38–73 [74–77] 78–104 [105–107] 108–135 [136–139] 140–155 [156–159] 160–180 [181–183] 184–199 [200–203] 204–218 [219–221] 222–245 [246–249] 250–266 [267–269] 270–286 [287–289] 290–303 [304]

[a]^4 1–12^{12} 13^8

Contents: pp. i–ii: blank; p. iii: 'ESSAYS.'; p. iv: blank; p. v: title page; p. vi: copyright page; pp. vii–viii: contents; p. 1: 'HISTORY. | [rule] | [four lines of verse]'; p. 2: four lines of verse; pp. 3–33: "Essay I. History."; p. 34: blank; p. 35: 'SELF-RELIANCE. | [rule] | Ne te quæsiveris extra. | [rule] | [six lines of verse] | *Epilogue to Beaumont and Fletcher's Honest Man's Fortune.*'; p. 36: four lines of verse; pp. 37–73: "Essay II. Self-Reliance."; p. 74: blank; p. 75: 'COMPENSATION.'; p. 76: blank; pp. 77–104: "Essay III. Compensation."; p. 105: 'SPIRITUAL LAWS.'; p. 106: blank; pp. 107–135: "Essay IV. Spiritual Laws."; p. 136: blank; p. 137: 'LOVE.'; p. 138: blank; pp. 139–155: "Essay V. Love."; p. 156: blank; p. 157: 'FRIENDSHIP.'; p. 158: blank; p. 159–180: "Essay VI. Friendship."; p. 181: 'PRUDENCE.'; p. 182: blank; pp. 183–199: "Essay VII. Prudence."; p. 200: blank; p. 201: 'HEROISM. | [rule] | "Paradise is under the shadow of swords." | *Mahomet.*'; p. 202: blank; pp. 203–218: "Essay VIII. Heroism."; p. 219: 'THE OVER-SOUL. | [rule] | [five lines of verse] | *Henry More.*'; p. 220: blank; pp. 221–245: "Essay IX. The Over-Soul."; p. 246: blank; p. 247: 'CIRCLES.'; p. 248: blank; pp. 249–266: "Essay X. Circles."; p. 267: 'INTELLECT.'; p. 268: blank; pp. 269–286: "Essay XI. Intellect."; p. 287: 'ART.'; p. 288: blank; pp. 289–303: "Essay XII. Art."; p. 304: blank.

Essays: "History" #, "Self-Reliance" #, "Compensation" #, "Spiritual Laws" #, "Love" #, "Friendship" #, "Prudence" #, "Heroism" #, "The Over-Soul" #, "Circles" #, "Intellect" #, "Art" #.

Typography and paper: 5″ (4³/₄″) × 2¹⁵/₁₆″; wove paper; 31 lines per page. Running heads: rectos: pp. 5–33, 39–73, 79–103, 109–135, 141–155, 161–179, 185–199, 205–217, 223–245, 251–265, 271–285, 291–303: titles of essays; versos: p. viii: 'CONTENTS.'; pp. 4–32, 38–72, 78–104, 108–134, 140–154, 160–180, 184–198, 204–218, 222–244, 250–266, 270–286, 290–302: 'ESSAY' and roman numeral.

Binding: Cloth and color variations listed below, priority undetermined. Front and back covers: stampings listed below, priority undetermined; spine: goldstamped 'EMERSON'S | ESSAYS.' Variations in flyleaves and endpapers listed below. All edges trimmed.

Binding A: Black or dark brown coarse T cloth (rib); black coarse horizontal T cloth (rib). Front and back covers: blindstamped triple-rule frame with 2¹/₈″ ornament in each corner; spine: blindstamped rules and boxes. Flyleaves. Yellow coated or cream coated endpapers.

Binding B: Black or brown coarse T cloth (rib); black coarse horizontal T cloth (rib). Front and back covers: blindstamped triple-rule frame with 2″ ornament in each corner; spine: blindstamped rules and boxes. Flyleaves. Yellow coated endpapers.

Binding C: Black or brown coarse horizontal T cloth (rib). Front and back covers: blindstamped triple-rule frame with 2⅛″ ornament in each corner; spine: blindstamped rules and filigrees. Flyleaves in some copies. Cream coated, yellow coated, or white endpapers.

Binding D: Black coarse T cloth (rib). Front and back covers: blindstamped double-rule frame with 2½″ ornament in each corner; spine: blindstamped horizontal rules. Yellow endpapers.

Binding E: Brown FL cloth (diagonal dotted line); brown H cloth (fine diaper); medium purple S cloth (diagonal fine rib); black or brown T cloth (rib); black TB cloth (net). Front and back covers: blindstamped triple-rule frame with 5⅞″ ornament in center; spine: blindstamped leafy ornament. Flyleaves. Cream coated or yellow coated endpapers.

Binding F: Dark gray green T cloth (rib). Front and back covers: blindstamped triple-rule frame with filigree in each corner and 3½″ filigree ornament in center; spine: blindstamped rules enclosing filigree ornaments. Flyleaves. Yellow endpapers.

Publication: On 12 January 1841, Emerson wrote Margaret Fuller that proofs were arriving (*L*, II, 376). In letters to William Emerson on 5 and 25 February 1841, and to Carlyle on 28 February 1841, Emerson mentions correcting proof (*L*, II, 378, 383; *CEC*, p. 291). According to James Munroe and Company's accounts with Emerson, printing was completed on 11 March 1841. Deposited for copyright: title, 12 March 1841; book, 27 March 1841. In a memorandum of 19 March 1841, Emerson notes that *Essays* is "this day published," and he entered in his journal on the same day the names of people to whom copies were to be sent (MH; *JMN*, VII, 546). Advertised as "This day published," in *Boston Daily Advertiser*, 20 March 1841, p. 2. Inscribed copies: Binding A: MH (from Emerson, 19 March 1841), NN (from Emerson, 22 March 1841); Binding B: InU (from Emerson, 19 March 1841), MH (from Emerson, 19 March 1841); Binding C: NN (from Emerson, 26 March 1841), NN (March 1841). On 14 October 1845, Emerson wrote Evert Duyckinck that 1,500 copies had been printed and all had sold (*L*, III, 308). Copies were bound for publication before 19 March 1841, and on 1 October, 14 December 1841, 29 April 1842, 1 January, and 1 July 1843; 109 copies were still in stock on 1 January 1844. Emerson wrote Duyckinck that "I print them at my own risk, & Munroe & Co have 30 per cent as their commission" (14 October 1845, *L*, III, 308). Price, $1.00. Publisher's commission, 29¢.

Locations: Binding A: CtY, JM, MH, NN, NNC, ViU; Binding B: InU, MH, TxU; Binding C: BE, CU, InU, JM, MB, MBAt, MCo, MH, MHi, MWA, MWiW-C, NN, NjP, PSt, RPB, TxU; Binding D: CSt, NN, ViU; Binding E: BL, DLC, JM, MCo, MH, NjP; Binding F: RPB, ViU, VtMiM.

Note: Copies have been located in a variant binding: black coarse T cloth (rib). Front and back covers: blindstamped triple-rule frame with 3″ leaf-and-vine designs at top and bottom; spine: blindstamped rules enclosing patterns of vertical lines, with gold-stamped 'EMERSON'S | ESSAYS | [rule] | FIRST SERIES'. Flyleaves or back flyleaf. Yellow or yellow coated endpapers. All edges trimmed. Probably a later binding, after the publication of *Essays: Second Series. Locations:* JM, VtMiM (25 April 1845).

A 10.1.b
First edition, second printing [1969]

Essays   *Essays: Second Series.* Columbus, Ohio: Charles E. Merrill, [1969].

Facsimile reprintings of the first editions. Cloth or wrappers. Introduction by Morse Peckham. *Charles E. Merrill Standard Editions*. Copyright, 6 January 1970. Prices: cloth, $6.95; wrappers, $1.35. *Locations:* JM (both).

A 10.2.a
First English edition, first printing (1841)

ESSAYS:

BY

R. W. EMERSON,

OF CONCORD, MASSACHUSETTS.

———

With Preface

By THOMAS CARLYLE.

———

LONDON:

JAMES FRASER, REGENT STREET.

———

MDCCCXLI.

A 10.2.a: 7¹/₂″ × 4³/₈″

[i–v] vi–xiii [xiv–xv] xvi [1–3] 4–41 [42–45] 46–90 [91–93] 94–127 [128–131] 132–166 [167–169] 170–189 [190–193] 194–219 [220–223] 224–243 [244–247] 248–266 [267–269] 270–299 [300–303] 304–324 [325–327] 328–349 [350–353] 354–371 [372]

[A]⁸ B–I¹² K–Q¹² R⁴ S²

Contents: p. i: 'ESSAYS.'; p. ii: printer's imprint; p. iii: title page; p. iv: blank; pp. v–xiii: "Preface by the English Editor," signed 'T. CARLYLE. | *London,* 11*th August,* 1841.'; p. xiv: blank; pp. xv–xvi: contents; p. 1: 'HISTORY. | [rule] | [four lines of verse]'; p. 2: four lines of verse; pp. 3–41: "Essay I. History."; p. 42: blank; p. 43: 'SELF-RELIANCE. | [rule] | Ne te quæsiveris extra. | [rule] | [six lines of verse] | *Epilogue to Beaumont and Fletcher's Honest Man's Fortune.*'; p. 44: four lines of verse; pp. 45–90: "Essay II. Self-Reliance."; p. 91: 'COMPENSATION.'; p. 92: blank; pp. 93–127: "Essay III. Compensation."; p. 128: blank; p. 129: 'SPIRITUAL LAWS.'; p. 130: blank; pp. 131–166: "Essay IV. Spiritual Laws."; p. 167: 'LOVE.'; p. 168: blank; pp. 169–189: "Essay V. Love."; p. 190: blank; p. 191: 'FRIENDSHIP.'; p. 192: blank; pp. 193–219: "Essay VI. Friendship."; p. 220: blank; p. 221: 'PRUDENCE.'; p. 222: blank; pp. 223–243: "Essay VII. Prudence."; p. 244: blank; p. 245: 'HEROISM. | [rule] | 'Paradise is under the shadow of swords.' | *Mahomet.*'; p. 246: blank; pp. 247–266: "Essay VIII. Heroism."; p. 267: 'THE OVER-SOUL. | [rule] | [five lines of verse] | Henry More.'; p. 268: blank; pp. 269–299: "Essay IX. The Over-Soul."; p. 300: blank; p. 301: 'CIRCLES.'; p. 302: blank; pp. 303–324: "Essay X. Circles."; p. 325: 'INTELLECT.'; p. 326: blank; pp. 327–349: "Essay XI. Intellect."; p. 350: blank; p. 351: 'ART.'; p. 352: blank; pp. 353–371: "Essay XII. Art."; p. 372: blank.

Typography and paper: 4¹⁵/₁₆″ (4¹¹/₁₆″) × 3⁷/₈″; wove paper; 28 lines per page. Running heads: rectos: pp. vii–xiii: 'EDITOR'S PREFACE.'; pp. 5–41, 47–89, 95–127, 133–165, 171–189, 195–219, 225–243, 249–265, 271–299, 305–323, 329–349, 355–371: titles of essays; versos: pp. vi–xii: 'EDITOR'S PREFACE.'; p. xvi: 'CONTENTS.'; pp. 4–40, 46–90, 94–126, 132–166, 170–188, 194–218, 224–242, 248–266, 270–298, 304–324, 328–348, 354–370: 'ESSAY' and roman numeral.

Binding: Three styles have been noted:

Binding A: Dark gray green H cloth (fine diaper). Front and back covers: blind-stamped leaf-and-vine border with 2″ floral urn ornament in center; spine: gold-stamped 'EMERSON'S | ESSAYS | [rule] | PREFACE BY | CARLYLE. | JAMES FRASER | LONDON.'. Yellow coated endpapers. All edges trimmed or edges untrimmed.

Binding B: Dark gray green S cloth (diagonal fine rib). Front and back covers: same as Binding A; spine: goldstamped 'EMERSON'S | ESSAYS | [rule] | PREFACE BY | CARLYLE. | NICKISSON | LONDON.'. Yellow or yellow coated endpapers. All edges trimmed. See *Note One,* below.

Binding C: Light green T cloth (rib). Front and back covers: ornate blindstamped vines-and-boxes frame; spine: ornate blindstamped boxes with goldstamped 'EMERSON'S | ESSAYS | [rule] | FIRST SERIES. | WITH PREFACE | BY | THO.ˢ CARLYLE | JOHN CHAPMAN | LONDON.'. Pale green endpapers. All edges trimmed. See *Note Two,* below.

Publication: On 25 June 1841, Carlyle wrote Emerson that Fraser would publish 750 copies and give Emerson half the profits (*CEC,* p. 302). On 18 August 1841, Carlyle wrote Emerson that he was reading proofs (*CEC,* p. 306). Listed in *Athenæum,* no. 721 (21 August 1841), 643. By 31 January 1844, 500 copies had been sold and Emerson received $121.02 (*CEC,* pp. 356–357). As late as May 1848, Emerson received £16 10s. "on a/c of First 'Essays'" from the publisher (*JMN,* X, 418). Price, 10s. Royalty, half profits.

Printing: "LONDON: | PRINTED BY ROBSON, LEVEY, AND FRANKLYN, | Great New Street, Fetter Lane" (p. [ii]).

Locations: Binding A: CtY, DLC, JM, NN, PSt, VtMiM; Binding B: MCo, TxU, ViU; Binding C: MBAt.

Note One: Fraser was succeeded in business by G. W. Nickisson in late 1842; see Nickisson's advertisement, *Publishers' Circular and Booksellers' Record,* 5 (1 October 1842), 285.

Note Two: Binding C is undoubtedly a later binding. The one located copy has a 24-page John Chapman catalogue dated 1 October 1847 inserted at the back. Nickisson's firm had failed in early 1847; see T. Bosworth's advertisement, *Athenæum,* no. 1030 (24 July 1847), p. 798. This book was advertised in *Athenæum,* no. 1047 (20 November 1847), p. 1204, and listed in *Literary Gazette,* no. 1629 (8 April 1848), p. 254.

LATER ENGLISH EDITIONS

A 10.3.a
Second English edition

London: William Smith, MDCCCXLIII.

64 pp., double columns. Cover title. Pamphlet. *Smith's Standard Library,* no. 53. Listed as published between 29 July and 14 August, in *Publishers' Circular and Booksellers' Record,* 6 (15 August 1843), 273, and advertised as "Just published" on p. 278. Carlyle wrote Emerson on 31 October 1843 about a pirated edition to be sold "on greyish paper . . . at two shillings," undoubtedly a reference to this edition (*CEC,* p. 349). Price, 2s. *Not seen.*

A 10.3.b
London: William Smith, MDCCCXLIV.

Cover title. Pamphlet. *Smith's Standard Library,* no. 53. Carlyle wrote Emerson on 17 November 1843 that the pirated *Essays* (see A 10.3.a) had "sold off, or nearly so," and the publisher was "preparing to print another" (*CEC,* p. 352). Advertised as "Just published," in *Athenæum,* no. 842 (16 December 1843), 1098; as "Recently Published," in *Athenæum,* no. 845 (6 January 1844), 2. Price, 2s. *Location:* MH.

A 10.3.c
Essays and Orations. [London: Ingram Cooke, 1853].

133–247 pp., double columns. Combined with *Nature: An Essay. And Orations* (C 1) in two-volumes-in-one format. Also numbered 64 pp. + 47 pp. Cover title. Pamphlet. *The Universal Library,* no. 13, *Essays,* vol. I, part 2. Advertised as "Essays," in *Publishers' Circular and Booksellers' Record,* 16 (15 April 1853), 154, and listed as published between 30 March and 14 April 1853 on p. 147. Price, 1s. *Location:* BL (18 April 1853).

Note: A copy has been noted bound in cloth: JM.

A 10.4.a
Third English edition

London: H. G. Clarke, 1845.

261 pp. Advertised as included in "Clarke's Cabinet Library," no. 36, in *Publishers' Circular and Booksellers' Record,* 7 (15 October 1844), 309. *Location:* MChB.

A 10.4.b
London: H. G. Clarke, 1849.

Listed in *Athenæum,* no. 1107 (13 January 1849), 13. Price, 1s. 6d. *Location:* BL (16 April 1849).

A 10.4.c–d
Twelve Essays. London: George Slater, 1849.

Slater's Shilling Series, no. 1. Listed in *Athenæum,* no. 1118 (31 March 1849), 327. Advertised as published "This day," in *Publishers' Circular and Booksellers' Record,* 12 (2 April 1849), 132. Price, 1s. Reprinted 1850. *Locations:* CtY, JM (26 October 1849), NNC, BE (1850), CtW (1850).

A 10.4.e
London: W. Tweedie, [1852].

Location: BL (24 August 1852).

A 10.5.a
Second American edition, first printing (1847)

ESSAYS:

BY

R. W. EMERSON.

FIRST SERIES.

NEW EDITION.

BOSTON:
JAMES MUNROE AND COMPANY.
1847.

A 10.5.a: $6^{15}/_{16}''$ × $4^{5}/_{16}''$

Entered according to Act of Congress, in the year 1847, by

JAMES MUNROE AND COMPANY,

in the Clerk's Office of the District Court of the District of Massachusetts.

CAMBRIDGE:

STEREOTYPED BY METCALF AND COMPANY,

PRINTERS TO THE UNIVERSITY.

[a–b] [i–v] vi [1–3] 4–36 [37–39] 40–79 [80–83] 84–113 [114–117] 118–149 [150–153] 154–171 [172–175] 176–198 [199–201] 202–219 [220–223] 224–240 [241–243] 244–270 [271–273] 274–292 [293–295] 296–314 [315–317] 318–333 [334–336]

[a]⁴ 1–21⁸

Contents: pp. a–b: blank; p. i: 'ESSAYS.'; p. ii: blank; p. iii: title page; p. iv: copyright page; pp. v–vi: contents; p. 1: 'HISTORY. | [rule] | [four lines of verse]'; p. 2; four lines of verse; pp. 3–36: "Essay I. History."; p. 37: 'SELF-RELIANCE. | [rule] | "Ne te quæsiveris extra." | [rule] | [six lines of verse] | *Epilogue to Beaumont and Fletcher's Honest Man's Fortune.*'; p. 38: four lines of verse; pp. 39–79: "Essay II. Self-Reliance."; p. 80: blank; p. 81: 'COMPENSATION. | [rule] | [14 lines of verse]'; p. 82: 14 lines of verse; pp. 83–113: "Essay III. Compensation."; p. 114: blank; p. 115: 'SPIRITUAL LAWS. | [rule] | [12 lines of verse]'; p. 116: blank; pp. 117–149: "Essay IV. Spiritual Laws."; p. 150: blank; p. 151: 'LOVE. | [rule] | [two lines of verse] | *Koran.*'; p.152: blank; pp. 153–171: "Essay V. Love."; p. 172: blank; p. 173: 'FRIEND-SHIP. | [rule] | [20 lines of verse]'; p. 174: blank; pp. 175–198: "Essay VI. Friendship."; p. 199: 'PRUDENCE. | [rule] | [six lines of verse]'; p. 200: blank; pp. 201–219: "Essay VII. Prudence."; p. 220: blank; p. 221: 'HEROISM. | [rule] | "Paradise is under the shadow of swords." | *Mahomet.* | [rule] | [10 lines of verse]'; p. 222: blank; pp. 223–240: "Essay VIII. Heroism."; p. 241: 'THE OVER-SOUL. | [rule] | [five lines of verse] | *Henry More.* | [11 lines of verse]'; p. 242: blank; pp. 243–270: "Essay IX. The Over-Soul."; p. 271: blank; p. 272: 'CIRCLES. | [rule] | [six lines of verse]'; p. 273–292: "Essay X. Circles."; p. 293: 'INTELLECT. | [rule] | [four lines of verse]'; p. 294: blank; pp. 295–314: "Essay XI. Intellect."; p. 315: 'ART. | [rule] | [28 lines of verse]'; p. 316: blank; pp. 317–333: "Essay XII. Art."; pp. 334–336: blank.

Typography and paper: 5″ (4³/₄″) × 3″; wove paper; 28 lines per page. Running heads: rectos: pp. 5–35, 41–79, 85–113, 119–149, 155–171, 177–197, 203–219, 225–239, 245–269, 275–291, 297–313, 319–333: titles of essays; versos: p. vi: 'CONTENTS.'; pp. 4–36, 40–78, 84–112, 118–148, 154–170, 176–198, 202–218, 224–240, 244–270, 274–292, 296–314, 318–332: 'ESSAY' and roman numeral.

Binding: Four styles have been noted:

Binding A: Brown or dark green A cloth (ribbed morocco); light green horizontal TF cloth (ripple). Front and back covers: blindstamped grolieresque frame with decorative lyre in each corner; spine: blindstamped rules with goldstamped 'EMERSON'S | ESSAYS | FIRST SERIES | [rule] | FOURTH EDITION | [gothic] Munroe & Co.'. Flyleaves. Cream coated or yellow endpapers. All edges trimmed.

Binding B: Brown, light brown, or light purple H cloth (fine diaper); black T cloth (rib). Stamping the same as Binding A, except the spine has goldstamped 'EMERSONS' [*sic*]' and 'MUNROE. [*sic*] & CO.'. Flyleaves. Cream coated or white endpapers. All edges trimmed.

Binding C: Black or medium brown H cloth (fine diaper). Front and back covers: blindstamped triple-rule frame with 6¹/₈″ oval ornament in center; spine: the same as Binding A, except the publisher's imprint is not present. Flyleaves. Yellow endpapers. All edges trimmed.

Binding D: Black T cloth (rib). Front and back covers: blindstamped double-rule frame surrounding frame of florets with floral design inside corners; spine: blindstamped bands with goldstamped 'ESSAYS | BY | EMERSON | [rule] | FIRST SERIES | [gothic] Munroe & Co.'. Flyleaves. Yellow endpapers. All edges trimmed.

Publication: Emerson returned proof of the title page on 31 May 1847 (MH). According to Emerson's journal, 500 copies were printed on 12 September 1847; 141 copies were sold through 1 January 1848, and an additional 323 copies through July 1848 (*JMN*, VII, 484). Deposited for copyright: title, 27 August 1847; book, unknown. Advertised as "just published," in *Boston Daily Advertiser*, 2 October 1847, p. 3. Listed as published between 2 and 9 October 1847, in *Literary World*, 2 (9 October 1847), 236. Inscribed copies: NN (from Emerson, September 1847, binding C), NN (October 1847, binding B), ViU (from Emerson, 1 October 1847, rebound). Emerson's contract called for him to pay for the plates and printing, and to retain the plates and copyright. As of 1 July 1852, Munroe had sold 1,048 copies. Price, unknown. Author's share, 50¢ per copy.

Locations: Binding A: JM, MBAt, MH, MWA; Binding B: CtY, NN, NjP; Binding C: JM, NN; Binding D: CSt.

Note one: Copies in Binding D were probably placed on sale in late 1849; see A 16.1.c, *Note one.*

Note two: The following intercalary poems are present: "History" # (retitled "The Informing Spirit"; see A 18.16), "Self-Reliance" ["Cast the bantling on the rocks"] # (retitled "Power"; see A 18.16), "Compensation" ["The wings of Time are black and white"] #, "Spiritual Laws" #, "Prudence" #, "Heroism" #, "The Over-Soul" # (retitled "Unity"; see A 28), "Circles" ["Nature centres into balls"] #, "Intellect" ["Go speed the stars of thought"] # (later incorporated into ["Pale genius roves alone"]; see A 18.16), and "Art"#.

LATER PRINTINGS WITHIN THE SECOND AMERICAN EDITION

A 10.5.b
Boston: James Munroe, 1850.

'NEW EDITION'. Price, 75¢. *Location:* JM.

A 10.5.c
Boston: Phillips, Sampson, 1850.

'NEW EDITION'. Price, 75¢. Royalty, 15¢. *Location:* NCH.

Note one: Publisher's records indicate copies were bound in half and full calf; no copies have been located.

Note two: Emerson "paid for the printing, & owned the stereotype plates," and was paid "in advance . . . 20 per cent on the retail price" of each printing (25 February 1867, *L*, V, 507).

A 10.5.d
Boston: Phillips, Sampson, 1852.

'NEW EDITION'. 500 copies printed 12 May 1852 (*JMN,* XIII, 479). Price, 75¢. Royalty, 15¢. *Location:* MH.

Note: Phillips, Sampson sold 701 copies of *Essays* between 1850 (when they assumed Munroe's stock) and mid-1852.

A 10.5.e
Boston: Phillips, Sampson, 1854.

'NEW EDITION'. 500 copies printed 17 January 1854 (Emerson's manuscript record [MH]). Price, $1.00. Royalty, 20¢. *Location:* JM.

A 10.5.f
Boston: Phillips, Sampson; New York: J. C. Derby, 1855.

'NEW EDITION.'. Price, $1.00. Royalty, 20¢. *Location:* JM.

A 10.5.g
Boston: Phillips, Sampson, 1856.

'[gothic] New Edition'. 1,000 copies printed February 1856 (*JMN,* XIV, 438). Price, $1.00. Royalty, 20¢. *Location:* OCIW.

A 10.5.h
Boston: Phillips, Sampson, 1857.

'[gothic] New Edition'. 1,000 copies printed 30 September 1856; 250 copies printed on "fine paper" December 1856 (*JMN,* XIV, 452). Price, $1.00. Royalty, 20¢. *Location:* CSt.

A 10.5.i
Boston: Phillips, Sampson, 1858.

'[gothic] New Edition'. 500 copies printed July 1858 (Account Books [MH]). Price, $1.00. Royalty, 20¢. *Location:* MMeT.

Note: Phillips, Sampson failed on 19 September 1859, apparently before selling any of the 500 copies printed on 6 August 1859 (Account Books [MH]).

A 10.5.j
Boston: Ticknor and Fields, M DCCC LX.

500 copies printed 27 September 1860. Price, $1.00. Royalty, 20¢. *Location:* JM.

Note one: Some copies of Phillips, Sampson sheets have been located in Ticknor and Fields bindings, with a cancel title leaf; these are from the 500 copies printed by Phillips, Sampson in August 1859 (see Note to A 10.5.i).

A 10.5.k
Boston: Ticknor and Fields, M DCCC LXI.

Price, $1.00. Royalty, 20¢. *Location:* MNoW.

A 10.5.l
Boston: Ticknor and Fields, M DCCC LXIII.

280 copies printed March–April 1863. Price, $1.25. Royalty, 25¢. *Location:* MH.

A 10.5.m
Boston: Ticknor and Fields, M DCCC LXIV.

280 copies printed 26 April 1864. Price, $1.50. Royalty, 30¢. *Location:* JM.

A 10.5.n
Boston: Ticknor and Fields, M DCCC LXV.

280 copies printed November 1864. Price, $1.50. Royalty, 30¢. *Location:* JM.

Note.   The copyright on *Essays* was renewed 13 May 1865.

A 10.5.o
Boston: Ticknor and Fields, M DCCC LXVI.

280 copies printed July–August 1866. Price, $1.50. Royalty, 30¢. *Location:* JM.

A 10.5.p
Boston: Ticknor and Fields, M DCCC LXVIII.

280 copies printed December 1867–March 1868; 280 copies printed March–May 1868. Price, $2.00. Royalty, 20¢. *Not seen.*

Note one: By a contract of 4 March 1868, Emerson's royalty was changed from 20 per cent to 20¢ per volume.

Note two: Ticknor and Fields was succeeded by Fields, Osgood in October 1868.

A 10.5.q
Boston: Fields, Osgood, 1869.

280 copies printed February 1869; 350 copies in April 1869 (Account Books [MH]). Price, $2.00. Royalty, 20¢. *Location:* OU.

Note one: Fields, Osgood was succeeded by James R. Osgood & Company in January 1871.

Note two: In a "Supplementary article of agreement" to the 4 March 1868 contract, dated 19 February 1870, Emerson's royalty was raised to 30¢ per copy when the price was $2.00 or above.

A 10.5.r
Boston: James R. Osgood, 1871.

Location: CSt.

A 10.5.s
Boston: James R. Osgood, 1873.

150 copies printed 11 June 1873. Price, $2.00. Royalty, 30¢. *Location:* MSaE.

A 10.5.t
Boston: James R. Osgood, 1874.

150 copies printed 27 May 1874. Price, $2.00. Royalty, 30¢. *Location:* MH.

A 10.5.u
Boston: James R. Osgood, 1875.

150 copies printed 21 May 1875. Price, $2.00. Royalty, 30¢. *Location:* JM.

A 10.5.v
Boston: James R. Osgood, 1876.

150 copies printed 18 March 1876. Price, $2.00. *Not seen.*

Note one: Emerson's 1 January 1876 contract with Osgood called for him to receive a flat annual fee of $1,500 for all his books, rather than a per copy royalty.

Note two: James R. Osgood was succeeded by Houghton, Osgood in February 1878.

A 10.5.w
Boston: Houghton, Osgood, 1878.

150 copies printed October–November 1877. Price, $1.50. *Not seen.*

A 10.5.x
Boston: Houghton, Osgood, 1880.

175 copies printed 4 November 1879. Price, $1.50. *Location:* MeWC.

Note: Houghton, Osgood was succeeded by Houghton, Mifflin in May 1880.

A 10.5.y
Boston: Houghton, Mifflin, 1882.

150 copies printed 29 May 1882 and 8 November 1882. Price, $1.50. *Not seen.*

Note: As of 15 January 1884, 15 copies of *Essays* were still in stock.

LATER EDITIONS

A 10.6.a
Fourth English edition

London: John Chapman, 1847.

191 pp. Advertised as included in "Chapman's Library for the People," no. 7. The "Fourth Edition" advertised in *Athenæum,* no. 1047 (20 November 1847), 1204. *Not seen.*

A 10.6.b
London: John Chapman, M.DCCC.LIII.

Cloth or wrappers. *Chapman's Library for the People,* no. 7. Advertised (wrappers) in *Athenæum,* no. 1340 (2 July 1853), 799. Listed (wrappers) as published between 30 June and 14 July 1853, in *Publishers' Circular and Booksellers' Record,* 16 (16 July 1853), 256. Price: wrappers, 2s. *Locations:* cloth, JM, RPB; wrappers, BL (29 June 1853), MCo.

A 10.7
First French edition (1851)

ESSAIS | DE | PHILOSOPHIE | AMÉRICAINE | PAR RALPH EMERSON | CITOYEN DES ETATS-UNIS D'AMÉRIQUE | Traduits en français | ET PRÉCÉDÉS D'UNE INTRODUCTION | PAR ÉMILE MONTÉGUT | [rule] | PARIS | CHARPENTIER, LIBRAIRE-ÉDITEUR | 19, RUE DE LILLE | 1851

311 pp. Wrappers. Contains *Essays* and "The Uses of Great Men." *Location:* MB.

A 10.8
First German edition (1858)

Versuche. Hannover: Carl Meyer, 1858.

448 pp. Translated by G. Fabricius. Contains *Essays* and *Essays: Second Series.* *Location:* ViU.

A 10.9.a–b
Essays First and Second Series. Boston: Ticknor and Fields, 1865.

515 pp. "Blue and Gold Edition." According to a contract of 2 January 1865, Ticknor and Fields paid for and retained the plates, and Emerson retained copyright. 3,000 copies printed. Deposited for copyright: title, 22 March 1865; book, 26 April 1865. Advertised for November-December 1864, in *Atlantic,* 14 (October 1864), wrappers; as "Published this day," in *Boston Daily Advertiser,* 6 April 1865, p. 3. Price, $1.50; also in various gift bindings at various prices. Royalty, 10¢. Reprinted 1866. All copies sold by 1 July 1883. *Locations:* JM, DLC (26 April 1865, 1866).

A 10.10.a
The Twenty Essays of Ralph Waldo Emerson. London: Bell & Daldy, 1870.

257 pp. *Bohn's Cheap Series.* Contains *Essays* and *Essays: Second* Series (except "New England Reformers"). Price, 1s. 6d. *Location:* CtY.

A 10.10.b–c
London: George Bell & Sons, 1876.

Bohn's Cheap Series. Reprinted 1883; listed in *Bookseller,* no. 308 (5 July 1883), 673. *Location:* CaOTU (1876).

PRINTINGS FROM THE "LITTLE CLASSIC EDITION" PLATES

A 10.11.a

[all within a double-rule frame; outer frame is red with boxed corners] [red] ESSAYS. | BY | RALPH WALDO EMERSON. | [red] *First Series.* | NEW AND REVISED EDITION. | [ornate rule] | [red] BOSTON: | JAMES R. OSGOOD AND COMPANY, | Late Ticknor & Fields, and Fields, Osgood, & Co. | [red] 1876.

290 pp. Vol. [II] of "Little Classic Edition" (see B 3). Listed in *Publishers' Weekly,* 9 (24 June 1876), 810. Copyright, 5 June 1876. Price, $1.50. Royalty: see Note to A 10.5.v. *Locations:* BL (12 April 1877), JM.

A 10.11.b
Boston: James R. Osgood, 1877.

280 copies printed June 1877 and 14 August 1877. Price, $1.50. *Not seen.*

A 10.11.c
Boston: James R. Osgood, 1878.

280 copies printed 8 December 1877. Price, $1.50. *Location:* MWC.

Note: James R. Osgood was succeeded by Houghton, Osgood in February 1878.

A 10.11.d
Boston: Houghton, Osgood, 1878.

280 copies printed 1 July 1878. Price, $1.50. *Not seen.*

A 10.11.e
Boston: Houghton, Osgood, 1879.

280 copies printed 3 October 1878 and July 1879; 520 copies on 15 February 1879. Price, $1.50. *Location:* MH.

A 10.11.f
Boston: Houghton, Osgood, 1879.

Combined with *Essays: Second Series* in two-volumes-in-one format as vol. I of the "Fireside Edition" (see B 4). 500 copies printed 15 August 1879. *Location:* KU.

A 10.11.g
Boston: Houghton, Osgood, 1880.

Combined with *Essays: Second Series* in two-volumes-in-one format as vol. I of the "Fireside Edition" (see B 4). 500 copies printed 6 February 1880. *Location:* JM.

Note: Houghton, Osgood was succeeded by Houghton, Mifflin in May 1880.

A 10.11.h
Boston: Houghton, Mifflin, 1880.

500 copies printed 13 May 1880. Price, $1.50. *Not seen.*

A 10.11.i
Boston: Houghton, Mifflin, 1881.

500 copies printed 24 January 1881. Price, $1.50. *Location:* MSaE.

A 10.11.j
Boston: Houghton, Mifflin, 1881.

Combined with *Essays: Second Series* in two-volumes-in-one format as vol. I of the "Fireside Edition" (see B 4). 500 copies printed 7 December 1880. *Location:* MWelC.

A10.11.k
Boston: Houghton, Mifflin, 1882.

500 copies printed 18 August 1881, 2 March 1882, 12 May 1882, and 26 July 1882. Price, $1.50. *Location:* OMC.

A 10.11.l
Boston: Houghton, Mifflin, 1882.

Combined with *Essays: Second Series* in two-volumes-in-one format as vol. I of the "Fireside Edition" (see B 4). 500 copies printed 4 October 1881, 13 May 1882, and 7 August 1882. *Location:* TSewU.

A 10.11.m
Boston: Houghton, Mifflin, 1883.

500 copies printed 20 November 1882, 27 January 1883, 24 April 1883, and 9 October 1883. *Location:* JM.

A 10.11.n
Boston: Houghton, Mifflin, 1883.

Combined with *Essays: Second Series* in two-volumes-in-one format as vol. I of the "Fireside Edition" (see B 4). 270 copies printed 12 January 1883. *Location:* JM.

A 10.11.o
Boston: Houghton, Mifflin, 1884.

Cloth or wrappers. Cloth: 500 copies printed 14 January 1884 and 22 August 1884. *Not seen.* Wrappers: 1,000 copies printed 12 June 1884, 19 June 1884, and 29 July 1884. *Revised Copyright Edition.* Advertised as "Cheap Edition," in *Publishers' Weekly,* 27 (14 March 1885), 299. According to the publisher's records, published 14 June 1884. Price, 15¢. *Location:* JM.

A 10.11.p
Boston: Houghton, Mifflin, 1885.

Wrappers. 1,000 copies printed 7 October 1884; 500 copies on 21 March 1885, 5 May 1885, 30 June 1885, 8 October 1885, and 12 November 1885. *Not seen.*

A 10.11.q
Boston: Houghton, Mifflin, 1886.

Cloth or wrappers. Cloth: 270 copies printed 30 November 1885 and 3 April 1886. *Not seen.* Wrappers: 500 copies printed 3 February 1886 and May–June 1886. *Not seen.*

A 10.11.r
Boston: Houghton, Mifflin, 1887.

Cloth or wrappers. Cloth: 270 copies printed 11 September 1886, 10 February 1887, and 3 August 1887; 500 copies on 27 October 1887. *Location:* JM. Wrappers: 500 copies printed 13 October 1886, 19 February 1887, and 9 August 1887. Referred to as "Chautauqua Edition" (see Edward Waldo Emerson to Houghton, Mifflin, 8 September 1887, Houghton Mifflin Company). *Not seen.*

A 10.11.s
Boston and New York: Houghton, Mifflin, 1888.

Cloth or wrappers. Cloth: 500 copies printed 27 January 1888, 13 July 1888, and 22 October 1888. Bound in medium blue V cloth (smooth), rather than "Little Classic Edition" binding, as are subsequent reprintings (see illustration at B 3). *Location:* NBuU. Wrappers: 500 copies printed 5 December 1887, 21 March 1888, and 20 August 1888; 1,000 copies on 12 November 1888. *Location:* JM.

A 10.11.t
Boston and New York: Houghton, Mifflin, 1889.

500 copies printed 30 April 1889. *Location:* NmU.

Note. Beginning in 1889, copies in wrappers were advertised as included in the "Riverside Paper Series," no. 12, for 50¢.

A 10.11.u
Boston and New York: Houghton, Mifflin, 1890.

500 copies printed 26 October 1889, ca. June 1890, and ca. September 1890. *Location:* JM.

A 10.11.v
Boston and New York: Houghton, Mifflin, 1891.

500 copies printed ca. May 1891. *Not seen.* Also in *Garnet Series, Chautauqua Edition:* 750 copies printed 19 June 1891. *Location:* MNoW.

A 10.11.w
Boston and New York: Houghton, Mifflin, 1892.

500 copies printed 31 October 1891, 26 February 1892, and 27 September 1892. *Location:* MHi.

A 10.11.x
Boston and New York: Houghton, Mifflin, 1893.

500 copies printed 24 March 1893 and 30 October 1893. *Location:* JM.

A 10.11.y
Boston and New York: Houghton, Mifflin, 1894.

500 copies printed 27 August 1894. *Not seen.*

A 10.11.z
Boston and New York: Houghton, Mifflin, 1895.

500 copies printed 23 July 1895. *Location:* ViU.

A 10.11.aa
Boston and New York: Houghton, Mifflin, 1896.

500 copies printed 31 July 1896. *Location:* JM.

A 10.11.bb
Boston and New York: Houghton, Mifflin, 1897.

500 copies printed 30 February 1897 and 9 September 1897. *Not seen.*

A 10.11.cc
Boston and New York: Houghton, Mifflin, 1898.

500 copies printed 19 August 1898. *Not seen.*

A 10.11.dd
Boston and New York: Houghton, Mifflin, 1899.

500 copies printed 26 September 1899. *Location:* MH.

A 10.11.ee
Boston and New York: Houghton, Mifflin, [n.d.].

Approximately 4,700 copies were sold between 1900 and 1923. *Location:* JM.

Note one: Approximately 22,000 copies of *Essays* printed from the "Little Classic Edition" plates were sold between 1876 and 1923, when the title was apparently allowed to go out of print in this format.

Note two: The "Little Classic Edition" plates were ordered destroyed 14 October 1929.

A 10.12.a–s
Essays. London: Macmillan, 1883.

538 pp. *Essays* and *Essays: Second Series.* Vol. II of the *Works* (see B 6). Reprinted (usually with dual New York imprint) 1884, 1885, 1888, 1891, 1893, 1895, 1897, 1899, 1900, 1901, 1903, 1906, 1910, 1920, 1924, 1929. Also reprinted in "Cheap Edition," 1911, 1921. *Locations:* BL (21 May 1883), CCC.

PRINTINGS FROM THE RIVERSIDE EDITION PLATES

A 10.13.a
Riverside Edition (trade), first printing (1883)

ESSAYS | by | RALPH WALDO EMERSON | *FIRST SERIES* | [gothic] New and Revised Edition | [publisher's logo] | BOSTON | HOUGHTON, MIFFLIN AND COMPANY | New York: 11 East Seventeenth Street | [gothic] The Riverside Press, Cambridge | 1883

343 pp. Vol. II of the *Riverside Edition,* trade printing (see B 7). 1,000 copies printed 22 August 1883; 500 copies on 6 October 1883. Listed in *Publishers' Weekly,* 24 (29 September 1883), 455. According to the publisher's records, published 8 September 1883. Copyright, 20 October 1883. Price, $1.75. *Locations:* DLC (6 October 1883), JM.

Note: Copies have been noted with a pine branch on the title page instead of the publisher's logo.

A 10.13.b
Riverside Edition (Copyright), second (English) printing (1883)

ESSAYS | BY | RALPH WALDO EMERSON | *FIRST SERIES* | [gothic] The Riverside Edition | (COPYRIGHT) | LONDON | GEORGE ROUTLEDGE AND SONS | BROADWAY, LUDGATE HILL | NEW YORK: 9, LAFAYETTE PLACE | 1883

Vol. II of the *Riverside Edition (Copyright),* English trade printing (see B 10). 1,000 copies printed 16 August 1883. Listed in *Athenæum,* no. 2916 (15 September 1883), 337; as published between 17 and 29 September 1883, in *Publishers' Circular and Booksellers' Record,* 46 (1 October 1883), 893. Price, 3s. 6d. *Locations:* BC (24 October 1883), BO (6 November 1883), BL (8 December 1883), CaBVaU.

A 10.13.c₁
Riverside Edition (large paper), third printing, American issue (1883)

[red] ESSAYS | BY | RALPH WALDO EMERSON | *FIRST SERIES* | [gothic] New and Revised Edition | [pine branch] | [red] CAMBRIDGE | [gothic] Printed at the Riverside Press | 1883

Vol. II of the *Riverside Edition,* large paper printing (see B 8). 500 copies printed 21 September 1883. Limited to 500 numbered copies. Sold out within a year. Price, $4.00. *Locations:* JM, TxU.

A 10.13.c₂
Riverside Edition (large paper), third printing, English issue (1883)

Title page is the same as in the American issue, except for publisher's imprint: 'LONDON | KEGAN PAUL, TRENCH, & CO., I, PATERNOSTER SQUARE | MDCCCLXXXIII'.

Vol. II of the *Riverside Edition,* large paper printing for English subscribers (see B 9). 25 title leaves printed 21 September 1883. Title leaf is a cancel. Limited to 25 signed and numbered copies. *Location:* JM.

A 10.13.d
Boston and New York: Houghton, Mifflin, 1884.

500 copies printed 14 December 1883, 3 January 1884, 26 March 1884, and 26 July 1884. *Location:* JM.

A 10.13.e
Boston and New York: Houghton, Mifflin, 1885.

500 copies printed 16 October 1884, 14 February 1885, 6 July 1885, and 19 October 1885. *Location:* JM.

A 10.13.f
London and New York: George Routledge and Sons, 1885.

1,000 copies printed 27 October 1885. *Not seen.*

A 10.13.g
Boston and New York: Houghton, Mifflin, 1886.

500 copies printed 26 January 1886 and 21 April 1886. *Location:* JM.

A 10.13.h
Boston and New York: Houghton, Mifflin, 1887.

500 copies printed 2 October 1886, 21 December 1886, 28 January 1887, 28 July 1887, and 22 October 1887. *Location:* JM.

A 10.13.i
Boston and New York: Houghton, Mifflin, 1888.

500 copies printed 31 December 1887, 17 April 1888, 8 August 1888, and 21 November 1888. *Location:* MiU.

Note: Edward Waldo Emerson wrote Houghton, Mifflin on 8 August 1888 that the copyright for *Essays* had expired (Houghton Mifflin Company).

A 10.13.j
Boston and New York: Houghton, Mifflin, 1889.

500 copies printed 7 March 1889 and 13 September 1889. *Location:* NBu.

A 10.13.k
London [&c.]: George Routledge and Sons, 1889.

500 copies printed 10 January 1889. *Location:* JM.

A 10.13.l
Essays First and Second Series. Boston and New York: Houghton, Mifflin, 1889.

Combined with *Essays: Second Series* in two-volumes-in-one format. Cloth or wrappers. Listed in the publisher's records as "Popular Edition." Listed in *Publishers' Weekly,* 36 (21 December 1889), 950. According to the publisher's records, published 16 November 1889. Price: cloth, $1.00; wrappers, 50¢. Numerous reprintings. *Not seen.*

Note: Allowed to go out of stock by 1 October 1898, by which time approximately 10,200 copies in cloth and 4,300 copies in wrappers had been sold.

A 10.13.m
Boston and New York: Houghton, Mifflin, 1890.

500 copies printed 18 January 1890 and ca. September 1890. *Location:* MH.

A 10.13.n
Boston and New York: Houghton, Mifflin, 1891.

500 copies printed ca. March 1891 and 27 July 1891. *Location:* JM.

A 10.13.o
Boston and New York: Houghton, Mifflin, 1892.

500 copies printed 6 January 1892, 12 May 1892, and 29 November 1892. *Location:* JM.

A 10.13.p
Essays. London, Manchester, and New York: George Routledge and Sons, 1893.

Combined with *Essays: Second Series* in two-volumes-in-one format. *Sir John Lubbock's Hundred Books,* no. 50. Published May 1893. Price, 3s. 6d. Undated reprints. *Locations:* BL (31 May 1893), BC (11 July 1893), BO (21 July 1893), JM (n.d.).

A 10.13.q
Boston and New York: Houghton, Mifflin, 1893.

500 copies printed 16 June 1893. *Location:* NcU.

A 10.13.r
Boston and New York: Houghton, Mifflin, 1894.

500 copies printed 18 January 1894 and 24 October 1894. *Location:* JM.

A 10.13.s
Standard Library Edition printing [1894]

ESSAYS | BY | RALPH WALDO EMERSON | *FIRST SERIES* | [pine branch] | BOSTON AND NEW YORK | HOUGHTON, MIFFLIN AND COMPANY | [gothic] The Riverside Press, Cambridge

Vol. II of the *Standard Library Edition* (see B 11). 1,000 copies printed 31 October 1894. Reprinted: 1,000 copies on 30 March 1895, 30 June 1896, and 31 December 1897. *Location:* JM.

A 10.13.t
Boston and New York: Houghton, Mifflin, 1895.

500 copies printed 13 August 1895. *Location:* JM.

A 10.13.u
Boston and New York: Houghton, Mifflin, 1896.

500 copies printed 19 May 1896. *Location:* RPB.

A 10.13.v
Boston and New York: Houghton, Mifflin, 1897.

500 copies printed 17 April 1897. *Location:* JM.

A 10.13.w
Boston and New York: Houghton, Mifflin, 1898.

500 copies printed 12 January 1898. *Location:* JM.

A 10.13.x
Essays First and Second Series. Boston and New York: Houghton, Mifflin, 1898.

Combined with *Essays: Second Series* in two-volumes-in-one format. *Cambridge Classics; Author's Edition Complete; The Riverside Library.* According to the publisher's records, published 1 October 1898. Price, $1.00. Reprinted 1899, 1900, [n.d.]; the latest reprinting noted is the 13th printing. *Locations:* JM (1898, 1899, n.d.), MnU (1900).

Note: By 2 January 1911, approximately 6,800 copies had been sold and 128 were still in stock.

A 10.13.y
Boston and New York: Houghton, Mifflin, 1899.

500 copies printed ca. December 1898; 270 copies on 25 May 1899. *Location:* MA.

A 10.13.z
Boston and New York: Houghton, Mifflin, 1900.

500 copies printed 10 November 1899. *Not seen.*

A 10.13.aa
London: George Routledge and Sons, 1900.

Location: BLdU.

A 10.13.bb
London: George Routledge and Sons, 1902.

Location: JM.

A 10.13.cc
London: George Routledge & Sons, 1903.

Combined with *Nature; Addresses, and Lectures* and *Essays: Second Series* in three-volumes-in-one format as vol. I of the "Sovereign Edition" (see B 12). 1,000 copies printed 16 September 1903. *Location:* InU.

A 10.13.dd
Fireside Edition printing (1909)

[all within red double-rule frame with red floral ornaments in each corner] THE WORKS OF | [red gothic] Ralph Waldo Emerson | ESSAYS | FIRST SERIES | [engraving of man reading book in chair before fireplace] | [gothic] Fireside Edition | BOSTON AND NEW YORK | MDCCCCIX

Vol. II of the *Fireside Edition* (see B 13). 500 copies printed 29 September 1909 and 9 February 1910. *Location:* JM.

A 10.13.ee
Boston and New York: Jefferson Press, [ca. 1912].

Combined with *Essays: Second Series* in two-volumes-in-one format as vol. [II] of the "Jefferson Press Edition" (see B 14). *Location:* CtW.

A 10.13.ff
New York: Sulley and Kleinteich, [ca. 1912].

Vol. II of the *University Edition* (see B 15). *Location:* JM.

A 10.13.gg
Boston and New York: Houghton, Mifflin, [n.d.].

Approximately 3,000 copies sold between 1901 and 1913. *Location:* JM.

Note: Approximately 21,000 copies of *Essays* in the *Riverside Edition* were sold between 1883 and 1913, when the title was apparently allowed to go out of print in this format.

A 10.13.hh
London: George Routledge and Sons, [n.d.].

Location: CaQMM.

A 10.13.ii
London: Waverley Book Company, [n.d.].

Vol. II of the "Waverley" *Riverside Edition* (see B 16). *Location:* JM.

LATER EDITIONS

A 10.14.a–c
NewYork: John B. Alden, 1884.

326 pp. Also advertised as included in "Brilliant Books" series. Reprinted 1885, [n.d.]. *Locations:* InNd (1884), JM (1885, n.d.).

A 10.14.d–e
New York: John W. Lovell, [1884].

Wrappers. *Lovell's Library,* vol. 7, no. 373, 29 April 1884. Advertised in *Publishers' Weekly,* 25 (14 June 1884), 684. Price, 20¢. *Location:* MCo. Cloth. Combined with *Essays: Second Series* in two-volumes-in-one format in *Lovell's Universal Series. Location:* JM. Reprinted 1890 in wrappers in *Lovell's Literature Series,* no. 83, 14 February 1890. Price, 25¢. *Location:* ViU.

A 10.14.f
New York: James B. Millar, 1884.

Location: JM.

A 10.14.g
Chicago: American Book Mart, 1888.

Location: JM.

A 10.14.h
New York: Merrill and Baker, [1896?].

Combined with *Essays: Second Series* in two-volumes-in-one format in *Levant Edition*. Also advertised as included in "Lotus Classics" and "World's Famous Books." *Location:* OCIW.

A 10.14.i
New York: American Publishers Corporation, [n.d.].

Combined with *Essays: Second Series* in two-volumes-in-one format. *Location:* CaB-VaU.

A 10.14.j
Chicago and New York: Belford, Clarke, [n.d.].

Household Edition. Location: JM.

A 10.14.k
New York: Clarke, Given, & Hooper, [n.d.].

Combined with *Essays: Second Series* in two-volumes-in-one format. Also advertised as included in "University Edition." *Location:* DCU.

A 10.14.l
Boston: Estes and Lauriat, [n.d.].

Advertised as combined with *Essays: Second Series* in two-volumes-in-one format. *Not seen.*

A 10.14.m
New York: Hovendon, [n.d.].

Location: JM.

A 10.14.n
New York: International Book Company, [n.d.].

Aldine Edition; Popular Edition. Locations: LNHT (*Aldine*), JM (*Popular*).

A 10.14.o
Boston: Joseph Knight, [n.d.].

Combined with *Essays: Second Series* in two-volumes-in-one format. *Location:* JM.

A 10.14.p
New York: Frank F. Lovell, [n,d.].

Location: JM.

A 10.14.q
New York: Lovell, Coryell, [n.d.].

Standard Edition. Also advertised combined with *Essays: Second Series* in two-volumes-in-one format. *Location:* JM.

A 10.14.r
Albany, N.Y.: James B. Lyon, [n.d.].

Location: N.

A 10.14.s
New York: National Book Company, [n.d.].

Combined with *Essays: Second Series* in two-volumes-in-one format. *Location:* JM.

A 10.14.t
New York: United States Book Company, Successors to John W. Lovell Company, [n.d.].

Stamped on spine is "Hovendon Company." *Location:* JM.

A 10.15.a–c
New York: John B. Alden, 1886.

254 pp. Reprinted 1891, 1892. *Locations:* JM (1886, 1891), MNoW (1892).

A 10.15.d
New York: Hurst, [n.d.].

Arlington Edition. Location: JM.

A 10.16.a
New York: Worthington, 1887.

320 pp. Also *Franklin Edition. Locations:* JM (both).

A 10.16.b
New York: Hurst, [n.d.].

Also *Arlington Edition. Locations:* JM, ViU (*Arlington*).

A 10.17.a–f
Philadelphia: David McKay, 1888.

396 pp. Also *American Classic Series.* Listed in *Publishers' Weekly,* 34 (22 September 1888), 291. Also advertised in a boxed set with *Essays: Second Series.* Price, $1.00. Reprinted 1889, 1890, 1891, 1892, [n.d.]. Also combined with *Essays: Second Series* in two-volumes-in-one format in 1891 and 1892. *Locations:* JM (1888, 1889, 1890, n.d.), MH (1891), MWC (1892), WaU (1891 combined), IdU (1892 combined).

A 10.18
New York: John B. Alden, 1890.

199 pp. *Location:* NNUT.

A 10.19.a
Essays First and Second Series. New York: A. L. Burt, [1890].

402 pp. Also *Cornell Series; Burt's Library of the World's Best Books.* Listed in *Publishers' Weekly,* 38 (4 October 1890), 490. Price, $1.00. *Locations:* JM, MH (*Library*).

A 10.19.b
New York: P. F. Collier and Son, [n.d.].

Combined with *Essays: Second Series* in two-volumes-in-one format in *American Authors in Prose and Poetry* series, *Emerson,* vol. I. *Location:* MH.

A 10.19.c
New York: F. M. Lupton, [n.d.].

Location: JM.

A 10.20
London: David Stott, 1890.

428 pp. Vol. I of *Emerson's Essays*. Edited by Ronald J. McNeill. *The Stott Library*. Published January 1890. Price, 3s. the set. Also advertised a large paper printing of 100 copies. *Locations:* BC (29 July 1890), JM.

A 10.21.a–d
Philadelphia: Henry Altemus, 1892.

322 pp. Advertised as included in "Altemus Library," no. 6, "Illustrated Vademecum Series," no. 51, "New Vademecum Series," and "Roycroft Series," no. 51, in various bindings at various prices. Reprinted 1894, 1895, [n.d.]. *Locations:* JM (1892, 1894, n.d.), MH (1895).

A 10.22.a
New York and Boston: H. M. Caldwell, [1892?].

307 pp. Also advertised as included in "Illustrated Library of Famous Books" and "Superb Series," no. 8. Price, 75¢. *Location:* JM.

A 10.22.b
New York: Home Book Company, [n.d.].

Also advertised as included in "New Beverly Edition." *Location:* JM.

A 10.22.c
New York: Lovell Brothers, [n.d.].

Hawthorn Series. Location: JM.

A 10.22.d
New York: F. M. Lupton, [n.d.].

Combined with *Essays: Second Series* in two-volumes-in-one format. *Location:* JM.

A 10.23.a–b
Chicago: Donohue, Henneberry, 1893.

304 pp. Reprinted [n.d.]. *Locations:* JM (1893), AzU (n.d.).

A 10.23.c
Chicago: Donohue Brothers, [n.d.].

Also advertised as included in "Dresden Edition." *Location:* JM.

A 10.23.d
Chicago: Monarch, [n.d.].

Location: KyL.

A 10.23.e
Chicago: Thompson & Thomas, [n.d.].

Noted with both "267 Wabash Ave." and "338 Wabash Ave." imprints. *Locations:* MH (267), IdU (338).

A 10.23.f
Chicago: Weeks, [n.d.].

Location: JM.

A 10.24.a
Essays. New York: Hurst, [1896].

208 pp. + 134 pp. of five essays from *Essays: Second Series.* Also advertised as included in "Cambridge Classics," no. 34. Price, 25¢. *Location:* JM.

A 10.24.b
Philadelphia: Rodgers, [n.d.].

Location: JM.

A 10.25
Emerson. London: Arthur L. Humphreys, [1899].

345 pp. Leather. *Location:* MH.

A 10.26.a
Chicago: W. B. Conkey, [1900].

306 pp. Combined with *Essays: Second Series* in two-volumes-in-one format; the same format in *Oxford Series. Locations:* DLC (18 August 1900), JM (*Oxford*).

A 10.26.b
Essays. Springfield, Ohio: Crowell Publishing Co., [n.d.].

My Lady's Library, vol. 6. Combined with the Homewood printing of *Essays: Second Series* (see A 16.17.h) in two-volumes-in-one format. *Location:* JM.

A 10.26.c
Emerson's Essays. Chicago and New York: Henneberry, [n.d.].

Combined with *Essays: Second Series* in two-volumes-in-one format. *Location:* RWe.

A 10.26.d
Chicago: Union School Furnishing Co., [n.d.].

Combined with *Essays: Second Series* in two-volumes-in-one format. *Location:* JM.

A 10.27.a–d
London: J. M. Dent, MDCCCCI.

288 pp. Cloth (with dust jacket) or flexible leather. Edited by Walter Jerrold. *The Temple Classics.* Published February 1901. Prices: cloth, 1s. 6d; leather, 2s. Reprinted July 1902, September 1903, September 1904. *Locations:* BL (27 February 1901), DeU (1903), JM (1904).

Note: Advertised as included in "The Temple Classics" in cloth and leather by Macmillan of New York in *Publishers' Weekly,* 59 (23 May 1901), 838. Probably an importation or, possibly, an American issue of the English sheets with a cancel title leaf. *Not seen.*

A 10.28.a–m
Essays. London: Grant Richards, 1901.

354 pp. Cloth (with dust jacket) or flexible leather. Contains *Essays* and *Essays: Second Series*. *The World's Classics,* no. 6 (also identified as vol. I of *Works*). Published October 1901. Reprinted (noted with the following imprints: London [&c.]: Henry Frowde and/or Oxford University Press; London [&c.]: Humphrey Milford, Oxford University Press; London, New York, Toronto: Geoffrey Cumberlege, Oxford University Press): 1902, 1903, 1904, 1905, 1906, 1909, 1912, 1919, 1921, 1927, 1936, 1950. *Locations:* BE (26 March 1902), BO (31 March 1902), JM.

A 10.29.a–c
Essays. London: Blackie and Son, [1903].

312 pp. Also noted with "London, Glasgow, Bombay" imprint. Introduction by Richard Whiteing. Notes by W. Keith Leask. *Red Letter Library*. Also advertised as included in "Wallet Library." Reprinted 1904, 1907. *Locations:* BL (4 January 1904), BE (26 January 1904), BO (28 January 1904), JM.

Note: Advertised as included in "Red Letter Library," no. 12, in cloth and leather, by H. M. Caldwell in *Publishers' Weekly,* 66 (22 October 1904), 961. Probably an importation or, possibly, an American issue of the English sheets with a cancel title leaf. *Not seen.*

A 10.29.d
London: Gresham, [n.d.].

Location: JM.

A 10.30.a
London: Isbister, 1903.

269 pp. *Isbister's Anglo Saxon Library*. Published April 1903. Price, 1s. 6d. *Locations:* BE (7 July 1903), BC (9 July 1903), BO (9 July 1903).

A 10.30.b
New York: Thomas Y. Crowell, [n.d.].

Flexible leather. Also combined with *Essays: Second Series* in two-volumes-in-one format. *Locations:* JM, CaBVaU (combined).

PRINTINGS FROM THE CENTENARY EDITION PLATES

A 10.31.a
Autograph Centenary Edition (large paper), first printing (1903)

RALPH WALDO EMERSON | [red] Essays | [red] First Series | [pine tree] | CAMBRIDGE | [red gothic] Printed at the Riverside Press | 1903

445 pp. Vol. II of the *Autograph Centenary Edition* (see B 19). Limited to 600 signed and numbered copies printed by 16 May 1903. Copyright, 16 May 1903. Sold out by 5 April 1906. Price, $6.00. *Locations:* DLC (20 May 1903), JM.

A 10.31.b$_1$
Centenary Edition (trade), second printing, American issue (1903)

ESSAYS | BY | RALPH WALDO EMERSON | FIRST SERIES | [pine tree] | BOSTON AND NEW YORK | HOUGHTON, MIFFLIN AND COMPANY, | [gothic] The Riverside Press, Cambridge | 1903

Dust jacket. Vol. II of the *Centenary Edition,* trade printing (see B 18). 1,000 copies printed 29 May 1903 and 5 November 1903. According to the publisher's records, published 23 May 1903. Listed in *Publishers' Weekly,* 63 (6 June 1903), 1324. Copyright, 16 May 1903. Price, $1.75. *Location:* JM.

Note: Numerous reprintings with undated title pages. Approximately 6,000 copies printed between 1 January 1904 and 31 December 1910. Approximately 10,900 copies sold through 1923.

A 10.31.b$_2$
English issue

London: A. P. Watt & Son, [1903].

Vol. II of the English *Centenary Edition* (see B 21). American sheets with Watt's label pasted on the title page. Price, 6s. *Locations:* BE (22 June 1903), BL (23 June 1903), BC (25 June 1903).

A 10.31.c
Boston and New York: Houghton, Mifflin, 1903.

Vol. II of the *Concord Edition* (see B 20). 1,000 copies printed 30 September 1903. *Location:* JM.

Note: Numerous reprintings with undated title pages. Approximately 3,100 copies sold by 31 December 1910.

A 10.31.d
Boston and New York: Houghton Mifflin, [1914].

Vol. II of the *Riverside Pocket Edition* (see B 22). Approximately 4,800 copies sold between 1914 and 1922. *Not seen.*

A 10.31.e
Boston and New York: Houghton Mifflin, 1921.

369 pp. (text without the notes). Combined with *Essays: Second Series* in two-volumes-in-one format as vol. I of *Emerson's Complete Works* (see B 23). *Location:* WaU.

A 10.31.f
New York: Wm. H. Wise, 1923.

Combined with *Nature; Addresses, and Lectures* in two-volumes-in-one format as vol. I of the *Current Opinion Edition* (see B 24). *Location:* JM.

A 10.31.g
Essays First and Second Series. Boston and New York: Houghton Mifflin, 1925.

Text without the notes. *Location:* MH.

A 10.31.h
Boston and New York: Houghton Mifflin, 1929.

Combined (text without the notes) with *Essays: Second Series* in two-volumes-in-one format as vol. [I] of the *Harvard Edition* (see B 25). *Location:* JM.

A 10.31.i
New York: Wm. H. Wise, 1929.

Combined with *Nature; Addresses, and Lectures* in two-volumes-in-one format as vol. I of the *Medallion Edition* (see B 26). *Location:* OC.

A 10.31.j–k
New York: AMS Press, [1968].

Vol. II of the "AMS Press" *Centenary Edition* (see B 27). Reprinted 1979. *Locations:* TxU, DLC (9 November 1979).

LATER EDITIONS

A 10.32
Essays. London: George Routledge & Sons; New York: E. P. Dutton, [1905].

391 pp. Dust jacket. Contains *Essays* and *Essays: Second Series. The New Universal Library* (also identified as vol. I of *Works*). Published August 1905. Price, 1s. *Locations:* BL (27 September 1905), JM.

A 10.33
Hammersmith [England]: Doves Press, MDCCCCVI.

312 pp. Stiff vellum wrappers. Printed on paper or vellum. Finished 5 January 1906. *Locations:* BL (14 June 1906; paper), MH (both).

A 10.34.a–r
Essays First and Second Series. London: J. M. Dent & Sons; New York: E. P. Dutton, [1906].

358 pp. Advertised in various bindings at various prices. *Everyman's Library,* no. 12. Published February 1906. Reprinted March 1906, August 1906, June 1907, November 1908, August 1909, October 1910, October 1912, June 1914, March 1916, February 1917, June 1920, 1924, 1927, 1930, 1934, 1938, 1947. *Locations:* BE (22 March 1906), BL (16 March 1906), BO (26 March 1906), MH.

A 10.34.s–w
Emerson's Essays. London: J. M. Dent & Sons; New York: E. P. Dutton, [1955].

Dust jacket. Introduction by Sherman Paul. *Everyman's Library,* no. 12. Published in England, 29 September 1955. Prices: 6s., $1.65. Reprinted 1961, 1963, 1967, 1971. 1971 reprinting seems to be in wrappers only. *Location:* JM.

A 10.35.a
Philadelphia: John D. Morris, [1906].

461 pp. Combined with *Essays: Second Series* as vol. V of the "John D. Morris Edition" (see B 29). Copyright, 13 February 1906. *Location:* JM.

A 10.35.b
Boston and New York: C. T. Brainard, [n.d.].

Vol. I of the *Works* (see B 30). *Location:* NHemH.

A 10.35.c
[New York]: A. L. Burt, [n.d.].

The Home Library. Location: JM.

A 10.35.d
New York: Caxton Society, [n.d.].

Vol. I of the *Works* (see B 31). *Location:* NjR.

A 10.35.e
New York: National Library Co., [n.d.].

Vol. I of the *Works* (see B 32). *Location:* CaOHM.

A 10.35.f
Philadelphia, New York, Chicago: Nottingham Society, [n.d.].

Vol. I of the *Works* (see B 33). *Location:* JM.

A 10.36.a–b
London: George G. Harrap, [1909].

277 pp. *The Harrap Library,* no. 1. Published September 1909. Reprinted November 1926. *Locations:* BL (2 September 1909), JM (both).

A 10.36.c
New York: Dodge, [n.d.].

The Dodge Library. Also advertised as included in "Green Book Series" and "Limp Leather Series." *Location:* JM.

A 10.36.d
New York: Robert M. McBride, [n.d.].

Introduction by Edward Everett Hale. *Chelsea College Classics. Location:* NFQC.

A 10.37.a
New York: Hearst's International Library Co., [1914].

423 pp. Combined with *Essays: Second Series* as vol. I of the *New National Edition* (see B 35). *Location:* DLC (24 June 1914).

A 10.37.b
New York: Tudor, [1942].

Combined with other volumes in the *New National Edition* in one-volume format as the *Works* (see B 36). *Locations:* DLC (12 February 1943), JM.

A 10.37.c
New York: Charles C. Bigelow, [n.d.].

Vol. I of the *Works* (see B 37). *Location:* IaU.

A 10.37.d–e
New York: Bigelow, Brown, [n.d.].

Vol. I of the *Works* (see B 38). Also as *Essays*, with no *Works* designation. *Locations:* JM (both).

A 10.37.f
New York: Bigelow, Smith, [n.d.].

Vol. I of the *Works* (see B 39). *Location:* CaQMM.

A 10.37.g
New York: Brentano's, [n.d.].

Vol. I of the *Writings* (see B 40). *Location:* In.

A 10.37.h
New York: Harper & Brothers, [n.d.].

Vol. I of the *Works* (see B 41). *Location:* JM.

A 10.37.i
Boston and New York: Jefferson Press, [n.d.].

Vol. I of the *Works* (see B 42). *Location:* JM.

A 10.37.j
[N.p.]: Library Society, [n.d.].

Vol. I of the *Works* (see B 43). *Location:* CaQMG.

A 10.37.k
New York: Three Sirens Press, [n.d.].

Vol. I of the *Works* (see B 44). *Location:* MdBE.

A 10.38
New York: Thomas Nelson and Sons, [1918?].

267 pp. Flexible leather. Combined with *Essays: Second Series* in two-volumes-in-one format. *New Century Library.* Also advertised as included in "Nelson Classics." *Location:* JM.

A 10.39.a–c
Essays First and Second Series. New York: Thomas Y. Crowell, [1926].

438 pp. Dust jacket. Introduction by Andrew J. George. Also *Large Type Edition.* Reprinted (with introduction by Irwin Edman) 1951; copyright, 17 August 1951. Reprinted in 1961 in wrappers as *Apollo Editions* A-1 at $1.95. *Locations:* JM (1926, 1961), MU (1951).

A 10.39.d
Essays. New York: Carlton House, [n.d.].

World's Great Thinkers. Location: JM.

A 10.40.a–b
Essays First and Second Series. New York: Macmillan, MCMXXVI.

360 pp. Cloth or half leather. Edited with an introduction by Harold Goddard. *The Modern Readers' Series.* Published November 1926. Copyright, 30 November 1926. Prices: cloth, 80¢; half leather, $1.25. Reprinted October 1937. *Locations:* PSt (1926), CSt (1937).

A 10.41
Washington: National Home Library Foundation, 1932.

172 pp. Wrappers. *Jacket Library,* no. 6. Price, 15¢. *Location:* JM.

A 10.42.a
The Essays of Ralph Waldo Emerson. San Francisco: Limited Editions Club, 1934.

262 pp. Boxed. Contains *Essays* and *Essays: Second Series.* Introduction by Edward F. O'Day. Printed by John Henry Nash. Limited to 1,500 numbered copies, signed by Nash. Copyright, 26 November 1934. *Location:* JM.

A 10.42.b
New York: Heritage Press, [1953].

Boxed. *Heritage Anniversary Edition.* Price, $5.00. *Location:* JM.

A 10.42.c
Norwalk, Conn.: Heritage Press, [1962].

Boxed. *Location:* JM.

A 10.43
Essays. [Reading, Penn.]: Spencer, [1936].

399 pp. Contains *Essays* and *Essays: Second Series. The World's Greatest Literature,* no. 13. *Location:* JM.

A 10.44.a
Emerson's Essays. Boston and New York: Books, Inc., [1943?].

252 pp. Dust jacket. Identified as both *Art-Type Edition* and *The World's Popular Classics.* Also advertised as included in "Duo-Tone Classics." *Location:* JM.

A 10.44.b
Boston and New York: Registered Editions Guild, [n.d.].

Identified as both *Art-Type Edition* and *The World's Popular Classics.* Also advertised as included in "Registered Editions Guild Classics," no. 13. *Location:* JM.

A 10.45
Essays First and Second Series. Mount Vernon, N.Y.: Peter Pauper, [1946].

314 pp. Boxed. Wood engravings by Hans Alexander Mueller. Price, $3.50. *Location:* JM.

A 10.46.a
Essays. New York: Grolier, [1969].

504 pp. Contains *Essays* and *Essays: Second Series.* Introduction by F. B. Sanborn. *The World's Great Classics.* Large type edition. *Location:* MWal.

A 10.46.b
New York: Franklin Watts, [n.d.].

A Watts Ultratype Edition. Price, $7.00. Location: RP.

A 10.47
Cambridge, Mass., and London: The Belknap Press of Harvard University Press, 1979.

368 pp. Dust jacket. Introduction and notes by Joseph Slater. Text established by Alfred R. Ferguson and Jean Ferguson Carr. Vol. II of *Collected Works* (see B 46). Published 3 March 1980. Price, $25.00. *Location:* JM.

UNDATED EDITIONS

A 10.48.a
New York: Wm. L. Allison, [n.d.].

364 pp. *Arundel Series*. Also combined with *Essays: Second Series* in two-volumes-in-one format. *Locations:* JM, NmU (combined).

A 10.48.b
New York: A. L. Burt, [n.d.].

Also combined with *Essays: Second Series* in two-volumes-in-one format. Also advertised as included in "Columbia Series," "Cornell Series," "Home Library," and "New Pocket Edition of Standard Classics." *Locations:* MH (both).

A 10.48.c
New York: Edward, [n.d.].

Location: CaQMBM.

A 10.49
New York: A. L. Burt, [n.d.].

311 pp. *Location:* JM.

A 10.50
New York: Grosset & Dunlap, [n.d.].

302 pp. Combined with *Essays: Second Series* in two-volumes-in-one format. *Location:* JM.

A 10.51
New York: Hurst, [n.d.].

197 pp. Cloth or wrappers. *Locations:* JM (both).

A 10.52
New York: F. M. Lupton, [n.d.].

226 pp. *Location:* JM.

A 10.53.a
Essays. New York and London: Merrill and Baker, [n.d.].

408 pp. Dust jacket. Contains *Essays* and *Essays: Second Series*. *World's Famous Books,* no. 18. *Location:* JM.

A 10.53.b
Chicago: Rand, McNally, [n.d.].

Location: JM.

SEPARATE PUBLICATIONS OF INDIVIDUAL ESSAYS

A 10.54
Art. New York: John B. Alden, [1886].

Wrappers. Advertised as included in "Elzevir Library," no. 214. Price, 2¢. *Not seen.*

Note: Probably from the plates of *Essays* (A 10.15.a).

A 10.55
Compensation. New York: Thomas Y. Crowell, [1902?].

28 pp. Limp leather. *Location:* JM.

A 10.56
Compensation. [Cambridge, Mass.]: Riverside Press, 1903.

70 pp. Boxed. Designed by Bruce Rogers. 530 numbered copies, of which 500 were for sale. Listed in *Publishers' Weekly,* 64 (4 July 1903), 7. According to the publisher's records, published 25 April 1903. Copyright, 20 April 1903. Sold out before publication. Price, $2.00. *Location:* JM.

A 10.57
Compensation. East Aurora, N.Y.: Roycrofters, MCMIV.

44 pp. Limp suede. Completed January 1904. Also advertised 100 copies on Japan vellum in three-quarter leather. *Location:* JM.

A 10.58
Emerson's Essay on Compensation. Sewanee, Tenn.: University Press, 1906.

30 pp. Boards or wrappers. Introduction by Lewis Nathaniel Chase. Prices: boards, $1.00; wrappers, 50¢. *Locations:* TU, InU (wrappers).

A 10.59
Compensation. New York: Platt & Peck, [1910?].

32 pp. Also advertised as included in "Keep-sake Books." Published August 1910. Price, 50¢. *Location:* JM.

A 10.60
Compensation. New York: Barse & Hopkins, [1910?].

29 pp. *The Golden Books.* Also advertised as included in the "Ardsley," "Embassy," "Relyea Classics," "Rockingham," "Savoy," "Shelburne," and "Traymore" series. *Location:* JM.

A 10.61
Compensation. New York: New York Book Company, [1912?].

Advertised as included in "Aurora Edition" series. Price, 40¢. *Not seen.*

A 10.62
Essay on Compensation. East Aurora, N.Y.: Roycrofters, [1917].

69 pp. Boards or limp leather. The colophon is erroneously dated 'MCMXXVII'. *Location:* JM.

A 10.63
Compensation. Baltimore: Norman T. A. Munder, MCMXXIII.

52 pp. Boards. Price, $1.00. *Location:* MNS.

A 10.64
Compensation. New York: Printed for William R. Scott, Publisher, by the Powgen Press, [1936].

41 pp. Designs by C. Barney Moore. Published July 1936. Price, $1.25. Also sold as one of six volumes in the boxed set *American Renaissance Series. Locations:* JM, DLC (set).

A 10.65
Compensation. [Eugene]: University of Oregon, John Henry Nash Fine Arts Press, MCM XXX VII.

27 pp. Limited to 100 copies. *Location:* ICarbS.

A 10.66
Ralph Waldo Emerson's Essay on Compensation. [Washington, D.C.]: Rufus H. Darby Printing Company, [1951].

38 pp. Published Christmas 1951. *Location:* MnU.

A 10.67
Compensation. New York: Kindle Press, 1956.

36 pp. *Location:* MA.

A 10.68
Compensation. Logan, Iowa: Perfection Form, 1971.

Single leaf folded twice to make six pages, printed on five pages only. Head title. *Pamph-lit, The Notebook Reader Series. Location:* JM.

A 10.69
Compensation. New York: H. M. Caldwell, [n.d.].

Advertised as included in "Words of Help" series, no. 33, at various prices. *Not seen.*

Note: Possibly the same as *Compensation [and Spiritual Laws]* (A 10.158).

A 10.70
Compensation. South Framingham, Mass.: Caxton Society, [n.d.].

Unpaged (15 leaves). Cover title. Pamphlet. *The Caxton Brochures,* series A, no. 2. *Location:* MH.

A 10.71
Compensation. New York: Thomas Y. Crowell, [n.d.].

36 pp. Advertised as included in the "Elzevir," "Hollywood," "Laurel," and "San Rafael" series. *Location:* JM.

A 10.72
Compensation. New York: Grosset & Dunlap, [n.d.].

29 pp. *Location:* JM.

A 10.73
Compensation. London: George G. Harrap, [n.d.].

36 pp. Wrappers. *Location:* CU.

A 10.74
Compensation. Philadelphia: George W. Jacobs, [n.d.].

37 pp. Self-wrappers. *Cadogan Booklets,* no. 29. *Location:* ViU.

Note: An English printing (in Glasgow) for American sale, undoubtedly preceded by an English printing for domestic sale, possibly by either Astolat or Gowans & Gray.

A 10.75
Compensation. Farmington, Maine: D. H. Knowlton, [n.d.].

32 pp. Wrappers. *Excelsior 5c Classics.* Price, 5¢. *Location:* MeHi.

A 10.76
Compensation. New York: Maynard, Merrill, [n.d.].

Advertised as included in "Maynard's English Classics Series," no. 194. Price, 12¢. *Not seen.*

A 10.77
Compensation. New York: Newton and Cartwright, [n.d.].

32 pp. *Location:* VtJC.

A 10.78
Friendship. New York: John B. Alden; Chicago: Alden Book Co., 1886.

[149]–167 pp. Wrappers. *The Elzevir Library,* vol. 5, no. 212, 22 June 1886. Price, 3¢. *Location:* IdPS.

Note: From the plates of *Essays* (A 10.15.a).

A 10.79
Friendship. London: n.p., 1894.

48 pp. Illustrated by Arthur A. Dixon and Maude Angell. Listed in *British Museum Catalogue* as included in "Laurel Wreath" series. *Not seen.*

A 10.80
The Essay on Friendship. East Aurora, N.Y.: Roycrofters, [1899].

53 pp. Boards or limp leather. Completed 10 July 1899. Also 50 numbered copies "specially illuminated by hand" and signed by Elbert Hubbard and the illustrator, Minnie Gardner. Also advertised 25 copies on Japan vellum. *Locations:* JM, MH (illuminated).

A 10.81
Friendship and Other Essays. New York: Dodge, [1902].

56 pp. Self-wrappers. Contains "Friendship" only. Also advertised as included in "Dodge Classics," "Green Book Series," and "Vine Tree Series." *Location.* JM.

A 10.82.a
Friendship. London: Astolat, MDCCCCIII.

25 pp. *Locations:* BL (25 February 1904), BC (26 February 1904), BE (26 February 1904), JM.

A 10.82.b
Philadelphia: George W. Jacobs, [n.d.].

Also advertised as included in "Cadogan Booklets." *Location:* CtY.

A 10.82.c
London: Siegle, Hill, [n.d.].

Cloth or limp leather. Also advertised as included in "Oakleaf Series." *Location:* JM.

A 10.83
Friendship. New York and San Francisco: Morgan Shepard, 1906.

38 pp. Decorations designed by Fred W. Goudy. *The Birdalone Series of Essays*. Completed October 1906. *Location:* DLC (7 December 1906).

A 10.84
Friendship. London and Glasgow: Gowans & Gray, 1907.

30 pp. Wrappers. *Cadogan Booklets*, no. 12. *Locations:* BC (22 May 1908), BE (22 May 1908).

A 10.85
An Essay on Friendship. London: George G. Harrap, [1908].

61 pp. Limp leather or wrappers. Miniature book. *Sesame Booklets*, no. 16. *Locations:* BC (10 December 1908), BL (10 December 1908), BO (12 December 1908), JM.

A 10.86
Friendship. [London]: Siegle, Hill, [1908].

83 pp. Cloth or leather. *Langham Booklets*. Prices: cloth, 6d.; leather, 1s. *Location:* BL (30 September 1908).

Note: Possible reprint advertised as included in "Langham Booklets, Cheap Edition" by Bailey Brothers of London for April 1935 in *English Catalogue*.

A 10.87
Friendship. London: Henry Frowde, [1911].

Unpaged (22 leaves). Miniature book. *Location:* BL (2 November 1911).

Note: Possibly the same as that advertised as included in "Oxford Monument" series by Oxford University Press in *Cumulative Book Index*.

A 10.88
Friendship. New York: Barse & Hopkins, [1912?].

Advertised as included in "Christmas Classics." *Not seen*.

A 10.89
Friendship. London and Edinburgh: T. N. Foulis, [1913].

42 pp. Self-wrappers or silk. Illustrated by H. C. Preston Macgoun. *Friendship Booklets,* no. 1. Prices: wrappers, 6d.; silk, 2s. 6d. *Locations:* BL (12 January 1914), BE (30 January 1914), JM.

A 10.90
Friendship. [N.p.]: Phillips, Le Roy, [1918?].

Advertised as included in "Friendship Booklets." *Not seen.*

A 10.91
Friendship. Boston and New York: Houghton Mifflin, 1922.

29 pp. Wrappers. *Merry Christmas Booklets.* Price, 25¢. Location: CtW.

Note: Printed from the *Centenary Edition* plates (A 10.31).

A 10.92
On Friendship. London: C. W. Daniel, [1926].

19 pp. Wrappers. *The People's Classics,* n.s. no. 3. Price, 2d. *Location:* BC (30 December 1926).

A 10.93
Friendship. Pittsburgh: privately printed, 1927.

18 pp. Printed by Harry Thompson at the Carnegie Institute of Technology in December 1927. Limited to 40 copies. *Location:* TU.

A 10.94
Friendship. New York: Privately printed by Samuel Graydon for His Friends, Christmas 1927.

43 pp. Printed by the Stillson Press. *Location:* JM.

A 10.95
Friendship. London: Lothian, 1929.

28 pp. Wrappers. Advertised as included in "Remembrance Booklets." *Not seen.*

A 10.96
Friendship. Worcester [Mass.]: Achille J. St. Onge, 1939.

82 pp. Leather. Boxed. Miniature book. Printed by D. B. Updike, The Merrymount Press. Limited to 950 copies. Price, $2.50. *Location:* MH.

A 10.97
Friendship. Old Tappan, N.J.: Fleming H. Revell, [1957].

55 pp. Dust jacket. Introduction by Brooks Atkinson. *A Revell Inspirational Classic.* Published October 1957. Price, $1.00. *Locations:* DLC (4 November 1957), JM.

A 10.98.a–b
Friendship. New York: Pyramid, [1966].

54 pp. Wrappers. *A Little Paperback Classic,* LP3. Published September 1966. Price, 35¢. Reprinted June 1967. *Location:* MB (1967).

A 10.99
Friendship. St. Louis: Ronart, [1972].

36 pp. Completed 16 July 1972. "About two hundred [numbered] copies were printed."
Location: NN.

A 10.100
Friendship. [N.p.: n.p., n.d.].

Unpaged (19 leaves). Page size: 7¹/₂" × 5". *Location:* JM.

Note: This may be the same as the copy illustrated by W. E. B. Starkweather listed in
the *National Union Catalog* (CLIX, 325).

A 10.101
Friendship. [N.p.]: Biddle, [n.d.].

43 pp. Leather. Advertised as included in "Holiday Edition" series. Price, $1.25. *Not
seen.*

A 10.102
Friendship. New York: Thomas Y. Crowell, [n.d.].

Advertised in various bindings. *Not seen.*

A 10.103
Friendship. New York: Dodd, Mead, [n.d.].

55 pp. Self-wrappers. *Location:* MH.

A 10.104
Friendship. New York: E. P. Dutton, [n.d.].

Advertised in various bindings. *Not seen.*

A 10.105
Friendship. New York: R. F. Fenno, [n.d.].

Advertised in various bindings. *Not seen.*

A 10.106
Friendship. Philadelphia: David McKay, [n.d.].

Advertised as included in "Sesame Booklets." *Not seen.*

A 10.107
Friendship. New York: Putnams, [n.d.].

Advertised as included in "Vest Pocket" series. *Not seen.*

A 10.108
The Gift of Friends. [San Francisco?: Florence Keene?, n.d.].

Broadside, printed on recto only. Selections from "Friendship." *Location:* RPB.

A 10.109
Heroism. New York: John B. Alden, 1885.

[5]–18 pp. Wrappers. Identified as in both *The Elzevir Library,* vol. 4, no. 164, 8 September 1885, and *The Book-Worm,* vol. 2, no. 15, September 1885. Price: 3¢. *Location:* MB.

Note: From the plates of *Essays* (A 10.15.a).

A 10.110
Heroism. Boston: H. M. Caldwell, [1906?].

83 pp. Cloth or leather. Prices: cloth, 30¢; leather, 60¢. *Location:* KyU.

A 10.111
Heroism. New York and San Francisco: Morgan Shepard, 1906.

28 pp. Decorations designed by Fred W. Goudy. Completed October 1906. *The Birda-lone Series of Essays. Location:* DLC (7 December 1906).

A 10.112
History. New York: John B. Alden; Chicago: Alden Book Co., 1886.

[35]–62 pp. Wrappers. *The Elzevir Library,* vol. 5, no. 210, 8 June 1886. Price, 3¢. *Location:* MH.

Note: From the plates of *Essays* (A 10.15.a).

A 10.113
Intellect. New York: John B. Alden; Chicago: Alden Book Co., 1886.

[224]–240 pp. Wrappers. *The Elzevir Library,* vol. 5, no. 213, 29 June 1886. Price, 2¢. *Location:* OO.

Note: From the plates of *Essays* (A 10.15.a).

A 10.114
Intellect. Philadelphia: Henry Altemus, [1896].

41 pp. Advertised as included in "Belles-Lettres" and "Love and Friendship," no. 2, series. *Location:* DLC (17 June 1896).

A 10.115
Love. New York: John B. Alden, [1885].

Wrappers. Advertised as included in "Elzevir Library," no. 168. Price, 2¢. *Not seen.*

Note: Probably from the plates of *Essays* (A 10.15.a).

A 10.116
Love. Boston and New York: Houghton Mifflin, 1922.

22 pp. Wrappers. *Merry Christmas Booklets.* Price. 25¢. *Location:* CtW.

Note: Printed from the *Centenary Edition* plates (A 10.31).

A 10.117
An Essay on Love. London, Calcutta, Sydney: G. G. Harrap, [1923].

61 pp. Limp cloth. Miniature book. *Sesame Booklets,* no. 49. *Location:* BL (1 October 1923).

A 10.118
Love. Philadelphia: David McKay, [n.d.].

Advertised as included in "Sesame Booklets." *Not seen.*

A 10.119
The Over-Soul. London: [John M. Watkins], 1910.

51 pp. Cover title. *The Porch*, vol. 1, no. 1, May 1910. *Location:* CaBViV.

A 10.120
The Over-Soul. New York: New York Book Company, [1912?].

Advertised as included in "Aurora Edition" series. *Not seen.*

A 10.121
Emerson's Essay on the Over-Soul. [N.p.: n.p., 1977].

44 pp. Wrappers. Introduction and notes by Vaidyanatha Sastri. *Sastri's Studies*, no. 1. *Location:* DLC.

A 10.122
Over-Soul. New York: R. F. Fenno, [n.d.].

30 pp. Wrappers. *Location:* CLU.

A 10.123.a
Prudence. New York and San Francisco: Morgan Shepard, 1906.

29 pp. Decorations designed by Fred W. Goudy. *The Birdalone Series of Essays*. Completed October 1906. *Location:* DLC (7 December 1906).

A 10.123.b
New York: Ivan Somerville, [1906].

Unprinted glassine dust jacket. Boxed. *The Birdalone Series of Essays. Location:* JM.

A 10.124
Prudence. New York: New York Book Company, [1912?].

Advertised as included in "Aurora Edition" series. *Not seen.*

A 10.125
Self-Reliance. New York: John B. Alden, 1888.

[63]–96 pp. Wrappers. *The Elzevir Library*, vol. 7, no. 323, 13 February 1888. Price, 3¢. *Location:* CLSU.

Note: Printed from the plates of *Essays* (A 10.15.a).

A 10.126
Self-Reliance. Philadelphia: Henry Altemus, [1896].

41 pp. Dust jacket. *Life of Service Series*, no. 12. Also advertised as included in "Belles-Lettres" and "Love and Friendship," no. 3, series. Price, 25¢. *Location* JM.

A 10.127
Self-Reliance. Boston: L. C. Page, MDCCCC.

47 pp. Dust jacket. *The Day's Work Series,* no. 15. Listed in *Publishers' Weekly,* 58 (8 December 1950), 1603. Price, 35¢. *Location:* JM.

A 10.128
Self-Reliance. [Wausau, Wisc.: Philosopher Press, 1901].

63 pp. Limited to 370 numbered copies. Completed 21 November 1901. Price, $3.00. *Location:* DLC (3 November 1902).

A 10.129
So This Then is the Essay on Self-Reliance. [East Aurora, N.Y.: Roycrofters, 1902].

46 pp. Limp suede. Listed in *Publishers' Weekly,* 64 (12 December 1903), 1439. Completed 28 July 1902. Also advertised 100 copies printed on Japan vellum bound in three-quarter leather. Prices: $2.00; vellum, $10.00. *Locations:* DLC (8 August 1902), JM.

A 10.130
Self-Reliance. New York: Maynard, Merrill, 1903.

58 pp. Wrappers. *Maynard's English Classics Series,* no. 193, n.s. no. 137, 1 February 1903. Price, 12¢. *Location:* OO.

A 10.131
Self-Reliance. New York: H. M. Caldwell, [1904?].

Advertised as included in "Character and Wisdom" series in various bindings at various prices. *Not seen.*

A 10.132
Pitfalls. London: Guilbert Pitman, [1904?].

Cover title. Contains "Self-Reliance" transcribed by T. A. Reed in the "Semi-Brief Style of Pitman's Shorthand," pp. 13–32. *Shorthand Library,* no. 5. Price, 6d. *Location:* BL (25 January 1905).

A 10.133
Self-Reliance. London: C. W. Daniel, [1905].

55 pp. Wrappers. *Threepenny Booklets.* Price, 3d. *Location:* BC (29 December 1905).

A 10.134
The Essay on Self-Reliance. East Aurora, N.Y.: Roycrofters, MCMV.

51 pp. Boards or limp leather. Completed 11 August 1905. Also 100 numbered copies printed on Imperial Japan vellum, signed by Elbert Hubbard. *Locations:* JM (both).

A 10.135
The Essay on Self-Reliance. East Aurora, N.Y.: Roycrofters, Nineteen Hundred Eight.

59 pp. Advertised in various bindings at various prices. *Locations:* DLC (26 December 1908), JM.

A 10.136
Self-Reliance. [South Framingham, Mass.]: Caxton Society, Nineteen Hundred Nine.

Unpaged (15 leaves). Cover title. Pamphlet. *The Caxton Brochures,* series A, no. 12, February 1909. *Location:* MH.

A 10.137
Self-Reliance. New York: Thomas Y. Crowell, [1911?].

43 pp. Cloth (with dust jacket) or limp leather. *Hollywood Series.* Also advertised as included in "Laurel" and "San Rafael" series. *Location:* JM, NeU (leather).

A 10.138
Self-Reliance. New York: New York Book Company, [1912?].

Advertised as included in "Aurora Edition" series. *Not seen.*

A 10.139
Excerpts from Self Reliance. [Montreal]: privately printed, 1922.

17 pp. Printed for Charles Corbett Ronalds for the Ronalds Press & Advertising Agency in December 1922. Limited to 350 copies. *Location:* CStbS.

A 10.140
Essay on Self-Reliance. East Aurora, N.Y.: Roycrofters, [1927].

82 pp. *Not seen.*

A 10.141
An Essay on Self-Reliance. Los Angeles: Frank Myrle Cushing, MCMXXXII.

55 pp. Printed at the Garden View Press. Limited to 150 numbered copies. *Location:* PSC.

A 10.142
Self-Reliance. Mount Vernon, N.Y.: Peter Pauper, [1949].

58 pp. Wood engravings by Boyd Hanna. Price, $1.00. *Location:* AzU.

A 10.143
Self-Reliance. Mount Vernon, N.Y.: Peter Pauper, [1967].

59 pp. Dust jacket. Illustrations by Stanley Clough. Copyright, 1 April 1967. *Location:* JM.

A 10.144
Self-Reliance. Logan, Iowa: Perfection Form, 1971.

Single sheet folded twice to make six pages, printed on all pages. Head title. *Pamphlit, The Notebook Reader Series. Location:* JM.

A 10.145
Essay on Self-Reliance. [N.p.]: Pyramid, [1973?].

Wrappers. Price, 50¢. *Not seen.*

A 10.146
Self-Reliance. New York: Funk & Wagnalls, [1975].

96 pp. Cloth (with dust jacket) or wrappers. Photographs by Gene Dekovic. Published 30 July 1975. Copyright, 5 June 1975. Prices: cloth, $6.95; wrappers, $4.95. *Location:* JM.

A 10.147
Self-Reliance. [N.p.: n.p., n.d.].

Unpaged (33 leaves). Page size: 7½″ × 5″. *Location:* JM.

A 10.148
Self-Reliance. New York: Barse & Hopkins, [n.d.].

44 pp. *The Golden Books.* Also advertised as included in the "Savoy" series. *Location:* MH.

A 10.149
Self-Reliance. New York: Dodge, [n.d.].

80 pp. Self-wrappers. Also advertised as included in "Brown Book" and "Leathercraft Library" series. *Location:* JM.

A 10.150
Self-Reliance. New York: R. F. Fenno, [n.d.].

Advertised in various bindings at various prices. *Not seen.*

A 10.151
Self-Reliance. Farmington, Maine: D. H. Knowlton, [n.d.].

Advertised as included in "Excelsior 5c Classics" and "School World Readings," no. 317. *Not seen.*

A 10.152
Spiritual Laws. Philadelphia: Henry Altemus, [1896].

33 pp. *Belles-Lettres Series.* Price, 25¢. Also advertised as included in "Love and Friendship" series, no. 6. *Locations:* DLC (17 June 1896), JM.

A 10.153
Essays on Art and Self-Reliance. Girard, Kansas: Haldeman-Julius, [n.d.].

56 pp. Wrappers. *Little Blue Book,* no. 550. *Location:* JM.

A 10.154
Essays on Compensation and Friendship. Girard, Kansas: Haldeman-Julius, [n.d.].

64 pp. Wrappers. *Little Blue Book,* no. 60. *Location:* KU.

A 10.155
Compensation and Heroism. New York: Dodge, [n.d.].

70 pp. Also advertised as included in "Autumn Leaf Classics," "Brown Book," "Dodge Classics," and "Rose" series. *Location:* InLP.

A 10.156
Emerson's Essays. Girard, Kansas: Haldeman-Julius, [n.d.].

58 pp. Wrappers. Contains "Compensation" and "Love." *Ten Cent Pocket Series,* no. 60. *Location:* JM.

A 10.157
Compensation and Self-Reliance. [Westwood, N.J.]: Fleming H. Revell, [1962].

63 pp. Price, $1.00. *Location:* JM.

A 10.158
Compensation [and Spiritual Laws]. New York: H. M. Caldwell, [n.d.].

108 + 140 pp. *Location:* CaBViV.

A 10.159
Friendship and Character. New York: Century, 1906.

131 pp. With "Emerson's Personality" by Emma Lazarus. Also advertised as included in "Thumb-nail Series." Published 3 November 1906. *Location:* JM.

A 10.160.a–b
Friendship and Love. New York and Boston: H. M. Caldwell, [1900].

84 pp. Also advertised as included in "Remarque Edition" series. Published 8 December 1900. Listed in *Publishers' Weekly*, 58 (8 December 1900), 1630. Copyright, 7 September 1900. Also a large paper printing. *Locations:* DLC (both).

A 10.160.c
San Francisco: Paul Elder and Morgan Shepard, 1902.

Also advertised as included in "Impression Classics." *Location:* MiU.

A 10.160.d
Philadelphia: David McKay, [n.d.].

Flexible cloth. Boxed. *The Pocket Classics.* Price, 75¢. *Location:* JM.

A 10.161
Friendship and Love. New York: Barse & Hopkins, [1910].

57 pp. Cloth or limp leather. Also boxed. Also advertised as included in "Blackstone," "Embassy," "Golden Book," "Savoy," and "Traymore" series. Advertised in *Publishers' Weekly*, 78 (2 July 1910), 6. Price, 50¢. *Location:* JM.

A 10.162
Friendship and Love. New York: Grosset & Dunlap, [n.d.].

57 pp. *Location:* OOxM.

A 10.163
Friendship and Other Essays. New York: Dodge, [1900].

90 pp. Self-wrappers. Boxed. Also contains "Prudence" and "Heroism." *Brown Book Series*. Published 17 November 1900. Listed in *Publishers' Weekly*, 58 (17 November 1900), 1295. Also advertised as included in "Alexandrian Series," "Almac Series," and "Remarque Editions of Literary Masterpieces." *Location:* JM.

A 10.164
Friendship and Self-Reliance. Edinburgh and London: T. N. Foulis, MDCCCCVIII.

85 pp. *The Holyrood Books*, no. 3. *Location:* BE (20 January 1909).

A 10.165
Heroism and Character. New York: Dodge, [n.d.].

Advertised as included in "Remarque Editions of Literary Masterpieces." *Not seen.*

A 10.166
Heroism and Character. San Francisco: Paul Elder and Morgan Shepard, [n.d.].

Advertised as included in "Impression Classics." *Not seen.*

A 10.167
Heroism, Love and Manners. Edinburgh and London: T. N. Foulis, MDCCCCIX.

93 pp. Boards or leather. *The Holyrood Books*, no. 6. Published November 1909. Prices: boards, 1s.; leather, 2s. 6d. *Locations:* BL (9 December 1909), JM.

A 10.168
Essays on History and Intellect. Girard, Kansas: Haldeman-Julius, [n.d.].

64 pp. Wrappers. *Little Blue Book*, no. 548. *Location:* KU.

A 10.169
Love and Friendship. Philadelphia: Henry Altemus, [1896].

47 pp. *Belles-Lettres Series*. Price, 25¢. Also advertised as included in "Life of Service," no. 9, and "Love and Friendship," no. 1, series. *Location:* JM.

A 10.170
Love and Friendship. New York: Thomas Y. Crowell, [1902?].

46 pp. Also noted with Boston and New York imprint in wrappers. Also advertised as included in "Hollywood," "Laurel," "San Rafael," and "What is Worth While" series. *Locations:* JM (both).

A 10.171
On Love and Friendship. Mount Vernon, N.Y.: Peter Pauper, [1967?].

61 pp. Dust jacket. Illustrations by Stanley Clough. *Location:* JM.

A 10.172
Love, Friendship, Domestic Life. Boston: James R. Osgood, 1877.

93 pp. *Vest-Pocket Series*, 1,000 copies printed 10 May 1877; 500 copies on 5 and 12 June 1877. Listed in *Publishers' Weekly*, 11 (26 May 1877), 559. Price, 50¢. *Location:* MB.

A 10.173
Love and Friendship. New York: Dodge, [n.d.].

203 pp. Also contains "Prudence." *Location:* UPB.

A 10.174
Essays on Love, Heroism and Prudence. Girard, Kansas: Haldeman-Julius, [n.d.].

60 pp. Wrappers. *Little Blue Book*, no. 546. *Location:* KU.

A 10.175
Self-Reliance and Character. New York: Dodge, [1910?].

59 + 94 pp. Flexible leather. Also advertised as included in "Leathersmith Library." *Location:* MB.

A 10.176
Self-Reliance and Character. New York: Robert M. McBride, [n.d.].

Listed in RWe catalogue but now lost. *Not seen.*

A 10.177.a
Essays. New York: Little Leather Library, [n.d.].

96 pp. Flexible leather. Contains "Self-Reliance," "Love," and "Friendship." *Miniature Library.* Also advertised in "Little Leather Library," no. 2. *Location:* JM.

A 10.177.b
New York: Robert K. Haas, [n.d.].

Flexible leather. *Little Luxart Library. Location:* JM.

A 10.178
Self-Reliance and The Poet. [N.p.]: Expression, [1933?].

Edited by Annie H. Allen. *Not seen.*

A 10.179
Essays on Spiritual Laws and Circles. Girard, Kansas: Haldeman-Julius, [n.d.].

57 pp. Wrappers. *Little Blue Book,* no. 547. *Location:* KU.

A 10.180
Spiritual Laws. New York: New York Book Company, [1912?].

39 + 23 pp. Also includes "Love." Advertised as included in "Aurora Edition" series. *Location:* MH.

A 11 THE METHOD OF NATURE

A 11.1
First edition, only printing (1841)

THE METHOD OF NATURE.

AN

ORATION,

DELIVERED BEFORE THE

SOCIETY OF THE ADELPHI,

IN WATERVILLE COLLEGE, IN MAINE,

AUGUST 11, 1841.

BY

RALPH WALDO EMERSON.

BOSTON:
SAMUEL G. SIMPKINS.

1841.

A 11.1: $9^{5}/_{16}$″ × $5^{3}/_{4}$″

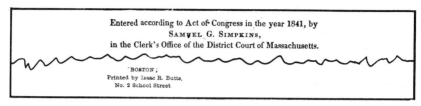

[1–3] 4–30

[1]⁴ 2–3⁴ 4¹ [5]²

Contents: p. 1: title page; p. 2: copyright page; pp. 3–30: text.

Typography and paper: 6″ × 3½″; wove paper; 31 lines per page. No running
heads.

Binding: Light brown wrappers: front recto: the same as the title page within a single
wavy-rule frame, all within a double-rule frame with heart-and-crown-like designs in
each corner; front verso, back recto and verso: blank. All edges trimmed.

Publication: Emerson wrote C. P. Cranch on 10 October 1841 that the oration was "in
press," and his manuscript "Notebook Δ" has entries for 3 and 11 October noting that
he had sent packets to the publisher (Scott, *Life and Letters of Christopher Pearse
Cranch* [D 196], pp. 61–63; MH). On 17 October 1841, Emerson wrote his brother
William that Simpkins was sending him copies of the oration (*L*, II, 459–460). Deposited
for copyright: title and book, 18 October 1841. Announced as received in *Boston Daily
Transcript,* 21 October 1841, p. 2. Possibly 500 copies printed. 62 copies were still in
stock on 1 January 1844. Price, unknown. Author's share, 12½¢.

Locations: CtY, JM, MH, MHi, MWA, NN, NNC, NjP, RPB, TxU, ViU, VtMiM.

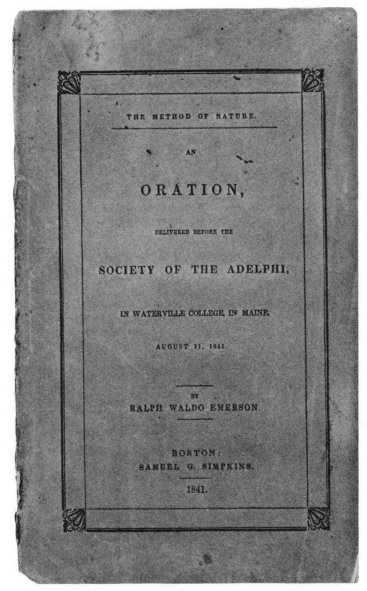

THE METHOD OF NATURE.

AN

ORATION,

DELIVERED BEFORE THE

SOCIETY OF THE ADELPHI,

IN WATERVILLE COLLEGE, IN MAINE,

AUGUST 11, 1841.

BY

RALPH WALDO EMERSON.

BOSTON:
SAMUEL G. SIMPKINS.

1841.

Wrapper for A 11.1

A 11.2
First English edition, only printing (1844)

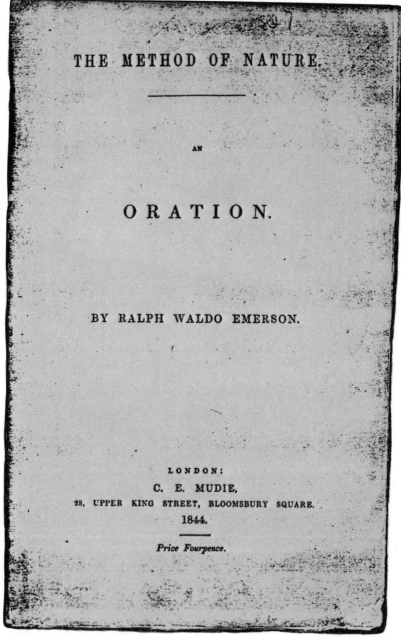

THE METHOD OF NATURE.

AN

ORATION.

BY RALPH WALDO EMERSON.

LONDON:
C. E. MUDIE,
28, UPPER KING STREET, BLOOMSBURY SQUARE.
1844.

Price Fourpence.

A 11.2: Cover title, 7^{15}/$_{16}$″ × 4^{13}/$_{16}$″

[1–3] 4–24

[a]^{12}

Contents: p. 1: cover title; p. 2: printer's imprint; pp. 3–24: text.

Typography and paper: 6″ × 3½″; wove paper; 35 lines per page. No running heads.

Binding: Cover title. All edges trimmed.

Publication: Advertised as "just Published," in *Athenæum,* no. 849 (3 February 1844), 120. Price, 4d.

Printing: "RICHARD KINDER, PRINTER, GREEN ARBOUR COURT, OLD BAILEY" (p. [2]).

Locations: BE, BL, BO, MBAt.

LATER EDITION

A 11.3
Second American edition (1886)

New York: John B. Alden; Chicago: Alden Book Co., 1886.

55–78 pp. Wrappers. *The Elzevir Library,* vol. 5, no. 209, 1 June 1886. Price, 3¢. *Location:* MeWC.

Note: From the plates of *Nature and Other Addresses* (C 16).

A 12 MAN THE REFORMER

A 12.1
Presumed first English edition, only printing [1842]

MAN THE REFORMER;

A LECTURE

ON SOME OF THE PROMINENT FEATURES OF
THE PRESENT AGE,

READ BEFORE THE MECHANICS' APPRENTICES' LIBRARY ASSOCIATION,

AT THE MASONIC TEMPLE,

BOSTON, U. S.,

BY R. W. EMERSON.

LONDON:
SIMPKIN, MARSHALL, & Co., STATIONERS' HALL COURT.
BOLTON: H. BRADBURY, JUN., & CO.
SOLD BY ALL BOOKSELLERS.

A 12.1: Cover title, 7^1/$_2$″ × 4^1/$_4$″

[1–3] 4–16

[a^6 b^2]

Contents: p. 1: cover title; p. 2: 'PREFACE.' about Emerson; pp. 3–16: text.

Typography and paper: 5^{15}/$_{16}$″ × 3^1/$_8$″; wove paper; 46 lines per page. No running heads.

Binding: Cover title. All edges trimmed.

Publication: Listed in *Athenæum*, no. 779 (1 October 1842), 850; as "Just published," *Athenæum*, no. 780 (8 October 1842), 878; as published between 1 and 14 October, *Publishers' Circular and Booksellers' Record,* 5 (15 October 1842), 304. Carlyle wrote Emerson on 17 November 1842 that the visiting Bronson Alcott was distributing copies, and Thomas Ballantyne sent a copy to Emerson on 3 December 1842; both copies may have been the first edition (*CEC*, p. 334; see *CEC*, p. 334n.). Price, 3d. Inscribed copy: MH (1842).

Printing: "H. Bradbury, Jun., & Co." (p. 16).

Locations: BL, BO, MH, NcD.

A 12.2
Presumed second English edition, only printing (1842)

MAN THE REFORMER.

A LECTURE,

Read before the Mechanics' Apprentices' Library
Association, at the Masonic Temple, Boston, 25th
January, 1841, and now published at their request.

BY R. W. EMERSON.

Published in ' The Dial: a Magazine for Literature,
Philosophy, and Religion, Boston, U. S.
April, 1841.

London:

SIMPKIN, MARSHALL, & CO.

DEARDEN, NOTTINGHAM.

1842,

A 12.2: Cover title, 4$^{1}/_{4}$″ × 2$^{11}/_{16}$″

[1–3] 4–32

[a]¹⁶

Contents: p. 1: cover title; p. 2: printer's imprint; pp. 3–32: text.

Typography and paper: 3³/₁₆″ × 2″; wove paper; 30 lines per page. No running heads.

Binding: Cover title. All edges trimmed.

Publication: Advertised in *Publishers' Circular and Booksellers' Record*, 5 (1 December 1842), 343. Price, 2d.

Printing: "W. DEARDEN, PRINTER, NOTTINGHAM" (p. [2]).

Locations: CtY, NcD.

LATER EDITIONS

A 12.3
Manchester: Abel Heywood, 1843.

8 pp., double columns. Cover title. *Locations:* BL, CtY, NN.

A 12.4
London: Simple Life Press, 1903.

40 pp. Wrappers. *The Simple Life Series*, no. 6. Published August 1903. 4,000 copies printed by 1904. Price, 3d. *Locations:* BL (30 November 1904), DLC.

A 13 [NATURE AND LECTURES ON THE TIMES]

A 13.1.a
First English edition, first printing (1844)

NATURE; AN ESSAY.

AND

LECTURES ON THE TIMES.

BY

R. W. EMERSON.

LONDON:

H. C. CLARKE AND CO., 66, OLD BAILEY.

—

1844.

A 13.1.a: 5⁷/₁₆″ × 3⁵/₈″

[i–v] vi [7] 8–40 43–64 [65–66] 65–89 [90] 91–138 [139–144]

[A]⁴ B–I⁸ K⁴

Contents: p. i: 'NATURE; AN ESSAY. | AND | LECTURES ON THE TIMES.'; p. ii: blank; p. iii: title page; p. iv: blank; pp. v–vi: contents; pp. 7–64: *Nature;* p. 65: 'LECTURES | ON THE TIMES.'; p. 66: blank; pp. 65–89: "Introductory Lecture"; p. 90: blank; pp. 91–114: "II. The Conservative"; pp. 115–138: "III. The Transcendentalist"; pp. 139–144: advertisements for Clarke's publications.

Includes: *Nature;* "Introductory Lecture [to "Lectures on the Times"] †; "The Conservative" †; "The Transcendentalist" †.

Typography and paper: 4″ (3¹¹/₁₆″) × 2¹/₂″; wove paper; 32 lines per page. Running heads: rectos: p. 9: 'INTRODUCTION.'; p. 11: 'INTRODUCTORY.'; p. 13: 'COMMODITY.'; pp. 17–21: 'BEAUTY.'; pp. 23–31: 'LANGUAGE.'; pp. 33–41: 'DISCIPLINE.'; pp. 43–53: 'IDEALISM.'; p. 55: 'SPIRIT.'; pp. 57–63: 'PROSPECTS.'; pp. 67–89: 'INTRODUCTORY LECTURE.'; pp. 93–113: 'THE CONSERVATIVE.'; pp. 117–137: 'THE TRANSCENDENTALIST.'; versos: p. vi: 'CONTENTS.'; p. 8: 'INTRODUCTION.'; pp. 10–40: 'NATURE.'; p. 42: 'IDEALISM; pp. 44–64: 'NATURE.'; pp. 66–88, 92–138: 'LECTURES ON THE TIMES.'.

Binding: Cream wrappers: front recto: gold, blue, red, and green—see *Note four* below and illustration; front verso and back recto: blank; back verso: all in green: single-rule frame with design in each corner with 'CLARKE'S | CABINET SERIES.' in center; spine: within green single-rule rectangular frame '[green] CLARKE'S | CABINET | SERIES. | Price 1s'. White flyleaves. All edges trimmed.

Publication: Listed in *Publishers' Circular and Booksellers' Record,* 7 (15 March 1844), 82; *Athenæum,* no. 855 (16 March 1844), p. 247. Deposit copy: BL (10 April 1844). Inscribed copy: MH (25 May 1844). Possibly 3,000 copies of all printings (see *JMN,* X, 427). *Clarke's Cabinet Series,* no. 14. Price, 1s.

Locations: MH, NcD.

Note one: In the contents, "Prospects" is listed on p. 56 and "The Conservative" is listed on p. 91.

Note two: There is no printer's imprint on p. 138.

Note three: The sequence for the advertisements, which are integral with the last gathering, is: p. 139: five volumes in "Clarke's English Helicon" series; p. 140: four volumes in "Clarke's English Helicon" American series; p. 141: six volumes of "Bremer's Novels"; p. 142: four "New Works"; p. 143: nine titles in "Clarke's Ladies' Hand-Books" series, ending with *The Ladies' Hand-Book of the Toilet;* p. 144: sixteen volumes in "Clarke's Cabinet Series."

Note four: The wrapper has been noted in two styles:

Wrapper A: At the lower left front recto: '*Printed in Colors, by Gregory & Collins.*': MH.

Wrapper B: At the lower left front recto: 'PRINTED IN COLORS BY GREGORY & COLLINS | 76 ST. JAMES'S STREET CLERKENWELL': NcD.

Note five: The errors in pagination (41–42 omitted and 65–66 repeated) were corrected in the second printing (A 13.1.b).

A 13.1.b
First English edition, second printing (1844)

London: H. G. Clarke and Co., 1844.

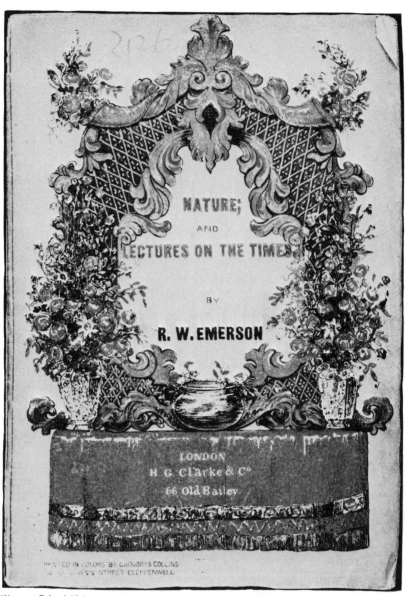

NATURE;

AND

LECTURES ON THE TIMES

BY

R. W. EMERSON

LONDON
H. G. Clarke & Cº
66 Old Bailey.

PRINTED IN COLORS BY GREGORY & COLLINS
ST JAMES'S STREET CLERKENWELL

Wrapper B for A 13 1 a

The title page, which has been reset, reads the same as in the first printing, except: 'ESSAY. [ESSAY,'. Collation, contents, and typography and paper are the same as in the first printing.

[i–v] vi [7] 8–62 [63–64] 65–89 [90] 91–138 [139–144]

Binding: Cream wrappers; front recto: black, blue, green, red, and gold—see illustration; front verso and back recto: blank; back verso: green double-rule frame with ornate design in each corner, with red gothic 'Clarke's | Cabinet Series.' in center; spine: unknown [only located copy lacks spine]. White flyleaves. All edges trimmed.

Publication: See first printing information.

Printing: "H. G. Clarke & Co. Printers, 66, Old Bailey" (p. 138).

Location: NcD.

Note one: In the contents, "Prospects" is listed on p. 54 and "The Conservative" is listed without page reference number.

Note two: The printer's imprint is present on p. 138.

Note three: The sequence for the advertisements, which are integral with the last gathering, is: p. 139: *The Ladies' Hand-Book of the Language of Flowers,* ed. Lucy Hooper; p. 140: 12 volumes of "Bremer's Novels"; p. 141: Louisa Stuart Costello's *The Falls, Lakes, and Mountains of North Wales;* p. 142: nine volumes of "Clarke's Ladies' Hand-Books" series, ending with Hooper's *The Language of Flowers;* p. 143: vols. 1–23 in "Clarke's Cabinet Series" listed; p. 144: vols. 24–40 in "Clarke's Cabinet Series" listed.

Note four: The errors in pagination for pp. 41–42 and 65–66 in the first printing have been corrected and pagination throughout the second printing is affected accordingly.

A 13.1.c
First English edition, third printing (1845) .

London: Henry G. Clarke, 1845.

Wrappers. *Location:* MCo.

LATER EDITION

A 13.2.a
Second English edition (1850)

Nature, An Essay: Lectures on the Times; and on War. London: George Slater, 1850.

157 pp. "Memoir" by Rufus Wilmot Griswold. *Slater's Shilling Series,* no. 11. Listed in *Athenæum,* no. 1152 (24 November 1849), 1179. Advertised for 1 December 1849 publication. Price, 1s. *Locations:* JM, MCo.

Note: Contains "War" (see D 18).

A 13.2.b
Orations, Lectures, and Addresses: To Which is Added, Nature; An Essay.   London: William Tweedie, 1853.

Combined with *Orations, Lectures, and Addresses* (A 14.1.c) in two-volumes-in-one format. *Location:* CaOLU.

Wrapper for A 13.1.b

A 14 ORATIONS, LECTURES, AND ADDRESSES

A 14.1.a
First English edition, first printing (1844)

ORATIONS,

LECTURES, AND ADDRESSES.

BY

RALPH WALDO EMERSON.

LONDON:

H. G. CLARKE AND CO., 66, OLD BAILEY.

—

1844.

A 14.1.a: $5^3/8''$ × $3^9/16''$

[a–b] [i–v] vi [7] 8–165 [166]

[A]⁴ B–H⁸ I⁴ K–L⁸ M⁴

Contents: p. a: 'ORATIONS, | LECTURES, AND ADDRESSES.'; p. b: blank; p. i: title page; p. ii: blank; p. iii: contents; p. iv: blank; pp. v–vi: 'MEMOIR.'; pp. 7–33: "Man Thinking: An Oration"; pp. 34–58: Divinity School Address; pp. 59–84: "Literary Ethics"; pp. 85–110: "The Method of Nature"; pp. 111–132: "Man the Reformer"; pp. 133–165: "The Young American"; p. 166: blank.

Addresses, lectures, and orations: "Man Thinking" [American Scholar Address] †; Divinity School Address †; "Literary Ethics" †; "The Method of Nature" †; "Man the Reformer" †; "The Young American" †.

Typography and paper: $4^{1}/_{16}''$ $(3^{13}/_{16}'')$ × $2^{1}/_{2}''$; wove paper; 32 lines per page. Running heads: rectos: pp. 9–33: 'MAN THINKING.'; pp. 35–57: 'AN ADDRESS.'; pp. 61–83: 'LITERARY ETHICS.'; pp. 87–109: 'THE METHOD OF NATURE.'; pp. 113–131: 'MAN THE REFORMER.'; pp. 135–165: 'THE YOUNG AMERICAN.'; versos: p. vi: 'MEMOIR.'; pp. 8–32: 'ORATIONS.'; pp. 36–54: 'AN ADDRESS.'; pp. 56–164: 'ORATIONS.'.

Binding: Cream wrappers: front recto: gold, green, red, blue, and black design—see illustration; front verso and back recto: blank; back verso: all in blue: all within a double-rule frame with intersecting corners: 'CLARKE'S | CABINET SERIES'; spine: all in blue: all within a single-rule rectangular frame: 'CLARKE'S | CABINET | SERIES | PRICE 1S'. White flyleaves. All edges trimmed.

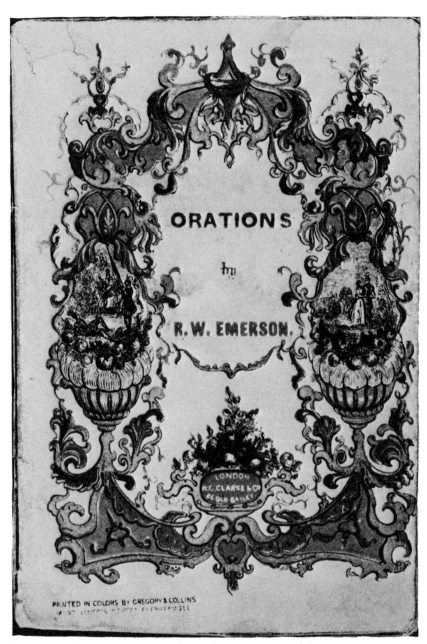

ORATIONS

by

R. W. EMERSON.

LONDON
H.C. CLARKE & Co.
66 OLD BAILEY

PRINTED IN COLORS BY GREGORY & COLLINS

Wrapper for A 14.1.a

Publication: *Clarke's Cabinet Series,* no. 31. Deposit copy: BL (3 August 1844). Price, 1s.

Printing: "Printed by H. G. Clarke & Co., 66, Old Bailey" (p. 165).

Locations: BL, CtY, NcD.

Note one: Copies have been noted with a six-page catalogue of Clarke's publications inserted at the back: NcD, VtMiM (lacking wrappers).

Note two: A copy has been noted with a seven-page catalogue of Clarke's publications inserted at the back: JM (lacking back wrapper).

A 14.1.b
First English edition, second printing (1845)

London: H. G. Clarke & Co., 1845.

Clarke's Cabinet Library, no. 31. Advertised in *Publishers' Circular and Booksellers' Record,* 7 (15 October 1844), 309. Price, 1s. *Location:* DLC.

A 14.1.c
Orations, Lectures, and Addresses: To Which is Added, Nature; An Essay. London: William Tweedie, 1853.

Combined with *Nature, An Essay: Lectures on the Times; and on War* in two-volumes-in-one format; see A 13.2.b.

OTHER EDITION

A 14.2
Second English edition, only printing (1849)

London: George Slater, 1849.

228 pp. *Slater's Shilling Series,* no. 7. Listed in *Athenæum,* no. 1139 (25 August 1849), 862. Listed as published between 14 and 29 August, in *Publishers' Circular and Booksellers' Record,* 12 (1 September 1849), 294. Price, Is. *Locations:* BL, CLU, CtW, NNC.

Note: Contains "Emancipation in the West Indies" (A 17).

A 15 THE YOUNG AMERICAN

A 15
First English edition, only printing (1844)

THE YOUNG AMERICAN.

A LECTURE

READ BEFORE THE MERCANTILE LIBRARY ASSOCIATION, IN
BOSTON, AT THE ODEON, WEDNESDAY, FEBRUARY 7, 1844.

BY

RALPH WALDO EMERSON.

LONDON:

JOHN CHAPMAN, 121, NEWGATE STREET.

1844.

A 15: Cover title, $8^7/8''$ × $5^7/16''$

[1–3] 4–23 [24]

[a]¹²

Contents: p. 1: cover title; p. 2: printer's imprint; pp. 3–23: text; p. 24: advertisement for Chapman's publications.

Typography and paper: $6^{7}/_{16}$″ × $3^{5}/_{8}$″; wove paper; 45 lines per page. No running heads.

Binding: Cover title. All edges trimmed.

Publication: Advertised as "Lately published," in *Athenæum,* no. 887 (26 October 1844), 984. Price, 6d.

Printing: "R. KINDER, PRINTER, | GREEN ARBOUR COURT, OLD BAILEY" (p. [2]).

Locations: BE, BL, CSt, MBAt, NNC, VtMiM.

A 16.1.a–b
First edition, first and second printings (1844)

E S S A Y S :

SECOND SERIES.

BY

R. W. EMERSON.

———◆———

BOSTON.
JAMES MUNROE AND COMPANY.

———

MDCCCXLIV.

A 16.1.a: 7″ × 4¹/₂″

Entered according to Act of Congress, in the year 1844, by
JAMES MUNROE & Co., in the Clerk's Office of the District
Court of the District of Massachusetts.

BOSTON:
PRINTED BY THURSTON, TORRY, AND CO.
31 Devonshire Street.

[i–iv] [1–3] 4–46 [47–49] 50–93 [94–97] 98–126 [127–129] 130–169 [170–173] 174–
180 [181–183] 184–213 [214–217] 218–242 [243–245] 246–256 259–273 [274–276]
[275] 276–313 [314–316]

[a]^2 1–19^8 20^4 21^2

Contents: p. i: title page; p. ii: copyright page; p. iii: contents; p. iv: blank; p. 1: 'THE
POET. | [rule] | [10 lines of verse]'; p. 2: four lines of verse; pp. 3–46: "Essay I. The
Poet."; p. 47: 'EXPERIENCE. | [rule] | [21 lines of verse]'; p. 48: blank; pp. 49–93:
"Essay II. Experience."; p, 94: blank; p. 95: 'CHARACTER. | [rule] | [10 lines of verse]';
p. 96: five lines of verse; pp. 97–126: "Essay III. Character."; p. 127: 'MANNERS. |
[rule] | [14 lines of verse] | BEN JONSON.'; p. 128: blank; pp. 129–169: "Essay IV.
Manners."; p. 170: blank; p. 171: 'GIFTS. | [rule] | [four lines of verse]'; p. 172: blank;
pp. 173–180: "Essay V. Gifts."; p. 181: 'NATURE. | [rule] | [10 lines of verse]'; p. 182:
blank; pp. 183–213: "Essay VI. Nature."; p. 214: blank; p. 215: 'POLITICS. | [rule] | [26
lines of verse]'; p. 216: blank; pp. 217–242: "Essay VII. Politics."; p. 243: 'NOMINALIST
AND REALIST. | [rule] | [10 lines of verse]'; p. 244: blank; pp. 245–273: "Essay VIII.
Nominalist and Realist."; p. 274: blank; p. 275: 'NEW ENGLAND REFORMERS.'; p. 276:
blank; pp. 275–313: "New England Reformers."; p. 314: blank; pp. 315–316: advertisements for Munroe's publications.

Essays: "The Poet" #; "Experience" #; "Character" #; "Manners" #; "Gifts" #; "Nature" #; "Politics" #; "Nominalist and Realist" #; "New England Reformers" #.

Typography and paper: 4^7/$_8$″ (4^5/$_8$″) × 2^7/$_8$″; wove paper; 26 lines per page. Running
heads: rectos: pp. 5–45: 'THE POET.'; pp. 51–53: 'ILLUSION.'; pp. 55–59: 'TEMPERA-
MENT.'; p. 61: 'SUCCESSION.'; pp. 63–71: 'SURFACE.'; pp. 73–75: 'SURPRISE.'; pp.
77–81: 'REALITY.'; pp. 83–89: 'SUBJECT OR THE ONE.'; pp. 91–93: 'EXPERIENCE.';
pp. 99–125, 131–169, 175–179, 185–213, 219–241, 247–273, 277–313: titles of essays; versos: pp. 4–46: 'ESSAY I.'; pp. 50–88: 'ESSAY II. EXPERIENCE.'; pp. 90–92,
98–126, 130–168, 174–180, 184–212, 218–242, 246–272: 'ESSAY' and roman numeral; pp. 276–312: 'LECTURE AT AMORY HALL.'.

Binding: Four styles have been noted; order of B and C is undetermined:

Binding A: Grayish green or light purple A cloth (ribbed morocco); medium brown FL
cloth (diagonal dotted line); dark brown H cloth (fine diaper); dark brown T cloth
(rib). Front and back covers: blindstamped triple-rule frame with 2^3/$_4$″ ornament in
each corner; spine: blindstamped rules and decorative bands with goldstamped
'EMERSON'S | ESSAYS | [rule] | 2D. SERIES'. Single or triple flyleaves. Yellow coated
endpapers. All edges trimmed.

Binding B: Black, light brown, or medium purple T cloth (rib). Front and back covers:
blindstamped triple-rule frame enclosing two horizontal filigree ornaments at top and
bottom; spine: blindstamped rules and decorative bands with goldstamped 'EMER-
SON'S | ESSAYS | [rule] | SECOND SERIES'. Flyleaves. Yellow or yellow coated
endpapers. All edges trimmed.

Binding C: Brown A cloth (ribbed morocco); medium brown T cloth (rib); black horizontal TF cloth (ripple). Front and back covers: blindstamped triple-rule frame with 6⁵/₁₆″ filigree ornament in center; spine: blindstamped rules and decorative bands with goldstamped 'EMERSON'S | ESSAYS. | [rule] | SECOND SERIES'. Flyleaves. Yellow coated endpapers. All edges trimmed.

Binding D: Black or dark green A cloth (ribbed morocco). Front and back covers: blindstamped grolieresque frame with decorative lyre in each corner; spine: blindstamped rules with goldstamped 'EMERSON'S | ESSAYS | SECOND SERIES | [rule] | THIRD EDITION | [gothic] Munroe & Co.'. Flyleaves. Yellow endpapers. All edges trimmed.

Publication: On 1 January 1844, Emerson entered in his journal that "I begin the year by sending my little book of Essays to the press," but on 20 July he wrote Caroline Sturgis "I carried my book to the printers, the other day . . . and they discovered it was not large enough . . . & I brought it back to deliberate whether I would add a chapter or two" (*JMN,* VII, 411; MH). In September 1844, Emerson sent a set of proofs to John Chapman for use in setting the English edition of *Essays: Second Series* (1 September, *CEC,* p. 364, and see 13 September, *L,* III, 260). On 4 October 1844 (Friday), Emerson wrote his brother William that he expected to receive copies on the following Monday or Tuesday (*L,* III, 263). However, on 14? October, Emerson wrote again to report that a fire at the bookbinder's "has delayed all binding of new books. In a day or two more, they say now, it shall be out" (*L,* III, 264). And on 15 October, Emerson entered in his journal a list of people to whom copies should be sent (*JMN,* IX, 128). Emerson's contract with Munroe called for him to pay for composition and printing costs, and to retain copyright. Deposited for copyright: title, 1 October 1844; book, 18 October 1844. Advertised as "This day published," in *Boston Daily Advertiser,* 19 October 1844, p. 3. Deposit copy: DLC (Binding A, 18 October 1844). Inscribed copies: Binding A: InU (from Emerson, 15 October 1844), MH (from Emerson, 15 October 1844), NN (from Emerson, 15 October 1844), MH (17 October 1844), NjP (from Emerson, 19 October 1844), NN (from Emerson, 22 October 1844); Binding B: MH (from Emerson, October 1844), NN (October 1844), ViU (from Emerson, October 1844). 2,000 copies were printed. Price, $1.00. Publisher's commission, 30¢.

Locations: Binding A: CtY, DLC, InU, JM, MH, MHi, MWA, MWiW-C, NjP, NN, NNC, ViU, VtMiM; Binding B: BE, DLC, JM, MH, NN, TxU, ViU; Binding C: CSt, InU, JM, MCo, MH, NN, PSt, ViU; Binding D: JM, MH.

Note one: Pages 257–258 are not accounted for in the pagination sequence, and pp. [275–276] are repeated in the pagination sequence.

Note two: Because *Essays: Second Series* was printed from standing type rather than from stereotype plates, there are variant readings. Moreover, nearly every copy examined is composed of mixed sheets from the first and second printings. Usually, copies in Binding A have the most first printing sheets and copies in Binding D have the most second printing sheets; copies in Bindings B and C usually have more first and second printing sheets, respectively. A list of variants between the printings follows:

1.1	'P' in 'POET' is over the second 'l' in 'wildly'	['P' in 'POET' is over the 'i' in 'wildly'
3.11	artsis	[arts is
5.4	whence	[when
7.4	is	[its
7.19–20	his | own	[his own
10.15	'f' in 'of' is defective	['f' in 'of' is correct

18.25	everything [every thing
26.15	tell, [tell
33	signature number '3' is under the space between 'and' and 'Timæus' [signature number '3' is under the 'i' in 'Timæus'
44.7–8	by | virtue [by vir- | tue
49.3	series, [series
49.17	glimmer [glitter
49	signature number '4' is under the 'e' in 'place' [signature number '4' is under the 'la' in 'place'
52.20	grieve [give
57.5	moment, [moment
59.1	neighborhood, [neighborhood
60.23	turn [I turn
62	running head starts over the space between 'the' and 'artist' [running head starts over the first 't' in 'artist'
63.5	is it [it is
116.26	prior to [prior ot
200.4–5	continua- | on [continua- | tion
309.5	'There's ['There's a
313.4	an [and

Some copies have been noted with the following reading at 200.4–5: 'continua- | [blank]'.

Note three: The following intercalary poems are present: "The Poet" ["A moody child and wildly wise"] #, "Experience" #, "Character" ["The sun set; but set not his hope"] #, "Character" ["Work of his hand"] # (later incorporated into "In Memoriam, E. B. E."; see A 28), "Gifts" #, "Nature" ["The rounded world is fair to see"] #, "Politics" #, and "Nominalist and Realist" # (retitled "Promise"; see A 18.16).

A 16.1.b
First American edition, second printing (1844)

Boston: James Munroe and Company, 1844.

Note: Copies composed exclusively of first or second printing sheets are scarce; the following have been noted: 1st printing: MH (A); 2nd printing: JM (C, D), MH (C, D).

A 16.1.c
First American edition, third printing (1845)

Boston: James Munroe and Company, MDCCCXLV. Pagination, collation, contents, and typography and paper are the same as in the first printing; see also *Note* below.

Binding: Four styles have been noted; priority undetermined:

Binding A: Light green horizontal TF cloth (ripple); medium green T cloth (rib); all else the same as the first printing, Binding D.

Binding B: Brown T cloth (rib). Front and back covers: blindstamped triple-rule frame; spine: blindstamped rules with goldstamped 'EMERSON'S | ESSAYS | [rule] | SECOND SERIES | MUNROE & CO.'. Flyleaves. Yellow endpapers. All edges trimmed.

Binding C: Light greenish gray or light brown wrappers. Front recto: all within a triple-rule frame: 'No. I [upper left] | SECOND SERIES. | [rule] | [rule] | BOSTON LIBRARY | OF | AMERICAN AND FOREIGN LITERATURE. | [rule] | [rule] | ESSAYS |

BY | RALPH WALDO EMERSON. | ONE VOLUME. | [rule] | BOSTON: | JAMES MUN-
ROE AND COMPANY. | 134 WASHINGTON STREET. | [rule] | *Price Fifty Cents*.'; front verso
and back recto: blank; back verso: advertisement for books in "Boston Library"
series; spine: top to bottom: 'EMERSON'S ESSAYS.'. All edges trimmed.

Binding D: Black T cloth (rib). Front and back covers: blindstamped double-rule
frame surrounding frame of florets with floral design inside corners; spine: blind-
stamped bands with goldstamped 'ESSAYS | BY | EMERSON | [rule] | SECOND
SERIES | [gothic] Munroe & Co.'. Flyleaves. Yellow endpapers. All edges trimmed.

No. I.

SECOND SERIES.

BOSTON LIBRARY

OF

AMERICAN AND FOREIGN LITERATURE.

ESSAYS

BY

R. W. EMERSON.

ONE VOLUME.

BOSTON:
JAMES MUNROE AND COMPANY,
134 WASHINGTON STREET.

Price Fifty Cents.

Wrapper for A 16.1.c

Publication: Back wrapper advertisement for *Memoirs of Fichte* in Binding C states that it will be published "early in April." A copy in Binding C reviewed in *New York Mirror,* 4 (18 July 1846), 234.

Locations: Binding A: JM; Binding B: JM, MH; Binding C: JM, MWA; Binding D: CSt.

Note one: A copy in Binding D has been noted with an eight-page catalogue of Munroe's publications, dated September 1849, inserted at the back: CSt. The date of this catalogue and the fact that the cover stamping in Binding D is identical to that in *Nature* (A 3.2, Binding B) and *Nature; Addresses, and Lectures* (A 21.1.a, Binding A), both published in 1849, probably indicates that copies of *Essays: Second Series* in Binding D were placed on sale in late 1849 to be sold as a set with copies of *Essays: First Series* in similar bindings (see A 10.5.a, Binding D).

Note two: Copies with an 1845 title page are composed of gatherings with both the first and second printing readings. This gives rise to speculation that perhaps only the preliminary gathering (containing the title page) was newly printed, and then bound with the remaining sheets from the first two printings.

A 16.1.d
Essays   Essays: Second Series. Columbus, Ohio: Charles E. Merrill, [1969].

Facsimile reprinting in two-volumes-in-one format; see A 10.1.b.

A 16.2.a
First English edition, first printing (1844)

E S S A Y S.

Second Series.

BY

R. W. EMERSON.

~~~~~~~~~~~~

" That which befits us, embosomed in beauty and wonder as we are, is
cheerfulness and courage, and the endeavour to realise our aspirations."—
Page 190.

LONDON :

JOHN CHAPMAN, 121, NEWGATE STREET.

M.DCCC.XLIV.

STEREOTYPE]   [EDITION.

A 16.2.a: $7^7/_8''$ × $4^3/_4''$

```
┌─────────────────────────────────────────────────────────────┐
│                                                               │
│            [ ENTERED AT STATIONERS' HALL. ]                   │
│                                                               │
│   ∿∿∿∿∿∿∿∿∿∿∿∿∿∿∿∿∿∿∿∿∿∿∿∿∿∿∿∿∿∿∿∿∿∿∿∿∿∿∿∿∿∿∿∿∿∿∿∿∿∿∿∿   │
│                        LONDON :                               │
│                                                               │
│     PRINTED BY RICHARD KINDER, GREEN ARBOUR COURT,            │
│                                                               │
│                      OLD BAILEY.                              │
│                                                               │
└─────────────────────────────────────────────────────────────┘
```

[i–v] vi [vii–viii] [1–3] 4–27 [28–31] 32–56 [57–59] 60–75 [76–79] 80–101 [102–105] 106–109 [110–113] 114–130 [131–133] 134–147 [148–151] 152–165 [166–169] 170–190 [191–192]

[A]⁴ B–I¹²

Contents: p. i: '[gothic] The Catholic Series.'; p. ii: 'TO PRINTERS, PUBLISHERS, AND OTHERS. | *The Publisher notifies that this Work is Copyright; and all persons | are hereby cautioned against printing, or causing to be printed, the | same. | Proceedings in Equity will be instituted against all persons so | offending after this notice. | London, 121 Newgate Street, | October* 26, 1844.'; p. iii: title page; p. iv: printer's imprint; pp. v–vi: 'NOTICE.'; p. vii: contents; p. viii: blank; p. 1: 'THE POET. | [10 lines of verse]'; p. 2: four lines of verse; pp. 3–27: "Essay I. The Poet."; p. 28: blank; p. 29: 'EXPERIENCE. | [rule] | [21 lines of verse]'; p. 30: blank; pp. 31–56: "Essay II. Experience."; p. 57: 'CHARACTER. | [rule] | [10 lines of verse]'; p. 58: blank; pp. 59–75: "Essay III. Character."; p. 76: blank; p. 77: 'MANNERS. | [rule] | [14 lines of verse] | BEN JONSON.'; p. 78: five lines of verse; pp. 79–101: "Essay IV. Manners."; p. 102: blank; p. 103: 'GIFTS. | [rule] | [four lines of verse]'; p. 104: blank; pp. 105–109: "Essay V. Gifts."; p. 110: blank; p. 111: 'NATURE. | [rule] | [ten lines of verse]'; p. 112: blank; pp. 113–130: "Essay VI. Nature."; p. 131: 'POLITICS. | [rule] | [26 lines of verse]'; p. 132: blank; pp. 133–147: "Essay VII. Politics."; p. 148: blank; p. 149: 'NOMINALIST AND REALIST. | [rule] | [10 lines of verse]'; p. 150: blank; pp. 151–165: "Essay VIII. Nominalist and Realist."; p. 166: blank; p. 167: 'NEW ENGLAND REFORMERS.'; p. 168: blank; pp. 169–190: 'New England Reformers.'; pp. 191–192: advertisements for Chapman's publications.

Typography and paper: 5¹³/₁₆″ (5¹/₂″) × 3³/₁₆″; wove paper; 35 lines per page. Running heads: rectos: pp. 5–27, 33–55, 61–75, 81–101, 107–109, 115–129, 135–147, 153–165, 171–189: titles of essays; versos: p. vi: 'NOTICE.'; pp. 4–26, 32–56, 60–74, 80–100, 106–108, 114–130, 134–146, 152–164: 'ESSAY' and roman numeral; pp. 170–190: 'LECTURE AT AMORY HALL.'.

Binding: Three styles have been noted, priority undertermined:

Binding A: Black, medium brown, or medium green T cloth (rib). Front and back covers: blindstamped leaf-and-vine ornamental frame; spine: blindstamped rules with goldstamped 'EMERSON'S | ESSAYS. | 2ⁿᵈ SERIES.'. Yellow or yellow coated endpapers. All edges trimmed.

Binding B: Medium brown or medium green T cloth (rib). All else the same as Binding A, except: blindstamped 1¹⁵/₁₆″ circular leaf-and-vine ornament in the center of front and back covers.

Binding C: Printed paper wrapper (no copies have been located).

Publication: In early September 1844, Emerson sent a set of American proofs—"ten or more signatures"—to Chapman for use in setting the English edition (Emerson to Chapman, 31 August 1844 [BLU]; and see 13 September, *L*, III, 260). He followed on

15 September with a shipment of three more signatures (ViU). On 3 November 1844, Carlyle wrote Emerson that he had seen an advertisement for the book "yesterday" (*CEC*, pp. 369–370). Advertised as "This day is published," in *Athenæum*, no. 889 (9 November 1844), 1011. Listed in *Literary Gazette*, no. 1451 (9 November 1844), 724. Advertised, with reviews from the *League* (n.d.) and the *Inquirer* (n.d.), in *Athenæum*, no. 892 (30 November 1844), 1101. Inscribed copies: CtY (13 November 1844), MB (Christmas 1844), MH (Christmas 1844). On 30 December 1844, Emerson wrote Chapman ackowledging receipt of a copy (*L*, III, 273). Prices: cloth, 3s. 6d; wrappers, 3s.

Locations: Binding A: CtY, JM, MCo; Binding B: JM, MB, MCo, NNC.

Note one: Advertisements end with *The Young American*.

Note two: Page 121 prints as '12' (CtY, JM [B], MH, NNC), '21' (JM [A], MCo), or '121' (MB).

A 16.2.b.
First English edition, second printing (1845)

London: John Chapman, M.DCCC.XLV.

Title page has a gray background with an engraving of Christ's head in an oval frame in the center; other slight changes from the first printing, not affecting wording. Contents the same as the first printing. Advertisements end with *The Autobiography of Joseph Blanco White*. Page 121 is numbered correctly.

Locations: DLC, JM.

A 16.2.c
First English edition, third printing (1845)

London: John Chapman, M.DCCC.XLV.

Title page is the same as the first printing, except for date. Contents the same as the first printing, except: p. i: a three-line reference to the publisher's catalogue at the end of the book is present; pp. 191–192: blank. Page 121 is numbered correctly. A 24-page catalogue of Chapman's publications, dated 30 April 1847, is inserted at the back.

Location: JM.

Note: The following textual changes were made between the second and third printings:

   [58]   [blank]   [[five lines of verse, beginning "Work of his hand"]

   [78]   [five lines of verse, beginning "Work of his hand"]   [[blank]

Emerson wrote to Chapman on 26 March 1845 that the mottoes to "Character" and "Manners" had been reversed in the first printing and requested correction (BLU).

A 16.2.d
First English edition, fourth printing (1845)

London: John Chapman, M.DCCC.XLV.

Title page is the same as the first printing, except: the date is changed; wavy rules are above and below '[gothic] Second Series.'; the epigram is in three lines, not two. Contents the same as the third printing, except: p. iv: blank. Page 121 is numbered correctly. A 32-page catalogue of Chapman's publications, dated 5 May 1848, is inserted at the back.

Location: VtMiM.

Note: The 1845 printings were advertised in cloth for 3s. 6d and in wrappers for 3s.

LATER PRINTINGS WITHIN THE FIRST ENGLISH EDITION

A 16.2.e
London: John Chapman, M.DCCC.XLVI.

Locations: BBP, MCo.

A 16.2.f
London: John Chapman, M.DCCC.XLVIII.

Cloth or wrappers. Prices: cloth, 3s. 6d; wrappers: 6d. *Location:* NNC.

A 16.2.g
London: John Chapman, M.DCCC.XLIX.

Copies have been noted with a 36-page catalogue for Chapman's publications, dated either 1 February 1853 or 20 April 1853, inserted at the back. *Locations:* BE (February), JM (April).

LATER EDITIONS

A 16.3.a
Second English edition, first printing (1850)

Eight Essays. London: George Slater, 1850.

208 pp. *Slater's Shilling Series,* no. 10. Listed in *Athenæum,* no. 1152 (24 November 1849), 1179. Advertised for 1 December 1849 publication. Price, 1s. *Location:* BL.

A 16.3.b–c
London: W. Tweedie, [1852].

Reprinted 1853. *Locations:* BL (24 August 1852), CaQMBN (1853).

A 16.4.a
Second American edition, first printing (1850)

Boston: Phillips, Sampson & Co., 1850.

274 pp. '[gothic] Second Edition'. 575 copies printed 20 November 1850 (Account Books [MH]). Price, 75¢. Royalty, 15¢. *Location:* DLC.

Note one: The following intercalary poem is added on p. 240: "New England Reformers" (reprinted as "Caritas"; see A 18.16).

Note two: Publisher's records indicate copies were bound in half and full calf; no copies have been located.

Note three: Emerson "paid for the printing & owned the stereotype plates," and was paid "in advance . . . 20 percent on the retail price" of each printing (25 February 1867, *L,* V, 507).

A 16.4.b
Boston: Phillips, Sampson, 1852.

'[gothic] Second Edition'. 500 copies printed 12 May 1852 (*JMN,* XIII, 479). Price, 75¢. Royalty, 15¢. *Location:* JM.

A 16.4.c
Boston: Phillips, Sampson, 1854.

'[gothic] Second Edition'. 500 copies printed 17 January 1854 (Account Books [MH]). Price, 75¢. Royalty, 15¢. *Location:* RPB.

A 16.4.d
Boston: Phillips, Sampson; New York: J. C. Derby, 1855.

'[gothic] Second Edition'. Price, $1.00. Royalty, 20¢. *Location:* JM.

A 16.4.e
Boston: Phillips, Sampson, 1856.

'[gothic] Second Edition'. 1,000 copies printed February 1856; 250 copies printed on "fine paper" December 1856 (*JMN,* XIV, 438, 452). Price, $1.00. Royalty, 20¢. *Not seen.*

A 16.4.f
Boston: Phillips, Sampson, 1857.

'[gothic] Third Edition'. 1,000 copies printed 30 September 1856 (*JMN,* XIV, 452). Price, $1.00. Royalty, 20¢. *Location:* ViU.

A 16.4.g
Boston: Phillips, Sampson, 1858.

'[gothic] Third Edition'. 500 copies printed July 1858 (Account Books [MH]). Price, $1.00. Royalty, 20¢. *Location:* JM.

Note: Phillips, Sampson failed on 19 September 1859.

A 16.4.h
Boston: Ticknor and Fields, M DCCC LX.

500 copies printed 13 January 1860. Price, $1.00. Royalty, 20¢. *Location:* JM.

Note: Some copies of Phillips, Sampson sheets may be in Ticknor and Fields bindings, with a cancel title leaf.

A 16.4.i
Boston: Ticknor and Fields, M DCCC LXII.

280 copies printed June–July 1862. Price, $1.00. Royalty, 20¢. *Not seen.*

A 16.4.j
Boston: Ticknor and Fields, MDCCCLXIII.

280 copies printed 10 August 1863. Price, $1.25. Royalty, 25¢. *Location:* JM

A 16.4.k
Boston: Ticknor and Fields, MDCCCLXV.

280 copies printed December 1864–January 1865. Price, $1.50. Royalty, 30¢. *Location:* JM.

Note: The copyright on *Essays: Second Series* was renewed 13 May 1865.

A 16.4.l
Boston: Ticknor and Fields, MDCCCLXVI.

Price, $1.50. Royalty, 30¢. *Location:* JM.

A 16.4.m
Boston: Ticknor and Fields, MDCCCLXVII.

280 copies printed October–November 1866. Price, $1.50. Royalty, 30¢. *Location:* JM.

A 16.4.n
Boston: Ticknor and Fields, MDCCCLXVIII.

280 copies printed December 1867–March 1868 and 20 May 1868. Price, $2.00. Royalty, 20¢. *Not seen.*

Note one: By a contract of 4 March 1868, Emerson's royalty was changed from 20 percent to 20¢ per volume.

Note two: Ticknor and Fields was succeeded by Fields, Osgood in October 1868.

A 16.4.o
Boston: Fields, Osgood, 1869.

280 copies printed April 1869 (Account Books [MH]). Price, $2.00. Royalty, 20¢. *Location:* JM.

Note one: In a "Supplementary article of agreement" to the 4 March 1868 contract, dated 19 February 1870, Emerson's royalty was raised to 30¢ per copy when the price was $2.00 or above.

Note two: Fields, Osgood was succeeded by James R. Osgood & Company in January 1871.

A 16.4.p
Boston: James R. Osgood, 1871.

150 copies printed 18 July 1871. Price, $2.00. Royalty, 30¢. *Not seen.*

A 16.4.q
Boston: James R. Osgood, 1873.

150 copies printed 11 June 1873. Price, $2.00. Royalty, 30¢. *Not seen.*

A 16.4.r
Boston: James R. Osgood, 1874.

150 copies printed 25 July 1874. Price, $2.00. Royalty, 30¢. *Location:* CtY.

A 16.4.s
Boston: James R. Osgood, 1875.

150 copies printed 21 May 1875. Price, $2.00. Royalty, 30¢. *Location:* MH.

A 16.4.t
Boston: James R. Osgood, 1876.

150 copies printed 31 August 1876. Price, $2.00. *Location:* JM.

Note one: Emerson's 1 January 1876 contract with Osgood called for him to receive a flat annual fee of $1,500 for all his books, rather than a per copy royalty.

Note two: James R. Osgood was succeeded by Houghton, Osgood in February 1878.

A 16.4.u
Boston: Houghton, Osgood, 1878.

164 copies printed 11 October 1878. Price, $1.50. *Not seen.*

A 16.4.v
Boston: Houghton, Osgood, 1880.

175 copies printed 21 January 1880. Price, $1.50. *Location:* MH.

Note: Houghton, Osgood was succeeded by Houghton, Mifflin in May 1880. Some copies of Houghton, Osgood sheets (including the title leaf) have been noted in Houghton, Mifflin bindings.

A 16.4.w
Boston: Houghton, Mifflin, 1882.

150 copies printed 9 September 1882. Price, $1.50. *Location:* MeWC.

A 16.4.x
Boston: Houghton, Mifflin, 1883.

150 copies printed 6 February 1883. Price, $1.50. *Location:* MMeT.

Note: As of 15 January 1884, 10 copies of *Essays: Second Series* were still in stock.

LATER EDITIONS

A 16.5
First German edition (1858)

Versuche. Hannover: Carl Meyer, 1858.

Combined with *Essays: First Series;* see A 10.8.

A 16.6.a–b
Essays   First and Second Series. Boston: Ticknor and Fields, 1865.

See A 10.9.a–b.

A 16.7.a
The Twenty Essays of Ralph Waldo Emerson. London: Bell & Daldy, 1870.

See A 10.10.a

A 16.7.b–c
London: George Bell & Sons, 1876.

See A 10.10.b–c.

PRINTINGS FROM THE "LITTLE CLASSIC EDITION" PLATES

A 16.8.a

[all within a double-rule frame; outer frame is red with boxed corners] [red] ESSAYS. | BY | RALPH WALDO EMERSON. | [red] *Second Series.* | NEW AND REVISED EDITION. | [ornate rule] | [red] BOSTON: | JAMES R. OSGOOD AND COMPANY, | Late Ticknor & Fields, and Fields, Osgood, & Co. | [red] 1876.

228 pp. Vol. [III] of the "Little Classic Edition" (see B 3). Listed in *Publishers' Weekly,* 10 (29 July 1876), 260. Copyright, 14 June 1876. Price, $1.50. Royalty: see *Note one* to A 16.4.t. *Locations:* BL (12 April 1877), PBL.

A 16.8.b
Boston: James R. Osgood, 1877.

500 copies printed 26 September 1877. Price, $1.50. *Not seen.*

Note: James R. Osgood was succeeded by Houghton, Osgood in February 1878.

A 16.8.c
Boston: Houghton, Osgood, 1879.

500 copies printed 21 October 1878 and 17 July 1879. Price, $1.50. *Location:* IaCrC.

A 16.8.d
Boston: Houghton, Osgood, 1879.

Combined with *Essays: First Series* in two-volumes-in-one format as vol. I of the "Fireside Edition" (see B 4). 500 copies printed 15 August 1879. *Location:* KU.

A 16.8.e
Boston: Houghton, Osgood, 1880.

Combined with *Essays: First Series* in two-volumes-in-one format as vol. I of the "Fireside Edition" (see B 4). 500 copies printed 6 February 1880. *Location:* JM.

Note: Houghton, Osgood was succeeded by Houghton, Mifflin in May 1880.

A 16.8.f
Boston: Houghton, Mifflin, 1880.

500 copies printed 9 June 1880. Price, $1.50. *Not seen.*

A 16.8.g
Boston: Houghton, Mifflin, 1881.

Combined with *Essays: First Series* in two-volumes-in-one format as vol. I of the "Fireside Edition" (see B 4). 500 copies printed 7 December 1880. *Location:* MWelC.

A 16.8.h
Boston: Houghton, Mifflin, 1881.

500 copies printed 9 March 1881. Price, $1.50. *Not seen.*

A 16.8.i
Boston: Houghton, Mifflin, 1882.

Combined with *Essays: First Series* in two-volumes-in-one format as vol. I of the "Fire-side Edition" (see B 4). 500 copies printed 4 October 1881, 13 May 1882, and 7 August 1882. *Location:* TSewU.

A 16.8.j
Boston: Houghton, Mifflin, 1882.

150 copies printed 17 November 1881; 500 copies on 25 November 1881, 12 May 1882, and 31 August 1882. Price, $1.50. *Location:* MH.

A 16.8.k
Boston: Houghton, Mifflin, 1883.

500 copies printed 20 November 1882 and 31 January 1883. *Location:* JM.

A 16.8.l
Boston: Houghton, Mifflin, 1883.

Combined with *Essays: First Series* in two-volumes-in-one format as vol. I of the "Fire-side Edition" (see B 4). 270 copies printed 12 January 1883. *Location:* JM.

A 16.8.m
Boston: Houghton, Mifflin, 1884.

500 copies printed 7 September 1883, 15 January 1884, and 26 August 1884. *Location:* JM.

A 16.8.n
Boston: Houghton, Mifflin, 1886.

270 copies printed 29 January 1886. Bound in medium blue V cloth (smooth), rather than "Little Classic Edition" binding, as are subsequent reprintings (see illustration at B 3). *Location:* TxHR.

A 16.8.o
Boston and New York: Houghton, Mifflin, 1887.

500 copies printed 2 October 1886; 270 copies on 4 August 1887. *Location:* MiD.

A 16.8.p
Boston and New York: Houghton, Mifflin, 1888.

500 copies printed 27 October 1887, 14 February 1888, and 13 July 1888. *Location:* JM.

A 16.8.q
Boston and New York: Houghton, Mifflin, 1889.

270 copies printed 18 February 1889; 500 copies on 18 July 1889. *Location:* JM.

A 16.8.r
Boston and New York: Houghton, Mifflin, 1890.

500 copies printed 14 January 1890 and ca. September 1890. *Location:* CtY.

A 16.8.s
Boston and New York: Houghton, Mifflin, 1891.

500 copies printed ca. February 1891 and 9 October 1891. *Not seen.*

A 16.8.t
Boston and New York: Houghton, Mifflin, 1892.

500 copies printed 29 February 1892 and 19 November 1892. *Location:* MHi.

A 16.8.u
Boston and New York: Houghton, Mifflin, 1893.

500 copies printed 15 August 1893. *Not seen.*

A 16.8.v
Boston and New York: Houghton, Mifflin, 1894.

500 copies printed 20 August 1894. *Not seen.*

A 16.8.w
Boston and New York: Houghton, Mifflin, 1895.

500 copies printed 18 October 1895. *Not seen.*

A 16.8.x
Boston and New York: Houghton, Mifflin, 1897.

500 copies printed 1 February 1897. *Not seen.*

A 16.8.y
Boston and New York: Houghton, Mifflin, 1898.

270 copies printed 9 February 1898. *Location:* JM.

A 16.8.z
Boston and New York: Houghton, Mifflin, 1899.

500 copies printed 28 January 1899. *Location:* MH.

A 16.8.aa
Boston and New York: Houghton, Mifflin, [n.d.].

Approximately 3,500 copies were sold between 1900 and 1923. *Location:* JM.

Note one: Approximately 21,600 copies of *Essays: Second Series* printed from the "Little Classic Edition" plates were sold between 1876 and 1923, when the title was apparently allowed to go out of print in this format.

Note two: The "Little Classic Edition" plates were ordered destroyed 5 October 1929.

LATER EDITION

A 16.9.a–s
Essays. London: Macmillan, 1883.

Combined with *Essays: First Series;* see A 10.12.a–s.

PRINTINGS FROM THE RIVERSIDE EDITION PLATES

A 16.10.a
Riverside Edition (trade), first printing (1883)

ESSAYS | BY | RALPH WALDO EMERSON | *SECOND SERIES* | [gothic] New and Revised Edition | [publisher's logo] | BOSTON | HOUGHTON, MIFᶜLIN AND COMPANY | New York: 11 East Seventeenth Street | [gothic] The Riverside Press, Cambridge | 1883

270 pp. Vol. III of the *Riverside Edition*, trade printing (see B 7). 1,000 copies printed 18 July 1883; 500 copies on 18 October 1883 and 18 December 1883. Listed in *Publishers' Weekly*, 24 (6 October 1883), 485. Copyright, 23 July 1883. According to the publisher's records, published 22 September 1883. Price, $1.75. *Location:* DLC (26 September 1883).

Note: Copies have been noted with a pine branch on the title page instead of the publisher's logo.

A 16.10.b
Riverside Edition (Copyright), second (English) printing (1883)

ESSAYS | BY | RALPH WALDO EMERSON | *SECOND SERIES* | [gothic] The Riverside Edition | (COPYRIGHT) | LONDON | GEORGE ROUTLEDGE AND SONS | BROADWAY, LUDGATE HILL | NEW YORK: 9, LAFAYETTE PLACE | 1883

Vol. III of the *Riverside Edition (Copyright)*, English trade printing (see B 10). 1,000 copies printed 1 September 1883. Listed as published between 17 and 29 September, in *Publishers' Circular and Booksellers' Record*, 46 (1 October 1883), 893. Price, 3s. 6d. *Locations:* BC (12 October 1883), BO (18 October 1883), BL (8 December 1883), CaBVaU.

A 16.10.c$_1$
Riverside Edition (large paper), third printing, American issue (1883)

[red] ESSAYS | BY | RALPH WALDO EMERSON | *SECOND SERIES* | [gothic] New and Revised Edition | [pine branch] | [red] CAMBRIDGE | [gothic] Printed at the Riverside Press | 1883

Vol. III of the *Riverside Edition*, large paper printing (see B 8). 500 copies printed 21 September 1883. Limited to 500 numbered copies. Price, $4.00. Sold out within a year. *Locations:* JM, TxU.

A 16.10.c$_2$
Riverside Edition (large paper), second printing, English issue (1883)

Title page is the same as in the American issue, except for publisher's imprint: 'LONDON | KEGAN PAUL, TRENCH, & CO., I, PATERNOSTER SQUARE | MDCCCLXXXIII'.

Vol. III of the *Riverside Edition*, large paper printing for English subscribers (see B 9). Limited to 25 signed and numbered copies. 25 title leaves printed 21 September 1883. Title leaf is a cancel. *Location:* JM.

A 16.10.d
Boston and New York: Houghton, Mifflin, 1884.

500 copies printed 4 January 1884, 7 March 1884, and 21 August 1884. *Location:* JM.

A 16.10.e
Boston and New York: Houghton, Mifflin, 1885.

500 copies printed 1 January 1885, 7 April 1885, and 23 September 1885. *Location:* JM.

A 16.10.f
Boston and New York: Houghton, Mifflin, 1886.

500 copies printed 30 January 1886 and 29 April 1886. *Location:* JM.

A 16.10.g
London and New York: George Routledge and Sons, 1887.

500 copies printed 22 September 1886. *Location:* JM.

A 16.10.h
Boston and New York: Houghton, Mifflin, 1887.

500 copies printed 2 October 1886, 25 April 1887, and 29 July 1887. *Location:* JM.

A 16.10.i
Boston and New York: Houghton, Mifflin, 1888.

500 copies printed 24 December 1887, 19 April 1888, 14 August 1888, and 27 November 1888. *Location:* JM.

Note: Edward Waldo Emerson wrote Houghton, Mifflin on 8 August 1888 that the copyright for *Essays: Second Series* had expired (Houghton Mifflin Company).

A 16.10.j
Boston and New York: Houghton, Mifflin, 1889.

500 copies printed 15 July 1889. *Location:* MH.

A 16.10.k
Essays First and Second Series. Boston and New York: Houghton, Mifflin, 1889.

See A 10.13.l.

A 16.10.l
Boston and New York: Houghton, Mifflin, 1890.`

500 copies printed 12 November 1889 and ca. September 1890. *Not seen.*

A 16.10.m
Boston and New York: Houghton, Mifflin, 1891.

500 copies printed ca. March, 1891 and 31 July 1891. *Location:* JM.

A 16.10.n
London [&c.]: George Routledge and Sons, 1891.

Location: MNoW.

A 16.10.o
Boston and New York: Houghton, Mifflin, 1892.

500 copies printed 9 January 1892 and 4 August 1892. *Location:* JM.

A 16.10.p
Essays. London, Manchester, New York: George Routledge and Sons, 1893.

Combined with *Essays: First Series;* see A 10.13.p.

A 16.10.q
Boston and New York: Houghton, Mifflin, 1893.

500 copies printed 14 November 1892. *Location:* JM.

A 16.10.r
Boston and New York: Houghton, Mifflin, 1894.

500 copies printed 10 October 1893 and 22 August 1894. *Location:* NBu.

A 16.10.s
Standard Library Edition printing [1894]

ESSAYS | BY | RALPH WALDO EMERSON | *SECOND SERIES* | [pine branch] | BOS-
TON AND NEW YORK | HOUGHTON, MIFFLIN AND COMPANY | [gothic] The River-
side Press, Cambridge

Vol. III of the *Standard Library Edition* (see B 11). 1,000 copies printed 31 October
1894, 30 March 1895, and 29 May 1896; 500 copies on 31 January 1898. *Location:* JM.

A 16.10.t
Boston and New York: Houghton, Mifflin, 1895.

500 copies printed 13 April 1895. *Location:* DeU.

A 16.10.u
Boston and New York: Houghton, Mifflin, 1896.

500 copies printed 29 February 1896. *Location:* VtSta.

A 16.10.v
Boston and New York: Houghton, Mifflin, 1897.

500 copies printed 27 February 1897. *Location:* JM.

A 16.10.w
Boston and New York: Houghton, Mifflin, 1898.

500 copies printed 10 January 1898. *Location:* LNHT.

A 16.10.x
Essays First and Second Series. Boston and New York: Houghton, Mifflin, 1898.
See A 10.13.x.

A 16.10.y
Boston and New York: Houghton, Mifflin, 1899.

500 copies printed 20 January 1899 and 30 September 1899. *Location:* MB.

A 16.10.z
London: George Routledge and Sons, 1900.

Location: CaQMM.

A 16.10.aa
London: George Routledge and Sons, 1903.

Location: JM.

A 16.10.bb
London: George Routledge and Sons, 1903.

Combined with *Nature; Addresses, and Lectures* and *Essays: First Series* in three-volumes-in-one format as vol. I of the "Sovereign Edition" (see B 12). 1,000 copies printed 16 September 1903. *Location:* InU.

A 16.10.cc
Fireside Edition printing (1909)

[all within double-rule frame with red floral ornaments in each corner] THE WORKS OF | [red gothic] Ralph Waldo Emerson | ESSAYS | SECOND SERIES | [engraving of man reading book in chair before fireplace] | [gothic] Fireside Edition | BOSTON AND NEW YORK | MDCCCCIX

Vol. III of the *Fireside Edition* (see B 13). 500 copies printed 30 September 1909 and 15 February 1910. *Location:* JM.

A 16.10.dd
Boston and New York: Jefferson Press, [ca. 1912].

Combined with *Essays: First Series;* see A 10.13.ee.

A 16.10.ee
New York: Sully and Kleinteich, [ca. 1912].

Vol. III of the *University Edition* (see B 15). *Location:* JM.

A 16.10.ff
Boston and New York: Houghton, Mifflin, [n.d.].

Approximately 3,200 copies sold between 1900 and 1913. *Location:* JM.

Note: Approximately 21,000 copies of *Essays: Second Series* in the *Riverside Edition* were sold between 1883 and 1913, when the title was apparently allowed to go out of print in this format.

A 16.10.gg
London: Waverley Book Company, [n.d.].

Vol. III of the "Waverley" *Riverside Edition* (see B 16). *Location:* JM.

LATER EDITIONS

A 16.11
New York: John B. Alden, 1886.

199 pp. Listed in *Publishers' Weekly,* 30 (6 November 1886), 638. Price, 50¢. Reprinted 1889, 1891, 1892. *Locations:* NcD (1886), JM (1889), InU (1891), MNoW (1892).

A 16.12.a
New York: John W. Lovell, [1888].

248 pp. Cloth or wrappers. Listed in *Publishers' Weekly,* 33 (23 January 1888), 957. Also advertised in wrappers as included in "Lovell's Library," no. 1167, for 20¢. Also

combined with *Essays: First Series* in two-volumes-in-one format in *Lovell's Universal Series. Locations:* JM (both).

A 16.12.b
New York: Merrill and Baker, [1896?].

Combined with *Essays: First Series;* see A 10.14.h.

A 16.12.c
New York: American Publishers Corporation, [n.d.].

Also combined with *Essays: First Series* in two-volumes-in-one format. *Locations:* CaPCL, CaBVaU (combined).

A 16.12.d
New York: Clarke, Given, & Hooper, [n.d.].

Also advertised as included in "University Edition." Also combined with *Essays: First Series* in two-volumes-in-one format. *Locations:* CaOTW, DCU (combined).

A 16.12.e
Boston: Estes and Lauriat, [n.d.].

Combined with *Essays: First Series* in two-volumes-in-one format. *Not seen.*

A 16.12.f
New York: Grosset & Dunlap, [n.d.].

Combined with *Essays: First Series;* see A 10.50.

A 16.12.g
New York: Hovendon, [n.d.].

Location: JM.

A 16.12.h
New York: International Book Company, [n.d.].

Aldine Edition; Popular Edition. Locations:

LNHT (*Aldine*), JM (*Popular*).

A 16.12.i
Boston: Joseph Knight, [n.d.].

Combined with *Essays: First Series;* see A 10.14.o.

A 16.12.j
New York: Frank F. Lovell, [n.d.].

Location: JM.

A 16.12.k
New York: Lovell, Coryell, [n.d.].

Also *Standard Edition.* Also advertised combined with *Essays: First Series* in two-volumes-in-one format. *Locations:* JM, NcU (*Standard*).

A 16.12.l
Albany [N.Y.]: James B. Lyon, [n.d.].

Location: N.

A 16.12.m
New York: National Book Company, [n.d.].

Combined with *Essays: First Series;* see A 10.14.s.

A 16.12.n
New York: United States Book Company, Successors to John W. Lovell Company, [n.d.].

Also advertised as included in "Lovell's Literaure Series," no. 100. Stamped on spine is "Hovendon Company." *Location:* JM.

A 16.13.a–g
Philadelphia: David McKay, 1888.

307 pp. Also *American Classic Series.* Listed in *Publishers' Weekly,* 34 (22 September 1888), 291. Price, $1.00. Reprinted 1889, 1890, 1891, 1892, 1893, [n.d.]. Also advertised in boxed set with *Essays: First Series.* Also combined with *Essays: First Series* in two-volumes-in-one format in 1891 and 1892. *Locations:* JM, PPT (1891), WaU (combined, 1891), IdU (combined, 1892).

A 16.13.h
Cleveland: Burrows Brothers, [n.d.].

Location: JM.

A 16.14.a
Essays First and Second Series. New York: A. L. Burt, [1890].

See A 10.19.a.

A 16.14.b
New York: F. M. Lupton, [1892].

Cloth or wrappers. *Avon Edition* (cloth); *Bijou Series,* no. 35, 4 May 1892 (wrappers). Price: wrappers, 25¢. Also combined with *Essays: First Series* in two-volumes-in-one format. *Locations:* JM (*Avon,* combined), MH (*Bijou*).

A 16.14.c
New York: P. F. Collier and Son, [n.d.].

See A 10.19.b.

A 16.15
London: David Stott, 1890.

338 pp. Vol. II of *Emerson's Essays;* see A 10.20.

A 16.16.a–e
Philadelphia: Henry Altemus, 1892.

245 pp. Advertised as included in "Altemus Library," no. 7, "Illustrated Vademecum Series," no. 52, "New Vademecum Series," and "Roycroft Series," no. 52. Reprinted 1894, 1895, 1896, [n.d.]. *Locations:* JM, VtU (1895), MWat (1896).

A 16.17.a–b
Chicago: Donohue, Henneberry, 1893.

315 pp. Reprinted [n.d.]. *Locations:* JM, AzU (n.d.).

A 16.17.c
Chicago: Geo. M. Hill, 1898.

Location: VtNoh.

A 16.17.d
Chicago: W. B. Conkey, [1900].

Combined with *Essays: First Series;* see A 10.26.a.

A 16.17.e
Chicago: M. A. Donohue, [n.d.].

Location: CaMWU.

A 16.17.f
Chicago: Donohue Brothers, [n.d.].

Also advertised as included in "Dresden Edition." *Location:* JM.

A 16.17.g
Emerson's Essays. Chicago and New York: Henneberry, [n.d.].

Combined with *Essays: First Series;* see A 10.26.c.

A 16.17.h
Chicago: Homewood, [n.d.].

Combined with the Crowell printing of *Essays: First Series;* see A 10.26.b.

A 16.17.i
Chicago: Monarch, [n.d.].

Location: KyL.

A 16.17.j
Chicago: Thompson & Thomas, [n.d.].

Noted with "267 Wabash Ave." and "338 Wabash Ave." imprints. *Locations:* JM (267), IdU (338).

A 16.17.k
Chicago: Union School Furnishing Co., [n.d.].

Combined with *Essays: First Series;* see A 10.26.d.

A 16.17.l
Chicago: Weeks, [n.d.].

Location: JM.

A 16.18.a
New York: H. M. Caldwell, [1896?].

234 pp. Also noted with Boston and New York imprint. Also advertised as included in "Superb Series," no. 8, for 75¢. *Locations:* JM (both).

A 16.18.b
Character and Other Essays. New York and Boston: H. M. Caldwell, [n.d.].

Price, 75¢. *Location:* JM.

A 16.18.c
New York: Home Book Company, [n.d.].

Also advertised as included in "New Beverly Edition." *Location:* JM.

A 16.18.d
New York: F. M. Lupton, [n.d.].

Combined with *Essays: First Series;* see A 10.22.d.

A 16.19
Emerson. London: Arthur L. Humphreys, 1899.

363 pp. Leather. *Location:* MH.

A 16.20.a–d
Essays Second Series & Nature. London: J. M. Dent, MDCCCCI.

279 pp. Cloth or flexible leather. Edited by Walter Jerrold. *The Temple Classics*. Published February 1901. Prices: cloth, 1s. 6d; leather, 2s. Reprinted August 1902, October 1903, January 1905. *Locations:* BL (27 February 1901), CtY (1903), JM (1905).

Note: Advertised as included in "The Temple Classics" in cloth and leather by Macmillan of New York in *Publishers' Weekly*, 59 (23 May 1901), 838. Probably an importation or, possibly, an American issue of the English sheets with a cancel title leaf. *Not seen.*

A 16.21.a–m
Essays. London: Grant Richards, 1901.

Combined with *Essays: First Series;* see A 10.28.a–m.

A 16.22.a
London: Isbister, 1903.

223 pp. *Isbister's Anglo Saxon Library*. Published April 1903. Price, 1s. 6d. *Locations:* BE (7 July 1903), BC (9 July 1903), BO (9 July 1903), CtW.

A 16.22.b
New York: T. Y. Crowell, [n.d.].

Advertised in various bindings at various prices. Also noted with Thomas Y. Crowell imprint. Also combined with *Essays: First Series* in two-volumes-in-one format. *Locations:* JM, CaBVaU (combined).

PRINTINGS FROM THE CENTENARY EDITION PLATES

A 16.23.a₁
Centenary Edition (trade), first printing, American issue (1903)

ESSAYS | BY | RALPH WALDO EMERSON | SECOND SERIES | [pine tree] | BOSTON AND NEW YORK | HOUGHTON, MIFFLIN AND COMPANY | [gothic] The Riverside Press, Cambridge | 1903

358 pp. Dust jacket. Vol. III of the *Centenary Edition,* trade printing (see B 18). 1,000 copies printed 8 June 1903; 500 copies on 31 December 1903. Listed in *Publishers' Weekly,* 63 (27 June 1903), 1445. Copyright, 1 June 1903. According to the publisher's records, published 1 June 1903 (but note first printing date above). Price, $1.75. *Location:* JM.

Note: Numerous reprintings with undated title pages. Approximately 6,500 copies printed between 1 January 1904 and 30 December 1910. Approximately 10,900 copies sold through 1923.

A 16.23.a$_2$
English issue

London: A. P. Watt & Son, [1903].

Vol. III of the English *Centenary Edition* (see B 21). American sheets with Watt's label pasted on the title page. Price, 6s. *Locations:* BL (3 June 1903), BE (1 July 1903), BC (3 July 1903).

A 16.23.b
Autograph Centenary Edition (large paper), second printing (1903)

RALPH WALDO EMERSON | [red] Essays | [red] Second Series | [pine tree] | CAMBRIDGE | [red gothic] Printed at the Riverside Press | 1903

Vol. III of the *Autograph Centenary Edition* (see B 19). Limited to 600 signed and numbered copies printed 8 June 1903. Price, $6.00. Sold out by 5 April 1906. *Locations:* DLC (12 June 1903), JM.

A 16.23.c
Boston and New York: Houghton, Mifflin, 1903.

Vol. III of the *Concord Edition* (see B 20). 1,000 copies printed 30 September 1903. *Location:* JM.

Note: Numerous reprintings with undated title pages. Approximately 3,000 copies sold by 1 April 1907.

A 16.23.d
Boston and New York: Houghton Mifflin, [1914].

Vol. III of the *Riverside Pocket Edition* (see B 22). Approximately 4,000 copies sold between 1914 and 1922. *Location:* NcCuW.

A 16.23.e
Boston and New York: Houghton Mifflin, 1921.

285 pp. (text without the notes). Combined with *Essays: First Series* in two-volumes-in-one format as vol. I of *Emerson's Complete Works* (see B 23). *Location:* WaU.

A 16.23.f
New York: Wm. H. Wise, 1923.

Combined with *Representative Men* in two-volumes-in-one format as vol. II of the *Current Opinion Edition* (see B 24). *Location:* JM.

A 16.23.g
Essays First and Second Series. Boston and New York: Houghton Mifflin, 1925.

See A 10.31.g.

A 16.23.h
Boston: Houghton Mifflin, 1929.

Combined (text without the notes) with *Essays: First Series* in two-volumes-in-one format as vol. [I] of the *Harvard Edition* (see B 25). *Location:* JM.

A 16.23.i
New York: Wm. H. Wise, 1929.

Combined with *Representative Men* in two-volumes-in-one format as vol. II of the *Medallion Edition* (see B 26). *Location:* OC.

A 16.23.j–k
New York: AMS Press, [1968].

Vol. III of the "AMS Press" *Centenary Edition* (see B 27). Reprinted 1979. *Locations:* TxU, DLC (9 November 1979).

LATER EDITIONS

A 16.24
Essays. London: George Routledge & Sons; New York: E. P. Dutton, [1905].

Combined with *Essays: First Series;* see A 10.32.

A 16.25.a–r
Essays First and Second Series. London: J. M. Dent & Sons; New York: E. P. Dutton, [1906].

See A 10.34.a–r.

A 16.25.s–w
Emerson's Essays. London: J. M. Dent & Sons; New York: E. P. Dutton, [1955].

See A 10.34.s–w.

A 16.26.a
Philadelphia: John D. Morris, [1906].

Combined with *Essays: First Series;* see A 10.35.a.

A 16.26.b
Boston and New York: C. T. Brainard, [n.d.].

Vol. I of the *Works;* see A 10.35.b.

A 16.26.c
[New York]: A. L. Burt, [n.d.].

See A 10.35.c.

A 16.26.d
New York: Caxton Society, [n.d.].

Vol. I of the *Works;* see A 10.35.d.

A 16.26.e
New York: National Library Co., [n.d.].

Vol. I of the *Works;* see A 10.35.e.

A 16.26.f
Philadelphia, New York, Chicago: Nottingham Society, [n.d.].

Vol. I of the *Works;* see A 10.35.f.

A 16.27.a
London: George G. Harrap, [1909].

229 pp. Also noted with London, Calcutta, Sydney imprint. *The Harrap Library,* no. 2. *Locations:* BL (2 September 1909), JM (both).

A 16.27.b
New York: Dodge, [n.d.].

The Dodge Library. Also advertised as included in "Green Book" and "Ooze Leather" series. *Location:* JM.

A 16.27.c
New York: Robert M. McBride, [n.d.].

Introduction by Edward Everett Hale. *Chelsea College Classics. Location:* NFQC.

A 16.28
New York: E. P. Dutton, [1912?].

Advertised as included in "Best Books," "Coniston Library," "New Commercial Library," and "Temple Classics." *Not seen.*

A 16.29.a
New York: Hearst's International Library Co., [1914].

Combined with *Essays: First Series* in the *New National Edition;* see A 10.37.a.

A 16.29.b
New York: Tudor, [1942].

The *Works;* see A 10.37.b.

A 16.29.c
New York: Charles C. Bigelow, [n.d.].

Vol. I of the *Works;* see A 10.37.c.

A 16.29.d–e
New York: Bigelow, Brown, [n.d.].

Vol. I of the *Works;* see A 10.37.d–e.

A 16.29.f
New York: Bigelow, Smith, [n.d.].

Vol. I of the *Works;* see A 10.37.f.

A 16.29.g
New York: Brentano's, [n.d.].

Vol. I of the *Writings;* see A 10.37.g.

A 16.29.h
New York: Harper & Brothers, [n.d.].

Vol. I of the *Works;* see A 10.37.h.

A 16.29.i
Boston and New York: Jefferson Press, [n.d.].

Vol. I of the *Works;* see A 10.37.i.

A 16.29.j
[N.p.]: Library Society, [n.d.].

Vol. I of the *Works;* see A 10.37.j.

A 16.29.k
New York: Three Sirens Press, [n.d.].

Vol. I of the *Works;* see A 10.37.k.

A 16.30
Essays First and Second Series. New York: Thomas Nelson and Sons, [1918?].

See A 10.38.

A 16.31.a–c
Essays First and Second Series. New York: Thomas Y. Crowell, [1926].

See A 10.39.a–c.

A 16.31.d
Essays. New York: Carlton House, [n.d.].

See A 10.39.d.

A 16.32.a–b
Essays First and Second Series. New York: Macmillan, MCMXXVI.

See A 10.40.a–b.

A 16.33.a
The Essays of Ralph Waldo Emerson. San Francisco: Limited Editions Club, 1934.

Combined with *Essays: First Series;* see A 10.42.a.

A 16.33.b
New York: Heritage Press, [1953].

See A 10.42.b.

A 16.33.c
Norwalk, Conn.: Heritage Press, [1962].

See A 10.42.c.

A 16.34
Essays. [Reading, Penn.]: Spencer, [1936].

Combined with *Essays: First Series;* see A 10.43.

A 16.35
Essays First and Second Series. Mount Vernon, N.Y.: Peter Pauper, [1946].

See A 10.45.

A 16.36.a
Essays. New York: Grolier, [1969].

Combined with *Essays: First Series;* see A 10.46.a.

A 16.36.b
New York: Franklin Watts, [n.d.].

See A 10.46.b.

UNDATED EDITIONS

A 16.37.a
New York: Wm. L. Allison, [n.d.].

280 + 100 pp. *Life* by Richard Garnett and 4 pp. bibliography by John P. Anderson. Also combined with *Essays: First Series* in two-volumes-in-one format. *Locations:* JM, NmU (combined).

A 16.37.b
New York: A. L. Burt, [n.d.].

The Home Library. Also advertised as included in "Columbia Series," "Cornell Series," and "New Pocket Edition of Standard Classics." Also combined with *Essays: First Series* in two-volumes-in-one format. *Locations:* MH (both).

A 16.37.c
Philadelphia: Porter & Coates, [n.d.].

Price, 75¢. *Location:* JM.

A 16.38
New York: A. L. Burt, [n.d.].

319 pp. *Location:* JM.

A 16.39
[N.p.]: Federal Book Company, [n.d.].

Advertised in various bindings at various prices. *Not seen.*

A 16.40
New York: Hurst, [n.d.].

151 pp. Advertised in various bindings at various prices. *Location:* JM.

A 16.41.a
Essays. New York and London: Merrill and Baker, [n.d.].

248 pp. Combined with *Essays: First Series;* see A 10.53.a.

A 16.41.b
Chicago: Rand, McNally, [n.d.].

See A 10.53.b.

A 16.42
Rahway, N.J.: Mershon, [n.d.].

Advertised in various bindings at various prices. *Not seen.*

A 16.43
[N.p.]: Wessell, [n.d.].

Price, $7.50. *Not seen.*

SEPARATE PUBLICATIONS OF INDIVIDUAL ESSAYS

A 16.44
Character. New York: John B. Alden; Chicago: Alden Book Co., 1886.

61–79 pp. Wrappers. *The Elzevir Library,* vol. 5, no. 238, 9 November 1886. Price, 3¢. *Location:* OO.

Note: From the plates of *Essays: Second Series* (A 16.11).

A 16.45
Character. Philadelphia: Henry Altemus, [1896].

27 pp. Dust jacket. *Life of Service Series,* no. 3. Price, 25¢. Also advertised as included in "Belles-Letters" and "Love and Friendship," no. 5, series. *Locations:* DLC (17 June 1896), JM.

A 16.46
Character. New York: H. M. Caldwell, [1900].

47 pp. *Location:* JM.

A 16.47.a
Character. London: Astolat, MDCCCCV.

25 pp. Published May 1905. Price, 1s. *Locations:* BL (3 July 1905), BC (10 July 1905), BE (10 July 1905), JM.

A 16.47.b–d
Character. London: Siegle, Hill, [1907].

Oakleaf Series. Published September 1907. Price, 1s. Reprinted twice [n.d.]. *Location:* CaQQLA (3rd printing).

A 16.48
Character. [London]: Siegle, Hill, [1909].

87 pp. Leather. Miniature book. *Langham Booklets.* Published September 1909. Price: 1s. *Location:* BL (18 January 1910).

A 16.49
Character. New York: H. M. Caldwell, [n.d.].

Advertised in various bindings at various prices. Advertised as included in "Words of Help" series. *Not seen.*

A 16.50
Character. New York: Dodge, [n.d.].

48 pp. *The Little Masterpieces.* Also advertised as included in "Booklover's Gems," "Florentine Classics," and "Handcraft" series. *Location:* CaOWtU.

A 16.51
Character. Philadelphia: George W. Jacobs, [n.d.].

Advertised in various bindings at various prices. *Not seen.*

A 16.52
Character. Philadelphia: David McKay, [n.d.].

Price, 50¢. *Not seen.*

A 16.53
Character. New York: Putnams, [n.d.].

Price, 50¢. *Not seen.*

A 16.54
Character. Philadelphia: Privately printed and presented with the compliments of Edward Stern & Company Incorporated, [n.d.].

36 pp. *Location:* NBu.

A 16.55
Experience. New York: John B. Alden; Chicago: Alden Book Co., 1886.

[33]–60 pp. Wrappers. *The Elzevir Library,* vol. 5, no. 237, 9 November 1886. Price, 3¢. *Location:* DLC.

Note: From the plates of *Essays: Second Series* (A 16.11).

A 16.56
Experience. New York: New York Book Company, [1912?].

Advertised as included in "Aurora Edition" series. Price, 40¢. *Not seen.*

A 16.57
Gifts. [Brooklyn, N.Y.]: Bewick Press, 1903.

15 leaves, printed on rectos only. Limited to 75 signed and numbered copies. *Location:* JM.

A 16.58
Gifts. New York: Hobby Press, MCMXIII.

15 pp. Wrappers. *Brushwood Classics*. Completed May 1913. Limited to 50 copies on Japanese handmade paper. *Location:* NN.

A 16.59
An Essay on Gifts. Boston: Seaver-Howland, [1914].

16 pp. Wrappers. *The Waverley Chap-books*, no. 6. *Location:* CStbS.

Note: Possible reprint advertised as included in "Waverley Chap-books" by Cornhill in 1918 *Cumulative Book Index*.

A 16.60
Manners. New York: John B. Alden, 1886.

[81]–106 pp. Wrappers. *The Elzevir Library*, vol. 5, no. 239, 16 November 1886. Price, 3¢. *Location:* OO.

Note: From the plates of *Essays: Second Series* (A 16.11).

A 16.61
Manners. Philadelphia: Henry Altemus, [1896].

35 pp. *Life of Service Series*, no. 10. Also *Belle-Lettres Series*. Price, 25¢. Also advertised as included in "Love and Friendship" series, no. 4. *Locations:* DLC (17 June 1896), JM (*Belle-Lettres*).

A 16.62
Manners. New York: H. M. Caldwell, [1912?].

Leather. Price, 60¢. *Not seen.*

A 16.63
The Essay on Nature. Ridgewood, N.J.: Press of Alwil Shop, MCMII.

Unpaged (33 leaves). Boards. Completed April 1903. Also 50 copies handcolored on Dutch handmade paper. Prices: $1.00; limited printing, $5.00. *Location:* NjHi.

A 16.64
Nature. [Croton Falls, N.Y.: Spiral Press, 1932].

28 pp. Limited to 100 numbered copies. *Location:* MH.

A 16.65
The Poet. New York: John B. Alden; Chicago: Alden Book Co., 1899.

Wrappers. Advertised as included in "Irving Library," vol. 6, no. 848, 9 October 1899. *Not seen.*

Note: Probably from the plates of *Essays: Second Series* (A 16.11).

A 16.66.a
Character and Heroism. New York and Boston: H. M. Caldwell, [1900].

83 pp. Advertised in various bindings at various prices. Listed in *Publishers' Weekly*, 58 (8 December 1900), 1630. Published 8 December 1900. Also advertised as included in "Remarque Editions" and "Remarque Literary Classics." *Location:* N.

A 16.66.b
San Francisco: Paul Elder, [1901?].

Limp leather. *Impression Classics*. Price, $1.00. *Location:* CtY.

A 16.67
Character and Heroism. New York: Putnams, [n.d.].

Limp leather. Price, $1.00. *Not seen.*

A 16.68
Essays on Character and Manners. Girard, Kansas: Haldeman-Julius, [n.d.].

63 pp. Wrappers. *Little Blue Book,* no. 545. *Location:* KU.

A 16.69
Character   Self-Reliance. London: John M. Watkins, 1917.

71 pp. Published August 1917. Price, 9d. *Location:* BL (20 March 1918).

A 16.70
Essays on Experience and Politics. Girard, Kansas: Haldeman-Julius, [n.d.].

57 pp. Wrappers. *Little Blue Book,* no. 543. *Location:* KU.

A 16.71
Nature and Art. Philadelphia: Henry Altemus, [1896].

46 pp. Also advertised as included in "Belles-Lettres" series in leatherette for 25¢. *Locations:* DLC (21 February 1896), JM.

A 16.72
Ralph Waldo Emerson   his Essay on Nature also Essay on Friendship. Pittsfield, Mass.: Caxton Society, nineteen hundred and nine.

Unpaged (32 leaves). Completed August 1909. *Location:* JM.

A 16.73.a
Love and Other Essays. New York: Dodge, [1901].

106 pp. Cloth or wrappers. Also contains "Nature" and "Character." Listed as "Love, Nature, and Other Essays," in *Publishers' Weekly,* 60 (28 December 1901), 1492. Also advertised as included in "Burnt Leather Classics," "Chettenham Nuggets," "Green Book Series," and "Vine Tree Series." Price: wrappers, 25¢. *Location:* CtY.

A 16.73.b
Love Nature and Other Essays. New York: Dodge, [1901].

Cloth or self-wrappers. Published 28 December 1901. *Location:* JM.

A 16.73.c
Nature and Other Essays. New York: Dodge, [1901].

Flexible leather. Also advertised as included in "Dodge Library" and "Flexible Suede Leather" series. *Location:* JM.

A 16.73.d
Nature—Love—Character. New York: Robert M. McBride, [n.d.].

Chelsea Classics. Location: OBgU.

A 16.74
Essays on Nominalist and Realist, Gifts and The Over-Soul. Girard, Kansas: Haldeman-Julius, [n.d.].

62 pp. Wrappers. *Little Blue Book,* no. 549. *Location:* KU.

A 16.75
Essays on the Poet and Nature. Girard, Kansas: Haldeman-Julius, [n.d.].

60 pp. Wrappers. *Little Blue Book,* no. 544. *Location:* KU.

A 17 [EMANCIPATION IN THE WEST INDIES]

A 17.1.a
First American edition, first printing (1844)

AN

ADDRESS

DELIVERED IN

THE COURT-HOUSE IN CONCORD, MASSACHUSETTS,

ON 1st AUGUST, 1844,

ON THE

ANNIVERSARY OF THE EMANCIPATION

OF THE

NEGROES IN THE BRITISH WEST INDIES.

By R. W. EMERSON.

Published by Request.

——◆——

BOSTON:
JAMES MUNROE AND COMPANY.
1844.

A 17.1.a: 9^{1}/$_{4}$″ × 5^{3}/$_{4}$″

Entered, according to Act of Congress, in the year 1844, by
JAMES MUNROE AND COMPANY,
in the Clerk's Office of the District Court of the District of Massachusetts.

BOSTON:
PRESS OF THURSTON, TORRY, AND CO.
31 Devonshire Street.

[1–3] 4–34

[1]⁴ 2–4⁴ 5¹

Contents: p. 1: title page; p. 2: copyright page; pp. 3–34: text.

Typography and paper: 6³/₈″ × 3¹/₂″; wove paper; 35 lines per page. No running heads.

Binding: Two styles have been noted, priority undetermined:

Binding A: Sewn but unbound sheets. All edges rough trimmed.

Binding B: Light brown wrappers. Front recto: the same as the title page within a triple-rule frame; front verso, back recto and verso: blank. All edges trimmed.

Publication: On 30 August 1844, Emerson wrote to Margaret Fuller that the address was "just getting through the press," and to Caroline Sturgis that it would be ready within the next two weeks (*L*, III, 259; MH). On 1 September 1844, Emerson wrote Carlyle that he had sent a set of the American proofs to John Chapman to use in setting the English edition (*CEC*, p. 364). Deposited for copyright: title, 4 September 1844; book, 18 October 1844. Advertised as "Is published," in *Boston Daily Advertiser*, 9 September 1844, p. 3. Deposit copy: DLC (18 October 1844). Price, 12¹/₂¢. Author's share, unknown.

Locations: Binding A: JM, NN; Binding B: CSt, DLC, InU, JM, MB, MH, MHi, NN, NNC, NcD, NjP, PSt, TxU, ViU.

AN

ADDRESS

DELIVERED IN

THE COURT-HOUSE IN CONCORD, MASSACHUSETTS,

ON 1st AUGUST, 1844,

ON THE

ANNIVERSARY OF THE EMANCIPATION

OF THE

NEGROES IN THE BRITISH WEST INDIES.

BY R. W. EMERSON.

Published by Request.

———◆———

BOSTON:
JAMES MUNROE AND COMPANY.
1844.

Wrapper for A 17.1.a

A 17.1.b
First edition, second printing (1844)

Boston: James Munroe and Company, 1844.

All the same as the first printing, except: front wrapper recto: ' . . . [gothic] Request. |
[rule] | SECOND THOUSAND. | [rule with dot in center] | BOSTON: . . . '.

Locations: DLC, JM, MHi, MWA, NjP, RPB, TxU.

Note: Some copies of the second printing are distinguished by type slippage: in the
first printing, the 'w' of 'will' (34.13) is to the left of the 'o' in 'of' (34.12); in the second
printing, the 'w' in 'will' is to the right of the 'o' in 'of'.

A 17.2
First English edition, only printing (1844)

THE

EMANCIPATION OF THE NEGROES

IN THE

BRITISH WEST INDIES.

AN ADDRESS DELIVERED AT CONCORD, MASSACHUSETTS,
ON 1st AUGUST, 1844

BY

R. W. EMERSON.

" Fetters, chains, monopolies, thefts, sales, statutes, all engines of tyranny,
men have found insufficient to annihilate freedom, for the good reason, that
they cannot annihilate the Soul whose first law of being is freedom. Despite
of lies which the ages have told, of tyrannies which the ages have established,
Freedom lives imperishable."

LONDON:
JOHN CHAPMAN, 121, NEWGATE STREET.

M.DCCC.XLIV.

A 17.2: 7⁷/₈″ × 4³/₄″

[1–3] 4–32

[A]⁶ B⁶ C⁴

Contents: p. 1: title page; p. 2: printer's imprint; pp. 3–32: text.

Typography and paper: $5^{13}/_{16}''$ ($5^9/_{16}''$) × $3^3/_{16}$; wove paper; 35 lines per page. Running heads. rectos: pp. 5–31: 'IN THE BRITISH WEST INDIES.'; versos: pp. 4–30: 'ON NEGRO EMANCIPATION'; p. 32: 'ON NEGRO EMANCIPATION, ETC.'.

Binding: Light brown wrappers. Front recto: same as the title page within a single-rule frame with designs in each corner and in the center on each side, with at bottom '[at left] STEREOTYPE] [at right] [EDITION. | PRICE SIXPENCE.'; front verso and back recto: blank; back verso: advertisements for Chapman's publications. All edges trimmed.

Publication: On 1 September 1844, Emerson wrote Carlyle that he had sent a set of American proofs to Chapman for setting the English edition (*CEC,* p. 364). Listed as published between 28 September and 4 October, in *Publishers' Circular and Booksellers' Record,* 7 (15 October 1844), 298; advertised as "already published," in *Publishers' Circular and Booksellers' Record,* 7 (15 October 1844), 301; advertised as "Already published," in *Athenæum,* no. 887 (26 October 1844), 984; advertised in *Athenæum,* no. 889 (9 November 1844), 1011, and *Literary Gazette,* no. 1451 (9 November 1844), 726. On 30 December 1844, Emerson wrote Chapman acknowledging receipt of a copy (*L,* III, 273). Price, 6d. Royalty, half profits.

Printing: "LONDON: | PRINTED BY RICHARD KINDER, GREEN ARBOUR COURT, | OLD BAILEY" (p. [2]).

Location: NcD.

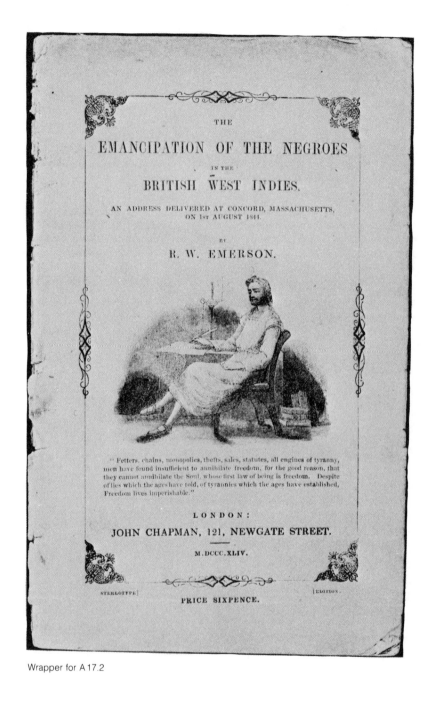

THE

EMANCIPATION OF THE NEGROES

IN THE

BRITISH WEST INDIES.

AN ADDRESS DELIVERED AT CONCORD, MASSACHUSETTS,
ON 1st AUGUST 1844.

BY

R. W. EMERSON.

" Fetters, chains, monopolies, thefts, sales, statutes, all engines of tyranny,
men have found insufficient to annihilate freedom, for the good reason, that
they cannot annihilate the Soul, whose first law of being is freedom. Despite
of lies which the ages have told, of tyrannies which the ages have established,
Freedom lives imperishable."

LONDON:

JOHN CHAPMAN, 121, NEWGATE STREET.

M.DCCC.XLIV.

[STEREOTYPE]　　　　　　　　　　　　　　　[EDITION.

PRICE SIXPENCE.

Wrapper for A 17.2

A 18 POEMS

A 18.1.a
First English edition, first printing (1847)

POEMS.

BY

RALPH WALDO EMERSON.

LONDON:

CHAPMAN, BROTHERS, 121, NEWGATE STREET.

M.DCCC.XLVII.

A 18.1.a: $7^{3}/_{4}''$ × $4^{11}/_{16}''$

NOTICE.

The Publishers of this work, which is printed from the Author's manuscript, beg to state that it is Copyright, according to the late Copyright, Act 5 & 6 Victoria; and all persons are hereby cautioned against printing or causing to be printed the same. Proceedings in Equity will be instituted against all persons so offending after this notice.

[i–v] vi–vii [viii] [1] 2–6 [7] 8–12 [13] 14–17 [18] 19–20 [21] 22–25 [26] 27–29 [30] 31 [32] 33–38 [39] 40–41 [42] 43 [44–45] 46–47 [48–49] 50–56 [57] 58–72 [73] 74–90 [91–92] 93–98 [99] 100 [101–104] 105 [106–107] 108–113 [114] 115 [116–117] 118 [119] 120–122 [123] 124–129 [130] 131–141 [142] 143–146 [147] 148–152 [153–155] 156–163 [164] 165 [166] 167–172 [173] 174 [175–176] 177 [178] 179–180 [181] 182–184 [185] 186–187 [188] 189–199 [200–202]

[a]² [A]² B–I¹² K⁴ [L]¹

Contents: p. i: 'POEMS.'; p. ii: notice of copyright protection; p. iii: title page; p. iv: printer's imprint; pp. v–vii: contents; p. viii: blank; pp. 1–200: poems; p. 201: 'MORTON AND CHAPMAN, | PRINTERS, | 2, CRANE-COURT, FLEET-STREET, LONDON.'; p. 202: blank.

Poems: "The Sphinx" †; "Each and All" †; "The Problem" †; "To Rhea" †; "The Visit" †; "Uriel" #; "The World-Soul" †; "Alphonso of Castile" #; "Mithridates" #; "To J. W." #; "Fate" ["That you are fair or wise is vain"] †; "Guy" #; "Tact" †; "Hamatreya" #; "Good-Bye" †; "The Rhodora" †; "The Humble-Bee" †; "Berrying" †; "The Snow-Storm" †; "Woodnotes. I." †; "Woodnotes. II." †; "Monadnoc" #; "Fable" †; "Ode, Inscribed to W. H. Channing" #; "Astræa" #; "Etienne de la Boéce" #; "Suum Cuique" †; "Compensation" #; "Forbearance" †; "The Park" †; "The Forerunners" †; "Sursum Corda" #; "Ode to Beauty" †; "Give All to Love" #; "To Ellen, at the South" †; "To Eva" †; ["Thine eyes still shined . . . "] #; "The Amulet" †; "Eros" ["The sense of the world is short"] †; "Hermione" #; "The Initial Love" #; "The Dæmonic and the Celestial Love" #; "The Apology" #; "Merlin. I." #; "Merlin. II." #; "Bacchus" #; "Loss and Gain" †; "Merops" #; "The House" #; "Saadi" †; "Holidays" †; "Painting and Sculpture" †; "From the Persian of Hafiz [1]" #; "From the Persian of Hafiz [2]" #; "Xenophanes" #; "The Day's Ration" #; "Blight" †; "Musketaquid" #; "Dirge" †; "Threnody" #; "Hymn, Sung at the Completion of the Concord Monument" †.

Typography and paper: 5¹⁵/₁₆″ (5⁵/₈″) × 3³/₁₆″; wove paper; 26 lines per page. Running heads: rectos: p. vii: 'CONTENTS.'; pp. 3–5, 9–11, 15–19, 23–37, 41–43, 47, 51–55, 59–71, 75–89, 93–97, 105, 109–115, 121, 125–145, 149–151, 157–171, 177–179, 183, 187–199: titles of poems; versos: p. vi: 'CONTENTS.'; pp. 2–16, 20–24, 28, 34–40, 46, 50–90, 94–100, 108–112, 118–128, 132–140, 144–152, 156–162, 168–174, 180–186, 190–198: titles of poems.

Binding: Two styles have been noted:

Binding A: Light green horizontal T cloth (rib). Front cover: blindstamped intersecting triple-rule frame with goldstamped 3¹/₂″ floral oval ornament and 'EMERSON'S | POEMS' in center; back cover: blindstamped intersecting triple-rule frame with 3¹/₂″ oval floral ornament in center; spine: goldstamped leaf-vine-and-flower design with 'EMERSON'S | POEMS | [two lines in script] *Chapman,* | *Brothers.* | LONDON.'. Yellow coated endpapers. All edges trimmed.

Binding B: Same as Binding A, except: front and back covers have blindstamped intersecting double-rule frame; back cover has blindstamped 'EMERSON'S | POEMS' in the center of the ornament; spine has goldstamped '[script] *J. Chapman* | LON-DON' at the bottom. Back flyleaf in some copies. Light brown coated or yellow coated endpapers. All edges trimmed.

Publication: Emerson sent his manuscript to John Chapman on 13 October 1846 (see *L*, III, 356). Advertised as "To be published early in December," in *Athenæum*, no. 994 (14 November 1846), 1155. Advertised as "This day is published," in *Athenæum*, no. 998 (12 December 1846), 1277. Listed as published between 28 November and 14 December, in *Publishers' Circular and Booksellers' Record*, 9 (15 December 1846), 378. Listed in *Athenæum*, no. 999 (19 December 1846), 1298. Advertised by John Chapman as "This day published," in *Athenæum*, no. 1005 (30 January 1847), 115. Inscribed copy: Binding A: InU (January 1847). Price, 6s. Royalty, unknown.

Printing: "[rule] | Morton & Chapman, Printers, 2, Crane-Court, Fleet-street" (p. [iv]).

Locations: Binding A: BE, BO, DLC, InU, JM, MH, NN, PSt, RPB, TxU, ViU; Binding B: JM, MH, MHi, NjP.

Note one: A 20-line errata slip, printed on the recto, is present in some copies: tipped to p. v: JM (B), PSt; tipped to p. 1: MH (B), NN, NjP, TxU.

Note two: Copies have been noted (all in Binding A) with a 24-page catalogue of Chapman's publications, dated 16 November 1846, inserted at the back: BO, DLC, InU, JM, MH, NN, RPB, TxU, ViU.

Note three: Copies have been noted (all in Binding A) with a 24-page catalogue of Chapman's publications, dated 1 January 1847, inserted at the back: BE, BO.

Note four: A copy has been noted (in Binding A) with a 24-page catalogue of Chapman's publications, dated 20 February 1847, inserted at the back: PSt.

Note five: A copy has been noted (in Binding B) with a 32-page catalogue of Chapman's publications, dated 12 January 1848, inserted at the back: JM.

Note six: Copies have been noted (all in Binding B) with a 24-page catalogue of Chapman's publications, dated September 1849, inserted at the back: MH, MHi.

Note seven: Copies have been noted (all in Binding B) lacking gathering [A], containing the contents: MH, MHi, NjP.

Note eight: Copies have been noted (all in Binding B) lacking the final leaf, with the printer's imprint: JM, MH, MHi.

Note nine: A copy has been noted lacking the half title leaf, gathering [A], and the final leaf; with the errata slip tipped to p. 1; and in a presumed remainder binding: purple AR cloth (coarse ribbed morocco); front and back covers: blank; spine: leather label with goldstamped '[rule] | EMERSON'S | POEMS | [rule]'; yellow endpapers; all edges trimmed. *Location:* MCo.

Note ten: A copy has been noted with gathering [A] folded in the reverse order (p. i: title page; p. ii: printer's imprint; p. iii: 'POEMS.'; p. iv: notice of copyright protection); lacking the final leaf; and in a presumed remainder binding: purple T cloth (rib); front and back covers: blank; spine: goldstamped '[rule] | [rule] | EMERSON'S | POEMS | [rule] | [rule]'; white endpapers; all edges trimmed. *Location:* JM.

A 18.1.b
First English edition, second printing (1850)

London: George Routledge & Co., MDCCCL.

'[gothic] Second Edition.'. Listed in *Literary Gazette,* no. 1770 (21 December 1850), 955. Price, 2s. 6d. *Locations:* BL, CtW, NNC, VtMiM, WU.

A 18.2.a
First American edition, first, second, and third printings (1847)

P O E M S.

B Y

R. W. E M E R S O N.

B O S T O N:

J A M E S   M U N R O E   A N D   C O M P A N Y.

1 8 4 7.

A 18.2.a: 7″ × 4^1/$_2$″

Entered according to act of Congress, in the year 1846, by

JAMES MUNROE AND COMPANY,

in the Clerk's office of the District Court of the District of Massachusetts.

STEREOTYPED AT THE
BOSTON TYPE AND STEREOTYPE FOUNDRY.

CAMBRIDGE:

METCALF AND COMPANY,

PRINTERS TO THE UNIVERSITY.

The first three printings within this edition cannot be distinguished.

Two issues have been noted:

1st issue: [i–viii] [1–3] 4–251 [252–256]

                 [a]^4 [1]^8 2–16^8

2nd issue: [1–3] 4–251 [252–256]

                 [1]^8 2–16^8

Contents: 1st issue: pp. i ii: blank; pp. iii–vi: catalogue for Munroe's publications, dated 1 January 1847; p. vii: 'POEMS.'; p. viii: blank; p. 1: title page; p. 2: copyright page; pp. 3–6: contents; pp. 7–251: poems; pp. 252–256: blank; 2nd issue: pp. 1–256 are the same as in the first issue.

Poems: The same contents as the English edition, except: the order of "The Amulet" and ["Thine eyes still shined . . . "] is reversed; "From the Persian of Hafiz [2]" is retitled "Ghaselle."

Typography and paper: 5″ (4^{11}/₁₆″) × 3^{1}/₁₆″; wove paper; 21 lines per page. Running heads: rectos: p. 5: 'CONTENTS.'; pp. 9–15, 19, 23, 29–39, 47–49, 55, 61–63, 69–73, 77–113, 119–121, 125–127, 137–139, 143–145, 153–183, 187–193, 199–207, 211–215, 225, 229–251: titles of poems; versos: pp. 4–6: 'CONTENTS.'; pp. 8–12, 16–28, 32–34, 38–46, 50–58, 62, 66–92, 96–124, 132–134, 138–142, 146, 152–154, 158–176, 182–186, 190, 196–204, 210–230, 234, 238–248: titles of poems.

Binding: Two styles have been noted:

Binding A: Cream, light olive gray, or yellow glazed boards. Spine: paper label with '[rule] | EMERSON'S | POEMS. | [rule] | 1847. | [rule]'. Single front, double front, or front and back flyleaves. Cream or yellow endpapers. All edges trimmed.

Binding B: Black T cloth (rib). Front and back covers: blindstamped single-rule frame surrounding ornate leaf-and-vine design rectangular frame; spine: blindstamped bands with goldstamped 'POEMS | BY | EMERSON | MUNROE & CO'. Flyleaves. Pale pink coated endpapers. All edges trimmed.

Publication: On 30 October 1846, Emerson wrote his brother William that *Poems* "goes to press here, I think, next week" (*L*, III, 352). Advertised as "will be published in about ten days," in *Boston Daily Advertiser*, 10 December 1846, p. 3; as "This day published," in *Christian Register*, 26 December 1846, p. 207. According to Emerson's contract with Munroe, dated 10 October 1846, he would pay composition and printing costs, and retain the plates and copyright. Emerson sent his brother William a copy of

Poems on Christmas Day, and on the 26th Henry Wadsworth Longfellow acknowledged receiving his copy (see *L*, III, 366, 364n.). Inscribed copies, all Binding A: InU (from Emerson, 25 December 1846), MH (from Emerson, 25 December 1846), NNC (25 December 1846), ViU (from Emerson, 25 December 1846), NN (from Emerson, 1 January 1847). Deposited for copyright: title and book, 7 January 1847. Deposit copy: now at OKentU (7 January 1847). Listed as a January publication in *Literary World*, 1 (13 February 1847), 42. 1,500 copies were printed. Price, 87¢. Publisher's commission, 30%.

Locations: 1st issue: Binding A: BE, JM, MWiW-C, NjP; *2nd issue:* Binding A: DLC, InU, JM, MCo, MH, MHi, NN, NNC, NjP, OKentU, TxU, ViU; Binding B: MH, RPB, ViU.

Note one: In some copies of the second issue, a four-page catalogue of Munroe's publications, dated 1 January 1847, is inserted at the front: InU, JM, MCo, MH (A), MHi, NNC, NjP, OKentU, TxU, ViU (A).

Note two: In some copies leaf 16_8 is cancelled and the stub pasted under the rear endpaper: BE, DLC, InU, JM (2nd), MCo, MH (A), NN, NNC, NjP (2nd), OKentU, TxU, ViU (A).

A 18.2.b
First American edition, second printing (1847)

Boston: James Munroe and Company, 1847.

Unknown number of copies printed April 1847 (Account Books [MH]; *JMN*, VII, 489).

A 18.2.c
First American edition, third printing (1847)

Boston: James Munroe and Company, 1847.

Unknown number of copies printed 28 December 1847 (see *JMN*, VII, 483).

LATER PRINTINGS WITHIN THE FIRST AMERICAN EDITION

A 18.2.d
First American edition, fourth printing (1847)

Boston: James Munroe and Company, 1847.

The same as the first three printings, except: the title page has '[gothic] Fourth Edition.' under Emerson's name; textual variants are present. Cloth or glazed boards. Price, 87¢. *Locations:* CtY, JM, MWiW, NNC, RPB.

Note one: Copies have been noted with a 12-page catalogue of Munroe's publications, dated 1 January 1847, inserted at the back: CtY, JM, NNC.

Note two: A copy has been noted with an eight-page catalogue of Munroe's publications, dated September 1849, inserted at the back: MWiW.

A 18.2.e
Boston: Phillips, Sampson, 1850.

'[gothic] Fourth Edition.'. Price, $1.00. Royalty, 20¢. *Locations:* DLC, JM, RPB.

Note one: Publisher's records indicate copies were bound in half and full calf; no copies have been located.

Note two: Some copies of James Munroe sheets have been located in Phillips, Sampson bindings, with a cancel title leaf.

Note three: Phillips, Sampson sold approximately 260 copies of *Poems* between 1850 (when they assumed Munroe's stock) and July 1852 (Account Books [MH]).

Note four: Emerson "paid for the printing, & owned the stereotype plates," and was paid "in advance . . . 20 per cent on the retail price" of each printing (25 February 1867, *L*, V, 507).

A 18.2.f
Boston: Phillips, Sampson, 1856.

'[gothic] Fifth Edition.'. 500 copies printed September 1856 (*JMN*, XIV, 452). Price, $1.00. Royalty, 20¢. *Location:* MH-AH.

A 18.2.g
Boston: Phillips, Sampson, 1857.

'[gothic] Sixth Edition.'. 250 copies printed on "fine paper" December 1856; 500 copies on 2 April 1857 (Account Books [MH]; *JMN*, XIV, 452). Listed in the *English Catalogue* as an importation at 4s. Price, $1.00. Royalty, 20¢. *Location:* JM.

A 18.2.h
Boston: Phillips, Sampson, 1858.

'[gothic] Seventh Edition.'. 500 copies printed July 1858 (Account Books [MH]). Price, $1.00. Royalty, 20¢. *Location:* MMeT.

Note: Phillips, Sampson failed on 19 September 1859.

A 18.2.i
Boston: Ticknor and Fields, M DCCC LX.

Price, $1.00. Royalty, 20¢. *Location:* JM.

Note: Some copies of Phillips, Sampson sheets have been located in Ticknor and Fields bindings, with a cancel title leaf.

A 18.2.j
Boston: Ticknor and Fields, M DCCC LXIII.

280 copies printed 3 March 1863. Price, $1.25. Royalty, 25¢. *Location:* JM.

A 18.2.k
Boston: Ticknor and Fields, M DCCC LXIV.

280 copies printed April 1864. Price, $1.50. Royalty, 30¢. *Location:* JM.

Note: The copyright on *Poems* was renewed 13 May 1865.

A 18.2.l
Boston: Ticknor and Fields, M DCCC LXVI.

Price, $1.50. Royalty, 30¢. *Location:* JM.

A 18.2.m
Boston: Ticknor and Fields, M DCCC LXVIII.

280 copies printed December 1867–March 1868. Price, $2.00. Royalty, 20¢. *Location:* JM.

Note one: By a contract of 4 March 1868, Emerson's royalty was changed from 20% to 20¢ per volume.

Note two: Ticknor and Fields was succeeded by Fields, Osgood in October 1868. Some copies of Ticknor and Fields sheets (including the title leaf) have been noted in Field, Osgood bindings.

A 18.2.n
Boston: Fields, Osgood, 1868.

280 copies printed 2 May 1868. Price, $2.00. Royalty, 20¢. *Not seen.*

A 18.2.o
Boston: Fields, Osgood, 1869.

Price, $2.00. Royalty, 20¢. *Location:* JM.

Note: Fields, Osgood was succeeded by James R. Osgood & Company in January 1871.

A 18.2.p
Boston: James R. Osgood, 1872.

150 copies printed 30 March 1872. Price, $2.00. Royalty, 30¢. *Not seen.*

Note: In a "Supplementary article of agreement" to the 4 March 1868 contract, dated 19 February 1870, Emerson's royalty was raised to 30¢ per copy when the price was $2.00 or above.

A 18.2.q
Boston: James R. Osgood, 1874.

150 copies printed 27 May 1874. Price, $2.00. Royalty, 30¢. *Location:* RPB.

A 18.2.r
Boston: James R. Osgood, 1876.

150 copies printed 26 October 1875. Price, $2.00. *Location:* JM.

Note: Emerson's 1 January 1876 contract with Osgood called for him to receive a flat annual fee of $1,500 for all his books, rather than a per copy royalty.

A 18.2.s
Boston: James R. Osgood, 1877.

150 copies printed 23 March 1877. Price, $1.50. *Location:* RPB.

Note: James R. Osgood was succeeded by Houghton, Osgood in February 1878.

A 18.2.t
Boston: Houghton, Osgood, 1879.

140 copies printed 23 May 1879. Price, $1.50. *Location:* MLy.

Note: Houghton, Osgood was succeeded by Houghton, Mifflin in May 1880.

A 18.2.u
Boston: Houghton, Mifflin, 1881.

150 copies printed 6 December 1880. Price, $1.50. *Location:* JM.

A 18.2.v
Boston: Houghton, Mifflin, 1882.

150 copies printed 25 May 1882. Price, $1.50. *Location:* JM.

A 18.2.w
Boston: Houghton, Mifflin, 1883.

270 copies printed 8 September 1882. Price, $1.50. *Location:* JM.

Note: As of 15 January 1884, 10 copies of *Poems* were still in stock.

LATER EDITION

A 18.3
Boston: Ticknor and Fields, 1865.

254 pp. "Blue and Gold Edition." According to a contract of 4 March 1868, Ticknor and Fields paid for and retained the plates, and Emerson retained copyright. 2,800 copies printed December 1864–January 1865; 280 copies in March–April 1865. Advertised for November December 1864, in *Atlantic*, 14 (October 1864), wrappers; as "Published this day," in *Boston Daily Advertiser*, 25 March 1865; p. 3. Deposited for copyright: title, 22 March 1865; book, 26 April 1865. Price, $1.50. Royalty, 10¢. Listed in the *English Catalogue* as an importation at 5s. All copies sold by 1 July 1883. *Locations:* InU (April 1865), MH, PSt.

PRINTINGS FROM THE "LITTLE CLASSIC EDITION" SELECTED POEMS PLATES

A 18.4.a

[all within a double-rule frame; outer frame is red with boxed corners] [red] SELECTED POEMS. | BY | RALPH WALDO EMERSON. | NEW AND REVISED EDITION. | [ornate rule] | [red] BOSTON: | JAMES R OSGOOD AND COMPANY, | Late Ticknor & Fields, and Fields, Osgood, & Co. | [red] 1876.

218 pp. Vol. [IX] of the "Little Classic Edition" (see B 3). 1,500 copies printed 30 October 1876. Advertised in *Publishers' Weekly*, 10 (16 September 1876), 438; in *Boston Daily Advertiser*, 4 November 1876, p. 2. Listed in *Publishers' Weekly*, 10 (11 November 1876), 770. Copyright, 21 October 1876. Price, $1.50. Royalty: see *Note* to A 18.2.r. *Location:* NcD.

Contents: "The Sphinx"; "Each and All"; "The Problem"; "The Visit"; "Uriel"; "To Rhea"; "The World-Soul"; "Alphonso of Castile"; "Mithridates"; "Saadi"; "May-Day"; "The Rhodora"; "The Humblebee"; "The Titmouse"; "The Snow-Storm"; "Forerunners"; "Hamatreya"; "Brahma"; "Astræa"; "Etienne de la Boéce"; "Forbearance"; "Letters"; "Sursum Corda"; "Ode to Beauty"; "Give All to Love"; "The Romany Girl"; "Fate"; "Guy"; "To Eva"; "The Amulet"; "Herminone"; "The Initial Love"; "The Dæmonic Love"; "The Celestial Love"; "Sea-Shore"; "Merlin. I."; "Merlin. II."; "Bacchus"; "The Harp" #; "April" #; "Woodnotes. I."; "Woodnotes. II"; "Monadnoc"; "Fable"; "Two Rivers"; "Waldeinsamkeit"; "Song of Nature"; "Xenophanes"; "Musketaquid"; "The Day's Ration"; "Experience"; "Wealth"; "Days"; "My Garden"; "Maiden Speech of the Æolian Harp" #; "Friendship" ["A ruddy drop of manly blood"]; "Beauty"; "Manners"; "Cupido" #; "Art"; "Worship"; "The Nun's Aspiration" #; "Terminus"; "Dirge"; "Threnody"; "Hymn Sung at the Second Curch, Boston, at the Ordination of Rev. Chandler Robbins" †; "Concord Fight" ["Concord Hymn"]; "Boston Hymn"; "Fourth of July Ode"; "Voluntaries"; "Boston" †. All poems not marked (by "†" or "#") are reprinted from *Poems* (A 18.2).

A 18.4.b
Boston: James R. Osgood, 1878.

280 copies printed 6 December 1877 and 18 December 1877. Price, $1.50. *Location:* MNS.

Note: James R. Osgood was succeeded by Houghton, Osgood in February 1878.

A 18.4.c
Boston: Houghton, Osgood, 1879.

280 copies printed 31 July 1879. Price, $1.50. *Location:* JM.

A 18.4.d
Boston: Houghton, Osgood, 1879.

Combined with *Letters and Social Aims* in two-volumes-in-one format as vol. IV of the "Fireside Edition" (see B 4). 500 copies printed 15 August 1879. *Location:* KU.

A 18.4.e
Boston: Houghton, Osgood, 1880.

Combined with *Letters and Social Aims* in two-volumes-in-one format as vol. IV of the "Fireside Edition" (see B 4). 500 copies printed 6 February 1880. *Location:* JM.

A 18.4.f
Boston: Houghton, Osgood, 1880.

270 copies printed 27 March 1880 and 1 October 1880. Price, $1.50. *Location:* MB.

Note: Houghton, Osgood was succeeded by Houghton, Mifflin in May 1880.

A 18.4.g
Boston: Houghton, Mifflin, 1881.

Combined with *Letters and Social Aims* in two-volumes-in-one format as vol. IV of the "Fireside Edition" (see B 4). 500 copies printed 7 December 1880. *Location:* MWelC.

A 18.4.h
Boston: Houghton, Mifflin, 1881.

270 copies printed 26 February 1881. Price, $1.50. *Location:* MH.

A 18.4.i
Boston: Houghton, Mifflin, 1882.

Combined with *Letters and Social Aims* in two-volumes-in-one format as vol. IV of the "Fireside Edition" (see B 4). 500 copies printed 27 October 1881, 12 May 1882, and 15 August 1882. *Location:* JM.

A 18.4.j
Boston: Houghton, Mifflin, 1882.

500 copies printed 19 November 1881, 17 May 1882, and 9 August 1882. Price, $1.50. *Location:* JM.

A 18.4.k
Boston: Houghton, Mifflin, 1883.

500 copies printed 20 November 1882 and 2 March 1883. Price, $1.50. *Location:* JM.

A 18.4.l
Boston: Houghton, Mifflin, 1883.

Combined with *Letters and Social Aims* in two-volumes-in-one format as vol. IV of the "Fireside Edition" (see B 4). 270 copies printed 13 January 1883. *Not seen.*

A 18.4.m
Boston: Houghton, Mifflin, 1884.

270 copies printed 7 November 1883. *Location:* MH.

LATER EDITION

A 18.5.a–f
London: Macmillan, 1883.

326 pp. Vol. III of the *Works* (see B 6). Price, 5s. Reprinted (usually with dual New York imprint) 1884, 1890, 1897, 1902, 1908. *Locations:* BL (21 May 1883), MB.

PRINTINGS FROM THE RIVERSIDE EDITION PLATES

A 18.6.a₁
Riverside Edition (trade), first printing, American issue (1884)

POEMS | BY | RALPH WALDO EMERSON | [gothic] New and Revised Edition | [publisher's logo] | BOSTON | HOUGHTON, MIFFLIN AND COMPANY | New York: 11 East Seventeenth Street | [gothic] The Riverside Press, Cambridge | 1884

315 pp. Vol. IX of the *Riverside Edition,* trade printing (see B 7). 1,500 copies printed 30 November 1883; 500 copies on 27 December 1883, 3 March 1884, 5 May 1884, and 7 August 1884. Listed in *Publishers' Weekly,* 24 (22 December 1883), 910. Copyright, 30 November 1883. According to the publisher's records, published 15 December 1883. Price, $1.75. *Locations:* DLC (18 December 1883), JM.

Contents: The same as in *Poems* (A 18.2), except: "Fate" is retitled "Destiny"; "The Celestial Love" is given its own title; and the following poems are not present: "Tact," "Suum Cuique," "The Amulet," "Loss and Gain," "The House," "Painting and Sculpture," and both "From the Persian of Hafiz"; the same as in *May-Day* (A 28), except: "From Omar Chiam" is retitled "From Omar Khay Yam"; the following poems are not present: "Nemesis," "Love and Thought," "Lover's Petition," "Una," and "Merlin's Song"; the following poems are added from *Selected Poems* (A 18.4): "Boston," "Hymn Sung at the Second Church, Boston, at the Ordination of Rev. Chandler Robbins," "The Harp," "The Nun's Aspiration," "April," and "Maiden Speech of the Æolian Harp"; and the following poems are added: "The Poet" ["Right upward on the road of fame"] #; "Fragments on the Poet and the Poetic Gift" #; ["The free winds told him what they knew"] #; ["Pale genius roves alone"] #; ["A dull uncertain brain"] #; ["I grieve that better souls than mine"] #; ["For thought, and not praise"] #; ["Try the might the Muse affords"] #; ["For Fancy's gift"] #; ["But over all his crowning grace"] #; ["Let me go where'er I will"] #; ["By thoughts I lead"] #; ["Shun passion, fold the hands of thrift"] #; ["The rules to men made evident"] #; ["I framed his tongue to music"] #; ["For every God"] #; ["For art, for music over-thrilled"] #; ["Hold of the Maker, not the Made"] #; ["That book is good"] #; ["Like vaulters in a circus round"] #; ["For Genius made his cabin wide"] #; ["The atom displaces all atoms beside"] #; ["To transmute crime to wisdom, so to stem"] #; ["Forebore the ant-hill, shunned to tread"] #; ["I have no brothers and no peers"] #; ["The brook sings on, but sings in vain"] #; ["On bravely through the sunshine and the showers!"] #; ["He planted where the deluge ploughed"] #; ["For what need I of book or priest"] #; ["Thou shalt not try"] #; ["Ah, not to me those dreams belong!"] #; ["Teach me your mood, O patient stars!"] #; ["The Muse's hill by fear is guarded"] #; ["His instant thought a poet spoke"] #; ["If bright the sun, he tarries"] #; ["The Asmodian feat is mine"] #; ["Slighted Minerva's learned tongue"] #; ["Best book of life is presence of a Muse"] #; "Fragments on Nature and Life": ["Daily the bending skies solicit man"] #; ["For Nature, true and like in every place"] #; ["The patient Pan"] #; ["What all the books of ages paint, I have"] #; ["But never yet the man was found"] #; ["Atom from atom yawns as far"] #; ["The sun athwart the cloud thought it no sin"] #; ["For joy and beauty planted it"] #; ["What central flowing forces, say"] #; ["Day by day for her darlings to her much she added more"] #; ["Samson stark at Dagon's knee"] #; ["She paints with red and white the moors"] #; ["A score of airy miles will smooth"] #; ["The mountain utters the same sense"] #; "The Earth" #; ["See yonder leafless trees against the sky"] #; ["Parks and ponds are good by day"] #; ["The low December vault in June be lifted high"] #; ["Solar insect on the wing"]; "Birds" #; "Water" #; ["All day the waves assailed the rock"] #; "Sunrise" #; ["He lives not who can refuse me"]; ["Seems, though the soft sheen all enchants"] #; ["Illusions like the tints of pearl"] #; ["The cold gray down upon the quinces lieth"] #; ["Put in, drive home the sightless wedges"] #; "Circles" ["Nature centers into balls"] †; ["But Nature whistled with all her winds"] #; "Life" #; ["No fate, save by the victim's fault, is low"] #; ["Around the man who seeks a noble end"] #; ["From high to higher forces"] #; ["The passing moment is an edifice"] #; ["Roomy Eternity"] #; ["The beggar begs by God's command"] #; ["Easy to match what others do"] #; ["In the chamber, on the stairs"] #; ["Of the wit's uses the main one"] #; ["The tongue is prone to lose the way"] #; ["She walked in flowers around my field"] #; ["Such another peerless queen"] #; ["I bear in youth the sad infirmities"] #; ["Be of good cheer brave spirit, steadfastly"] #; ["Friends to me are frozen wine"] #; ["Day by day returns"] #; ["Vast the realm of Being is"] #; ["Leave me, Fear, thy throbs are base"] #; ["Has God on thee conferred"] #; ["You shall not love me for what daily spends"] #; ["To and fro the genius flies"] #; "Love" #; ["Go if thou wilt, ambrosial flower"] #; ["Tell men what they knew before"] #; ["Him strong genius urged to roam"] #; ["Thou shalt make thy house"] #; ["As the drop feeds its fated flower"] #; ["Ever the Rock of Ages melts"] #; ["Yes, sometimes to the sorrow-stricken"] #; ["The archangel Hope"] #; ["But if thou do thy best"] #; ["From the stores of eldest matter"] #; ["Ascending through just degrees"] #; ["The bard and mystic held me for their own"] #; ["With the key of the secret he marches faster"] #; ["Oh what is Heaven but the fellowship"] #; ["That each should in his house abide"] #; ["If curses be the wage of love"] #; ["When wrath and terror changed Jove's regal port"] #; "The Bohemian Hymn" #; "Prayer" #; "Grace" #; "Eros" ["They put their finger on their lip"] †; "Written in Naples, March, 1833" #; "Written at Rome, 1833" #; "Peter's Field" #; "The Walk" #; "May Morning" #; "The Miracle" #; "The Waterfall" #; "Walden" #; "Pan" #; "Monadnoc from Afar" #; "The South Wind" #; "Fame" †; "Webster" #; "Written in a Volume of Goethe" #; "The Enchanter" #; "Philosopher" #; "Limits" #; "Inscription for a Well in Memory of the Martyrs of the War" #; "The Exile. (After Taliessin.)" #; ["I have an arrow that will find its mark"] #.

Note: Some copies have been noted with a pine branch on the title page instead of the publisher's logo.

A 18.6.a$_2$
Riverside Edition (trade), first printing, English issue (1884)

POEMS | BY | RALPH WALDO EMERSON | [gothic] The Riverside Edition | (COPY-RIGHT) | LONDON | GEORGE ROUTLEDGE AND SONS | BROADWAY, LUDGATE HILL | NEW YORK: 9, LAFAYETTE PLACE

The title leaf is a cancel. Vol. IX of the *Riverside Edition (Copyright),* English trade printing (see B 10). Copies have been noted in American *Riverside Edition* bindings with the works half title leaf cancelled. Listed in *Athenæum,* no. 2931 (29 December 1883), 865. Price, 3s. 6d. *Locations:* BC (31 December 1883), BE (8 January 1884), BO (8 January 1884).

A 18.6.b
Riverside Edition (Copyright), second (English) printing (1884)

Title page is the same as in the first printing, English issue, with '1884' added on a new line after 'PLACE'.

Vol. IX of the *Riverside Edition (Copyright),* English trade printing (see B 10). 1,000 copies printed 5 December 1883. Listed in *Athenæum,* no. 2931 (29 December 1883), 865. Price, 3s. 6d. *Location:* BL (15 March 1884), CaQMM.

A 18.6.c$_1$
Riverside Edition (large paper), third printing, American issue (1884)

[red] POEMS | BY | RALPH WALDO EMERSON | [gothic] New and Revised Edition | [pine branch] | [red] CAMBRIDGE | [gothic] Printed at the Riverside Press | 1884

Vol. IX of the *Riverside Edition,* large paper printing (see B 8). Limited to 500 numbered copies printed 23 January 1884. Price, $4.00. Sold out within a year. *Locations:* JM, TxU.

A 18.6.c$_2$
Riverside Edition (large paper), third printing, English issue [1884]

Title page is the same as in the American issue, except for the publisher's imprint: 'LONDON | KEGAN PAUL, TRENCH, & CO., I, PATERNOSTER SQUARE | MDCCCLXXXIII'.

Vol. IX of the *Riverside Edition,* large paper printing for English subscribers (see B 9). Limited to 25 signed and numbered copies. 25 title leaves printed 23 January 1884. Title leaf is a cancel; the date is in error. *Location:* JM.

A 18.6.d
Boston and New York: Houghton, Mifflin, 1884.

Household Edition. Various bindings. 500 copies printed 2 September 1884 and 25 September 1884. Advertised in *Atlantic,* 54 (October 1884), wrappers. Listed in *Publishers' Weekly,* 26 (16 October 1884), 534. According to the publisher's records, published 27 September 1884. Prices: cloth, $2.00; half calf, $4.00; morocco or tree calf, $5.00. *Location:* JM.

A 18.6.e
Boston and New York: Houghton, Mifflin, 1885.

Household Edition. 1,000 copies printed 4 October 1884. *Location:* JM.

A 18.6.f
Boston and New York: Houghton, Mifflin, 1885.

500 copies printed 10 October 1884, 4 December 1884, 13 January 1885, 30 June 1885, and 22 October 1885. *Location:* JM.

A 18.6.g
Boston and New York: Houghton, Mifflin, 1886.

1,000 copies printed 2 April 1886 and 2 October 1886. *Location:* JM.

A 18.6.h
Boston and New York: Houghton, Mifflin, 1886.

Household Edition. 500 copies printed 22 June 1886. *Location:* CLSU.

A 18.6.i
Boston and New York: Houghton, Mifflin, 1887.

Household Edition. 500 copies printed 8 March 1887 and 22 September 1887. *Location:* JM.

A 18.6.j
Boston and New York: Houghton, Mifflin, 1887.

500 copies printed 8 March 1887 and 15 September 1887. *Location:* JM.

A 18.6.k
Boston and New York: Houghton, Mifflin, 1888.

Household Edition. 500 copies printed 20 January 1888; 1,000 copies printed 31 July 1888. *Location:* JM.

A 18.6.l
London, Glasgow, New York: George Routledge and Sons, 1888.

500 copies printed 24 January 1888. *Location:* JM.

A 18.6.m
Boston and New York: Houghton, Mifflin, 1888.

500 copies printed 25 February 1888 and 12 September 1888. *Location:* MWin.

A 18.6.n
Boston and New York: Houghton, Mifflin, 1889.

500 copies printed 3 April 1889; 270 copies printed 26 August 1889. *Location:* NBu.

A 18.6.o
Boston and New York: Houghton, Mifflin, 1889.

Household Edition. 500 copies printed 31 July 1889. *Location:* AzU.

A 18.6.p
Boston and New York: Houghton, Mifflin, 1890.

500 copies printed 18 February 1890. *Not seen.*

A 18.6.q
Boston and New York: Houghton, Mifflin, 1890.

Household Edition. 500 copies printed April–June 1890 and July–September 1890. *Location:* RPB.

A 18.6.r
Boston and New York: Houghton, Mifflin, 1891.

500 copies printed ca. December 1890 and 30 September 1891. *Location:* JM.

A 18.6.s
Boston and New York: Houghton, Mifflin, 1891.

324 pp. (contains an index). *Household Edition.* 500 copies printed 29 June 1891 and 21 October 1891. *Location:* JM.

Note: All subsequent reprintings contain an index.

A 18.6.t
Boston and New York: Houghton, Mifflin, 1892.

Household Edition. 750 copies printed 9 April 1892; 1,000 copies on 28 October 1892. *Location:* KU.

A 18.6.u
Boston and New York: Houghton, Mifflin, 1892.

500 copies printed 19 May 1892. *Not seen.*

A 18.6.v
Boston and New York: Houghton, Mifflin, 1893.

500 copies printed 11 February 1893. *Location:* NhR.

A 18.6.w
Boston and New York: Houghton, Mifflin, 1893.

Household Edition. 500 copies printed 24 May 1893 and 14 October 1893. *Location:* MSom.

A 18.6.x
Boston and New York: Houghton, Mifflin, 1894.

500 copies printed 20 December 1893. *Location:* PPLas.

A 18.6.y
Boston and New York: Houghton, Mifflin, 1894.

Household Edition. 500 copies printed 8 August 1894. *Not seen.*

A 18.6.z
Standard Library Edition printing [1894]

POEMS | BY | RALPH WALDO EMERSON | [pine branch] | BOSTON AND NEW YORK | HOUGHTON, MIFFLIN AND COMPANY | [gothic] The Riverside Press, Cambridge

Vol. IX of the *Standard Library Edition* (see B 11). 1,000 copies printed 19 November 1894, 31 May 1895, and 26 June 1896; 500 copies on 28 February 1898. *Location:* JM.

A 18.6.aa
Boston and New York: Houghton, Mifflin, 1895.

Household Edition. 500 copies printed 9 January 1895 and 26 July 1895. *Location:* JM.

A 18.6.bb
Boston and New York: Houghton, Mifflin, 1895.

500 copies printed 28 January 1895. *Location:* NBu.

A 18.6.cc
Boston and New York: Houghton, Mifflin, 1896.

Household Edition. 500 copies printed 17 December 1895, 15 July 1896, and 17 November 1896. *Location:* JM.

A 18.6.dd
Boston and New York: Houghton, Mifflin, 1896.

500 copies printed 9 April 1896. *Not seen.*

A 18.6.ee
Boston and New York: Houghton, Mifflin, 1897.

Household Edition. 500 copies printed 6 May 1897 and 15 October 1897. *Location:* JM.

A 18.6.ff
Boston and New York: Houghton, Mifflin, 1897.

270 copies printed 6 July 1897. *Not seen.*

A 18.6.gg
Boston and New York: Houghton, Mifflin, 1898.

Household Edition. 500 copies printed 21 December 1897, 24 May 1898, and 24 October 1898. *Location:* JM.

A 18.6.hh
Boston and New York: Houghton, Mifflin, 1898.

270 copies printed 28 February 1898. *Location:* ScU.

A 18.6.ii
Boston and New York: Houghton, Mifflin, 1899.

500 copies printed 17 December 1898. *Not seen.*

A 18.6.jj
Boston and New York: Houghton, Mifflin, 1899.

Household Edition. 500 copies printed 13 March 1899 and 28 September 1899. *Location:* IHi.

A 18.6.kk
Boston and New York: Houghton, Mifflin, 1900.

250 copies printed January–March 1900. *Location:* MGro.

A 18.6.ll
Boston and New York: Houghton, Mifflin, 1900.

Household Edition. 500 copies printed January–March 1900; 1,000 copies in April–June 1900. *Location:* MH.

A 18.6.mm
London: George Routledge & Sons, 1903.

Combined with *Society and Solitude* and *Letters and Social Aims* in three-volumes-in-one format as vol. III of the "Sovereign Edition" (see B 12). 1,000 copies printed 16 September 1903. *Location:* InU.

A 18.6.nn
Fireside Edition printing (1909)

[all within red double-rule frame with red floral ornaments in each corner] THE WORKS OF | [red gothic] Ralph Waldo Emerson | POEMS | [engraving of man reading book in chair before fireplace] | [gothic] Fireside Edition | BOSTON AND NEW YORK | MDCCCCIX

Vol. IX of the *Fireside Edition* (see B 13). 500 copies printed 1 October 1909 and 15 February 1910. *Location:* JM.

A 18.6.oo
Boston and New York: Jefferson Press, [ca. 1912].

Combined with *Lectures and Biographical Sketches* in two-volumes-in-one format as vol. V of the "Jefferson Press Edition" (see B 14). *Location:* JM.

A 18.6.pp
New York: Sully and Kleinteich, [ca. 1912].

Vol. IX of the *University Edition* (see B 15). *Location:* JM.

A 18.6.qq
Boston and New York: Houghton, Mifflin, [n.d.].

Approximately 1,800 copies sold between 1901 and 1913. *Location:* JM.

Note: Approximately 15,000 copies of *Poems* in the *Riverside Edition* were sold between 1883 and 1913, when the title was apparently allowed to go out of print in this format.

A 18.6.rr
Boston and New York: Houghton, Mifflin, [n.d.].

Household Edition. Approximately 12,600 copies sold between 1901 and 1923. *Location:* JM.

Note: Approximately 29,000 copies of the *Household Edition* of *Poems* (including those printed from the *Centenary Edition* plates—see A 18.16 below) were sold between 1884 and 1923, when the title was apparently allowed to go out of print in this format.

A 18.6.ss
London: George Routledge and Sons, [n.d.].

Location: JM.

A 18.6.tt
London: Waverley Book Company, [n.d.].

Vol. IX of the "Waverley" *Riverside Edition* (see B 16). *Location:* JM.

PRINTINGS FROM THE "LITTLE CLASSIC EDITION" PLATES

A 18.7.a

POEMS | BY | RALPH WALDO EMERSON | [gothic] New and Revised Edition | [publisher's logo] | BOSTON | HOUGHTON, MIFFLIN AND COMPANY | New York: 11 East Seventeenth Street | [gothic] The Riverside Press, Cambridge | 1884

368 pp. Vol. [IX] of the "Little Classic Edition," replacing *Selected Poems* (see B 3). 500 copies printed 12 March 1884. Advertised in *Atlantic,* 53 (March 1884), wrappers. Price, $1.50. *Location:* JM.

Contents: The same as the *Riverside Edition* (A 18.6).

A 18.7.b
Boston and New York: Houghton, Mifflin, 1886.

270 copies printed 8 February 1886. *Not seen.*

A 18.7.c
Boston and New York: Houghton, Mifflin, 1887.

270 copies printed 4 November 1886; 250 copies on 22 September 1887. Bound in medium blue V cloth (smooth), rather than the "Little Classic Edition" binding, as are subsequent reprintings (see illustration at B 3). *Location:* JM.

A 18.7.d
Boston and New York: Houghton, Mifflin, 1888.

270 copies printed 27 November 1887 and 10 May 1888; 500 copies on 14 September 1888. *Location:* UU.

A 18.7.e
Boston and New York: Houghton, Mifflin, 1889.

270 copies printed 24 July 1889. *Location:* NcU.

A 18.7.f
Boston and New York: Houghton, Mifflin, 1890.

500 copies printed ca. December 1889 and July–September 1890. *Location:* JM.

A 18.7.g
Boston and New York: Houghton, Mifflin, 1891.

500 copies printed 18 June 1891. *Location:* JM.

A 18.7.h
Boston and New York: Houghton, Mifflin, 1892.

500 copies printed 5 March 1892. *Not seen.*

A 18.7.i
Boston and New York: Houghton, Mifflin, 1893.

500 copies printed 13 December 1892 and 30 October 1893. *Location:* MHi.

A 18.7.j
Boston and New York: Houghton, Mifflin, 1895.

500 copies printed 20 December 1894 and 21 October 1895. *Location:* JM.

A 18.7.k
Boston and New York: Houghton, Mifflin, 1897.

270 copies printed 26 July 1897. *Location:* NBu.

A 18.7.l
Boston and New York: Houghton, Mifflin, 1898.

270 copies printed 31 March 1898. *Location:* DeU.

A 18.7.m
Boston and New York: Houghton, Mifflin, 1899.

500 copies printed ca. December 1898; 270 copies on 5 May 1899. *Not seen.*

A 18.7.n
Boston and New York: Houghton, Mifflin, [n.d.].

Approximately 2,400 copies sold between 1900 and 1923. *Location:* OO.

Note one: Approximately 10,000 copies of *Poems* printed from the "Little Classic Edition" plates were sold between 1884 and 1923, when the title was apparently allowed to go out of print in this format.

Note two: The "Little Classic Edition" plates were ordered destroyed 14 October 1929.

LATER EDITIONS

A 18.8.a–c
The Poems of Ralph Waldo Emerson. London and Newcastle-on-Tyne: Walter Scott, 1886.

270 pp. Advertised in various bindings at various prices. Introduction by Walter Lewin. *The Canterbury Poets,* vol. 30. Reprinted 1888 (with New York: Thomas Whittaker; Toronto: W. J. Gage imprint), [n.d.] (with London, Felling-on-Tyne; New York: Walter Scott imprint). *Locations:* BL (15 July 1886), JM (1886, 1888), MnU (n.d.).

A 18.9.a–d

London [&c.]: George Routledge and Sons, 1890.

319 pp. *Routledge's Pocket Library*. 5,000 copies printed 20 August 1899; 3,000 copies on 16 July 1891 and 20 January 1893. Price, 1s. Reprinted 1894. *Locations:* BL (11 December 1889), BC (29 May 1890), BO (1 July 1890), CaNFSM (1894).

A 18.9.e
London: George Routledge & Sons; New York: E. P. Dutton, [n.d.].

Location: JM.

A 18.10
The Snow Storm. And Other Poems. Boston: Samuel E. Cassino, 1892.

Unpaged (12 leaves), printed on rectos only. Wrappers or linen over foam-covered boards. Illustrations by Louis K. Harlow. *Locations:* JM, NcD (wrappers).

A 18.11.a
Poems from the Writings of Ralph Waldo Emerson. Boston, New York, Chicago: Houghton, Mifflin, [1897].

94 pp. Wrappers. Introduction and notes by George H. Browne. *The Riverside Literature Series*, no. 113, 7 April 1897. According to the publisher's records, published 20 August 1897. Price, 15¢. *Location:* JM.

A 18.11.b–e
Poems and Essays. Boston, New York, Chicago: Houghton, Mifflin, [1897].

Combined with *The Fortune of the Republic and Other American Addresses* (C 22) in two-volumes-in-one format in cloth. Price, 40¢. Reprinted 1904, 1906, 1911. *Locations:* MH, ICU (1911).

Note: Numerous reprintings with undated title pages. Approximately 600 copies were sold in the *Riverside School Library* by 1 October 1907, and 6,600 copies in the *Riverside Literature Series* by 2 October 1911, when 307 copies were still in stock.

A 18.12.a
Poems of Ralph Waldo Emerson. New York: Thomas Y. Crowell, [1899].

386 pp. Introduction by Nathan Haskell Dole. *Location:* OU.

A 18.12.b
Poems of Ralph Waldo Emerson. New York: Thomas Y. Crowell, [1899].

302 pp. Introduction by Nathan Haskell Dole. Also advertised as included in "Cragmere," "Gladstone," and "Woodbine" series. *Location:* MeWC.

A 18.12.c
The Early Poems of Ralph Waldo Emerson. New York: T. Y. Crowell, [1899].

220 pp. Introduction by Nathan Haskell Dole. *Astor Edition*. Also advertised as included in "Faience Library," "Gladstone," "Westminster," and "Woodbine" series. Listed in *Publishers' Weekly*, 56 (23 September 1899), 385. Copyright, 15 June 1899. *Locations:* DLC (15 June 1899), JM.

A 18.13.a
The Early Poems of Ralph Waldo Emerson. New York: A. L. Burt, [1900].

244 pp. Cloth or cloth over foam-covered boards. Introduction by Henry Ketcham. *The Home Library*. Also advertised as included in "Berkshire Poets" and "New Century

Poets" series. Listed in *Publishers' Weekly*, 58 (28 July 1900), 280. Price, $1.00. *Locations:* DLC (15 February 1900), JM.

A 18.13.b
Representative Men   Poems. New York: P. F. Collier & Son, MCMIII.

Combined in two-volumes-in-one format in *American Authors in Prose and Poetry* series, *Emerson*, vol. II. Reprinted [n.d.]. *Locations:* PPT (1903), MH (n.d.).

A 18.13.c
Philadelphia: John D. Morris, [1906].

Vol. VI of the "John D. Morris Edition" (see B 29). Also noted with introduction by J. Ellis Burdick. Copyright, 13 February 1906. *Locations:* DLC, JM (Burdick).

A 18.13.d
Boston and New York: C. T. Brainard, [n.d.].

Vol. III of the *Works* (see B 30). *Location:* CaOTV.

A 18.13.e
New York: Caxton Society, [n.d.].

Vol. III of the *Works* (see B 31). *Location:* NjR.

A 18.13.f
New York: National Library Co., [n.d.].

Vol. III of the *Works* (see B 32). *Location:* CaOHM.

A 18.13.g
Philadelphia, New York, Chicago: Nottingham Society, [n.d.].

Vol. III of the *Works* (see B 33). *Location:* JM.

A 18.14.a
Chicago: W. B. Conkey, [1901].

150 pp. Also noted containing "The Poet" (43 pp.) at the back. *Locations:* CaNBS, JM (Poet).

A 18.14.b
Emerson's Poems. Chicago: Henneberry, [n.d.].

Location: MoU.

A 18.14.c
Chicago: Homewood, [n.d.].

Combined with four essays (129 pp.) in two-volumes-in-one format. Also advertised as included in "Abbey Series," no. 119, at 18¢. *Location:* JM.

A 18.15
Earlier Poems. Rahway, N.J.: Mershon, [1902?].

Not seen.

A 18.16.a₁

POEMS | BY | RALPH WALDO EMERSON | [pine tree] | BOSTON AND NEW YORK | HOUGHTON, MIFFLIN AND COMPANY, | [gothic] The Riverside Press, Cambridge | 1904

531 pp. Dust jacket. Vol. IX of the *Centenary Edition,* trade printing (see B 18). 1,000 copies printed 17 May 1904 and 21 October 1904; 500 copies on 21 December 1904. Listed in *Publishers' Weekly,* 65 (4 June 1904), 1429. Copyright, 16 May 1904. According to the publisher's records, published 28 May 1904. Price, $1.75. *Locations:* DLC (9 September 1904), JM.

Contents: The same as in *Poems* (A 18.2), except: "Fate" is retitled "Destiny"; the following poems are not present: "Tact," "Loss and Gain," "Painting and Sculpture," and both "From the Persian of Hafiz"; "The Celestial Love" is given its own title; and the following poems by Ellen Tucker Emerson are added: "Lines" and "The Violet"; the same as *May-Day* (A 28), except: the following poem is not present: "Lover's Petition"; the following poems are added: "Boston," "Hymn, Sung at the Second Church, Boston, at the Ordination of Rev. Chandler Robbins," "The Harp," "The Nun's Aspiration," "April," "Maiden Speech of the Æolian Harp," and "Cupido"; and the same as in the *Riverside Edition* (A 18.6), except: the following poems are not present: ["Thou shalt not try"], ["Teach me your mood, O patient stars"], ["Best book of life is presence of a Muse"], ["The mountain utters the same sense"], ["Leave me, Fear, thy throbs are base"], and ["Has God on thee conferred"]; the following poems have been retitled: ["He who has a thousand friends has not a friend at all"] is "From Ali Ben Abu Taleb"; ["See yonder leafless trees against the skies"] is "Transition"; ["All day the waves assailed the rock"] is "Nahant"; ["The bard and mystic hold me for their own"] is "Rex"; ["Daily the bending skies solicit man"] is included in "The Adirondacs"; "May Morning" is "Cosmos"; and "The South Wind" is "September"; and the following poems have been added; "Prudence" †; "Nature" ["A subtle chain of countless rings"]; "The Informing Spirit" †; "Intellect" ["Go, speed the stars of thought"] †; "Gifts" †; "Promise" †; "Caritas" †; "Power" †; "Wealth" †; "Illusions" †; ["And as the light divides the dark"] #; ["He could condense cerulean ether"] #; ["Coin the day-dawn into lines"] #; "The Heavens" #; "The Garden" #; "Night in June" #; "Maia" #; ["The brave Empedocles, defying fools"] #; "October" #; "Music" #; ["In Walden wood the cherubic"] #; "Riches" #; "Intellect" ["Gravely it broods apart on joy"] #; "The Bell" #; "Thought" #; "To-Day" #; "The Summons" #; "The River" #; "Good Hope" #; "Lines to Ellen" #; "Security" #; "A Mountain Grave" #; "A Letter" #; "Hymn" ["There is in all the sons of men"] #; "Self-Reliance" ["Henceforth, please God, forever I forego"] #.

Note one: Numerous reprintings with undated title pages. Approximately 3,000 copies printed between 1 July 1905 and 30 September 1910. Approximately 5,700 copies sold through 1923.

Note two: The copyright on *Poems* was renewed 9 September 1904.

A 18.16.a₂
English issue

London: A. P. Watt & Son, [1904].

Vol. IX of the English *Centenary Edition* (see B 21). American sheets with Watt's label pasted on the title page. Price, 6s. *Locations:* BL (30 May 1904), BC (7 June 1904), BE (7 June 1904).

A 18.16.b
Autograph Centenary Edition (large paper), second printing (1904)

RALPH WALDO EMERSON | [red] Poems | [pine tree] | CAMBRIDGE | [red gothic] Printed at the Riverside Press | 1904

Vol, IX of the *Autograph Centenary Edition* (see B 19). Limited to 600 signed and numbered copies printed 17 May 1904. Copyright, 16 May 1904. Price, $6.00. Sold out by 5 April 1906. *Locations:* DLC (21 May 1904), JM.

A 18.16.c
Boston and New York: Houghton Mifflin, 1904.

Vol. IX of the *Concord Edition* (see B 20). 2,000 copies printed 23 May 1904. *Location:* JM.

Note: Numerous reprintings with undated title pages. Approximately 3,000 copies sold by 31 December 1910.

A 18.16.d
The Complete Poetical Works of Ralph Waldo Emerson. Boston and New York: Houghton, Mifflin, [1904].

409 pp. (text and index without the notes). *Autograph Poets. Location:* NcU.

A 18.16.e
Boston and New York: Houghton, Mifflin, [1904].

409 pp. *Household Edition. Location:* JM.

A 18.16.f
The Poems of Ralph Waldo Emerson. Boston and New York: Houghton, Mifflin, [1904].

409 pp. *Popular Edition. Location:* MNoW.

Note: Approximately 1,000 copies of the *Popular Edition* were sold between 1907 and 1923.

A 18.16.g
Boston and New York: Houghton Mifflin, [1911].

Vol. IX of the *Centenary Edition,* trade printing (see B 18). *Location:* NbU.

A 18.16.h
The Complete Poetical Works of Ralph Waldo Emerson. Boston and New York: Houghton Mifflin, [1911].

409 pp. *Autograph Poets. Location:* MnU.

A 18.16.i$_1$
Boston and New York: Houghton Mifflin, [1911].

409 pp. *Household Edition. Location:* JM.

A 18.16.i$_2$
The Complete Poetical Works of Ralph Waldo Emerson. London: George G. Harrap, [1913].

409 pp. *Authorised Copyright Edition.* The title leaf is a cancel. *Location:* BL (12 September 1913).

A 18.16.j
Boston and New York: Houghton Mifflin, [1914].

Vol. IX of the *Riverside Pocket Edition* (see B 22). Approximately 1,300 copies sold between 1914 and 1922. *Not seen.*

A 18.16.k
Boston and New York: Houghton Mifflin, [1918].

409 pp. *Household Edition. Location:* MH.

A 18.16.l
The Complete Poetical Works of Ralph Waldo Emerson. Boston and New York: Houghton Mifflin, [1918].

409 pp. *Autograph Poets. Location:* NcU.

Note: Approximately 2,100 copies of the *Autograph Poets* were sold between 1910 and 1923.

A 18.16.m
Boston and New York: Houghton Mifflin, [1918].

Vol. IX of the *Centenary Edition,* trade printing (see B 18). *Location:* MeU.

A 18.16.n
Boston and New York: Houghton Mifflin, 1921.

Combined (text and index without the notes) with *Society and Solitude* in two-volumes-in-one format as vol. VI of *Emerson's Complete Works* (see B 23). *Location:* JM.

A 18.16.o
New York: Wm. H. Wise, 1923.

Combined with *Lectures and Biographical Sketches* in two-volumes-in-one format as vol. V of the *Current Opinion Edition* (see B 24). *Location:* JM.

A 18.16.p
The Complete Poetical Works of Ralph Waldo Emerson. Boston and New York: Houghton Mifflin, 1924.

409 pp. *Fireside Poets. Location:* MiEM.

A 18.16.q
Boston and New York: Houghton Mifflin, 1929.

Combined (text and index without the notes) with *Society and Solitude* in two-volumes-in-one format as vol. [VI] of the *Harvard Edition* (see B 25). *Location:* JM.

A 18.16.r
New York: Wm. H. Wise, 1929.

Combined with *Lectures and Biographical Sketches* in two-volumes-in-one format as vol. V of the *Medallion Edition* (see B 26). *Location:* OC.

A 18.16.s
Boston and New York: Houghton Mifflin, [1932].

Vol. IX of the *Centenary Edition,* trade printing (see B 18). *Location:* Nm.

A 18.16.t–u
New York: AMS Press, [1968].

Vol. IX of the "AMS Press" *Centenary Edition* (see B 27). Reprinted 1979. *Locations:* TxU, DLC (9 November 1979).

LATER EDITIONS

A 18.17
Select Poems. London, Glasgow, Dublin: Blackie & Son, 1904.

36 pp. Cloth or wrappers. Edited by F. G. Phillips. *Blackie's English Classics*. Prices: cloth, 3d.; wrappers, 2d. *Location:* BL (23 January 1905).

A 18.18.a–f
London: George Bell and Sons, 1905.

281 pp. Vol. V of the *York Library Edition* (see B 28). *The York Library*. Published July 1905. Reprinted April 1906, March 1914, 1919, 1924. *Bohn's Standard Library; Bohn's Popular Library*. *Locations:* BL (22 December 1905), MiU.

A 18.19
Emerson's Earlier Poems. New York: Macmillan, 1908.

161 pp. Introduction and notes by Oscar Charles Gallagher. *Macmillan's Pocket American and English Classics*. Copyright, 20 July 1908. Published 8 August 1908. Price, 24¢. *Location:* MiU.

A 18.20.a
Poems of Ralph Waldo Emerson. London: George G. Harrap, [1910].

231 pp. Also includes "The Poet." *The Choice Books*, no. 6. Published September 1910. Price, 1s. *Location:* BC (23 January 1911).

A 18.20.b
New York: Dodge, [1912?].

Advertised in various bindings at various prices. Also advertised as included in "Choice Books" series. *Location:* MH.

A 18.20.c–d
Poems. London and Toronto: J. M. Dent & Sons; New York: E. P. Dutton, [1914].

Dust jacket. Introduction by Charles M. Bakewell. Advertised in various bindings at various prices. *Everyman's Library*, no. 715. Reprinted 1936. Price, 1s. *Locations:* BO (9 May 1914), JM, MWal (1936).

A 18.21
Threnody and Other Poems. Portland, Maine: Thomas B. Mosher, MDCCCCXI.

44 pp. Boards or self-wrappers. Foreword by T. B. M[osher]. Advertised as included in "Golden Text Series," no. 8. Published September 1911. Limited to 925 copies on Van Gelder handmade paper and 100 copies on Japan vellum. Prices: boards, 60¢; wrappers, 40¢; vellum, $1.00. *Locations:* JM (both).

A 18.22.a–b
Poems of Ralph Waldo Emerson. London [&c.]: Humphrey Milford, Oxford University Press, 1914.

316 pp. Dust jacket. *Oxford Edition; Oxford Edition, Thin Paper.* Also advertised as included in "Oxford Editions of Standard Authors," "Oxford India Paper," and "Oxford Poets" series. Published May 1914. Price, 2s. Reprinted 1921. *Locations:* BO (1 May 1914, *Oxford*), JM (all).

A 18.23.a
New York: Hearst's International Library Co., [1914].

326 pp. Combined with Richard Garnett's *Life* and the index as vol. V of the *New National Edition* (see B 35). *Location:* CaOH.

A 18.23.b
New York: Charles C. Bigelow, [n.d.].

Vol. V of the *Works* (see B 37). *Not seen.*

A 18.23.c
Poems   Addresses. New York: Bigelow, Brown, [n.d.].

428 pp. Vol. V of the *Works* (see B 38). *Location:* MoSU.

A 18.23.d
New York: Bigelow, Smith, [n.d.].

322 pp. (no index). Vol. V of the *Works* (see B 39). *Location:* CaQMM.

A 18.23.e
New York: Brentano's. [n.d.].

322 pp. Vol. V of the *Writings* (see B 40). *Location:* ViNO.

A 18.23.f
New York: Harper & Brothers, [n.d.].

322 pp. Vol. V of the *Works* (see B 41). *Location:* JM.

A 18.23.g
Boston and New York: Jefferson Press, [n.d.].

322 pp. Vol. V of the *Works* (see B 42). *Location:* JM.

A 18.23.h
[N.p]: Library Society, [n.d.].

322 pp. Vol. V of the *Works* (see B 43). *Location:* CaQMG.

A 18.24
Poems of Ralph Waldo Emerson. Girard, Kansas: Haldeman-Julius, [1925].

64 pp. Wrappers. Edited with an introduction by Nelson Antrim Crawford. *Little Blue Book,* no. 742. Copyright, 13 April 1925. *Location:* KU.

A 18.25
Ralph Waldo Emerson. London: Ernest Benn, [1926].

31 pp. Wrappers. *The Augustan Books of Modern Poetry.* Published September 1926. Price, 6d. *Locations:* BL (21 September 1926), MH.

A 18.26
New York: Simon and Schuster, [1927].

31 pp. Cover title. Introduction by John Erskine. *The Pamphlet Poets.* Price, 25¢. *Location:* JM.

A 18.27.a
The Poems of Ralph Waldo Emerson. New York: Limited Editions Club, 1945.

238 pp. Full leather. Boxed. Edited by Louis Untermeyer. Illustrated by Richard and Doris Beer. Limited to 1,500 numbered copies, signed by the Beers. Copyright, 23 April 1945. *Location:* JM.

A 18.27.b
New York: Heritage Press, [1945].

Boxed. Price, $3.75. *Locations:* DLC (3 July 1945), JM.

A 18.28.a–b
Poems of Ralph Waldo Emerson. New York: Thomas Y. Crowell, [1965].

112 pp. Selected by J. Donald Adams. Drawings by Virgil Burnett. Copyright, 10 September 1965. Price, $2.95. Reprinted 1971 in wrappers in *Apollo Editions* A-309 at $1.45. *Locations:* JM (1971), NcD.

UNDATED EDITIONS

A 18.29
Cleveland: Goldsmith, [n.d.].

112 pp. Advertised as included in "Little Leather Classics," no. 11. *Not seen.*

A 18.30.a
New York: Hurst, [n.d.].

165 pp. *Location:* JM.

A 18.30.b
New York: E. A. Lawson, [n.d.].

Location: MU.

A 18.30.c
Chicago: Thompson & Thomas, [n.d.].

Location: CaOLH.

A 18.31
New York: Hurst, [n.d.].

252 pp. *Knickerbocker Classics.* Also advertised as included in "Cambridge Classics," no. 35. *Location:* JM.

A 18.32
[N.p.]: Kennedy, [n.d.].

Not seen.

A 18.33
Edinburgh: W. P. Nimmo, [n.d.].

Advertised as included in "Nimmo's Thin Paper Poets Pocket Editions," no. 8, in various bindings at various prices. *Not seen.*

SEPARATE PUBLICATIONS OF INDIVIDUAL POEMS

A 18.34
The Apology. New York: G. Schirmer, 1882.

5 pp. Wrappers. Music by Georgina Schuyler. Price, 35¢. *Location:* ViU.

A 18.35
Earth-Song. New York: G. Schirmer, 1969.

24 pp. Wrappers. Music by Frank Erickson only; Emerson's poem [from "Hamatreya"] is printed on p. 3. *Location:* NN.

A 18.36
The Humble Bee. [N.p.]: Parker Publishing Co., [1928?].

Advertised as included in "Eight Page Classics." Price, 2¢. *Not seen.*

A 18.37
The Mountain and the Squirrel. [N.p.]: Parker Publishing Co., [1928?].

Advertised as included in "Eight Page Classics." Reprinting of "A Fable." Price, 2¢. *Not seen.*

A 18.38
The Rhodora. [N.p.]: Parker Publishing Co., [1928?].

Advertised as included in "Eight Page Classics." Price, 2¢. *Not seen.*

A 18.39
The Seer. New York: J. Fischer & Bro., [1946].

29 pp. Wrappers. Music by George Frederick McKay. Sheet music. From "Woodnotes." Price, 60¢. *Location:* WaU.

A 18.40
Sky-born Music. [N.p.: n.p., n.d.].

Broadside, printed on recto only. Reprinting of "Music." *Location:* RPB.

A 18.41
The Snowstorm. [N.p.]: Parker Publishing Co., [1928?].

Advertised as included in "Eight Page Classics." Price, 2¢. *Not seen.*

A 18.42
The Snowstorm. Leicester [England]: Toni Savage, 1974.

Unpaged (six leaves). Wrappers. Illustrated by Rigby Graham. Printed at the New Broom Press. Completed Christmas 1974. Limited to 50 copies, not for sale. *Location:* JM.

A 18.43
Thine Eyes Still Shined. New York: G. Ricordi, [1918].

4 pp. Cover title. Music by Edwin Schneider; sung by John McCormack. Sheet music. Price, 40¢. *Location:* MB.

A 18.44
To Ellen at the South. New York: G. Schirmer, 1882.

7 pp. Wrappers. Music by Georgina Schuyler. Price, 50¢. *Location:* ViU.

A 19 [TOWN AND COUNTRY CLUB PROSPECTUS]

A 19
First edition, only printing [1849]

TOWN AND COUNTRY CLUB.

1. The Town and Country Club is formed to establish better acquaintance between men of scientific, literary, and philanthropic pursuits.

2. After the names of a hundred subscribers shall have been procured, the name of any person may be proposed by any member, and ballotted for. No ballot shall be valid, unless ten members actually ballot. One black ball in five shall exclude. On admission, the member shall pay his annual subscription.

3. The annual subscription of each member shall be five dollars.

4. There shall be a Secretary chosen, whose duty it shall be to take charge of the Club-Room, to notify the members of special meetings, and to preside at meetings.

5. There shall be a Treasurer, who shall take charge of all moneys, and disburse them under the direction of the Committee.

6. The economies of the Club shall be managed by an Executive Committee of three members, who shall, from time to time, make such regulations as they think fit, which shall be binding, unless set aside by a general meeting.

7. The Club shall hold an ordinary meeting on the first (Wednesday) of every month. Its quarterly meetings, on the first (Wednesdays) of January, April, July, and October, shall be occasions for the offering of papers or oral communications on literary and general questions.

8. The Club-Room shall be open every day, for the reception of members, from   o'clock, A. M. till   o'clock, P. M.

A 19: 10³/₁₆″ × 7³/₄″

[1–4]

[a]²

Contents: p. 1: text: pp. 2–4: blank.

Typography and paper: 6³/₁₆″ × 6¹/₂″; pale gray-blue wove paper; 21 lines. No running head.

Binding: Single sheet, folded once; unbound.

Publication: On 11 April 1849, Emerson wrote James Munroe and Company that he expected to have 100 copies printed (*L*, IV, 139).

Locations: MH, NcD.

Note one: The following notation in Emerson's hand appears on page 3 of the NcD copy: 'meeting for choice of | officers, determination | of place, &c holden next | Tuesday Apr 17 at 10 o'c A M | 12 West Street. | R. W. E.'; and, again in Emerson's hand, it is addressed on page 4: 'J. R. Lowell, Esq. | Cambridge, | Mass.'. Lowell has endorsed page 4: 'Town & Country Club | 1849.'.

Note two: In his manuscript records of the Town and Country Club, Bronson Alcott calls this the 'Draft of Constitution' (MH).

A 20 [TOWN AND COUNTRY CLUB CONSTITUTION]

A 20.1
First edition, only printing [1849]

TOWN AND COUNTRY CLUB.

Club Room, No. 15 Tremont Row.

CONSTITUTION.

ARTICLE 1. The Town and Country Club is formed to establish better acquaintance between men of scientific, literary and philanthropic pursuits.

ARTICLE 2. The name of a candidate for membership may be proposed by any member at any monthly meeting, (by entering the same in a book to be provided for the purpose) and being seconded in writing, shall be balloted for at the next monthly meeting. No ballot shall be valid unless ten members actually ballot. One black ball in ten shall exclude. Every person, on admission, shall sign the Constitution, and thereupon pay the annual subscription, which shall be five dollars.

ARTICLE 3. The officers of the Club shall be, a Corresponding Secretary, a Recording Secretary, a Treasurer, and an Executive Committee of three members. These officers shall be chosen at each annual meeting.

ARTICLE 4. The Executive Committee shall manage the economies of the Club, and shall, from time to time, make such regulations as they shall think fit, which shall be binding, unless set aside by a vote of the Club, at a monthly meeting.

ARTICLE 5. The Corresponding Secretary shall take charge of the Club Room and Library, and notify members of all meetings. He shall open all stated meetings by selecting a Chairman, who shall preside during the meeting.

ARTICLE 6. The duties of the Recording Secretary shall be to keep a record of the transactions of the Club.

ARTICLE 7. The Treasurer shall collect the subscriptions of members, take charge of all moneys, and disburse the same under the direction of the Executive Committee, and present a report of his doings at the annual meeting.

ARTICLE 8. The annual meeting of the Club shall be held on the first Thursday of May, and ordinary meetings on the first Thursday of each month. Its quarterly meetings, on the first Thursday of January, April, July and October, shall be occasions for the offering of papers or oral communications on literary or general questions. Special meetings of the Club may be called by the Corresponding Secretary, whenever requested so to do by five members. A quorum shall consist of ten members.

ARTICLE 9. The Club Room shall be open every day for the reception of members from   A. M. to   P. M.

ARTICLE 10. For the introduction of men of letters or distinction not residing within thirty miles of Boston, each member shall have the privilege of introducing one such person at a time, to the privileges of the Club Room without charge, for the term of thirty days. The Executive Committee may extend this privilege to residents whom they may think it desirable to interest in the Club, for a term of thirty days, provided the number of such residents do not exceed five at one time.

ARTICLE 11. This Constitution may be altered or amended at any regular monthly meeting by a vote of two-thirds of the members present. Provided notice be given of such amendment at the previous monthly meeting.

MEMBERS.

R. WALDO EMERSON,
J. ELLIOT CABOT, } *Executive Committee,*
JAMES T. FISHER,

A. BRONSON ALCOTT, *Corresponding Secretary.*
JAMES W. STONE, *Recording Secretary.*
JOHN W. BROWNE, *Treasurer.*

C. Allen Browne,
Walter Channing,
George P. Bradford,
J. Earl Williams,
Samuel G. Ward,
Edmund L. Benzon,
A. Burlingame,
S. H. Phillips,
C. B. Fairbanks,
J. F. Flagg,
Allen C. Spooner,
Alpheus C. Morse,
C. H. A. Dall,
Edward Bang,
Theodore Parker,
George S. Hillard,
John T. Sargent,
Samuel D. Robbins,
Charles C. Shackford,
Le Baron Russell,
Chandler Robbins,
S. G. Howe,
William Silsbee,
Richard Soule, Jr.,
John S. Dwight,
O. B. Frothingham,
Alfred Norton,
William A. Alcott,
W. R. Alger,
Francis Jackson,
Bernard Roelker,
Jno. O. Choules,

A. L. Stimson,
James Bunker Congdon,
J. R. Lowell,
Benjamin Rodman,
Edmund Jackson,
Elizur Wright,
R. E. Apthorp,
Ephraim Peabody,
James Egan,
James F. Clarke,
John B. Willard,
Charles K. Whipple,
C. A. Bartol,
John Flint,
E. Rockwood Hoar,
William A. White,
E. P. Clark,
Charles Sumner,
S. E. Sewall,
Joseph Willard,
Horatio Woodman,
George Bemis,
Ellis Gray Loring,
John G. King,
Otis Clapp,
W. H. Dennet,
James Tolman,
James T. Fields,
W. D. Ticknor,
T. P. Chandler,
F. Haven,

E. P. Whipple,
Wm. B. Greene,
Ben: Perley Poore,
Geo. B. Loring,
John Cheney,
Geo. W. Light,
A. B. Mussey,
Samuel Johnson,
Stephen C. Phillips,
John G. Palfrey,
Charles Kraitsir,
Convers Francis,
Robert Townley,
W. F. Channing,
Geo. C. Ward,
Henry W. Longfellow,
T. Wentworth Higginson,
H. I. Bowditch,
E. E. Hale,
John C. Wyman,
Frederic H. Hedge,
Wm. H. Channing,
Gilbert L. Streeter,
John Orvis,
Thomas Hill,
J. F. Flagg,
E. L. Frothingham,
Frederic Beck,
H. Perabeau,
J. A. Andrew,
John S. Holmes.

A 20.1: 8¼″ × 6⅞″; page 2

Broadside, printed on both sides

Contents: p. 1: constitution; p. 2: list of members.

Typography and paper: p. 1: 7¾″ × 6⅜″; p. 2; 7″ × 6⅜″; pale gray-blue wove paper; 41 lines on recto; 32 lines on verso. No running heads.

Publication: According to Alcott's manuscript journal for 27 March 1849, "R. W. Emerson was requested to draft a Constitution and present the same at the next meeting" (MH). In his manuscript records of the Town and Country Club for 10 April 1849, Alcott states: "R. W. Emerson read a Preamble of Reasons for organizing a Society . . . with a Constitution for the same, which was adopted, and 100 copies ordered to be printed" (MH). On 11 April 1849, Emerson wrote his publisher, James Munroe: "Will you have the goodness, to have the enclosed paper printed on a neat letter sheet, & send me the proof. It is important that it should be done immediately[.] I think I will have 100 copies when the proof comes back" (*L*, IV, 139).

Location: MH.

A 20.2
Second edition, only printing [1849]

TOWN AND COUNTRY CLUB.

Club Room, No. 15 Tremont Row.

CONSTITUTION.

ARTICLE 1.   The Town and Country Club is formed to establish better acquaintance between men of scientific, literary and philanthropic pursuits.

ARTICLE 2.   The name of a candidate for membership may be proposed by any member at any monthly meeting, (by entering the same in a book to be provided for the purpose) and being seconded in writing, shall be balloted for at the next monthly meeting.   No ballot shall be valid unless ten members actually ballot.   One black ball in ten shall exclude.   Every person, on admission, shall sign the Constitution, and thereupon pay the annual subscription, which shall be five dollars.

ARTICLE 3.   The officers of the Club shall be, a Corresponding Secretary, a Recording Secretary, a Treasurer, and an Executive Committee of three members.   These officers shall be chosen at each annual meeting.

ARTICLE 4.   The Executive Committee shall manage the economies of the Club, and shall, from time to time, make such regulations as they shall think fit, which shall be binding, unless set aside by a vote of the Club at a monthly meeting.

ARTICLE 5.   The Corresponding Secretary shall take charge of the Club Room and Library, and notify members of all meetings.   He shall open all stated meetings by selecting a Chairman, who shall preside during the meeting.

ARTICLE 6.   The duties of the Recording Secretary shall be to keep a record of the transactions of the Club.

ARTICLE 7.   The Treasurer shall collect the subscriptions of members, take charge of all moneys, and disburse the same under the direction of the Executive Committee, and present a report of his doings at the annual meeting.

ARTICLE 8.   The annual meeting of the Club shall be held on the first Thursday of May, and ordinary meetings on the first Thursday of each month.   Its quarterly meetings, on the first Thursday of January, April, July and October, shall be occasions for the offering of papers or oral communications on literary or general questions. Special meetings of the Club may be called by the Corresponding Secretary, whenever requested so to do by five members.   A quorum shall consist of ten members.

ARTICLE 9.   The Club Room shall be open every day for the reception of members from 8 A. M. till 7 P. M. between April 1, and October 1, and from 8 A. M. till 10 P. M., the remainder of the year.

ARTICLE 10.   For the introduction of men of letters or distinction not residing within thirty miles of Boston, each member shall have the privilege of introducing one such person at a time, to the privileges of the Club Room without charge, for the term of thirty days.   The Executive Committee may extend this privilege to residents

A 20.2: 10″ × 7⁷/₈″; page 1

whom they may think it desirable to interest in the Club, for a term of thirty days, provided the number of such residents do not exceed five at one time.

ARTICLE 11. This Constitution may be altered or amended at any regular monthly meeting by a vote of two-thirds of the members present; provided notice be given of such amendment at the previous monthly meeting.

MEMBERS.

APTHORP ROBERT E., Esq., Boston,
CABOT, J. ELLIOT, Esq., Boston, *Executive Committee.*
FISHER, JAMES T. Esq., Boston,

ALCOTT, A. BRONSON, Esq., Boston, *Corresponding Secretary.*
STONE, DR. JAMES W., Boston, *Recording Secretary.*
BROWNE, JOHN W., Esq., Boston, *Treasurer.*

Alcott, Dr. William A., West Newton,
Alger, Rev. William R., Roxbury,
Andrew, John A., Esq., Boston,
Bangs, Edward, Esq. "
Bartol, Rev. Cyrus A., "
Beck, Frederic, Esq., "
Bemis, George, Esq., "
Benzon, Edmund L., Esq., "
Bowditch, Dr. Henry I., "
Bradford, George P., Esq., Jamaica Plain,
Browne, C. Allen, Esq., Boston,
Buffum, James N., Esq., Lynn,
Burlingame, Anson, Esq., Boston,
Chamberlain, H. H., Esq., Worcester,
Chandler, Theophilus P., Esq., Boston,
Channing, Dr. Walter, "
Channing, Dr. William F., "
Channing, Rev. William H., "
Cheney, John, Esq., "
Choules, Rev. Jno. O., Newport, R. I.
Clapp, Otis, Esq., Boston,
Clark, E. P., Esq., "
Clarke, Rev. James F., Boston,
Congdon, James Bunker, Esq., New Bedford,
Dall, Rev. C. H. A., Needham,
Dennet, W. H., Esq., Boston,
Dwight, John S., Esq., Boston,
Egan, James, Esq., "
Emerson, Ralph Waldo, Esq., Concord,
Fairbanks, Charles B., Esq., Boston,
Farley, James P., Esq., Chelsea,
Fields, James T., Esq., Boston,
Flagg, Dr. Josiah F., "
Flint, Dr. John, "
Francis, Rev. Convers, Cambridge,
Frothingham, E. L., Esq., Boston,
Frothingham, Rev. Octavius B., Salem,

Greene, Rev. William B., West Brookfield,
Hale, Rev. Edward E., Worcester,
Haven, Franklin, Esq., Boston,
Hawthorne, Hon. Nathaniel, Salem,
Hedge, Rev. Frederic H., Bangor, Me.,
Higginson, Rev. T. Wentworth, Newburyport,
Hill, Rev. Thomas, Waltham,
Hillard, George S., Esq., Boston,
Holmes, John S., Esq., "
Hoar, Hon. E. Rockwood, Concord,
Hollingsworth, Lyman, Esq., Boston,
Howe, Dr. Samuel G., Boston,
Jackson, Edmund, Esq., "
Jackson, Francis Esq., "
Johnson, Rev. Samuel, Salem,
King, John G., Esq., Boston,
King, Rev. Thomas Starr, Boston,
Light, Geo. W., Esq., "
Longfellow, Prof. Henry W., Cambridge,
Loring, Ellis Gray, Esq., Boston,
Loring, Dr. Geo. B., Chelsea,
Lowell, James Russell, Esq., Cambridge,
Mack, David, Esq., Watertown,
May, Rev. Samuel, Jr., Leicester,
Miller, Ephraim F., Esq., Salem,
Morse, Alpheus C., Esq., Boston,
Muzzey, Rev. Artemas B., Cambridgeport,
Norton, Alfred, Esq., Medford,
Orvis, John, Esq., Boston,
Palfrey, Hon. John G., Cambridge,
Parker, Rev. Theodore, Boston,
Peabody, Rev. Ephraim, Boston,
Perabeau, H, Esq., "
Phillips, Hon. Stephen C., Salem,
Phillips, Stephen H., Esq., "
Pike, William B., Esq., Boston,
Poore, Benjamin Perley, Esq., Boston,

A 20.2: 10″ × 7⁷/₈″; page 2

[1–4]

[a]²

Contents: p. 1: constitution; p. 2: constitution continued and list of members; p. 3: list of members and notice of election; p. 4: blank.

Typography and paper: pp. 1–2: 8¹/₁₆″ × 6¹/₂″; p. 3: 6″ × 6¹/₂″; pale gray-blue wove paper; 33 lines on p. 1; 48 lines on p. 2; 22 lines on p. 3. No running heads.

Robbins, Rev. Chandler, Boston,
Robbins, Rev. Samuel D., Chelsea,
Rodman, Benjamin, Esq., New Bedford,
Roelker, Bernard, Esq., Boston,
Russell, Dr. Le Baron,   "
Sargent, Rev. John T.,   "
Sewall, Samuel E., Esq.,   "
Shackford, Rev. Charles C., Lynn.
Silsbee, Rev. William, Salem,
Soule, Richard, Jr., Esq., East Boston,
Spooner, Allen C., Esq., Boston,
Stimson, Alexander, L., Esq., Boston.
Stone, Rev. Thomas T., Salem,
Streeter, Gilbert L., Esq., "
Sumner, Charles, Esq., Boston,

Ticknor, William D., Esq , Boston.
Tolman, James, Esq ,   "
Townley, Rev. Robert, Charlestown,
Ward, George C., Esq., Boston,
Ward, Samuel G., Esq , Lenox,
Westall, John, Esq., Fall River,
Whipple, Charles K., Esq , Boston,
Whipple, Edwin P., Esq ,   "
White, William A., Esq , Watertown,
Willard, Rev. John B., Westford,
Willard, Joseph, Esq., Boston,
Williams, J. Earl, Esq.,   "
Woodman, Horatio, Esq., Boston,
Wright, Elizur, Esq.,   "
Wyman, John, C. Esq., Worcester.

N. B. The above is a list of those who had signed the Constitution at the date of the monthly meeting in July.

Boston,   18

Sir:

    At the monthly meeting of the Town and Country Club,   18

you were elected a member of the same.

    You are respectfully requested to sign the Constitution at the next meeting of the Club.

     18   at 15 Tremont Row.

Recording Secretary.

A 20.2: 10″ × 7⁷/₈″; page 3

Binding: Head title. Single sheet, folded once; unbound.

Publication: After July 1849.

Location: MH.

A 21.1.a
First American edition, first printing (1849)

NATURE;

ADDRESSES, AND LECTURES.

BY

R. W. EMERSON.

———————

BOSTON AND CAMBRIDGE:
JAMES MUNROE AND COMPANY.
M DCCC XLIX.

A 21.1.a₁: 7^{1}/₄″ × 4^{9}/₁₆″

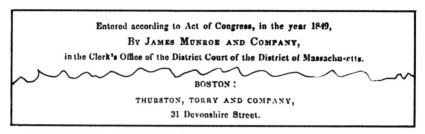

Two issues have been noted:

A 21.1.a₁
First issue

[i–v] vi [vii–viii] [1] 2–3 [4–5] 6–8 [9–10] 11–12 [13] 14–22 [23] 24–33 [34] 35–44 [45] 46–58 [59] 60–63 [64] 65–74 [75–77] 78–111 [112–115] 116–146 [147–149] 150–180 [181–183] 184–215 [216–219] 220–248 [249–251] 252–282 [283–285] 286–315 [316–319] 320–348 [349–351] 352–383 [384]

[a]⁴ 1–24⁸

Contents: p. i: 'NATURE. | ADDRESSES, AND LECTURES.'; p. ii: blank; p. iii: title page; p. iv: copyright page; pp. v–vi: contents; p. vii: 'NATURE. | [rule] | [six lines of verse]'; p. viii: blank; pp. 1–3: "Introduction to Nature"; p. 4: blank; pp. 5–74: text of *Nature;* p. 75: 'THE AMERICAN SCHOLAR. | AN ORATION DELIVERED BEFORE THE PHI BETA KAPPA SOCIETY, | AT CAMBRIDGE, AUGUST 31, 1837.'; p. 76: blank; pp. 77–111: text; p. 112: blank; p. 113: 'AN ADDRESS | DELIVERED BEFORE THE SEN- IOR CLASS IN DIVINITY COLLEGE, | CAMBRIDGE, SUNDAY EVENING, JULY 15, 1838.'; p. 114: blank; pp. 115–146: text; p. 147: 'LITERARY ETHICS. | AN ORATION DELIVERED BEFORE THE LITERARY SOCIETIES OF | DARTMOUTH COLLEGE, JULY 24, 1838.'; p. 148: blank; pp. 149–180: text; p. 181: 'THE METHOD OF NATURE. | AN ORATION DELIVERED BEFORE THE SOCIETY OF THE ADELPHI, | IN WATERVILLE COLLEGE, MAINE, AUGUST 11, 1841.'; p. 182: blank; pp. 183–215: text; p. 216: blank; p. 217: 'MAN THE REFORMER. | A LECTURE READ BEFORE THE MECHANICS' APPRENTICES' | LIBRARY ASSOCIATION, BOSTON, JANUARY 25, 1841.'; p. 218: blank; pp. 219–248: text; p. 249: 'LECTURE ON THE TIMES. | READ AT THE MASONIC TEMPLE, BOSTON, DECEMBER 2, 1841.'; p. 250: blank; pp. 251–282: text; p. 283: 'THE CONSERVATIVE. | A LECTURE DELIVERED AT THE MASONIC TEMPLE, BOS- TON, | DECEMBER 9, 1841.'; p. 284: blank; pp. 285–315: text; p. 316: blank; p. 317: 'THE TRANSCENDENTALIST. | A LECTURE READ AT THE MASONIC TEMPLE, BOS- TON, JAN- | UARY, 1841.'; p. 318: blank; pp. 319–348: text; p. 349: 'THE YOUNG AMERICAN. | A LECTURE READ BEFORE THE MERCANTILE LIBRARY ASSO- | CIA- TION, BOSTON, FEBRUARY 7, 1844.'; p. 350: blank; pp. 351–383: text; p. 384: blank.

Includes: *Nature;* "The American Scholar"; Divinity School Address; "Literary Ethics"; "The Method of Nature"; "Man the Reformer"; "Introductory Lecture" [to "Lectures on the Times"]; "The Conservative"; "The Transcendentalist"; "The Young American."

Typography and paper: 5¼" (4¹⁵/₁₆") × 3"; wove paper; 28 lines per page. Running heads: rectos: pp. 3, 7–11, 15–21, 25–43, 47–57, 61–73: chapter titles from *Nature;* pp. 79–111, 117–145, 151–179, 185–215, 221–247, 253–281, 287–315, 321–347, 353–383: titles of selections; versos: p. vi: 'CONTENTS.'; pp. 2, 6–8, 12–32, 36–62, 66–74: chapter titles from *Nature;* pp. 78–110, 116–146, 150–180, 184–214, 220– 248, 252–282, 286–314, 320–348, 352–382: titles of selections.

Binding: Four styles have been noted, priority undetermined:

Binding A: Medium brown A cloth (ribbed morocco); black, dark blue, or medium brown T cloth (rib). Front and back covers: blindstamped double-rule frame outside of a frame of florets with a floral design inside of each corner; spine: blindstamped rules with goldstamped 'NATURE. | ADDRESSES | AND | LECTURES | [rule] | EMERSON | [gothic] Munroe & Co.'. Flyleaves. Yellow endpapers. All edges trimmed.

Binding B: Black, dark brown, medium brown, or green gray T cloth (rib). Front and back covers: blindstamped ornate cartouche forming 4½" grilled area in center; spine: the same as Binding A, except: 'MUNROE & CO.' at bottom. Flyleaves. Yellow endpapers. All edges trimmed.

Binding C: Light brown, light green, or purple A cloth (ribbed morocco); medium brown T cloth (rib). Front and back covers: blindstamped grolieresque frame with 2¹¹/₁₆" rococo ornament in the center; spine: the same as Binding B. Flyleaves (with conjugate leaf pasted under pastedown endpaper). Cream, pink, or yellow endpapers. All edges trimmed.

Binding D: Light green A cloth (ribbed morocco). Front and back covers: blindstamped grolieresque frame with 4⅝" blank space in the center; spine: the same as Binding B, except: blindstamped rules and boxes with florets in the center. Flyleaves. Yellow endpapers. All edges trimmed.

Publication: On 23 May 1849, Emerson wrote John Chapman "I am just printing 'Nature' again, & the Orations" (CLU). On 29 May 1849, Emerson wrote his brother William that he was "just reprinting" his earlier works (*L*, IV, 149). Munroe advertised the book as "Nature, Orations, Addresses, &c" and as "In press . . . will shortly be published," in *Boston Daily Advertiser*, 13 June 1849, p. 3. On 18 August 1849, Emerson announced to William that the book "comes out next week," but on that same date Munroe sent Emerson more proofs and asked for additional information (*L*, IV, 158; MH). According to Emerson's contract with Munroe, he paid for the composition and printing costs, and retained the copyright. 1,500 copies were printed and the book was apparently published on 7 September 1849 (see *JMN*, XI, 156). A "few copies" were trimmed and bound "to match the Essays," but the idea was discarded because "the larger size book looks better" (Munroe to Emerson, [September 1849] [MH]). Only 596 copies were bound at first. Deposited for copyright: title, 22 August 1849; book, 19 October 1849. Advertised as "This day published," in *Boston Daily Advertiser*, 11 September 1849, p. 3. Listed as published between 22 and 29 September, in *Literary World*, 5 (29 September 1849), 285. Inscribed copies: Binding A: MH (from Emerson, September 1849); Binding B: DLC (from Emerson, September 1849), MH (from Emerson, September 1849), NN (from Emerson, September 1849). The entire printing was sold out by February 1854. Price, $1.00. Publisher's commission, 33⅓¢.

Locations: Binding A: CU, CtY, JM, MB, MBAt, MCo (2 copies), MH, NNC, PSt, ViU; Binding B: DLC, MH, NN, NNC; Binding C: JM, MWA, NN; Binding D: JM, MH, NNC, ViU.

Note one: In some copies, p. 9 is not numbered: CtY, JM (C, D), MCo, MH (A, B, D), NNC (B, D).

Note two: A copy has been noted with a 6-page catalogue of Munroe's publications, dated September 1849, inserted at the front: MH (D).

Note three: Copies have been noted with an 8-page catalogue of Munroe's publications, dated September 1849, inserted at the front: DLC, JM (D), MBAt, MH (B), NN (B), NNC (B, D), ViU (D).

Note four: Copies have been noted with an 8-page catalogue of Munroe's publications, dated September 1849, inserted at the back: CU, CtY, JM (A, C), MCo, MH (A), MWA, NN (C), NNC (A), PSt, ViU (A).

Note five: 250 copies of *Nature* were printed from these plates and bound as a separate publication; see A 3.2.

A 21.1.a₂
Second issue

NATURE; | ADDRESSES AND LECTURES. | BY | R. W. EMERSON. | [rule] | BOSTON: | PHILLIPS, SAMPSON & CO. | 110 WASHINGTON STREET. | 1850.

The title leaf is a cancel. The title leaf verso contains only the copyright information. Price, $1.00.

Locations: CtY, GAE.

Note one: Publisher's records indicate copies were bound in half and full calf; no copies have been located.

Note two: Emerson's usual agreement with Phillips, Sampson called for a 20% royalty (see *Note three* to A 21.1.b).

Note three: Phillips, Sampson sold 577 copies of *Nature; Addresses, and Lectures* between 1850 (when they assumed most of Munroe's stock, purchasing another 100 copies in sheets in September 1854) and November 1854 (Account Books and Emerson's manuscript memorandum [MH]).

A 21.1.b
First American edition, second printing (1856)

MISCELLANIES;

EMBRACING

NATURE, ADDRESSES, AND LECTURES.

BY

R. W. EMERSON.

BOSTON:
PHILLIPS, SAMPSON, AND COMPANY.
M.DCCC.LVI.

A 21.1.b: 7$1/4$″ × 4$9/16$″

```
┌─────────────────────────────────────────────────────────────┐
│   Entered according to Act of Congress, in the year 1855, by  │
│   PHILLIPS, SAMPSON, AND COMPANY, in the Clerk's Office of the │
│   District Court of the District of Massachusetts.            │
│                                                               │
│                  RIVERSIDE,  CAMBRIDGE:                        │
│                                                               │
│         STEREOTYPED BY H. O. HOUGHTON AND COMPANY.            │
└─────────────────────────────────────────────────────────────┘
```

500 copies printed December 1855 (Account Books [MH]). Advertised in *Boston Daily Advertiser,* 18 July 1856, p. 3. Listed as an importation in *Publishers' Circular and Booksellers' Record,* 19 (16 June 1856), 246, at 6s. 6d. Copyright, 14 December 1855. Price, $1.00. Royalty, 20¢. *Locations:* CtY, InU, JM.

Note one: The first stereotype printing.

Note two: Publisher's records indicate copies were bound in half and full calf; no copies have been located.

Note three: Emerson "paid for the printing, & owned the stereotype plates," and was paid "in advance . . . 20 per cent on the retail price" of each printing (25 February 1867, *L,* V, 507).

Note four: The *Miscellanies* title appears on all subsequent reprintings from the first edition plates.

A 21.1.c
Boston: Phillips, Sampson, M.DCCC.LVII.

500 copies printed 22 December 1856; 250 copies on "fine paper" December 1856 (*JMN,* XIV, 452). Price, $1.00. Royalty, 20¢. *Location:* JM.

A 21.1.d
Boston: Phillips, Sampson, M.DCCC.LVIII.

500 copies printed July 1858 (Account Books [MH]). Price, $1.00. Royalty, 20¢. *Location:* JM.

Note: Phillips, Sampson failed on 19 September 1859, after printing 1,000 copies after 29 August 1859. Of this last printing, 627 copies in sheets and 111 bound copies were turned over to Ticknor and Fields (see *Note* to A 21.1.e). The disposition of the remaining 262 copies is unknown; no copies have been located with an 1859 Phillips, Sampson title page.

A 21.1.e
Boston: Ticknor and Fields, M DCCC LX.

Price, $1.00. Royalty, 20¢. *Location:* JM.

Note: Some copies of Phillips, Sampson sheets have been located in Ticknor and Fields bindings, with a cancel title leaf; these are from the 1,000 copies printed by Phillips, Sampson after 29 August 1859 (see *Note* to A 21.1.d).

A 21.1.f
Boston: Ticknor and Fields, M DCCC LXV.

280 copies printed March–June 1865. Price, $1.50. Royalty, 30¢. *Location:* JM.

Note: The copyright on *Nature; Addresses, and Lectures* was renewed 13 May 1865.

A 21.1.g
Boston: Ticknor and Fields, M DCCC LXVI.

280 copies printed 20 July 1866. Price, $1.50. Royalty, 30¢. *Location:* LNHT.

A 21.1.h
Boston: Ticknor and Fields, M DCCC LXVIII.

280 copies printed July 1868. Price, $2.00. Royalty, 20¢. *Location:* JM.

Note one: By a contract of 4 March 1868, Emerson's royalty was changed from 20% to 20¢ per volume.

Note two: Ticknor and Fields was succeeded by Fields, Osgood in October 1868. Some copies of Ticknor and Fields sheets (including the title leaf) have been noted in Fields, Osgood bindings.

A 21.1.i
Boston: Fields, Osgood, 1870.

280 copies printed 21 September 1870. Price, $2.00. Royalty, 30¢. *Location:* JM.

Note one: In a "Supplementary article of agreement" to the 4 March 1868 contract, dated 19 February 1870, Emerson's royalty was raised to 30¢ per copy when the price was $2.00 or above.

Note two: Fields, Osgood was succeeded by James R. Osgood & Company in January 1871.

A 21.1.j
Boston: James R. Osgood, 1875.

180 copies printed 26 March 1875. Price, $2.00. Royalty, 30¢. *Location:* JM.

A 21.1.k
Boston: James R. Osgood, 1877.

'NEW AND REVISED EDITION'. 150 copies printed 23 March 1877. Price, $1.50. *Location:* MLy.

Note one: Emerson's 1 January 1876 contract with Osgood called for him to receive a flat annual fee of $1,500 for all his books, rather than a per copy royalty.

Note two: James R. Osgood was succeeded by Houghton, Osgood in February 1878. Some copies of James R. Osgood sheets (including the title leaf) have been noted in Houghton, Osgood bindings.

Note three: All subsequent reprintings are designated 'NEW AND REVISED EDITION' on the title page.

A 21.1.l
Boston: Houghton, Osgood, 1880.

175 copies printed 26 January 1880. Price, $1.50. *Not seen.*

Note: Houghton, Osgood was succeeded by Houghton, Mifflin in May 1880.

A 21.1.m
Boston: Houghton, Mifflin, 1880.

270 copies printed 10 June 1880. Price, $1.50. *Not seen.*

A 21.1.n
Boston: Houghton, Mifflin, 1882.

150 copies printed 12 April 1882. Price, $1.50. *Location:* InNd.

A 21.1.o
Boston: Houghton, Mifflin, 1883.

150 copies printed 10 January 1883. Price, $1.50. *Location:* JM.

Note one: The copyright on *Nature; Addresses, and Lectures* was renewed 19 July 1883.

Note two: As of 10 January 1884, 10 copies of *Nature; Addresses, and Lectures* were still in stock.

PRINTINGS FROM THE "LITTLE CLASSIC EDITION" PLATES

A 21.2.a

[all within a double-rule frame; outer frame is red with boxed corners] [red] MISCELLA-NIES; | EMBRACING | [red] NATURE, ADDRESSES, AND LECTURES. | BY | RALPH WALDO EMERSON. | NEW AND REVISED EDITION. | [ornamental rule] | [red] BOS-TON: | JAMES R. OSGOOD AND COMPANY, | Late Ticknor & Fields, and Fields, Osgood, & Co. | [red] 1876.

315 pp. Vol. [I] of the "Little Classic Edition" (see B 3). 2,000 copies printed 29 May 1876. Listed in *Publishers' Weekly,* 9 (24 June 1876), 810. Copyright, 5 June 1876. Price, $1.50. Royalty: see *Note one* to A 21.1.k. *Locations:* BL (12 April 1877), JM.

Note: James R. Osgood was succeeded by Houghton, Osgood in February 1878.

A 21.2.b
Boston: Houghton, Osgood, 1879.

280 copies printed 31 July 1879. Price, $1.50. *Location:* MH.

A 21.2.c
Boston: Houghton, Osgood, 1879.

Vol. V of the "Fireside Edition" (see B 4). 500 copies printed 15 August 1879. *Location:* JM.

A 21.2.d
Boston: Houghton, Osgood, 1880.

Vol. V of the "Fireside Edition" (see B 4). 500 copies printed 6 February 1880. *Location:* JM.

Note: Houghton, Osgood was succeeded by Houghton, Mifflin in May 1880.

A 21.2.e
Boston: Houghton, Mifflin, 1880.

Price, $1.50. *Location:* MAsh.

A 21.2.f
Boston: Houghton, Mifflin, 1881.

Vol. V of the "Fireside Edition" (see B 4). 500 copies printed 7 December 1880. *Location:* KyU.

A 21.2.g
Boston: Houghton, Mifflin, 1881.

270 copies printed 25 February 1881. Price, $1.50. *Location:* DLC.

A 21.2.h
Boston: Houghton, Mifflin, 1882.

270 copies printed 19 August 1881; 500 copies on 23 February 1882. Price, $1.50. *Location:* ICarbS.

A 21.2.i
Boston: Houghton, Mifflin, 1882.

Vol. V of the "Fireside Edition" (see B 4). 500 copies printed 26 October 1881, 13 May 1882, and 10 August 1882. *Location:* TSewU.

A 21.2.j
Boston: Houghton, Mifflin, 1883.

500 copies printed 20 September 1882; 270 copies on 10 April 1883. *Location:* MH.

A 21.2.k
Boston: Houghton, Mifflin, 1883.

Vol. V of the "Fireside Edition" (see B 4). 270 copies printed 11 January 1883. *Location:* JM.

A 21.2.l
Nature Addresses, and Lectures. Boston: Houghton, Mifflin, 1883.

270 copies printed 18 October 1883. *Not seen.*

Note: The title *Miscellanies* was dropped because the original title was being used in the *Riverside Edition,* and because *Miscellanies* would become the title of a later volume in the *Riverside Edition* (see A 40).

A 21.2.m
Boston: Houghton, Mifflin, 1884.

270 copies printed 3 December 1883, 22 January 1884, and 2 October 1884; 500 copies on 18 August 1884. *Location:* JM.

A 21.2.n
Boston: Houghton, Mifflin, 1886.

270 copies printed 12 July 1886. *Not seen.*

A 21.2.o
Boston: Houghton, Mifflin, 1887.

270 copies printed 14 October 1887. *Not seen.*

A 21.2.p
Boston and New York: Houghton, Mifflin, 1888.

270 copies printed 31 March 1888 and 20 November 1888. Bound in medium blue V cloth (smooth), rather than "Little Classic Edition" binding, as are subsequent reprintings (see illustration at B 3). *Location:* JM.

A 21.2.q
Boston and New York: Houghton, Mifflin, 1889.

270 copies printed 23 July 1889. *Not seen.*

A 21.2.r
Boston and New York: Houghton, Mifflin, 1890.

500 copies printed 28 December 1889. *Location:* JM.

A 21.2.s
Boston and New York: Houghton, Mifflin, 1891.

270 copies printed 27 July 1891. *Not seen.*

A 21.2.t
Boston and New York: Houghton, Mifflin, 1892.

270 copies printed 4 January 1892 and 9 August 1892; 500 copies on 30 July 1892. *Location:* JM.

A 21.2.u
Boston and New York: Houghton, Mifflin, 1893.

500 copies printed 17 August 1893. *Location:* MH.

A 21.2.v
Boston and New York: Houghton, Mifflin, 1894.

250 copies printed 19 January 1894. *Not seen.*

A 21.2.w
Boston and New York: Houghton, Mifflin, 1895.

500 copies printed 30 March 1895. *Not seen.*

A 21.2.x
Boston and New York: Houghton, Mifflin, 1897.

500 copies printed 5 January 1897. *Location:* JM.

A 21.2.y
Boston and New York: Houghton, Mifflin, 1900.

270 copies printed 29 November 1899. *Not seen.*

A 21.2.z
Boston and New York: Houghton, Mifflin, [n.d.].

Approximately 1,600 copies sold between 1901 and 1923. *Location:* NNS.

Note: Approximately 11,000 copies of *Nature; Addresses, and Lectures* (including *Miscellanies*) printed from the "Little Classic Edition" plates were sold between 1876 and 1923, when the title was apparently allowed to go out of print in this format.

PRINTINGS FROM THE RIVERSIDE EDITION PLATES

A 21.3.a
Riverside Edition (trade), first printing (1883)

NATURE, ADDRESSES, AND | LECTURES | BY | RALPH WALDO EMERSON | [gothic] New and Revised Edition | [publisher's logo] | BOSTON | HOUGHTON, MIFFLIN AND COMPANY | New York: 11 East Seventeenth Street | [gothic] The Riverside Press, Cambridge | 1883

372 pp. Vol. I of the *Riverside Edition,* trade printing (see B 7). 1,000 copies printed 29 June 1883 and 22 August 1883. Listed in *Publishers' Weekly,* 24 (29 September 1883), 455. Copyright, 16 July 1883. According to the publisher's records, published 20 September 1883. Price, $1.75. *Location:* DLC (18 December 1883).

Note: Copies have been noted with a pine branch on the title page instead of the publisher's logo.

A 21.3.b
Riverside Edition (Copyright), second (English) printing (1883)

NATURE, ADDRESSES, AND | LECTURES | BY | RALPH WALDO EMERSON | [gothic] The Riverside Edition | (COPYRIGHT) | LONDON | GEORGE ROUTLEDGE AND SONS | BROADWAY, LUDGATE HILL | NEW YORK: 9, LAFAYETTE PLACE | 1883

Vol. I of the *Riverside Edition (Copyright),* English trade printing (see B 10). 1,000 copies printed 18 August 1883. Listed in *Athenæum,* no. 2916 (15 September 1883), 337. Listed as published between 17 and 29 September, in *Publishers' Circular and Booksellers' Record,* 46 (1 October 1883), 893. Price, 3s. 6d. *Locations:* BC (24 October 1893), BO (6 November 1883), BL (8 December 1883), CaBVaU.

A 21.3.c$_1$
Riverside Edition (large paper), third printing, American issue (1883)

[red] NATURE | ADDRESSES, AND LECTURES | BY | RALPH WALDO EMERSON | [gothic] New and Revised Edition | [pine branch] | [red] CAMBRIDGE | [gothic] Printed at the Riverside Press | 1883

Vol. I of the *Riverside Edition,* large paper printing (see B 8). Limited to 500 numbered copies printed 17 September 1883. Price, $4.00. Sold out within a year. *Locations:* JM, TxU.

A 21.3.c$_2$
Riverside Edition (large paper), third printing, English issue (1883)

Title page is the same as in the American issue, except for publisher's imprint: 'LONDON | KEGAN PAUL, TRENCH, & CO., I, PATERNOSTER SQUARE | MDCCCLXXXIII'.

Vol. I of the *Riverside Edition,* large paper printing for English subscribers (see B 9). 25 title leaves printed 17 September 1883. Title leaf is a cancel. Limited to 25 signed and numbered copies. *Location:* JM.

A 21.3.d
Boston and New York: Houghton, Mifflin, 1884.

500 copies printed 19 February 1884 and 2 July 1884. *Location:* JM.

A 21.3.e
Boston and New York: Houghton, Mifflin, 1885.

500 copies printed 3 January 1885 and 31 July 1885. *Location:* CoU.

A 21.3.f
London and New York: George Routledge and Sons, 1886.

500 copies printed 1 January 1886. *Location:* JM.

A 21.3.g
Boston and New York: Houghton, Mifflin, 1886.

500 copies printed 17 March 1886 and 2 October 1886. *Location:* JM.

A 21.3.h
Boston and New York: Houghton, Mifflin, 1887.

500 copies printed 20 January 1887 and 12 September 1887. *Location:* JM.

A 21.3.i
Boston and New York: Houghton, Mifflin, 1888.

500 copies printed 13 March 1888 and 9 October 1888. *Location:* MBAt.

A 21.3.j
Boston and New York: Houghton, Mifflin, 1889.

270 copies printed 3 May 1889; 500 copies on 12 August 1889. *Location:* JM.

A 21.3.k
Boston and New York: Houghton, Mifflin, 1890.

500 copies printed April–June 1890. *Location:* JM.

A 21.3.l
Representative Men   Nature, Addresses, and Lectures. Boston and New York: Houghton, Mifflin, 1890.

Combined in two-volumes-in-one format. *Popular Edition.* Advertised in *Atlantic,* 66 (September 1890), advertising section. Listed as an importation for September 1890 at 5s. in the *English Catalogue.* According to the publisher's records, published 6 September 1890. Price, $1.00. Numerous undated reprintings. *Location:* JM (n.d.).

Note: Allowed to go out of stock by 1902, by which time approximately 4,700 copies had been sold.

A 21.3.m
Boston and New York: Houghton, Mifflin, 1891.

500 copies printed January–March 1891. *Location:* JM.

A 21.3.n
Boston and New York: Houghton, Mifflin, 1892.

500 copies printed 2 January 1892 and 13 September 1892. *Location:* JM.

A 21.3.o
Boston and New York: Houghton, Mifflin, 1893.

500 copies printed 13 August 1893. *Location:* OC.

A 21.3.p
London, Manchester, New York: George Routledge and Sons, 1894.

1,000 copies printed 11 January 1894. *Location:* JM.

A 21.3.q
Boston and New York: Houghton, Mifflin, 1894.

500 copies printed 21 June 1894. *Location:* NBu.

A 21.3.r
Standard Library Edition printing [1894]

NATURE, ADDRESSES, AND | LECTURES | BY | RALPH WALDO EMERSON | [pine branch] | BOSTON AND NEW YORK | HOUGHTON, MIFFLIN AND COMPANY | [gothic] The Riverside Press, Cambridge

Vol. I of the *Standard Library Edition* (see B 11). 1,000 copies printed 31 October 1894, 30 March 1895, 29 May 1896; 500 copies on 31 December 1897. *Location:* JM.

A 21.3.s
Boston and New York: Houghton, Mifflin, 1895.

500 copies printed 31 August 1895. *Location:* JM.

A 21.3.t
Boston and New York: Houghton, Mifflin, 1897.

250 copies printed April–June 1897. *Location:* MH.

A 21.3.u
Boston and New York: Houghton, Mifflin, 1898.

250 copies printed January–March 1898 and June–September 1898. *Location:* MNoW.

A 21.3.v
Representative Men   Nature, Addresses, and Lectures. Boston and New York: Houghton, Mifflin, 1898.

Combined in two-volumes-in-one format. *Cambridge Classics.* According to the publisher's records, published 1 October 1898. Price, $1.00. Reprinted 1900. Numerous undated reprints. *Locations:* ICarbS (1900), JM (n.d.).

Note: By 2 October 1911, approximately 2,800 copies had been sold and 68 were still in stock.

A 21.3.w
Boston and New York: Houghton, Mifflin, 1899.

500 copies printed 9 June 1899. *Location:* OCIW.

A 21.3.x
London: George Routledge and Sons, 1903.

Location: JM.

A 21.3.y
London: George Routledge & Sons, 1903.

Combined with *Essays: First Series* and *Essays: Second Series* in three-volumes-in-one format as vol. I of the "Sovereign Edition" (see B 12). 1,000 copies printed 16 September 1903. *Location:* InU.

A 21.3.z
Fireside Edition printing (1909)

[all within red double-rule frame with red floral ornaments in each corner] THE WORKS OF | [red gothic] Ralph Waldo Emerson | NATURE, ADDRESSES, AND | LECTURES | [engraving of man reading book in chair before fireplace] | [gothic] Fireside Edition | BOSTON AND NEW YORK | MDCCCCIX

Vol. I of the *Fireside Edition* (see B 13). 500 copies printed 29 September 1909 and 15 February 1910. *Location:* JM.

A 21.3.aa
Boston and New York: Jefferson Press, [ca. 1912].

Combined with *Representative Men* in two-volumes-in-one format as vol. [I] of the "Jefferson Press Edition" (see B 14). *Location:* CtW.

A 21.3.bb
New York: Sully and Kleinteich, [ca. 1912].

Vol. I of the *University Edition* (see B 15). *Location:* JM.

A 21.3.cc
Boston and New York: Houghton, Mifflin, [n.d.].

Approximately 1,900 copies sold between 1900 and 1913. *Location:* JM.

Note: Approximately 13,800 copies of *Nature; Addresses, and Lectures* in the *Riverside Edition* were sold between 1883 and 1913, when the title was apparently allowed to go out of print in this format.

A 21.3.dd
London: Waverley Book Co., [n.d.].

Vol. I of the "Waverley" *Riverside Edition* (see B 16). *Location:* JM.

A 21.4.a
First English edition, first printing (1884)

MISCELLANIES

BY

RALPH WALDO EMERSON

WITH AN INTRODUCTION BY

JOHN MORLEY

𝕷𝖔𝖓𝖉𝖔𝖓

MACMILLAN AND CO.

1884

A 21.4.a: 7^1/₁₆″ × 4^{13}/₁₆″

[a–b] [i–vii] viii–lix [lx] [lxi–lxii] [1] 2–3 [4–5] 6–62 [63–65] 66–93 [94–97] 98–123 [124–127] 128–152 [153–155] 156–181 [182–185] 186–208 [209–211] 212–236 [237–239] 240–263 [264–267] 268–291 [292–295] 296–321 [322–324]

[a]⁸ *b–d* ⁸ B–I⁸ K–U⁸ X⁸ [Y]²

Contents: pp. a–b: blank; p. i: 'THE WORKS | OF | RALPH WALDO EMERSON | VOL. I.'; p. ii: publisher's device; p. iii: title page; p. iv: printer's imprint; p. v: contents; p. vi: blank; pp. vii–lix: 'INTRODUCTORY.', signed 'J[ohn]. M[orley]. | *December* 24, 1883.'; p. lx: blank; p. lxi: 'NATURE | [six lines of verse]'; p. lxii: blank; pp. 1–62: text; p. 63: 'THE AMERICAN SCHOLAR | AN ORATION DELIVERED BEFORE THE PHI BETA KAPPA | SOCIETY, AT CAMBRIDGE, AUGUST 31, 1837.'; p. 64: blank; pp. 65–93: text; p. 94: blank; p. 95: 'AN ADDRESS | DELIVERED BEFORE THE SENIOR CLASS IN | DIVINITY COLLEGE, CAMBRIDGE, SUNDAY EVENING, | JULY 15, 1838.'; p. 96: blank; pp. 97–123: text; p. 124: blank; p. 125: 'LITERARY ETHICS | AN ORATION | DE-LIVERED BEFORE THE LITERARY SOCIETIES OF | DARTMOUTH COLLEGE, JULY 24, 1838.'; p. 126: blank; pp. 127–152: text; p. 153: 'THE METHOD OF NATURE | AN ORATION DELIVERED BEFORE THE SOCIETY OF | THE ADELPHI, IN WATERVILLE COLLEGE, | MAINE, AUGUST 11, 1841.'; p. 154: blank; pp. 155–181: text; p. 182: blank; p. 183: 'MAN THE REFORMER | A LECTURE | READ BEFORE THE MECHANICS' APPRENTICES' | LIBRARY ASSOCIATION, BOSTON, | JANUARY 25, 1841.'; p. 184: blank; pp. 185–208: text; p. 209: 'LECTURE ON THE TIMES | READ AT THE MASONIC TEMPLE, BOSTON, | DECEMBER 2, 1841.'; p. 210: blank; pp. 211–236: text; p. 237: 'THE CONSERVATIVE | A LECTURE DELIVERED AT THE MASONIC TEMPLE, | BOS-TON, DECEMBER 9, 1841.'; p. 238: blank; pp. 239–263: text; p. 264: blank; p. 265: 'THE TRANSCENDENTALIST | A LECTURE | READ AT THE MASONIC TEMPLE, BOS-TON, | JANUARY 1842.'; p. 266: blank; pp. 267–291: text; p. 292: blank; p. 293: 'THE YOUNG AMERICAN | A LECTURE | READ BEFORE THE MERCANTILE LIBRARY AS-SOCIATION, | BOSTON, FEBRUARY 7, 1844.'; p. 294: blank; pp. 295–321: text; p. 322: blank; pp. 323–324: publisher's advertisements.

Typography and paper: 5⁷/₁₆″ (5¹/₈″) × 3″; wove paper; 31 lines per page. Running heads: rectos: pp. ix–lix: '*INTRODUCTORY.*'; pp. 3, 7–61: chapter titles from *Nature;* pp. 67–93, 99–123, 129–151, 157–181, 187–207, 213–235, 241–263, 269–291, 297–321: titles of selections; versos: pp. viii–lviii: '*INTRODUCTORY.*';; pp. 2, 6–62: 'NA-TURE.'; pp. 66–92, 98–122, 128–152, 156–180, 186–208, 212–236, 240–262, 268–290, 296–320: titles of selections.

Binding: Very deep red V cloth (smooth). Front and back covers: blindstamped single-rule frame; spine: goldstamped '[rule] | MISCELLANIES | EMERSON | MACMILLAN & C° | [rule]'. Cream endpapers. All edges trimmed.

Publication: Advertised as "now ready," in *Publishers' Circular and Booksellers' Re-cord,* 47 (18 January 1884), 23. Listed in *Athenæum,* no. 2934 (19 January 1884), 88. Listed as published between 18 and 31 January, in *Publishers' Circular and Book-sellers' Record,* 47 (1 February 1884), 114. According to *Publishers' Circular and Booksellers' Record,* this volume was delayed pending the receipt of John Morley's introduction (46 [2 April 1883], 280). Deposit copies: BL (20 February 1884), BC (17 March 1884), BO (17 March 1884). Price, 5s.

Printing: "*Printed by* R. & R. Clark, *Edinburgh*" (p. [iv]).

Locations: BC, BL, BO, JM, MCo.

Note one: Vol. I of the *Works* (see B 6).

Note two: Copies have been noted with a one-line errata slip, printed on the recto, inserted before p. vii: BL, BO, MCo.

A 21.4.b–h
London and New York: Macmillan, 1884.

Vol. I of the *Works* (see B 6). Reprinted July 1884, 1890, 1896, 1900, 1905; with London imprint only, 1912. *Locations:* JM (1890), BRU (1896), MH (1900), CaOSuL (1905), BLdU (1912).

LATER EDITIONS

A 21.5.a–d
Philadelphia: David McKay, 1892.

346 pp. *American Classic Series.* Also combined with *Representative Men* in two-volumes-in-one format. Also advertised in a boxed set with *Representative Men.* Reprinted 1893, 1894, [n.d.]. *Locations:* KyU, JM (1893, 1894), SdU (n.d.), IdU (combined).

A 21.5.e
Chicago: Hooper, Clarke, [n.d.].

Combined with *Representative Men* in two-volumes-in-one format in *Century Series.* Stamped on spine is "American Publishers Corporation." *Location:* ScU.

A 21.6
Philadelphia: Henry Altemus, [1899].

294 pp. Also advertised as included in "Illustrated Vademecum Series," no. 141. *Location:* JM.

A 21.7
New York: Maynard, Merrill, 1901.

Wrappers. Advertised as included in "Maynard's English Classics Series." Price, 12¢. *Not seen.*

A 21.8.a
New York: A. L. Burt, [1902].

368 pp. *Cornell Series.* Also advertised as included in "Home Library" by itself or combined with *Representative Men* in two-volumes-in-one format. Listed in *Publishers' Weekly*, 62 (12 July 1902), 36. Price, $1.00. *Location:* JM.

A 21.8.b
Philadelphia: John B. Morris, [1906].

Vol. III of the "John D. Morris Edition" (see B 29). Copyright, 13 February 1906. *Location:* JM.

A 21.8.c
Boston and New York: C. T. Brainard, [n.d.].

Vol. II of the *Works* (see B 30). *Location:* NHemH.

A 21.8.d
New York: Caxton Society, [n.d.].

Vol. II of the *Works* (see B 31). *Location:* NjR.

A 21.8.e
New York: National Library Co., [n.d.].

Vol. II of the *Works* (see B 32). *Location:* CaOHM.

A 21.8.f
Philadelphia, New York, Chicago: Nottingham Society, [n.d.].

Vol. II of the *Works* (see B 33). *Location:* JM.

A 21.9
Nature and Other Addresses and Lectures. London: Isbister, 1903.

298 pp. *Isbister's Anglo Saxon Library.* Advertised with *Essays: First Series* and *Essays: Second Series* as "Essays: Third Series." Published April 1903. Price, 1s. 6d. *Locations:* BC (9 July 1903), BO (9 July 1903), CtW.

A 21.10.a–b
The Conduct of Life   Nature, Addresses, and Lectures. New York: P. F. Collier & Son, MCMIII.

210 pp. Combined in two-volumes-in-one format in *American Authors in Prose and Poetry* series, *Emerson,* vol. III. Reprinted [n.d.]. *Location:* JM (n.d.).

PRINTINGS FROM THE CENTENARY EDITION PLATES

A 21.11.a
Autograph Centenary Edition (large paper), first printing (1903)

RALPH WALDO EMERSON | [red] Nature | [red] Addresses and Lectures | [pine tree] | CAMBRIDGE | [red gothic] Printed at the Riverside Press | 1903

461 pp. Vol. I of the *Autograph Centenary Edition* (see B 19). Limited to 600 signed and numbered copies printed 11 May 1903. Copyright, 16 May 1903. Price, $6.00. Sold out by 5 April 1906. *Locations:* DLC (20 May 1903), JM.

A 21.11.b$_1$
Centenary Edition (trade), second printing, American issue (1903)

NATURE | ADDRESSES AND LECTURES | BY | RALPH WALDO EMERSON | [pine tree] | BOSTON AND NEW YORK | HOUGHTON, MIFFLIN AND COMPANY | [gothic] The Riverside Press, Cambridge | 1903

Dust jacket. Vol. II of the *Centenary Edition,* trade printing (see B 18). 1,000 copies printed 29 May 1903. Listed in *Publishers' Weekly,* 63 (6 June 1903), 1324. Copyright, 16 May 1903. According to the publisher's records, published 23 May 1903. Price, $1.75. *Location:* JM.

Note: Numerous reprintings with undated title pages. Approximately 4,000 copies printed between 1 January 1904 and 1 October 1910. Approximately 6,300 copies sold through 1923.

A 21.11.b$_2$
English issue

London: A. P. Watt & Son, [1903].

Vol. I of the English *Centenary Edition* (see B 21). American sheets with Watt's label pasted on the title page. Price, 6s. *Locations:* BL (3 June 1903), BE (22 June 1903), BC (25 June 1903).

A 21.11.c
Boston and New York: Houghton, Mifflin, 1903.

Vol. I of the *Concord Edition* (see B 20). 1,000 copies printed 30 September 1903. *Location:* JM.

Note: Numerous reprintings with undated title pages. Approximately 3,100 copies sold by 31 December 1910.

A 21.11.d
Boston and New York: Houghton Mifflin, [1914].

Vol. I of the *Riverside Pocket Edition* (see B 22). Approximately 1,100 copies sold between 1914 and 1922. *Not seen.*

A 21.11.e
Boston and New York: Houghton Mifflin, 1921.

395 pp. (text without the notes). Combined with *Letters and Social Aims* in two-volumes-in-one format as vol. II of *Emerson's Complete Works* (see B 23). *Location:* RP.

A 21.11.f
New York: Wm. H. Wise, 1923.

Combined with *Essays: First Series* in two-volumes-in-one format as vol. I of the *Current Opinion Edition* (see B 24). *Location:* JM.

A 21.11.g
Boston and New York: Houghton Mifflin, 1929.

Combined (text without the notes) with *Letters and Social Aims* in two-volumes-in-one format as vol. [II] of the *Harvard Edition* (see B 25). *Location:* JM.

A 21.11.h
New York: Wm. H. Wise, 1929.

Combined with *Essays: First Series* in two-volumes-in-one format as vol. I of the *Medallion Edition* (see B 26). *Location:* OC.

A 21.11.i–j
New York: AMS Press, [1968].

Vol. I of the "AMS Press" *Centenary Edition* (see B 27). Reprinted 1979. *Locations:* TxU, DLC (9 November 1979), JM.

LATER EDITIONS

A 21.12.a
London: George G. Harrap, [1911].

265 pp. *The Harrap Library,* no. 14. *Location:* BL (16 August 1911).

A 21.12.b
New York: Dodge, [n.d.].

Location: InU.

A 21.12.c
Nature, The American Scholar, and Other Essays and Addresses. New York: Robert M. McBride, [n.d.].

Chelsea College Classics. Location: JM.

A 21.13
Nature and Other Miscellanies. London [&c.]: Humphrey Milford, Oxford University Press, [1922].

278 pp. Advertised in various bindings at various prices. *The World's Classics*, no. 236. Published June 1922. *Locations:* BL (24 May 1922), MH.

A 21.14.a–b
Cambridge: The Belknap Press of Harvard University Press, 1971.

333 pp. Dust jacket. Edited by Alfred R. Ferguson and Robert E. Spiller. Vol. I of the *Collected Works* (see B 46). Price, $15.00. Reprinted (283 pp., without textual apparatus) in wrappers, 1979. Price, $7.95. *Locations:* JM (both).

UNDATED EDITION

A 21.15
New York and Boston: Thomas Y. Crowell, [n.d.].

298 pp. Also noted with New York imprint only. Advertised in various bindings at various prices. *Locations:* MH (both).

A 22.1.a
First edition, first printing (1850)

REPRESENTATIVE MEN:

SEVEN LECTURES.

BY R. W. EMERSON

——————— ————

BOSTON:

PHILLIPS, SAMPSON AND COMPANY,

110 WASHINGTON STREET.

1850.

A 22.1.a: $7^5/16'' \times 4^5/8''$

```
┌─────────────────────────────────────────────────────────────────┐
│          Entered according to Act of Congress, in the year 1849,  │
│                                                                   │
│                 BY PHILLIPS, SAMPSON AND COMPANY,                 │
│                                                                   │
│        In the Clerk's Office of the District Court of Massachusetts. │
│                                                                   │
│                         STEREOTYPED BY                            │
│                      CHARLES W. COLTON,                           │
│                        No. 2 Water Street.                        │
└─────────────────────────────────────────────────────────────────┘
```

[1–9] 10–40 [41–43] 44–81 [82] 83–91 [92–95] 96–145 [146–149] 150–184 [185–187] 188–216 [217–219] 220–253 [254–257] 258–285 [286–290]

[1]⁶ 2–18⁶ [19]⁶ 20–23⁶ 24⁶ (+24₅)   The inserted leaf contains p. 285 of the text.

Contents: p. 1: 'REPRESENTATIVE MEN.'; p. 2: blank; p. 3: title page; p. 4: copyright page; p. 5: contents; p. 6: blank; p. 7: 'USES OF GREAT MEN.'; p. 8: blank; pp. 9–40: "I. Uses of Great Men."; p. 41: 'PLATO; | OR, | THE PHILOSOPHER.'; p. 42: blank; pp. 43–81: "II. Plato; or, the Philosopher."; pp. 82–91: "Plato: New Readings."; p. 92: blank; p. 93: 'SWEDENBORG; | OR, | THE MYSTIC.'; p. 94: blank; pp. 95–145: "III. Swedenborg; or, the Mystic."; p. 146: blank; p. 147: 'MONTAIGNE | OR, | THE SKEPTIC.'; p. 148: blank; pp. 149–184: "IV. Montaigne; or, the Skeptic."; p. 185: 'SHAKSPEARE | OR, | THE POET.'; p. 186: blank; pp. 187–216: "V. Shakspeare; or, the Poet."; p. 217: 'NAPOLEON; | OR, | THE MAN OF THE WORLD.'; p. 218: blank; pp. 219–253: "VI. Napoleon; or, the Man of the World."; p. 254: blank; p. 255: 'GOETHE; | OR, | THE WRITER.'; p. 256: blank; pp. 257–285: "VII. Goethe; or, the Writer."; pp. 286–290: blank.

Essays: "Uses of Great Men" #; "Plato; or, the Philosopher" #; "Swedenborg; or, the Mystic" #; "Montaigne; or, the Skeptic" #; "Shakspeare; or, the Poet" #; "Napoleon; or, the Man of the World" #; "Goethe; or, the Writer" #.

Typography and paper: 4¹⁵/₁₆″ (4¹¹/₁₆″) × 3″; wove paper; sheets bulk ¹¹/₁₆″; 28 lines per page. Running heads: rectos: pp. 11–39, 45–91, 97–145, 151–183, 189–215, 221–253, 259–285: titles of chapters; versos: pp. 10–40, 44–80, 84–90, 96–144, 150–184, 188–216, 220–252, 258–284: 'REPRESENTATIVE MEN.'.

Binding: Black, brown, or light brown T cloth (rib). Front and back covers: blind-stamped fasceslike frame with decorative lyre in each corner, and 1⁵/₈″ hourglass design in the center; spine: blindstamped bands and goldstamped 'REPRESENTATIVE | MEN | [rule] | EMERSON | BOSTON.'. Flyleaves. Pale yellow endpapers. All edges trimmed.

Publication: Emerson wrote John Chapman on 10 October 1849 that "I shall not get any copy delivered to the printers before 1 November" (NN). On 8 December 1849, Phillips, Sampson wrote Emerson to acknowledge receiving proofs, and to state that the book would not be published before Christmas (MH). Advertised as "In Press" and "in the course of speedy preparation, and will be published in a few days," in *Literary World*, 5 (10 November 1849), 413; as "just ready," in *Literary World*, 5 (17 November 1849), 427. Announced as ready "about the first of January" in a Boston newsletter dated 20 December 1849, reprinted in *Literary World*, 5 (29 December 1849), 566. Deposited for copyright: title, 28 December 1849; book, unknown. Emerson sent Henry Wadsworth Longfellow a copy on 30 December 1849, and his brother William one on 31 December 1849 (MH; see *L*, IV, 174). Advertised as "received and for sale," in *Boston Daily Advertiser*, 1 January 1850, p. 3. Emerson "paid for the printing, & owned the stereotype plates," and was paid "in advance . . . 20 percent on the retail price" of each printing (25 February 1867, *L*, V, 507). Inscribed copies: NN (from Emerson, 30

December 1849), DLC (from Emerson, December 1849), InU (from Emerson, December 1849), MH (from Emerson, December 1849), NN (two copies from Emerson, December 1849). Price, $1.00. Royalty, 20¢.

Locations: BE, CtY, DLC, InU, JM, MB, MH, MHi, MWA, MWiW-C, NN, NNC, NcD, NjP, TxU, VtMiM.

A 22.1.b
First edition, second printing (1850)

Boston: Phillips, Sampson, and Company, 1850.

Pagination is the same as the first printing, except: the last page of gathering 24 is p. [288].

[1]^6 2–8^6 [19]^6 20–24^6

Contents: The same as the first printing, except: p. 286: blank; pp. 287–288: publisher's advertisements.

Typography and paper: The same as the first printing, except: sheets bulk $^7/_8''$.

Binding: Three styles have been noted, priority undertermined:

Binding A: Black or medium brown T cloth (rib). Front and back covers: blindstamped frame of parallel double-rules with floret in each boxed corner; spine: blindstamped boxes with florets in the center and goldstamped 'REPRESENTATIVE | MEN | [rule] | EMERSON | BOSTON.'. Flyleaves. Yellow or ornate white with blueprinted publisher's advertisements endpapers. All edges trimmed.

Binding B: The same as Binding A, except: front and back covers have blindstamped 1$^5/_8''$ hourglass design in the center.

Binding C: Black or dark brown T cloth (rib). Front and back covers: blindstamped frame of fluted columns with ornamental corners with 1$^5/_8''$ hourglass design in the center; spine: blindstamped rules with the same goldstamping as Binding A. Flyleaves. Yellow endpapers. All edges trimmed.

Publication: Apparently published soon after the first printing.

Locations: Binding A: CtY, JM, MB, MH, NNC; Binding B: DLC, MWA; Binding C: MCo, MH.

Note one: Publisher's records indicate copies were bound in half and full calf; no copies have been located.

Note two: Approximately 3,100 copies of *Representative Men* were sold by January 1851 (Emerson's manuscript memorandum [MH]).

LATER PRINTINGS WITHIN THE FIRST AMERICAN EDITION

A 22.1.c
Boston: Phillips, Sampson, 1852.

500 copies printed 11 September 1852 (see *JMN,* XIII, 479). Price, $1.00. Royalty, 20¢.
Location: JM.

A 22.1.d
Boston: Phillips, Sampson; New York: James C. Derby, [1854].

500 copies printed May 1854 (Account Books [MH]). Price, $1.00. Royalty, 20¢. *Location:* JM.

A 22.1.e
Boston: Phillips, Sampson, 1856.

500 copies printed December 1855 (*JMN,* XIV, 452). Price, $1.00. Royalty, 20¢. *Not seen.*

A 22.1.f
Boston: Phillips, Sampson, 1857.

500 copies and 250 copies on "fine paper" printed December 1856 (*JMN,* XIV, 452; Account Books [MH]). Price, $1.00. Royalty, 20¢. *Location:* JM.

A 22.1.g
Boston: Phillips, Sampson, 1858.

500 copies printed October 1858 (Account Books [MH]). Price, $1.00. Royalty, 20¢. *Location:* LNHT.

A 22.1.h
Boston: Phillips, Sampson, 1859.

500 copies printed August 1859 (Account Books [MH]). Price, $1.00. Royalty, 20¢. *Location:* MMeT.

Note: Phillips, Sampson failed on 19 September 1859.

A 22.1.i
Boston: Ticknor and Fields, M DCCC LX.

Price, $1.00. Royalty, 20¢. *Location:* JM.

Note: Some copies of Phillips, Sampson sheets have been located in Ticknor and Fields bindings, with a cancel title leaf; these are from the 500 copies printed by Phillips, Sampson in August 1859 (see A 22.1.h).

A 22.1.j
Boston: Ticknor and Fields, M DCCC LXI.

500 copies printed 24 December 1860. Price, $1.00. Royalty, 20¢. *Location:* JM.

A 22.1.k
Boston: Ticknor and Fields, M DCCC LXIII.

280 copies printed April 1863 (Account Books [MH]). Price, $1.25. Royalty, 25¢. *Location:* JM.

A 22.1.l
Boston: Ticknor and Fields, M DCCC LXIV.

280 copies printed April 1864 (Account Books [MH]). Price, $1.25. Royalty, 25¢. *Location:* JM.

A 22.1.m
Boston: Ticknor and Fields, M DCCC LXV.

280 copies printed March–May 1865. Price, $1.50. Royalty, 30¢. *Location:* NSchU.

Note: The copyright on *Representative Men* was renewed 13 May 1865.

A 22.1.n
Boston: Ticknor and Fields, M DCCC LXVI.

280 copies printed July–August 1866. Price, $1.50. Royalty, 30¢. *Location:* JM.

A 22.1.o
Boston: Ticknor and Fields, M DCCC LXVIII.

280 copies printed December 1867–March 1868. Price, $2.00. Royalty, 20¢. *Location:* CaNbU.

Note one: By a contract of 4 March 1868, Emerson's royalty was changed from 20% to 20¢ per volume.

Note two: Ticknor and Fields was succeeded by Fields, Osgood in October 1868.

A 22.1.p
Boston: Fields, Osgood, 1868.

280 copies printed March–May 1868. Price, $2.00. Royalty, 20¢. *Not seen.*

A 22.1.q
Boston: Fields, Osgood, 1869.

280 copies printed February 1869 (Account Books [MH]). Price, $2.00. Royalty, 20¢. *Location:* JM.

Note: Fields, Osgood was succeeded by James R. Osgood & Company in January 1871.

A 22.1.r
Boston: James R. Osgood, 1871.

280 copies printed 18 March 1871. Price, $2.00. Royalty, 30¢. *Location:* Nv.

Note: In a "Supplementary article of agreement" to the 4 March 1868 contract, dated 19 February 1870, Emerson's royalty was raised to 30¢ per copy when the price was $2.00 or above.

A 22.1.s
Boston: James R. Osgood, 1873.

140 copies printed 1 June 1873. Price, $2.00. Royalty, 30¢. *Location:* LNHT.

A 22.1.t
Boston: James R. Osgood, 1874.

150 copies printed 30 April 1874. Price, $2.00. Royalty, 30¢. *Not seen.*

A 22.1.u
Boston: James R. Osgood, 1875.

150 copies printed 30 January 1875. Price, $2.00. Royalty, 30¢. *Location:* JM.

A 22.1.v
Boston: James R. Osgood, 1876.

150 copies printed 26 November 1875. Price, $2.00. *Not seen.*

Note: Emerson's 1 January 1876 contract with Osgood called for him to receive a flat annual fee of $1,500 for all his books, rather than a per copy royalty.

A 22.1.w
Boston: James R. Osgood, 1877.

150 copies printed 26 January 1877. Price, $1.50. *Location:* ICarbS.

Note: James R. Osgood was succeeded by Houghton, Osgood in February 1878.

A 22.1.x
Boston: Houghton, Osgood, 1879.

180 copies printed 18 December 1878. Price, $1.50. *Location:* NIC.

Note: Houghton, Osgood was succeeded by Houghton, Mifflin in May 1880.

A 22.1.y
Boston: Houghton, Mifflin, 1881.

150 copies printed 8 December 1880. Price, $1.50. *Location:* MH.

A 22.1.z
Boston: Houghton, Mifflin, 1882.

150 copies printed 13 May 1882 and 20 November 1882. Price, $1.50. *Location:* JM.

Note: As of 15 January 1884, 10 copies of *Representative Men* were still in stock.

A 22.2.a
First English edition, first printing (1850)

REPRESENTATIVE MEN.

SEVEN LECTURES.

BY

R. W. EMERSON.

LONDON:

JOHN CHAPMAN, 142, STRAND.

MDCCCL.

A 22.2.a: 7^{11}/$_{16}$″ × 4^3/$_4$″

[i–iv] [1] 2–26 [27] 28–65 [66–67] 68–108 [109] 110–138 [139] 140–163 [164–165] 166–192 [193] 194–215 [216]

[A]² B–I¹² K¹²

Contents: p. i: title page; p. ii: printer's imprint; p. iii: contents; p. iv: blank; pp. 1–26: "Uses of Great Men."; pp. 27–65: "Plato; or, the Philosopher."; p. 66: blank; pp. 67–108: "Swedenborg; or, the Mystic."; pp. 109–138: "Montaigne; or, the Skeptic."; pp. 139–163: "Shakspeare; or, the Poet."; p. 164: blank; pp. 165–192: "Napoleon; or, the Man of the World."; pp. 193–215: "Goethe; or, the Writer."; p. 216: 'PRINTED BY RICHARD KINDER, | GREEN ARBOUR COURT, OLD BAILEY.'.

Typography and paper: 5¹¹/₁₆″ (5⁷/₁₆″) × 3³/₁₆″; wove paper; 32 lines per page. Running heads: rectos: pp. 3–25, 29–65, 69–107, 111–137, 141–163, 167–191, 195–215: titles of essays; versos: pp. 2–64, 68–162, 166–214: 'REPRESENTATIVE MEN.'.

Binding: Three styles have been noted, priority undetermined:

Binding A: Black, dark brown, or dark green T cloth (rib). Front and back covers: blindstamped leaf-and-vine ornamental frame with 2⁵/₁₆″ circular Catholic Series logo in center; spine: blindstamped rules with goldstamped 'REPRESENTATIVE | MEN | BY | R. W. EMERSON | [script] *J. Chapman* | LONDON.'. Pale yellow or yellow coated endpapers. All edges trimmed.

Binding B: The same as Binding A, except: goldstamped 'LONDON.' is not present at the bottom of the spine.

Binding C: "Ornamental" paper wrappers (information from contemporary advertisements); no copies have been located.

Publication: Advertised as "*Lectures on Representative Men*" for 1 January 1850, in *Athenæum,* no. 1154 (8 December 1849), 1254. Advertised as *Representative Men* and "Will be published in early January," in *Athenæum,* no. 1156 (22 December 1849), 1316; for 1 January in *Athenæum,* no. 1157 (29 December 1849), 1324; as "Just published," in *Athenæum,* no. 1158 (5 January 1850), 5. Listed in *Athenæum,* no. 1158 (5 January 1850), 18; *Literary Gazette,* no. 1720 (5 January 1850), p. 22; and as published between 29 December and 14 January, in *Publishers' Circular and Booksellers' Record,* 13 (15 January 1850), 19. *The Catholic Series.* Advertised in contemporary John Chapman publications in cloth in "The Catholic Series" and in paper as no. 3 in "Chapman's Library for the People." Price, cloth 5s; paper 6d.

Printing: "LONDON | PRINTED BY RICHARD KINDER, | GREEN ARBOUR COURT, OLD BAILEY" (p. [ii]).

Locations: Binding A: BC, BE, CU, CtY, InU, JM, MB, MCo, MH, MWA, NNC, VtMiM; Binding B: DLC.

Note one: Advertised by Chapman in the *Athenæum* as follows: "This edition will be printed from an original MS. revised and forwarded to England for the purpose; and alone possesses the sanction of the Author" (no. 1154 [8 December 1849], 1254). This statement is repeated in advertisements for Chapman's books inserted in some copies of *Representative Men.*

Note two: All copies have an additional leaf describing the *Catholic Series* inserted at the front: p. i: '[gothic] The Catholic Series' half title and a three-line reference to the series advertisements in the back of the book; p. ii: blank.

Note three: Copies have been noted with a 24-page catalogue of Chapman's publications, dated September 1849, inserted: at the front: CtY; at the back: DLC.

Note four: Copies have been noted with a 24-page catalogue of Chapman's publications, dated 1 January 1850, inserted at the back: BC, BE, CU, InU, JM, MB, MCo, MH, MWA, NNC, VtMiM.

LATER PRINTING WITHIN THE FIRST ENGLISH EDITION

A 22.2.b
First English edition, second printing (1851)

London: John Chapman, M.DCCC.LI.

Chapman's Library for the People, no. 3. Advertised for "immediate publication," in *Literary Gazette,* no. 1816 (8 November 1851), 754. Listed as published between 29 November and 13 December, in *Publishers' Circular and Booksellers' Record,* 14 (15 December 1851), 434. Listed in *Athenæum,* no. 1258 (6 December 1851), 1280; *Literary Gazette,* no. 1820 (6 December 1851), 845; *Publishers' Circular and Booksellers' Record,* 14 (15 December 1851), 434. Price, 1s. 6d. *Location:* BL (20 December 1851).

A 22.3.a
Second English edition, first printing (1850)

REPRESENTATIVE MEN.

Seben Lectures.

BY

R. W. EMERSON.

LONDON:
GEORGE ROUTLEDGE & CO., SOHO SQUARE.
1850.

A 22.3.a: 6⁵⁄₈″ × 4¹⁄₈″

[i–iv] [1] 2–21 [22] 23–53 [54] 55–88 [89] 90–114 [115] 116–136 [137] 138–161 [162] 163–182 [183–188]

[A]² B–I⁸ K–M⁸ N⁶

Contents: p. i: title page; p. ii: blank; p. iii: contents; p. iv: blank; pp. 1–182: the same chapters as the first American edition; pp. 183–188: publisher's advertisements.

Typography and paper: 5³/₁₆″ (4¹⁵/₁₆″) × 2¹³/₁₆″; wove paper; 36 lines per page. Running heads: rectos: pp. 3–87, 91–113, 117–135, 139–181: titles of essays; versos: pp. 2–20, 24–52, 56–160, 164–182: 'REPRESENTATIVE MEN.'.

Binding: Glazed paper-covered boards with light blue printing. Front cover: '[single-rule frame surrounding ornate leaf-and-vine design background] [gothic] The | [ornate lettering] POPULAR LIBRARY | REPRESENTATIVE | MEN. | [wavy rule] | BY | R. W. EMER-SON | [wavy rule] | ONE SHILLING. | LONDON: | GEO. ROUTLEDGE & CO. | SOHO SQUARE.'; back cover: advertisements for the *Railway Library* series; spine: ornate rectangular frame with grolieresque designs at top and bottom with '[from bottom to top] REPRESENTATIVE MEN.' in center. Endpapers are imprinted on front and back pastedowns and front free recto and back free verso with publisher's advertisements. All edges trimmed.

Publication: Advertised as "just ready," in *Athenæum,* no. 1160 (19 January 1850), 85. Listed in *Athenæum,* no. 1161 (26 January 1850), 100; as published between 29 January and 14 February, in *Publishers' Circular and Booksellers' Record,* 13 (15 February 1850), 74. *The Popular Library,* no. 2. Price, 1s.

Location: DLC.

Note: Routledge may have done four printings by July 1851, when approximately 1,800 copies were still in stock.

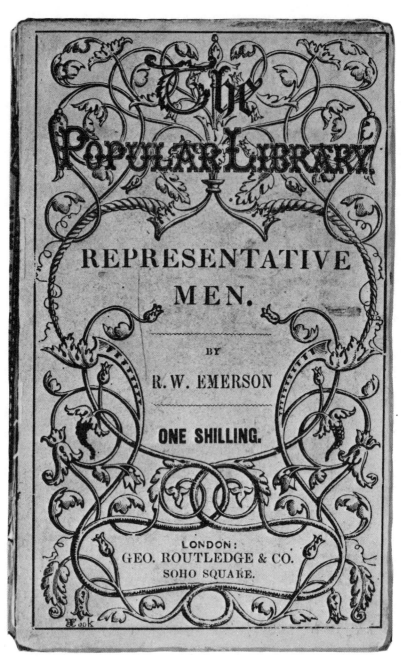

The Popular Library.

REPRESENTATIVE MEN.

BY

R. W. EMERSON

ONE SHILLING.

LONDON:
GEO. ROUTLEDGE & CO.
SOHO SQUARE.

LATER PRINTINGS WITHIN THE SECOND ENGLISH EDITION

A 22.3.b
Second English edition, second printing (1853)

London: George Routledge & Co., 1853.

2,000 copies printed August 1853. *Not seen.*

A 22.3.c
London: George Routledge & Co., 1855.

Advertised as included in "Routledge's Cheap Series," no. 35, in "Twelfth Thousand."
Not seen.

A 22.3.d
London and New York: George Routledge and Sons, 1882.

Listed as published between 16 and 31 May, in *Publishers' Circular and Booksellers'
Record,* 45 (1 June 1882), 484. Price, 1s. *Location:* BL (8 June 1882).

A 22.4.a
Third English edition, first printing (1850)

REPRESENTATIVE MEN:

SEVEN LECTURES.

BY

RALPH WALDO EMERSON.

LONDON:

HENRY G. BOHN, YORK STREET, COVENT GARDEN.

1850.

A 22.4.a: $6^{15}/_{16}'' \times 4^3/_8''$

[i–v] vi [vii–viii] [1] 2–17 [18] 19–38 [39] 40–44 [45] 46–72 [73] 74–92 [93] 94–108 [109] 110–127 [128] 129–143 [144]

[A]⁴ [B]⁸ C–I⁸ K⁸

Contents: p. i: 'BOHN'S SERIES. | [rule] | EMERSON'S REPRESENTATIVE MEN.'; p. ii: blank; p. iii: title page; p. iv: printer's imprint; pp. v–vi: 'ADVERTISEMENT.'. signed 'HENRY G. BOHN. | *Feb.* 1, 1850.'; p. vii: contents; p. viii: blank; pp. 1–143: the same chapters as the first American edition; p. 144: printer's imprint, the same as on p. iv.

Typography and paper: 5¹/₂″ (5¹/₄″) × 3¹/₄″; wove paper; 41 lines per page. Running heads: rectos: pp. 3–37, 41–43, 47–71, 75–91, 95–107, 111–143: titles of essays; versos: p. vi: 'ADVERTISEMENT.'; pp. 2–16, 20–126, 130–142: 'REPRESENTATIVE MEN.'.

Binding: Two styles have been noted, priority undetermined:

> *Binding A:* Medium red AR cloth (coarse ribbed morocco). Front and back covers: blank; spine: goldstamped '[ornate leaf-and-vine design] | [rule] | [rule] | EMER-SON'S | REPRESENTATIVE | MEN | [rule] | [rule] | [ornate leaf-and-vine design]'. Yellow endpapers. All edges trimmed.

> *Binding B:* Light green glazed paper-covered boards. Front cover: green lettering over ornate blue background, all within ornate leaf-and-vine design frame: 'BOHN'S | SHILLING SERIES | [three lines on red background] EMERSON'S | REPRESENTA-TIVE | MEN. | COMPLETE | IN | ONE VOLUME | LONDON. | HENRY. [*sic*] G. BOHN, YORK STREET, | COVENT GARDEN | 1850'; back cover: ornate blue and red frame surrounding a field of diagonal designs with flowers on it; spine: missing in the only copy located. Endpapers imprinted in blue with publisher's advertisements.

Publication: Advertised for February, in *Athenæum,* no. 1163 (9 February 1850), 145; in *Publishers' Circular and Booksellers' Record,* 13 (1 March 1850), 96. Listed in *Athenæum,* no. 1163 (9 February 1850), 157; as published between 29 January and 14 February, in *Publishers' Circular and Booksellers' Record,* 13 (15 February 1850), 74. *Bohn's Shilling Series,* no. 1. Price, 1s.

Printing: "LONDON: | PRINTED BY HARRISON AND SON, | ST. MARTIN'S LANE" (p. [iv]).

Locations: Binding A: MCo; Binding B: NNC.

Note: The "Advertisement" states: "The revised [American] sheets reached me . . . but a few days before the whole came to hand, the work had already been published here . . . at five times the price of the present volume. . . . Besides this, other editions were forthwith announced as in preparation" (p. vi).

LATER PRINTINGS WITHIN THE THIRD ENGLISH EDITION

A 22.4.b
Third English edition, second printing (1870)

London: Bell and Daldy, 1870.

Advertised as included in "Bohn's Cheap Series." Listed as published between 16 and 31 January, in *Publishers' Circular and Bookseller's Record,* 34 (1 February 1871), 77. Price, 1s. 6d. *Not seen,*

A 22.4.c
London: George Bell and Sons, 1878.

Advertised as included in "Bohn's Cheap Series." Listed as published between 16 and 31 May, in *Publishers' Circular and Booksellers' Record*, 41 (1 June 1878), 383. Price, 1s. *Not seen.*

A 22.4.d
London and New York: George Bell & Sons, 1894.

Location: BRU.

OTHER EDITIONS

A 22.5
First German edition, only printing (1856)

REPRESENTATIVE MEN: | SEVEN LECTURES | BY | RALPH WALDO EMERSON. | [rule] | AUTHORIZED EDITION. | [rule] | LEIPZIG: ALPHONS DÜRR. | 1856. | ROME: SPITHÖVER. HAMBURGH: PERTHES-BESSER & MAUKE. VIENNA: | W. BRAUMÜLLER. AMSTER-DAM: J. MÜLLER. BRUSSELS: C. MUQUARDT. | BASLE: H. GEORG. PARIS: C. REINWALD. TUR-IN: CH. SCHIEPATTI.

214 pp. English text. *Dürr's Collection of Standard American Authors*, vol. 22. *Location:* JM.

A 22.6
Second German edition, only printing [ca. 1856]

[all gothic] Repräsentanten | des | Menschengeschlechts | von | Ralph Waldo Emerson. | [rule] | Aus dem Englischen übersetzt und mit | biographischer Einleitung versehen | von | Oskar Dähnert. | [rule] | Leipzig. | Druck und Verlag von Philipp Reclam jun.

225 pp. *Locations:* CU, WaU.

A 22.7
First Danish edition, only printing (1857)

Menneskehedens Repræsentanter. | Syv Forelæsninger | af | Ralph Waldo Emerson. | Paa Dansk udgivne | af | [gothic] F. M. Thorson. | Med Forfatterens Portræt. | [ornate rule] | Kjøbenhavn. | Forlagt af og trykt hos S. Trier. | 1857.

199 pp. *Locations:* MB, NNC.

A 22.8
First Swedish edition, only printing [1862]

REPRESENTANTER AF MENSKLIGHETEN. | (REPRESENTATIVE MEN). | Plato eller Filosofen, Svedenborg eller Mystikern, Montaigne | eller Skeptikern, Shakspeare eller Skalden, Napolean eller | Verldsmannen, Goethe eller Skriftställeren. | AF | RALPH WALDO EMERSON. | [rule] | Öfversättning från engelskan | af | VICTOR PFEIFF. | UPSALA | ESAIAS EDQUIST.

162 pp. Wrappers. *Location:* MH.

A 22.9
First French edition, only printing (1863)

Les Représentants de l'humanité.   Bruxelles: Lacroix, Verboeckhoven et Cie, 1863.

Translated by P. de Boulogne. *Not seen.*

A 22.10
Second Swedish edition, only printing [1875]

Title page is basically the same as in the first Swedish edition. Translated by Victor Pfeiff. Published by Esaias Edquist of Upsala.

175 pp. *Location:* NNC.

PRINTINGS FROM THE "LITTLE CLASSIC EDITION" PLATES

A 22.11.a

[all within a double-rule frame; outer frame is red with boxed corners] [red] REPRESEN-TATIVE MEN: | *Seven Lectures.* | BY | RALPH WALDO EMERSON. | NEW AND REVISED EDITION. | [ornate rule] | [red] BOSTON: | JAMES R. OSGOOD AND COMPANY, | Late Ticknor & Fields, and Fields, Osgood, & Co. | [red] 1876.

231 pp. Vol. [IV] of the "Little Classic Edition" (see B 3). Advertised in *Atlantic*, 38 (August 1876), wrappers. Listed in *Publishers' Weekly*, 10 (5 August 1876), 302. Copyright, 1 July 1876. Price, $1.50. Royalty: see Note to A 22.1.v. *Location:* DLC (2 August 1876), MH.

A 22.11.b
Boston: James R. Osgood, 1878.

280 copies printed 8 December 1877. Price, $1.50. *Location:* JM.

Note: James R. Osgood was succeeded by Houghton, Osgood in February 1878.

A 22.11.c
Boston: Houghton, Osgood, 1879.

520 copies printed 4 December 1878; 280 copies on 31 July 1879 and 12 August 1879. Price, $1.50. *Location:* JM.

A 22.11.d
Boston: Houghton, Osgood, 1879.

Combined with *Society and Solitude* in two-volumes-in-one format as vol. II of the "Fireside Edition" (see B 14). 500 copies printed 15 August 1879. *Location:* KU.

A 22.11.e
Boston: Houghton, Osgood, 1880.

Combined with *Society and Solitude* in two-volumes-in-one format as vol. II of the "Fireside Edition" (see B 4). 500 copies printed 6 February 1880. *Location:* JM.

Note: Houghton, Osgood was succeeded by Houghton, Mifflin in May 1880.

A 22.11.f
Boston: Houghton, Mifflin, 1880.

270 copies printed 1 October 1880. Price, $1.50. *Not seen.*

A 22.11.g
Boston: Houghton, Mifflin, 1881.

270 copies printed 25 February 1881 and 19 August 1881. Price, $1.50. *Location:* JM.

A 22.11.h

Boston: Houghton, Mifflin, 1881.

Combined with *Society and Solitude* in two-volumes-in-one format as vol. II of the "Fireside Edition" (see B 4). 500 copies printed 7 December 1880. *Not seen.*

A 22.11.i
Boston: Houghton, Mifflin, 1882.

Combined with *Society and Solitude* in two-volumes-in-one format as vol. II of the "Fireside Edition" (see B 4). 500 copies printed 17 October 1881 and 8 May 1882. *Location:* JM.

A 22.11.j
Boston: Houghton, Mifflin, 1882.

500 copies printed 22 February 1882, 13 June 1882, and 20 September 1882. Price, $1.50. *Location:* ViU.

A 22.11.k
Boston: Houghton, Mifflin, 1883.

Combined with *Society and Solitude* in two-volumes-in-one format as vol. II of the "Fireside Edition" (see B 4). 270 copies printed 9 January 1883. *Not seen.*

A 22.11.l
Boston: Houghton, Mifflin, 1883.

270 copies printed 20 February 1883; 500 copies on 24 July 1883. *Location:* MH.

A 22.11.m
Boston and New York: Houghton, Mifflin, 1884.

270 copies printed 22 January 1884; 500 copies on 22 August 1884. *Location:* JM.

A 22.11.n
Boston and New York: Houghton, Mifflin, 1886.

270 copies printed 2 October 1886. Presumably bound in medium blue V cloth (smooth), rather than "Little Classic Edition" binding, as are subsequent reprintings (see illustration at B 3). *Not seen.*

A 22.11.o
Boston and New York: Houghton, Mifflin, 1887.

270 copies printed 23 September 1887. *Location:* JM.

A 22.11.p
Boston and New York: Houghton, Mifflin, 1888.

270 copies printed 4 February 1888 and 14 August 1888. *Location:* NmU.

A 22.11.q
Boston and New York: Houghton, Mifflin, 1889.

270 copies printed 2 October 1888; 500 copies on 29 July 1889. *Location:* JM.

A 22.11.r
Boston and New York: Houghton, Mifflin, 1890.

500 copies printed ca. March 1890. *Not seen.*

A 22.11.s
Boston and New York: Houghton, Mifflin, 1891.

500 copies printed January–March 1891. *Location:* JM.

A 22.11.t
Boston and New York: Houghton, Mifflin, 1892.

500 copies printed 23 December 1891. *Location:* MHi.

A 22.11.u
Boston and New York: Houghton, Mifflin, 1893.

500 copies printed 14 November 1892. *Not seen.*

A 22.11.v
Boston and New York: Houghton, Mifflin, 1894.

500 copies printed 30 October 1893. *Not seen.*

A 22.11.w
Boston and New York: Houghton, Mifflin, 1895.

500 copies printed 22 July 1895. *Location:* OCIWHi.

A 22.11.x
Boston and New York: Houghton, Mifflin, 1897.

270 copies printed 30 July 1897. *Not seen.*

A 22.11.y
Boston and New York: Houghton, Mifflin, 1898.

270 copies printed 31 August 1898. *Location:* JM.

A 22.11.z
Boston and New York: Houghton, Mifflin, 1900.

270 copies printed 27 October 1899. *Not seen.*

A 22.11.aa
Boston and New York: Houghton, Mifflin, [n.d.].

Approximately 1,500 copies sold between 1900 and 1923. *Location:* MiYEM.

Note: Approximately 10,500 copies of *Representative Men* printed from the "Little Classic Edition" plates were sold between 1876 and 1923, when the title was apparently allowed to go out of print in this format.

LATER EDITION

A 22.12.a–h
English Traits and Representative Men. London: Macmillan, 1883.

476 pp. Vol. IV of the *Works* (see B 6). Listed in *Athenæum,* no. 2899 (19 May 1883), 635. Listed as published between 16 and 31 May, in *Publishers' Circular and Booksellers' Record,* 46 (1 June 1883), 485. Price, 5s. Reprinted (usually with dual New York imprint) 1884, 1888, 1893, 1899, 1902, 1906, 1911. *Locations:* BL (26 June 1883), JM.

PRINTINGS FROM THE RIVERSIDE EDITION PLATES

A 22.13.a
Riverside Edition (trade), first printing (1883)

REPRESENTATIVE MEN | SEVEN LECTURES | BY | RALPH WALDO EMERSON | [gothic] New and Revised Edition | [publisher's logo] | BOSTON | HOUGHTON, MIFFLIN AND COMPANY | New York: 11 East Seventeenth Street | [gothic] The Riverside Press, Cambridge | 1883

276 pp. Vol. IV of the *Riverside Edition,* trade printing (see B 7). 1,000 copies printed 25 August 1883. Advertised as "now ready," in *Atlantic,* 52 (October 1883), wrappers. Listed in *Publishers' Weekly,* 24 (6 October 1883), 485. According to the publisher's records, published 22 September 1883. Copyright, 25 August 1883. Price, $1.75. *Locations:* DLC (26 September 1883), JM.

Note: Copies have been noted with a pine branch on the title page instead of the publisher's logo.

A 22.13.b
Riverside Edition (Copyright), second (English) printing (1883)

REPRESENTATIVE MEN | SEVEN LECTURES | BY | RALPH WALDO EMERSON | [gothic] The Riverside Edition | (COPYRIGHT) | LONDON | GEORGE ROUTLEDGE AND SONS | BROADWAY, LUDGATE HILL | NEW YORK: 9, LAFAYETTE PLACE | 1883

Vol. IV of the *Riverside Edition (Copyright),* English trade printing (see B 10). 1,000 copies printed 1 September 1883. Listed as published between 17 and 29 September, in *Publishers' Circular and Booksellers' Record,* 46 (1 October 1883), 893. Price, 3s. 6d. *Locations:* BC (12 October 1883), BO (18 October 1883), BL (8 December 1883), CaQMM.

A 22.13.c$_1$
Riverside Edition (large paper), third printing, American issue (1883)

[red] REPRESENTATIVE MEN | SEVEN LECTURES | BY | RALPH WALDO EMERSON | [gothic] New and Revised Edition | [pine branch] | [red] CAMBRIDGE | [gothic] Printed at the Riverside Press | 1883

Vol. IV of the *Riverside Edition,* large paper printing (see B 8). 500 copies printed 21 September 1883. Limited to 500 numbered copies. Price, $4.00. Sold out within a year. *Locations:* JM, TxU.

A 22.13.c$_2$
Riverside Edition (large paper), third printing, English issue (1883)

Title page is the same as in the American issue, except for publisher's imprint: 'LONDON | KEGAN PAUL, TRENCH, & CO., I, PATERNOSTER SQUARE | MDCCCLXXXIII'.

Vol. IV of the *Riverside Edition,* large paper printing for English subscribers (see B 9). 25 title leaves printed 21 September 1883. Title leaf is a cancel. Limited to 25 signed and numbered copies. *Location:* JM.

A 22.13.d
Boston and New York: Houghton, Mifflin, 1884.

500 copies printed 22 October 1883, 19 December 1883, 9 February 1884, and 19 May 1884. *Location:* JM.

A 22.13.e
Boston and New York: Houghton, Mifflin, 1885.

500 copies printed 13 October 1884, 3 April 1885, and 15 September 1885. *Location:* JM.

A 22.13.f
Boston and New York: Houghton, Mifflin, 1886.

500 copies printed 6 March 1886 and 9 April 1886. *Location:* JM.

A 22.13.g
London, Glasgow, New York: George Routledge and Sons, 1887.

500 copies printed 16 December 1886. *Location:* JM.

A 22.13.h
Boston and New York: Houghton, Mifflin, 1887.

500 copies printed 12 January 1887 and 3 August 1887. *Location:* MH.

A 22.13.i
Boston and New York: Houghton, Mifflin, 1888.

500 copies printed 16 December 1887 and 19 April 1888. *Location:* JM.

A 22.13.j
Boston and New York: Houghton, Mifflin, 1889.

500 copies printed 10 October 1888 and 27 April 1889. *Not seen.*

A 22.13.k
Boston and New York: Houghton, Mifflin, 1890.

500 copies printed 7 November 1889 and ca. June 1890. *Location:* JM.

A 22.13.l
Representative Men   Nature, Addresses, and Lectures. Boston and New York: Houghton, Mifflin, 1890.

Combined in two-volumes-in-one format; see A 21.3.l.

A 22.13.m
Boston and New York: Houghton, Mifflin, 1891.

500 copies printed ca. March 1891 and 31 July 1891. *Location:* NbOM.

A 22.13.n
Boston and New York: Houghton, Mifflin, 1892.

500 copies printed 9 May 1892 and 9 August 1892. *Location:* JM.

A 22.13.o
Boston and New York: Houghton, Mifflin, 1893.

500 copies printed 14 March 1893. *Location:* JM.

A 22.13.p
Boston and New York: Houghton, Mifflin, 1894.

500 copies printed 11 June 1894. *Location:* NBu.

A 22.13.q
Standard Library Edition printing [1894]

REPRESENTATIVE MEN | SEVEN LECTURES | BY | RALPH WALDO EMERSON | [pine branch] | BOSTON AND NEW YORK | HOUGHTON, MIFFLIN AND COMPANY | [gothic] The Riverside Press, Cambridge

Vol. IV of the *Standard Library Edition* (see B 11). 1,000 copies printed 31 October 1894, 30 April 1895, 29 May 1896; 500 copies on 31 January 1898. *Location:* JM.

A 22.13.r
Boston and New York: Houghton, Mifflin, 1895.

500 copies printed 22 August 1895. *Location:* LNHT.

A 22.13.s
Boston and New York: Houghton, Mifflin, 1896.

500 copies printed 22 July 1896. *Location:* JM.

A 22.13.t
Boston and New York: Houghton, Mifflin, 1897.

500 copies printed 13 September 1897. *Location:* MH.

A 22.13.u
Representative Men   Nature, Addresses, and Lectures. Boston and New York: Houghton, Mifflin, 1898.

Combined in two-volumes-in-one format; see A 21.3.v.

A 22.13.v
Boston and New York: Houghton, Mifflin, 1899.

270 copies printed 24 February 1899; 250 copies on 21 October 1899. *Location:* NcD.

A 22.13.w
London: George Routledge and Sons, 1902.

Location: JM.

A 22.13.x
London: George Routledge & Sons, 1903.

Combined with *English Traits* and *The Conduct of Life* in three-volumes-in-one format as vol. II of the "Sovereign Edition" (see B 12). 1,000 copies printed 16 September 1903. *Location:* InU.

A 22.13.y
Fireside Edition printing (1909)

[all within red double-rule frame with red floral ornaments in each corner] THE WORKS OF | [red gothic] Ralph Waldo Emerson | REPRESENTATIVE MEN | [engraving of man reading book in chair before fireplace] | [gothic] Fireside Edition | BOSTON AND NEW YORK | MDCCCCIX

Vol. IV of the *Fireside Edition* (see B 13). 500 copies printed 30 September 1909 and 15 February 1910. *Location:* JM.

A 22.13.z
Boston and New York: Jefferson Press, [ca. 1912].

Combined with *Nature; Addresses, and Lectures* in two-volumes-in-one format as vol. [I] of the "Jefferson Press Edition"; see A 21.3.aa.

A 22.13.aa
New York: Sully and Kleinteich, [ca. 1912].

Vol. IV of the *University Edition* (see B 15). *Location:* JM.

A 22.13.bb
Boston and New York: Houghton, Mifflin, [n.d.].

Approximately 2,300 copies sold between 1900 and 1913. *Location:* JM.

Note: Approximately 16,500 copies of *Representative Men* in the *Riverside Edition* were sold between 1883 and 1913, when the title was apparently allowed to go out of print in this format.

A 22.13.cc
London: Waverley Book Company, [n.d.].

Vol. IV of the "Waverley" *Riverside Edition* (see B 16). *Location:* JM.

LATER EDITIONS

A 22.14
Representative Men and English Traits. London and New York: Ward, Lock, [1886].

128 pp., double columns. Cloth or wrappers. Introduction by G. T. Bettany. *Popular Library of Literary Treasures*, no. 1. Listed as published between 16 and 31 May 1886, in *Publishers' Circular and Booksellers' Record*, 49 (1 April 1886), 334. Prices: cloth, 6d; wrappers: 3d. *Locations:* BL (13 April 1886), N.

A 22.15.a
New York: John B. Alden, 1892.

211 pp. *Location:* CtY.

A 22.15.b–c
New York: Hurst, [n.d.].

Also in *Cosmos Series*. Also undated reprint as *Representative of Man* [sic] in *The Companion Books*. *Locations:* JM (all).

A 22.15.d
Chicago: Thompson & Thomas, [n.d.].

Location: MH.

A 22.16.a–e
Philadelphia: Henry Altemus, 1892.

294 pp. Advertised as included in "Altemus Library," No. 18, "Illustrated Vademecum Series," no. 173, and "New Vademecum Series." Reprinted 1894, 1895, 1902, [n.d.]. *Locations:* JM (1892, 1894, n.d.). NcD (1895).

A 22.16.f
Boston: E. P. Harlow, [n.d.].

Location: JM.

A 22.17.a–d
Philadelphia: David McKay, 1892.

296 pp. *American Classic Series.* Also combined with *Nature; Addresses, and Lectures* in two-volumes-in-one format. Also advertised in boxed set with *Nature; Addresses, and Lectures.* Reprinted 1893, 1894, [n.d.]. *Locations:* JM, (1892, 1893, 1894), FTaSu (n.d.), IdU (combined).

A 22.17.e
Chicago: Hooper, Clarke, [n.d.].

Combined with *Nature; Addresses, and Lectures;* see A 21.5.e.

A 22.18
New York: Merrill and Baker, 1896.

Advertised as included in "Coates Classics." Price, 75¢. *Not seen.*

A 22.19.a
Chicago: W. B. Conkey, [1900].

251 pp. Advertised in various bindings at various prices. *Location:* DLC (13 August 1900).

A 22.19.b
Chicago and New York: Henneberry, [n.d.].

Location: JM.

A 22.19.c
Chicago: Homewood, [n.d.].

Also advertised as included in "Abbey Series," no. 305. Price, 18¢. *Location:* JM.

A 22.20.a–b
London: J. M. Dent, MDCCCCI.

224 pp. Cloth or flexible leather. Edited by Walter Jerrold. *The Temple Classics.* Published February 1901. Prices: cloth, 1s. 6d; leather, 2s. Reprinted November 1904. *Locations:* BL (13 May 1901), CU-I, JM (1904).

Note: Advertised as included in "The Temple Classics" in cloth and leather by Macmíl-lan of New York in *Publishers' Weekly,* 59 (8 June 1901), 1366. Probably an importation or, possibly, an American issue of the English sheets with a cancel title leaf. *Not seen.*

A 22.21.a
[New York]: A. L. Burt, [1902].

267 pp. Cloth or flexible leather. Also noted with New York: A. L. Burt imprint. Also *Cornell Series; The Home Library.* Listed in *Publishers' Weekly,* 61 (17 May 1902), 1124. Published 17 May 1902. Price, \$1.00. Also advertised combined with *Nature; Addresses, and Lectures* in two-volumes-in-one format as included in "Home Library." *Locations:* JM (all).

A 22.21.b
Representative Men   Poems. New York: P. F. Collier & Son, MCMIII.

Combined in two-volumes-in-one format; see A 18.13.b.

A 22.21.c
Philadelphia: John D. Morris, [1906].

Vol. I of the "John D. Morris Edition" (see B 29). Contains Richard Garnett's *Life. Location:* JM.

A 22.21.d
Boston and New York: C. T. Brainard, [n.d.].

Vol. IV of the *Works* (see B 30). Contains Garnett's *Life. Location:* JM.

A 22.21.e
New York and Boston: H. M. Caldwell, [n.d.].

Advertised in various bindings at various prices. Also noted with New York imprint only. *Locations:* NNF, JM (N.Y.).

A 22.21.f
New York: Caxton Society, [n.d.].

Vol. IV of the *Works* (see B 31). Contains Garnett's *Life. Location:* NjR.

A 22.21.g
Chicago: M. A. Donohue, [n.d.].

Advertised in various bindings at various prices. *Location:* JM.

A 22.21.h
Chicago: Donohue, Henneberry, [n.d.].

Location: JM.

A 22.21.i
Chicago: Geo. M. Hill, [n.d.].

Location: JM.

A 22.21.j
New York: Home Book Company, [n.d.].

Location: LNHT.

A 22.21.k
Rahway, N.J., and New York: Mershon, [n.d.].

Advertised in various bindings at various prices. Also advertised as included in the "Standard Series." Price, 15¢. *Location:* JM.

A 22.21.l
New York: National Library Co., [n.d.].

Vol. IV of the *Works* (see B 32). Contains Garnett's *Life. Location:* CaOHM.

A 22.21.m
Philadelphia, New York, Chicago: Nottingham Society, [n.d.].

Vol. IV of the *Works* (see B 33). Contains Garnett's *Life. Location:* JM.

A 22.21.n
New York: George Routledge & Sons, [n.d.].

Location: JM.

A 22.21.o
New York and Chicago: Siegel, Cooper, [n.d.].

Location: CaOPAL.

A 22.22.a
English Traits and Representative Men. London: Grant Richards, 1903.

349 pp. Cloth (with dust jacket) or leather. *The World's Classics,* no. 30 (also identified as vol. II of *Works*). Published March 1903. *Locations:* BE (10 June 1903), BC (13 June 1903), BO (13 June 1903), MH.

A 22.22.b
London [&c.]: Henry Frowde, [1903].

The World's Classics, no. 30. *Location:* JM.

A 22.22.c–d
London [&c.]: Henry Frowde, Oxford University Press, [1905].

The World's Classics, no. 30. Reprinted 1911. *Location:* CaOOCC (1911).

A 22.22.e–f
London [&c.]: Humphrey Milford, Oxford University Press, [1923].

The World's Classics, no. 30. Reprinted 1934. *Locations:* CaMWU, TxU (1934).

Note: Advertised as included in "The World's Classics," no. 30, in cloth and leather by Turner for 26 March 1904 in the *American Catalog.* Probably an importation. *Not seen.*

PRINTINGS FROM THE CENTENARY EDITION PLATES

A 22.23.a$_1$
Centenary Edition (trade), first printing, American issue (1903)

REPRESENTATIVE MEN | SEVEN LECTURES | BY | RALPH WALDO EMERSON | [pine tree] | BOSTON AND NEW YORK | HOUGHTON, MIFFLIN AND COMPANY | [gothic] The Riverside Press. Cambridge | 1903

378 pp. Dust jacket. Vol. IV of the *Centenary Edition*, trade printing (see B 18). 1,000 copies printed 30 September 1903. Listed in *Publishers' Weekly*, 64 (7 August 1903), 1001. According to the publisher's records, published 28 October 1903. Price, $1.75. *Location:* JM.

Note: Numerous reprintings with undated title pages. 3,000 copies printed between 1 July 1904 and 1 October 1910. Approximately 5,200 copies sold through 1923.

A 22.23.a$_2$
English issue

London: A. P. Watt & Son, [1903].

Vol. IV of the English *Centenary Edition* (see B 21). American sheets with Watt's label pasted on the title page. Price, 6s. *Locations:* BL (28 October 1903), BE (11 November 1903), BC (13 November 1903).

A 22.23.b
Concord Edition, second printing (1903)

Boston and New York: Houghton, Mifflin, 1903.

Vol. IV of the *Concord Edition* (see B 20). 1,000 copies printed 30 September 1903. *Location:* JM.

Note: Numerous reprintings with undated title pages. Approximately 3,000 copies sold by 31 December 1910.

A 22.23.c
Autograph Centenary Edition (large paper), third printing (1903)

RALPH WALDO EMERSON | [red] Representative Men | [red] Seven Lectures | [pine tree] | CAMBRIDGE | [red gothic] Printed at the Riverside Press | 1903

Vol. IV of the *Autograph Centenary Edition* (see B 19). Limited to 600 signed and numbered copies printed 15 October 1903. Price, $6.00. Sold out by 5 April 1906. *Locations:* DLC (20 October 1903), JM.

A 22.23.d
Boston and New York: Houghton Mifflin, [1914].

Vol. IV of the *Riverside Pocket Edition* (see B 22). Approximately 1,200 copies sold between 1914 and 1922. *Location:* JM.

A 22.23.e
Boston and New York: Houghton Mifflin, 1921.

290 pp. (text without the notes). Combined with *Miscellanies* in two-volume-in-one format as vol. III of *Emerson's Complete Works* (see B 23). *Location:* JM.

A 22.23.f
New York: Wm. H. Wise, 1923.

Combined with *Essays: Second Series* in two-volumes-in-one format as vol. II of the *Current Opinion Edition* (see B 24). *Location:* JM.

A 22.23.g
Boston and New York: Houghton Mifflin, 1929.

Combined (text without the notes) with *Miscellanies* in two-volumes-in-one format as vol. [III] of the *Harvard Edition* (see B 25). *Location:* JM.

A 22.23.h
New York: Wm. H. Wise, 1929.

Combined with *Essays: Second Series* in two-volumes-in-one format as vol. II of the *Medallion Edition* (see B 26). *Location:* OC.

A 22.23.i
Boston and New York: Houghton Mifflin, 1930.

The Riverside Library. Location: JM.

A 22.23.j–k
New York: AMS Press, [1968].

Vol. IV of the "AMS Press" *Centenary Edition* (see B 27). Reprinted 1979. *Locations:* TxU, DLC (9 November 1979).

LATER EDITIONS

A 22.24.a
London: George G. Harrap, MCMVI.

234 pp. *Location:* CaBViV.

A 22.24.b
New York: Thomas Y. Crowell, [n.d.].

Handy Volume Classics. Also noted with New York and Boston imprint. Also advertised in various bindings at various prices. *Locations:* JM (both).

A 22.25.a–c
New York: Macmillan Company; London: Macmillan & Co., 1906.

221 pp. Edited with introduction and notes by Philo Melvyn Buck, Jr. *Macmillan's Pocket American and English Classics.* Published September 1906. Copyright, 3 October 1906. Price, 25¢. Reprinted 1919, 1926. *Locations:* UU (1906), NbU (1919), CU-D (1926).

A 22.26
Leipzig: Bernhard Tauchnitz, 1907.

287 pp. Wrappers. *Authorized Edition. Collection of British Authors,* vol. 3962. *Location:* JM.

A 22.27
London: George G. Harrap, [1910].

223 pp. *The Harrap Library,* no. 7. Published November 1910. Price, 2s. 6d. *Locations:* BC (9 February 1911), BE (9 February 1911), JM.

A 22.28
New York: Dodge, [1911].

Advertised in various bindings at various prices. Advertised as included in "Dodge Library." *Not seen.*

A 22.29
Heidelberg: Carl Winter, 1912.

135 pp. English text. Edited by Otto Dost. *Location:* CtHT-W.

A 22.30
London, Glasgow, Bombay: Blackie and Son, 1923.

216 pp. Edited with introduction and notes by David Frew. *Standard English Classics.* Published November 1923. Price, 2s. *Location:* BL (11 December 1923).

A 22.31
[Malibu, Cal.]: Joseph Simon, [1980].

204 pp. Boxed. Introduction by Myron Simon. Advertised as included in "The Mind of Man Series." Price, $25.00. *Location:* JM.

UNDATED EDITION

A 22.32
Girard, Kansas: Haldeman-Julius, [n.d.].

Four parts of 61, 53, 58, and 55 pp. Wrappers. *Little Blue Book,* nos. 423–426. *Location:* JM.

SEPARATE PUBLICATIONS OF INDIVIDUAL ESSAYS

A 22.33
Napoleon or the Man of the World. New York: William Bradford, [1930].

63 pp. Wrappers. *The Big Type Library,* no. 43. Copyright, 26 May 1930. *Location:* CtY.

A 22.34.a
Napoleon or The Man of the World. Bloomington: Indiana University, [1947].

63 pp. Wrappers. Introduction and notes by Frank Davidson. *Indiana University Publications, Humanities Series,* no. 16. Price, $1.00. *Locations:* DLC (27 January 1948), JM.

A 22.34.b
New York: Kraus Reprint, 1969.

Wrappers. Price, $3.00. *Location:* JM.

A 22.35
Napoleon. Cincinnati: Jennings & Graham; New York: Eaton & Mains, [n.d.].

45 pp. *The Hero Series,* no. 7. Price, 25¢. *Location:* JM.

Note: Possibly reprinted in the "Hero Series" at 25¢ by the Methodist Book Company in 1912.

A 22.36
Shakespeare. New York: John B. Alden, [1899].

Wrappers. Advertised as included in "The Irving Library," vol. 6, no. 661, 4 March 1899. *Not seen.*

Note: Probably from the plates of *Representative Men* (A 22.15.a).

A 22.37
Emerson on Shakespeare from His Essays on Representative Men. London: De La More Press, 1904.

38 pp. Wrappers or leather. *The De La More Booklets*. In a three-volume boxed set with essays on Shakespeare by Carlyle and Goethe. Published November 1904. Prices: wrappers, 1s. 6d; leather, 2s. 6d. *Location:* BL (5 October 1904).

A 22.38
Swedenborg. Boston: B. A. Whittemore, [1927?].

55 pp. Wrappers. Abridged. *Location:* DLC (5 March 1927).

A 22.39
Some Thoughts of a Definitely Non-Swedenborgian   Ralph Waldo Emerson. New York: Charles E. Witzell, Jr., [n.d.].

26 leaves. Mimeographed. Selections from "Swedenborg." *Location:* NNUT.

A 22.40
Uses of Great Men. New York: John B. Alden, 1892.

[3]–15 pp. Wrappers. *The Elzevir Library*, vol. 11, no. 580, 6 August 1892. Price, 2¢. *Location:* IU.

Note: From the plates of *Representative Men* (A 22.15.a).

A 22.41
Uses of Great Men. New York: Little Leather Library, [n.d.].

149 pp. Limp leather. Also contains "Goethe," "Shakespeare," and "Napoleon." *Little Leather Library*, no. 47. *Location:* JM.

A 22.42
Über Goethe und Shakespeare. Hannover: Carl Rümpler, 1857.

116 pp. Wrappers. Translated by Herman Grimm. *Location:* MB.

A 22.43
Shakespeare and the Over-soul. Los Angeles: Thumb, [n.d.].

32 pp. *Not seen.*

A 23 [LETTER TO WHITMAN]

A 23
First edition, only printing [1855]

[Copy for the convenience of private, reading only.]

Concord. Mass'tts, 21 July, 1855.

DEAR SIR, I am not blind to the worth of the wonderful gift of "LEAVES OF GRASS." I find it the most extraordinary piece of wit and wisdom that America has yet contributed. I am very happy in reading it, as great power makes us happy. It meets the demand I am always making of what seemed the sterile and stingy nature, as if too much handiwork, or too much lymph in the temperament, were making our western wits fat and mean.

I give you joy of your free and brave thought. I have great joy in it. I find incomparable things said incomparably well, as they must be. I find the courage of treatment which so delights us, and which large perception only can inspire.

I greet you at the beginning of a great career, which yet must have had a long foreground somewhere, for such a start. I rubbed my eyes a little, to see if this sunbeam were no illusion; but the solid sense of the book is a sober certainty. It has the best merits, namely, of fortifying and encouraging.

I did not know until I last night saw the book advertised in a newspaper that I could trust the name as real and available for a post-office. I wish to see my benefactor, and have felt much like striking my tasks and visiting New-York to pay you my respects.

R. W. EMERSON..

WALT WHITMAN.

A 23: Broadside, $6^{1}/_{8}'' \times 4^{7}/_{8}''$

Broadside, printed on recto only.

Typography and paper: $5^1/_8'' \times 3^5/_8''$; wove paper; 32 lines. No running head.

Publication: Printed in Brooklyn, N.Y.

Locations: InU, MWA, NN, NjP, RPB, ViU.

A 24.1.a
First American edition, first printing (1856)

ENGLISH TRAITS.

BY

R. W. EMERSON.

BOSTON:
PHILLIPS, SAMPSON, AND COMPANY.
1856.

A 24.1.a: $7^1/_2''$ × $4^{13}/_{16}''$

1 [2–4] 5–7 [8] 9–312

[1]⁶ 2–26⁶

Contents: p. 1: 'ENGLISH TRAITS.'; p. 2: blank; p. 3: title page; p. 4: copyright page; pp. 5–7: contents; p. 8: blank; pp. 9–30: "Chapter I. First Visit to England."; pp. 31–39: "Chapter II. Voyage to England."; pp. 40–49: "Chapter III. Land."; pp. 50–78: "Chapter IV. Race."; pp. 79–105: "Chapter V. Ability."; pp. 106–118: "Chapter VI. Manners."; pp. 119–129: "Chapter VII. Truth."; pp. 130–145: "Chapter VIII. Character."; pp. 146–155: "Chapter IX. Cockayne."; pp. 156–173: "Chapter X. Wealth."; pp. 174–199: "Chapter XI. Aristocracy."; pp. 200–214: "Chapter XII. Universities."; pp. 215–231: "Chapter XIII. Religion."; pp. 232–259: "Chapter XIV. Literature."; pp. 260–271: "Chapter XV. The 'Times.'"; pp. 272–289: "Chapter XVI. Stonehenge."; pp. 290–297: "Chapter XVII. Personal."; pp. 298–306: "Chapter XVIII. Result."; pp. 307–312: "Chapter XIX. Speech at Manchester."

Typography and paper: $4^{15}/_{16}''$ ($4^{11}/_{16}''$) × 3″; wove paper; 27 lines per page. Running heads: rectos: p. 7: 'CONTENTS.'; pp. 11–29, 33–77, 81–97: chapter titles; pp. 99–101: 'FACTITIOUS.'; pp. 103–105: 'SOLIDARITY.'; pp. 107–117, 121–213, 217–305, 309–311: chapter titles; versos: p. 6: 'CONTENTS.'; pp. 10–38, 42–48, 52–104, 108–128, 132–144, 148–154, 158–172, 176–198, 202–230, 234–258, 262–270, 274–288, 292–296, 300–312: 'ENGLISH TRAITS.'.

Binding: Black, medium brown, or dark brown T cloth (rib). Front and back covers: blindstamped frame of parallel double-rules with floret in each boxed corner; spine: blindstamped rules and boxes with florets in boxes and goldstamped 'ENGLISH | TRAITS | [rule] | EMERSON | BOSTON'. Flyleaves. Yellow endpapers. All edges trimmed.

Publication: On 26 December 1855, Emerson wrote Thoreau that there was "one chapter ["Stonehenge"] yet to go to the printer; perhaps two, if I decide to send the second," and asked for his help in reading proofs for these chapters (*The Correspondence of Henry David Thoreau* [D 214], pp. 403–404). Although Emerson had sent the first chapter to the printer on 9 October 1855, he was not through reading proofs until mid-June 1856 (see *L*, IV, 533, V, 24). 3,000 copies printed and probably published on 6 August 1856 (see *JMN*, XIV, 31). Deposited for copyright: title, 8 July 1856; book: 12 August 1856. Advertised as "in Press," in *Knickerbocker*, 48 (July 1856), advertising section; as published on 6 August, in *Boston Daily Advertiser*, 5 August 1856, p. 2; as "in Press," in *Knickerbocker*, 48 (August 1856), advertising section; as "This day issued," in *Boston Daily Advertiser*, 6 August 1856, p. 2. Emerson "paid for the printing, & owned the stereotype plates," and was paid "in advance . . . 20 percent on the retail price" of each printing (25 February 1867, *L*, V, 507). S. J. May wrote Emerson on 13 August praising the book (MH). Inscribed copies: NNC (12 August 1856), MBAt (14 August 1856), CtY (15 August 1856), JM (Evert A. Duyckinck, 20 August 1856), VtMiM (August 1856). On 12 August 1856, Emerson reported to his brother William that 1,700 copies "had gone in four days," and on 2 September he wrote that the first printing had sold out (*L,* V, 30, 34). Price, $1.00. Royalty, 20¢.

Locations: BE, CSt, CtY, DLC, InU, JM, MB, MBAt, MCo, MH, MWA, NN, NNC, NcD, NjP, RPB, TxU, ViU, VtMiM.

Note one: A rebound copy has been noted with calendered wove paper measuring $7^7/_8'' \times 4^7/_8''$, top edges gilded (NNC). This may be one of the "fine paper" copies of the Phillips, Sampson printings that Emerson often mentions.

Note two: Publisher's records indicate that copies were bound in half and full calf; no copies have been located.

Note three: Listed as an importation at 6s., in *Publishers' Circular and Booksellers' Record,* 19 (15 October 1856), 414. The same importation listed as published between 30 October and 14 November by Sampson Low, in *Publishers' Circular and Book-sellers' Record,* 19 (15 November 1856), 459.

LATER PRINTINGS WITHIN THE FIRST EDITION

A 24.1.b
Boston: Phillips, Sampson, 1856.

'FIFTH THOUSAND'. 2,000 copies printed late October 1856 (see *L,* V, 34). Price, $1.00. Royalty, 20¢. *Location:* JM,

Note: The following textual changes are present:

4	[the stereotype information is present] [[the stereotype information is not present]
5–7	[the dots are closed up, the page numbers are in a small font, and the chapter titles are in large capitals] [[the dots are spaced out, the page numbers are in a large font, and the chapter titles are in large and small capitals]
82.14	temperature [temperament
90.21	dpended [depended
278.20	"London Library," [London Library.

A 24.1.c
Boston: Phillips, Sampson, 1857.

'SIXTH THOUSAND'. 1,000 copies printed November 1856; 250 copies on "fine paper" December 1856 (Account Books [MH]). Price, $1.00. Royalty, 20¢. *Location:* JM.

A 24.1.d
Boston: Phillips, Sampson, 1857.

'SEVENTH THOUSAND'. 1,000 copies printed March–April 1857 and July 1857 (Account Books [MH]; *JMN,* XIV, 452). Price, $1.00. Royalty, 20¢. *Location:* JM.

Note one: The following additional textual changes are present:

73.20	James [Edward
120.20–27	plaindealing of others. We will not have to do | with a man in a mask. Let us know the truth. | Draw a straight line, hit whom and where it will. | Alfred, whom the affection of the nation makes the | type of their race, is called by his friend Asser, | the *truth-speaker; Aluered us veridicus.* Geoffrey | of Monmouth says of King Aurelius, uncle of | Arthur, that

"above all things he hated a lie." [plaindealing of others. We will not have to do with | a man in a mask. Let us know the truth. Draw a | straight line, hit whom and where it will. Alfred, | whom the affection of the nation makes the type | of their race, is called by a writer at the Norman | Conquest, *the truth-speaker; Alueredus veridicus.* | Geoffrey of Monmouth says of King Aurelius, uncle | of Arthur, that "above all things he hated a lie."

124.19   make [makes
124.20   they would instantly, [it would instantly

Note two: 650 copies of the July 1857 printing were sold to an "Illinois Library Agent" at a discount, with Emerson's royalty being reduced to 10¢ (Account Books [MH]).

A 24.1.e
Boston: Phillips, Sampson, 1858.

'SEVENTH THOUSAND'. 1,000 copies printed October 1858 (Account Books [MH]). Price, $1.00. Royalty, 20¢. *Location:* MH.

Note: Phillips, Sampson failed on 19 September 1859, apparently before selling any of the 1,000 copies printed ca. 29 August 1859.

A 24.1.f
Boston: Ticknor and Fields, M DCCC LX.

Price, $1.00. Royalty, 20¢. *Location:* JM.

Note: Some copies of Phillips, Sampson sheets have been located in Ticknor and Fields bindings, with a cancel title leaf; these are from the 1,000 copies printed by Phillips, Sampson in August 1859 (see Note to A 24.1.e).

A 24.1.g
Boston: Ticknor and Fields, M DCCC LXIII.

'EIGHTH THOUSAND'. 280 copies printed 5 November 1862 and April 1863 (Account Books [MH]). Price, $1.25. Royalty, 25¢. *Location:* MH.

A 24.1.h
Boston: Ticknor and Fields, M DCCC LXIII.

280 copies printed 10 August 1863. Price, $1.25. Royalty, 25¢. *Location:* MH.

A 24.1.i
Boston: Ticknor and Fields, M DCCC LXV.

280 copies printed March 1865. Price, $1.50. Royalty, 30¢. *Location:* JM.

Note: The copyright on *English Traits* was renewed 13 May 1865.

A 24.1.j
Boston: Ticknor and Fields, M DCCC LXVI.

280 copies printed July–August 1866. Price, $1.50. Royalty, 30¢. *Location:* NhU.

Note one: By a contract of 4 March 1868, Emerson's royalty was changed from 20% to 20¢ per volume.

Note two: Ticknor and Fields was succeeded by Fields, Osgood in October 1868.

A 24.1.k
Boston: Fields, Osgood, 1869.

280 copies printed March–May 1869. Price, $2.00. Royalty, 20¢. *Location:* JM.

Note: Fields, Osgood was succeeded by James R. Osgood & Company in January 1871.

A 24.1.l
Boston: James R. Osgood, 1872.

Price, $2.00. Royalty, 30¢. *Location:* NIC.

Note: In a "Supplementary article of agreement" to the 4 March 1868 contract, dated 19 February 1870, Emerson's royalty was raised to 30¢ per copy when the price was $2.00 or above.

A 24.1.m
Boston: James R. Osgood, 1874.

150 copies printed 1 April 1874. Price, $2.00. Royalty, 30¢. *Location:* NCH.

A 24.1.n
Boston: James R. Osgood, 1876.

150 copies printed 20 November 1875. Price, $2.00. *Not seen.*

Note one: Emerson's 1 January 1876 contract with Osgood called for him to receive a flat annual fee of $1,500 for all his books, rather than a per copy royalty.

Note two: James R. Osgood was succeeded by Houghton, Osgood in February 1878.

A 24.1.o
Boston: Houghton, Osgood, 1878.

170 copies printed 18 June 1878. Price, $1.50. *Location:* MH.

Note: Houghton, Osgood was succeeded by Houghton, Mifflin in May 1880. Some copies of Houghton, Osgood sheets (including the title leaf) have been noted in Houghton, Mifflin bindings.

A 24.1.p
Boston: Houghton, Mifflin, 1881.

150 copies printed 8 December 1880. Price, $1.50. *Not seen.*

A 24.1.q
Boston: Houghton, Mifflin, 1882.

150 copies printed 16 June 1882. Price, $1.50. *Location:* InNd.

A 24.1.r
Boston: Houghton, Mifflin, 1883.

150 copies printed 12 January 1883. *Not seen.*

Note one: As of 10 January 1884, 10 copies of *English Traits* were still in stock.

Note two: The copyright on *English Traits* was renewed 31 May 1884.

A 24.2.a–d
First English edition, first through fourth printings (1856)

ENGLISH   TRAITS.

BY

R. W. EMERSON,

AUTHOR OF "REPRESENTATIVE MEN," ETC.

LONDON:

G. ROUTLEDGE & CO., FARRINGDON STREET.

1856.

A 24.2.a: $6^3/_8'' \times 4''$

The first four printings within this edition cannot be distinguished.

[i–viii] [1] 2–176

[A]⁴ B–I⁸ K–M⁸

Contents: pp. i–ii: pastedown endpaper with publisher's advertisements; pp. iii–iv: free endpaper with publisher's advertisements; p. v: title page; p. vi: printer's imprint; pp. vii–viii: contents; pp. 1–176: text.

Typography and paper: $5^9/_{16}''$ $(5^5/_{16}'')$ × $3^3/_{16}''$; wove paper; 40 lines per page. Running heads: rectos: pp. 3–53: chapter titles; p. 55: 'FACTITIOUS.'; p. 57: 'SOLIDARITY.'; pp. 59–175: chapter titles; versos: p. iv: 'CONTENTS.'; pp. 2–176: 'ENGLISH TRAITS.'.

Binding: Light green glazed paper-covered boards with blue printing. Front cover: 'ONE SHILLING. | [rule] | ENGLISH TRAITS | BY | R. W. EMERSON, | Author of "REPRESENTATIVE MEN," &c. | [rule] | (PRINTED BY ARRANGEMENT WITH THE AUTHOR.) | [rule] | LONDON: | GEO. ROUTLEDGE & CO., FARRINGDON ST.' within double-rule frame; back cover: 36-line advertisement for *Austrian Dungeons of Italy;* spine: from bottom to top '[floral device] ENGLISH TRAITS, BY R. W. Emerson. [floral device]' within single-rule frame. White endpapers, imprinted with advertisements for Routledge's "Railway and Home Reading" books (see "Contents" above). All edges trimmed.

Publication: On 5 October 1855, Routledge wrote Emerson promising £20 on credit for the advance American proof sheets for *English Traits.* On 17 October 1856, Emerson received $100 from Phillips, Sampson as Routledge's advance (MH). Advertised as "Printed by arrangement with the Author," in *Athenæum,* no. 1505 (30 August 1856), 1077. Listed in *Athenæum,* no. 1506 (6 September 1856), 1117. 6,000 copies printed early September 1856. Deposit copy: BL (rebound, 6 September 1856). Price, 1s.

Printing: "LONDON: | SAVILL AND EDWARDS, PRINTERS | CHANDOS STREET, | COVENT GARDEN" (p. [ii]).

Locations: MH, NN.

Note one: Copies have been noted with a 4-page catalogue of Routledge's publications, dated September 1856, inserted at the back: MH, NN.

Note two: A Richard Bentley advertisement in the *Athenæum* promises "English Notes; or, Impressions of Europe" for July 1853, and a later advertisement reports "Mr. Emerson's work on England is still in promise" (no. 1341 [9 July 1853], 833; no. 1387 [27 May 1854], 655). No Bentley edition has been located.

Note three: Copies have been noted with defective spines: JM, MCo.

A 24.2.b
First English edition, second printing (1856)

London: G. Routledge & Co., 1856.

6,000 copies printed 22 September 1856.

A 24.2.c
First English edition, third printing (1856)

London: G. Routledge & Co., 1856.

6,000 copies printed 15 October 1856.

ONE SHILLING.

ENGLISH TRAITS

BY

R. W. EMERSON,

Author of " REPRESENTATIVE MEN," &c.

(PRINTED BY ARRANGEMENT WITH THE AUTHOR.)

LONDON:
GEO. ROUTLEDGE & CO., FARRINGDON ST.

Boards for A 24.2.a

A 24.2.d
First English edition, fourth printing (1856)

London: G. Routledge & Co., 1856.

6,000 copies printed 19 October 1856.

A 24.2.e
First English edition, presumed fifth printing [1856]

ENGLISH TRAITS.

BY

R. W. EMERSON,

AUTHOR OF " REPRESENTATIVE MEN," ETC.

REPRINTED VERBATIM FROM THE AUTHOR'S EDITION.

LONDON:

PUBLISHED BY KNIGHT AND SON,

CLERKENWELL CLOSE.

A 24.2.e: 6³/₈″ × 4″

The same as the first English (Routledge) printing, except: p. i: Knight title page; p. ii: blank; p. 176: printer's imprint is at the page bottom.

Binding: Light yellow green glazed boards with blue printing. Front cover: all within double-rule frame 'ONE SHILLING | [rule] | English Traits. | BY | R. W. EMERSON, | Author of "Representative Men," etc. | [ornate rule] | LONDON: | PUBLISHED BY KNIGHT AND SON, | CLERKENWELL CLOSE.'; back cover: publisher's advertisement; spine: from bottom to top within single-rule frame 'EMERSON'S ENGLISH TRAITS.——1s.'. Blue printed endpapers with publisher's advertisements. All edges trimmed.

Publication: Listed as published between 30 October and 14 November, in *Publishers' Circular and Booksellers' Record,* 19 (15 November 1856), 459, and *Literary Gazette,* no. 2087 (17 January 1857), 60. Price, 1s.

Printing: "LONDON: KNIGHT AND SON, PRINTERS, CLERKENWELL CLOSE" (p. 176).

Location: BC.

A 24.2.f
London: G. Routledge & Co., 1857.

'NEW EDITION'. Location: NNC.

A 24.2.g
London and New York: George Routledge and Sons, 1882.

1,000 copies printed 2 May 1882. Price, 1s. *Locations:* BL (8 June 1882), CtY.

A 24.2.h
London and New York: George Routledge and Sons, 1884.

1,000 copies printed 1 October 1884. *Not seen.*

LATER EDITIONS

A 24.3
First German edition, only printing (1857)

[all gothic except date] Ralph Waldo Emerson. | Englische Characterzüge. | [rule] | Deutsch | von | Friedrich Spielhagen. | (Verfasser von "Clara Bere".) | [ornate rule] | Hannover. | Carl Meyer. | 1857.

239 pp. Glazed paper-covered boards or wrappers, both dated '1857'. *Locations:* CtY, MB, NNC.

Note: A copy has been located in wrappers which are imprinted '1858' (BL).

A 24.4.a
London: George Bell and Sons, 1874.

139 pp. Listed as published between 16 and 28 February, in *Publishers' Circular and Booksellers' Record,* 37 (2 March 1874), 138. Price, 1s. *Not seen.*

A 24.4.b
English Traits   England and English Characteristics. London: George Bell and Sons, 1877.

Location: BMP.

ONE SHILLING.

English Traits.

BY

R. W. EMERSON,

Author of "Representative Men," etc.

LONDON:
PUBLISHED BY KNIGHT AND SON,
CLERKENWELL CLOSE.

Boards for A 24.2.a

A 24.5
First Swedish edition, only printing [1875]

Engleska Karaktärsdrag | af | Ralph Waldo Emerson | Öfversättning | af | A. F. Åkerberg | [rule] | UPSALA | ESAIAS EDQUIST.

229 pp. *Locations:* MH, NNC.

PRINTINGS FROM THE "LITTLE CLASSIC EDITION" PLATES

A 24.6.a

[all within a double-rule frame; outer frame is red with boxed corners] [red] ENGLISH TRAITS. | BY | RALPH WALDO EMERSON. | NEW AND REVISED EDITION. | [ornate rule] | [red] BOSTON: | JAMES R. OSGOOD AND COMPANY, | Late Ticknor & Fields, and Fields, Osgood, & Co. | [red] 1876.

236 pp. Vol. [V] of the "Little Classic Edition" (see B 3). 1,500 copies printed July–August 1876. Listed in *Publishers' Weekly,* 10 (16 September 1876), 446. Copyright, 26 July 1876. Price, $1.50. Royalty: see *Note One* to A 24.1.n. *Location:* MBAt.

A 24.6.b
Boston: James R. Osgood, 1877.

280 copies printed January 1877. Price, $1.50. *Not seen.*

A 24.6.c
Boston: James R. Osgood, 1878.

Price, $1.50. *Location:* MMeT.

Note: James R. Osgood was succeeded by Houghton, Osgood in February 1878.

A 24.6.d
Boston: Houghton, Osgood, 1879.

520 copies printed 15 February 1879. Price, $1.50. *Location:* CSt.

A 24.6.e
Boston: Houghton, Osgood, 1879.

Combined with *The Conduct of Life* in two-volumes-in-one format as vol. III of the "Fireside Edition" (see B 4). *Location:* JM.

A 24.6.f
Boston: Houghton, Osgood, 1880.

Combined with *The Conduct of Life* in two-volumes-in-one format as vol. III of the "Fireside Edition" (see B 4). 500 copies printed 6 February 1880. *Location:* JM.

Note: Houghton, Osgood was succeeded by Houghton, Mifflin in May 1880.

A 24.6.g
Boston: Houghton, Mifflin, 1881.

270 copies printed 1 October 1880 and 26 May 1881. Price, $1.50. *Location:* JM.

A 24.6.h
Boston: Houghton, Mifflin, 1881.

Combined with *The Conduct of Life* in two-volumes-in-one format as vol. III of the "Fireside Edition" (see B 4). 500 copies printed 7 December 1880. *Location:* MWelC.

A 24.6.i
Boston: Houghton, Mifflin, 1882.

Combined with *The Conduct of Life* in two-volumes-in-one format as vol. III of the "Fireside Edition" (see B 4). 500 copies printed 19 October 1881, 12 May 1882, and 8 August 1882. *Location:* JM.

A 24.6.j
Boston: Houghton, Mifflin, 1882.

270 copies printed 26 January 1882, 20 May 1882, and 31 August 1882. Price, $1.50. *Location:* MH.

A 24.6.k
Boston: Houghton, Mifflin, 1883.

500 copies printed 27 November 1882; 270 copies on 14 July 1883. *Location:* JM.

A 24.6.l
Boston: Houghton, Mifflin, 1883.

Combined with *The Conduct of Life* in two-volumes-in-one format as vol. III of the "Fireside Edition" (see B 4). 270 copies printed 10 January 1883. *Location:* JM.

A 24.6.m
Boston and New York: Houghton, Mifflin, 1884.

270 copies printed 12 January 1884; 500 copies on 13 August 1884. Bound in medium blue V cloth (smooth), rather than "Little Classic Edition" binding, as are subsequent reprintings (see illustration at B 3). *Location:* KyL.

A 24.6.n
Boston and New York: Houghton, Mifflin, 1887.

270 copies printed 7 January 1887. *Location:* JM.

A 24.6.o
Boston and New York: Houghton, Mifflin, 1888.

270 copies printed 10 March 1888 and 23 October 1888. *Location:* JM.

A 24.6.p
Boston and New York: Houghton, Mifflin, 1889.

270 copies printed 20 July 1889. *Location:* JM.

A 24.6.q
Boston and New York: Houghton, Mifflin, 1890.

270 copies printed 29 November 1889. *Location:* JM.

A 24.6.r
Boston and New York: Houghton, Mifflin, 1891.

250 copies printed ca. December 1890; 270 copies on 24 June 1891. *Location:* JM.

A 24.6.s
Boston and New York: Houghton, Mifflin, 1892.

500 copies printed 16 March 1892. *Location:* JM.

A 24.6.t
Boston and New York: Houghton, Mifflin, 1893.

500 copies printed 22 September 1893. *Not seen.*

A 24.6.u
Boston and New York: Houghton, Mifflin, 1895.

500 copies printed 5 April 1895. *Location:* MoU.

A 24.6.v
Boston and New York: Houghton, Mifflin, 1898.

270 copies printed 30 June 1898. *Location:* JM.

A 24.6.w
Boston and New York: Houghton, Mifflin, 1899.

270 copies printed 30 April 1899. *Location:* DeU.

A 24.6.x
Boston and New York: Houghton, Mifflin, [n.d.].

Approximately 1,400 copies sold between 1900 and 1923. *Location:* JM.

Note: Approximately 10,000 copies of *English Traits* printed from the "Little Classic Edition" plates were sold between 1876 and 1923, when the title was apparently allowed to go out of print in this format.

LATER EDITIONS

A 24.7.a–h
English Traits and Representative Men. London: Macmillan, 1883.

See A 22.12.a–h.

A 24.7.i
English Traits. London and New York: Macmillan, 1889.

253 pp. Cloth or wrappers. *Macmillan's Colonial Library,* no. 101. Intended for circulation only in India and the British colonies. *Location:* CtY.

Note: Printed from the plates of A 22.12.

PRINTINGS FROM THE RIVERSIDE EDITION PLATES

A 24.8.a
Riverside Edition (trade), first printing (1883)

ENGLISH TRAITS | BY | RALPH WALDO EMERSON | [gothic] New and Revised Edition | [publisher's logo] | BOSTON | HOUGHTON, MIFFLIN COMPANY | New York: 11 East Seventeenth Street | [gothic] The Riverside Press, Cambridge | 1883

296 pp. Vol. V of the *Riverside Edition,* trade printing (see B 7). 1,000 copies printed 31 July 1883; 500 copies on 31 October 1883. Listed in *Publishers' Weekly,* 24 (27 October 1883), 574. According to the publisher's records, published 6 October 1883. Copyright, 15 October 1883. Price, $1.75. *Location:* DLC (15 October 1883).

Note: Copies have been noted with a pine branch on the title page instead of the publisher's logo.

A 24.8.b
Riverside Edition (Copyright), second (English) printing (1883)

ENGLISH TRAITS | BY | RALPH WALDO EMERSON | [gothic] The Riverside Edition | (COPYRIGHT) | LONDON | GEORGE ROUTLEDGE AND SONS | BROADWAY, LUDGATE HILL | NEW YORK: 9, LAFAYETTE PLACE | 1883

Vol. V of the *Riverside Edition (Copyright),* English trade printing (see B 10). 1,000 copies printed 12 September 1883. Listed as published between 1 and 15 October, in *Publishers' Circular and Booksellers' Record,* 46 (15 October 1883), 1000. Price, 3s. 6d. *Locations:* BC (12 October 1883), BO (18 October 1883), BL (8 December 1883), CaQMM.

A 24.8.c$_1$
Riverside Edition (large paper), third printing, American issue (1883)

[red] ENGLISH TRAITS | BY | RALPH WALDO EMERSON | [gothic] New and Revised Edition | [pine branch] | [red] CAMBRIDGE | [gothic] Printed at the Riverside Press | 1883

Vol. V of the *Riverside Edition,* large paper printing (see B 8). Limited to 500 numbered copies printed 30 November 1883. Price, $4.00. Sold out within a year. *Locations:* JM, TxU.

A 24.8.c$_2$
Riverside Edition (large paper), second printing, English issue (1883)

Title page is the same as in the American issue, except for publisher's imprint: 'LONDON | KEGAN PAUL, TRENCH, & CO., I, PATERNOSTER SQUARE | MDCCCLXXXIII'.

Vol. V of the *Riverside Edition,* large paper printing for English subscribers (see B 9). 25 title leaves printed 30 November 1883. Title leaf is a cancel. Limited to 25 signed and numbered copies. *Location:* JM.

A 24.8.d
Boston and New York: Houghton, Mifflin, 1884.

500 copies printed 22 December 1883, 7 April 1884, and 2 October 1884. *Location:* JM.

Note: The copyright on *English Traits* was renewed 29 May 1884.

A 24.8.e
Boston and New York: Houghton, Mifflin, 1885.

500 copies printed 7 April 1885 and 22 September 1885. *Location:* JM.

A 24.8.f
Boston and New York: Houghton, Mifflin, 1886.

500 copies printed 2 April 1886. *Location:* MBAt.

A 24.8.g
Boston and New York: Houghton, Mifflin, 1887.

500 copies printed 16 November 1886 and ca. June 1887. *Location:* JM.

A 24.8.h
Boston and New York: Houghton, Mifflin, 1888.

500 copies printed 19 December 1887; 270 copies on 14 August 1888. *Location:* JM.

A 24.8.i
London, Glasgow, New York: George Routledge and Sons, 1888.

500 copies printed 24 January 1888. *Location:* JM.

A 24.8.j
Boston and New York: Houghton, Mifflin, 1889.

500 copies printed 26 November 1888 and 27 July 1889. *Location:* OrP.

A 24.8.k
Boston and New York: Houghton, Mifflin, 1890.

500 copies printed 14 January 1890. *Location:* VtMo.

A 24.8.l
Boston and New York: Houghton, Mifflin, 1891.

500 copies printed January–March 1891. *Location:* JM.

A 24.8.m
Boston and New York: Houghton, Mifflin, 1892.

500 copies printed 17 December 1891 and 27 August 1892. *Location:* JM.

A 24.8.n
Boston and New York: Houghton, Mifflin, 1893.

500 copies printed 5 September 1893. *Location:* RNR.

A 24.8.o
Boston and New York: Houghton, Mifflin, 1894.

500 copies printed 29 October 1894. *Location:* JM.

A 24.8.p
Standard Library Edition printing [1894]

ENGLISH TRAITS | BY | RALPH WALDO EMERSON | [pine branch] | BOSTON AND NEW YORK | HOUGHTON, MIFFLIN AND COMPANY | [gothic] The Riverside Press, Cambridge

Vol. V of the *Standard Library Edition* (see B 11). 1,000 copies printed 31 October 1894, 30 April 1895, 29 May 1896; 500 copies on 31 January 1898. *Location:* JM.

A 24.8.q
Boston and New York: Houghton, Mifflin, 1896.

500 copies printed 11 May 1896. *Location:* MH.

A 24.8.r
Boston and New York: Houghton, Mifflin, 1898.

270 copies printed 23 October 1897 and 29 August 1898. *Location:* JM.

A 24.8.s
London: George Routledge and Sons, 1898.

Location: CaNfSM.

A 24.8.t
Boston and New York: Houghton, Mifflin, 1899.

270 copies printed 31 May 1899. *Location:* ICM.

A 24.8.u
Boston and New York: Houghton, Mifflin, 1900.

250 copies printed April–June 1900. *Location:* MF.

A 24.8.v
London: George Routledge and Sons, 1902.

Location: JM.

A 24.8.w
London: George Routledge & Sons, 1903.

Combined with *Representative Men* and *The Conduct of Life* in three-volumes-in-one format as vol. II of the "Sovereign Edition" (see B 12). 1,000 copies printed 16 September 1903. *Location:* InU.

A 24.8.x
Fireside Edition printing (1909)

[all within red double-rule frame with red floral ornaments in each corner] THE WORKS OF | [red gothic] Ralph Waldo Emerson | ENGLISH TRAITS | [engraving of man reading book in chair before fireplace] | [gothic] Fireside Edition | BOSTON AND NEW YORK | MDCCCCIX

Vol. V of the *Fireside Edition* (see B 13). 500 copies printed 30 September 1909 and 14 February 1910. *Location:* JM.

A 24.8.y
Boston and New York: Jefferson Press, [ca. 1912].

Combined with *The Conduct of Life* in two-volumes-in-one format as vol. [III] of the "Jefferson Press Edition" (see B 14). *Not seen.*

A 24.8.z
New York: Sully and Kleinteich, [ca. 1912].

Vol. V of the *University Edition* (see B 15). *Location:* JM.

A 24.8.aa
Boston and New York: Houghton, Mifflin, [n.d.].

Approximately 1,400 copies sold between 1901 and 1923. *Location:* JM.

Note: Approximately 13,000 copies of *English Traits* in the *Riverside Edition* were sold between 1883 and 1913, when the title was apparently allowed to go out of print in this format.

A 24.8.bb
London: Waverley Book Company, [n.d.].

Vol. V of the "Waverley" *Riverside Edition* (see B 16). *Location:* JM.

LATER EDITIONS

A 24.9
Representative Men and English Traits. London and New York: Ward, Lock, [1886].

See A 22.14.

A 24.10
New York: T. Y. Crowell, [1899].

248 pp. Introduction by Andrew J. George. *Handy Volume Classics.* Also advertised as included in "Faience Library" and "Photogravure Series." Listed in *Publishers' Weekly,* 56 (23 September 1899), 385. Copyright, 20 June 1899. *Locations:* DLC (21 June 1899), JM.

A 24.11
London and New York: Unit Library, 1902.

183 pp. Cloth, leather, or wrappers. *The Unit Library,* no. 4. *Locations:* BL (1 May 1902), JM.

A 24.12.a
English Traits and Representative Men. London: Grant Richards, 1903.

See A 22.22.a.

A 24.12.b
London [&c.]: Henry Frowde, [1903].

See A 22.22.b.

A 24.12.c–d
London [&c.]: Henry Frowde, Oxford University Press, [1905].

See A 22.22.c–d.

A 24.12.e–f

London [&c.]: Humphrey Milford, Oxford University Press, [1923].

See A 22.22.e–f.

PRINTINGS FROM THE CENTENARY EDITION PLATES

A 24.13.a$_1$
Centenary Edition (trade), first printing, American issue (1903)

ENGLISH TRAITS | BY | RALPH WALDO EMERSON | [pine tree] | BOSTON AND NEW YORK | HOUGHTON, MIFFLIN AND COMPANY, | [gothic] The Riverside Press, Cambridge | 1903

406 pp. Dust jacket. Vol. V of the *Centenary Edition,* trade printing (see B 18). 1,000 copies printed 16 October 1903. Listed in *Publishers' Weekly,* 64 (7 November 1903), 1001. According to the publisher's records, published 28 October 1903. Copyright, 17 October 1903. *Location:* JM.

Note: Numerous reprintings with undated title pages. 2,500 copies printed between 1 October 1904 and 30 March 1910. Approximately 4,300 copies sold through 1923.

A 24.13.a$_2$
English issue

London: A. P. Watt & Son, [1903].

Vol. V of the English *Centenary Edition* (see B 21). American sheets with Watt's label pasted on the title page. Price, 6s. *Locations:* BL (28 October 1903), BE (11 November 1903), BC (13 November 1903).

A 24.13.b
Autograph Centenary Edition (large paper), second printing (1903)

RALPH WALDO EMERSON | [red] English Traits | [pine tree] | CAMBRIDGE | [red gothic] Printed at the Riverside Press | 1903

Vol. V of the *Autograph Centenary Edition* (see B 19). Limited to 600 signed and numbered copies printed 16 October 1903. Copyright, 17 October 1903. Price, $6.00. Sold out by 5 April 1906. *Locations:* DLC (20 October 1903), JM.

A 24.13.c
Boston and New York: Houghton, Mifflin, 1903.

Vol. V of the *Concord Edition* (see B 20). 1,000 copies printed mid-october 1903. *Location:* JM.

Note: Numerous reprintings with undated title pages. Approximately 3,100 copies sold by 31 December 1910.

A 24.13.d
Boston and New York: Houghton Mifflin, [1914].

Vol. V of the *Riverside Pocket Edition* (see B 22). Approximately 900 copies sold between 1914 and 1922. *Not seen.*

A 24.13.e
Boston and New York: Houghton Mifflin, 1921.

314 pp. (text without the notes). Combined with *Lectures and Biographical Sketches* in two-volumes-in-one format as vol. IV of *Emerson's Complete Works* (see B 23). *Location:* RP.

A 24.13.f
New York: Wm. H. Wise, 1923.

Combined with *The Conduct of Life* in two-volumes-in-one format as vol. III of the *Current Opinion Edition* (see B 24). *Not seen.*

A 24.13.g
Boston and New York: Houghton Mifflin, 1929.

Combined (text without the notes) with *Lectures and Biographical Sketches* in two-volumes-in-one format as vol. [IV] of the *Harvard Edition* (see B 25). *Location:* JM.

A 24.13.h
New York: Wm. H. Wise, 1929.

Combined with *The Conduct of Life* in two-volumes-in-one format as vol. III of the *Medallion Edition* (see B 26). *Location:* OC.

A 24.13.i–j
New York: AMS Press, [1968].

Vol. V of the "AMS Press" *Centenary Edition* (see B 27). Reprinted 1979. *Locations:* TxU, DLC (9 November 1979).

LATER EDITIONS

A 24.14
London: H. R. Allenson, 1906.

103 pp., double columns. Wrappers. *Allenson's Sixpenny Series.* Published April 1906. Price, 6d. *Location:* BL (10 May 1906).

A 24.15.a
Philadelphia: John B. Morris, [1906].

304 pp. Vol. II of the "John D. Morris Edition" (see B 29). Copyright, 13 February 1906. *Location:* JM.

A 24.15.b
New York: A. L. Burt, [1906].

Cornell Series. Also advertised as included in "Home Library." Published 19 May 1906. *Location:* JM.

A 24.15.c
Boston and New York: C. T. Brainard, [n.d.].

Vol. V of the *Works* (see B 30). *Location:* NHemH.

A 24.15.d
New York: Caxton Society, [n.d.].

Vol. V of the *Works* (see B 31). *Location:* NjR.

A 24.15.e
New York: National Library Co., [n.d.].

Vol. V of the *Works* (see B 32). *Location:* CaOHM.

A 24.15.f
Philadelphia, New York, Chicago: Nottingham Society, [n.d.].

Vol. V of the *Works* (see B 33). *Location:* JM.

A 24.16.a
London: George G. Harrap, [1910].

238 pp. *The Harrap Library*, no. 8. Price, 2s. 6d. *Locations:* BC (9 February 1911), BE (9 February 1911), BO (14 February 1911), CCC.

A 24.16.b
New York: Robert M. McBride, [n.d.].

Chelsea College Classics. Location: NAIU.

A 24.17
New York: Dodge, [1912?].

Advertised in various bindings at various prices. Also advertised in "Dodge Library." *Not seen.*

A 24.18
Leipzig: Bernhard Tauchnitz, 1917.

255 pp. Wrappers. *Collection of British Authors*, vol. 4519. *Location:* JM.

A 24.19
Cambridge: The Belknap Press of Harvard University Press, 1966.

267 pp. Dust jacket. Edited by Howard Mumford Jones. *The John Harvard Library.* Copyright, 23 November 1966. Price, $5.00. *Locations:* BL (12 June 1967), JM.

UNDATED EDITIONS

A 24.20
Presumed first French edition, only printing [n.d.]

R. W. EMERSON | [rule] | ENGLISH TRAITS | SELECTED AND ANNOTATED | BY | GEORGES ROTH | [rule] | PARIS | LIBRAIRIE HATIER | 8, Rue d'Assas, 8

64 pp. Wrappers. In English. *Location:* CaOOSJ.

A 24.21
Presumed second French edition, only printing [n.d.]

Title page is the same as in the first French edition.

77 pp. Wrappers. *Les Classiques Pour Tous*, no. 10. In English. *Location:* MH.

A 24.22.a
New York: Hurst, [n.d.].

234 pp. Advertised in various bindings at various prices. Also *The Companion Books*. *Locations:* JM (both).

A 24.22.b
Chicago: Thompson & Thomas, [n.d.].

Location: MtU.

A 24.23
Philadelphia: David McKay, [n.d.].

333 pp. *American Classic Series*. Also advertised as combined with *The Conduct of Life* in two-volumes-in-one format and in a boxed set with *The Conduct of Life*. *Location:* JM.

SEPARATE PUBLICATIONS OF INDIVIDUAL ESSAYS

A 24.24.
Britain. London: People's Refreshment House, [n.d.].

Broadside, printed on recto only. Selection from "Speech at Manchester." *Location:* MCo.

A 24.25
English Traits. Westport, Conn.: Redcoat Press, MCMXXXXI.

19 pp. Wrappers. Selections. Printed September 1941. Limited to 150 copies. *Location:* JM.

A 24.26
First Visit to England. Kent, England: Sign of the Hop-pole, MDCCCCII.

29 pp. Wrappers. Limited to 500 copies. *Location:* MCo.

A 24.27
Literature. [London]: London County Council Central School of Arts and Crafts, MCMXII.

23 pp. Full leather. According to Bertram Rota booksellers, "we understand that no more than fifteen copies were produced of any book [from this press], sometimes considerably fewer" (catalogue 209, winter 1977–1978). *Location:* JM.

A 25 [FOURTH OF JULY ODE]

A 25.1
First edition, only printing [1857]

FOURTH OF JULY BREAKFAST
—AND—
FLORAL EXHIBITION,
—AT THE—
Town Hall, Concord,
FOR THE BENEFIT OF
SLEEPY HOLLOW CEMETERY.

ODE.

O tenderly the haughty day
Fills his blue urn with fire,
One morn is in the mighty heaven,
And one in our desire.

The cannon booms from town to town,
Our pulses are not less,
The joy-bells chime their tidings down,
Which children's voices bless.

For He that flung the broad blue fold
O'er-mantling land and sea,
One third part of the sky unrolled
For the banner of the free.

The men are ripe of Saxon kind
To build an equal state;
To take the statute from the mind,
And make of duty fate.

United States! the ages plead,—
Present and Past in under-song,—
Go put your creed into your deed,
Nor speak with double tongue.

For sea and land don't understand,
Nor skies without a frown.
See rights for which the one hand fights
By the other cloven down.

Be just at home; then reach beyond
Your charter o'er the sea,
And make the broad Atlantic pond
A ferry of the free.

And, henceforth, there shall be no chain,
Save, underneath the sea,
The wires shall murmur thro' the main
Sweet songs of LIBERTY.

The conscious stars accord above,
The waters wild below
And under, thro' the cable wove,
Her fiery errands go.

For He that worketh high and wise,
Nor pauses in his plan,
Will take the sun out of the skies
Ere freedom out of man.

A 25: 8¹/₄″ × 5⁵/₁₆″; 1st state

Two states have been noted:

  1st state: Emerson's name is not present

  2nd state: Emerson's name is present

[1–4]

[a]^2

Contents: p. 1: text; pp. 2–4: blank.

Typography and paper: 1st state: 6^5/$_{16}$″ × 3^1/$_8$″; 2nd state: 6^9/$_{16}$″ × 3^1/$_8$″; wove paper; 1st state: 49 lines; 2nd state: 52 lines. No running head.

Binding: Single sheet, folded once; unbound.

Publication: Probably printed in Concord and distributed on 4 or 5 July 1857. The copy at MHi is enclosed with a letter from James J. Higginson to George Higginson of 5 July 1857, stating: "We had a real pleasant day here yesterday . . . Mr. Emerson wrote an ode for the occasion which was sung during the afternoon. I send you a copy of it here."

Locations: 1st state: MHi; 2nd state: MCo, MH, ViU.

FOURTH OF JULY BREAKFAST
—AND—
FLORAL EXHIBITION,
—AT THE—
Town Hall, Concord,
FOR THE BENEFIT OF
SLEEPY HOLLOW CEMETERY.

ODE.

BY R. W. EMERSON.

O tenderly the haughty day
  Fills his blue urn with fire,
One morn is in the mighty heaven,
  And one in our desire.

The cannon booms from town to town,
  Our pulses are not less,
The joy-bells chime their tidings down,
  Which children's voices bless.

For He that flung the broad blue fold
  O'er-mantling land and sea,
One third part of the sky unrolled
  For the banner of the free.

The men are ripe of Saxon kind
  To build an equal state;
To take the statute from the mind,
  And make of duty fate.

United States! the ages plead,—
  Present and Past in under-song,—
Go put your creed into your deed,
  Nor speak with double tongue.

For sea and land don't understand,
  Nor skies, without a frown,
See rights for which the one hand fights
  By the other cloven down.

Be just at home; then reach beyond
  Your charter o'er the sea,
And make the broad Atlantic pond
  A ferry of the free.

And, henceforth, there shall be no chain,
  Save, underneath the sea,
The wires shall murmur thro' the main
  Sweet songs of LIBERTY.

The conscious stars accord above,
  The waters wild below,
And under, thro' the cable wove,
  Her fiery errands go.

For He that worketh high and wise,
  Nor pauses in his plan,
Will take the sun out of the skies
  Ere freedom out of man.

A 25: 8³/₈″ × 5⁵/₁₆″; 2nd state

Note: Kenneth Walter Cameron facsimiles a reprinting of the "Ode" as "The Atlantic Cable" from an unidentified newspaper (30 July or 1 August 1866) in "Emerson, Thoreau, and the Atlantic Cable," *Emerson Society Quarterly,* no. 26 (1st Quarter 1962), 55.

LATER EDITION

A 25.2
["Concord Hymn" and "Fourth of July Ode"]

Anonymous. Broadside, laid paper, printed on recto only. Page size: 10$\frac{1}{2}$" × 5". *Location:* MH.

A 26 THE CONDUCT OF LIFE

A 26.1.a
First American edition, first printing (1860)

THE

CONDUCT OF LIFE.

BY

R. W. EMERSON.

BOSTON:
TICKNOR AND FIELDS.
M DCCC LX.

A 26.1.a: $7^{1}/_{8}''$ × $4^{1}/_{2}''$

> Entered according to Act of Congress, in the year 1860, by
>
> R. W. EMERSON,
>
> in the Clerk's Office of the District Court of the District of Massachusetts.
>
> RIVERSIDE, CAMBRIDGE:
> STEREOTYPED AND PRINTED BY H. O. HOUGHTON.

Three sequences of pagination, collation, and contents, resulting from the binder's positioning of preliminary material, have been noted:

Sequence 1: [i–x] [xi–xii] [1] 2–42 [43–45] 46–70 [71] 72 [73] 74–110 [111–113] 114–144 [145–147] 148–172 [173–175] 176–211 [212–215] 216–244 [245–247] 248–270 [271] 272 [273] 274–288

[a]^2 [b]^4 [1]^{12} 2–12^{12}

Contents: pp. i–iii: blank; p. iv: publisher's advertisements; p. v: 'CONDUCT OF LIFE.'; p. vi: blank; p. vii: title page; p. viii: copyright page; p. ix: contents; p. x: blank; p. xi: 'I. | FATE. | [rule] | [14 lines of verse]'; p. xii: blank; pp. 1–42: "Fate"; p. 43: 'II. | POWER. | [rule] | [four lines of verse]'; p. 44: blank; pp. 45–70: "Power"; p. 71: 'III. | WEALTH. | [rule] | [23 lines of verse]'; p. 72: 26 lines of verse; pp. 73–110: "Wealth"; p. 111: 'IV. | CULTURE. | [rule] | [11 lines of verse]'; p. 112: blank; pp. 113–144: "Culture"; p. 145: 'V. | BEHAVIOR. | [rule] | [20 lines of verse]'; p. 146: blank; pp. 147–172: "Behavior"; p. 173: 'VI. | WORSHIP. | [rule] | [23 lines of verse]'; p. 174: blank; pp. 175–211: "Worship"; p. 212: blank; p. 213: 'VII. | CONSIDERATIONS BY THE WAY. | [rule] | [33 lines of verse]'; p. 214: blank; pp. 215–244: "Considerations by the Way"; p. 245: 'VIII. | BEAUTY. | [rule] | [26 lines of verse]'; p. 246: blank; pp. 247–270: "Beauty"; p. 271: 'IX. | ILLUSIONS. | [rule] | [21 lines of verse]'; p. 272: 16 lines of verse; pp. 273–288: "Illusions."

Sequence 2: [i–vi]; all else the same as in Sequence 1.

[a]^4 [1]^{12} 2–12^{12}

Contents: p. i: half title; p. ii: blank; p. iii: title page; p. iv: copyright page; p. v: contents; p. vi: blank; all else the same as in Sequence 1.

Sequence 3: [i–viii]; all else the same as in Sequence 1.

[a]^4 (+a$_2$) [1]^{12} 2–12^{12} The inserted leaf contains the publisher's advertisements.

Contents: p. i: half title; p. ii: blank; p. iii: blank; p. iv: publisher's advertisements; p. v: title page; p. vi: copyright page; p. vii: contents; p. viii: blank; all else the same as in Sequence 1.

Essays: "Fate" #; "Power" #; "Wealth" #; "Culture" †; "Behavior" #; "Worship" #; "Considerations by the Way" #; "Beauty" #; "Illusions" #.

Typography and paper: 5^1/$_2$″ (5^1/$_4$″) × 3^1/$_{16}$″; wove paper; 29 lines per page. Running heads: rectos: pp. 3–41, 47–69, 75–109, 115–143, 149–171, 177–211, 217–243, 249–269, 275–287: chapter titles; versos: pp. 2–42, 46–70, 74–110, 114–144, 148–172, 176–210, 216–244, 248–270, 274–288: 'CONDUCT OF LIFE.'.

Binding: Two styles have been noted, priority undetermined:

Binding A: Light brown T cloth (rib). Front and back covers: blindstamped triple-rule frame with small leaf design in each corner and 3^1/$_2$″ ornament in center; spine:

blindstamped rules with goldstamped 'CONDUCT | OF | LIFE | [rule] | EMERSON | TICKNOR & CO.'. Flyleaves. Brown coated endpapers. All edges trimmed.

Binding B: The same as Binding A, except: dark brown or light medium brown cloth; spine: blindstamped rules with goldstamped 'EMERSON'S | WRITINGS | CONDUCT | OF LIFE | TICKNOR & CO.'; flyleaves in some copies.

Publication: Part of *The Conduct of Life* was in proof as early as March 1860 (see Ticknor and Fields to Emerson, 24 March 1860 [MH]). In October 1860, Ticknor and Fields was still sending proof (Account Books [MH]). Emerson's contract, dated 21 November 1859, called for him to retain the plates and copyright. Advertised as "In Press, and shortly to be published," in *Norton's Literary Letter*, n.s. 1 (1860), 51; for 8 December, in *Bookseller's Medium and Publisher's Advertiser*, 8 December 1860; for 8 December on printed advertising slips for the book (JM); as "This day published," in *Boston Daily Advertiser*, 8 December 1860, p. 2. Listed in *Bookseller's Medium and Publisher's Advertiser*, 15 December 1860. 2,500 copies printed November 1860. Deposited for copyright: title and book, 1 December 1860. According to the publisher's records, published 8 December 1860. William Emerson received his copy on 8 December (*L*, V, 233n.). Inscribed copies: NjP (rebound, from Emerson, 6 November 1860), Carroll A. Wilson copy (3B; from Emerson, 6 November 1860; see *Thirteen Author Collections of the Nineteenth Century* [D 213], I, 30–31), MH (3B; from Emerson, 6 November 1860), ViU (1A; from Emerson, 8 December 1860), JM (3B; 12 December 1860), NN (2A; 12 December 1860), CtY (2B; 25 December 1860), JM (2B, December 1860). Price, $1.00. Royalty, 20¢.

Locations: Sequence 1: DLC (B), JM (B), MB (B), MH (B), MWA (B), NN (A, B), NNC (A), ViU (A); Sequence 2: CSt (B), CU (B), CtY (A), JM (B), MH (B), MWA (B), MWiW-C (B), NN (A), NNC (A, B), RPB (B), TxU (B), ViU (A, B), VtMiM (B); Sequence 3: CtY (A, B), DLC (B), InU (B), JM (B), MCo (B), MH (B), MHi (B), MWiW-C (A), NN (A, B), NNC (B), PSt (B), TxU (A), ViU (B).

Note one: In Sequence 1 and 3 advertisements, *The Conduct of Life* is described as "nearly ready," as having seven sections, and as costing "$1.00" (p. [iv]).

Note two: All copies have a 16-page catalogue of Ticknor and Fields's publications, dated December 1860, inserted at the back.

Note three: Copies have been noted containing mixed sheets from the first and subsequent printings. These copies are clearly created by the arrangement of the gatherings in binding and do not represent separate printings. *Locations:* CtY, JM.

Note four: The following intercalary poems are present: "Fate" ["Delicate omens traced in air"] # (later incorporated into "Fragments on the Poet and the Poetic Gift"; see A 18.6), "Power" ["His tongue is framed to music"] # (later incorporated into "Fragments on the Poet and the Poetic Gift"; see A 18.6), "Wealth" #, "Culture" #, "Behavior" # (retitled "Manners"; see A 28), "Worship" #, "Considerations by the Way" # (later incorporated into "Merlin's Song"; see A 18.6), "Beauty" #, and "Illusions" †.

A 26.1.b
First American edition, second printing (1860)

Boston: Ticknor and Fields, M DCCC LX. Pagination and typography and paper are the same as in the first printing, Sequence 2; binding is the same as in the first printing, in two forms.

[a]⁴ 1–12¹²

Contents: The same as in the first printing, Sequence 2, except: p. ii: publisher's advertisements.

Publication: 500 copies printed December 1860. Inscribed copies: NNC (25 December 1860), MH (January 1861).

Locations: CSt (B), CtY (B), JM (A, B), MCo (B), MH (B), MWA (B), NNC (A, B), NjP (B), TxU (A, B), VtMiM (B).

Note one: In all advertisements, *The Conduct of Life* is described as having seven sections and costing "$1.00"; the statement "nearly ready" is not present (p. [ii]).

Note two: Copies have been noted with a 16-page catalogue of Ticknor and Fields's publications, dated December 1860, inserted at the back: JM (B), MH, NNC (B).

A 26.1.c
First American edition, third printing (1860)

Boston: Ticknor and Fields, M DCCC LX. Pagination, collation, and typography and paper are the same as in the second printing; binding is the same as in the first printing, Binding A.

Contents: The same as in the second printing, except: p. 213: 'VII. | CONSIDERA-TIONS BY THE WAY. | [rule] | [25 lines of verse]'; p. 214: eight lines of verse.

Publication: 1,500 copies printed 18 December 1860. Advertised as "The third Edition in two weeks from the day of publication," in *Atlantic,* 7 (January 1861), wrappers. Inscribed copy: NN (from Emerson, January 1861).

Location: NN.

Note one: In all advertisements, *The Conduct of Life* is described as having seven sections and costing "$1.00"; the statement "nearly ready" is not present (p. [ii]).

Note two: All copies have a 16-page catalogue of Ticknor and Fields's publications, dated January 1861, inserted at the back.

Note three: All the intercalary verse has been reset in a larger font of type.

A 26.1.d
First American edition, fourth printing (1860)

Boston: Ticknor and Fields, M DCCC LX. Pagination, contents, and typography and paper are the same as in the third printing; binding is the same as in the first printing, Binding A.

$[a]^4$ $1-6^{12}$ 10^{12} $8-12^{12}$

Publication: 1,500 copies printed 22 December 1860.

Locations: DLC, JM.

Note one: In all advertisements, *The Conduct of Life* is described as having nine sections and costing "$.100"; the statement "nearly ready" is not present (p. [ii]).

Note two: All copies have a 16-page catalogue of Ticknor and Fields's publications, dated January 1861, inserted at the back.

Note three: A number of copies with an 1860 title page have been noted containing mixed sheets from the first four printings.

A 26.1.e
Boston: Ticknor and Fields, M DCCC LXI.

1,000 copies printed in mid-January 1861. Advertised as the "fifth Edition," in *Atlantic*, 7 (April 1861), wrappers. *Location:* JM (23 March 1861).

Note: It is possible that 2,000 more copies were printed in 1861; advertisements for the sixth and seventh thousands of *The Conduct of Life* are in the *Atlantic*, 7 (May 1861), wrappers, and 8 (October 1861), wrappers.

A 26.1.f
Boston: Ticknor and Fields, M DCCC LXIII.

Price, $1.25. Royalty, 25¢. *Location:* P.

A 26.1.g
Boston: Ticknor and Fields, M DCCC LXIV.

280 copies printed April 1864. Price, $1.25. Royalty, 25¢. *Location:* MH.

A 26.1.h
Boston: Ticknor and Fields, M DCCC LXV.

1,000 copies printed December 1864–January 1865. Price, $1.50. Royalty, 30¢. *Location:* JM.

A 26.1.i
Boston: Ticknor and Fields, M DCCC LXVI.

280 copies printed April–May 1866. Price, $1.50. Royalty, 30¢. *Location:* JM.

A 26.1.j
Boston: Ticknor and Fields, M DCCC LXVII.

280 copies printed April–May 1867. Price, $1.50. Royalty, 30¢. *Location:* JM.

A 26.1.k
Boston: Ticknor and Fields, M DCCC LXVIII.

280 copies printed December 1867–March 1868 and March–May 1868. Price, $2.00. Royalty, 20¢. *Location:* JM.

Note one: By a contract of 4 March 1868, Emerson's royalty was changed from 20% to 20¢ per volume.

Note two: Ticknor and Fields was succeeded by Fields, Osgood in October 1868.

A 26.1.l
Boston: Fields, Osgood, 1869.

280 copies printed February 1869 (Account Books [MH]). Price, $2.00. Royalty, 20¢. *Location:* JM.

Note: Fields, Osgood was succeeded by James R. Osgood & Company in January 1871.

A 26.1.m

Boston: James R. Osgood, 1871.

280 copies printed March 1871 (Account Books [MH]). Price, $2.00. Royalty, 30¢. *Location:* Nv.

Note one: In a "Supplementary article of agreement" to the 4 March 1868 contract, dated 19 February 1870, Emerson's royalty was raised to 30¢ per copy when the price was $2.00 or above.

Note two: Copies have been noted with James R. Osgood sheets in Fields, Osgood bindings.

A 26.1.n

Boston: James R. Osgood, 1873.

280 copies printed 16 December 1872. Price, $2.00. Royalty, 30¢. *Location:* MH-AH.

A 26.1.o

Boston: James R. Osgood, 1875.

150 copies printed October–November 1874. Price, $2.00. Royalty, 30¢. *Location:* VtVe.

A 26.1.p

Boston: James R. Osgood, 1876.

150 copies printed 6 December 1875. Price, $2.00. *Location:* JM.

Note: Emerson's 1 January 1876 contract with Osgood called for him to receive a flat annual fee of $1,500 for all his books, rather than a per copy royalty.

A 26.1.q

Boston: James R. Osgood, 1877.

150 copies printed January 1877. Price, $1.50. *Location:* MWiW-C.

Note: James R. Osgood was succeeded by Houghton, Osgood in February 1878.

A 26.1.r

Boston: Houghton, Osgood, 1879.

140 copies printed 2 April 1879. Price, $1.50. *Not seen.*

Note: Houghton, Osgood was succeeded by Houghton, Mifflin in May 1880.

A 26.1.s

Boston: Houghton, Mifflin, 1881.

150 copies printed 7 December 1880. Price, $1.50. *Location:* MH.

A 26.1.t

Boston: Houghton, Mifflin, 1882.

150 copies printed 18 May 1882. Price, $1.50. *Not seen.*

A 26.1.u

Boston: Houghton, Mifflin, 1883.

150 copies printed 23 November 1882. *Not seen.*

Note: As of 15 January 1884, 10 copies of *The Conduct of Life* were still in stock.

A 26.2
Presumed first English edition, only printing (1860)

THE

CONDUCT OF LIFE.

BY

RALPH WALDO EMERSON,

AUTHOR OF " REPRESENTATIVE MEN," " TRAITS OF ENGLISH LIFE,"
ETC. ETC.

AUTHOR'S EDITION.

LONDON:
SMITH, ELDER AND CO., 65, CORNHILL.

M.DCCC.LX.

A 26.2: 7¹³/₁₆″ × 5″

[i–iv] [1–3] 4–43 [44–47] 48–72 [73] 74 [75] 76–111 [112–115] 116–145 [146–150] 151–173 [174–176] 177–212 [213] 214–244 [245–247] 248–269 [270–271] 272 [273] 274–287 [288]

[a]^2 1–18^8

Contents: p. i: title page; p. ii: blank; p. iii: contents; p. iv: blank; pp. 1–287: the same as in the first American edition; p. 288: printer's imprint.

Typography and paper: 5^5/$_8$″ (5^3/$_8$″) × 3^3/$_{16}$″; wove paper; 29 lines per page. Running heads: rectos: pp. 5–43, 49–71, 77–111, 117–145, 151–173, 179–211, 217–243, 249–269, 275–287: chapter titles; versos: pp. 4–42, 48–110, 116–144, 150–172, 178–244, 248–268, 272–286: 'CONDUCT OF LIFE.'.

Binding: Purple-blue coarse TR cloth (wavy). Front and back covers: blindstamped ornamental frame of stylized flowers; spine: goldstamped '[band] | [next five lines within an ornate design, each word within a box, and each word in raised letters in purple-blue cloth] THE | CONDUCT | OF | LIFE | R. W. EMERSON | LONDON | SMITH, ELDER & CO. | [band]'. Yellow coated endpapers. All edges trimmed.

Publication: In an advertisement dated 30 August 1860, Smith, Elder announced that they will "publish, contemporaneously with the publication in America, an Edition, in which the Author is interested, of the forthcoming Work, entitled, 'ON THE CONDUCT OF LIFE'" (*Athenæum,* no. 1714 [1 September 1860], 300). Advertised as "In the press," in *Athenæum,* no. 1719 (6 October 1860), 464; in *Publishers' Circular and Booksellers' Record,* 24 (16 October 1860), 511, and 24 (15 November 1860), 581; as to be published "On the 8th," in *Athenæum,* no. 1727 (1 December 1860), 768. Listed in *Athenæum,* no. 1728 (8 December 1860), 790; as published between 1 and 14 December, in *Publishers' Circular and Booksellers' Record,* 24 (15 December 1860), 732. Deposit copy: BL (rebound, 5 January 1861). Price, 6s.

Printing: "LONDON: | PRINTED BY SMITH, ELDER AND CO., | LITTLE GREEN ARBOUR COURT, OLD BAILEY, E.C." (p. [288]).

Locations: BC, BO, CSt, CtY, JM, MWA, NNC, VtMiM.

Note one: All copies have a 16-page catalogue of Smith, Elder's publications, dated December 1860, inserted at the back.

Note two: Inserted opposite the title page is a slip, printed on the verso, stating that Emerson receives "a pecuniary benefit from this Edition" (see illustration).

Note three: Emerson received $462.22 on 10 January 1861 for an "early copy" (probably advance proof sheets) of *The Conduct of Life* (Account Books [MH]).

*** *The Publishers think it right to state that the Author derives a pecuniary benefit from this Edition.*

Inserted slip for A 26.2

A 26.3.a
Presumed second English edition, first printing (1860)

Author's Edition.

THE

CONDUCT OF LIFE.

BY

RALPH WALDO EMERSON,

AUTHOR OF " REPRESENTATIVE MEN," "TRAITS OF ENGLISH LIFE,"
ETC. ETC.

LONDON:

SMITH, ELDER AND CO., 65, CORNHILL.

M.DCCC.LX.

A 26.3.a: $6^{13}/_{16}$" × $4^{1}/_{4}$"

[i–iv] [1] 2–4 [5] 6–203 [204]

[a² 1–6¹⁶ 7⁶]   Signed [a]² 1–12⁸ 13⁶

Contents: p. i: title page; p. ii: blank; p. iii: contents; p. iv: blank; pp. 1–203: the same as in the first American edition; p. 204: printer's imprint.

Typography and paper: 5³/₄″ (5¹/₂″) × 3³/₁₆″; wove paper; 38 lines per page. Running heads: rectos: pp. 2–203: chapter titles; versos: pp. 2–202: 'CONDUCT OF LIFE.'.

Binding: Light brown B cloth (linen). Front cover: all within a double-rule frame surrounding a single-rule frame with a bow in each corner, except the last line, which is between the two frames: 'AUTHOR'S EDITION. | [rule] | THE | CONDUCT OF LIFE. | BY | RALPH WALDO EMERSON, | AUTHOR OF "REPRESENTATIVE MEN," "TRAITS OF ENGLISH LIFE," | "ESSAYS," ETC. ETC. | LONDON: | SMITH, ELDER, AND CO., 65, CORNHILL. | [rule] | 1861. | PRICE ONE SHILLING.'; back cover: same frames as on the front cover enclosing a 20-line advertisement for the *Cornhill Magazine;* spine: '[rule] | THE | CONDUCT | OF | LIFE. | [rule] | [star-like design] | [rule] | BY R.W. | EMERSON. | [rule] | [star-like design] | [rule] | AUTHOR'S | EDITION. | [rule]'. Yellow endpapers imprinted with publisher's advertisements.

Publication: Advertised simultaneously with the first English edition; see publication information for A 26.2. Price, 1s.

Printing: The same printer's imprint as in A 26.2.

Locations: JM, MBAt, MCo, MH.

Note one: Page 5 is unnumbered, even though it contains text.

Note two: Inserted opposite the title page is a slip, printed on the verso, stating that Emerson receives "a pecuniary benefit from this Edition" (see the illustration at A 26.2).

A 26.3.b
Second English edition, second printing (1861)

The title page is the same as in the first printing, except it has '*SECOND EDITION.*' and '1861.' All else is the same is in the first printing, except: the author's slip is not present; p. 5 is numbered; the printer's imprint on p. 204 is in large and small capitals; the binding is cream-colored linen; yellow unprinted endpapers.

Publication: Listed as published between 15 and 31 December, in *Publishers' Circular and Booksellers' Record,* 24 (31 December 1861), 764. Price, 1s.

Location: VtU.

OTHER EDITIONS

A 26.4
Third English edition, only printing (1861)

London: Routledge, Warne, and Routledge, 1861.

189 pp. Listed as published between 1 and 14 January, in *Publishers' Circular and Booksellers' Record,* 25 (15 January 1861), 6. Price, 1s. *Locations:* BE, BL (8 February 1861), MNtS.

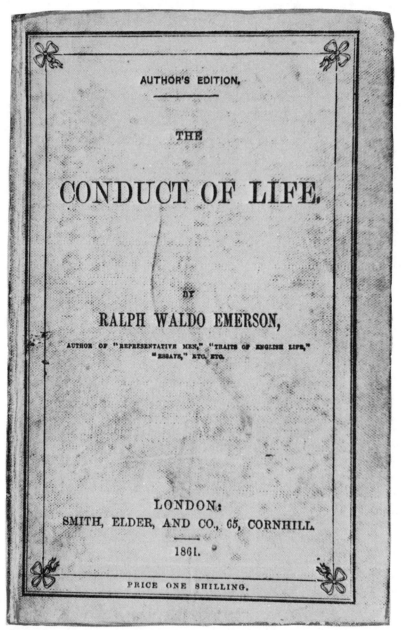

AUTHOR'S EDITION.

THE

CONDUCT OF LIFE.

BY

RALPH WALDO EMERSON,

AUTHOR OF "REPRESENTATIVE MEN," "TRAITS OF ENGLISH LIFE,"
"ESSAYS," ETC. ETC.

LONDON:
SMITH, ELDER, AND CO., 65, CORNHILL.

1861.

PRICE ONE SHILLING.

Binding for A 26.3.a

A 26.5
First German edition, only printing (1862)

[all gothic except date] Die | Führung des Lebens. | Gedanken and Studien | von | Ralph Waldo Emerson. | [rule] | Ins Deutsche übertragen | von | E. S. v. Mühlberg. | [rule] | Autorisirte Ausgabe. | [ornamental rule] | Leipzig: | F. J. Steinnacher. | 1862.

227 pp. *Locations:* CaOWtL, LNHT.

A 26.6
First French edition, only printing [1864?]

R. W. EMERSON | [rule] | LES | LOIS DE LA VIE | TRADUIT DE L'ANGLAIS | PAR | XAVIER EYMA | [rule] | PARIS | LIBRAIRE INTERNATIONALE | 13, RUE DE GRAM-MONT, 13 | A. LACROIX, VERBOECKHOVEN ET Cie, ÉDITEURS | A. BRUXELLES, A LIVOURNE ET A LEIPZIG | [rule] | Droits de reproduction réservés

395 pp. Wrappers. *Location:* MiU.

PRINTINGS FROM THE "LITTLE CLASSIC EDITION" PLATES

A 26.7.a

[all within a double-rule frame; outer frame is red with boxed corners] [red] THE CONDUCT OF LIFE. | BY | RALPH WALDO EMERSON. | [ornate rule] | [red] BOSTON: | JAMES R. OSGOOD AND COMPANY, | Late Ticknor & Fields, and Fields, Osgood, & Co. | [red] 1876.

256 pp. Vol. [VI] of the "Little Classic Edition" (see B 3). 2,000 copies printed 27 April 1876. Listed in *Publishers' Weekly*, 8 (27 May 1876), 700. Price, $1.50. Royalty: see *Note* to A 26.1.p. *Locations:* BL (12 April 1877), MBAt.

A 26.7.b
Boston: James R. Osgood, 1878.

280 copies printed 7 December 1877 and 18 December 1877. Price, $1.50. *Not seen.*

Note: James R. Osgood was succeeded by Houghton, Osgood in February 1878.

A 26.7.c
Boston: Houghton, Osgood, 1879.

510 copies printed 23 May 1879; 280 copies on 12 August 1879. Price, $1.50. *Location:* NcU.

A 26.7.d
Boston: Houghton, Osgood, 1879.

Combined with *English Traits* in two-volumes-in-one format as vol. III of the "Fireside Edition" (see B 4). *Location:* JM.

A 26.7.e
Boston: Houghton, Osgood, 1880.

Combined with *English Traits* in two-volumes-in-one format as vol. III of the "Fireside Edition" (see B 4). 500 copies printed 6 February 1880. *Location:* JM.

Note: Houghton, Osgood was succeeded by Houghton, Mifflin, in May 1880.

A 26.7.f
Boston: Houghton, Mifflin, 1880.

500 copies printed 3 June 1880. Price, $1.50. *Location.* MAsh.

A 26.7.g
Boston: Houghton, Mifflin, 1881.

Combined with *English Traits* in two-volumes-in-one format as vol. III of the "Fireside Edition" (see B 4). 500 copies printed 7 December 1880 and 19 October 1881. *Location:* MWelC.

A 26.7.h
Boston: Houghton, Mifflin, 1881.

500 copies printed 18 February 1881. Price, $1.50. *Not seen.*

A 26.7.i
Boston: Houghton, Mifflin, 1882.

Combined with *English Traits* in two-volumes-in-one format as vol. III of the "Fireside Edition" (see B 4). 500 copies printed 12 May 1882 and 8 August 1882. *Location:* JM.

A 26.7.j
Boston: Houghton, Mifflin, 1882.

500 copies printed 14 January 1882 and 17 May 1882; 1,000 copies on 19 September 1882. Price, $1.50. *Location:* MBAt.

A 26.7.k
Boston: Houghton, Mifflin, 1883.

Combined with *English Traits* in two-volumes-in-one format as vol. III of the "Fireside Edition" (see B 4). 270 copies printed 10 January 1883. *Location:* JM.

A 26.7.l
Boston: Houghton, Mifflin, 1883.

500 copies printed 20 July 1883. *Location:* JM.

A 26.7.m
Boston: Houghton, Mifflin, 1884.

270 copies printed 21 February 1884; 500 copies on 25 September 1884. *Location:* JM.

A 26.7.n
Boston: Houghton, Mifflin, 1886.

270 copies printed 5 June 1886. *Not seen.*

A 26.7.o
Boston: Houghton, Mifflin, 1887.

270 copies printed 10 January 1887; 500 copies on 24 October 1887. Bound in medium blue V cloth (smooth), rather than "Little Classic Edition" binding, as are subsequent reprintings (see illustration at B 3). *Location:* JM.

A 26.7.p
Boston and New York: Houghton, Mifflin, 1888.

270 copies printed 17 April 1888 and 17 November 1888. *Location:* NmU.

Note: The copyright on *The Conduct of Life* was renewed 27 June 1888.

A 26.7.q
Boston and New York: Houghton, Mifflin, 1889.

250 copies printed ca. March 1889; 270 copies on 26 July 1889. *Not seen.*

A 26.7.r
Boston and New York: Houghton, Mifflin, 1890.

500 copies printed ca. December 1889. *Location:* JM.

A 26.7.s
Boston and New York: Houghton, Mifflin, 1891.

500 copies printed 30 November 1890 and ca. June 1891. *Not seen.*

A 26.7.t
Boston and New York: Houghton, Mifflin, 1892.

500 copies printed 2 January 1892 and 28 September 1892. *Location:* JM.

A 26.7.u
Boston and New York: Houghton, Mifflin, 1893.

500 copies printed 26 September 1893. *Location:* JM.

A 26.7.v
Boston and New York: Houghton, Mifflin, 1894.

500 copies printed 16 August 1894. *Location:* MH.

A 26.7.w
Boston and New York: Houghton, Mifflin, 1895.

500 copies printed 22 October 1895. *Location:* MoU.

A 26.7.x
Boston and New York: Houghton, Mifflin, 1897.

270 copies printed 10 May 1897. *Not seen.*

A 26.7.y
Boston and New York: Houghton, Mifflin, 1898.

270 copies printed 12 April 1898 and 29 April 1898. *Location:* NbCrD.

A 26.7.z
Boston and New York: Houghton, Mifflin, 1899.

270 copies printed 27 October 1899. *Not seen.*

A 26.7.aa
Boston and New York: Houghton, Mifflin, [n.d.].

Approximately 2,400 copies sold between 1900 and 1923. *Location:* NNS.

Note one: Approximately 17,000 copies of *The Conduct of Life* printed from the "Little Classic Edition" plates were sold between 1876 and 1923, when the title was apparently allowed to go out of print in this format.

Note two: The "Little Classic Edition" plates were ordered destroyed 14 October 1929.

LATER EDITIONS

A 26.8
London: George Bell and Sons, 1883.

141 pp. Wrappers. *Bohn's Cheap Series of Standard Works.* Listed as published between 16 and 30 April 1883, in *Publishers' Circular and Booksellers' Record,* 46 (1 May 1883), 382. Price, 1s. *Location:* BL (31 August 1883).

A 26.9.a–h
The Conduct of Life and Society and Solitude. London: Macmillan, 1883.

520 pp. Vol. V of the *Works* (see B 6). Listed as published between 1 and 15 June 1883, in *Publishers' Circular and Booksellers' Record,* 46 (15 June 1883), 528; in *Athenæum,* no. 2903 (16 June 1883), 762; in *Bookseller,* no. 308 (5 July 1883), 673. Price, 5s. Reprinted (usually with dual New York imprint) 1884, 1888, 1892, 1896, 1900, 1905, 1910. *Locations:* BL (26 June 1883), CaBViV.

A 26.9.i
The Conduct of Life. London and New York: Macmillan, [ca. 1889].

Cloth or wrappers. Advertised as included in "Macmillan's Colonial Library," no. 9. Intended for circulation only in India and the British colonies. *Not seen.*

Note: Probably printed from the plates of A 26.9.a.

PRINTINGS FROM THE RIVERSIDE EDITION PLATES

A 26.10.a
Riverside Edition (trade), first printing (1883)

THE | CONDUCT OF LIFE | BY | RALPH WALDO EMERSON | [gothic] New and Revised Edition | [publisher's logo] | BOSTON | HOUGHTON, MIFFLIN AND COMPANY | New York: 11 East Seventeenth Street | [gothic] The Riverside Press, Cambridge | 1883

308 pp. Vol. VI of the *Riverside Edition,* trade printing (see B 7). 1,000 copies printed 16 August 1883; 500 copies on 16 October 1883. Listed in *Publishers' Weekly,* 24 (27 October 1883), 574. According to the publisher's records, published 6 October 1883. Copyright, 15 October 1883. Price, $1.75. *Locations:* DLC (13 October 1883), JM.

Note: Copies have been noted with a pine branch on the title page instead of the publisher's logo.

A 26.10.b
Riverside Edition (Copyright), second (English) printing (1883)

THE | CONDUCT OF LIFE | BY | RALPH WALDO EMERSON | [gothic] The Riverside

Edition | (COPYRIGHT) | LONDON | GEORGE ROUTLEDGE AND SONS | BROADWAY, LUDGATE HILL | NEW YORK: 9, LAFAYETTE PLACE | 1883

Vol. VI of the *Riverside Edition (Copyright),* English trade printing (see B 10). 1,000 copies printed 18 September 1883. Listed as published between 1 and 15 October 1883, in *Publishers' Circular and Booksellers' Record,* 46 (15 October 1883), 1000. Price, 3s. 6d. *Locations:* BC (12 October 1883), BO (20 October 1883), BL (8 December 1883), CaBVaU.

A 26.10.c$_1$
Riverside Edition (large paper), third printing, American issue (1883)

THE | [red] CONDUCT OF LIFE | BY | RALPH WALDO EMERSON | [gothic] New and Revised Edition | [pine branch] | [red] CAMBRIDGE | [gothic] Printed at the Riverside Press | 1883

Vol. VI of the *Riverside Edition,* large paper printing (see B 8). Limited to 500 numbered copies printed 30 November 1883. Price, $4.00. Sold out within a year. *Locations:* JM, TxU.

A 26.10.c$_2$
Riverside Edition (large paper), third printing, English issue (1883)

Title page is the same as in the American issue, except for publisher's imprint: 'LONDON | KEGAN PAUL, TRENCH, & CO., I, PATERNOSTER SQUARE | MDCCCLXXXIII'.

Vol. VI of the *Riverside Edition,* large paper printing for English subscribers (see B 9). 25 title leaves printed 30 November 1883. Title leaf is a cancel. Limited to 25 signed and numbered copies. *Location:* JM.

A 26.10.d
Boston and New York: Houghton, Mifflin, 1884.

500 copies printed 26 December 1883, 30 April 1884, and 1 October 1884; 270 copies on 5 March 1884. *Location:* JM.

A 26.10.e
Boston and New York: Houghton, Mifflin, 1885.

500 copies printed 13 February 1885 and 23 July 1885. *Location:* JM.

A 26.10.f
Boston and New York: Houghton, Mifflin, 1886.

500 copies printed 16 December 1885 and 26 April 1886. *Location:* NNF.

A 26.10.g
London and New York: George Routledge and Sons, 1886.

500 copies printed 1 January 1886. *Location:* JM.

A 26.10.h
Boston and New York: Houghton, Mifflin, 1887.

500 copies printed 26 November 1886, 12 March 1887, and ca. September 1887. *Location:* JM.

A 26.10.i
Boston and New York: Houghton, Mifflin, 1888.

500 copies printed 1 December 1887, 25 April 1888, and ca. September 1888. *Location:* DLC (16 July 1888).

Note: The copyright on *The Conduct of Life* was renewed 25 June 1888.

A 26.10.j
Boston and New York: Houghton, Mifflin, 1889.

270 copies printed 27 February 1889; 500 copies on 30 March 1889. *Location:* MB.

A 26.10.k
Boston and New York: Houghton, Mifflin, 1890.

500 copies printed 30 January 1890 and ca. September 1890. *Not seen.*

A 26.10.l
Boston and New York: Houghton, Mifflin, 1891.

500 copies printed ca. March 1891 and 5 October 1891. *Location:* JM.

A 26.10.m
Boston and New York: Houghton, Mifflin, 1892.

500 copies printed 5 May 1892. *Location:* JM.

A 26.10.n
Boston and New York: Houghton, Mifflin, 1893.

500 copies printed 23 November 1892 and 30 August 1893. *Location:* RNR.

A 26.10.o
Boston and New York: Houghton, Mifflin, 1894.

500 copies printed 11 September 1894. *Location:* JM.

A 26.10.p
Standard Library Edition printing [1894]

THE | CONDUCT OF LIFE | BY | RALPH WALDO EMERSON | [pine branch] | BOSTON AND NEW YORK | HOUGHTON, MIFFLIN AND COMPANY | [gothic] The Riverside Press, Cambridge

Vol. VI of the *Standard Library Edition* (see B 11). 1,000 copies printed 31 October 1894, 30 April 1895, and 29 May 1896; 500 copies on 31 January 1898. *Location:* JM.

A 26.10.q
Boston and New York: Houghton, Mifflin, 1895.

500 copies printed 4 September 1895. *Location:* DeU.

A 26.10.r
Boston and New York: Houghton, Mifflin, 1896.

500 copies printed 22 September 1896. *Location:* MH.

A 26.10.s
Boston and New York: Houghton, Mifflin, 1898.

500 copies printed 1 January 1898. *Location:* JM.

A 26.10.t
Boston and New York: Houghton, Mifflin, 1899.

270 copies printed 27 April 1899; 500 copies on 31 October 1899. *Location:* JM.

A 26.10.u
London: George Routledge and Sons, 1902.

Location: CaQMM.

A 26.10.v
London: George Routledge & Sons, 1903.

Combined with *Representative Men* and *English Traits* in three-volumes-in-one format as vol. II of the "Sovereign Edition" (see B 12). 1,000 copies printed 16 September 1903. *Location:* InU.

A 26.10.w
Fireside Edition printing (1909)

[all within red double-rule frame with red floral ornaments in each corner] THE WORKS OF | [red gothic] Ralph Waldo Emerson | THE CONDUCT OF LIFE | [engraving of man reading book in chair before fireplace] | [gothic] Fireside Edition | BOSTON AND NEW YORK | MDCCCCIX

Vol. VI of the *Fireside Edition* (see B 13). 500 copies printed 29 September 1909 and 15 February 1910. *Location:* JM.

A 26.10.x
Boston and New York: Jefferson Press, [ca. 1912].

Combined with *English Traits* in two-volumes-in-one format as vol. III of the "Jefferson Press Edition" (see B 14). *Not seen.*

A 26.10.y
New York: Sully and Kleinteich, [ca. 1912].

Vol. VI of the *University Edition* (see B 15). *Location:* JM.

A 26.10.z
Boston and New York: Houghton, Mifflin, [n.d.].

Approximately 2,300 copies sold between 1900 and 1913. *Location:* JM.

Note: Approximately 17,000 copies of *The Conduct of Life* in the *Riverside Edition* were sold between 1883 and 1913, when the title was apparently allowed to go out of print in this format.

A 26.10.aa
London: George Routledge and Sons, [n.d.].

Location: JM.

A 26.10.bb
London: Waverley Book Company, [n.d.].

Vol. VI of the "Waverley" *Riverside Edition* (see B 16). *Location:* JM.

LATER EDITIONS

A 26.11.a
New York: A. L. Burt, [1903].

319 pp. *The Home Library.* Also advertised as included in the "Cornell Series." Listed in *Publishers' Weekly,* 63 (16 May 1903), 1158. Published 16 May 1903. Price, $1.00. *Location:* JM.

A 26.11.b
The Conduct of Life   Nature, Addresses and Lectures. New York: P. F. Collier & Son, MCMIII.

See A 21.10.

A 26.11.c
Philadelphia: John D. Morris, [1906].

Vol. IV of the "John D. Morris Edition" (see B 29). *Locations:* DLC (13 February 1906), JM.

A 26.11.d
Boston and New York: C. T. Brainard, [n.d.].

Vol. VI of the *Works* (see B 30). *Location:* JM.

A 26.11.e
New York: Caxton Society, [n.d.].

Vol. VI of the *Works* (see B 31). *Location:* NjR.

A 26.11.f
New York: Hurst, [n.d.].

Also advertised as included in "Gilt Top Library" and "Laurelhurst" series. *Location:* Sd.

A 26.11.g
Rahway, N.J., and New York: Mershon, [n.d.].

Location: JM.

A 26.11.h
New York: National Library Co., [n.d.].

Vol. VI of the *Works* (see B 32). *Location:* CaOHM.

A 26.11.i
Philadelphia, New York, Chicago: Nottingham Society, [n.d.].

Vol. VI of the *Works* (see B 33). *Location:* JM.

A 26.12

New York: Thomas Y. Crowell, [1903].

260 pp. Introduction by Andrew J. George. Also advertised as included in "Astor Library," "Handy Volume Classics," and "Handy Volume Classics, Pocket Edition." Listed in *Publishers' Weekly,* 64 (19 September 1903), 444. Published September 1903. Price, 35¢. *Locations:* DLC (9 July 1903), JM.

A 26.13

London: George Bell and Sons, 1903.

231 pp. *Light and Life Books.* Published November 1903. Price, 1s. *Locations:* BC (6 May 1904), BE (6 May 1904).

Note: Advertised as included in "Light and Life Books" at 35¢ by Macmillan of New York in *Cumulative Book Index.* Probably an importation or, possibly, an American issue of the English sheets with a cancel title leaf. *Not seen.*

A 26.14

New York: Scott-Thaw, 1903.

287 pp. Printed in England by the Chiswick Press. Limited to 350 copies. *Location:* JM.

PRINTINGS FROM THE CENTENARY EDITION PLATES

A 26.15.a

Autograph Centenary Edition (large paper), first printing (1904)

RALPH WALDO EMERSON | [red] The Conduct of Life | [pine tree] | CAMBRIDGE | [red gothic] Printed at the Riverside Press | 1904

435 pp. Vol. VI of the *Autograph Centenary Edition* (see B 19). Limited to 600 signed and numbered copies printed 29 January 1904. Copyright, 1 February 1904. Price, $6.00. Sold out by 5 April 1906. *Locations:* DLC (15 February 1904), JM.

A 26.15.b₁

Centenary Edition (trade), second printing, American issue (1904)

THE CONDUCT OF LIFE | BY | RALPH WALDO EMERSON | [pine tree] | BOSTON AND NEW YORK | HOUGHTON, MIFFLIN AND COMPANY | [gothic] The Riverside Press, Cambridge | 1904

Dust jacket. Vol. VI of the *Centenary Edition,* trade printing (see B 18). 1,000 copies printed 30 January 1904. Listed in *Publishers' Weekly,* 65 (5 May 1904), 715. According to the publisher's records, published 27 February 1904. Copyright, 1 February 1904. Price, $1.75. *Location:* JM.

Note: Numerous reprintings with undated title pages. 3,000 copies printed between 25 November 1904 and 31 March 1910. Approximately 5,500 copies sold through 1923.

A 26.15.b₂

English issue

London: A. P. Watt and Son, [1904.].

Vol. VI of the English *Centenary Edition* (see B 21). American sheets with Watt's label pasted on the title page. Price, 6s. *Locations:* BL (27 February 1904), BC (11 March 1904), BE (11 March 1904).

A 26.15.c
Boston and New York: Houghton, Mifflin, 1904.

Vol. VI of the *Concord Edition* (see B 20). 1,000 copies printed 29 February 1904 and 21 July 1904. *Location:* JM.

Note: Numerous reprintings with undated title pages. Approximately 3,000 copies sold by 31 March 1907.

A 26.15.d
Boston and New York: Houghton Mifflin, [1914].

Vol. VI of the *Riverside Pocket Edition* (see B 22). Approximately 1,400 copies sold between 1914 and 1922. *Not seen.*

A 26.15.e
Boston and New York: Houghton Mifflin, 1921.

325 pp. (text without the notes). Combined with *Natural History of Intellect* in two-volumes-in-one format as vol. V of *Emerson's Complete Works* (see B 23). *Location:* JM.

A 26.15.f
New York: Wm. H. Wise, 1923.

Combined with *English Traits* in two-volumes-in-one format as vol. III of the *Current Opinion Edition* (see B 24). *Location:* JM.

A 26.15.g
Boston and New York: Houghton Mifflin, [1927].

Vol. VI of the *Centenary Edition,* trade printing (see B 18). Title leaf verso has 'TWELFTH IMPRESSION, AUGUST, 1927'. *Location:* MB.

A 26.15.h
Boston and New York: Houghton Mifflin, 1929.

Combined (text without the notes) with *Natural History of Intellect* in two-volumes-in-one format as vol. V of the *Harvard Edition* (see B 25). *Location:* JM.

A 26.15.i
New York: Wm. H. Wise, 1929.

Combined with *English Traits* in two-volumes-in-one format as vol. III of the *Medallion Edition* (see B 26). *Location:* OC.

A 26.15.j
Boston and New York: Houghton Mifflin, [1931].

Vol. VI of the *Centenary Edition,* trade printing (see B 18). Title leaf verso has 'THIRTEENTH IMPRESSION, FEBRUARY, 1931'. *Location:* TMM.

A 26.15.k–l
New York: AMS Press, [1968].

Vol. VI of the "AMS Press" *Centenary Edition* (see B 27). Reprinted 1979. *Locations:* TxU, DLC (9 November 1979).

LATER EDITIONS

A 26.16
Edinburgh: Otto Schulze, [1904].

366 pp. Cloth or leather. *The Lighthouse Library of Great Thinkers*. Published November 1904. Also 42 copies printed on Japan vellum. Prices: cloth, 16s.; leather, 25s. *Locations:* BE (2 June 1906), BL (2 June 1906), JM, NN (vellum).

A 26.17
The Conduct of Life and Society and Solitude. London: George Routledge & Sons; New York: E. P. Dutton, [1906].

400 pp. *The New Universal Library*, vol. 3 (also identified as vol. II of the *Works*). Published July 1906. *Locations:* BL (15 November 1906), JM.

A 26.18.a
London: George G. Harrap, [1911].

241 pp. *The Harrap Library*, no. 13. *Location:* BL (16 August 1911).

A 26.18.b
New York: Robert M. McBride, [n.d.].

Chelsea College Classics. Location: NFQC.

A 26.19
Leipzig: Bernhard Tauchnitz, 1918.

280 pp. Wrappers. *Tauchnitz Edition, Collection of British and American Authors*, vol. 4525. *Location:* Collection of William B. Todd.

A 26.20
Washington, D.C.: National Home Library Foundation, 1935.

205 pp. *National Home Library Edition*, no. 8. Price, 25¢. *Location:* JM.

A 26.21.a
Garden City, N.Y.: Doubleday & Company, [1960].

200 pp. Wrappers. *Dolphin Books*, C2. Price, 95¢. *Location:* MtU.

Note: Listed as an importation for 27 September 1960 at 8s. by Mayflower in the *English Catalogue. Not seen.*

A 26.21.b
Garden City, N.Y.: The Masterworks Program, [n.d.].

Location: NNC.

UNDATED EDITIONS

A 26.22
New York: Dodge, [n.d.].

Advertised as included in the "Dodge Library." Price, $1.50. *Not seen.*

A 26.23
Philadelphia: David McKay, [n.d.].

346 pp. Also advertised as included in "American Classics Series." Also advertised as combined with *English Traits* in two-volumes-in-one format. *Location:* JM.

SEPARATE PUBLICATIONS OF INDIVIDUAL ESSAYS

A 26.24
Emerson's Essay on Beauty   A Class Study in English Composition. Shaldon, South Devon [England]: E. E. Speight, The Norland Press; London: Simpkin, Marshall, [1901].

87 pp. Wrappers. Edited by Susan Cunnington. *Locations:* BL (3 February 1902), BE (7 February 1902), BC (10 February 1902).

A 26.25
Culture. New York: Barse & Hopkins, [1910].

30 pp. *The Golden Books*. Also advertised as included in "Ardsley," "Greylock," "Rockingham," "Savoy," and "Shelburne" series. *Location:* JM.

A 26.26
Culture. New York: Thomas Y. Crowell, [n.d.].

41 pp. *Verona Edition*. Also advertised as included in "Hollywood," "Laurel," and "San Rafael" series. *Location:* JM.

A 26.27
Essays on Beauty and Worship. Girard, Kansas: Haldeman-Julius, [n.d.].

62 pp. Wrappers. *Little Blue Book*, no. 551. *Location:* KU.

A 26.28
Culture and Behavior. Tokyo: Tokio Daigaku, 1882.

76 pp. *Not seen*.

A 26.29.a–e
Culture, Behavior, Beauty. Boston: James R. Osgood, 1875.

108 pp. *Vest-Pocket Series*, no. 4. 3,000 copies printed 26 October 1875. Advertised in *Boston Daily Advertiser*, 18 December 1875, p. 2; in *Publishers' Weekly*, 8 (25 December 1875), 948. Price, 50¢. Reprinted 1876 (James R. Osgood; 2,000 copies printed 5 December 1875), 1877 (James R. Osgood; 1,000 copies printed March–April 1877), 1879 (Houghton, Osgood), 1880 (Houghton, Osgood). *Locations:* JM (1875, 1876, 1877), MWA (1879), NNC (1880).

A 26.30
Culture and Character. London and Edinburgh: T. N. Foulis, [1910].

111 pp. Limp suede. Also contains "Compensation." *The Holyrood Books*, no. 9. Printed September 1910. *Location:* BL (5 November 1910).

A 26.31
Culture: And "Education by Nature, Books, and Action." London: Arthur C. Fifield, Simple Life Press, 1904.

38 pp. Cloth or wrappers. *The Simple Life Series,* no. 13. The second selection is from "The American Scholar." Published July 1904. Prices: cloth, 6d; wrappers, 3d. *Location:* BL (30 November 1904).

A 26.32
Essays on Fate and Illusions. Girard, Kansas: Haldeman-Julius, [n.d.].

59 pp. Wrappers. *Little Blue Book,* no. 552. *Location:* KU.

A 26.33
Essays on Power and Behavior. Girard, Kansas: Haldeman-Julius, [n.d.].

64 pp. Wrappers. *Little Blue Book,* no. 542. *Location:* JM.

A 26.34
Power and Wealth. London: L. N. Fowler; Holyoke, Mass.: Elizabeth Towne, 1918.

123 pp. Miniature book. *Little Sun-Books. Location:* NNUT.

A 26.35
Power, Wealth, Books. Boston: Houghton, Mifflin, 1881.

85 + 39 pp. Wrappers. *Location:* ViU.

Note: From the plates of A 26.36 and A 31.15.

A 26.36.a–c
Power, Wealth, Illusions. Boston: James R. Osgood, 1875.

107 pp. *Vest-Pocket Series,* no. 3. 3,000 copies printed 26 October 1875. Advertised in *Boston Daily Adveriser,* 18 December 1875, p. 2; in *Publishers' Weekly,* 8 (25 December 1875), 948. Price, 50¢. Reprinted 1876 (2,000 copies printed 13 December 1875), 1877. *Locations:* JM (all).

A 26.37
Essays on Wealth and Culture. Girard, Kansas: Haldeman-Julius, [n.d.].

64 pp. Wrappers. *Little Blue Book,* no. 553. *Location:* JM.

A 27 ADDITIONAL TESTIMONIAL IN FAVOUR OF JAMES HUTCHISON STIRLING

A 27
First edition, only printing [1866?]

ADDITIONAL TESTIMONIAL

IN FAVOUR OF

JAMES HUTCHISON STIRLING,

CANDIDATE FOR THE CHAIR OF MORAL PHILOSOPHY IN THE
UNIVERSITY OF GLASGOW.

From RALPH WALDO EMERSON, Esq.

CONCORD, MASSACHUSETTS, *8th May* 1866.

I HAVE learned that the Chair of Moral Philosophy in the University of Glasgow is vacant, and that James Hutchison Stirling, Esq., is a candidate. I have not the advantage of any personal acquaintance with Mr. Stirling, nor any knowledge of him, except through his book, 'The Secret of Hegel'; nor am I much a reader of metaphysical works. But I have never seen any modern British book which appears to me to show such competence to analyse the most abstruse problems of the Science, and, much more, such singular vigour and breadth of view in treating the matter in relation to literature and humanity. It exhibits a general power of dealing with the subject, which, I think, must compel the attention of readers in proportion to their strength and subtlety. One of the high merits of the book is its healthy moral perceptions. I have had the pleasure of introducing the work to the atten

A 27: 8⁵/₈″ × 5⁷/₁₆″; page 1

2

tion of some experts in the science here- whence I look for good results in their own minds and in those of their students. If the Electors in the University of Glasgow can secure the services of such a teacher as Mr. Stirling, I believe they will be most fortunate in their choice. If there can be any question, when such an incumbent can be found, I shall be glad to believe that Intellectual and Moral Science is richer in masters than I have had opportunity to know.

R. W. EMERSON.

A 27: 8⁵⁄₈″ × 5⁷⁄₁₆″; page 2

[1] 2 [3–4]

[a]²

Contents: pp. 1–2: text of Emerson's letter; pp. 3–4: blank.

Typography and paper: 5¹⁄₁₆″ × 3³⁄₄″; wove paper; 23 lines on recto; nine lines on verso. No running heads.

Binding: Head title. Single sheet, folded once; unbound.

Publication: Possibly printed by Stirling when he was an applicant for the chair of moral philosophy at the University of Glasgow in 1866 (see his letter to Emerson, 24 May 1866 [MH]). Stirling also applied for the chair of moral philosophy at the University of Edinburgh in 1868 (see his letter to Emerson, 16 April 1868 [MH]), and planned to use Emerson's letter again for this position. He may have, therefore, printed the letter for use at this later date.

Location: BEU.

A 28 MAY-DAY AND OTHER PIECES

A 28.1.a
First American edition, first printing (1867)

MAY–DAY

AND OTHER PIECES.

BY

RALPH WALDO EMERSON.

BOSTON:
TICKNOR AND FIELDS.
1867.

A 28.1.a: 6^{15}/$_{16}$″ × 4^{5}/$_{8}$″

[i–iii] iv [1–3] 4–39 [40–43] 44–62 [63–65] 66 [67] 68 [69–70] 71 [72] 73–74 [75] 76–80 [81] 82–88 [89–90] 91 [92] 93 [94–98] 99–102 [103–105] 106 [107] 108 [109] 110 [111–112] 113 [114] 115–118 [119] 120–124 [125] 126–127 [128] 129–133 [134] 135 [136] 137–139 [140] 141–142 [143] 144 [145] 146–147 [148] 149–154 [155–157] 158 [159] 160 [161] 162 [163–166] 167 [168] 169 [170] 171 [172] 173 [174–176] 177 [178–181] 182–191 [192–195] 196–205 [206–208]

[a]^2 A–M^8 Also signed [a]^2 1–3^{12} [4]^{12} 5–8^{12} 9^8

Contents: p. i: title page; p. ii: copyright page; pp. iii–iv: contents; p. 1: 'MAY-DAY.'; p. 2: blank; pp. 3–39: "May-Day"; p. 40: blank; p. 41: 'THE ADIRONDACS. | A JOUR-NAL. | DEDICATED TO MY FELLOW-TRAVELLERS IN AUGUST, 1858. | [four lines of verse]'; p. 42: blank; pp. 43–62: "The Adirondacs"; p. 63: 'OCCASIONAL AND MIS-CELLA- | NEOUS PIECES.'; p. 64: blank; pp. 65–102: poems; p. 103: 'NATURE AND LIFE.'; p. 104: blank; pp. 105–154: poems; p. 155: 'ELEMENTS.'; p. 156: blank; pp. 157–177: poems; p. 178: blank; p. 179: 'QUATRAINS.'; p. 180: blank; pp. 181–191: poems; p. 192: blank; p. 193: 'TRANSLATIONS.'; p. 194: blank; pp. 195–205: translations; pp. 206–208: blank.

Poems: "May-Day" #; "The Adirondacs" #; "Brahma" †; "Nemesis" #; "Fate" ["Deep in the man sits fast his fate"] #; "Freedom" †; "Ode Sung in the Town Hall, Concord, July 4, 1857" †; "Boston Hymn" †; "Voluntaries" †; "Love and Thought" #; "Lover's Petition" †; "Una" #; "Letters" #; "Rubies" #; "Merlin's Song" #; "The Test" †; "Solution" #; "Nature. I." #; "Nature. II." #; "The Romany Girl" †; "Days" †; "The Chartist's Complaint" †; "My Garden" †; "The Titmouse" †; "Sea-Shore" †; "Song of Nature" †; "Two Rivers" †; "Waldeinsamkeit" †; "Terminus" †; "The Past" #; "The Last Farewell" [identified correctly as by Edward Bliss Emerson] †; "In Memoriam, E[dward]. B[liss]. E[merson]." #; "Experience" †; "Compensation" ["The wings of time are black and white"] †; "Politics" †; "Heroism" †; "Character" ["The sun set; but set not his hope"] †; "Culture" †; "Friendship" ["A ruddy drop of manly blood"] †; "Beauty" †; "Manners" †; "Art" †; "Spiritual Laws" †; "Unity" †; "Worship" †; "S[amuel]. H[oar]." #; "A. H." #; "Suum Cuique" ["Will thou seal up the avenues of ill?"] #; "Hush!" #; "Orator" †; "Artist" †; "Poet" ["Ever the Poet *from* the land"] †; "Poet" ["To clothe the fiery thought"] †; "Botanist" †; "Gardener" †; "Forester" †; "Northman" †; "From Alcuin" †; "Excelsior" #; "Borrowing. From the French" †; "Nature" ["Boon Nature yields each day … "] †; "Fate" ["Her planted eye to-day controls"] #; "Horoscope" #; "Power" ["Cast the bantlings on the rocks"] †; "Climacteric" †; "Heri, Cras, Hodie" †; "Memory" #; "Love" #; "Sacrifice" #; "Pericles" #; "Casella" #; "Shakspeare" #; "Hafiz" #; "Nature in Leasts" †; "ΑΔΑΚΡΥΝ ΝΕΜΟΝΤΑΙ ΑΙΩΝΑ" #; "Sonnet of Michel Angelo Buonaroti" #; "The Exile. From the Persian of Kermani" #; "From Hafiz" #; ["If my darling should depart"] #; "Epitaph" #; "Friendship" ["Thou foolish Hafiz!"] #; ["Dearest, where thy shadow falls"] #; ["On prince or bride no diamond stone"] #; "From Omar Chiam" #; ["He who has a thousand friends has not a friend to spare"] #; ["On two days it steads not to run from thy grave"] #; "From Ibn Jemin" #; "The Flute. From Hilali" #; "To the Shah. From Hafiz" #; "To the Shah. From Enweri" ["Not in their houses stand the stars"] #; "To the

Shah. From Enweri" ["From thy worth and weight the stars gravitate"] #; "Song of Seid Nimetollah of Kuhistan" †.

Typography and paper: 4⁷/₈" (4⁹/₁₆") × 3"; laid paper with 1¹/₈" vertical chain marks; 19 lines per page. Running heads: rectos: pp. 5–39: 'MAY-DAY.'; pp. 45–61: 'THE ADIRONDACS.'; pp. 71–73, 77–79, 83–87, 91–93, 99–101, 113–117, 121–123, 127–141, 147–153, 167–173, 177: titles of poems; pp. 183–191: 'QUATRAINS.'; pp. 197–205: 'TRANSLATIONS.'; versos: p. iv: 'CONTENTS.'; pp. 4–38: 'MAY-DAY.'; pp. 44–62: 'THE ADIRONDACS.'; pp. 66–68, 74–88, 100–102, 106–110, 116–126, 130–132, 138, 142–146, 150–154, 158–162: titles of poems; pp. 182–190: 'QUATRAINS.'; pp. 196–204: 'TRANSLATIONS.'.

Binding: Two styles have been noted:

Binding A: Dark brown, medium green, dark reddish orange, or medium purple C cloth (sand); bevelled edges. Front cover: goldstamped 2" design of three ferns in center; back cover: blindstamped 2" design of three ferns in center; spine: goldstamped '[ornate 'M'] MAY-DAY | [ornamental rule | EMERSON | [fern design] | [publisher's logo]'. Laid flyleaves. Brown coated endpapers. All edges trimmed. Top edges gilded.

Binding B: The same as Binding A, except: white linen cloth; edges are not bevelled; back cover is blank; publisher's logo not present at spine bottom.

Publication: Although Emerson wrote Anne C. L. Botta on 7 December 1866 that *May-Day* was printed, he was receiving proofs as late as 24 February 1867 (CtY; see *L*, V, 505). Advertised for April 1867 in *Atlantic*, 19 (February 1867), wrappers. On 26 March 1867, Emerson wrote James T. Fields "I have no keen edge now to publish" (Isabella Stuart Gardner Museum). Emerson finally gave Ticknor and Fields his permission to publish *May-Day* on 2 April 1867 (NN). Advertised as "Published this day," in *Boston Daily Advertiser*, 29 April 1867, p. 2. Listed as "Just Ready," in *American Literary Gazette and Publishers' Circular*, 9 (1 May 1867), 18. On 1 May 1867, Emerson listed in his journal those people to whom he had sent presentation copies ("Journal LN," p. 182 [MH]). 2,000 copies printed April 1867. According to Emerson's contract, dated 4 May 1868 (a written version of another agreement reached soon after publication), he retained the plates and copyright. Deposited for copyright: title, 22 April 1867; book, 27 April 1867. Inscribed copies: Binding A: MH (from Ticknor and Fields, 27 April 1867); Binding B (all from Emerson, 1 May 1867): CtY, DLC, JM, MB, MH, NN, NjP, ViU; rebound: MBAt (30 April 1867). Deposit copies: Binding A: BL (25 July 1867), DLC (3 August 1867). Price, $2.00. Royalty, $400 for the first 2,000 copies and 25¢ per copy thereafter.

Locations: Binding A: BL, CtY, DLC, InU, JM, MB, MBAt, MCo, MH, MHi, MWiW-C, NN, NNC, NjP, PSt, TxU, VtMiM; Binding B: CtY, DLC, JM, MB, MH, NN, NjP, ViU.

Note one: A copy at MH in Binding A (medium purple) is inscribed "For Mrs Emerson from J. T. F[ields]. | (the first copy bound of | this lovely Spring volume.)"

Note two: 100 copies in Binding B, apparently a special presentation binding for Emerson's friends, were prepared (Account Books [MH]).

A 28.1.b
First American edition, second printing (1868)

Boston: Ticknor and Fields, 1868.

[i–iii] iv . . . 182–191 [192] [195] 196–205 [206]

[a²] A–L⁸ [M]⁶ Also signed [a]² 1–3¹² [4]¹² 5–8¹² [9]⁶

Contents: pp. i–192: the same as in the first printing; pp. 195–205: translations; p. 206: blank.

Typography and paper: The same as in the first printing.

Binding: Light brown T cloth (rib). Front and back covers: blindstamped triple-rule frame with small leaf design in each corner and 3¹/₂″ ornament in center; spine: blind-stamped rules with goldstamped 'EMERSON'S | WRITINGS | MAY-DAY | AND OTHER PIECES | TICKNOR & CO.'. Flyleaves. Brown coated endpapers. All edges trimmed.

Publication: 280 copies printed July 1868 (Account Books [MH]). Price, $2.00. Royalty, 25¢.

Location: JM.

Note one: A copy of the second printing has been noted inscribed by Lidian Emerson, 22 April 1869, and bound in full red leather with gold tooling, and with a gold-stamped fern design on the front cover identical to that in the first printing, Binding A (JM).

Note two: Ticknor and Fields was succeeded by Fields, Osgood in October 1868, and Fields, Osgood was succeeded by James R. Osgood & Company in January 1871.

LATER PRINTINGS WITHIN THE AMERICAN EDITION

A 28.1.c
Boston: James R. Osgood, 1871.

280 copies printed 1 April 1871. Price, $2.00. Royalty, 25¢. *Location:* CSt.

A 28.1.d
Boston: James R. Osgood, 1874.

130 copies printed 27 April 1874. Price, $2.00. Royalty, 25¢. *Location:* ICM.

A 28.1.e
Boston: James R. Osgood, 1875.

150 copies printed 27 August 1875. Price, $2.00. Royalty, 25¢. *Location:* JM.

Note: James R. Osgood was succeeded by Houghton, Osgood in February 1878.

A 28.1.f
Boston: Houghton, Osgood, 1878.

175 copies printed 19 June 1878. Price, $1.50. *Location:* RNR.

Note one: Emerson's 1 January 1876 contract with James R. Osgood called for him to receive a flat annual fee of $1,500 for all his books, rather than a per copy royalty.

Note two: Houghton, Osgood was succeeded by Houghton, Mifflin in May 1880.

A 28.1.g
Boston: Houghton, Mifflin, 1881.

150 copies printed 7 December 1880. Price, $1.50. *Location:* MH.

A 28.1.h
Boston: Houghton, Mifflin, 1882.

Price, $1.50. *Location:* MMeT.

A 28.1.i
Boston: Houghton, Mifflin, 1883.

150 copies printed 23 December 1882. Price, $1.50. *Not seen.*

Note one: As of 15 January 1884, 10 copies of *May-Day* were still in stock.

Note two: The plates of *May-Day* were ordered destroyed on 24 February 1906.

A 28.2
First English edition, only printing (1867)

MAY-DAY

AND OTHER PIECES.

BY

RALPH WALDO EMERSON.

LONDON:

GEORGE ROUTLEDGE AND SONS,

THE BROADWAY, LUDGATE.

1867.

A 28.2: 6^1/$_2$″ × 4^1/$_8$″

[i–iii] iv [5] 6–37 83 39–41 [42] 43–61 [62] 63 [64] 65 [66–67] 68 [69] 70–71 [72] 73–77 [78] 79–85 [86–87] 88 [89] 90 [91–95] 96–99 [100] 101 [102] 103 [104] 105 [106–107] 108 [109] 110–113 [114] 115–119 [120] 121–122 [123] 124–128 [129] 130 [131] 132–134 [135] 136–137 [138] 139 [140] 141–142 [143] 144–149 [150] 151 [152] 153 [154] 155 [156–159] 160 [161] 162 [163]164 [165] 166 [167–169] 170 [171] 172–181 [182] 183–192

[A]⁸ B–I⁸ K–M⁸

Contents: p. i: title page; p. ii: printer's imprint; pp. iii–iv: contents; pp. 5–41: "May-Day"; pp. 42–61: "The Adirondacs"; pp. 62–99: "Occasional and Miscellaneous Poems"; pp. 100–149: "Nature and Life"; pp. 150–170: "Elements"; pp. 171–181: "Quatrains"; pp. 182–192: "Translations."

Typography and paper: 4⁷/₈″ (4⁹/₁₆″) × 3″; wove paper; 19 lines per page. Running heads: rectos: pp. 7–41: 'MAY-DAY.'; pp. 43–61: 'THE ADIRONDACS.'; pp. 63–65, 71–85, 97–105, 111–121, 125–127, 133, 137–141, 145–155: titles of poems; pp. 173–181: 'QUATRAINS.'; pp. 183–191: 'TRANSLATIONS.'; versos: p. iv: 'CONTENTS.'; pp. 6–40: 'MAY-DAY.'; pp. 44–60: 'THE ADIRONDACS.'; pp. 68–70, 74–76, 80–84, 88–90, 96–98, 108–112, 116–118, 122–136, 142–148, 160–166, 170: titles of poems; pp. 172–180: 'QUATRAINS.'; pp. 184–192: 'TRANSLATIONS.'.

Binding: Four styles have been noted, priority approximate:

Binding A: Light gray wrappers. Front recto: 'ONE SHILLING. | MAY-DAY | AND OTHER PIECES. | BY | RALPH WALDO EMERSON. | [leaf-and-vine rule] | LONDON: | GEORGE ROUTLEDGE AND SONS, | THE BROADWAY, LUDGATE. | 1867.' with all but price within a double-rule frame with vine-and-flower design in each corner; front verso and back recto have pastedown endpapers over them; back verso: advertisement for Longfellow's translations of Dante. Cream endpapers imprinted with publisher's advertisements. All edges trimmed.

Binding B: Deep green C cloth (sand); bevelled edges. Front and back covers: blindstamped double-rule frame with 2″ circular publisher's logo in center; spine: blindstamped triple rules at top and bottom, with goldstamped 'MAY | DAY | [rule] | EMERSON | ROUTLEDGE'. Gray coated endpapers. All edges trimmed. Top edges gilded.

Binding C: Dark green H cloth (fine diaper). Front cover: background of blindstamped parallel vertical lines with blindstamped ornate frame of rules and circles, with goldstamped "MAY-DAY | AND OTHER PIECES. | [rule] | Emerson.' in center; back cover: the same as the front cover, except the title and author are not present; spine: blindstamped parallel vertical lines. Pale yellow coated endpapers. All edges trimmed.

Binding D: Light gray wrappers of Binding A over boards. Front and back covers: the same printed wrappers as Binding A; spine: from bottom to top 'MAY DAY. BY R. W. EMERSON.'. Light brown endpapers imprinted with advertisements for Chapman and Hall's publications. All edges trimmed. Possibly a remainder binding.

Publication: Listed in *Athenæum,* no. 2067 (8 June 1867), 758; in *American Literary Gazette and Publishers' Circular,* 9 (1 July 1867), 145. Deposit copy: Binding A: BL (bound; 10 July 1867). Prices: cloth, unknown; wrappers, 1s.

Printing: "LONDON: | SAVILL, EDWARDS AND CO., PRINTERS, CHANDOS STREET, | COVENT GARDEN" (p. [ii]).

ONE SHILLING.

MAY-DAY

AND OTHER PIECES.

BY

RALPH WALDO EMERSON.

LONDON:
GEORGE ROUTLEDGE AND SONS,
THE BROADWAY, LUDGATE.
1867.

Wrapper for A 28.2

Locations: Binding A: BC, DLC, MCo, PSt, VtMiM; Binding B: CtY, JM, MCo, TxU; Binding C: NNC; Binding D: MH, NNC.

Note one: In all copies, p. 38 prints as '83'; in some copies, p. 136 prints as '13'.

Note two: Binding A is probably the first binding offered for sale; the BL deposit copy is in Binding A (bound). Binding D, with advertisements by a publisher other than Routledge, the original publisher, is probably a later, remainder binding.

Note three: An importation (undoubtedly of the American edition) at 8s. by Trübner listed in *Publishers' Circular and Booksellers' Record,* 30 (1 June 1867), 319.

SEPARATE PUBLICATIONS OF INDIVIDUAL POEMS

A 28.3
"Already blushes in thy cheek . . . " [N.p.: n.p., n.d.].

Single leaf folded once to make four pages, printed on p. 1 only. From "Nemesis." *Location:* MHi.

A 28.4
Letters. [Austin, Texas]: privately printed, 1932.

French fold, printed on pp. 1–3 only. Text and facsimile of manuscript poem. Printed by Charles C. Raines. Published ca. December 1932. *Location:* TxU.

A 28.5
Poet . . . Orator . . . Artist. [N.p.: n.p., n.d.].

Single leaf folded once to make four pages, printed on p. 1 only. "The Poet" is ["To clothe the fiery thought"]. *Location:* MHi.

A 28.6
Spring Vision from Emerson's Poems. Brooklyn, N.Y.: Hugh & Margaret Eaton, 1908.

French fold, printed on pp. 1, 4, 5, and 8. Hand-lettered and decorated text by Hugh and Margaret Eaton. Stanza 17 from "May-Day." *Location:* DLC (13 March 1908).

A 29 MRS. SARAH A. RIPLEY

A 29
First edition, only printing (1867)

MRS. SARAH A. RIPLEY.

Died, in Concord, on the 26th instant, Mrs. Sarah A. Ripley, aged seventy-four years. The death of this lady, widely known and beloved, will be sincerely deplored by many persons, scattered in distant parts of the country, who have known her rare accomplishments, and the singular loveliness of her character. A lineal descendant of the first governor of Plymouth colony, she was happily born and bred. Her father, Gamaliel Bradford, was a sea-captain of marked ability, with heroic traits which old men will still remember, and, though a man of action, yet adding a taste for letters. Her brothers were scholars, so that from childhood up she lived in an atmosphere of science and literature. Her own taste for study was even more decided, and she enjoyed from youth to age unusual advantages for gratifying it. Her brothers early inspired her with a love of botany, which endured as long as life. Her sympathy with their studies also made her acquainted with the genius of the French physiologists, Bichat and Biot, and with the chemists Lavoisier and Fourcroy, so that no one better appreciated the new nomenclature. At a time when perhaps no other young women read Greek, she acquired the language with ease, and read Plato, adding soon the advantage of German commentators.

After her marriage, when her husband, long the well-known clergyman of Waltham, received boys in his home to be fitted for college, she assumed the advanced instruction in Greek and Latin, and did not fail to turn it to account by extending her studies in the literature of both languages. It soon happened that students from Cambridge were put under her private instruction and oversight. If the young men shared her delights in the book, she was interested at once to lead them to higher steps, and more difficult but not less engaging authors, and they soon learned to prize the new world of thought and history thus opened. Her best pupils became her lasting friends. She became one of the best Greek scholars in the country, and continued, in recent years, the habit of reading Homer, the tragedians, and Plato. But her studies took a wide range in mathematics, in natural philosophy, in psychology, in theology, as well as in ancient and modern literature.

She had always a keen ear open to whatever new facts, astronomy, chemistry, or the theories of light and heat had to furnish. She had so vast a curiosity that it made little difference what book or department was offered. Any knowledge, all knowledge was welcome. The thirst for knowledge would not let her sleep. Her stores increased day by day. She was absolutely without pedantry. Nobody ever heard of her learning until a necessity came for its use, and then nothing could be more simple than her solution of the problem proposed to her. Her studies so occupied her that she naturally preferred the society of men, as usual the better scholars; and the most intellectual gladly conversed with one whose knowledge, however rich and varied, was always with her only the means of new acquisition. Meantime her mind was purely receptive. She had no ambition to propound a theory, or to write her own name on any book, or plant, or opinion. Her delight in books was not tainted by any wish to shine, or any appetite for praise or influence. She seldom and unwillingly used a pen, and only for necessity or affection.

But this wide and successful study was, during all the years of middle life, only the work of hours stolen from sleep, or was combined with some household task which occupied the hands and left the eyes free. She was faithful to all the duties of wife and mother in a well-ordered and eminently hospitable household wherein she was dearly loved, and where "her heart life's lowliest duties on itself did lay." She was not only the most amiable but the tenderest of women, wholly sincere, thoughtful for others, and though careless of appearances submitting with docility to the better arrangements which her children or friends insisted on supplementing to her own negligence of dress; for her own part, indulging her children without stint, assured that their own reflection, as it opened, would supply all needed checks.

She was absolutely without a disposition to any vice, no appetite for luxury, or display, or praise, or influence, with entire indifference to trifles. Not long before her marriage, one of her intimate friends in the city, whose family were removing, proposed to her to go with her to the new house, and taking some articles in her own hand, by way of trial artfully put into her hand a broom, whilst she kept her in free conversation on some speculative points, and this she faithfully carried across Boston common, from Summer street to Hancock street, without hesitation or remark.

Though entirely domestic in her habit and inclination, she was everywhere a welcome visitor and a favorite of society, when she rarely entered it. The elegance of her tastes commended her to the elegant, who were swift to distinguish her, as they found her simple manners faultless. With her singular simplicity and purity,—such that society could not spoil, not much affect,—she was only entertained by it, and really went into it as children into a theatre, to be diverted, while her ready sympathy enjoyed whatever beauty of person, manners, or ornaments, it had to show. If there was conversation, if there was thought or learning, her interest was commanded, and she gave herself up to the happiness of the hour.

As she advanced in life, her personal beauty, not remarked in her youth, drew the notice of all, and age brought no fault but the sudden decay or eclipse of her intellectual powers.   E.

—[From the Boston Daily Advertiser of July 31, 1867.

A 29: Broadside, 8^{7}/$_{16}$″ × 6^{7}/$_{8}$″

Broadside, printed on recto only.

Typography and paper: 7″ × 4⅝″; wove paper; column 1, 64 lines; column 2, 65 lines. No running head.

Publication: Possibly printed soon after 31 June 1867, the date on which this obituary appeared in the *Boston Daily Advertiser* (see E 172).

Locations: MBAt, MCo, MH.

Note: This may be a late nineteenth-century edition, but no conclusive evidence exists. The MCo copy is inserted into a scrapbook compiled in 1883.

A 30 ADDRESS [AT THE DEDICATION OF THE SOLDIERS' MONUMENT]

A 30
First edition, only printing [1867]

ADDRESS,

BY R. W. EMERSON.

A 30: Cover title, 7³/₈″ × 4⁷/₈″

[27–29] 30–55 [56] 57–60

$[3]^6 (_{-3_1})$ 4–5^6 See *Note Two* below for a description of the cancelled leaf.

Contents: p. 27: 'ADDRESS, | BY R. W. EMERSON.'; p. 28: blank; pp. 29–52: text; pp. 53–55: 'APPENDIX.'; p. 56: blank; pp. 57–60: 'POEM, | BY F. B. SANBORN.'.

Typography and paper: $5^3/_{16}''$ ($4^7/_8''$) × $3^3/_{16}''$; uncalendered wove paper; 27 lines per page. Running heads: rectos: pp. 31–59: 'SOLDIERS' MONUMENT.'; versos: pp. 30–54, 58–60: 'SOLDIERS' MONUMENT.'.

Binding: Cover title. All edges trimmed.

Publication: *Ceremonies at the Dedication of the Soldiers' Monument* (see *Note one* below) reviewed in *Boston Daily Advertiser*, 28 June 1867.

Printing: Benjamin Tolman, Concord.

Locations: MH, ViU.

Note one: Apparently a separate printing, not an offprint, from *Ceremonies at the Dedication of the Soldiers' Monument, in Concord, Mass.* (see D 67), which is printed on calendered wove paper.

Note two: The cancelled leaf contains text from the preceding contribution in the complete volume.

A31 SOCIETY AND SOLITUDE

A31.1.a
First edition, presumed first printing (1870)

SOCIETY AND SOLITUDE.

TWELVE CHAPTERS.

BY

RALPH WALDO EMERSON.

BOSTON:
FIELDS, OSGOOD, & CO.
1870.

A31.1.a: 7″ × 4¹/₄″

> **Entered according to Act of Congress, in the year 1870, by**
>
> **RALPH WALDO EMERSON,**
>
> **in the Clerk's Office of the District Court of the District of Massachusetts.**
>
> **UNIVERSITY PRESS: WELCH, BIGELOW, & CO.,**
> **CAMBRIDGE.**

The first nine printings within this edition cannot be distinguished.

[i–iv] [1–3] 4–14 [15–17] 18–30 [31–33] 34–51 [52–55] 56–89 [90–93] 94–119 [120–123] 124–138 [139–141] 142–166 [167–169] 170–197 [198–201] 202–223 [224–227] 228–250 [251–253] 254–278 [279–281] 282–300

[1^2 $2-19^8$ 20^6]

Contents: p. i: title page; p. ii: copyright page; p. iii: contents; p. iv: blank; p. 1: 'SOCIETY AND SOLITUDE.'; p. 2: blank; pp. 3–14: "Society and Solitude"; p. 15: 'CIVILIZATION.'; p. 16: blank; pp. 17–30: "Civilization"; p. 31: 'ART.'; p. 32: blank; pp. 33–51: "Art"; p. 52: blank; p. 53: 'ELOQUENCE.'; p. 54: blank; pp. 55–89: "Eloquence"; p. 90: blank; p. 91: 'DOMESTIC LIFE.'; p. 92: blank; pp. 93–119: "Domestic Life"; p. 120: blank; p. 121: 'FARMING.'; p. 122: blank; pp. 123–138: "Farming"; p. 139: 'WORKS AND DAYS.'; p. 140: blank; pp. 141–166: "Works and Days"; p. 167: 'BOOKS.'; p. 168: blank; pp. 169–197: "Books"; p. 198: blank; p. 199: 'CLUBS.'; p. 200: blank; pp. 201–223: "Clubs"; p. 224: blank; p. 225: 'COURAGE.'; p. 226: blank; pp. 227–250: "Courage"; p. 251: 'SUCCESS.'; p. 252: blank; pp. 253–278: "Success"; p. 279: 'OLD AGE.'; p. 280: blank; pp. 281–300: "Old Age."

Essays: "Society and Solitude" †; "Civilization" #; "Art" #; "Eloquence" †; "Domestic Life" †; "Farming" †; "Works and Days" #; "Books" †; "Clubs" #; "Courage" #; "Success" #; "Old Age" †.

Typography and paper: $5^3/8''$ ($5^1/8''$) × $3^1/16''$; wove paper; 29 lines per page. Running heads: rectos: pp. 5–13, 19–29, 35–51, 57–89, 95–119, 125–137, 143–176, 181–197, 203–223, 229–249, 255–277, 283–299: chapter titles; versos: pp. 4–14, 18–30, 34–50, 56–88, 94–118, 124–138, 142–166, 170–196, 202–222, 228–250, 254–278, 282–300: chapter titles.

Binding: Medium green, dark reddish orange, or medium purple C cloth (sand); bevelled edges. Front and back covers: blindstamped single-rule frame; spine: blindstamped bands at top and bottom with goldstamped 'SOCIETY | AND | SOLITUDE | [rule] | R. W. EMERSON | [publisher's logo]'. Wove or laid flyleaves. Brown coated endpapers. All edges trimmed.

Publication: Emerson carried the "copy of the first four chapters of my so-called new book" to Fields, Osgood on 19 October 1869 ("Journal New York," p. 193 [MH]). He began receiving proofs by 22 November 1869, and had received proofs for all but four pages by 28 January 1870 (*L*, VI, 92; letter to Fields, Osgood, *Pittsburgh Index*, 2 May 1903, p. 9 [see E 241]). On 3 February 1870, the "last proof-sheet" came back "for correction," and the next day Emerson wrote James Elliot Cabot that "The poor little book has come to an end of all demands on me" ("Journal New York," p. 213 [MH]; *L*, VI, 101). Advertised as "in Press," in *Atlantic*, 25 (January 1870), wrappers. Noted for "the current month," in *American Bibliopolist*, 2 (February 1870), 79. On 3 March 1870, Emerson wrote James T. Fields that "The new books came last night" (MH). Advertised as "Published This Day," in *Boston Daily Advertiser*, 5 March 1870, p. 2. 1,500 copies printed mid-February 1870. According to Emerson's contract, he paid for the plates, and retained the plates and copyright. Deposited for copyright: title, 9 February 1870; book, 10 March 1870. Inscribed copies: MH (from Fields, Osgood, 4 March 1870), MH (from Emerson, 4 March 1870), NNC (from Emerson, 7 March 1870), JM (7 March 1870), CtY (17 March 1870), InU (from Emerson, March 1870), MHi (March 1870), NN (from Emerson, March 1870), TxU (from Emerson, March 1870). Price, $2.00. Royalty, 30¢ per copy after the first 300 copies.

Locations: BL, CSt, CtY, InU, JM, MB, MBAt, MCo, MH, MHi, MWA, MWiW-C, NN, NNC, NjP, PSt, TxU, ViU, VtMiM.

Note one: The poem "George Nidiver," at the end of the "Courage" chapter (pp. 248–250), is by Elizabeth Hoar.

Note two: A copy has been noted in dark reddish orange C cloth (sand) with a slip (identical to that in the English editions of *The Conduct of Life*) tipped on to the title page, stating "The Publishers think it right to state that the Author derives a pecuniary benefit from this Edition" (see illustration at A 26.2). Also, a holograph note is inserted stating "an unusual copy, with the slip which was inserted for copies sent to England and France." *Location:* JM.

A 31.1.b–i
First American edition, presumed second through ninth printings (1870)

Boston: Fields, Osgood, & Co., 1870.

450 copies printed March 1870; 500 copies in March 1870 (twice), March–April 1870 (twice), April–May 1870, June 1870, and September 1870.

A 31.1.j
First American edition, presumed tenth printing (1870)

Boston: Fields, Osgood, & Co., 1870.

The same as the first printing, except: [1^2 $2–19^8$ 20^4 21^2]. Copies have been noted in medium green C cloth (sand) and dark reddish brown FL cloth (dotted line). 500 copies printed October–November 1870. Deposit copy: DLC (10 December 1870). *Locations:* CtY, DLC, JM, RPB, ViU.

Note: Fields, Osgood was succeeded by James R. Osgood & Company in January 1871.

LATER PRINTINGS WITHIN THE FIRST AMERICAN EDITION

A 31.1.k
Boston: James R. Osgood, 1871.

500 copies printed March 1871. Price, $2.00. Royalty, 30¢. *Location:* MeSaco.

A 31.1.l
Boston: James R. Osgood, 1872.

280 copies printed 12 February 1872; 500 copies in August 1872. Price, $2.00. Royalty, 30¢. *Location:* JM.

A 31.1.m
Boston: James R. Osgood, 1873.

500 copies printed 5 August 1873. Price, $2.00. Royalty, 30¢. *Location:* JM.

A 31.1.n
Boston: James R. Osgood, 1875.

280 copies printed October–November 1874; 430 copies on 15 July 1875. Price, $2.00. Royalty, 30¢. *Location:* JM.

A 31.1.o
Boston: James R. Osgood, 1876.

500 copies printed 12 June 1876. Price, $2.00. *Location:* JM.

Note one: Emerson's 1 January 1876 contract with Osgood called for him to receive a flat annual fee of $1,500 for all his books, rather than a per copy royalty.

Note two: James R. Osgood was succeeded by Houghton, Osgood in February 1878.

A 31.1.p
Boston: Houghton, Osgood, 1879.

180 copies printed 3 May 1879. Price, $1.50. *Location:* JM.

Note: Houghton, Osgood was succeeded by Houghton, Mifflin, in May 1880. Copies of Houghton, Osgood sheets (including the title leaf) have been noted in Houghton, Mifflin bindings.

A 31.1.q
Boston: Houghton, Mifflin, 1882.

150 copies printed 4 May 1882 and 7 September 1882. Price, $1.50. *Not seen.*

Note: As of 15 January 1884, 10 copies of *Society and Solitude* were still in stock.

A 31.2.a
First English edition, first printing (1870)

SOCIETY AND SOLITUDE.

TWELVE CHAPTERS.

BY

RALPH WALDO EMERSON.

(Low's Copyright Cheap Editions of American Books.)

LONDON:
SAMPSON LOW, SON, & MARSTON,
CROWN BUILDINGS, 188 FLEET STREET.
1870.

A 31.2.a: 6³/₁₆″ × 4¹/₄″

[i–iv] [1] 2–13 [14–15] 16–29 [30–31] 32–49 [50–51] 52–86 [87] 88–114 [115] 116–130 [131] 132–156 [157] 158–186 [187] 188–210 [211] 212–235 [236–237] 238–263 [264–265] 266–284

[a]² A–I⁸ K–R⁸ S⁶

Contents: p. i: title page; p. ii: printer's imprint; p. iii: contents; p. iv: blank; pp. 5–284: same chapters as the first edition.

Typography and paper: 5¹/₁₆″ (4¹³/₁₆″) × 3¹/₈″; wove paper; 26 lines per page. Running heads: rectos: pp. 3–13, 17–29, 33–49, 53–85, 89–113, 117–129, 133–155, 159–185, 189–209, 213–225, 239–263, 267–283: chapter titles; versos: pp. 2–12, 16–28, 32–48, 52–234, 238–262, 266–284: chapter titles.

Binding: Two styles have been noted, priority undetermined:

Binding A: Deep blue B cloth (linen). Front cover: blindstamped double-rule frame with goldstamped 'Society & Solitude | [rule] | Twelve Chapters | By Ralph Waldo Emerson | [next two lines within rectangular frame] LOW'S COPYRIGHT SERIES | OF AMERICAN AUTHORS | LONDON | SAMPSON LOW SON & MARSTON | [rule]'; back cover: blindstamped double-rule frame with 1¹/₁₆″ ornament in center; spine: goldstamped '[rule] | [rule] | [from bottom to top] Society & Solitude | 2/- | [rule] | [rule]'. White endpapers. All edges trimmed.

Binding B: Printed glazed paper-covered boards of medium green background with white frame and black printing. Front cover: see illustration; back cover: same as front cover, except: publisher's name and address, and price are not present, and the book's title has been replaced with an advertisement for seven books in *Low's Copyright Series of American Authors;* spine: all on green background '[floral design] | [from bottom to top on white background] SOCIETY AND SOLITUDE | [floral design]' all within rules-and-dots frame on white background. White endpapers. All edges trimmed.

Publication: Apparently published simultaneously with the American edition. Carlyle wrote Emerson that he had seen it advertised on 24 February 1870 (*CEC*, p. 563). Advertised for "Next week," in *Athenæum*, no. 2209 (26 February 1870), 304. Advertised for 3 March 1870, with the statement "Published simultaneously in London and Boston . . . by arrangement with the Author," in *Publishers' Circular and Booksellers' Record*, 33 (1 March 1870), 154. Listed in *Athenæum*, no. 2210 (5 March 1870), 325. Advertised for "This day," in *Athenæum*, no. 2210 (5 March 1870), 336. Listed as published between 1 and 14 March 1870, in *Publishers' Circular and Booksellers' Record*, 33 (5 March 1870), 169. Deposit copy: Binding A: BL (3 March 1870). Prices: cloth 2s.; glazed paper-covered boards, 1s. 6d.

Printing: "PRINTED BY BALLANTYNE AND COMPANY | EDINBURGH AND LONDON" (p. [ii]).

Locations: Binding A: BL, JM, MCo; Binding B: CtY, MCo, MB, MH.

Note one: *Low's Copyright Cheap Editions of American Authors*, no. 8.

Note two: A copy has been noted with a 4-page undated catalogue for Sampson Low, Son, & Marston's publications inserted at the back: JM.

Note three: On 31 March 1870, Emerson assigned the copyright to *Society and Solitude* to Sampson Low, Sampson Low the Younger, and Edward Marston (Routledge Archives), but the English copyright was apparently not officially registered until 22 April 1870.

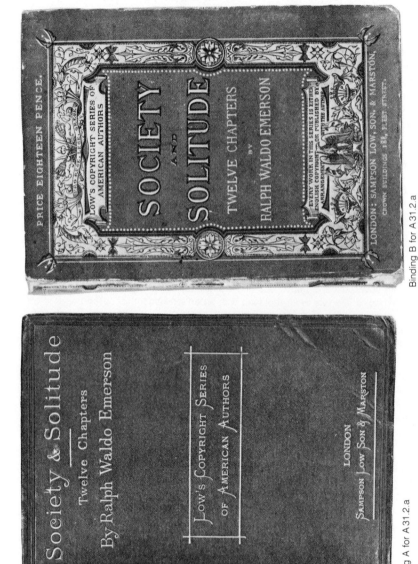

Binding B for A31.2.a

Binding A for A31.2.a

A 31.2.b
London: Sampson Low, Marston, Low, & Searle, 1874.

Low's Copyright Cheap Editions of American Books. Locations: BMP, NRU.

A 31.2.c
London and New York: George Routledge and Sons, 1883.

Locations: BL (21 August 1883), BC (25 September 1883), BO (12 October 1883).

A 31.2.d
London and New York: George Routledge and Sons, 1884.

Location: CaOPeT.

GERMAN EDITION

A 31.3.a
First German edition, first printing (1871)

[all gothic except the date] Gesellschaft und Einsamkeit | [wavy rule] | Zwölf Kapitel | von | Ralph Waldo Emerson. | [rule] | Aus den Englischen | von | Selma Mohnicke. | [ornate rule] | Bremen, 1871. | Verlag von J. Kühtmann's Buchhandlung. | U. L. Fr. Kirchhof Dr. 4.

410 pp. *Location:* NNC.

A 31.3.b
Bremen: Auflage, 1875.

Not seen.

A 31.3.c
Norden: Titelausgabe, 1885.

Not seen.

PRINTINGS FROM THE "LITTLE CLASSIC EDITION" PLATES

A 31.4.a

[all within a double-rule frame; outer frame is red with boxed corners] [red] SOCIETY AND SOLITUDE. | *Twelve Chapters.* | BY | RALPH WALDO EMERSON. | [ornate rule] | [red] BOSTON: | JAMES R. OSGOOD AND COMPANY, | Late Ticknor & Fields, and Fields, Osgood, & Co. | [red] 1876.

269 pp. Vol. [VII] of the "Little Classic Edition" (see B 3). 2,000 copies printed 5 April 1876. Listed in *Publishers' Weekly,* 9 (27 May 1876), 700. Price, $1.50. Royalty: see *Note one* to A 31.1.o. *Locations:* BL (12 April 1877), JM.

A 31.4.b
Boston: James R. Osgood, 1878.

280 copies printed 21 December 1877. Price, $1.50. *Not seen.*

Note: James R. Osgood was succeeded by Houghton, Osgood in February 1878.

A 31.4.c
Boston: Houghton, Osgood, 1879.

280 copies printed 20 December 1878; 500 copies on 17 July 1879. Price, $1.50. *Location:* NcU.

A 31.4.d
Boston: Houghton, Osgood, 1879.

Combined with *Representative Men* in two-volumes-in-one format as vol. II of the "Fireside Edition" (see B 4). 500 copies printed 15 August 1879. *Location:* KU.

A 31.4.e
Boston: Houghton, Osgood, 1880.

Combined with *Representative Men* in two-volumes-in-one format as vol. II of the "Fireside Edition" (see B 4). 500 copies printed 6 February 1880. *Location:* JM.

Note: Houghton, Osgood was succeeded by Houghton, Mifflin in May 1880.

A 31.4.f
Boston: Houghton, Mifflin, 1881.

Combined with *Representative Men* in two-volumes-in-one format as vol. II of the "Fireside Edition" (see B 4). 500 copies printed 7 December 1880. *Not seen.*

A 31.4.g
Boston: Houghton, Mifflin, 1881.

500 copies printed 23 July 1881. Price, $1.50. *Location:* MAsh.

A 31.4.h
Boston: Houghton, Mifflin, 1882.

Combined with *Representative Men* in two-volumes-in-one format as vol. II of the "Fireside Edition" (see B 4). 500 copies printed 17 October 1881 and 8 May 1882. *Location:* JM.

A 31.4.i
Boston: Houghton, Mifflin, 1882.

500 copies printed 23 February 1882 and 7 June 1882. Price, $1.50. *Location:* NNC.

A 31.4.j
Boston: Houghton, Mifflin, 1883.

500 copies printed 23 November 1882 and 26 April 1883. *Location:* JM.

A 31.4.k
Boston: Houghton, Mifflin, 1883.

Combined with *Representative Men* in two-volumes-in-one format as vol. II of the "Fireside Edition" (see B 4). 270 copies printed 9 January 1883. *Not seen.*

A 31.4.l
Boston: Houghton, Mifflin, 1884.

270 copies printed 7 January 1884; 500 copies on 31 May 1884. *Location:* JM.

A 31.4.m
Boston: Houghton, Mifflin, 1886.

270 copies printed 27 January 1886. *Not seen.*

A 31.4.n
Boston and New York: Houghton, Mifflin, 1887.

270 copies printed 16 February 1887. Bound in medium blue V cloth (smooth), rather than "Little Classic Edition" binding, as are subsequent reprintings (see illustration at B 3). *Location:* OCIW.

A 31.4.o
Boston and New York: Houghton, Mifflin, 1888.

270 copies printed 8 November 1887 and 30 April 1888. *Location:* JM.

A 31.4.p
Boston and New York: Houghton, Mifflin, 1889.

270 copies printed 15 November 1888 and 6 August 1889. *Location:* JM.

A 31.4.q
Boston and New York: Houghton, Mifflin, 1890.

270 copies printed 27 November 1889; 250 copies ca. June 1890. *Not seen.*

A 31.4.r
Boston and New York: Houghton, Mifflin, 1891.

Location: JM.

A 31.4.s
Boston and New York: Houghton, Mifflin, 1892.

500 copies printed 14 December 1891 and 17 November 1892. *Location:* JM.

A 31.4.t
Boston and New York: Houghton, Mifflin, 1893.

500 copies printed 30 October 1893. *Location:* MH.

A 31.4.u
Boston and New York: Houghton, Mifflin, 1895.

500 copies printed 11 June 1895. *Location:* NjP.

A 31.4.v
Boston and New York: Houghton, Mifflin, 1897.

270 copies printed 6 May 1897. *Location:* JM.

Note: The copyright on *Society and Solitude* was renewed 30 November 1897.

A 31.4.w
Boston and New York: Houghton, Mifflin, 1898.

270 copies printed 23 December 1897. *Not seen.*

A 31.4.x
Boston and New York: Houghton, Mifflin, 1899.

270 copies printed 30 April 1899. *Not seen.*

A 31.4.y
Boston and New York: Houghton Mifflin, [1912].

Location: MH.

A 31.4.z
Boston and New York: Houghton, Mifflin, [n.d.].

Approximately 1,900 copies sold between 1900 and 1923. *Location:* JM.

Note: Approximately 13,500 copies of *Society and Solitude* printed from the "Little Classic Edition" plates were sold between 1876 and 1923, when the title was apparently allowed to go out of print in this format.

LATER EDITION

A 31.5.a–h
The Conduct of Life and Society and Solitude. London: Macmillan, 1883.

Vol. V of the *Works;* see A 26.9.a–h.

PRINTINGS FROM THE RIVERSIDE EDITION PLATES

A 31.6.a
Riverside Edition (trade), first printing (1883)

SOCIETY AND SOLITUDE | TWELVE CHAPTERS | BY | RALPH WALDO EMERSON | [gothic] New and Revised Edition | [publisher's logo] | BOSTON | HOUGHTON, MIF-FLIN AND COMPANY | New York: 11 East Seventeenth Street | [gothic] The Riverside Press, Cambridge | 1883

316 pp. Vol. VII of the *Riverside Edition,* trade printing (see B 7). 1,000 copies printed 31 August 1883; 500 copies on 25 October 1883. Listed in *Publishers' Weekly,* 24 (27 October 1883), 574. According to the publisher's records, published 20 October 1883. Copyright, 13 September 1883. Price, $1.75. *Locations:* DLC (24 October 1883), JM.

Note: Copies have been noted with a pine branch on the title page instead of the publisher's logo.

A 31.6.b
Riverside Edition (Copyright), second (English) printing (1883)

SOCIETY AND SOLITUDE | TWELVE CHAPTERS | BY | RALPH WALDO EMERSON | [gothic] The Riverside Edition | (COPYRIGHT) | GEORGE ROUTLEDGE AND SONS | BROADWAY, LUDGATE HILL | NEW YORK: 9, LAFAYETTE PLACE | 1883

Vol. VII of the *Riverside Edition (Copyright),* English trade printing (see B 10). 1,000 copies printed 18 September 1883. Listed as published between 16 and 31 October 1883, in *Publishers' Circular and Booksellers' Record,* 46 (1 November 1883), 1060. Price, 3s. 6d. *Locations:* BL (8 December 1883), BC (26 March 1884), BO (3 April 1884), CaQMM.

A 31.6.c₁
Riverside Edition (large paper), third printing, American issue (1883)

[red] SOCIETY AND SOLITUDE | TWELVE CHAPTERS | BY | RALPH WALDO EMER-SON | [gothic] New and Revised Edition | [pine branch] | [red] CAMBRIDGE | [gothic] Printed at the Riverside Press | 1883

Vol. VII of the *Riverside Edition,* large paper printing (see B 8). Limited to 500 numbered copies printed 30 November 1883. Price, $4.00. Sold out within a year. *Locations:* JM, TxU.

A 31.6.c₂
Riverside Edition (large paper), third printing, English issue (1883)

Title page is the same as in the American issue, except for publisher's imprint: 'LON-DON | KEGAN PAUL, TRENCH, & CO., I, PATERNOSTER SQUARE | MDCCCLXXXIII'.

Vol. VII of the *Riverside Edition,* large paper printing for English subscribers (see B 9). 25 title leaves printed 30 November 1883. Title leaf is a cancel. Limited to 25 signed and numbered copies. *Location:* JM.

A 31.6.d
Boston and New York: Houghton, Mifflin, 1884.

500 copies printed 31 December 1883, 26 March 1884, and 12 August 1884. *Location:* JM.

A 31.6.e
Boston and New York: Houghton, Mifflin, 1885.

500 copies printed 2 January 1885 and 8 July 1885. *Location:* JM.

A 31.6.f
Boston and New York: Houghton, Mifflin, 1886.

500 copies printed 27 October 1885 and 14 April 1886. *Location:* NGenoU.

A 31.6.g
Boston and New York: Houghton, Mifflin, 1887.

500 copies printed 30 October 1886 and 25 January 1887; 270 copies on 5 August 1887. *Location:* JM.

A 31.6.h
London, Glasgow, New York: George Routledge and Sons, 1887.

500 copies printed 1 July 1887. *Location:* JM.

A 31.6.i
Boston and New York: Houghton, Mifflin, 1888.

500 copies printed 14 December 1887 and 21 April 1888. *Location:* JM.

A 31.6.j
Boston and New York: Houghton, Mifflin, 1889.

500 copies printed ca. December 1888 and 7 August 1889; 270 copies on 30 April 1889. *Not seen.*

A 31.6.k
Boston and New York: Houghton, Mifflin, 1890.

500 copies printed ca. June 1890 and ca. September 1890. *Not seen.*

A 31.6.l
Boston and New York: Houghton, Mifflin, 1891.

500 copies printed ca. February 1891 and 7 August 1891. *Location:* JM.

A 31.6.m
Boston and New York: Houghton, Mifflin, 1892.

500 copies printed 3 February 1892. *Location:* MNew.

A 31.6.n
Boston and New York: Houghton, Mifflin, 1893.

500 copies printed 23 November 1892 and 11 September 1893. *Location:* MH.

A 31.6.o
Boston and New York: Houghton, Mifflin, 1894.

500 copies printed 17 September 1894. *Location:* NBu.

A 31.6.p
Standard Library Edition printing [1894]

SOCIETY AND SOLITUDE | TWELVE CHAPTERS | BY | RALPH WALDO EMERSON | [pine branch] | BOSTON AND NEW YORK | HOUGHTON, MIFFLIN AND COMPANY | [gothic] The Riverside Press, Cambridge

Vol. VII of the *Standard Library Edition* (see B 11). 1,000 copies printed 31 October 1894, 30 April 1895, and 29 May 1896; 500 copies on 31 January 1898. *Location:* JM.

A 31.6.q
Boston and New York: Houghton, Mifflin, 1895.

500 copies printed 9 August 1895. *Location:* NcRS.

A 31.6.r
London, Manchester, and New York: George Routledge and Sons, 1895.

Location: CaQMM.

A 31.6.s
Boston and New York: Houghton, Mifflin, 1897.

500 copies printed 9 January 1897. *Location:* MH.

Note: The copyright on *Society and Solitude* was renewed 30 November 1897.

A 31.6.t
Boston and New York: Houghton, Mifflin, 1898.

500 copies printed 20 June 1898. *Location:* JM.

A 31.6.u
Boston and New York: Houghton, Mifflin, 1899.

500 copies printed 20 June 1899. *Not seen.*

A 31.6.v
London: George Routledge & Sons, 1903.

Combined with *Letters and Social Aims* and *Poems* in three-volumes-in-one format as vol. III of the "Sovereign Edition" (see B 12). 1,000 copies printed 16 September 1903. *Location:* InU.

A 31.6.w
Fireside Edition printing (1909)

[all within red double-rule frame with red floral ornaments in each corner] THE WORKS OF | [red gothic] Ralph Waldo Emerson | SOCIETY AND SOLITUDE | [engraving of man reading book in chair before fireplace] | [gothic] Fireside Edition | BOSTON AND NEW YORK | MDCCCCIX

Vol. VII of the *Fireside Edition* (see B 13). 500 copies printed 29 September 1909 and 14 February 1910. *Location:* JM.

A 31.6.x
Boston and New York: Jefferson Press, [ca. 1912].

Combined with *Letters and Social Aims* in two-volumes-in-one format as vol. IV of the "Jefferson Press Edition" (see B 14). *Location:* CtW.

A 31.6.y
New York: Sully and Kleinteich, [ca. 1912].

Vol. VII of the *University Edition* (see B 15). *Location:* JM.

A 31.6.z
Boston and New York: Houghton, Mifflin, [n.d.].

Approximately 2,100 copies sold between 1900 and 1913. *Location:* JM.

Note: Approximately 15,500 copies of *Society and Solitude* in the *Riverside Edition* were sold between 1883 and 1913, when the title was apparently allowed to go out of print in this format.

A 31.6.aa
London: George Routledge and Sons, [n.d.].

Location: JM.

A 31.6.bb
London: Waverley Book Company, [n.d.].

Vol. VII of the "Waverley" *Riverside Edition* (see B 16). *Location:* JM.

LATER EDITION

A 31.7
London: George Bell and Sons, 1895.

Advertised as included in "Bohn's Standard Library." Published February 1895. Price, 1s. *Not seen.*

PRINTINGS FROM THE CENTENARY EDITION PLATES

A 31.8.a
Autograph Centenary Edition (large paper), first printing (1904)

RALPH WALDO EMERSON | [red] Society and Solitude | Twelve Chapters | [pine tree] | CAMBRIDGE | [red gothic] Printed at the Riverside Press | 1904

451 pp. Vol. VII of the *Autograph Centenary Edition* (see B 19). Limited to 600 signed and numbered copies printed 5 February 1904. Copyright, 1 February 1904. Price, $6.00. Sold out by 5 April 1906. *Locations:* DLC (15 February 1904), JM.

A 31.8.b₁
Centenary Edition (trade), second printing, American issue (1904)

SOCIETY AND SOLITUDE | TWELVE CHAPTERS | BY | RALPH WALDO EMERSON | [pine tree] | BOSTON AND NEW YORK | HOUGHTON, MIFFLIN AND COMPANY, | [gothic] The Riverside Press, Cambridge | 1904

Dust jacket. Vol. VII of the *Centenary Edition*, trade printing (see B 18). 1,000 copies printed 8 February 1904; 500 copies on 26 November 1904. Listed in *Publisher's Weekly*, 65 (5 March 1904), 715. According to the publisher's records, published 27 February 1904. Copyright, 1 February 1904. Price, $1.75. *Location:* JM.

Note: Numerous reprintings with undated title pages. 2,500 copies printed between 1 April 1905 and 30 September 1910. Approximately 5,000 copies sold through 1923.

A 31.8.b₂
English issue

London: A. P. Watt & Son, [1904].

Vol. VII of the English *Centenary Edition* (see B 21). American sheets with Watt's label pasted on the title page. Price, 6s. *Locations:* BL (27 February 1904), BC (11 March 1904), BE (11 March 1904).

A 31.8.c
Boston and New York: Houghton, Mifflin, 1904.

Vol. VII of the *Concord Edition* (see B 20). 1,000 copies printed 10 February 1904 and 23 July 1904. *Location:* JM.

Note: Numerous reprintings with undated title pages. Approximately 3,100 copies sold by 31 December 1910.

A 31.8.d
Boston and New York: Houghton Mifflin, [1912].

Vol. VII of the *Centenary Edition*, trade printing (see B 18). *Location:* JM.

A 31.8.e
Boston and New York: Houghton Mifflin, [1914].

Vol. VII of the *Riverside Pocket Edition* (see B 22). Approximately 1,100 copies sold between 1914 and 1922. *Location:* JM.

A 31.8.f
Boston and New York: Houghton Mifflin, 1921.

336 pp. (text without the notes). Combined with *Poems* in two-volumes-in-one format as vol. VI of *Emerson's Complete Works* (see B 23). *Location:* JM.

A 31.8.g
New York: Wm. H. Wise, 1923.

Combined with *Letters and Social Aims* in two-volumes-in-one format as vol. IV of the *Current Opinion Edition* (see B 24). *Location:* JM.

A 31.8.h
Boston and New York: Houghton, Mifflin, 1929.

Combined (text without the notes) with *Poems* in two-volumes-in-one format as vol. VI of the *Harvard Edition* (see B 25). *Location:* JM.

A 31.8.i
New York: Wm. H. Wise, 1929.

Combined with *Letters and Social Aims* in two-volumes-in-one format as vol. IV of the *Medallion Edition* (see B 26). *Location:* OC.

A 31.8.j
Boston and New York: Houghton Mifflin, [1930].

Vol. VII of the *Centenary Edition,* trade printing (see B 18). The title leaf verso reads 'ELEVENTH IMPRESSION, APRIL, 1930.' *Location:* PSC.

A 31.8.k–l
New York: AMS Press, [1968].

Vol. VII of the "AMS Press" *Centenary Edition* (see B 27). Reprinted 1979. *Locations:* TxU, DLC (9 November 1979).

LATER EDITION

A 31.9
The Conduct of Life and Society and Solitude. London: George Routledge and Sons; New York: E. P. Dutton, [1906].

See A 26.17.

SEPARATE PUBLICATIONS OF INDIVIDUAL ESSAYS

A 31.10
Ueber Buecher. Bremen: J. Kühtmann, 1875.

61 pp. Wrappers. "Books," translated by Selma Mohnicke. *Not seen.*

Note: Probably from the plates of *Gesellschaft und Einsamkeit* (A 31.3.a).

A 31.11
Courage. New York: New York Book Company, [1912].

Advertised as included in "Aurora Editions." Price, 40¢. *Not seen.*

A 31.12
Ueber häusliches Leben. Bremen: J. Kühtmann, 1876.

59 pp. Wrappers. "Domestic Life," translated by Selma Mohnicke. *Not seen.*

Note: Probably from the plates of *Gesellschaft und Einsamkeit* (A 31.3.a).

A 31.13
Old Age. [Cleveland: Caxton Company], 1939.

28 pp. Printed December 1939. Limited to 30 numbered copies. *Location:* CtHT-W.

A 31.14
Success. Boston and New York: Houghton Mifflin, 1912.

65 pp. Designed by Bruce Rogers. Printed November 1912. Limited to 540 numbered copies, of which 500 were for sale. Listed in *Publishers' Weekly*, 85 (14 February 1914), 528. According to the publisher's records, published 9 November 1912. Price, $2.00. *Location:* JM.

A 31.15
Books, Art, Eloquence. Boston: James R. Osgood, 1877.

104 pp. *Vest-Pocket Series*, no. 21. 1,000 copies printed 4 May 1877; 500 copies on June 1877. Listed in *Publishers' Weekly*, 11 (26 May 1877), 559. Price, 50¢. *Location:* N.

A 31.16
Civilization, Art, Eloquence, and Books. Tokyo: Tokio Publishing Company, 1886.

Translated by Masakazu Toyama. *Not seen.*

A 32 REMARKS ON THE CHARACTER OF GEORGE L. STEARNS

A 32.1
First edition, only printing [1872]

REMARKS

ON THE CHARACTER OF

GEORGE L. STEARNS,

AT MEDFORD, APRIL 14, 1867,

BY R. W. EMERSON.

WE do not know how to prize good men until they depart. High virtue has such an air of nature and necessity that to thank its possessor would be to praise the water for flowing or the fire for warming us. But, on the instant of their death, we wonder at our past insensibility, when we see how impossible it is to replace them. There will be other good men, but not these again. And the painful surprise which the last week brought us, in the tidings of the death of Mr. Stearns, opened all eyes to the just consideration of the singular merits of the citizen, the neighbor, the friend, the father, and the husband, whom this assembly mourns. We recall the all but exclusive devotion of this excellent man during the last twelve years to public and patriotic interests. Known until that time in no very wide circle as a man of skill and perseverance in his business; of pure life; of retiring and affectionate habits; happy in his domestic relations, — his extreme interest in the national politics, then growing more anxious year by year, engaged him to scan the fortunes of freedom with keener attention. He was an early laborer in the resistance to slavery. This brought him into sympathy with the people of Kansas. As early as 1855 the Emigrant Aid Society was formed; and in 1856 he organized the Massachusetts State Kansas Committee, by means of which a large amount of money was obtained for the "free-State men," at times of the greatest need. He was the more engaged to this cause by making in 1857 the acquaintance of Captain John Brown, who was not only an extraordinary man, but one who had a rare magnetism for men of character, and attached some of the best and noblest to him, on very short acquaintance, by lasting ties. Mr. Stearns made himself at once necessary to Captain Brown as one who respected his inspirations, and had the magnanimity to trust him entirely, and to arm his hands with all needed help.

For the relief of Kansas, in 1856–57, his own contributions were the largest and the first. He never asked any one to give so much as he himself gave, and his interest was so manifestly pure and sincere that he easily obtained eager offerings in quarters where other petitioners failed. He did not hesitate to become the banker of his clients, and to furnish them money and arms in advance of the subscriptions which he obtained. His first donations were only entering wedges of his later; and, unlike other benefactors, he did not give money to excuse his entire preoccupation in his own pursuits, but as an earnest of the dedication of his heart and hand to the interests of the sufferers, — a pledge kept until the success he wrought and prayed for was consummated. In 1862, on the President's first or preliminary Proclamation of Emancipation, he took the first steps for organizing the Freedman's Bureau, — a department which has since grown to great proportions. In 1863, he began to recruit colored soldiers in Buffalo; then at Philadelphia and Nashville. But these were only parts of his work. He passed his time in incessant consultations with all men whom he could reach, to suggest and urge the measures needed for the hour. And there are few men of real or supposed influence, North or South, with whom he has not at some time communicated. Every important patriotic measure in this region has had his sympathy, and of many he has been the prime mover. He gave to each his strong support, but uniformly shunned to appear in public. For himself or his friends he asked no reward: for himself, he asked only to do the hard work. His transparent singleness of purpose, his freedom from all by-ends, his plain good sense, courage, adherence, and his romantic generosity disarmed first or last all gainsayers. His examination before the United States Senate Committee on the Harper's Ferry Invasion, in January, 1860, as reported in the public documents, is a chapter well worth reading, as a shining example of the manner in which a truth-speaker baffles all statecraft, and extorts at last a reluctant homage from the bitterest adversaries.

I have heard, what must be true, that he had great executive skill, a clear method, and a just attention to

---

A 32: 12¹⁄₈″ × 9¹⁄₄″; 'GEORGE L. STEARNS.' and 'BY R. W. EMERSON.' are in red

[1–4]

[a]^2

Contents: p. 1: text; p. 2: blank; p. 3: text; p. 4: blank.

Typography and paper: 9^1/$_4$″ × 6^1/$_2$″; very light brown laid paper with 1^1/$_4$″ vertical chain marks; 40 lines per column on p. 1, 41 lines per column on p. 2. No running heads.

Binding: Single leaf, folded once; unbound.

Locations: InU, JM, MB, MH, MWA, NN, NNC, NcD, NjP, PSt, ViU.

OTHER EDITION

A 32.2
Second American edition, only printing [n.d.].

Mr. R. W. Emerson's Remarks | —AT THE— | UNITARIAN CHURCH AT MEDFORD, | ——ON THE CHARACTER OF—— | MR. GEORGE L. STEARNS, | Sunday, April 14, 1867. | [rule] | [text]

Broadside, printed on recto only. Limited to about 110 copies printed by William T. Newton. *Location:* MBAt.

A 33 SONG

A 33
First edition, only printing (1875)

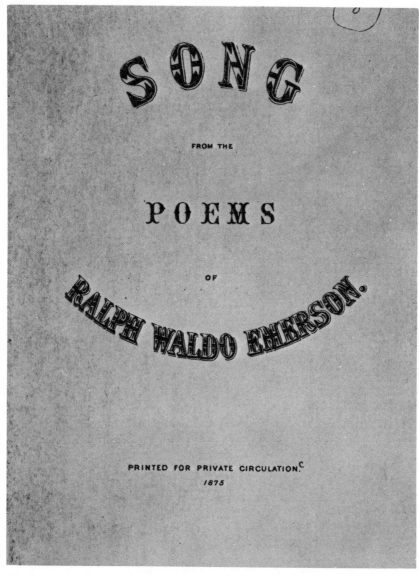

A 33: Cover title, 13^9/₁₆″ × 10^3/₁₆″

Text of A 33

[i–ii] [1] 2–5 [6]

[a]⁴

Contents: p. i: title page; p. ii: blank; p. 1: "The Apology" printed in five stanzas; pp. 2–5: sheet music; p. 6: blank.

Typography and paper: 10⁵/₁₆″ × 7⁷/₈″; wove paper; 12 staves of music per page. No running heads.

Binding: Cover title. All edges trimmed.

Location: MB.

Note: Listed in the MB catalogue as published in '[London]'.

A 34 LETTERS AND SOCIAL AIMS

A 34.1.a
First American edition, first printing (1876)

LETTERS

AND

SOCIAL AIMS.

BY

RALPH WALDO EMERSON.

BOSTON:
JAMES R. OSGOOD AND COMPANY,
LATE TICKNOR & FIELDS, AND FIELDS, OSGOOD, & Co.
1876.

A 34.1.a₁: 7″ × 4⁷/₁₆″

```
COPYRIGHT, 1875.
By RALPH WALDO EMERSON.

UNIVERSITY PRESS: WELCH, BIGELOW, & CO.,
CAMBRIDGE.
```

Two issues have been noted:

A 34.1.a₁
First American edition, first printing, American issue (1876)

[i–iv] [1–3] 4–67 [68–71] 72–96 [97–99] 100–118 [119–121] 122–136 [137–139] 140–154 [155–157] 158–181 [182–185] 186–209 [210–213] 214–238 [239–241] 242–266 [267–269] 270–286 [287–289] 290–314 [315–316]

$[a]^2 1–10^{12} [11]^{12} 12–13^{12} [14]^2$ Falsely signed $[a]^2 A–O^8 Q^8 Q–S^8 T^6$

Contents: p. i: title page; p. ii: copyright page; p. iii: contents; p. iv: blank; p. 1: 'POETRY AND IMAGINATION.'; p. 2: blank; pp. 3–67: "Poetry and Imagination"; p. 68: blank; p. 69: 'SOCIAL AIMS.'; p. 70: blank; pp. 71–96: "Social Aims"; p. 97: 'ELO-QUENCE.'; p. 98: blank; pp. 99–118: "Eloquence"; p. 119: 'RESOURCES.'; p. 120: blank; pp. 121–136: "Resources"; p. 137: 'THE COMIC.'; p. 138: blank; pp. 139–154: "The Comic"; p. 155: 'QUOTATION AND ORIGINALITY.'; p. 156: blank; pp. 157–181: "Quotation and Originality"; p. 182: blank; p. 183: 'PROGRESS OF CULTURE.'; p. 184: blank; pp. 185–209: "Progress of Culture"; p. 210: blank; p. 211: 'PERSIAN POETRY.'; p. 212: blank; pp. 213–238: "Persian Poetry"; p. 239: 'INSPIRATION.'; p. 240: blank; pp. 241–266: "Inspiration"; p. 267: 'GREATNESS.'; p. 268: blank; pp. 269–286: "Greatness"; p. 287: 'IMMORTALITY.'; p. 288: blank; pp. 289–314: "Immortality"; pp. 315–316: blank.

Essays: "Poetry and Imagination" #; "Social Aims" #; "Eloquence" #; "Resources" #; "The Comic" †; "Quotation and Originality" †; "Progress of Culture" #; "Persian Poetry" †; "Inspiration" #; "Greatness" #; "Immortality" #.

Typography and paper: $5^5/_{16}''$ ($5^1/_{16}''$) × $3^1/_{16}''$; wove paper; 29 lines per page. Running heads: rectos: pp. 5–9: 'INTRODUCTORY.'; pp. 11–15: 'POETRY.'; pp. 17–25: 'IMAGINATION.'; pp. 27–33: 'VERACITY.'; pp. 35–39: 'CREATION.'; pp. 41–49: 'MELODY, RHYME, FORM.'; pp. 51–55: 'BARDS AND TROUVEURS.'; pp. 57–61: 'MORALS.'; pp. 63–67: 'TRANSCENDENCY.'; pp. 73–95, 101–117, 123–135, 141–153, 159–181, 187–209, 215–237, 243–265, 271–285, 291–313: titles of chapters; versos: pp. 4–68, 72–96, 100–118, 122–136, 140–154, 158–180, 186–208, 214–238, 242–266, 270–286, 290–314: titles of chapters.

Binding: Medium green or dark reddish orange C cloth (sand); dark reddish orange or medium purple FL cloth (dotted-line); grayish brown or medium green S cloth (diagonal rib); bevelled edges. Front and back covers: blindstamped single-rule frame; spine: blindstamped double rules on top and bottom with goldstamped 'LETTERS | AND | SOCIAL AIMS | [rule] | R. W. EMERSON | [publisher's logo]'. Flyleaves. Brown coated endpapers. All edges trimmed.

Publication: Emerson wrote Osgood on 13 August 1875 that the title of his new book would be "Poetry & Criticism" (MiD; see also I 13). On 31 August 1875, Emerson noted in his "Pocket Diary," "Proofs sent to Osgood," undoubtedly meaning that he had sent his manuscript (MH). 5,000 copies printed 15 December 1875. Advertised as "Published This Day," in *Boston Daily Advertiser,* 15 December 1875, p. 2. Listed in *Publishers' Weekly,* 8 (25 December 1875), 948. *Publishers' Weekly* reported that "the fifth thousand was in the market before January 1st, and . . . a second edition has been called for" (9 [1 April 1870], 448). Copyright, 6 December 1875. MBAt copy received 16 December 1875. Inscribed copies: CtY (from Emerson, 25 December 1875), JM (from Ellen Emerson Forbes, 25 December 1875), MB (25 December 1875), InU (from Emerson, December 1875), JM (December 1875), MCo (from Emerson, December 1875), NN (from Emerson, December 1875), TxU (from Emerson, December 1875), ViU (from Emerson, December 1875, two copies). Price, $2.00. Royalty, 40¢ per copy after the first 300 copies.

Locations: CSt, CtY, DLC, JM, MB, MBAt, MCo, MH, MH-AH, MHi, NN, NNC, PSt, TxU, ViU.

Note one: Emerson's contract, dated 1 January 1876, called for him to pay for and retain the plates, with Osgood paying him $2,500 for costs, and to retain copyright. Emerson would receive a 40¢ per copy royalty after 300 copies had been sold; this would remain in effect until 1 September 1876, when *Letters and Social Aims* would come under the flat fee of $1,500 which Emerson would receive annually for all his books.

Note two: Emerson was greatly assisted in compiling this volume by James Elliot Cabot and Ellen Emerson.

Note three: The period after '1876' on the title page is to the left of 'FIELDS' in the line above.

Note four: The following readings are present:

     308.5   inviolate
     308.19   choices

A 34.1.a₂
First edition, first printing, English issue (1876)

LETTERS

AND

SOCIAL   AIMS.

BY

RALPH   WALDO   EMERSON.

𝕃𝕠𝕟𝕕𝕠𝕟:

CHATTO   AND   WINDUS,   PICCADILLY.

1876.

A 34.1.a₂: 7⁵/₁₆″ × 4³/₄″

[i–vi] [1–3] . . . 290–314

[a–b²] (–b₁) 1–10¹² [11]¹² 12–13¹² [14]² (–14₂)   Falsely signed [a]³ A–O⁸ Q⁸ Q–S⁸ T⁵
The cancelled leaf in gathering b is the American title leaf; in gathering [14], a blank
leaf.

Contents: p. i: '*LETTERS* | AND | *SOCIAL AIMS*.'; p. ii: blank; p. iii: title page; p. iv:
blank; p. v: contents; p. vi: blank; pp. 1–314: the same as in the American issue.

Typography and paper: The same as in the American issue.

Binding: Grayish brown S cloth (diagonal rib). Front cover: blackstamped ornate
design and boxes (see illustration); spine: blackstamped leaf-and-vine design with
goldstamped 'LETTERS | AND | SOCIAL | AIMS | [rule] | EMERSON | [urn-and-flower
publisher's logo]'. Dark gray-green coated endpapers. All edges rough trimmed.

Publication: Osgood shipped 500 copies to Chatto & Windus on 10 [*sic*] December
1875. Advertised as "Essays and Social Aims" to be ready "In a few days," in
Athenæum, no. 2514 (1 January 1876), 10. Listed in *Athenæum*, no. 2515 (8 January
1876), 54; as "Essays on Poetry and Imagination, Eloquence, Persian Poetry, Greatness, Immortality, &c." and published between 1 and 17 January 1876, in *Publishers'
Circular and Booksellers' Record*, 39 (18 January 1876), 12. Deposit copy: BL (6
January 1876). Price, 7s. 6d.

Locations: BL, JM, MCo, MH, MWA, NN, NNC.

Binding for A 34.1.a₂

Note one: Copies have been noted with a 32-page catalogue of Chatto & Windus's publications, dated October 1875, inserted at the back: BL, MH, NNC.

Note two: Copies have been noted with a 32-page catalogue of Chatto & Windus's publications, dated January 1876, inserted at the back: JM, MCo, MWA, NN.

Note three: Copies have been noted with inserted presentation slips from Emerson: dated 5 December 1875 (NN); dated 25 December 1875 (NNC).

LATER PRINTINGS WITHIN THE FIRST AMERICAN EDITION

A 34.1.b
First American edition, second printing (1876)

Boston: James R. Osgood and Company, 1876. Pagination, collation, contents, and typography and paper are the same as in the first printing.

Binding: Medium green or dark reddish orange C cloth (sand); dark reddish brown or dark reddish orange FL cloth (dotted line); grayish brown S cloth (diagonal rib); all else the same as in the first printing binding.

Publication: 450 copies printed 15 January 1876. Inscribed copy: ViU (June 1876).

Locations: CtY, InU, JM, MH, NNC, NjP, RPB, ViU.

Note one: Falsely signed the same as in the first printing.

Note two: Title page line registration is the same as in the first printing.

Note three: The following readings are present:

    308.5   inviolable
    308.19   choices

A 34.1.c$_1$
First American edition, third printing, American issue (1876)

Boston: James R. Osgood and Company, 1876. Pagination, collation, contents, and typography and paper are the same as in the first printing.

Binding: Purple FL cloth (dotted line); medium green S cloth (diagonal rib); all else the same as in the first printing binding.

Publication: 2,000 copies printed 1 February 1876.

Locations: MH, MWA, RPB.

Note one: Falsely signed the same as in the first printing.

Note two: Title page line registration is the same as in the first printing.

Note three: The following readings are present:

    308.5   inviolable
    308.19   choice

These readings are present in subsequent reprintings.

A 34.1.c$_2$
First American edition, third printing, English issue (1876)

London: Chatto and Windus, 1876.

Osgood shipped 500 copies to Chatto and Windus on 1 February 1876. No copies of this issue (with the third printing readings on p. 308) have been located.

A 34.1.d
First American edition, fourth printing (1876)

Boston: James R. Osgood and Company, 1876.

Pagination, contents, and typography and paper are the same as in the first printing. Gathering 1 is unsigned; collation is affected accordingly.

Binding: Two styles have been noted:

Binding A: Dark reddish orange C cloth (sand); dark reddish orange or medium purple FL cloth (dotted line); medium green S cloth (diagonal rib); all else the same as in the first printing binding.

Binding B: Light brown T cloth (rib); bevelled edges. Front and back covers: blind-stamped triple-rule frame with 3½″ ornate leaf-and-vine design in the center; spine: blindstamped rules with goldstamped 'EMERSON'S | WRITINGS | LETTERS | AND | SOCIAL AIMS | JAMES R. OSGOOD & Cᵒ'. Front flyleaf. Yellow endpapers. All edges trimmed.

Publication: 1,000 copies printed 5 June 1876. MH-AH copy received 6 September 1876.

Locations: Binding A: JM, MH-AH, NN, NNC; Binding B: MH.

Note one: Signature marks 'A' on p. 1 and 'N' on p. 209 are not present; the way the book is falsely signed is affected accordingly.

Note two: The period after '1876' on the title page is under the 'FI' of 'FIELDS' in the line above.

Note three: Copies have been noted in medium green C cloth (sand) and medium purple FL cloth (dotted line) with a goldstamped Houghton, Osgood logo at the spine bottom (JM, ViU).

A 34.1.e
Boston: Houghton, Mifflin, 1882.

150 copies printed 8 November 1882. Price, $1.50. *Location:* MH.

Note: As of 15 January 1884, 10 copies of *Letters and Social Aims* were still in stock.

A 34.2.a
Second American edition, first printing (1876)

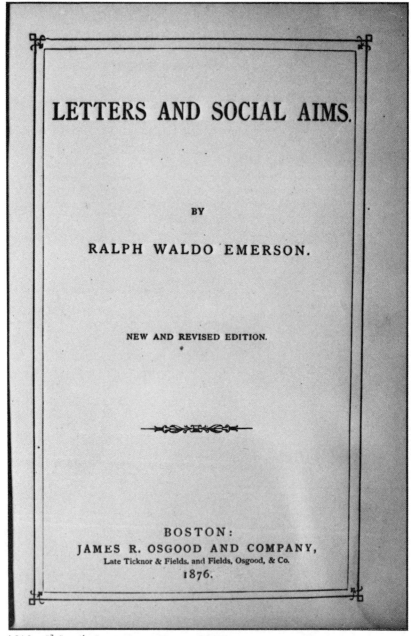

LETTERS AND SOCIAL AIMS.

BY

RALPH WALDO EMERSON.

NEW AND REVISED EDITION.

BOSTON:
JAMES R. OSGOOD AND COMPANY,
Late Ticknor & Fields, and Fields, Osgood, & Co.
1876.

A 34.2.a: 5⁷/₈″ × 4¹/₁₆″; outer frame, title, and 'BOSTON:' are in red

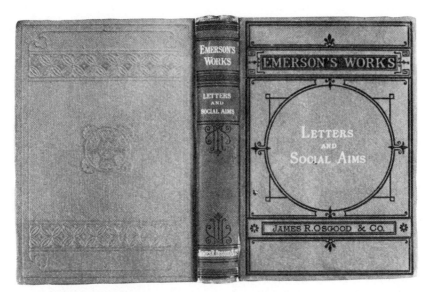

"Little Classic Edition" binding for A 34.2.a

[1–9] 10–64 [65–67] 68–88 [89–91] 92–107 [108–111] 112–123 [124–127] 128–140 [141–143] 144–163 [164–167] 168–187 [188–191] 192–215 [216–219] 220–241 [242–245] 246–260 [261–263] 264–285 [286–288]

[1² 2–18⁸ 19⁴ 20²]   Falsely signed [1]¹² 2–12¹² and [A]⁸ B–R⁸

Contents: p. 1: blank; p. 2: publisher's advertisement; pp. 3–285: basically the same as in the first edition; pp. 286–288: blank.

Typography and paper: 4³/₄″ (4¹/₂″) × 2¹¹/₁₆″; wove paper; 31 lines per page. Running heads basically the same as in the first edition.

Binding: Grayish brown, medium green, or dark reddish orange S cloth (diagonal fine rib). "Little Classic Edition" binding (see illustration) with 'EMERSON'S WORKS' outlined in primary cloth color against black background, goldstamped 'LETTERS | AND | SOCIAL | AIMS', and blackstamped 'JAMES R. OSGOOD & CO.' on front cover, and gold-stamped 'EMERSON'S WORKS | LETTERS | AND | SOCIAL AIMS | JAMES R. OSGOOD & Cº' on spine. Front flyleaf. Dark green coated endpapers. All edges trimmed. All edges stained red.

Publication: Advertised in *Publishers' Weekly*, 10 (16 September 1876), 438. Listed in *Publishers' Weekly*, 10 (23 September 1876), 526. 1,500 copies printed 31 August 1876. Price, $1.50. Royalty: see *Note one* to A 34.1.a₁.

Printing: The same printer's imprint as in A 34.1.a.

Locations: JM, MWiW-C, VtMiM.

Note: Vol. [VIII] of the "Little Classic Edition" (see B 3).

LATER PRINTINGS FROM THE "LITTLE CLASSIC EDITION" PLATES

A 34.2.b
Boston: James R. Osgood, 1877.

500 copies printed 14 August 1877. Price, $1.50. *Location:* NcU.

Note: James R. Osgood was succeeded by Houghton, Osgood in February 1878.

A 34.2.c
Boston: Houghton, Osgood, 1878.

280 copies printed 12 August 1878. Price, $1.50. *Not seen.*

A 34.2.d
Boston: Houghton, Osgood, 1879.

500 copies printed 15 February 1879. Price, $1.50. *Location:* MH.

A 34.2.e
Boston: Houghton, Osgood, 1879.

Combined with *Poems* in two-volumes-in-one format as vol. IV of the "Fireside Edition" (see B 4). 500 copies printed 15 August 1879. *Location:* KU.

A 34.2.f
Boston: Houghton, Osgood, 1880.

Combined with *Poems* in two-volumes-in-one format as vol. IV of the "Fireside Edition" (see B 4). 500 copies printed 6 February 1880. *Location:* JM.

A 34.2.g
Boston: Houghton, Osgood, 1880.

500 copies printed 10 June 1880. Price, $1.50. *Location:* RNR.

Note: Houghton, Osgood was succeeded by Houghton, Mifflin in May 1880.

A 34.2.h
Boston: Houghton, Mifflin, 1881.

Combined with *Poems* in two-volumes-in-one format as vol. IV of the "Fireside Edition" (see B 4). 500 copies printed 7 December 1880. *Location:* MWelC.

A 34.2.i
Boston: Houghton, Mifflin, 1881.

500 copies printed 22 August 1881. Price, $1.50. *Not seen.*

A 34.2.j
Boston: Houghton, Mifflin, 1882.

Combined with *Poems* in two-volumes-in-one format as vol. IV of the "Fireside Edition" (see B 4). 500 copies printed 27 October 1881 and 10 August 1882. *Location:* JM.

A 34.2.k
Boston: Houghton, Mifflin, 1882.

150 copies printed 18 November 1881; 500 copies on 26 May 1882 and 19 September 1882. Price, $1.50. *Not seen.*

A 34.2.l
Boston: Houghton, Mifflin, 1883.

Combined with *Poems* in two-volumes-in-one format as vol. IV of the "Fireside Edition" (see B 4). 270 copies printed 13 January 1883. *Not seen.*

A 34.2.m
Boston: Houghton, Mifflin, 1883.

270 copies printed 22 February 1883 and 7 September 1883. *Location:* JM.

A 34.2.n
Boston and New York: Houghton, Mifflin, 1884.

270 copies printed 16 February 1884. *Location:* MiU.

A 34.2.o
Boston and New York: Houghton, Mifflin, 1885.

270 copies printed 20 February 1885. *Not seen.*

A 34.2.p
Boston and New York: Houghton, Mifflin, 1887.

270 copies printed 4 November 1886. Bound in medium blue V cloth (smooth), rather than "Little Classic Edition" binding, as are subsequent reprintings (see illustration at B 3). *Location:* JM.

A 34.2.q
Boston and New York: Houghton, Mifflin, 1888.

270 copies printed 31 October 1887 and 17 April 1888. *Location:* JM.

A 34.2.r
Boston and New York: Houghton, Mifflin, 1889.

270 copies printed 15 November 1888 and 29 July 1889. *Location:* JM.

A 34.2.s
Boston and New York: Houghton, Mifflin, 1890.

250 copies printed ca. March 1890. *Not seen.*

A 34.2.t
Boston and New York: Houghton, Mifflin, 1891.

250 copies printed ca. December 1890; 500 copies on 14 October 1891. *Location:* JM.

A 34.2.u
Boston and New York: Houghton, Mifflin, 1893.

500 copies printed 30 November 1892. *Location:* MHi.

A 34.2.v
Boston and New York: Houghton, Mifflin, 1894.

500 copies printed 21 December 1893. *Location:* MH.

A 34.2.w
Boston and New York: Houghton, Mifflin, 1895.

270 copies printed 10 October 1895. *Not seen.*

A 34.2.x
Boston and New York: Houghton, Mifflin, 1898.

270 copies printed 21 January 1898. *Location:* NbPerT.

A 34.2.y
Boston and New York: Houghton, Mifflin, [n.d.].

Approximately 1,300 copies sold between 1900 and 1923. *Location:* JM.

Note: Approximately 12,000 copies of *Letters and Social Aims* printed from the "Little Classic Edition" plates were sold between 1876 and 1923, when the title was apparently allowed to go out of print in this format.

GERMAN EDITION

A 34.3.a
First German edition, first printing (1876)

[all but English title and date in gothic] Neue Essays | (LETTERS AND SOCIAL AIMS) | von | R. W. Emerson. | [wavy rule] | Autorisirte Uebersetzung. | Mit einer Einleitung | von | Julian Schmidt. | [ornate rule] | Stuttgart: | Verlag von Aug. Berth. Auerbach. | 1876.

324 pp. Contains a facsimile of Emerson's manuscript "Authors Note," dated Concord, 24 February 1876, after p. xlii. Introduction dated March 1876. Auerbach had sent Emerson $100 on 25 August 1875 for advance sheets of *Letters and Social Aims* (*L,* VI, 282n.). *Location:* NNC.

A 34.3.b
Stuttgart: Abenheim'iche Verlagsbuchhandlung, [n.d.].

Wrappers. *Location:* NNC, OCl.

A 34.4
First English edition, only printing (1877)

LETTERS

AND

SOCIAL AIMS.

BY

RALPH WALDO EMERSON.

London:
CHATTO AND WINDUS, PICCADILLY.
1877.

A 34.4: 6¼″ × 4½″

```
┌─────────────────────────────────────────────────────┐
│                    LONDON                             │
│      PRINTED BY J. OGDEN AND CO.,                     │
│            172, ST. JOHN STREET, E.C.                 │
└─────────────────────────────────────────────────────┘
```

Two issues have been noted:

A 34.4.a₁
First English edition, only printing, first issue (1877)

[1–8] 9–64 [65] 66–87 [88] 89–105 [106] 107–119 [120] 121–133 [134] 135–156
[157] 158–179 [180] 181–203 [204] 205–227 [228] 229–243 [244] 245–267 [268–
272]

[B]⁸ C–I⁸ K–S⁸

Contents: p. 1: 'LETTERS | AND | SOCIAL AIMS.'; p. 2: advertisement for "The
Golden Library" series; p. 3: title page; p. 4: printer's imprint; p. 5: 'CONTENTS.'; p. 6:
blank; pp. 7–64: "Poetry and Imagination"; pp. 65–87: "Social Aims"; pp. 88–105:
"Eloquence"; pp. 106–119: "Resources"; pp. 120–133: "The Comic"; pp. 134–156:
"Quotation and Originality"; pp. 157–179: "Progress of Culture"; pp. 180–203: "Persian
Poetry"; pp. 204–227: "Inspiration"; pp. 228–243: "Greatness"; pp. 244–267: "Immor-
tality"; p. 268: blank; p. 269: publisher's device; p. 270: blank; p. 271: '[ornamental
band] | *CHATTO & WINDUS'S* | *List of Books.* | [design]'; p. 272: blank.

Typography and paper: 5″ (4³⁄₄″) × 3″; wove paper; 31 lines per page. Running
heads: rectos: pp. 9–11: '*INTRODUCTORY.*'; pp. 13–19: '*POETRY.*'; pp. 21–27:
'*IMAGINATION.*'; pp. 29–35: '*VERACITY.*'; pp. 37–39: '*CREATION.*'; pp. 41–49: '*MEL-
ODY, RHYME, FORM.*'; pp. 51–53: '*BARDS AND TROUVEURS.*'; pp. 55–59: '*MO-
RALS.*'; pp. 61–63: '*TRANSCENDENCY.*'; pp. 67–155, 159–267: chapter titles; versos:
pp. 8–86, 90–104, 108–118, 122–132, 136–178, 182–202, 206–226, 230–242, 246–
266: chapter titles.

Binding: Brown orange S cloth (diagonal rib). Front cover: blackstamped ornate
design (see illustration) with 'THE GOLDEN LIBRARY | EMERSON'S | LETTERS AND SOCIAL |
AIMS. | CHATTO & WINDUS'; back cover: blindstamped double-rule frame with boxes in
each corner; spine: blackstamped ornate design (see illustration) with goldstamped
'EMERSON'S | LETTERS | AND | SOCIAL AIMS | 5 | [curved] CHATTO & WINDUS'. Pale
yellow endpapers. All edges trimmed.

Publication: Listed as published between 1 and 15 November 1876, in *Publishers'
Circular and Booksellers' Record*, 39 (16 November 1876), 924. Price, 2s.

Printing: "LONDON | PRINTED BY J. OGDEN AND CO., | 172, ST. JOHN STREET,
E.C." (p. [4]).

Location: JM.

Note one: *The Golden Library*, no. 5.

Note two: A 36-page catalogue of Chatto and Windus's publications, dated October
1876, is inserted at the back.

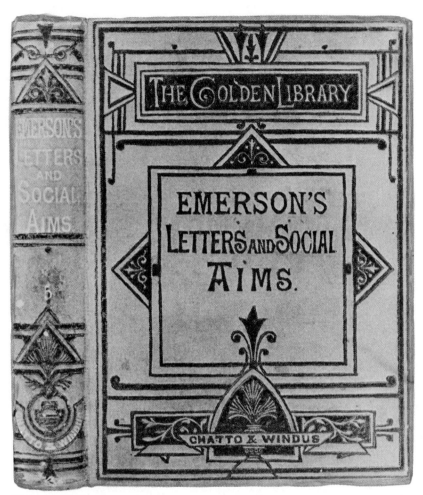

Binding for A 34.4.a₁

A 34.4.a₂
First English edition, only printing, second issue (1879?)

London: Chatto and Windus, 1877.

[1–7] . . . 245–267 [268–270]

[B]⁸ C–I⁸ K–S⁸ (–S₈)   The cancelled leaf contained the half title for the publisher's advertisements

Contents: pp. 1–270: the same as in the first issue.

Typography and paper: The same as in the first issue.

Binding: The same as the first issue, except: medium yellow brown S cloth (diagonal rib); the '5' on the spine is not present; yellow coated endpapers.

Publication: After the first issue, as evidenced by the cancellation, which was done to permit the insertion of a new catalogue of Chatto and Windus's publications (see *Note* below).

Location: JM.

Note: A 40-page catalogue of Chatto and Windus's publications, dated February 1879, is inserted at the back.

LATER EDITION

A 34.5.a–f
London: Macmillan, 1883.

260 pp. Vol. VI of the *Works* (see B 6). Listed in *Athenæum,* no. 2904 (23 June 1883), 795; as published between 16 and 30 June, *Publishers' Circular and Booksellers' Record,* 46 (1 July 1883), 571; in *Bookseller,* no. 308 (5 July 1883), 673. Published June 1903. Price, 5s. Reprinted (usually with dual New York imprint) 1885, 1891, 1898, 1903, 1910. *Locations:* BL (26 June 1883), BC (4 August 1883), BO (14 August 1883).

PRINTINGS FROM THE RIVERSIDE EDITION PLATES

A 34.6.a
Riverside Edition (trade), first printing (1883)

LETTERS AND SOCIAL AIMS | BY | RALPH WALDO EMERSON | [gothic] New and Revised Edition | [publisher's logo] | BOSTON | HOUGHTON, MIFFLIN AND COMPANY | New York: 11 East Seventeenth Street | [gothic] The Riverside Press, Cambridge | 1883

333 pp. Vol. VIII of the *Riverside Edition,* trade printing (see B 7). 1,500 copies printed 8 October 1883. Listed in *Publishers' Weekly,* 24 (27 October 1883), 574. According to the publisher's records, published 20 October 1883. Copyright, 10 October 1883. Price, $1.75. *Locations:* DLC (24 October 1883), JM.

Note: Copies have been noted with a pine branch on the title page instead of the publisher's logo.

A 34.6.b
Riverside Edition (Copyright), second (English) printing (1883)

LETTERS AND SOCIAL AIMS | BY | RALPH WALDO EMERSON | [gothic] The Riverside Edition | (COPYRIGHT) | LONDON | GEORGE ROUTLEDGE AND SONS | BROADWAY, LUDGATE HILL | NEW YORK: 9, LAFAYETTE PLACE | 1883

Vol. VIII of the *Riverside Edition (Copyright),* English trade printing (see B 10). 1,000 copies printed 8 October 1883. Listed as published between 16 and 31 October, in *Publishers' Circular and Booksellers' Record,* 46 (1 November 1883), 1060. Price, 3s. 6d. *Locations:* BC (15 November 1883), BO (16 November 1883), BL (8 December 1883), JM.

A 34.6.c$_1$
Riverside Edition (large paper), third printing, American issue (1883)

[red] LETTERS AND SOCIAL AIMS | BY | RALPH WALDO EMERSON | [gothic] New and Revised Edition | [pine branch] | [red] CAMBRIDGE | [gothic] Printed at the Riverside Press | 1883

Vol. VIII of the *Riverside Edition,* large paper printing (see B 8). Limited to 500 numbered copies printed 31 December 1883. Price, $4.00. Sold out within a year. *Locations:* JM, TxU.

A 34.6.c$_2$
Riverside Edition (large paper), third printing, English issue (1883)

Title page is the same as in the American issue, except for publisher's imprint: 'LONDON | KEGAN PAUL, TRENCH, & CO., I, PATERNOSTER SQUARE | MDCCCLXXXIII'.

Vol. VIII of the *Riverside Edition,* large paper printing for English subscribers (see B 9). 25 title leaves printed 31 December 1883. Title leaf is a cancel. Limited to 25 signed and numbered copies. *Location:* JM.

A 34.6.d
Boston and New York: Houghton, Mifflin, 1884.

500 copies printed 31 December 1883, 11 April 1884, and 30 October 1884. *Location:* JM.

A 34.6.e
Boston and New York: Houghton, Mifflin, 1885.

500 copies printed 3 April 1885 and 23 September 1885. *Location:* JM.

A 34.6.f
Boston and New York: Houghton, Mifflin, 1886.

500 copies printed 15 April 1886. *Location:* MH.

A 34.6.g
Boston and New York: Houghton, Mifflin, 1887.

500 copies printed 4 November 1886 and 11 May 1887. *Location:* MBAt.

A 34.6.h
Boston and New York: Houghton, Mifflin, 1888.

500 copies printed 13 December 1887, 21 April 1888, and 27 October 1888. *Location:* JM.

A 34.6.i
Boston and New York: Houghton, Mifflin, 1889.

500 copies printed 20 July 1889. *Not seen.*

A 34.6.j
Boston and New York: Houghton, Mifflin, 1890.

500 copies printed 21 February 1890 and ca. September 1890. *Location:* JM.

A 34.6.k
Boston and New York: Houghton, Mifflin, 1892.

500 copies printed 18 November 1891 and 4 June 1892. *Location:* MNew.

A 34.6.l
Boston and New York: Houghton, Mifflin, 1893.

500 copies printed 6 June 1893. *Location:* JM.

A 34.6.m
Boston and New York: Houghton, Mifflin, 1894.

500 copies printed 30 April 1894. *Location:* MH.

A 34.6.n
Standard Library Edition printing [1894]

LETTERS AND SOCIAL AIMS | BY | RALPH WALDO EMERSON | [pine branch] | BOSTON AND NEW YORK | HOUGHTON, MIFFLIN AND COMPANY | [gothic] The Riverside Press, Cambridge

Vol. VIII of the *Standard Library Edition* (see B 11). 1,000 copies printed 17 November 1894, 30 April 1895, and 29 May 1896; 500 copies on 31 January 1898. *Location:* JM.

A 34.6.o
Boston and New York: Houghton, Mifflin, 1895.

Location: JM.

A 34.6.p
Boston and New York: Houghton, Mifflin, 1896.

500 copies printed 30 November 1895. *Not seen.*

A 34.6.q
Boston and New York: Houghton, Mifflin, 1897.

270 copies printed 27 February 1897. *Location:* JM.

A 34.6.r
Boston and New York: Houghton, Mifflin, 1898.

270 copies printed 17 January 1898. *Location:* Ia.

A 34.6.s
Boston and New York: Houghton, Mifflin, 1899.

270 copies printed 10 January 1899 and 22 June 1899. *Location:* CtY.

A 34.6.t
London: George Routledge and Sons, 1899.

Location: CaQMM.

A 34.6.u
Boston and New York: Houghton, Mifflin, 1900.

250 copies printed July–September 1900. *Location:* MAt.

A 34.6.v
London: George Routledge and Sons, 1903.

Location: JM.

A 34.6.w
London: George Routledge & Sons, 1903.

Combined with *Society and Solitude* and *Poems* in three-volumes-in-one format as vol. III of the "Sovereign Edition" (see B 12). 1,000 copies printed 16 September 1903. *Location:* InU.

A 34.6.x
Fireside Edition printing (1909)

[all within red double-rule frame with red floral ornaments in each corner] THE WORKS OF | [red gothic] Ralph Waldo Emerson | LETTERS AND SOCIAL AIMS | [engraving of man reading book in chair before fireplace] | [gothic] Fireside Edition | BOSTON AND NEW YORK | MDCCCCIX

Vol. VIII of the *Fireside Edition* (see B 13). 500 copies printed 6 October 1909 and 15 May 1910. *Location:* JM.

A 34.6.y
Boston and New York: Jefferson Press, [ca. 1912].

Combined with *Society and Solitude* in two-volumes-in-one format as vol. [IV] of the "Jefferson Press Edition" (see B 14). *Location:* CtW.

A 34.6.z
New York: Sully and Kleinteich, [ca. 1912].

Vol. VIII of the *University Edition* (see B 15). *Location:* JM.

A 34.6.aa
Boston and New York: Houghton, Mifflin, [n.d.].

Approximately 1,500 copies sold between 1901 and 1913. *Location:* JM.

Note one: The copyright on *Letters and Social Aims* was renewed 11 November 1903.

Note two: Approximately 13,500 copies of *Letters and Social Aims* in the *Riverside Edition* were sold between 1883 and 1913, when the title was apparently allowed to go out of print in this format.

A 34.6.bb
London: Waverley Book Company, [n.d.].

Vol. VIII of the "Waverly" *Riverside Edition* (see B 16). *Location:* JM.

A 34.7
London: George Bell and Sons, 1897.

Advertised as included in "Bohn's Standard Library." Published September 1897. Price, 1s. *Not seen.*

PRINTINGS FROM THE CENTENARY EDITION PLATES

A 34.8.a
Autograph Centenary Edition (large paper), first printing (1904)

RALPH WALDO EMERSON | [red] Letters and Social | [red] Aims | [pine tree] | CAM-BRIDGE | [red gothic] Printed at the Riverside Press | 1904

441 pp. Vol. VIII of the *Autograph Centenary Edition* (see B 19). Limited to 600 signed and numbered copies printed 13 May 1904. Copyright, 16 May 1904. Price, $6.00. Sold out by 5 April 1906. *Locations:* DLC (21 May 1904), JM.

A 34.8.b$_1$
Centenary Edition (trade), second printing, American issue (1904)

LETTERS AND SOCIAL AIMS | BY | RALPH WALDO EMERSON | [pine tree] | BOSTON AND NEW YORK | HOUGHTON, MIFFLIN AND COMPANY, | [gothic] The Riverside Press, Cambridge | 1904

Dust jacket. Vol. VIII of the *Centenary Edition,* trade printing (see B 18). 1,000 copies printed 14 May 1904. Listed in *Publishers' Weekly,* 65 (4 June 1904), 1429. According to the publisher's records, published 28 May 1904. Copyright, 16 May 1904. Price, $1.75. *Locations:* DLC (21 May 1904), JM.

Note: Numerous reprintings with undated title pages. 2,000 copies printed between 30 December 1904 and 30 September 1908. Approximately 4,100 copies sold through 1923.

A 34.8.b$_2$
English issue

London: A. P. Watt & Son, [1904].

Vol. VIII of the English *Centenary Edition* (see B 21). American sheets with Watt's label pasted on the title page. Price, 6s. *Locations:* BL (30 May 1904), BC (7 June 1904), BO (7 June 1904).

A 34.8.c
Boston and New York: Houghton, Mifflin, 1904.

Vol. VIII of the *Concord Edition* (see B 20). 2,000 copies printed 19 May 1904. *Location:* JM.

Note: Numerous reprintings with undated title pages. Approximately 3,100 copies sold by 31 December 1910.

A 34.8.d
Boston and New York: Houghton Mifflin, [1914].

Vol. VIII of the *Riverside Pocket Edition* (see B 22). Approximately 900 copies sold between 1914 and 1922. *Not seen.*

A 34.8.e
Boston and New York: Houghton Mifflin, [1917].

Vol. VIII of the *Centenary Edition*, trade printing (see B 18). *Location:* PSC.

A 34.8.f
Boston and New York: Houghton Mifflin, 1921.

352 pp. (text without the notes). Combined with *Nature; Addresses, and Lectures* in two-volumes-in-one format as vol. II of *Emerson's Complete Works* (see B 23). *Location:* RP.

A 34.8.g
New York: Wm. H. Wise, 1923.

Combined with *Society and Solitude* in two-volumes-in-one format as vol. VI of the *Current Opinion Edition* (see B 24). *Location:* JM.

A 34.8.h
Boston and New York: Houghton Mifflin, 1929.

Combined (text without the notes) with *Nature; Addresses, and Lectures* in two-volumes-in-one format as vol. [II] of the *Harvard Edition* (see B 25). *Location:* JM.

A 34.8.i
New York: Wm. H. Wise, 1929.

Combined with *Society and Solitude* in two-volumes-in-one format as vol. IV of the *Medallion Edition* (see B 26). *Location:* OC.

A 34.8.j–k
New York: AMS Press, [1968].

Vol. VIII of the "AMS Press" *Centenary Edition* (see B 27). Reprinted 1979. *Locations:* TxU, DLC (9 November 1979).

SEPARATE PUBLICATIONS OF INDIVIDUAL ESSAYS

A 34.9.a–b
Success, Greatness, Immortality. Boston: James R. Osgood, 1877.

96 pp. *Vest-Pocket Series*, no. 20. 1,000 copies printed 1 May 1877; 500 copies in June 1877. Listed in *Publishers' Weekly*, 11 (26 May 1877), 559. Price, 50¢. Reprinted by Houghton, Osgood in 1880. *Locations:* MB (21 May 1877), N (1880).

A 35
First edition, only printing (1876)

REMARKS
BY
R. W. EMERSON
AT THE
Centennial Celebration of the Latin School,

NOVEMBER 8, 1876.

I dare not attempt to say anything to
you, because, in my old age, I am forget-
ting the word that I should speak. I
can't remember anybody's name, not
even my recollections of the Latin school.
I have, therefore, guarded against abso-
lute silence by bringing you a few reminiscences which I have written. [Ap-
plause.] When I entered the Latin school,
nine or ten years old, William Bigelow
was master. The schoolhouse was very
old and shabby, and it was decided to
pull it down and rebuild it on the same
ground. In wintering, the scholars were
removed to the old wooden block on the
Milldam, and soon after to a loft on Pem-
berton Hill. You need not seek for the
places, for you cannot find them. One
was where the Boston and Maine depot now
stands, and the other was where Scollay's
building stood, now called Tremont row.
We are now coming to the new schoolhouse, rebuilt where the Parker House
now stands. In Mr. William Bigelow's
reign the boys discovered his habit of

A 35: Broadside, 16³/₄" × 4¹/₈"; partial reproduction

Broadside, printed on recto only

Typography and paper: 14⁵/₁₆″ × 2¹/₄″; wove paper; 108 lines. No running head.

Publication: Possibly printed soon after 9 November 1876, the date on which these remarks appeared in the *Boston Daily Advertiser* (see E 185).

Locations: MBAt, MCo, MH.

Note: This may be a late nineteenth-century edition, but no conclusive evidence exists. The MCo copy is inserted into a scrapbook compiled in 1883.

A 36 FORTUNE OF THE REPUBLIC

A 36.1.a
First edition, first printing (1878)

FORTUNE OF THE REPUBLIC.

LECTURE

DELIVERED AT THE OLD SOUTH CHURCH,

March 30, 1878.

BY

RALPH WALDO EMERSON.

BOSTON:

HOUGHTON, OSGOOD AND COMPANY.

The Riverside Press, Cambridge.

1878.

A 36.1.a: Cloth, $6^{13}/_{16}"$ × $4^{1}/_{4}"$; Wrappers, $7^{7}/_{8}"$ × $4^{1}/_{4}"$

Copyright, 1878,

By RALPH WALDO EMERSON.

All rights reserved.

RIVERSIDE, CAMBRIDGE:

STEREOTYPED AND PRINTED BY

H. O. HOUGHTON AND COMPANY.

[i–iv] [1] 2–44

[1–3]^8 Signed [a]^2 1–2^8 3^6

Contents: pp. i–ii: blank; p. iii: title page; p. iv: copyright page; pp. 1–44: text.

Typography and paper: 4^3/$_4$″ (4^1/$_2$″) × 2^{13}/$_{16}$″; laid paper with 1^1/$_4$″ vertical chain marks; 22 lines per page. Running heads: rectos: pp. 3–43: 'FORTUNE OF THE REPUBLIC.'; versos: pp. 2–44: 'FORTUNE OF THE REPUBLIC.'.

Binding: Two styles have been noted, priority undetermined:

Binding A: Dark brown, medium brown, or dark reddish orange S cloth (diagonal fine-rib); dark reddish orange FL cloth (dotted-line). Front cover: blindstamped single-rule frame with goldstamped '*Fortune* | OF THE | *Republic* | [next three lines blindstamped] [rule] | [oval ornament] | [rule] | *Ralph Waldo Emerson*'; back cover: same blindstamped frame, rules, and ornament as the front cover; spine: blank. Laid paper double flyleaves or laid paper double front and wove paper double back flyleaves. Brown coated endpapers. All edges trimmed.

Binding B: Gray or light greenish gray stiff wrappers. Front recto: same as the title page, except: triple-rule above title, rule after '*Republic*', publisher's device is not present, rule after 'EMERSON.', and triple-rule after '1878.'; front verso, back recto and verso: blank; spine: blank. Stapled. All edges trimmed.

FORTUNE OF THE REPUBLIC.

LECTURE

DELIVERED AT THE OLD SOUTH CHURCH,

March 30, 1878.

BY

RALPH WALDO EMERSON.

BOSTON:

HOUGHTON, OSGOOD AND COMPANY.

The Riverside Press, Cambridge.

1878.

Wrapper for A 36.1.a

Publication: 504 copies in cloth and 300 copies in wrappers printed 17 July 1878. Listed in cloth in *Publishers' Weekly*, 14 (10 August 1878), 156, and noted in cloth and wrappers, p. 164. According to Emerson's contract, dated 17 August 1878, he paid for and retained the plates, and retained copyright. Copyright, 22 July 1878. MB copy received 9 August 1878. Inscribed copies: Binding A: NNC (from Emerson, 26 August 1878), NN (7 August 1878), JM (August 1878). Prices: cloth, 50¢; wrappers, 25¢. Royalty, 10¢ per copy in cloth and 5¢ per copy in wrappers after the first 300 copies.

Locations: Binding A: BL, CSt, CtY, DLC, InU, JM, MB, MCo, MH, NN, NNC, NjP, PSt, TxU, ViU, VtMiM; Binding B: CtY, JM, MWA, NN, NcD.

Note one: Advertised as an importation in cloth at 1s. by Walter Lewin.

Note two: Contrary to the title page information, the lecture was actually delivered 25 February 1878 (see *L*, VI, 309).

LATER PRINTINGS WITHIN THE FIRST EDITION

A 36.1.b–d
First edition, second through fourth printings (1878)

Boston: Houghton, Osgood, and Company, 1878.

200 copies in cloth and 322 copies in wrappers printed 27 August 1878; 222 copies in cloth and 300 copies in wrappers on 4 September 1878; 300 copies in cloth and 200 copies in wrappers on 23 October 1878.

Note: The second through fourth printings cannot be distinguished.

A 36.1.e
Boston: Houghton, Osgood, 1879.

Location: JM.

Note: A copy of the 1879 sheets in wrappers imprinted 1878 has been noted: MHi.

A 36.1.f
Boston: Houghton, Osgood, 1880.

Location: KU.

Note one: Copies in wrappers were sold out by 1886; copies in cloth were sold out by 1888.

Note two: The plates of *Fortune of the Republic* were melted by 1 July 1906.

Note three: The copyright on *Fortune of the Republic* was renewed 22 July 1906.

A 37
First edition, only printing (1879)

GENERAL INTRODUCTION

TO

THE HUNDRED GREATEST MEN.

[LONDON: 1879.]

A 37: Cover title, $8^3/8'' \times 5^5/8''$

[1-4]

[a]^2

Contents: p. 1: cover title; pp. 2-4: text.

Typography and paper: 6″ × 3^{11}/$_{16}$″; wove paper; 34 lines per page. No running heads.

Binding: Cover title. Single sheet, folded once; unbound. All edges trimmed.

Publication: The Hundred Greatest Men (see D 109) was advertised in *Publishers' Circular and Booksellers' Record,* 43 (6 December 1880), 1194-1195.

Printing: Sampson Low, Marston, Searle, and Rivington.

Locations: MCo, MH.

Note: Really the work of James Elliot Cabot and Ellen Emerson, working from Emerson's journals (see *L,* VI, 318-319); the manuscript draft of the introduction is in both their hands (MH).

A 38
First edition, only printing (1880)

THE PREACHER.

BY

RALPH WALDO EMERSON.

REPRINTED FROM "THE UNITARIAN REVIEW."

BOSTON :
GEORGE H. ELLIS, PRINTER, 101 MILK STREET.
1880.

A 38: 9$\frac{1}{2}$″ × 5$\frac{7}{8}$″

[1–3] 4–15 [16]

[a]⁸

Contents: p. 1: title page; p. 2: blank; pp. 3–15: text; p. 16: blank.

Typography and paper: 6⁷/₈″ (6⁵/₈″) × 3⁷/₈″; wove paper; 38 lines per page. Running heads: rectos: pp. 5–15: 'THE PREACHER.'; versos: pp. 4–14: 'THE PREACHER.'.

Binding: Reddish–brown wrappers. Front recto: 'THE PREACHER. | BY | RALPH WALDO EMERSON.'; front verso, back recto and verso: blank. All edges trimmed.

Publication: Listed in *Publishers' Weekly,* 17 (27 March 1880), 332. Deposit copy: BL (bound, 8 July 1880). Price, 15¢.

Locations: CtY, DLC, JM, MH, MHi, MWA, MWiW-C, NN, NNC, NcD, NjP, RPB, ViU, VtMiM.

Note one: Advertised as an importation at 5d. by Walter Lewin.

Note two: A copy has been noted with a slip of paper, printed on the recto, tipped to p. 1: all within a single-rule frame: 'TO THE EDITOR OF | [line of dots] | [line of dots] | Published by GEORGE H. ELLIS, | 101 MILK STREET, BOSTON. | [flush left] *Price,* $ [line of dots]   [flush right] Please send any paper containing notice.'. The price written in here is 10¢. *Location:* NN.

THE PREACHER.

BY

RALPH WALDO EMERSON.

A 39 THE CORRESPONDENCE OF THOMAS CARLYLE AND RALPH WALDO EMERSON

A 39.1.a
First American edition, first printing (1883)

Two issues have been noted:

A 39.1.a₁
First edition, first printing, American issue (1883)

THE CORRESPONDENCE

OF

THOMAS CARLYLE

AND

RALPH WALDO EMERSON

1834—1872

"To my friend I write a letter, and from him I receive a letter. It is a
spiritual gift, worthy of him to give, and of me to receive." — EMERSON

"What the writer did actually mean, the thing he then thought of, the
thing he then was." — CARLYLE

VOLUME I

BOSTON
JAMES R. OSGOOD AND COMPANY
1883

A 39.1.a₁: 7⅝″ × 5″

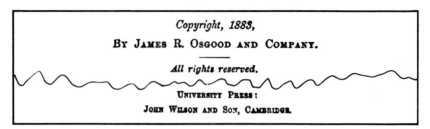

I: [a–b] [i–iii] iv [v] vi–xii 1–9 [10–11] 12–368

II: [a–b] [i–iii] iv–xiii [xiv] 1–354 [355] 356–370 [371] 372–383 [384]

I: [1^8(-1_1) 2–31^6 32^4] Signed [a]^7 1–23^8

II: [1^8 2–29^6 30^4 31–32^6 33^8] Signed [a]^8 1–20^8 [21]^8 22–24^8

Contents: I: pp. a–b: blank; inserted leaf with drawing of Carlyle printed on verso; p. i: title page; p. ii: copyright page; pp. iii–iv: 'EDITORIAL NOTE.' signed 'CHARLES ELIOT NORTON. | CAMBRIDGE, MASSACHUSETTS, | January 29, 1883.'; pp. v–xii: contents of vol. I; pp. 1–368: text; II: pp. a–b: blank; inserted leaf with drawing of Emerson printed on verso; p. i: title page; p. ii: copyright page; pp. iii–xiii: contents of vol. II; p. xiv: blank; pp. 1–354: text; pp. 355–370: index to Carlyle's letters; pp. 371–383: index to Emerson's letters; p. 384: blank.

Typography and paper: 5⁷/₁₆″ (5¹/₈″) × 3³/₁₆″; wove paper; 26 lines per page. Running heads: I: verso: p. iv: '*Editorial Note.*'; rectos and versos: pp. vi–xii: '*Contents of Volume I.*'; versos: pp. 2–8: '*Correspondence of*'; rectos: pp. 3–9: '*Carlyle and Emerson.*'; rectos and versos: pp. 12–17, 27–35, 47–62, 80–89, 95–99, 117–122, 129–137, 144–150, 158–163, 170–174, 181–184, 208–210, 218–225, 233–236, 238–241, 250–259, 268–272, 279–290, 297–300, 307–309, 319–323, 332–334, 340–347, 357–359, 365–368: '*Emerson to Carlyle.*'; rectos and versos: pp. 18–26, 36–46, 63–79, 90–94, 100–116, 123–128, 138–143, 151–157, 164–168, 175–180, 185–207, 211–217, 226–232, 242–249, 260–267, 273–278, 292–296, 301–306, 310–315, 324–331, 335–339, 348–356, 360–364: '*Carlyle to Emerson.*'; recto and versos: pp. 316–318: '*Carlyle to Mrs. Emerson.*'; II: rectos and versos: pp. iv–xiii: '*Contents of Volume II.*'; pp. 2–3, 13–15, 27–33, 36–38, 51–53, 58–60, 68–69, 75–77, 83–87, 97–108, 114–119, 128–129, 134–137, 142–143, 150–151, 156, 160–161, 164, 173–174, 200–203, 209–210, 216–219, 230–235, 241–244, 250–252, 263–265, 270–271, 277–281, 283–287, 293–299, 310–313, 317–319, 326–329, 334–337, 343–349: '*Emerson to Carlyle.*'; rectos and versos: pp. 4–12, 17–26, 34–35, 39–50, 54–57, 61–67, 70–74, 78–82, 88–96, 109–113, 120–127, 130–133, 138–141, 144–146, 152–155, 157–159, 162–163, 165–172, 175–199, 204–208, 211–215, 221–229, 236–240, 245–249, 253–262, 266–269, 272–276, 282, 288–292, 300–309, 314–316, 320–325, 330–333, 338–342, 350–354: '*Carlyle to Emerson.*'; rectos and verso: pp. 147–149: '*Extracts from Emerson's Diary.*'; rectos and versos: pp. 356–370: '*Index to Carlyle's Letters.*'; rectos and versos: pp. 372–383: '*Index to Emerson's Letters.*'.

Binding: Medium brown S cloth (diagonal rib). Front and back covers: blank; spine: leather label with goldstamped '[rule] | [rule] | CORRESPONDENCE | OF | THOMAS CARLYLE | AND | RALPH WALDO EMERSON | [rule] | [rule]', with goldstamped '1834–1872 | * [**]' on cloth below. Vol. I: back flyleaf; Vol. II: flyleaves. Light brown or medium brown coated endpapers. All edges trimmed. Top edges gilded.

Publication: 2,500 copies printed 30 January 1883. Advertised as "Published this day," in *New York Daily Tribune,* 24 February 1883, p. 6. Noted for "this week," in

Publishers' Weekly, 23 (24 February 1883), 229. Advertised as "Just Published," in *Publishers' Weekly*, 23 (24 February 1883), 246. Listed in *Publishers' Weekly*, 23 (17 March 1883), 308. According to the publisher's records, published 24 February 1883. Inscribed copies: ViU (28 February 1883), RPB (February 1883). Prices: cloth, $4.00; half calf, $8.00.

Locations: JM, MCo, MH, NNC, ViU, VtMiM.

Note one: In vol. I, leaf [1]₁ is either cancelled or pasted under the front pastedown endpaper.

Note two: A set of uncut, untrimmed, and unbound sheets has been noted: CtY.

A 39.1.a₂
First edition, first printing, English issue (1883)

THE CORRESPONDENCE OF

THOMAS CARLYLE

AND

RALPH WALDO EMERSON

1834—1872/

IN TWO VOLUMES

VOL. I.

WITH PORTRAITS

𝔏𝔬𝔫𝔡𝔬𝔫

CHATTO & WINDUS, PICCADILLY

1883

A 39.1.a₂: 7⅝″ × 5″

I: [a–d] [i–iii]; all else is the same as in the American issue

II: the same as in the American issue

I: $[1^8 (\pm 1_3) \ 2-31^6 \ 32^4]$ The title leaf is a cancel

II: $[1^8 (\pm 1_2) \ 2-29^6 \ 30^4 \ 31-32^6 \ 33^8]$ The title leaf is a cancel

Contents: I: the same as in the American issue, except: pp. a–d: blank; p. i: English title page; p. ii: copyright page; II: the same as in the American issue, except: p. i: English title page; p. ii: the lines from Emerson and Carlyle that appear on the title page of the American issue.

Typography and paper: The same as in the American issue.

Binding: Medium brown H cloth (fine diaper). Front and back covers: four rules blindstamped at top and bottom; spine: four rules blindstamped at top and bottom with goldstamped 'THE | CORRESPONDENCE | OF | CARLYLE | AND | EMERSON | VOL. I [II] | CHATTO & WINDUS'. Dark blue or dark green coated endpapers. All edges trimmed.

Publication: Title leaves electroplated 13 February 1883. Advertised in *Athenæum*, no. 2886 (17 February 1883), 227. Listed in *Athenæum*, no. 2887 (24 February 1883), 246. Listed as received by BL, 13 February 1883. Price, 24s.

Locations: BC, BE, InU, JM (2 copies), MWA, ScU.

Note one: Copies have been noted with a 32-page catalogue of Chatto and Windus's publications, dated February 1882, inserted at the back of vol. I: BC, BE, InU, JM, MWA, ScU.

Note two: A copy has been noted with a 32-page catalogue of Chatto and Windus's publications, dated January 1883, inserted at the back of vol. I: JM.

A 39.1.b
First edition, second printing for English sale (1883)

THE CORRESPONDENCE

OF

THOMAS CARLYLE

AND

RALPH WALDO EMERSON

1834—1872

" To my friend I write a letter, and from him I receive a letter. It is a
spiritual gift, worthy of him to give, and of me to receive." — EMERSON

" What the writer did actually mean, the thing he then thought of, the
thing he then was." — CARLYLE

VOLUME I

LONDON
CHATTO AND WINDUS, PICCADILLY
1883

A 39.1.b: 7⁵/₈″ × 5″

I: [a–d] [i–iii]; all else is the same as in the first printing

II: the same as in the first printing

I: [1^8 2–31^6 32^4]

II: the same as in the first printing

Contents: I: pp. a–d: blank; [frontispiece not present]; p. i: English title page; all else is the same as in the first printing; II: pp. a–b: blank; [frontispiece not present]; p. i: English title page; all else is the same as in the first printing.

Typography and paper: The same as in the first printing.

Binding: The same as in the first printing, English issue, except: dark blue coated endpapers.

Publication: Inscribed copy: NNC (from M. D. Conway, 14 March 1883).

Printing: The same information as on p. [ii] of the first printing.

Location: NNC.

A 39.1.c
First edition, third (large paper) printing (1883)

THE

CORRESPONDENCE

OF

THOMAS CARLYLE

AND

RALPH WALDO EMERSON

1834 — 1872

" To my friend I write a letter, and from him I receive a letter. It is a
spiritual gift, worthy of him to give, and of me to receive." — EMERSON
" What the writer did actually mean, the thing he then thought of, the
thing he then was." — CARLYLE

VOLUME I

BOSTON
JAMES R. OSGOOD AND COMPANY
1883

A 39.1.c: $9^5/8''$ × $5^3/4''$; 'CORRESPONDENCE', '1834–1872', and 'JAMES R. OSGOOD
AND COMPANY' are in red

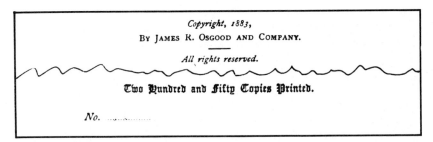

I: The same as in the first printing

II: [i–iii] iv–xiv; all else the same as in the first printing

I: [1^2 ($+1_2$) 2–48^4]   Signed the same as in the first printing; the title leaf is a cancel, pasted to the stub of the frontispiece

II: [1^1 2^2 3–51^4]   Signed [a]^7 1–20^8 [21]^8 22–24^8 The title leaf is pasted to the stub of the frontispiece

Contents: I: pp. a–b: blank; inserted leaf with drawing of Carlyle printed on verso, with protective tissue; p. i: title page, same as the first printing, except 'CORRESPON-DENCE', '1834–1872', and 'JAMES R. OSGOOD AND COMPANY' are in red; p. ii: copyright page, same as the first printing, except, instead of printer's imprint, appears '[gothic] Two Hundred and Fifty Copies Printed. | *No.* [19 dots]'; all else the same as the first printing; II: inserted leaf with a drawing of Emerson printed on verso, with protective tissue; p. i: title page—see vol. I information; p. ii: copyright page—see vol. I information; all else the same as the first printing, except: p. 384: printer's imprint.

Typography and paper: The same as the first printing, except: laid paper with 1^1/₁₆″ vertical chain marks.

Binding: White vellum with paper label on spine: '[gothic] Carlyle and Emerson | Large Paper | *CORRESPONDENCE OF* | *THOMAS CARLYLE* | AND | *RALPH WALDO EMERSON* | [rule with dot in center] | VOL. I. [II.]'. White laid endpapers. Top edges uncut; front and bottom edges trimmed.

Publication: 250 copies printed 9 October 1883. Price, $12.00.

Printing: "[gothic] Cambridge: | PRINTED BY JOHN WILSON AND SON, | UNIVER-SITY PRESS" (II, 384).

Locations: InU, JM, LNHT, RPB, ViU.

Note one: Probably sold in unprinted brown dust jackets; no copies have been located.

Note two: A copy has been noted with pp. 1–16 only, both frontispiece engravings, and unnumbered, bound in gray paper-covered boards, possibly a salesman's dummy: CtY.

LATER PRINTINGS WITHIN THE FIRST EDITION

A 39.1.d
Boston: James R. Osgood, 1883.

'SECOND EDITION'. 1,000 copies printed 27 March 1883. *Location:* JM.

A 39.1.e

Boston: James R. Osgood, 1883.

'THIRD EDITION'. 1,100 copies printed 1 May 1883. *Location:* JM.

A 39.2.a

Second American edition, first printing [1885]

The title page is the same as in the first edition, except: 'FIFTH EDITION, REVISED | BOSTON | TICKNOR AND COMPANY | 211 [gothic] Tremont Street'.

Vol. I: 399 pp.; vol. II: 422 pp. Cloth or leather. 280 copies printed September–October 1885. Advertised in *Atlantic* as "Enriched in 1885 by the addition of newly-found letters, covering 100 pages" (56 [December 1885], wrappers). Advertised as "New rev. enl. ed.," in *Publishers' Weekly,* 28 (5 December 1885), 878; in *Publishers' Weekly,* 29 (30 January 1886), 174. Advertised in *Supplementary Letters* (see A 43) as "New revised edition of 1885, with 100 additional pages of newly-found letters" (advertisements, p. [2]). Prices: cloth, $4.00; half calf, $8.00; half morocco, $8.00. *Location:* NCH.

Note one: Includes the material printed in *Supplementary Letters* (A 43).

Note two: The "Note to Revised Edition," dated 31 December 1884, is signed 'C[harles]. E[liot]. N[orton].' (pp. [iv–v]).

A 39.2.b

Boston: Ticknor and Company, 1886.

'REVISED EDITION'. 280 copies printed 26 November 1886. *Location:* JM.

A 39.2.c

Boston: Ticknor and Company, 1887.

500 copies printed 11 August 1887. *Not seen.*

A 39.2.d

Boston: Ticknor and Company, 1888.

'[gothic] Library Edition'. *Location:* MeWC.

Note: According to an advertisement in the May 1889 *Atlantic,* Houghton, Mifflin had purchased "the stereotype plates, stock, and copyright" of Ticknor's books, including the *Correspondence* (63, wrappers). From this stock, 190 copies were bound for sale in the *Riverside Edition* format and 742 in the *Library Edition* format. The stock from this sale was sold out by 1898.

A 39.2.e

Boston and New York: Houghton, Mifflin, 1892.

'[gothic] Library Edition'. *Location:* JM.

A 39.2.f

Boston and New York: Houghton, Mifflin, 1892.

'[gothic] Riverside Edition'. 250 copies printed 19 November 1891. *Location:* LNHT.

A 39.2.g
Boston and New York: Houghton, Mifflin, 1894.

'[gothic] Library Edition'. 250 copies printed 21 March 1894. *Location:* JM.

Note one: An additional letter from Carlyle to Emerson, dated 9 April 1859 and numbered 'CLXIII.*', is added on pp. 301*–301** (i.e., on the facing pages between pp. 301 and 302). The letter is described as "discovered in 1893."

Note two: Copies bound in half calf were added to specially-bound sets of the *Riverside Edition,* trade printing (see B 7, *Note four*).

A 39.2.h
Boston and New York: Houghton, Mifflin, 1896.

'[gothic] Riverside Edition'. 150 copies printed 28 December 1895; 270 copies on 30 April 1896. *Location:* NcU.

A 39.2.i
Boston and New York: Houghton, Mifflin, 1897.

'[gothic] Library Edition'. *Location:* OCIW.

A 39.2.j
Boston and New York: Houghton, Mifflin, 1899.

'[gothic] Riverside Edition'. 270 copies printed August–September 1899. *Location:* VtNorwU.

A 39.2.k
Boston and New York: Houghton, Mifflin, 1899.

'[gothic] Library Edition'. *Location:* ICM.

A 39.2.l
Boston and New York: Houghton, Mifflin, [n.d.].

'[gothic] Library Edition'. *Location:* JM.

A 39.2.m
Boston and New York: Houghton, Mifflin, [n.d.].

'[gothic] Riverside Edition'. *Location:* OBgU.

Note: The second edition apparently remained in print through 1916.

A 40 MISCELLANIES

A 40.1.a
First edition, first printing (1884)

MISCELLANIES

BY

RALPH WALDO EMERSON

BOSTON
HOUGHTON, MIFFLIN AND COMPANY
New York: 11 East Seventeenth Street
The Riverside Press, Cambridge
1884

A 40.1.a: $7^{7}/_{16}''$ × $4^{15}/_{16}''$

[i–vii] viii [7–9] 10–29 [30–33] 34–97 [98–101] 102–128 [129–131] 132–175 [176–179] 180–201 [202–205] 206–230 [231–233] 234–237 [238–241] 242–248 [249–251] 252–256 [257–259] 260–263 [264–267] 268–274 [275–277] 278–290 [291–293] 294–303 [304–307] 308–315 [316–319] 320–322 [323–325] 326–334 [335–337] 338–356 [357–359] 360–362 [363–365] 366–369 [370–373] 374–377 [378–381] 382–384 [385–387] 388–392 [393–395] 396–425 [426]

$[1–35^6 \ 36^4]$ Signed $[a]^1 \ [1]^8 \ 2–8^8 \ [9]^8 \ 10–11^8 \ [12]^8 \ 13–16^8 \ [17]^8 \ 18–19^8 \ [20]^8 \ 21–24^8 \ [25]^8 \ 26^8 \ 27^5$

Contents: p. i: '[gothic] Riverside Edition | [rule with dot in center] | MISCELLANIES | BEING VOLUME XI. | OF | EMERSON'S COMPLETE WORKS | [leaf device]'; p. ii: blank; p. iii: title page; p. iv: copyright page; p. v: 'NOTE' on the text, signed 'J. E. CABOT'; p. vi: blank; pp. vii–viii: contents; p. 7: 'THE LORD'S SUPPER. | SERMON DELIVERED BEFORE THE SECOND CHURCH IN BOSTON | SEPTEMBER 9, 1832.'; p. 8: blank; pp. 9–29: text; p. 30: blank; p. 31: 'HISTORICAL DISCOURSE, | AT CONCORD, ON THE SECOND CENTENNIAL ANNIVERSARY OF THE | INCORPORATION OF THE TOWN, SEPTEMBER 12, 1835.'; p. 32: blank; pp. 33–97: text; p. 98: blank; p. 99: 'ADDRESS | AT THE DEDICATION OF THE SOLDIERS' MONUMENT IN CONCORD, | APRIL 19TH, 1867.'; p. 100: blank; pp. 101–128: text; p. 129: 'ADDRESS | DELIVERED IN CON-CORD ON THE ANNIVERSARY OF THE EMAN- | CIPATION OF THE NEGROES IN THE BRITISH WEST | INDIES, AUGUST 1, 1844.'; p. 130: blank; pp. 131–175: text; p. 176: blank; p. 177: 'WAR. | [rule with dot in center] | [four lines of verse]'; p. 178: blank; pp. 179–201: text; p. 202: blank; p. 203: 'THE FUGITIVE SLAVE LAW. | LECTURE READ AT THE TABERNACLE, NEW YORK CITY, | MARCH 7, 1854.'; p. 204: blank; pp. 205–230: text; p. 231: 'THE ASSAULT UPON MR. SUMNER. | SPEECH AT A MEETING OF THE CITIZENS IN THE TOWN HALL, | IN CONCORD, MAY 26, 1856.'; p. 232: blank; pp. 233–237: text; p. 238: blank; p. 239: 'SPEECH | AT THE KANSAS RELIEF MEETING IN CAMBRIDGE, WEDNESDAY | EVENING, SEPTEMBER 10, 1856.'; p. 240: blank; pp. 241–248: text; p. 249: 'REMARKS | AT A MEETING FOR THE RELIEF OF THE FAMILY OF JOHN | BROWN, AT TREMONT TEMPLE, BOSTON, | NOVEMBER 18, 1859.'; p. 250: blank; pp. 251–256: text; p. 257: 'JOHN BROWN. | SPEECH AT SALEM, JANU-ARY 6, 1860.'; p. 258: blank; pp. 259–263: text; p. 264: blank; p. 265: 'THEODORE PARKER. | AN ADDRESS AT THE MEMORIAL MEETING AT THE MUSIC HALL, | BOSTON, JUNE 15, 1860.'; p. 266: blank; pp. 267–274: text; p. 275: 'AMERICAN CIVILIZATION.'; p. 276: blank; pp. 277–290: text; p. 291: 'THE EMANCIPATION PROC-LAMATION. | AN ADDRESS DELIVERED IN BOSTON IN SEPTEMBER, 1862.'; p. 292: blank; pp. 293–303: text; p. 304: blank; p. 305: 'ABRAHAM LINCOLN. | REMARKS AT THE FUNERAL SERVICES HELD IN CONCORD, | APRIL 19, 1865.'; p. 306: blank; pp. 307–315: text; p. 316: blank; p. 317: 'HARVARD COMMEMORATION SPEECH. | JULY 21, 1865.'; p. 318: blank; pp. 319–322: text; p. 323: 'EDITORS' ADDRESS. | MAS-SACHUSETTS QUARTERLY REVIEW, DECEMBER, 1847.'; p. 324: blank; pp. 325–334: text; p. 335: 'WOMAN. | A LECTURE READ BEFORE THE WOMAN'S RIGHTS CON-

VENTION, | BOSTON, SEPTEMBER 20, 1855.'; p. 336: blank; pp. 337–356: text; p. 357:
'ADDRESS TO KOSSUTH. | AT CONCORD, MAY 11, 1852.'; p. 358: blank; pp. 359–
362: text; p. 363: 'ROBERT BURNS. | SPEECH AT THE CELEBRATION OF THE BURNS
CENTENARY, | BOSTON, JANUARY 25, 1859.'; p. 364: blank; pp. 365–369: text; p.
370: blank; p. 371: 'WALTER SCOTT. | REMARKS AT THE CELEBRATION BY THE
MASSACHUSETTS HIS- | TORICAL SOCIETY OF THE CENTENNIAL ANNIVERSARY
OF HIS | BIRTH. BOSTON, AUGUST 15, 1871.'; p. 372: blank; pp. 373–377: text; p.
378: blank; p. 379: 'REMARKS | AT THE MEETING FOR ORGANIZING THE FREE
RELIGIOUS ASSO- | CIATION, BOSTON, MAY 30, 1867.'; p. 380: blank; pp. 381–384:
text; p. 385: 'SPEECH | AT THE SECOND ANNUAL MEETING OF THE FREE RELI-
GIOUS ASSO- | CIATION, AT TREMONT TEMPLE, FRIDAY, MAY 28, 1869.'; p. 386:
blank; pp. 387–392: text; p. 393: 'THE FORTUNE OF THE REPUBLIC. | A LECTURE
DELIVERED AT THE OLD SOUTH CHURCH, BOSTON, | MARCH 30, 1878.'; p. 394:
blank; pp. 395–425: text; p. 426: blank.

Selections: "The Lord's Supper" †; "Historical Discourse in Concord" †; "Address at
the Dedication of the Soldiers' Monument in Concord" †; "Address on Emancipation in
the British West Indies" †; "War" †; "The Fugitive Slave Law" #; "The Assault Upon Mr.
Sumner" †; "Speech on Affairs in Kansas" #; "Remarks at a Meeting for the Relief of
John Brown's Family" †; "John Brown: Speech at Salem" †; "Theodore Parker" †;
"American Civilization" †; "The Emancipation Proclamation" †; "Abraham Lincoln" †;
"Harvard Commemoration Speech" #; "Editors' Address: Massachusetts Quarterly Re-
view" †; "Woman" †; "Address to Kossuth" †; "Robert Burns" †; "Walter Scott" †;
"Remarks at the Organization of the Free Religious Association" †; "Speech at the
Annual Meeting of the Free Religious Association" †; "The Fortune of the Republic" †.

Typography and paper: 5³⁄₈″ (5¹⁄₈″) × 4¹⁵⁄₁₆″; laid paper with 2³⁄₁₆″ horizontal chain
marks; 28 lines per page. Running heads: rectos: pp. 11–29: *'THE LORD'S SUPPER.'*;
pp. 35–87: *'AT CONCORD.'*; pp. 89–97: *'APPENDIX.'*; pp. 103–123: *'SOLDIERS'
MONUMENT, CONCORD.'*; pp. 125–127: *'APPENDIX.'*; pp. 133–175: *'WEST INDIA EM-
ANCIPATION.'*; pp. 181–201: *'WAR.'*; pp. 207–229: *'FUGITIVE SLAVE LAW.'*; pp. 235–
237: *'ASSAULT UPON MR. SUMNER.'*; pp. 243–247: *'SPEECH ON AFFAIRS IN KAN-
SAS.'*; pp. 253–255: *'RELIEF OF JOHN BROWN'S FAMILY.'*; pp. 261–263: *'SPEECH AT
SALEM.'*; pp. 269–273: *'THEODORE PARKER.'*; pp. 279–289: *'AMERICAN CIVILIZA-
TION.'*; pp. 295–303: *'EMANCIPATION PROCLAMATION.'*; pp. 309–315: *'ABRAHAM
LINCOLN.'*; p. 321: *'HARVARD COMMEMORATION.'*; pp. 327–333: *'MASSACHUSETTS
QUARTERLY REVIEW.'*; pp. 339–355: *'WOMAN.'*; p. 361: *'ADDRESS TO KOSSUTH.'*;
pp. 367–369: *'ROBERT BURNS.'*; pp. 375–377: *'WALTER SCOTT.'*; pp. 383, 389–391:
'THE FREE RELIGIOUS ASSOCIATION.'; pp. 397–425: *'THE FORTUNE OF THE REPUB-
LIC.'*; versos: p. viii: *'CONTENTS.'*; pp. 10–28: *'SERMON ON'*; pp. 34–86: *'HISTORICAL
DISCOURSE'*; p. 88: *'HISTORICAL DISCOURSE.'*; pp. 90–96: *'APPENDIX.'*; pp. 102–
124: *'ADDRESS.'*; pp. 126–128: *'APPENDIX.'*; pp. 132–174: *'ADDRESS. '*; pp. 180–200:
'WAR.'; pp. 206–228: *'LECTURE ON THE'*; p. 230: *'THE FUGITIVE SLAVE LAW.'*; pp.
234–236: *'SPEECH ON THE'*; pp. 242–248: *'SPEECH ON AFFAIRS IN KANSAS.'*; pp.
252–254: *'REMARKS AT A MEETING FOR'*; p. 256: *'RELIEF OF JOHN BROWN'S
FAMILY.'*; pp. 260–262: *'JOHN BROWN:'*; pp. 268–274: *'THEODORE PARKER.'*; pp.
278–290: *'AMERICAN CIVILIZATION.'*; pp. 294–302: *'SPEECH ON THE'*; pp. 308–314:
'ABRAHAM LINCOLN.'; p. 320: *'SPEECH AT THE'*; p. 322: *'HARVARD COMMEMORA-
TION SPEECH.'*; pp. 326–334: *'EDITORS' ADDRESS.'*; pp. 338–356: *'WOMAN.'*; pp.
360–362: *'ADDRESS TO KOSSUTH.'*; pp. 366–368: *'ROBERT BURNS.'*; pp. 374–376:
'WALTER SCOTT.'; pp. 382–384: *'REMARKS AT THE ORGANIZATION OF'*; pp. 388–
390: *'SPEECH AT THE ANNUAL MEETING OF'*; p. 392: *'THE FREE RELIGIOUS ASSO-
CIATION.'*; pp. 396–424: *'THE FORTUNE OF THE REPUBLIC.'*.

Binding: Medium blue H cloth (fine diaper). Front and back covers: blank; spine: goldstamped 'MISCELLANIES | EMERSON | [publisher's logo]'. Laid paper flyleaves. Gray coated endpapers. All edges trimmed. Top edges gilded.

Publication: Listed in *Publishers' Weekly,* 24 (22 December 1883), 910. MB and MH copies listed as received 17 December 1883; DLC copy listed as received 18 December 1883. 1,500 copies printed 28 November 1883. According to the publisher's records, published 15 December 1883. Copyright, 11 November 1883. Price, $1.75.

Location: MWA.

Note one: Vol. XI of the *Riverside Edition,* trade printing (see B 7).

A 40.1.b
First edition, presumed second (English) printing (1884)

MISCELLANIES

BY

RALPH WALDO EMERSON

COPYRIGHT

LONDON
GEORGE ROUTLEDGE AND SONS
BROADWAY, LUDGATE HILL.
NEW YORK, 9, LAFAYETTE PLACE.
1884

A 40.1.b: $7^{3}/_{8}''$ × $4^{7}/_{8}''$

[iii–vii]; all else is the same as in the first printing

[1]⁸ 2–26⁸ 27⁴ 28¹

Contents: p. iii: title page; p. iv: printer's imprint; all else is the same as in the first printing.

Typography and paper: The same as in the first printing, except: calendered wove paper.

Binding: Gray green S cloth (diagonal rib). Front and back covers: blank; spine: goldstamped 'MISCELLANIES | EMERSON | ROUTLEDGE.'. Light gray green floral design endpapers. All edges trimmed.

Publication: Deposit copies: BC (31 December 1883), BO (7 May 1884).

Printing: "LONDON: | BRADBURY, AGNEW, & CO., PRINTERS, WHITEFRIARS" (p. [iv]).

Locations: BC, BE, BO.

A 40.1.c
First edition, presumed third (English) printing (1884)

The title page is the same as in the second printing, except: '[gothic] The Riverside Edition | (COPYRIGHT)' is under Emerson's name.

Vol. XI of the *Riverside Edition (Copyright),* English trade printing (see B 10). 1,000 copies printed late November 1883. Listed in *Athenæum,* no. 2929 (15 December 1883), 776. Price, 3s. 6d. *Locations:* BL (15 March 1884), CaQMM.

A 40.1.d
First edition, fourth printing (1884)

MISCELLANIES

BY

RALPH WALDO EMERSON

BOSTON
HOUGHTON, MIFFLIN AND COMPANY
New York : 11 East Seventeenth Street
𝔗𝔥𝔢 𝔑𝔦𝔳𝔢𝔯𝔰𝔦𝔡𝔢 𝔓𝔯𝔢𝔰𝔰, 𝔠𝔞𝔪𝔟𝔯𝔦𝔡𝔤𝔢
1884

A 40.1.d: $7^7/_{16}''$ × $4^{15}/_{16}''$

The same as the first printing. 500 copies printed early December 1883. MCo copy received December 1883. DLC copy received (by War Department Library) 17 January 1885. *Locations:* DLC, JM, MCo, MH-AH.

A 40.1.e
First edition, fifth printing (1884)

The title page is the same as in the fourth printing. The same as the first printing, except: collation is $[1–18]^{12}$; pagination is [i–vii] . . . 396–425 [426–430], with pp. 426–430 blank; laid paper front flyleaf. 500 copies printed February 1884. *Location:* JM.

LATER PRINTINGS FROM THE RIVERSIDE EDITION PLATES

A 40.1.f₁
Riverside Edition (large paper), sixth printing, American issue (1884)

[red] MISCELLANIES | BY | RALPH WALDO EMERSON | [pine branch] | [red] CAM-BRIDGE | [gothic] Printed at the Riverside Press | 1884

Vol. XI of the *Riverside Edition,* large paper printing (see B 8). Limited to 500 numbered copies printed 7 March 1884. Price, $4.00. Sold out within a year. *Locations:* JM, TxU.

A 40.1.f₂
Riverside Edition (large paper), sixth printing, English issue [1884]

Title page is the same as in the American issue, except for publisher's imprint: 'LON-DON | KEGAN PAUL, TRENCH, & CO., I, PATERNOSTER SQUARE | MDCCCLXXXIII'.

Vol. XI of the *Riverside Edition,* large paper printing for English subscribers (see B 9). 25 title leaves printed 15 July 1884. Title leaf is a cancel; the date on the title page is in error. Limited to 25 signed and numbered copies. *Location:* JM.

A 40.1.g
Boston and New York: Houghton, Mifflin, 1884.

500 copies printed 15 July 1884. *Not seen.*

A 40.1.h
Boston and New York: Houghton, Mifflin, 1885.

500 copies printed 24 January 1885 and 31 August 1885. *Location:* JM.

A 40.1.i
Boston and New York: Houghton, Mifflin, 1886.

500 copies printed 2 April 1886. *Location:* JM.

A 40.1.j
Boston and New York: Houghton, Mifflin, 1887.

500 copies printed 12 November 1886, ca. March 1887, and 16 May 1887. *Location:* JM.

A 40.1.k
London, Glasgow, New York: George Routledge and Sons, 1887.

500 copies printed 16 December 1886. *Location:* JM.

A 40.1.l
Boston and New York: Houghton, Mifflin, 1888.

500 copies printed 22 December 1887; 270 copies on 11 July 1888. *Location:* NCH.

A 40.1.m

270 copies printed 17 November 1888, 30 March 1889, and 25 July 1889. *Location:* JM.

A 40.1.n
Boston and New York: Houghton, Mifflin, 1890.

500 copies printed ca. February 1890. *Not seen.*

A 40.1.o
Boston and New York: Houghton, Mifflin, 1891.

500 copies printed October–December 1890. *Location:* VtSta.

A 40.1.p
Boston and New York: Houghton, Mifflin, 1892.

500 copies printed 3 November 1891 and 24 August 1892. *Location:* JM.

A 40.1.q
Boston and New York: Houghton, Mifflin, 1893.

500 copies printed 26 August 1893. *Location:* PSC.

A 40.1.r
Standard Library Edition printing [1894]

MISCELLANIES | BY | RALPH WALDO EMERSON | [pine branch] | BOSTON AND NEW YORK | HOUGHTON, MIFFLIN AND COMPANY | [gothic] The Riverside Press, Cambridge

Vol. XI of the *Standard Library Edition* (see B 11). 1,000 copies printed 20 November 1894, 31 May 1895, and 29 June 1896; 500 copies on 31 January 1898. *Location:* JM.

A 40.1.s
London and New York: George Routledge and Sons, 1894.

Published September 1894. *Not seen.*

A 40.1.t
Boston and New York: Houghton, Mifflin, 1895.

500 copies printed 24 April 1895. *Location:* PSC.

A 40.1.u
Boston and New York: Houghton, Mifflin, 1896.

270 copies printed 22 October 1896. *Not seen.*

A 40.1.v
Boston and New York: Houghton, Mifflin, 1897.

270 copies printed 5 October 1897. *Not seen.*

A 40.1.w
Boston and New York: Houghton, Mifflin, 1898.

270 copies printed 6 May 1898. *Not seen.*

A 40.1.x
London: George Routledge and Sons, 1898.

Location: CaQMM.

A 40.1.y
Boston and New York: Houghton, Mifflin, 1899.

270 copies printed 31 May 1899. *Not seen.*

A 40.1.z
London: George Routledge and Sons, 1902.

Location: JM.

A 40.1.aa
London: George Routledge & Sons, 1903.

Combined with *Lectures and Biographical Sketches* and *Natural History of Intellect* in three-volumes-in-one format as vol. IV of the "Sovereign Edition" (see B 12). 1,000 copies printed 16 September 1903. *Location:* InU.

A 40.1.bb
Fireside Edition printing (1909)

[all within red double-rule frame with red floral ornaments in each corner] THE WORKS OF | [red gothic] Ralph Waldo Emerson | MISCELLANIES | [engraving of man reading book in chair before fireplace] | [gothic] Fireside Edition | BOSTON AND NEW YORK | MDCCCCIX

Vol. XI of the *Fireside Edition* (see B 13). 500 copies printed 1 October 1909 and 9 February 1910. *Location:* JM.

Note: The copyright on *Miscellanies* was renewed 11 September 1911.

A 40.1.cc
Boston and New York: Jefferson Press, [ca. 1912].

Combined with *Natural History of Intellect* in two-volumes-in-one format as vol. [VI] of the "Jefferson Press Edition" (see B 14). *Location:* JM.

A 40.1.dd
New York: Sully and Kleinteich, [ca. 1912].

Vol. XI of the *University Edition* (see B 15). *Location:* JM.

A 40.1.ee
Boston and New York: Houghton, Mifflin, [n.d.].

Approximately 1,600 copies sold between 1900 and 1923. *Location:* JM.

Note: Approximately 12,000 copies of *Miscellanies* in the *Riverside Edition* were sold between 1884 and 1913, when the title was apparently allowed to go out of print in this format.

A 40.1.ff
London: George Routledge and Sons, [n.d.].

Location: JM.

A 40.1.gg
London: Waverley Book Company, [n.d.].

Vol. XI of the "Waverley" *Riverside Edition* (see B 16). *Location:* JM.

A 40.2.a
Second edition, first printing (1884)

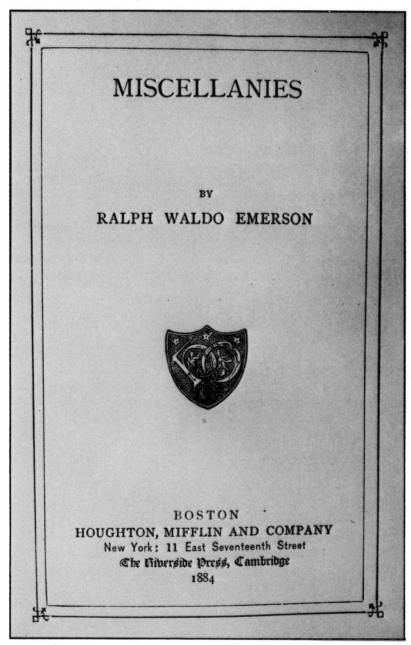

MISCELLANIES

BY

RALPH WALDO EMERSON

BOSTON ·
HOUGHTON, MIFFLIN AND COMPANY
New York: 11 East Seventeenth Street
The Riverside Press, Cambridge
1884

A 40.2.a: 5³/₄″ × 4¹/₈″; outer frame, title, and 'BOSTON:' are in red

[i–ii] [1–9] 10–25 [26–29] 30–80 [81–83] 84–105 [106–109] 110–143 [144–147]
148–165 [166–169] 170–188 [189–191] 192–194 [195–197] 198–203 [204–207]
208–211 [212–215] 216–218 [219–221] 222–226 [227–229] 230–239 [240–243]
244–251 [252–255] 256–261 [262–265] 266–268 [269–271] 272–278 [279–281]
282–296 [297–299] 300–302 [303–305] 306–308 [309–311] 312–314 [315–317]
318–320 [321–323] 324–327 [328–331] 332–354

$[1^2 2–23^8]$ Signed $[a]^1 [1]^8 2–5^8 [6]^8 7–9^8 [10]^8 11–15^8 [16]^8 17–22^8 23^1$

Contents: pp. i–ii: blank; pp. 1–354: basically the same as pp. iii–393 of the first edition.

Typography and paper: $4^3/_4''$ ($4^1/_2''$) × $2^{11}/_{16}''$; wove paper; 33 lines per page. Running heads basically the same as in the first edition.

Binding: Medium brown S cloth (diagonal fine-rib). "Little Classic Edition" binding (see illustration at A 34.2.a) with goldstamped 'MISCELLANIES' and blackstamped 'HOUGHTON, MIFFLIN & CO.' on front cover and goldstamped 'MISCELLANIES' and 'HOUGHTON, MIFFLIN & CO.' on spine. Back flyleaf. Black coated endpapers. All edges trimmed. All edges stained red.

Publication: 1,000 copies printed 17 December 1883. According to the publisher's records, published 15 December 1883, but note printing date. Price, $1.50.

Printing: The same printer's imprint as in A 40.1.a.

Locations: JM, VtMiM.

Note: Vol. [XI] of the "Little Classic Edition" (see B 3).

LATER PRINTINGS FROM THE "LITTLE CLASSIC EDITION" PLATES

A 40.2.b
Boston and New York: Houghton, Mifflin, 1887.

270 copies printed 7 January 1887. Bound in medium blue V cloth (smooth), rather than "Little Classic Edition" binding, as are subsequent reprintings (see illustration at B 3). *Location:* JM.

A 40.2.c
Boston and New York: Houghton, Mifflin, 1888.

270 copies printed 8 November 1887 and 5 May 1888. *Location:* UU.

A 40.2.d
Boston and New York: Houghton, Mifflin, 1889.

270 copies printed 30 April 1889. *Location:* JM.

A 40.2.e
Boston and New York: Houghton, Mifflin, 1890.

270 copies printed 11 January 1890. *Not seen.*

A 40.2.f
Boston and New York: Houghton, Mifflin, 1891.

250 copies printed January–March 1891. *Location:* JM.

A 40.2.g

Boston and New York: Houghton, Mifflin, 1892.

270 copies printed 3 December 1891 and 26 February 1892. *Location:* MHi.

A 40.2.h

Boston and New York: Houghton, Mifflin, 1893.

250 copies printed 2 June 1893. *Location:* MdBJ.

A 40.2.i

Boston and New York: Houghton, Mifflin, 1894.

270 copies printed 24 August 1894. *Not seen.*

A 40.2.j

Boston and New York: Houghton, Mifflin, 1896.

270 copies printed 25 February 1896. *Location:* DeU.

A 40.2.k

Boston and New York: Houghton, Mifflin, 1898.

270 copies printed 31 August 1898. *Location:* PBm.

A 40.2.l

Boston and New York: Houghton, Mifflin, 1899.

250 copies printed ca. December 1898. *Not seen.*

A 40.2.m

Boston and New York: Houghton, Mifflin, [n.d.].

Approximately 1,000 copies sold between 1900 and 1923. *Location:* NNS.

Note: Approximately 5,000 copies of *Miscellanies* printed from the "Little Classic Edition" plates were sold between 1884 and 1923, when the title was apparently allowed to go out of print in this format.

PRINTINGS FROM THE CENTENARY EDITION PLATES

A 40.3.a
Centenary Edition (trade), first printing (1904)

MISCELLANIES | BY | RALPH WALDO EMERSON | [pine tree] | BOSTON AND NEW YORK | HOUGHTON, MIFFLIN AND COMPANY, | [gothic] The Riverside Press, Cambridge | 1904

647 pp. Dust jacket. Vol. XI of the *Centenary Edition,* trade printing (see B 18). 1,000 copies printed 25 October 1904. Listed in *Publishers' Weekly,* 66 (10 December 1904), 1592. According to the publisher's records, published 30 November 1904. Copyright, 17 October 1904. Price, $1.75. *Locations:* DLC (9 November 1904), JM.

Note one: New items: "Letter to President Van Buren" †; "Fugitive Slave Law [Concord, 1851]" #; [Consecration of Sleepy Hollow Cemetery] #; "Shakespeare" #; "Humboldt" †; "Speech at Banquet in Honor of the Chinese Embassy" †; "Address at the Opening of the Concord Free Public Library" †.

Note two: Numerous reprintings with undated title pages. 1,500 copies printed between 1 January 1905 and 30 June 1907. Approximately 3,700 copies sold through 1923.

A 40.3.b
Boston and New York: Houghton, Mifflin, 1904.

Vol. XI of the *Concord Edition* (see B 20). 2,000 copies printed 28 October 1904. *Location:* JM.

Note: Numerous reprintings with undated title pages. Approximately 2,100 copies sold by 31 March 1907.

A 40.3.c
Autograph Centenary Edition (large paper), third printing (1904)

RALPH WALDO EMERSON | [red] MISCELLANIES | [pine tree] | CAMBRIDGE | [red gothic] Printed at the Riverside Press | 1904

Vol. XI of the *Autograph Centenary Edition* (see B 19). Limited to 600 signed and numbered copies printed 29 October 1904. Copyright, 17 October 1904. Price, $6.00. Sold out by 5 April 1906. *Locations:* DLC (9 November 1904), JM.

A 40.3.d
Boston and New York: Houghton Mifflin, [1906].

Vol. XI of the *Centenary Edition,* trade printing (see B 18). *Location:* DLC (20 June 1906).

A 40.3.e₂
English issue of the American sheets [1909]

London: Archibald Constable; Boston and New York: Houghton Mifflin, [1909].

Vol. XI of the English *Centenary Edition* (see B 21). Title leaf is a cancel. Price, 6s. *Locations:* BC (23 August 1909), BE (23 August 1909), BL (19 February 1915).

Note: Undoubtedly the sheets from an undated American reprinting (presumed A 40.3.e₁) of the *Centenary Edition,* trade printing.

A 40.3.f
Boston and New York: Houghton Mifflin, [1911].

Vol. XI of the *Centenary Edition,* trade printing (see B 18). *Location:* PSC.

A 40.3.g
Boston and New York: Houghton Mifflin, [1914].

Vol. XI of the *Riverside Pocket Edition* (see B 22). Approximately 900 copies sold between 1914 and 1922. *Not seen.*

A 40.3.h
Boston and New York: Houghton Mifflin, 1921.

544 pp. (text without the notes). Combined with *Representative Men* in two-volumes-in-one format as vol. III of *Emerson's Complete Works* (see B 23). *Location:* JM.

A 40.3.i
New York: Wm. H. Wise, 1923.

Combined with *Natural History of Intellect* in two-volumes-in-one format as vol. VI of the *Current Opinion Edition* (see B 24). *Location:* JM.

A 40.3.j
Boston and New York: Houghton Mifflin, 1929.

Combined (text without the notes) with *Representative Men* in two-volumes-in-one format as vol. [III] of the *Harvard Edition* (see B 25). *Location:* JM.

A 40.3.k
New York: Wm. H. Wise, 1929.

Combined with *Natural History of Intellect* in two-volumes-in-one format as vol. VI of the *Medallion Edition* (see B 26). *Location:* OC.

A 40.3.l
Boston and New York: Houghton Mifflin, [1932].

Vol. XI of the *Centenary Edition,* trade printing (see B 18). *Location:* RPB.

A 40.3.m–n
New York: AMS Press, [1968].

Vol. XI of the "AMS Press" *Centenary Edition* (see B 27). Reprinted 1979. *Locations:* TxU, DLC (9 November 1979).

SEPARATE PUBLICATIONS OF INDIVIDUAL ESSAYS

A 40.4
[*Abraham Lincoln*]. San Francisco: Wallace Kibbee & Son, [n.d.].

Single leaf folded once to make four pages, printed on pp. 2–3. Drawing by Laurence B. Haste. *Location:* MBU.

A 40.5.a
The Wisest Words Ever Written on War. [New York: De Vinne Press, 1916].

12 pp. Cover title. Preface by Henry Ford. Copyright, 20 June 1916. Price, 15¢. *Location:* IaHi.

A 40.5.b
On War. [New York: American News Co., 1916].

Cover title. *Location:* CSt.

A 40.6
War. Washington, D.C.: American Peace Society, [1924].

8 pp. Cover title. Reprinted from the February 1924 *Advocate of Peace.* Price, 15¢. *Location:* OOxM.

A 41 LECTURES AND BIOGRAPHICAL SKETCHES

A 41.1.a
First edition, first printing (1884)

LECTURES

AND

BIOGRAPHICAL SKETCHES

BY

RALPH WALDO EMERSON

BOSTON
HOUGHTON, MIFFLIN AND COMPANY
New York: 11 East Seventeenth Street
The Riverside Press, Cambridge
1884

A 41.1.a: $7^3/8'' \times 5''$

[i–ii] [1–9] 10–32 [33–35] 36–67 [68–71] 72–89 [90–93] 94–121 [122–125] 126–156 [157–159] 160–174 [175–177] 178–205 [206–209] 210–228 [229–231] 232–246 [247–249] 250–274 [275–277] 278–304 [305–307] 308–347 [348–351] 352–354 [355–357] 358–370 [371–373] 374–404 [405–407] 408–418 [419–421] 422–452 [453–455] 456–463 [464–466]

[1–39^6]   Signed [a]^1 [1]^8 2^8 [3]^8 4–19^8 [20]^8 21–29^8 [30]^1

Contents: p. i: '[gothic] Riverside Edition | [rule with dot in center] | LECTURES AND BIOGRAPHICAL | SKETCHES | BEING VOLUME X. | OF | EMERSON'S COMPLETE WORKS | [leaf design]'; p. ii: blank; p. 1: title page; p. 2: copyright page; p. 3: 'NOTE' on the text, signed 'J. E. CABOT.'; p. 4: blank; p. 5: contents; p. 6: blank: p. 7: 'DEMONOLOGY. | [rule with dot in center] | [four lines of verse]'; p. 8: four lines of verse; pp. 9–32: text; p. 33: 'ARISTOCRACY. | [rule with dot in center] | [11 lines of verse]'; p. 34: blank; pp. 35–67: text; p. 68: blank; p. 69: 'PERPETUAL FORCES. | [rule with dot in center] | [two lines of verse] | GEORGE HERBERT.'; p. 70: four lines of verse; pp. 71–89: text; p. 90: blank; p. 91: 'CHARACTER. | [rule with dot in center] | [six lines of verse]'; p. 92: seven lines of verse; pp. 93–121: text; p. 122: blank; p. 123: 'EDUCA-TION. | [rule with dot in center] | [four lines of verse]'; p. 124: blank; pp. 125–156: text; p. 157: 'THE SUPERLATIVE. | [rule with dot in center] | [two lines of verse]'; p. 158: two lines of verse; pp. 159–174: text; p. 175: 'THE SOVEREIGNTY OF ETHICS. | [rule with dot in center] | [four lines of verse]'; p. 176: three lines of verse; pp. 177–205: text; p. 206: blank; p. 207: 'THE PREACHER. | [rule with dot in center] | [four lines of verse]'; p. 208: blank; pp. 209–228: text; p. 229: 'THE MAN OF LETTERS. | [rule with dot in center] | [two lines of verse]'; p. 230: four lines of verse; pp. 231–246: text; p. 247: 'THE SCHOLAR. | [rule with dot in center] | [10 lines of verse]'; p. 248: three lines of verse; pp. 249–274: text; p. 275: 'PLUTARCH. | [rule with dot in center] | [six lines of verse]'; p. 276: blank; pp. 277–304: text; p. 305: 'HISTORIC NOTES OF LIFE AND LETTERS | IN NEW ENGLAND. | [rule with dot in center] | [four lines of verse]'; p. 306: four lines of verse; pp. 307–347: text; p. 348: blank; p. 349: 'THE CHARDON STREET CONVEN-TION.'; p. 350: blank; pp. 351–354: text; p. 355: 'EZRA RIPLEY, D.D. | [rule with dot in center] | [eight lines of verse]'; p. 356: blank; pp. 357–370: text; p. 371: 'MARY MOODY EMERSON. | [rule with dot in center] | [32 lines of verse]'; p. 372: 16 lines of prose; pp. 373–404: text; p. 405: 'SAMUEL HOAR. | [two lines of Latin verse] | [rule with dot in center] | [14 lines of verse] | F. B. SANBORN | April 1857.'; p. 406: blank; pp. 407–418: text; p. 419: 'THOREAU. | [rule with dot in center] | [eight lines of verse]'; p. 420: four lines of verse; pp. 421–452: text; p. 453: 'CARLYLE. | [rule with dot in center] | [two lines of verse]'; p. 454: blank; pp. 455–463: text; pp. 464–466: blank.

Selections: "Demonology" †; "Aristocracy" #; "Perpetual Forces" †; "Character" †; "Education" #; "The Superlative" †; "The Sovereignty of Ethics" †; "The Preacher" †; "The Man of Letters" #; "The Scholar" #; "Plutarch" †; "Historic Notes of Life and Letters in New England" †; "The Chardon Street Convention" †; "Ezra Ripley" †; "Mary Moody Emerson" †; "Samuel Hoar" †; "Thoreau" †; "Carlyle" †.

Typography and paper: 5³/₈″ (5¹/₈″) × 3¹/₁₆″; laid paper with 1¹/₈″ horizontal chain marks; 28 lines per page. Running heads: rectos: pp. 11–31, 37–67, 73–89, 95–121, 127–155, 161–173, 179–205, 211–227, 233–245, 251–273, 279–303: titles of selections; pp. 309–347: 'LIFE AND LETTERS IN NEW ENGLAND.'; pp. 353, 359–369, 375–403, 409–417, 423–451, 457–463: titles of selections; versos: pp. 10–32, 36–66, 72–88, 94–120, 126–156, 160–174, 178–204, 210–228, 232–246, 250–274, 278–304: titles of selections; pp. 308–346: 'HISTORIC NOTES OF'; pp. 352–354, 358–370, 374–404, 408–418, 422–452, 456–462: titles of selections.

Binding: Medium blue H cloth (fine diaper). Front and back covers: blank; spine: goldstamped 'LECTURES | AND | BIOGRAPHICAL | SKETCHES | EMERSON | [publisher's logo]'. Laid paper front flyleaf. Gray coated endpapers. All edges trimmed. Top edges gilded.

Publication: Listed in *Publishers' Weekly,* 24 (22 December 1883), 910. According to the publisher's records, published 15 December 1883. Copyright, 22 November 1883. Price, $1.75.

Location: OCIW.

Note: Vol. X of the *Riverside Edition,* trade printing (see B 7).

A 41.1.b
First edition, second printing (1884)

LECTURES

AND

BIOGRAPHICAL SKETCHES

BY

RALPH WALDO EMERSON

BOSTON
HOUGHTON, MIFFLIN AND COMPANY
New York: 11 East Seventeenth Street
𝕿𝖍𝖊 𝕽𝖎𝖛𝖊𝖗𝖘𝖎𝖉𝖊 𝕻𝖗𝖊𝖘𝖘, 𝕮𝖆𝖒𝖇𝖗𝖎𝖉𝖌𝖊
1884

A 41.1.b: $7^{3}/_{8}''$ × 5″

1,500 copies printed 30 November 1883. Deposit copy: DLC (18 December 1883). MCo copy received December 1883. *Locations:* DLC, JM, MCo, MH, MH-AH, MWA, PSt, RPB.

A 41.1.c
First edition, presumed third (English) printing (1884)

LECTURES

AND

BIOGRAPHICAL SKETCHES

BY

RALPH WALDO EMERSON

(COPYRIGHT)

LONDON
GEORGE ROUTLEDGE AND SONS
BROADWAY, LUDGATE HILL
NEW YORK: 9, LAFAYETTE PLACE

1884

A 41.1.c: $7^7/_{16}''$ × $4^{15}/_{16}''$

[3–9] . . . 456–463 [464]

[1]^8 (-1_1) 2–19^8 [20]^8 21–29^8 The cancelled leaf is probably the *Riverside Edition* series half title

Contents: p. 3: title page; p. 4: printer's imprint; p. 5: 'NOTE'; p. 6: contents; p. 7: 'DEMONOLOGY. | [four lines of verse]'; p. 8: four lines of verse; pp. 9–463: the same as in the first printing; p. 464: the same as p. 4.

Typography and paper: The same as in the first printing, except: calendered wove paper.

Binding: Gray green S cloth (diagonal rib). Front and back covers: blank; spine: goldstamped 'LECTURES | AND | BIOGRAPHICAL | SKETCHES | EMERSON | ROUTLEDGE.'. Light brown floral design endpapers. All edges trimmed.

Publication: Deposit copies: BC (4 January 1884), BO (4 February 1884).

Printing: "LONDON: | PRINTED BY WILLIAM CLOWES AND SONS, LIMITED, | STAMFORD STREET AND CHARING CROSS" (p. [4]).

Locations: BC, BE, BO.

A 41.1.d
First edition, presumed fourth (English) printing (1884)

Title page is the same as in the third printing.

Vol. X of the *Riverside Edition (Copyright)*, English trade printing (see B 10). 1,000 copies printed late November 1883. Listed in *Athenæum*, no. 2929 (15 December 1883), 776; as published between 1 and 15 January 1884, in *Publishers' Circular and Booksellers' Record*, 47 (18 January 1884), 18. Price, 3s. 6d. *Locations:* BL (15 March 1884), JM.

A 41.1.e
First edition, fifth printing (1884)

Boston and New York: Houghton, Mifflin, 1884.

The same as the second printing, except collation is [1–19^{12} 20^6]. 500 copies printed 29 December 1883. *Locations:* CtY, JM.

LATER PRINTINGS FROM THE RIVERSIDE EDITION PLATES

A 41.1.f₁
Riverside Edition (large paper), sixth printing, American issue (1884)

[red] LECTURES | AND | BIOGRAPHICAL SKETCHES | BY | RALPH WALDO EMERSON | [pine branch] | [red] CAMBRIDGE | [gothic] Printed at the Riverside Press | 1884

Vol. X of the *Riverside Edition*, large paper printing (see B 8). Limited to 500 numbered copies printed 13 March 1884. Price, $4.00. Sold out within a year. *Locations:* JM, TxU.

A 41.1.f₂
Riverside Edition (large paper), sixth printing, English issue [1884]

Title page is the same as in the American issue, except for publisher's imprint: 'LONDON | KEGAN PAUL, TRENCH, & CO., I, PATERNOSTER SQUARE | MDCCCLXXXIII'.

Vol. X of the *Riverside Edition,* large paper printing for English subscribers (see B 9). 25 title leaves printed 13 March 1884. Title leaf is a cancel; the date on the title page is in error. Limited to 25 signed and numbered copies. *Location:* JM.

A 41.1.g
Boston and New York: Houghton, Mifflin, 1885.

500 copies printed 2 January 1885 and 31 August 1885. *Location:* JM.

A 41.1.h
London and New York: George Routledge and Sons, 1886.

500 copies printed 1 January 1886. *Location:* JM.

A 41.1.i
Boston and New York: Houghton, Mifflin, 1886.

500 copies printed 11 March 1886. *Location:* JM.

A 41.1.j
Boston and New York: Houghton, Mifflin, 1887.

500 copies printed 9 November 1886 and ca. June 1887; 250 copies ca. September 1887. *Location:* JM.

A 41.1.k
Boston and New York: Houghton, Mifflin, 1888.

500 copies printed 6 March 1888 and 25 October 1888. *Location:* MWin.

A 41.1.l
Boston and New York: Houghton, Mifflin, 1889.

500 copies printed 2 August 1889. *Not seen.*

A 41.1.m
Boston and New York: Houghton, Mifflin, 1890.

500 copies printed April–June 1890. *Location:* MdBJ.

A 41.1.n
Boston and New York: Houghton, Mifflin, 1891.

500 copies printed ca. December 1890 and 13 August 1891. *Location:* JM.

A 41.1.o
Boston and New York: Houghton, Mifflin, 1892.

500 copies printed 3 September 1892. *Not seen.*

A 41.1.p
Boston and New York: Houghton, Mifflin, 1893.

500 copies printed 17 October 1893. *Location:* JM.

A 41.1.q
London, Manchester, New York: George Routledge and Sons, 1894.

Published August 1894. *Location:* JM.

A 41.1.r
Standard Library Edition printing [1894]

LECTURES | AND BIOGRAPHICAL SKETCHES | BY | RALPH WALDO EMERSON | [pine branch] | BOSTON AND NEW YORK | HOUGHTON, MIFFLIN AND COMPANY | [gothic] The Riverside Press, Cambridge

Vol. X of the *Standard Library Edition* (see B 11). 1,000 copies printed 17 November 1894, 31 May 1895, and 29 May 1896; 500 copies on 16 May 1898. *Location:* JM.

A 41.1.s
Boston and New York: Houghton, Mifflin, 1895.

500 copies printed 21 January 1895. *Location:* NcU.

A 41.1.t
Boston and New York: Houghton, Mifflin, 1896.

500 copies printed ca. December 1895 and 26 June 1896. *Location:* JM.

A 41.1.u
Boston and New York: Houghton, Mifflin, 1897.

500 copies printed ca. March 1897. *Not seen.*

A 41.1.v
Boston and New York: Houghton, Mifflin, 1898.

250 copies printed April–June 1898. *Location:* ScU.

Note: Contains a new selection, "George L. Stearns," pp. [465]–473 (see A 32).

A 41.1.w
Boston and New York: Houghton, Mifflin, 1899.

270 copies printed 20 February 1899. *Location:* MB.

A 41.1.x
Boston and New York: Houghton, Mifflin, 1900.

270 copies printed 8 November 1899. *Location:* MGro.

A 41.1.y
London: George Routledge & Sons, 1903.

Combined with *Miscellanies* and *Natural History of Intellect* in three-volumes-in-one format as vol. IV of the "Sovereign Edition" (see B 12). 1,000 copies printed 16 September 1903. *Location:* InU.

A 41.1.z
Fireside Edition printing (1909)

[all within red double-rule frame with red floral ornaments in each corner] THE WORKS OF | [red gothic] Ralph Waldo Emerson | LECTURES AND BIOGRAPHICAL | SKETCHES | [engraving of man reading book in chair before fireplace] | [gothic] Fireside Edition | BOSTON AND NEW YORK | MDCCCCIX

Vol. X of the *Fireside Edition* (see B 13). 500 copies printed 6 October 1909 and 9 February 1910. *Location:* JM.

Note: The copyright on *Lectures and Biographical Sketches* was renewed 11 September 1911.

A 41.1.aa
Boston and New York: Jefferson Press, [ca. 1912].

Combined with *Poems* in two-volumes-in-one format as vol. [V] of the "Jefferson Press Edition" (see B 14). *Location:* JM.

A 41.1.bb
New York: Sully and Kleinteich, [ca. 1912].

Vol. X of the *University Edition* (see B 15). *Location:* JM.

A 41.1.cc
Boston and New York: Houghton, Mifflin, [n.d.].

Approximately 1,400 copies sold between 1901 and 1913. *Location:* JM.

Note: Approximately 12,500 copies of *Lectures and Biographical Sketches* in the *Riverside Edition* were sold between 1884 and 1913, when the title was apparently allowed to go out of print in this format.

A 41.1.dd
London: George Routledge and Sons, [n.d.].

Location: JM.

A 41.1.ee
London: Waverley Book Company, [n.d.].

Vol. X of the "Waverley" *Riverside Edition* (see B 16). *Location:* JM.

A 41.2.a

Second edition, first printing (1884)

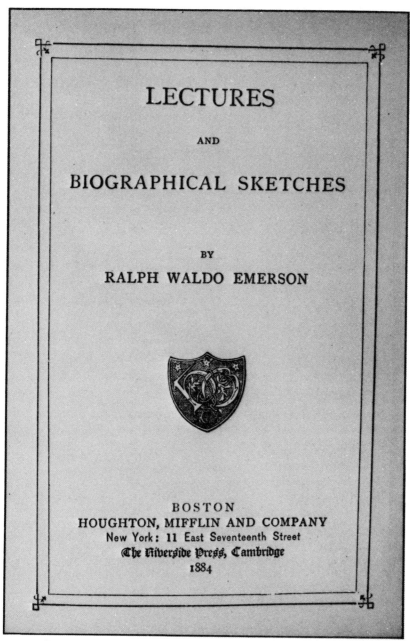

LECTURES

AND

BIOGRAPHICAL SKETCHES

BY

RALPH WALDO EMERSON

BOSTON
HOUGHTON, MIFFLIN AND COMPANY
New York: 11 East Seventeenth Street
The Riverside Press, Cambridge
1884

A 41.2.a: 5³/₄″ × 4¹/₄″; outer frame, 'LECTURES', and 'BOSTON:' are in red

[1–9] 10–27 [28–31] 32–56 [57–59] 60–73 [74–77] 78–99 [100–103] 104–127 [128–131] 132–142 [143–145] 146–167 [168–171] 172–186 [187–189] 190–201 [202–205] 206–225 [226–229] 230–250 [251–253] 254–285 [286–289] 290–292 [293–295] 296–305 [306–309] 310–333 [334–337] 338–346 [347–349] 350–373 [374–377] 378–383 [384]

$[1^1 2–25^8 (–25_8)]$ Signed $[1]^8 2–8^8 [9]^8 10–21^8 [22]^8 23–24^8$

Contents: Basically the same as pp. 1–464 of the first edition.

Typography and paper: $4^3/_4''$ $(4^1/_2'')$ × $2^{11}/_{16}''$; wove paper; 33 lines per page. Running heads: basically the same as in the first edition.

Binding: Medium brown S cloth (diagonal fine-rib). "Little Classic Edition" binding (see illustration at A 34.2.a) with goldstamped 'LECTURES | AND | BIOGRAPHICAL | SKETCHES' on front cover and 'LECTURES | AND | BIOGRAPHICAL | SKETCHES' on spine. Flyleaves. Black coated endpapers. All edges trimmed. All edges stained red.

Publication: 1,000 copies printed 17 December 1883. According to the publisher's records, published 15 December 1883. Price, $1.50.

Printing: The same printer's imprint as in A 41.1.a.

Locations: JM, VtMiM.

Note one: Vol. [X] of the "Little Classic Edition" (see B 3).

Note two: A copy has been noted with advertisements for Houghton, Mifflin and Company's publications on the verso of a leaf inserted before the title page: VtMiM.

Note three: In both copies, leaf 25_8 is cancelled; in one copy, the stub is pasted under the rear pastedown endpaper.

LATER PRINTINGS FROM THE "LITTLE CLASSIC EDITION" PLATES

A 41.2.b
Boston and New York: Houghton, Mifflin, 1886.

270 copies printed 11 June 1886. Probably bound in medium blue V cloth (smooth), rather than "Little Classic Edition" binding, as are subsequent reprintings (see illustration at B 3). *Not seen.*

A 41.2.c
Boston and New York: Houghton, Mifflin, 1888.

270 copies printed 8 November 1887 and 30 April 1888. *Location:* UU.

A 41.2.d
Boston and New York: Houghton, Mifflin, 1889.

270 copies printed 21 December 1888. *Location:* JM.

A 41.2.e
Boston and New York: Houghton, Mifflin, 1890.

270 copies printed 31 December 1889; 250 copies ca. September 1890. *Not seen.*

A 41.2.f
Boston and New York: Houghton, Mifflin, 1891.

270 copies printed 24 June 1891. *Not seen.*

A 41.2.g
Boston and New York: Houghton, Mifflin, 1892.

500 copies printed 15 March 1892. *Location:* MHi.

A 41.2.h
Boston and New York: Houghton, Mifflin, 1893.

500 copies printed 25 August 1893. *Location:* MH.

A 41.2.i
Boston and New York: Houghton, Mifflin, 1896.

270 copies printed 10 February 1896. *Location:* CU.

A 41.2.j
Boston and New York: Houghton, Mifflin, 1898.

270 copies printed 31 January 1898. *Location:* JM.

A 41.2.k
Boston and New York: Houghton, Mifflin, 1900.

270 copies printed 29 November 1899. *Not seen.*

A 41.2.l
Boston and New York: Houghton, Mifflin, [n.d.].

Approximately 900 copies sold between 1901 and 1923. *Location:* NNS.

Note: Approximately 5,500 copies of *Lectures and Biographical Sketches* printed from the "Little Classic Edition" plates were sold between 1884 and 1923, when the title was apparently allowed to go out of print in this format.

PRINTINGS FROM THE CENTENARY EDITION PLATES

A 41.3.a
Centenary Edition (trade), first printing (1904)

LECTURES AND | BIOGRAPHICAL SKETCHES | BY | RALPH WALDO EMERSON | [pine tree] | BOSTON AND NEW YORK | HOUGHTON, MIFFLIN AND COMPANY, | [gothic] The Riverside Press, Cambridge | 1904

623 pp. Dust jacket. Vol. X of the *Centenary Edition,* trade printing (see B 18). 1,000 copies printed 26 July 1904. Advertised as "now ready," in *Publishers' Weekly,* 66 (3 December 1904), 1573. Listed in *Publishers' Weekly,* 66 (10 December 1904), 1592. According to the publisher's records, published 30 November 1904. Copyright, 17 October 1904. Price, $1.75. *Locations:* DLC (9 November 1904), JM.

Note: Numerous reprintings with undated title pages. 2,000 copies printed between 1 January 1905 and 31 March 1909. Approximately 3,800 copies sold through 1923.

A 41.3.b
Boston and New York: Houghton, Mifflin, 1904.

Vol. X of the *Concord Edition* (see B 20). 2,000 copies printed 28 October 1904. *Location:* JM.

Note: Numerous reprintings with undated title pages. Approximately 3,100 copies sold by 31 December 1910.

A 41.3.c
Autograph Centenary Edition (large paper), third printing (1904)

RALPH WALDO EMERSON | [red] Lectures and | [red] Biographical Sketches | [pine tree] | CAMBRIDGE | [red gothic] Printed at the Riverside Press | 1904

Vol. X of the *Autograph Centenary Edition* (see B 19). Limited to 600 signed and numbered copies printed 31 October 1904. Copyright, 17 October 1904. Price, $6.00. Sold out by 5 April 1906. *Locations:* DLC (9 November 1904), JM.

A 41.3.d$_2$
English issue of the American sheets [1909]

London: Archibald Constable; Boston and New York: Houghton, Mifflin, [1909].

Vol. X of the English *Centenary Edition* (see B 21). The title leaf is a cancel. Price, 6s. *Locations:* BC (23 August 1909), BE (23 August 1909). BL (19 February 1915).

Note: Undoubtedly the sheets from an undated American reprinting (presumed A 41.3.d$_1$) of the *Centenary Edition,* trade printing.

A 41.3.e
Boston and New York: Houghton Mifflin, [1911].

Vol. X of the *Centenary Edition,* trade printing (see B 18). *Location:* PSC.

A 41.3.f
Boston and New York: Houghton Mifflin, [1914].

Vol. X of the *Riverside Pocket Edition* (see B 22). Approximately 900 copies sold between 1914 and 1922. *Not seen.*

A 41.3.g
Boston and New York: Houghton Mifflin, 1921.

507 pp. (text without the notes). Combined with *English Traits* in two-volumes-in-one format as vol. IV of *Emerson's Complete Works* (see B 23). *Location:* RP.

A 41.3.h
New York: Wm. H. Wise, 1923.

Combined with *Poems* in two-volumes-in-one format as vol. V of the *Current Opinion Edition* (see B 24). *Location:* JM.

A 41.3.i
Boston and New York: Houghton Mifflin, 1929.

Combined (text without the notes) with *English Traits* in two-volumes-in-one format as vol. [IV] of the *Harvard Edition* (see B 25). *Location:* JM.

A 41.3.j
New York: Wm. H. Wise, 1929.

Combined with *Poems* in two-volumes-in-one format as vol. V of the *Medallion Edition* (see B 26). *Location:* OC.

A 41.3.k–l
New York: AMS Press, [1968].

Vol. X of the "AMS Press" *Centenary Edition* (see B 27). Reprinted 1979. *Locations:* TxU, DLC (9 November 1979).

SEPARATE PUBLICATIONS OF INDIVIDUAL ESSAYS

A 41.4
Henry D. Thoreau. Boston [&c.]: Houghton, Mifflin, [1906].

xv–xl, 27–30 pp. Cover title. Pamphlet. *Location:* MH.

Note: Reprinted from the plates of the *Walden Edition* of Thoreau's works.

A 42
First English edition, only printing (1884)

THE SENSES AND THE SOUL,

AND

MORAL SENTIMENT IN RELIGION:

T W O   E S S A Y S

BY

RALPH   WALDO   EMERSON.

LONDON:

FOULGER & CO.,

THE MODERN PRESS, 13 & 14 PATERNOSTER ROW, E.C.

1884.

[*Price Twopence.*]

A 42: Cover title, 7⅝″ × 5″

[11–13] 14–20 [21] 22–24 [25–26]

[a]⁸

Contents: p. 11: cover title; p. 12: "Editor's Note," dated 14 February 1884, and publisher's advertisements; pp. 13–20: text of *The Senses and the Soul;* pp. 21–24: text of *Moral Sentiment in Religion;* pp. 25–26: publisher's advertisements.

Selections: "The Senses and the Soul" †; "Moral Sentiment in Religion" †.

Typography and paper: 5¹¹/₁₆″ (5³/₈″) × 3¹/₂″; wove paper; 31 lines per page. Running heads: rectos: pp. 15–19: '*THE SENSES AND THE SOUL.*'; p. 23: '*MORAL SENTIMENT IN RELIGION.*'; versos: pp. 14–20: '*THE SENSES AND THE SOUL.*'; pp. 22–24: '*MORAL SENTIMENT IN RELIGION.*'.

Binding: Cover title. All edges trimmed.

Publication: Probably published ca. March–April 1884. Price, 2d.

Locations: BL, MCo, MH, ViU.

Note one: Edited by Walter Lewin.

Note two: The previous year, Foulger had advertised as "In preparation" the following: "Two Addresses; I. Religious Needs of the Age. II. Religion," noting that "These two Papers have not, hitherto, appeared in any collection of Emerson's writings" (see John Fiske, *Evolution and Religion* [London: J. C. Foulger, 1883], p. [13]). The "Editor's Note" to the present title states that "The Senses and the Soul" was substituted for "Religious Needs of the Age," which "appears in a recent edition of Mr. Emerson's writings, and there is, therefore, no need to reproduce it" (p. [12]). There is no published work by Emerson with the title "Religious Needs of the Age"; Lewin is probably referring to either of the talks before the Free Religious Association collected for the first time in *Miscellanies* (see A 40).

Note three: "Moral Sentiment in Religion" is retitled from "Religion," in *Sketches and Reminiscences of the Radical Club* (see D 113).

A 43 THE CORRESPONDENCE OF THOMAS CARLYLE AND RALPH WALDO
EMERSON   SUPPLEMENTARY LETTERS

A 43
First edition, only printing (1886)

THE CORRESPONDENCE

OF

THOMAS CARLYLE

AND

RALPH WALDO EMERSON

1834—1872

SUPPLEMENTARY LETTERS

BOSTON
TICKNOR AND COMPANY
1886

A 43: 7⅝" × 4⅞"

[i–iii] iv–v [vi–viii] 1–80

[a]^4 [1]^8 2–5^8

Contents: p. i: title page; p. ii: copyright page; pp. iii–v: contents; p. vi: blank; p. vii: 'NOTE TO SUPPLEMENT.', signed 'C[harles]. E[liot]. N[orton]. | December 31, 1884.'; p. viii: blank; pp. 1–80: text of letters.

Typography and paper: 5^1/$_2$″ (5^1/$_8$″) × 3^3/$_{16}$″; laid paper with 1^3/$_{16}$″ vertical chain marks; 26 lines per page. Running heads: rectos: p. v: '*Contents.*'; pp. 3–5, 13–31, 37–61: '*Carlyle to Emerson.*'; pp. 7–11, 33–35, 63–79: '*Emerson to Carlyle.*'; versos: p. iv: '*Contents.*'; pp. 2–6, 12–32, 36–62: '*Carlyle to Emerson.*'; pp. 8–10, 34, 64–80: '*Emerson to Carlyle.*'.

Binding: Medium brown S cloth (diagonal fine-rib). Front and back covers: blank; spine: leather label with goldstamped '[rule] | [rule] | CORRESPONDENCE | OF | CAR-LYLE | AND | EMERSON | [rule] | [rule]' and goldstamped beneath it 'SUPPLEMEN-TARY'. Gray coated endpapers. All edges trimmed. Top edges gilded.

Publication: Advertised in *Publishers' Weekly*, 29 (30 January 1886), 174. MBAt copy received 15 December 1885. Deposit copy: DLC (16 December 1885). Price, $1.00.

Locations: CU, CtY, DLC, JM, MBAt, MCo, MH.

Note: All copies have a 24-page undated catalogue of Ticknor's publications inserted at the back.

A 44 NATURAL HISTORY OF INTELLECT

A 44.1.a
First edition, first printing (1893)

NATURAL HISTORY OF INTELLECT

AND OTHER PAPERS

BY

RALPH WALDO EMERSON

BOSTON AND NEW YORK
HOUGHTON, MIFFLIN AND COMPANY
The Riverside Press, Cambridge
1893

A 44.1.a: 6″ × 4⁵/₁₆″

[i–iii] iv [5–9] 10–53 [54–57] 58–71 [72–75] 76–95 [96–99] 100–120 [121–123] 124–146 [147–149] 150–224

[1-14⁸]

Contents: p. i: title page; p. ii: copyright page; pp. iii–iv: 'PREFATORY NOTE.', signed 'J. E. Cabot. | *September* 9, 1893.'; p. 5: contents; p. 6: blank; p. 7: 'NATURAL HISTORY OF INTELLECT.'; p. 8: blank; pp. 9–53: text; p. 54: blank; p. 55: 'MEMORY.'; p. 56: blank; pp. 57–71: text; p. 72: blank; p. 73: 'BOSTON. | [rule with dot in center] | [six lines of prose]'; p. 74: '[four lines of verse] | [dotted line] | [16 lines of verse]'; pp. 75–95: text; p. 96: blank; p. 97: 'MICHAEL ANGELO. | [rule with dot in center] | [five lines of verse] | Michael Angelo's *Sonnets.*'; p. 98: '[four lines of Italian verse] | M. Angelo, *Sonnetto primo.*'; pp. 99–120: text; p. 121: 'MILTON. | [rule with dot in center] | [four lines of verse]'; p. 122: blank; pp. 123–146: text; p. 147: 'PAPERS FROM THE DIAL. | [rule with dot in center] | [four lines of verse]'; p. 148: blank; pp. 149–168: "Thoughts on Modern Literature"; pp. 168–177: "Walter Savage Landor"; pp. 177–183: "Prayers"; pp. 183–187: "Agriculture of Massachusetts"; pp. 187–197: "Europe and European Books"; pp. 197–206: "Past and Present"; pp. 206–215: "A Letter"; pp. 216–224: "The Tragic."

Selections: "Natural History of Intellect" #; "Memory" #; "Boston" †; "Michael Angelo" †; "Milton" †; "Thoughts on Modern Literature" †; "Walter Savage Landor" †; "Prayers" †; "Agriculture of Massachusetts" †; "Europe and European Books" †; "Past and Present" †; "A Letter" †; "The Tragic" †.

Typography and paper: 4³/₄″ (4¹/₂″) × 2¹³/₁₆″; wove paper; 33 lines per page. Running heads: rectos: pp. 11–53, 59–71, 77–95, 101–119, 125–145, 151–223: titles of selections; versos: p. iv: 'PREFATORY NOTE.'; pp. 10–52, 58–70, 76–94, 100–120, 124–146: titles of selections; pp. 150–224: 'PAPERS FROM THE DIAL.'.

Binding: Medium blue V cloth (smooth). Front and back covers: blank; spine: gold-stamped '[rule] | [rule] | Emerson's | Works | [rule] | NATURAL | HISTORY | OF | INTELLECT | [rule] | [rule]'. Flyleaves. White laid endpapers. All edges trimmed. Top edges gilded.

Publication: Advertised as "In preparation and to be published during the Autumn of 1892," in *Atlantic,* 70 (September 1892), wrappers. Listed as received in *Publishers' Weekly,* 44 (9 December 1893), 960. 1,000 copies printed 19 October 1893. Inscribed copy: NNC (20 November 1893). Price, $1.25.

Locations: JM, MH, NNC, NjP.

Note: Vol. [XII] of the "Little Classic Edition" (see B 3).

A 44.1.b–c
Boston and New York: Houghton, Mifflin, 1894.

500 copies printed 30 November 1893, 14 March 1894, and 30 August 1894. *Not seen.*

A 44.1.d
Boston and New York: Houghton, Mifflin, 1897.

270 copies printed 15 September 1897. *Location:* DeU.

A 44.1.e
Boston and New York: Houghton, Mifflin, [n.d.].

Approximately 900 copies sold between 1900 and 1910. *Not seen.*

Note one: Approximately 3,000 copies of *Natural History of Intellect* printed from the "Little Classic Edition" plates were sold between 1893 and 1923, when the title was apparently allowed to go out of print in this format.

Note two: The "Little Classic Edition" plates were ordered destroyed 14 October 1929.

A 44.2.a
Second edition, first printing (1893)

NATURAL· HISTORY OF INTELLECT

AND OTHER PAPERS

BY

RALPH WALDO EMERSON

WITH A GENERAL INDEX TO EMERSON'S COLLECTED WORKS

BOSTON AND NEW YORK
HOUGHTON, MIFFLIN AND COMPANY
𝕿𝔥𝔢 𝕽𝔦𝔳𝔢𝔯𝔰𝔦𝔡𝔢 𝕻𝔯𝔢𝔰𝔰, 𝕮𝔞𝔪𝔟𝔯𝔦𝔡𝔤𝔢
1893

A 44.2.a: 7^{7}/₁₆″ × 5″

[a–b] [i–iii] iv [v–vi] [1–3] 4–59 [60–63] 64–81 [82–85] 86–111 [112–115] 116–142 [143–145] 146–174 [175–177] 178–272 [273] 274–350 [351] 352–353 [354]

[1^8 (+1$_5$) 2–22^8 23^4]   The inserted leaf contains the contents

Contents: Basically the same as the first edition (but with *Riverside Edition* half title), except: pp. 273–350: "General Index"; pp. 351–353: "Index of Quotations"; p. 354: blank.

Typography and paper: 5^3/$_8$" (5^3/$_{16}$") × 3^1/$_{16}$"; laid paper with 1^5/$_{16}$" vertical chain marks; 28 lines per page. Running heads are basically the same as in the first edition.

Binding: Medium blue H cloth (fine diaper). Front and back covers: blank; spine: goldstamped 'NATURAL | HISTORY | OF | INTELLECT | EMERSON | [publisher's logo]'. Laid paper flyleaves. Blue coated endpapers. All edges trimmed. Top edges gilded.

Publication: Advertised as "In preparation and to be published during the Autumn of 1892," in *Atlantic*, 70 (September 1892), wrappers. Listed as received in *Critic*, 23 (25 November 1893), 350; in *Publishers' Weekly*, 44 (9 December 1893), 960. 2,000 copies printed 28 October 1893. According to the publisher's records, published 15 November 1893. Copyright, 27 October 1893. Deposit copy: DLC (9 November 1893). MCo copy received December 1893. Price, $1.75.

Printing: The same printer's imprint as in A 44.1.a.

Locations: CtY, DLC, JM, MB, MCo, MH, MH-AH, MWA, NNC, RPB.

Note: Vol. XII of the *Riverside Edition,* trade printing (see B 7).

A 44.2.b
Riverside Edition (large paper), second printing (1893)

[red] NATURAL HISTORY OF | [red] INTELLECT | *AND OTHER PAPERS* | BY | RALPH WALDO EMERSON | *WITH A GENERAL INDEX TO EMERSON'S* | *COLLECTED WORKS* | [pine branch] | [red] CAMBRIDGE | [gothic] Printed at the Riverside Press | 1893

Vol. XII of the *Riverside Edition,* large paper printing (see B 8). Limited to 500 numbered copies printed 10 November 1893. Listed as received in *Critic*, 23 (25 November 1893), 350; in *Publishers' Weekly*, 44 (9 December 1893), 960. Price, $5.00. *Locations:* CtY, DLC (20 November 1893), JM, TxU.

Note: Only 248 copies of the large paper printing had been sold by 1912. According to the publisher's records, 200 copies were bound in half leather and sold in 1913 and 1914, possibly the remaining stock of the large paper printing; no copies bound in leather have been located.

A 44.2.c
Second edition, third printing for English sale (1893)

NATURAL HISTORY OF INTELLECT

AND OTHER PAPERS

BY

RALPH WALDO EMERSON

WITH A GENERAL INDEX TO EMERSON'S COLLECTED WORKS

LONDON
GEORGE ROUTLEDGE & SONS
1893

A 44.2.c: 7⁷/₁₆″ × 5″

[a–b] [i–iii] iv [v–vi] [3] 4–59; all else is the same as in the first printing

[1–22^8 23^4]

Contents: pp. a–b: blank; p. i: title page; p. ii: printer's information; pp. iii–vi, 3–354: the same as in the first printing.

Typography and paper: The same as in the first printing.

Binding: The same as in the first printing, except: publisher's logo on spine has been blotted out; no flyleaves.

Publication: Deposit copies: BC (23 November 1893), BO (29 November 1893).

Printing: "*The Riverside Press, Cambridge, Mass., U.S.A.* | Printed by H. O. Houghton & Company" (p. [ii]).

Locations: BC, BE, BO.

A 44.2.d
Second edition, fourth printing (1894)

Boston and New York: Houghton, Mifflin, 1894.

500 copies printed 27 December 1893. *Location:* MH.

A 44.2.e
Second edition, fifth (English) printing (1894)

Title page is the same as in the third printing, except: '[pine branch] | *COPYRIGHT* | LONDON | GEORGE ROUTLEDGE & SONS, Limited | BROADWAY, LUDGATE HILL | 1894 | *All rights reserved*'.

[i–iv] v . . . 352–353 [354–362]

[A]^4 B–H^8 [I]^8 K–U^8 X–Z^8 ZA^4

Contents: p. i: 'NATURAL HISTORY OF INTELLECT | AND OTHER PAPERS'; p. ii: blank; p. iii: title page; p. iv: printer's imprint; pp. v–354: the same as in the third printing; pp. 355–362: publisher's advertisements, dated December 1893.

Typography and paper: The same as in the third printing, except: page size is 7^7/$_{16}$" × 4^{15}/$_{16}$"; calendered wove paper.

Binding: Dark gray blue B cloth (linen). Front and back covers: blindstamped single-rule frame; spine: goldstamped '[four rules] | NATURAL | HISTORY OF | INTELLECT | AND | OTHER PAPERS | *RALPH WALDO EMERSON* | ROUTLEDGE | [four rules]'. Dark blue coated endpapers. All edges trimmed. Top edges gilded.

Publication: On 27 October 1893, Houghton, Mifflin wrote Routledge that "your set of plates for the new volume of Emerson" had been shipped, and four days later the cost of the plates was billed to Routledge, who also paid a £75 royalty to the Emerson heirs. Listed in *Publishers' Circular and Booksellers' Record*, 60 (3 February 1894), 137. Deposit copies: BC (1 June 1894), BO (6 June 1894). Price, 5s.

Printing: "LONDON: | PRINTED BY WILLIAM CLOWES AND SONS LIMITED, | STAMFORD STREET AND CHARING CROSS" (p. [iv]).

Locations: BC, BE, BO, NNF.

A 44.2.f
Second edition, sixth printing (1894)

Boston and New York: Houghton, Mifflin, 1894.

500 copies printed 12 May 1894. *Not seen.*

LATER PRINTINGS FROM THE RIVERSIDE EDITION PLATES

A 44.2.g
Standard Library Edition printing [1894]

NATURAL HISTORY OF | INTELLECT | AND OTHER PAPERS | BY | RALPH WALDO EMERSON | *WITH A GENERAL INDEX TO EMERSON'S* | *COLLECTED WORKS* | [pine branch] | BOSTON AND NEW YORK | HOUGHTON, MIFFLIN AND COMPANY | [gothic] The Riverside Press, Cambridge

Vol. XII of the *Standard Library Edition* (see B 11). 1,000 copies printed 19 November 1894, 31 May 1895, and 29 May 1896; 500 copies on 31 January 1898. *Location:* JM.

Note: There were other undated reprints: according to the publisher's records, approximately 4,700 copies were sold by 31 December 1904.

A 44.2.h
Boston and New York: Houghton, Mifflin, 1895.

500 copies printed 30 April 1895. *Location:* JM.

A 44.2.i
Boston and New York: Houghton, Mifflin, 1897.

270 copies printed 26 January 1897 and 9 October 1897. *Location:* MNoW.

A 44.2.j
Boston and New York: Houghton, Mifflin, 1899.

270 copies printed 31 December 1898 and 21 June 1899; 250 copies ca. March 1899. *Location:* JM.

A 44.2.k
London: George Routledge and Sons, 1903.

Location: JM.

A 44.2.l
London: George Routledge & Sons, 1903.

Combined with *Lectures and Biographical Sketches* and *Miscellanies* in three-volumes-in-one format as vol. IV of the "Sovereign Edition" (see B 12). 1,000 copies printed 16 September 1903. *Location:* InU.

A 44.2.m
Fireside Edition printing (1909)

[all within red double-rule frame with red floral ornaments in each corner] THE WORKS OF | [red gothic] Ralph Waldo Emerson | NATURAL HISTORY OF INTELLECT | AND OTHER PAPERS | [engraving of man reading book in chair before fireplace] | [gothic] Fireside Edition | BOSTON AND NEW YORK | MDCCCCIX

Vol. XII of the *Fireside Edition* (see B 13). 500 copies printed 5 October 1909 and 15 February 1910. *Location:* JM.

A 44.2.n
Boston and New York: Jefferson Press, [ca. 1912].

Combined with *Miscellanies* in two-volumes-in-one format as vol. [VI] of the "Jefferson Press Edition" (see B 14). *Location:* JM.

A 44.2.o
New York: Sully and Kleinteich, [ca. 1912].

Vol. XII of the *University Edition* (see B 15). *Location:* JM.

A 44.2.p
Boston and New York: Houghton, Mifflin, [n.d.].

Approximately 1,700 copies sold between 1900 and 1913. *Location:* JM.

Note one: Approximately 5,800 copies of *Natural History of Intellect* in the *Riverside Edition* were sold between 1893 and 1913, when the title was apparently allowed to go out of print in this format.

Note two: The copyright on *Natural History of Intellect* was renewed 14 January 1921.

A 44.2.q
London: Waverley Book Company, [n.d.].

Vol. XII of the "Waverley" *Riverside Edition* (see B 16). *Location:* JM.

PRINTINGS FROM THE CENTENARY EDITION PLATES

A 44.3.a
Autograph Centenary Edition (large paper), first printing (1904)

RALPH WALDO EMERSON | [red] Natural History of | [red] Intellect | And Other Papers | [pine tree] | CAMBRIDGE | [red gothic] Printed at the Riverside Press | 1904

612 pp. Vol. XII of the *Autograph Centenary Edition* (see B 19). Limited to 600 signed and numbered copies printed 31 October 1904. Copyright, 17 October 1904. Price, $6.00. Sold out by 5 April 1906. *Locations:* DLC (9 November 1904), JM.

Note: New items: "Instinct and Inspiration" #; "The Celebration of Intellect" #; "Country Life" †; "Concord Walks" #; "Art and Criticism" #.

A 44.3.b
Centenary Edition (trade), second printing (1904)

NATURAL HISTORY OF | INTELLECT | AND OTHER PAPERS | BY | RALPH WALDO EMERSON | [pine tree] | BOSTON AND NEW YORK | HOUGHTON, MIFFLIN AND COMPANY, | [gothic] The Riverside Press, Cambridge | 1904

Vol. XII of the *Centenary Edition,* trade printing (see B 18). 1,000 copies printed 5 November 1904. Advertised as "now ready," in *Publishers' Weekly,* 66 (3 December 1904), 1573. Listed in *Publishers' Weekly,* 66 (10 December 1904), 1592. According to the publisher's records, published 30 November 1904. Copyright, 17 October 1904. Price, $1.75. *Locations:* DLC (9 November 1904), JM.

Note: Numerous reprintings with undated title pages. 1,500 copies printed between 1 April 1905 and 30 September 1908. Approximately 4,000 copies sold through 1923.

A 44.3.c
Boston and New York: Houghton, Mifflin, 1904.

Vol. XII of the *Concord Edition* (see B 20). 2,000 copies printed 8 November 1904. *Location:* JM.

Note: Numerous reprintings with undated title pages. Approximately 2,900 copies sold by 31 December 1910.

A 44.3.d$_2$
English issue of American sheets [1909]

London: Archibald Constable; Boston and New York: Houghton Mifflin, [1909].

Vol. XII of the English *Centenary Edition* (see B 21). Title leaf is a cancel. *Locations:* BC (23 August 1909), BE (23 August 1909), BL (19 February 1915).

Note: Undoubtedly the sheets from an undated American reprinting (presumed A 44.3.d$_1$) of the *Centenary Edition,* trade printing.

A 44.3.e
Boston and New York: Houghton Mifflin, [1914].

Vol. XII of the *Riverside Pocket Edition* (see B 22). Approximately 1,000 copies sold between 1914 and 1922. *Not seen.*

A 44.3.f
Boston and New York: Houghton Mifflin, 1921.

Vol. XII of the *Centenary Edition,* trade printing (see B 18). *Location:* KU.

A 44.3.g
Boston and New York: Houghton Mifflin, 1921.

417 pp. (text without the notes). Combined with *The Conduct of Life* in two-volumes-in-one format as vol. V of *Emerson's Complete Works* (see B 23). *Location:* JM.

A 44.3.h
New York: Wm. H. Wise, 1923.

Combined with *Miscellanies* in two-volumes-in-one format as vol. VI of the *Current Opinion Edition* (see B 24). *Location:* JM.

A 44.3.i
Boston and New York: Houghton Mifflin, 1929.

Combined (text without the notes) with *The Conduct of Life* in two-volumes-in-one format as vol. [V] of the *Harvard Edition* (see B 25). *Location:* JM.

A 44.3.j
New York: Wm. H. Wise, 1929.

Combined with *Miscellanies* in two-volumes-in-one format as vol. VI of the *Medallion Edition* (see B 26). *Location:* OC.

A 44.3.k–l
New York: AMS Press, [1968].

Vol. XII of the "AMS Press" *Centenary Edition* (see B 27). Reprinted 1979. *Locations:* TxU, DLC (9 November 1979).

UNDATED EDITION

A 44.4
Philadelphia: Henry Altemus, [n.d.].

Price, 25¢. *Not seen.*

A 45 TWO UNPUBLISHED ESSAYS

A 45.1.a
First edition, first printing (1896)

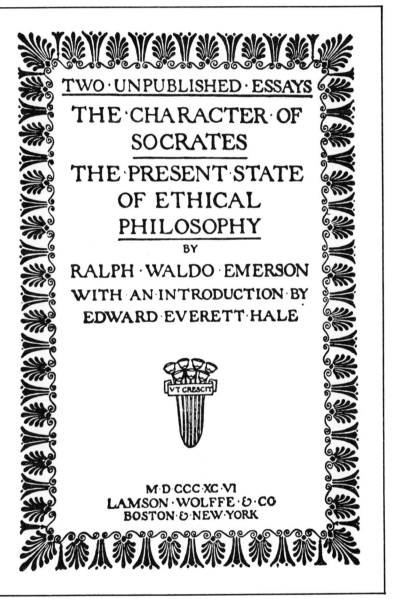

TWO · UNPUBLISHED · ESSAYS

THE · CHARACTER · OF
SOCRATES

THE · PRESENT · STATE
OF ETHICAL
PHILOSOPHY

BY

RALPH · WALDO · EMERSON

WITH · AN · INTRODUCTION · BY
EDWARD · EVERETT · HALE

VT CRESCIT

M · D · CCC · XC · VI
LAMSON · WOLFFE · & · CO
BOSTON · & · NEW · YORK

A 45.1.a: $6^9/_{16}$″ × $4^5/_{16}$″

[i–viii] [1–3] 4–39 [40–43] 44–81 [82–84]

[1⁴ 2–6⁸ 7²]

$[1^4 \ 2-6^8 \ 7^2]$

Contents: p. i: title page; p. ii: copyright page; pp. iii–viii: "Introduction"; p. 1: 'The Character of Socrates'; p. 2: blank; pp. 3–39: text; p. 40: blank; p. 41: 'The Present State of Ethical | Philosophy'; p. 42: blank; pp. 43–81: text; p. 82: printer's imprint; pp. 83–84: blank.

Essays: "The Character of Socrates" #; "The Present State of Ethical Philosophy" #.

Typography and paper: 4³/₈″ (4¹/₁₆″) × 2⁷/₈″; laid paper with 1¹/₄″ vertical chain marks; 23 lines per page. Running heads: rectos: pp. v–vii: 'Introduction'; pp. 5–39, 45–81: titles of essays; versos: pp. iv–viii: 'Introduction'; pp. 4–38, 44–80: titles of essays.

Binding: Very deep red V cloth (smooth). Front cover: goldstamped 'TWO·UNPUBLISHED·ESSAYS | RALPH·WALDO·EMERSON', variations listed below; back cover: blank; spine: two styles have been noted, priority undetermined, listed below. White laid endpapers. All edges trimmed. Top edges gilded.

> *Binding A:* Spine: goldstamped '[rule] | TWO | UNPUB· | LISHED | ESSAYS | [rule] | [rule] | EMER· | SON· | [rule] | [rule] | HALE | [rule] | [rule] | LAMSON | WOLFFE | AND·CO | [rule]'.

> *Binding B:* The same as Binding A, except: front cover: all within goldstamped single-rule frame; spine: goldstamped 'AND CO. | BOSTON | AND | NEW YORK | [rule]' at bottom.

Dust jacket: Unprinted glassine.

Publication: Noted as "just issued," in *Publishers' Weekly,* 49 (28 March 1896), 590. Listed in *Publishers' Weekly,* 49 (4 April 1896), 605. Copyright, 19 November 1895; renewed, 22 November 1912. Deposit copies: DLC (27 February 1896), BL (27 November 1896). MBAt copy received 10 March 1896. MH copy received 11 March 1896. Price. $1.00.

Printing: "PRINTED AT THE EVERETT PRESS BOSTON" (p. [82]).

Locations: Binding A: BL, CtY, DLC, JM, MB, MBAt, MCo, MH, MWA, NNC, NjP, TxU (dust jacket), VtMiM; Binding B: CtY, CU, MB, RPB, TxU.

A 45.2.a
Second edition, first printing (1899)

Ralph Waldo Emerson | BY | EDWARD EVERETT HALE | *TOGETHER WITH TWO EARLY ESSAYS* | *OF EMERSON* | [leaf design] | BOSTON | BROWN & COMPANY | 1899

135 pp. Emerson's essays are printed from the plates of the first edition, with new pagination, and the addition of "A paper read before the Brooklyn Institute" by Hale. *Locations:* DLC (28 October 1899), JM.

A 45.2.b–c
Boston: American Unitarian Association, 1902.

Reprinted 1904. *Locations:* JM (both).

A 45.2.d
[Folcroft, Penn.]: Folcroft Library Editions, 1972.

Facsimile reprinting. *Location:* ScU.

A 46 A CORRESPONDENCE BETWEEN JOHN STERLING AND RALPH
WALDO EMERSON

A 46.1.a
First edition, first printing (1897)

𝕬 Correspondence

BETWEEN

JOHN STERLING

AND

RALPH WALDO EMERSON

WITH A SKETCH OF
STERLING'S LIFE

BY

EDWARD WALDO EMERSON

BOSTON AND NEW YORK
HOUGHTON, MIFFLIN AND COMPANY
The Riverside Press, Cambridge
1897

A 46.1.a: Binding A, 7″ × 4¹¹/₁₆″; Binding B, 7⁵/₁₆″ × 4³/₄″

[i–vi] [1–2] 3–95 [96–98]

[1–6⁸ 7⁴]

Contents: p. i: blank; p. ii: publisher's advertisements for Emerson's works; p. iii: title page; p. iv: copyright page; p. v: 'PREFATORY NOTE', signed 'EDWARD W. EMERSON | CONCORD, *September, 1897.*'; p. vi: blank; p. 1: 'STERLING AND EMERSON'; p. 2: '[eight lines of verse in italics] | SIGURD THE VOLSUNG, WILLIAM MORRIS.'; pp. 3–24: 'JOHN STERLING'; pp. 25–91: 'THE CORRESPONDENCE'; pp. 92–96: 'CONCLUSION'; p. 97: printer's imprint; p. 98: blank.

Typography and paper: 4¹/₄″ (4¹/₁₆″) × 2¹/₂″; laid paper with 1¹/₄″ vertical chain marks; 24 lines per page. Running heads: rectos: pp. 5–23: 'JOHN STERLING'; pp. 27–91: 'THE CORRESPONDENCE'; pp. 93–95: 'CONCLUSION'; versos: pp. 4–24: 'JOHN STERLING'; pp. 26–90: 'THE CORRESPONDENCE'; pp. 94–96: 'CONCLUSION'.

Binding: Two styles have been noted, priority undetermined:

Binding A: Medium green B cloth (linen); medium green V cloth (smooth). Front cover: goldstamped single-rule frame with goldstamped 'CORRESPONDENCE | OF | EMERSON AND STERLING'; back cover: blank; spine: goldstamped '[rule] | LET-TERS | OF | EMERSON | AND | STERLING | [two lines in block handprinting] HOUGH-TON | MIFFLIN & C° [rule]'. Laid paper flyleaves. White laid endpapers. All edges trimmed. Top edges gilded.

Binding B: Medium red V cloth (smooth). Front and back covers: blank; spine: white paper label with '[yellow rule] | [yellow rule] | Letters | of | Emerson | and | Sterling | [yellow rule] | [yellow rule] | *First Edition*'. Laid paper flyleaves. White laid endpapers. Top edges trimmed; front and bottom edges rough trimmed.

Publication: 1,500 copies printed 6 October 1897. Advertised for 9 October 1897 in *Publishers' Weekly,* 52 (9 October 1897), 623. A delay in publication until 20 October 1897 noted in *Publishers' Weekly,* 25 (16 October 1897), 624. Listed in *Publishers' Weekly,* 25 (30 October 1897), 711. According to the publisher's records, published 20 October 1897. Copyright, unknown; renewed, 30 October 1924. Deposit copies: DLC (13 October 1897), BL (9 May 1898). MBAt copy received 26 October 1897. Inscribed copy: MCo (from Edward Waldo Emerson, November 1897). Price: Binding A, $1.00.

Printing: "[gothic] The Riverside Press | CAMBRIDGE, MASSACHUSETTS, U.S.A. | ELECTROTYPED AND PRINTED BY | H. O. HOUGHTON AND CO." (p. [97]).

Locations: Binding A: BL, CU, CtY, JM, MB, MBAt, MCo, MH, NN, NNC, NjP, VtU; Binding B: JM, MH, NNC.

Note one: 100 labels for Binding B printed 22 October 1897.

Note two: 1,183 copies were sold by 1922; 118 copies had been given to the editor for gratis distribution upon publication.

Note three: Listed as an importation at 4s. by Gay and Bird in *Athenæum,* no. 3664 (15 January 1898), 85. No copies with a Gay and Bird title page have been located.

Note four: The plates for *A Correspondence* were ordered destroyed 3 June 1931.

LATER PRINTING WITHIN THE FIRST EDITION

A 46.1.b
Port Washington, N.Y., and London: Kennikat, [1971].

Facsimile reprinting. *Location:* NcU.

A 47 LETTERS FROM RALPH WALDO EMERSON TO A FRIEND

A 47.1.a
First edition, first printing (1899)

LETTERS

FROM

RALPH WALDO EMERSON

TO

A FRIEND

1838–1853

EDITED BY

CHARLES ELIOT NORTON

BOSTON AND NEW YORK
HOUGHTON, MIFFLIN AND COMPANY
The Riverside Press, Cambridge
1899

A 47.1.a₁: Binding A, 7″ × 4¹¹/₁₆″; Binding B, 7¹/₈″ × 4¹¹/₁₆″

Two issues have been noted:

A 47.1.a₁
First edition, first printing, American issue (1899)

[i–ii] [1–2] 3–7 [8] 9–81 [82]

[1² 2⁶ 3–6⁸ 7²]

Contents: p. i: blank; p. ii: publisher's advertisements for Emerson's works; p. 1: title page; p. 2: copyright page; pp. 3–7: 'INTRODUCTION', signed 'C. E. NORTON. | MAY, 1899.'; p. 8: blank; pp. 9–81: 'LETTERS'; p. 82: printer's imprint.

Typography and paper: 4⁵/₁₆″ (4¹/₈″) × 2¹/₂″; laid paper with 1¹/₄″ vertical chain marks; 24 lines per page. Running heads: rectos: pp. 5–7: 'INTRODUCTION'; pp. 11–81: 'LETTERS'; versos: pp. 4–6: 'INTRODUCTION'; pp. 10–80: 'LETTERS'.

Binding: Two styles have been noted, priority undetermined:

Binding A: Medium green B cloth (linen); medium green V cloth (smooth). Front cover: goldstamped single-rule frame with goldstamped 'LETTERS OF EMERSON | TO | A FRIEND'; back cover: blank; spine: goldstamped '[rule] | LETTERS | OF | EMERSON | TO | A FRIEND | [two lines in block handprinting] HOUGHTON | MIFFLIN & C° | [rule]'. Laid paper flyleaves. White laid endpapers. All edges trimmed. Top edges gilded.

Binding B: Medium red V cloth (smooth). Front and back covers: blank; spine: white paper label with '[rule] | [rule] | Letters | from | Emerson | to | A Friend | [leaf design] | [rule] | [rule]'. Laid paper flyleaves. White laid endpapers. Top edges trimmed; front and bottom edges rough trimmed.

Dust jacket: Grayish yellow green paper. Front cover: all within a single-rule frame: 'LETTERS OF EMERSON | TO | A FRIEND'; back cover: blank; spine: '[rule] | LETTERS | OF | EMERSON | TO | A FRIEND | [two lines in block handprinting] HOUGHTON | MIFFLIN & C° | [rule]'; front and back flaps: blank.

Publication: 1,500 copies printed 31 August 1899. Advertised and noted in *Publishers' Weekly,* 56 (30 September 1899), 429, 463, 514. Listed in *Publishers' Weekly,* 56 (7 October 1899), 649. According to the publisher's records, published 23 September 1899. Copyright, 11 September 1899. Deposit copy: DLC (11 September 1899). MBAt copy received 19 September 1899. MCo copy received October 1899. Price: Binding A, $1.00.

Printing: "ELECTROTYPED AND PRINTED | BY H. O. HOUGHTON AND CO. | [rule] | [rule] | [gothic] The Riverside Press | [rule] | [rule] | CAMBRIDGE, MASS., U.S.A." (p. [82]).

Locations: Binding A: CU, CtY, JM, MB, MBAt, MCo, MH, NNC, NjP, RPB, TxU, ViU (dust jacket), VtMiM (partial dust jacket); Binding B: JM, MH.

Note one: 100 labels for Binding B printed 6 October 1899.

Note two: 1,500 dust jackets printed 14 September 1899.

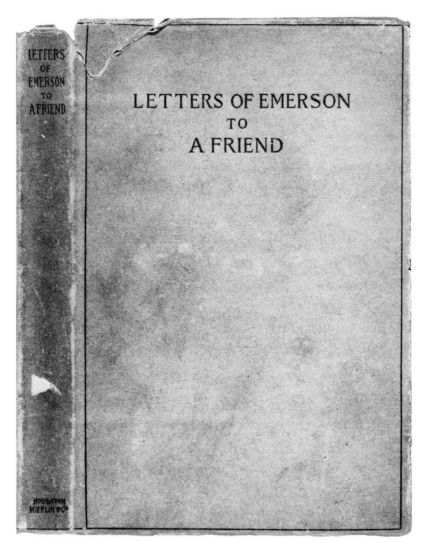

LETTERS
OF
EMERSON
TO
A FRIEND

LETTERS OF EMERSON
TO
A FRIEND

HOUGHTON
MIFFLIN CO

Dust jacket for A 47.1.a₁

Note three: 1,370 copies were sold by 1921; 114 copies had been given to the editor upon publication for gratis distribution.

Note four: The "friend" was Samuel Gray Ward.

Note five: The plates for *Letters to a Friend* were ordered destroyed 14 October 1929.

A 47.1.a₂
First edition, first printing, English issue (1899)

LETTERS

FROM

RALPH WALDO EMERSON

TO

A FRIEND

1838–1853

EDITED BY

CHARLES ELIOT NORTON

A. P. WATT & SON
Hastings House
NORFOLK STREET, STRAND
LONDON

A 47.1.a₂: 7″ × 4⁵⁄₈″

[1–2] 3–7 [8] 9–81 [82]

[1¹ 2⁶ 3–6⁸ 7²]   A new first gathering with the English title page replaces the first gathering of the American issue with the American title page

Contents: p. 1: title page; p. 2: blank; all else is the same as in the first printing.

Typography and paper: The same as in the first printing.

Binding: The same as in the first printing, except: the publisher's logo on the spine has been blotted out; the top edges are not gilded.

Publication: Houghton, Mifflin printed the title leaves 31 August 1899. Deposit copies: BL (23 September 1899), BE (18 October 1899), BC (20 October 1899).

Locations: BC, BE, BL.

LATER PRINTINGS WITHIN THE FIRST EDITION

A 47.1.b
Boston and New York: Houghton, Mifflin, 1900.

Location: PPT.

A 47.1.c
Port Washington, N.Y., and London: Kennikat, [1971].

Facsimile reprinting of A 47.1.a₁. Price, $6.00. *Location:* MB.

FOREIGN EDITION

A 47.2
Japanese edition

[Emerson no Shokan]. [Tokyo: Minyusha, 1901].

Unpaged. Wrappers. *Location:* RPB.

A 48 [SERMON ON GEORGE ADAMS SAMPSON]

A 48
First edition, only printing (1903)

PRINTED COPY

OF

PREACHED BY

RALPH WALDO EMERSON

ON THE DEATH OF

GEORGE ADAMS SAMPSON

1834

PRIVATELY PRINTED

1903

A 48: Cover title, 11″ × 8¹¹/₁₆″

[1–3] 4–13 [14–16]

[a]⁸

Contents: p. 1: cover title; p. 2: blank; pp. 3–13: text; pp. 14–16: blank.

Typography and paper: $6^1/_2''$ × 5''; laid paper with $1^3/_{16}''$ horizontal chain marks; 34 lines per page. No running heads.

Binding: Cover title. Unstitched sheets loosely laid together. All edges trimmed.

Publication: Tipped to p. 2 is this notice, printed on verso: 'Only thirty copies of this sermon are | printed, for private circulation, of which this | is No. ········ | *WILLIAM SAMPSON*'.

Locations: CSt, CtY, DLC, MB, MBAt, MH, MWA, NNC, ViU.

A 49 CORRESPONDENCE BETWEEN RALPH WALDO EMERSON AND
HERMAN GRIMM

A 49.1.a
First edition, first printing (1903)

CORRESPONDENCE BETWEEN

RALPH WALDO EMERSON

AND HERMAN GRIMM

EDITED BY

FREDERICK WILLIAM HOLLS

BOSTON AND NEW YORK

HOUGHTON, MIFFLIN AND COMPANY

The Riverside Press, Cambridge

1903

A 49.1.a: $6^{3}/4'' \times 4^{1}/_{16}''$

Reprinted — with the exception of the original German letters — from the "Atlantic Monthly," April, 1903

COPYRIGHT, 1903,
BY HOUGHTON, MIFFLIN & Co.
All rights reserved

Published May, 1903

[i–iv] [1–2] 3–14 [15] 16–19 [20–22] 23–24 [25–26] 27–28 [29–30] 31–35 [36–38] 39–44 [45] 46–53 [54–56] 57–63 [64–66] 67–68 [69] 70–77 [78–80] 81 [82–84] 85–86 [87–88] 89–90 [91–92]

[1–12⁴]

Contents: inserted leaf with picture of Emerson printed on verso, with protective tissue printed on recto '*Ralph Waldo Emerson*'; p. i: title page; p. ii: copyright page; p. iii: contents; p. iv: blank; p. 1: 'INTRODUCTION'; p. 2: blank; pp. 3–14: "Introduction"; p. 15: 'I | GRIMM TO EMERSON'; pp. 16–19: text of letter; p. 20: blank; p. 21: 'II | EMERSON TO GRIMM'; p. 22: blank; pp. 23–24: text of letter; p. 25: 'III | EMERSON TO THE FRÄULEIN GISELA | VON ARNIM, AFTERWARDS THE | WIFE OF HERMAN GRIMM'; p. 26: blank; pp. 27–28: text of letter; p. 29: 'IV | EMERSON TO GRIMM'; p. 30: blank; pp. 31–35: text of letter; p. 36: blank; p. 37: 'V | EMERSON TO GISELA VON ARNIM'; p. 38: blank; pp. 39–44: text of letter; inserted leaf with picture of Grimm printed on recto, with protective tissue printed on recto '*Herman Grimm*'; p. 45: 'VI | GRIMM TO EMERSON'; pp. 46–53: text of letter; p. 54: blank; p. 55: 'VII | EMERSON TO GRIMM'; p. 56: blank; pp. 57–63: text of letter; p. 64: blank; p. 65: 'VIII | EMERSON TO GRIMM'; p. 66: blank; pp. 67–68: text of letter; p. 69: 'IX | GRIMM TO EMERSON'; pp. 70–77: text of letter; p. 78: blank; p. 79: 'X | EMERSON TO GRIMM'; p. 80: blank; p. 81: text of letter; p. 82: blank; p. 83: 'XI | EMERSON TO GRIMM'; p. 84: blank; pp. 85–86: text of letter; p. 87: 'XII | EMERSON TO GRIMM'; p. 88: blank; pp. 89–90: text of letter; p. 91: blank; p. 92: printer's imprint.

Typography and paper: 4³/₁₆″ (4″) × 2³/₁₆″; wove paper; 25 lines per page. Running heads: rectos: pp. 3–13, 17–19, 23, 27, 31–35, 39–43, 47–53, 57–63, 67, 71–77, 81, 85, 89: 'EMERSON-GRIMM'; versos: pp. 4–14, 16–18, 24, 28, 32–34, 40–44, 46–52, 58–62, 68, 70–76, 86, 90: 'EMERSON-GRIMM'.

Binding: Cream stiff wrappers folded over unprinted off-white wrapper. Front cover: same as the title page within double-rule red frame, with publisher's logo in red; back cover and spine: blank. Front flyleaf. White laid endpapers. All edges trimmed. Top edges gilded.

Dust jacket: White stiff paper. Front cover: same as the title page, except publisher's logo is not present and '[gothic] The Riverside Press, Cambridge | 1903' is replaced with '$1.00, NET'; back cover, spine, and front and back flaps: blank.

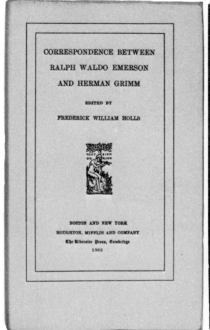

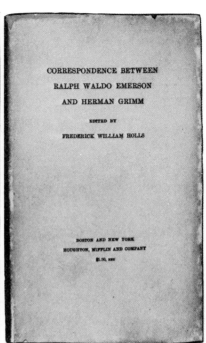

Wrapper for A 49.1.a   Dust jacket for A 49.1.a

Publication: 500 copies printed 30 April 1903. Listed in *Publishers' Weekly*, 63 (16 May 1903), 1158. According to the publisher's records, published 13 May 1903. Copyright, 30 April 1903. Deposit copy: DLC (6 May 1903). MBAt copy (bound) received 19 May 1903. Inscribed copy: ViU (from Holls, 18 May 1903). Copyright page states '*Published May, 1903*'. Published on a commission basis. Price, $1.00.

Printing: "[gothic] The Riverside Press | *Electrotyped and printed by H. O. Houghton & Co.* | *Cambridge, Mass., U.S.A.*" (p. [92]).

Locations: CtY (dust jacket), DLC, InU, JM (dust jacket), MCo, MH, NN, NNC, NjP (dust jacket), ViU (dust jacket), VtMiM.

Note one: 45 copies of a descriptive brochure printed on Old Berkshire laid paper were done 17 March 1903. *Not seen.*

Note two: 265 postal cards for advertising and ordering were printed 25 April 1903. *Not seen.*

Note three: Grimm's letters are printed in German and English on facing pages.

Note four: Reprinted from the April 1903 *Atlantic* (see E 238).

Note five: 498 copies were sold by 1907.

LATER PRINTING WITHIN THE FIRST EDITION

A 49.1.b
Port Washington, N.Y., and London: Kennikat, 1971.

Facsimile reprinting. Price, $6.00. *Locations:* DLC (4 September 1970), JM.

A 50 TANTALUS

A 50
First edition, only printing (1903)

T A N T A L U S

BY
RALPH WALDO
EMERSON

WITH A
MEMORIAL NOTE
BY
F. B. SANBORN

CANTON PENNSYLVANIA
THE KIRGATE PRESS

MCMIII

A 50: 6½″ × 3⅝″; 'TANTALUS', the strawberry, and 'THE KIRGATE PRESS' are in orange

> # NOTE copyrighted, 1903,
> ## By LEWIS BUDDY III

[i–ii] [1–9] 10–12 [13–15] 16–41 [42–46]

[1–6⁴]

Contents: pp. i–ii: blank; p. 1: 'TANTALUS'; pp. 2–3: blank; p. 4: statement of limitation; pp. 5–6: blank; p. 7: title page; p. 8: copyright page; pp. 9–12: 'NOTE', signed 'F. B. S[anborn].'; p. 13: 'TANTALUS'; p. 14: blank; pp. 15–41: text; pp. 42–46: blank.

Typography and paper: 4¹/₁₆″ (3⁷/₈″) × 2″; handmade wove paper watermarked 'KIRGATE | [strawberry] | L·B·3ʳᵈ' or Imperial Japan paper; 19 lines per page. Running heads: rectos: p. 11: 'NOTE'; pp. 17–41: 'TANTALUS'; versos: pp. 10–12: 'NOTE'; pp. 16–40: 'TANTALUS'.

Binding: Mottled light brown paper covered boards with white vellum shelfback. Front cover: goldstamped 'TANTALUS | EMERSON'; back cover: blank; spine: gold-stamped from bottom to top 'TANTALUS'. White endpapers of heavy stock. Top edges uncut and side and bottom edges trimmed; or top and bottom edges trimmed and side edges untrimmed. See *Note one* below.

Publication: Statement of limitation (p. 4): "Of this edition, one hundred copies have been printed from type,—90 copies on hand-made paper and 10 copies on Imperial Japan paper,—in commemoration of the one hundredth anniversary of the birth of RALPH WALDO EMERSON May 25th, 1903". Deposit copy: BL (22 January 1904).

Locations: BL, CtY, JM, MB, MH, NNC, PSt, ViU, VtMiM.

Note one: The only located copy on Imperial Japan paper is bound in red leather: NjP.

Note two: "Tantalus" was first published in the January 1844 *Dial* (see E 105).

A 51 HENRY D. THOREAU

A 51.1
First edition, only printing (1904)

Collectanea

HENRY D. THOREAU

EMERSON'S OBITUARY

NUMBER ONE

LAKELAND, MICHIGAN
EDWIN B. HILL.
1904

A 51.1: 6⁵/₁₆″ × 4¹³/₁₆″

[i–ii] [1–3] 4–5 [6–7] 8–10 [11–14]

[a]^8

Contents: pp. i–ii: blank; p. 1: title page; p. 2: blank; pp. 3–5: text; p. 6: blank; pp. 7–10: 'NOTE'; pp. 11–14: blank.

Typography and paper: 4$^7/_{16}$″ (4$^1/_8$″) × 3″; wove paper; 26 lines per page. Running heads: rectos: pp. 5, 9: 'HENRY D. THOREAU.'; versos: pp. 4, 8, 10: 'HENRY D. THOREAU.'.

Binding: Mottled gray blue laid paper wrapper with 1$^3/_{16}$″ vertical chain marks. Front recto: 'HENRY D. THOREAU | EMERSON'S OBITUARY'; front verso and back recto and verso: blank. Sheets are unstitched and loosely laid into wrapper. Top edges uncut and side and bottom edges trimmed; or all edges trimmed.

HENRY D. THOREAU

EMERSON'S OBITUARY

Wrapper for A 51.1

Locations: CtY, DLC, MH, NN, NcD, ViU.

Note one: The "Note" is by Samuel Arthur Jones.

Note two: "Henry D. Thoreau" was first published in the 8 May 1862 *Boston Daily Advertiser* (see E 158). This is not to be confused with "Thoreau" in the August 1862 *Atlantic* (see E 160).

A 51.2
Second edition, only printing (1942)

HENRY D. THOREAU | EMERSON'S OBITUARY | [hat] | YSLETA [Texas] | EDWIN B. HILL | 1942

3 leaves, folded once to make six pages. Unstitched, laid into paper wrapper. *Locations:* DLC (28 January 1944), JM, MH, TxU.

A52 JOURNALS OF RALPH WALDO EMERSON

VOLUME I

A52.I.1.a
First edition, first printing (1909)

JOURNALS

OF

RALPH WALDO EMERSON

WITH ANNOTATIONS

EDITED BY

EDWARD WALDO EMERSON

AND

WALDO EMERSON FORBES

1820–1824

BOSTON AND NEW YORK
HOUGHTON MIFFLIN COMPANY
The Riverside Press Cambridge
1909

A52.I.1.a: 7³/4″ × 5″

[a–d] [i–v] vi–xix [xx–xxi] xxii–xxv [xxvi–xxviii] [1–3] 4–9 [10] 11–51 [52] 53–62 [63] 64–91 [92–95] 96–110 [111] 112–131 [132] 133–159 [160] 161–175 [176] 177–204 [205] 206–231 [232] 233–266 [267] 268–298 [299] 300–337 [338] 339–394 [395–396]

[1⁴ 2–27⁸ 28²] Inserted leaves of coated paper, with photographs of manuscript pages, printed on the rectos, are positioned after pp. 4, 70, 138, 264

Contents: pp. a–c: blank; p. d: Houghton Mifflin advertisement for Emerson's writings; p. i: 'JOURNALS | OF | RALPH WALDO EMERSON | 1820–1872 | [rule] | VOL. I'; p. ii: blank; inserted leaf with portrait of Emerson and facsimile signature printed on recto, followed by protective tissue; p. iii: title page; p. iv: copyright page; pp. v–xix: 'INTRODUCTION'; p. xx: blank; pp. xxi–xxv: contents; p. xxvi: blank; p. xxvii: 'ILLUS-TRATIONS'; p. xxviii: blank; p. 1: 'JOURNAL | COLLEGE | [five lines of prose] | *Emerson's Journal, 1859.*'; p. 2: '[eight lines of prose] | *From a letter about Emerson by his earliest friend,* | *Dr. William H. Furness.*'; pp. 3–9: "Journal I. No. XVII"; pp. 10–51: "Journal II. The Wide World, No. 1"; pp. 52–62: "Journal III. No. XVIII"; pp. 63–91: "Journal IV. The Wide World, No. 2"; p. 92: blank; p. 93: 'JOURNAL | TEACHER'; p. 94: blank; pp. 95–110: "Journal V. The Wide World, No. 3"; pp. 111–131: "Journal VI. The Wide World, No. 4"; pp. 132–159: "Journal VII. The Wide World, No. 6"; pp. 160–175: "Journal VIII. The Wide World, No. 7"; pp. 176–204: "Journal IX. The Wide World, No. 8"; pp. 205–231: "Journal X. The Wide World, No. 9"; pp. 232–266: "Journal XI. The Wide World, No. 10"; pp. 267–298: "Journal XII. The Wide World, No. 11"; pp. 299–337: "Journal XIII. The Wide World, No. 12"; pp. 338–394: "Journal XIV. The Wide World, No. 13"; p. 395: blank; p. 396: printer's imprint.

Typography and paper: 5¹/₂" (5¹/₈") × 3¹/₈"; laid paper with vertical chain marks 1¹/₄" apart; 27 lines per page. Running heads: rectos: pp. vii–xix: 'INTRODUCTION'; pp. xxiii–xxv: 'CONTENTS'; pp. 5–61, 65–91, 97–109, 113–203, 207–265, 269–297, 301–393: years of entries and topical headings; versos: pp. vi–xviii: 'INTRODUCTION'; pp. xxii–xxiv: 'CONTENTS'; pp. 4–8, 12–50, 54–90, 96–130, 134–158, 162–174, 178–230, 234–336, 340–394: 'JOURNAL' and Emerson's age at the time of the entry.

Binding: Dark green T cloth (rib). Front cover: blindstamped double-ruled frame with goldstamped 'R. Waldo Emerson' facsimile signature in center; back cover: blind-stamped double-rule frame; spine: goldstamped '[rule] | [rule] | EMERSON'S | JOUR-NALS | 1820–1824 | I | HOUGHTON | MIFFLIN CO. | [rule] | [rule]'. White laid endpapers. All edges trimmed. Top edges gilded. See *Note one* below.

Dust jacket: See *Note two* below.

Publication: On the copyright page is '*Published November 1909*'. 1,000 copies and dust jackets printed 17 November 1909. Noted for 27 November 1909 in *Publishers' Weekly,* 76 (20 November 1909), 1399. Listed in *Publishers' Weekly,* 76 (4 December 1909), 1732. According to the publisher's records, published 27 November 1909. Copyright, 27 November 1909; renewed, 7 July 1937. Deposit copy: DLC (2 December 1909). Prices: cloth, $1.75; half calf, $3.00; half polished morocco, $3.50.

Bindings for A 52: Trade printing, green T cloth; trade printing, red T cloth; Constable; untrimmed trade printing; *Large Paper Edition*, first issue; *Large Paper Edition*, second issue

Printing: "[gothic] The Riverside Press | CAMBRIDGE·MASSACHUSETTS | U·S·A" (p. [396]).

Locations: DLC, MBAt, MH, MWA, RPB, ViU, VtU.

Note one: Subsequent volumes have the new volume number in roman numerals and the dates of the journals included in the volume (the same dates as appear on the title page) goldstamped on the spine. Bindings on later printings often lack the gold-stamped volume number in roman numerals on the spine. Flyleaves of laid paper may or may not be present: vol. I: no flyleaves; vol. II: front flyleaf; vol. III: flyleaves; vol. IV: no flyleaves; vol. V: back flyleaf; vol. VI: flyleaves; vol. VII: front flyleaf; vol. VIII: front flyleaf; vol. IX: no flyleaves; vol. X: no flyleaves. Some bindings lack the goldstamped volume number on the spine.

Note two: Dust jackets for the *Journals* have been noted as follows:
Vol. I: very light blue hair-vein (described in the *Costbooks* as "blue granite") paper; front cover: all within a single-rule frame 'The Journals | OF | Ralph Waldo Emerson | NOW PUBLISHED FOR THE | FIRST TIME AND EDITED BY | EDWARD W. EMERSON and | WALDO EMERSON FORBES | [notices from periodicals within a single-rule frame]'; back cover: advertisement for 13 Houghton Mifflin books, beginning with *The Problem of Freedom*; spine: '[rule] | [rule] | EMERSON'S | JOURNALS | 1820–1824 | $1.75 net | HOUGHTON | MIFFLIN CO. | [rule] | [rule]'; front and back flaps: blank;
Vol. II: the same as for vol. I, except: front cover has a blurb for vols. I and II in the box; back cover has advertisement for 10 Houghton Mifflin books;

Vol. III: the same as for vol. I, except: back cover has advertisement for nine Houghton Mifflin books;

Vol. IV: the same as for vol. III;

Vol. V: two styles noted: Jacket A: the same as for vol. IV, except: back cover has advertisement for 12 Houghton Mifflin books, beginning with *The Diary of Gideon Welles;* Jacket B: the same as for vol. I, except: the notices from periodicals are not on the front cover; the back cover is blank; the price is not on the spine (this may be a later style);

Vol. VI: the same as for vol. V, Jacket A;

Vol. VII: the same as for vol. VI, except: back cover has advertisement for 12 Houghton Mifflin books, beginning with *The Three Brontes;*

Vol. VIII: no jackets have been located;

Vol. IX: the same as for vol. VII, except: the notices from periodicals are not on the front cover; back cover has advertisement for 13 Houghton Mifflin books, beginning with *The Letters of Charles Eliot Norton;*

Vol. X: the same as for vol. IX, except: the front cover has blurbs for vols. IX and X within a single-rule frame.

Each dust jacket has the dates of the journals included in the volume (the same dates as appear on the title page) printed on the spine.

Note three: 1,500 copies of a circular, in red and black, were printed 5 November 1909. *Not seen.*

Note four: A set of the *Journals* has been noted bound in dark red T cloth (rib); stamping is the same as on copies bound in green cloth, except the facsimile signature on the front cover is not present. Possibly a later binding; the only located set is composed of later, undated printings for all volumes except vols. III and IV. *Location:* JM.

Note five: 2,589 copies of all printings in this format were sold by 1923.

A 52.I.1.b
First edition, second printing (1909)

The same as A 52.I.1.a, except: p. d is blank (Houghton Mifflin advertisements are omitted); page size is $7^{15}/_{16}$″ × 5″.

Binding: Gray olive green fine B cloth (linen). Front and back covers: blank; spine: white paper label with '[rule] | JOURNALS | OF | RALPH | WALDO | EMERSON | [leaf design] | WITH | *ANNOTATIONS* | [rule] | 1820–1824'.

Publication: 250 copies printed 19 November 1909, but only 200 copies advertised for sale. Price, $2.00.

Printing: The same printer's imprint as in A 52.I.1.a.

Locations: CtY, NNC, RPB, VtMiM.

Note one: Subsequent volumes have the dates of the journals included in the volume printed on the paper label on the spine; these are the same dates as appear on the title page.

Note two: According to the *Costbooks,* dust jackets of "Scotia laid" paper were printed for this particular set of the *Journals;* no copies have been located. Presumably, these jackets were unprinted with an aperture cut in the spine to allow the label to show.

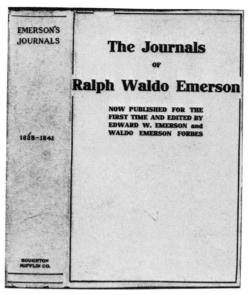

Dust jacket for A 52.V

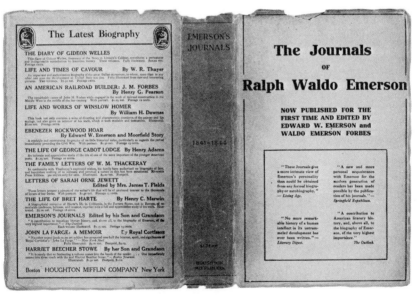

Dust jacket for A 52.VI

A 52.I.1.c
First edition, third printing (1909)

Boston and New York: Houghton Mifflin Company, The Riverside Press, 1909. The same as A 52.I.1.a, except:

[a–b] [i–v] . . . 339–394 [395–398]

[1–26⁸ 27⁶]

Contents: p. a: blank; p. b: Houghton Mifflin advertisements for Emerson's writings; pp. 1–396 the same as A 52.I.1.a; pp. 397–398: blank.

Publication: MB copy received 18 December 1909.

Locations: CtY, MB, MH-AH, ViU.

A 52.I.1.d
First edition, fourth (large paper) printing (1909)

RALPH WALDO EMERSON

Journals

1820-1824

CAMBRIDGE
𝔓𝔯𝔦𝔫𝔱𝔢𝔡 𝔞𝔱 𝔗𝔥𝔢 ℜ𝔦𝔳𝔢𝔯𝔰𝔦𝔡𝔢 𝔓𝔯𝔢𝔰𝔰
1909

A 52.I.1.d₁: 8¹⁵/₁₆″ × 6″; 'Journals' and '[gothic] Printed at the Riverside Press' are in red

Two issues have been noted:

A 52.I.1.d₁
First issue

Contents: pp. a–b: blank; p. c: statement of limitation; p. d: blank; p. i: '[two lines in red] JOURNALS OF | RALPH WALDO EMERSON | 1820–1872 | EDITED BY | EDWARD WALDO EMERSON AND | WALDO EMERSON FORBES | VOLUME | I'; p. ii: '[red gothic] Large Paper Edition | ILLUSTRATED WITH | PHOTOGRAVURES | [ornament]'; inserted leaf, the same as in A 52.I.1.a; p. iii: title page; p. iv: copyright page; pp. v–394: the same as A 52.I.1.a; pp. 395–396: blank.

Typography and paper: The same as A 52.I.1.a, except: laid paper with facsimile 'Emerson' signature watermark and with vertical chain marks ⅞" apart.

Binding: Light brown or grayish yellow green YR cloth (coarse linen). Front and back covers: blank; spine: cream paper label with double-rule frame around 'EMERSON | [rule] | The | Journals | [red] I | [rule] | 1909'. White laid endpapers. Untrimmed.

Publication: 630 copies printed 16 December 1909.

Printing: The Riverside Press, Cambridge.

Locations: JM, MB, TxU, VtMiM.

Note one: Subsequent volumes have the volume number in roman numerals and the dates of the journals included in the volume (the same dates as appear on the title page) printed on the paper label on the spine.

THIS

LARGE PAPER EDITION

OF THE JOURNALS OF

RALPH WALDO EMERSON

IS LIMITED

TO SIX HUNDRED

SIGNED AND NUMBERED

COPIES

OF WHICH THIS IS

NO. *475*

Statement of limitation for A 52.I.1.d₁

Note two: According to the *Costbooks,* dust jackets of "Kenesaw linen" paper were printed for the *Large Paper Edition* of the *Journals;* no copies have been located. Presumably, these jackets were unprinted with an aperture cut in the spine to allow the label to show.

A 52.I.1.d₂
Second issue

The same as the first issue, except: the leaves containing pp. c–d and i–ii (statement of limitation and *Large Paper Edition* half title) have been cancelled; the sheets have been trimmed to $8^3/8''$ × $5^5/16''$.

Binding: Medium red B cloth (linen). Front and back covers: blank; spine: gold-stamped '[band] | [rule] | [rule] | [band] | EMERSON'S | *Journals* | [leaf design] | 1820–1824 | I | HOUGHTON | MIFFLIN CO. | [band] | [rule] | [rule] | [band]'. Laid endpapers. All edges trimmed. Probably a remainder binding.

Publication: Placed on sale ca. 1930.

Location: JM.

Note: Subsequent volumes have the volume number in roman numerals and the dates of the journals included in the volume (the same dates as appear on the title page) goldstamped on the spine.

A 52.I.1.e
First edition, fifth printing (1909)

Two issues have been noted:

A 52.I.1.e₁
First issue

Boston and New York: Houghton Mifflin Company, The Riverside Press, 1909.

The same as A 52.I.1.a, except:

[a–b] [i–v] . . . 339–394

[1–26⁸ 27⁴]

Contents: p. a: blank; p. b: Houghton Mifflin advertisement for Emerson's writings; pp. i–394: the same as in A 52.I.1.a.

Locations: InU, JM, NN.

Note one: Copies of all volumes of the *Journals* printed after the initial year of publication have undated title pages.

Note two: Copies of the first and early printings of all volumes of the *Journals* have prices in the Houghton Mifflin advertisements; copies of the later printings of all volumes of the *Journals* do not have prices in the advertisements.

Note three: Copies of vol. I printed after 1937 have the following information on the copyright page: 'COPYRIGHT, 1937, BY RAYMOND EMERSON'.

A 52.I.1.e₂
Second (English) issue

JOURNALS

OF

RALPH WALDO EMERSON

WITH ANNOTATIONS

EDITED BY

EDWARD WALDO EMERSON

AND

WALDO EMERSON FORBES

1820–1824

London

CONSTABLE & CO. LIMITED

BOSTON AND NEW YORK

HOUGHTON MIFFLIN COMPANY

1909

A 52.I.1.e₂: 7¹¹/₁₆″ × 5″

The same as the first issue, except: the leaf containing pp. a–b (the Houghton Mifflin advertisements) has been cancelled; the title leaf is a cancel, with 'COPYRIGHT, 1909, BY EDWARD WALDO EMERSON | ALL RIGHTS RESERVED' on the verso; a leaf containing the printer's imprint (the same as p. 396 of the first printing) on the recto is inserted at the back.

Binding: Deep red T cloth (rib). Front and back covers: blank; spine: cream paper label with '[rule] | [rule] | [two lines in red] RALPH WALDO | EMERSON | [rule] | [rule] | JOURNALS | VOL. I | 1820–1824 | [rule] | [rule] | [two lines in red] CONSTABLE | LONDON | [rule] | [rule]'. Laid endpapers. All edges trimmed.

Publication: 100 sets of sheets sent to Constable before 2 April 1910. Listed in *Bookseller,* n.s. 55 (14 January 1910), 43. Deposit copies: BC (31 January 1910), BE (31 January 1910), BO (2 February 1910). Price, 6s.

Locations: BC, BE, BO, JM.

Note one: Subsequent volumes of the Constable *Journals* have the volume number in roman numerals and the dates of the journals included in the volume (the same dates as appear on the title page) printed on the paper label on the spine.

Note two: Partial dust jackets for the Constable *Journals* have been noted as follows:
Vol. I: no jackets have been located;
Vol. II: no jackets have been located;
Vol. III: very light blue hair-vein with medium blue printing; front: advertisement for *Centenary Edition* within a double-rule frame; spine: 'EMERSON'S | JOURNALS | III. | 1833–1835 | 6/- | NET | CONSTABLE | LONDON'; back and flaps: unknown;
Vol. IV: the same as for vol. III;
Vol. V: the same as for vol. IV, except: front cover has advertisement for *Centenary Edition* and vols. I–VI of *Journals,* all within a double-rule frame;
Vol. VI: the same as for vol. V;
Vol. VII: the same as for vol. VI, except: front cover has advertisement for *Centenary Edition* and vols. I–VIII of *Journals;*
Vol. VIII: the same as for vol. VII;
Vol. IX: the same as for vol. VIII, except: front cover has advertisement for *Centenary Edition* and vols. I–X of *Journals;*
Vol. X: the same as for vol. IX.

Each dust jacket has the volume number in roman numerals and the dates of the journals included in the volume (the same dates as appear on the title page) printed on the spine.

VOLUME II

A 52.II.1.a
First edition, first printing (1909)

The title page is the same as in A 52.I.1.a, except '1824–1832' is substituted for '1820–1824'.

[a–b] [i–v] vi–xvi [xvii–xviii] [1–3] 4–35 [36] 37–69 [70] 71–143 [144] 145–226 [227] 228–256 [256a–256b] [257] 258–280 [281] 282–352 [353] 354–443 [444] 445–542 [543–544]

[1^{10} 2–11^{12} 12^8 13^1 14–15^8 16–25^{12} 26^8]   Inserted leaves of coated paper, with portraits of Achille Murat and Ellen Tucker, and a drawing of the Second Church printed on the rectos, are positioned after pp. 188, 256, 424. The single-leaf gathering [13], here designated pp. 256a–256b, is not accounted for in the volume's pagination and is not present in all copies.

Contents: p. a: blank; p. b: Houghton Mifflin advertisements for Emerson's writings; p. i: half title, the same as in A 52.I.1.a, except 'II'; p. ii: blank; inserted leaf with portrait of Emerson's mother printed on verso, followed by protective tissue; p. iii: title page; p. iv: copyright page; pp. v–xvi: contents; p. xvii: 'ILLUSTRATIONS'; p. xviii: blank; p. 1: 'JOURNAL | TEACHER AND DIVINITY | STUDENT'; p. 2: blank; pp. 3–35: "Journal XV"; pp. 36–69: "Journal XVI. 1825"; pp. 70–143: "Journal XVII"; pp. 144–226: "Journal XVIII. 1827"; pp. 227–256: "Journal XIX"; p. 256a: 'JOURNAL | MINISTER OF THE SECOND | CHURCH OF BOSTON'; p. 256b: blank; pp. 257–280: "Journal XX. 1829"; pp. 281–352: "Journal XXI. 1830"; pp. 353–443: "Journal XXII from Ψ. 1831"; pp. 444–542: "Journal XXIII. 1832"; p. 543: blank; p. 544: printer's imprint, the same as in A 52.I.1.a.

Typography and paper: The same as in A 52.I.1.a. Running heads: rectos: pp. vii–xv: 'CONTENTS'; pp. 5–225, 229–255, 259–279, 283–351, 355–541: the same as in A 52.I.1.a; versos: pp. vi–xvi: 'CONTENTS'; pp. 4–34, 38–68, 72–142, 146–256, 258–442, 446–542: the same as in A 52.I.1.a.

Publication: On the copyright page is '*Published November 1909*'. 1,000 copies and dust jackets printed 17 November 1909. Noted for 27 November 1909 in *Publishers' Weekly,* 76 (20 November 1909), 1399. Listed in *Publishers' Weekly,* 76 (4 December 1909). According to the publisher's records, published 27 November 1909. Copyright, 27 November 1909; renewed, 7 July 1937. RPB copy received 30 November 1909. Inscribed copy: MH (30 November 1909). Deposit copy: DLC (2 December 1909). Same pricing schedule as for A 52.I.1.a.

Printing: The same printer's imprint as in A 52.I.1.a.

Locations: DLC, MB, MBAt, MH, MWA, NN (dust jacket), RPB, ViU, VtU.

Note one: 2,499 copies of all printings in this format sold by 1923.

Note two: Emerson's poem on St. Augustine (pp. 181–182) was reprinted by Max Cosman as "An Emerson Sonnet," *Saturday Review of Literature,* 21 (6 April 1940), 13.

A 52.II.1.b
First edition, second printing (1909)

The same as A 52.II.1.a, except: p. b is blank (Houghton Mifflin advertisements are omitted); page size is $7^{15}/_{16}'' \times 5''$; flyleaves.

Publication: 250 copies printed 19 November 1909, but only 200 copies advertised for sale. Price, $2.00.

Locations: CtY, NNC, RPB, VtMiM.

A 52.II.1.c
First edition, third printing for English sale (1909)

London: Constable & Co., Limited; Boston and New York: Houghton Mifflin Company, 1909.

The same as A 52.II.1.a, except: pp. a–b (the Houghton Mifflin advertisements) are blank; the title leaf verso has 'COPYRIGHT, 1909, BY EDWARD WALDO EMERSON | ALL RIGHTS RESERVED'.

Publication: 110 sets of sheets sent to Constable before 2 April 1910. Listed in *Bookseller,* n.s. 55 (14 January 1910), 43. Deposit copies: BC (31 January 1910), BE (31 January 1910), BO (2 February 1910). Price, 6s.

Locations: BC, BE, BO.

A 52.II.1.d
First edition, fourth printing (1909)

Boston and New York: Houghton Mifflin Company, The Riverside Press, 1909.

The same as A 52.II.1.a, except:

[a–b] [i–v] . . . [543–546]

$[1–23^{12}\,24^8]$

Contents: pp. a–544: the same as in A 52.II.1.a; pp. 545–546: blank.

Publication: MB copy received 18 December 1909.

Locations: CtY, JM, MB, MH-AH, ViU.

A 52.II.1.e
First edition, fifth printing (1909)

Boston and New York: Houghton Mifflin Company, The Riverside Press, 1909.

The same as A 52.II.1.a, except:

[a–b] [i–v] . . . 445–542

$[1–23^{12}\,24^6]$

Contents: pp. a–542: the same as in A 52.II.1.a.

Locations: JM, MB.

Note: Copies of later printings of this volume have 'ALL RIGHTS RESERVED IN-CLUDING THE RIGHT TO REPRODUCE | THIS BOOK OR PARTS THEREOF IN ANY FORM' on the copyright page.

A 52.II.1.f
First edition, sixth (large paper) printing (1909)

Two issues have been noted:

A 52.II.1.f₁
First issue

The title page is the same as in A 52.I.1.d₁, except '1824–1832' is substituted for '1820–1824'.

Contents: pp. a–d: the same as in A 52.I.1.d₁; pp. i–ii: the same as in A 52.I.1.d₁, except p. i has 'II'; inserted leaf, the same as in A 52.II.1.a; p. iii: title page; p. iv: copyright page, the same as in A 52.I.1.d₁; pp. v–542: the same as A 52.II.1.a.

Publication: 630 copies printed 17 December 1909.

Printing: The Riverside Press, Cambridge.

Locations: JM, MB, TxU, VtMiM.

A 52.II.1.f₂
Second issue

The same as vol. I (*Large Paper Edition*, A 52.I.1.d₂).

Location: JM.

VOLUME III

A 52.III.1.a
First edition, first printing (1910)

The title page is the same as in A 52.I.1.a, except '1833–1835' is substituted for '1820–1824' and '1910' for '1909'.

[a–b] [i–v] vi–xvi [xvii–xviii] [1–3] 4–241 [242–245] 246–428 [429–430] 431–575 [576]

[1¹⁴ 2–24¹² 25⁸] Inserted leaves of coated paper, with a silhouette of Edward Bliss Emerson, a photograph of the Old Manse, and drawings of the Concord Battleground in 1837 and the Emerson house, printed on the rectos, are positioned after pp. 346, 360, 508, 540.

Contents: p. a: blank; p. b: Houghton Mifflin advertisements for Emerson's writings; p. i: half title, the same as in A 52.I.1.a, except 'III'; p. ii: blank; inserted leaf with silhouette of Ezra Ripley printed on verso, followed by protective tissue; p. iii: title page; p. iv: copyright page, the same as in A 52.I.1.a, except '1910'; pp. v–xvi: 'CONTENTS'; p. xvii: 'ILLUSTRATIONS'; p. xviii: blank; p. 1: 'JOURNAL | VOYAGE TO EUROPE. | CITIES AND MEN. RETURN'; p. 2: blank; pp. 3–241: "Journal XXIV. 1833"; p. 242: blank; p. 243: 'JOURNAL | NEWTON | LECTURES IN BOSTON | PREACHING AT NEW BEDFORD | AND PLYMOUTH | THE OLD MANSE, CONCORD'; p. 244: blank; pp. 245–428: "Journal XXV. 1834"; p. 429: 'JOURNAL | THE NEW HOME IN CONCORD | MARRIAGE TO LIDIAN JACKSON | CHARLES EMERSON | COURSE OF LECTURES IN BOSTON | ALCOTT | PREACHING IN EAST LEXINGTON'; pp. 430–575: "Journal XXVI. 1835"; p. 576: printer's imprint, the same as in A 52.I.1.a.

Typography and paper: The same as in A 52.I.1.a. Running heads: rectos: pp. vii–xv: 'CONTENTS'; pp. 5–241, 247–427, 431–575: the same as in A 52.I.1.a; versos: pp. vi–xvi: 'CONTENTS'; pp. 4–240, 246–428, 432–574: the same as in A 52.I.1.a.

Publication: 1,500 copies printed 1 November 1910. On the copyright page is '*Published November 1910*'. According to the publisher's records, published 12 November 1910. Listed in *Publishers' Weekly*, 78 (3 December 1910), 2212. Copyright, 9 December 1910; renewed, 7 November 1938. MBAt copy received 21 November 1910. Deposit copy: DLC (19 December 1910). Same pricing schedule as for A 52.I.1.a.

Printing: The same printer's imprint as in A 52.I.1.a.

Locations: DLC, JM, MBAt, MH-AH, MWA, NN (dust jacket), RPB, ViU.

Note: 1,720 copies of all printings in this format sold by 1923.

A 52.III.1.b
First edition, second printing (1910)

The same as A 52.III.1.a, except page size is 7¹⁵/₁₆″ × 5″; flyleaves.

Publication: 200 copies advertised for sale. Price, $2.00.

Locations: CtY, NNC, RPB, TxU, VtMiM.

Note: Beginning with vol. III of this binding, it is unclear from publisher's records whether the sheets used in this binding were of a separate printing or merely sheets of a regular printing (the first?) that were not trimmed.

A 52.III.1.c
First edition, third printing for English sale (1910)

London: Constable & Co., Limited; Boston and New York: Houghton Mifflin Company, 1910.

The same as A 52.III.1.a, except: pp. a–b (the Houghton Mifflin advertisements) are blank; the title leaf verso has 'COPYRIGHT, 1910, BY EDWARD WALDO EMERSON | ALL RIGHTS RESERVED'.

Publication: 100 sets of sheets sent to Constable before 2 January 1911. Listed in *Athenæum*, no. 4346 (11 February 1911), 161. Advertised as though published, in *Athenæum*, no. 4388 (25 February 1911), 211. According to the publisher's records, published 12 November 1910. Copyright registered, 28 November 1910. Deposit copies: BL (31 January 1911), BC (9 February 1911), BE (9 February 1911), BO (14 September 1911). Price, 6s.

Locations: BC, BE, BL, BO (partial dust jacket).

A 52.III.1.d
First edition, fourth (large paper) printing (1910)

Two issues have been noted:

A 52.III.1.d₁
First issue

The title page is the same as in A 52.I.1.d₁, except '1833–1835' is substituted for '1820–1824' and '1910' for '1909'.

Contents: pp. a–d: the same as in A 52.I.1.d₁; pp. i–ii: the same as in A 52.I.1.d₁, except p. i has 'III'; inserted leaf, the same as in A 52.III.1.a; p. iii: title page; p. iv: copyright page, the same as in A 52.I.1.d₁, except '1910'; pp. v–575: the same as in A 52.III.1.a; pp. 576–578: blank.

Publication: 630 copies printed 1 November 1910.

Printing: The Riverside Press, Cambridge.

Locations: JM, MB, TxU, VtMiM.

A 52.III.1.d₂
Second issue

The same as vol. I (*Large Paper Edition*, A 52.I.1.d₂).

Location: JM.

A 52.III.1.e
First edition, fifth printing (1910)

Boston and New York: Houghton Mifflin Company, The Riverside Press, 1910.

The same as A 52.III.1.a, except:

$[1-24^{12}\ 25^{10}]$

Locations: CtY, JM, MB, MH, MHi, TxU, ViU, VtMiM.

VOLUME IV

A 52.IV.1.a
First edition, first printing (1910)

The title page is the same as in A 52.I.1.a, except '1836–1838' is substituted for '1820–1824' and '1910' for '1909'.

[a–d] [i–v] vi–xvi [xvii–xviii] [1–3] 4–175 [176–179] 180–383 [384–387] 388–499 [500–502]

$[1-21^{12}\ 22^{10}]$ Inserted leaves of coated paper, with silhouettes of Charles Emerson and Mary Moody Emerson printed on the rectos, are positioned after pp. 40, 480; an inserted leaf with a portrait of William Emerson printed on the recto is positioned after p. 234.

Contents: pp. a–c: blank; p. d: Houghton Mifflin advertisements for Emerson's writings; p. i: half title, the same as in A 52.I.1.a, except 'IV'; p. ii: blank; inserted leaf with photograph of Lidian Emerson and child printed on verso, followed by protective tissue; p. iii: title page; p. iv: copyright page, the same as in A 52.I.1.a, except '1910'; pp. v–xvi: 'CONTENTS'; p. xvii: 'ILLUSTRATIONS'; p. xviii: blank; p. 1: 'JOURNAL | NATURE | CHARLES'S DEATH | NEW FRIENDS | BIRTH OF WALDO'; p. 2: blank; pp. 3–175: "Journal XXVII. 1836"; p. 176: blank; p. 177: 'JOURNAL | THE CONCORD HOME AND | WOODS | LECTURING AND PREACHING | DEFENCE OF ALCOTT | PHI BETA KAPPA ORATION'; p. 178: blank; pp. 179–383: "Journal XXVIII. 1837"; p. 384: blank; p. 385: 'JOURNAL | BOSTON LECTURES | THE PULPIT FROM THE PEW | ADDRESS TO THE SENIOR CLASS | IN THE DIVINITY COLLEGE | THE RESULTING STORM | ORATION AT DARTMOUTH | COLLEGE'; p. 386: blank; pp. 387–499: "Journal XXIX. 1838"; p. 500: printer's imprint, the same as in A 52.I.1.a; pp. 501–502: blank.

Typography and paper: The same as in A 52.I.1.a. Running heads: rectos: pp. vii–xv: 'CONTENTS'; pp. 5–175, 181–383, 389–499: the same as in A 52.I.1.a; versos: pp. vi–xvi: 'CONTENTS'; pp. 4–174, 180–382, 388–498: the same as in A 52.I.1.a.

Publication: 1,500 copies printed 4 November 1910. On the copyright page is '*Published November 1910*'. According to the publisher's records, published 12 November 1910. Listed in *Publishers' Weekly*, 78 (3 December 1910), 2212. Copyright, 9 December 1910; renewed, 7 November 1938. MBAt copy received 21 November 1910. Deposit copy: DLC (19 December 1910). Same pricing schedule as for A 52.I.1.a.

Printing: The same printer's imprint as for A 52.I.1.a.

Locations: DLC, InU, JM, MB, MBAt, MH-AH, NN (dust jacket), RPB, TxU, ViU, VtU.

Note: 1,709 copies of all printings in this format sold by 1923.

A 52.IV.1.b
First edition, second printing (1910)

The same as A 52.IV.1.a, except the page size is $7^{15}/_{16}" \times 5"$.

Publication: 200 copies advertised for sale. Price, $2.00.

Locations: CtY, JM, NNC, RPB, TxU, VtMiM.

A 52.IV.1.c
First edition, third printing for English sale (1910)

London: Constable & Co., Limited; Boston and New York: Houghton Mifflin Company, 1910.

The same as A 52.IV.1.a, except: pp. c–d (the Houghton Mifflin advertisements) are blank; the title leaf verso has 'COPYRIGHT, 1910, BY EDWARD WALDO EMERSON | ALL RIGHTS RESERVED'.

Publication: 100 sets of sheets sent to Constable before 2 January 1911. Listed in *Athenæum*, no. 4346 (11 February 1911), 161. Advertised as though published, in *Athenæum*, no. 4348 (25 February 1911), 211. According to the publisher's records, published 12 November 1910. Copyright registered, 28 November 1910. Deposit copies: BL (31 January 1911), BC (9 February 1911), BE (9 February 1911), BO (14 September 1911). Price 6s.

Locations: BC, BE, BL, BO (partial dust jacket).

A 52.IV.1.d
First edition, fourth (large paper) printing (1910)

Two issues have been noted:

A 52.IV.1.d₁
First issue

The title page is the same as in A 52.I.1.d₁, except '1836–1838' is substituted for '1820–1824' and '1910' for '1909'.

Contents: pp. a-d: the same as in A 52.I.1.d₁; pp. i–ii: the same as in A 52.I.1.d₁, except p. i has 'IV'; inserted leaf, the same as in A 52.IV.1.a; p. iii: title page: p. iv: copyright page, the same as in A 52.I.1.d₁, except '1910'; pp. v–499: the same as in A 52.IV.1.a; pp. 500–502: blank.

Publication: 630 copies printed 4 November 1910.

Printing: The Riverside Press, Cambridge.

Locations: JM, MB, TxU, VtMiM.

A 52.IV.1.d₂
Second issue

The same as vol. I (*Large Paper Edition*, A 52.I.1.d₂).

Location: JM.

A 52.IV.1.e
First edition, fifth printing (1910)

Boston and New York: Houghton Mifflin Company, The Riverside Press, 1910.

The same as A 52.IV.1.a, except:

[1–21¹² 22⁸]

Contents: p. a: blank; p. b: Houghton Mifflin advertisements for Emerson's writings; pp. i–500: the same as in A 52.IV.1.a.

Locations: CtY, JM, MH, MHi, ViU.

VOLUME V

A 52.V.1.a
First edition, first printing (1911)

The title page is the same as in A 52.I.1.a, except '1838–1841' is substituted for '1820–1824' and '1911' for '1909'.

[a–d] [i–v] vi–xviii [xix–xx] [1–3] 4–155 [156–159] 160–364 [365–367] 368–502 [503–505] 506–571 [572]

[1^{12} 2–36^8 37^6] Inserted leaves of coated paper, with portraits of John Sterling and Bronson Alcott, and a drawing of Coleridge, printed on the rectos, are positioned after pp. 352, 388, 528.

Contents: pp. a–c: blank; p. d: Houghton Mifflin advertisements for Emerson's writings; p. i: half title, the same as in A 52.I.1.a, except 'V'; p. ii: blank; inserted leaf with drawing of Emerson in 1846 printed on recto, followed by protective tissue; p. iii: title page; p. iv: copyright page, the same as in A 52.I.1.a, except '1911' and new publication date; pp. v–xviii: 'CONTENTS'; p. xix: 'ILLUSTRATIONS'; p. xx: blank; p. 1: 'JOURNAL | DIVINITY SCHOOL ADDRESS | ABIDING THE STORM | DARTMOUTH ADDRESS | COURSE ON HUMAN LIFE'; p. 2: blank; pp. 3–155: "Journal XXIX (Continued). 1838"; p. 156: blank; p. 157: 'JOURNAL | BOSTON LECTURES | SYMPOSIA | VISITORS | JONES VERY. EDWARD PALMER | THE WHITE MOUNTAINS'; p. 158: blank; pp. 159–364: "Journal XXX. 1839"; p. 365: 'JOURNAL | PREPARATION OF ESSAYS | SYMPOSIA | FRIENDS | THE DIAL APPEARS | BROOK FARM PROJECT'; p. 366: blank; pp. 367–502: "Journal XXXI. 1840"; p. 503: 'JOURNAL | FIRST ESSAYS PRINTED | REFORMS'; p. 504: blank; pp. 505–571: "Journal XXXII. 1841"; p. 572: printer's imprint, the same as in A 52.I.1.a.

Typography and paper: The same as in A 52.I.1.a. Running heads: rectos: pp. vii–xvii: 'CONTENTS'; pp. 5–155, 161–363, 369–501, 507–571: the same as in A 52.I.1.a; versos: pp. vi–xviii: 'CONTENTS'; pp. 4–154, 160–364, 369–502, 506–570: the same as in A 52.I.1.a.

Publication: 1,500 copies printed 6 November 1911. On the copyright page is '*Published November 1911*'. According to the publisher's records, published 11 November 1911. Advertised as "Now Ready," in *Publishers' Weekly*, 80 (11 November 1911), 1933, and noted for "this week," on p. 1941. Listed in *Publishers' Weekly*, 80 (2 December 1911), 2306. Copyright, 11 November 1911; renewed, 5 October 1939. MBAt copy received 14 November 1911. Deposit copy: DLC (27 November 1911). Same pricing schedule as for A 52.I.1.a.

Printing: The same printer's imprint as in A 52.I.1.a.

Locations: CU, CtY, DLC, InU, JM (dust jacket), MB, MBAt, MH, MH-AH, MHi, MWA, NN (dust jacket), RPB, TxU, ViU, VtU.

Note: 1,392 copies of all printings in this format sold by 1923.

A 52.V.1.b
First edition, second printing (1911)

The same as A 52.V.1.a, except the page size is $7^{15}/_{16}$" × 5".

Publication: 200 copies advertised for sale. Price, $2.00.

Locations: CtY, RPB, VtMiM.

A 52.V.1.c
First edition, third printing for English sale (1911)

London: Constable & Co., Limited; Boston and New York: Houghton Mifflin Company, 1911.

The same as A 52.V.1.a, except: pp. c–d (the Houghton Mifflin advertisements) are blank; the title leaf verso has 'COPYRIGHT, 1911, BY EDWARD WALDO EMERSON | ALL RIGHTS RESERVED'; bound with back fly leaf.

Publication: Listed in *Athenæum*, no. 4390 (16 December 1911), 772. Deposit copies: BL (7 December 1911), BC (4 January 1912), BE (4 January 1912), BO (8 January 1912). Price, 6s.

Locations: BC, BE, BL, BO (partial dust jacket), PSt.

A 52.V.1.d
First edition, fourth (large paper) printing (1911)

Two issues have been noted:

A 52.V.1.d₁
First issue

The title page is the same as in A 52.I.1.d₁, except '1838–1841' is substituted for '1820–1824' and '1911' for '1909'.

Contents: pp. a–b: the same as pp. c–d in A 52.I.1.d₁; pp. i–ii: the same as in A 52.I.1.d₁, except p. i has 'V'; inserted leaf, the same as in A 52.V.1.a; p. iii: title page; p. iv: copyright page, the same as in A 52.I.1.d₁, except '1911'; pp. v–571: the same as in A 52.V.1.a; p. 572: blank.

Publication: 630 copies printed 14 November 1911.

Printing: The Riverside Press, Cambridge.

Locations: JM, MB, TxU, VtMiM.

A 52.V.1.d₂
Second issue

The same as vol. I (*Large Paper Edition*, A 52.I.1.d₂).

Location: JM.

VOLUME VI

A 52.VI.1.a
First edition, first printing (1911)

The title page is the same as in A 52.I.1.a, except '1841–1844' is substituted for '1820–1824' and '1911' for '1909'.

[i–v] vi–xxi [xxii–xxiv] [1–3] 4–146 [147–149] 150–332 [333–335] 336–484 [485–487] 488–551 [552]

[1¹² 2–35⁸ 36⁴] Inserted leaves of coated paper, with a portrait of Elizabeth Hoar, a photograph of a bust of Thoreau, and a drawing of Carlyle printed on the rectos, are positioned after pp. 86, 298, 410.

Contents: p. i: half title, the same as A 52.I.1.a, except 'VI'; p. ii: blank; inserted leaf with portrait of Waldo Emerson printed on verso, followed by protective tissue; p. iii: title page; p. iv: copyright page, the same as in A 52.I.1.a, except '1911' and new publication date: pp. v–xxi: 'CONTENTS'; p. xxii: blank; p. xxiii: 'ILLUSTRATIONS'; p. xxiv: blank; p. 1: 'JOURNAL | NANTASKET | WATERVILLE ADDRESS | LECTURES ON THE TIMES'; p. 2: blank; pp. 3–146: "Journal XXXII (Continued). 1841"; p. 147: 'JOURNAL | WALDO'S DEATH | COURSES IN PROVIDENCE AND | NEW YORK | ALCOTT VISITS ENGLAND | HAWTHORNE COMES TO CON- | CORD | ALCOTT'S RETURN'; p. 148: blank; pp. 149–332: "Journal XXXIII. 1842"; p. 333: 'JOURNAL | LECTURES IN NEW YORK AND | BALTIMORE | VISIT TO WASHINGTON | EDITING DIAL | WEBSTER IN CONCORD | BROOK FARM'; p. 334: blank; pp. 335–484: "Journal XXXIV. 1843"; p. 485: 'JOURNAL | LYCEUM LECTURES | ADDRESSES | END OF THE DIAL | WEST INDIAN EMANCIPATION | THE SECOND ESSAYS'; p. 486: blank; pp. 487–551: "Journal XXXV. 1844"; p. 552: printer's imprint, the same as in A 52.I.1.a.

Typography and paper: The same as in A 52.I.1.a. Running heads: rectos: pp. vii–xxi: 'CONTENTS'; pp. 5–145, 151–331, 337–483, 489–551: the same as in A 52.I.1.a; versos: pp. vi–xx: 'CONTENTS'; pp. 4–146, 150–332, 336–484, 448–550: the same as in A 52.I.1.a.

Publication: 1,500 copies printed 6 November 1911. On the copyright page is '*Published November 1911*'. According to the publisher's records, published 11 November 1911. Advertised as "Now Ready," in *Publishers' Weekly,* 80 (11 November 1911), 1933, and noted for "this week," on p.1941. Listed in *Publishers' Weekly,* 80 (2 December 1911), 2306. Copyright, 11 November 1911; renewed, 5 October 1939. MBAt copy received 14 November 1911. Same pricing schedule as for A 52.I.1.a.

Printing: The same printer's imprint as in A 52.I.1.a.

Locations: CU, CtY, JM, MB, MBAt, MH, MH-AH, MHi, MWA, NN (dust jacket), RPB, ViU, VtU.

Note one: A leaf with Houghton Mifflin advertisements for Emerson's writings printed on the verso has been noted in some copies inserted before p. i: CU, CtY, JM, MWA, RPB, ViU.

Note two: 1,376 copies of all printings in this format sold by 1923.

A 52.VI.1.b
First edition, second printing (1911)

The same as A 52.VI.1.a, except the page size is 7¹⁵/₁₆″ × 5″; flyleaves.

Publication: 200 copies advertised for sale. Price, $2.00.

Locations: CtY, RPB, VtMiM.

Note: All copies examined have a single leaf, with Houghton Mifflin advertisements for Emerson's writings printed on the verso, inserted before p. i.

A 52.VI.1.c
First edition, third printing for English sale (1911)

London: Constable & Co., Limited; Boston and New York: Houghton Mifflin Company, 1911.

The same as A 52.VI.1.a, except: the title leaf verso has 'COPYRIGHT, 1911, BY EDWARD WALDO EMERSON | ALL RIGHTS RESERVED'; bound with flyleaves.

Publication: Deposit copies: BL (7 December 1911), BC (4 January 1912), BE (4 January 1912), BO (8 January 1912).

Locations: BC, BE, BL, BO (partial dust jacket).

A 52.VI.1.d
First edition, fourth (large paper) printing (1911)

Two issues have been noted:

A 52.VI.1.d₁
First issue

The title page is the same as in A 52.I.1.d₁, except '1841–1844' is substituted for '1820–1824' and '1911' for '1909'.

Contents: pp. a–b: the same as pp. c–d in A 52.I.1.d₁; pp. i–ii: the same as in A 52.I.1.d₁, except p. i has 'VI'; inserted leaf, the same as in A 52.VI.1.a; p. iii: title page; p. iv: copyright page, the same as in A 52.I.1.d₁, except '1911'; pp. v–551: the same as in A 52.VI.1.a; p. 552: blank.

Publication: 630 copies printed 14 November 1911.

Printing: The Riverside Press, Cambridge.

Locations: JM, MB, TxU, VtMiM.

A 52.VI.1.d₂
Second issue

The same as vol. I (*Large Paper Edition*, A 52.I.1.d₂).

Location: JM.

VOLUME VII

A 52.VII.1.a
First edition, first printing (1912)

The title page is the same as in A 52.I.1.a, except '1845–1848' is substituted for '1820–1824' and '1912' for '1909'.

[a–b] [i–v] vi–xix [xx–xxii] [1–3] 4–144 [145–147] 148–236 [237–239] 240–371 [372–375] 376–565 [566–568]

[1⁴ 2–37⁸ 38⁴] Inserted leaves of coated paper, with a photograph of Carlyle and a portrait of Samuel Gray Ward printed on the rectos, are positioned after pp. 196, 272.

Contents: p. a: blank; p. b: Houghton Mifflin advertisements for Emerson's writings; p. i: half title, the same as in A 52.I.1.a, except 'VII'; p. ii: blank; inserted leaf with portrait of Emerson in 1846 and facsimile signature printed on verso, followed by protective tissue; p. iii: title page; p. iv: copyright page, the same as in A 52.I.1.a, except '1912' and new publication date; pp. v–xix: 'CONTENTS'; p. xx: blank; p. xxi: 'ILLUSTRATIONS'; p. xxii: blank; p. 1: 'JOURNAL | SLAVERY | NAPOLEON | WEBSTER IN CONCORD | FATHER TAYLOR | ADDRESS AT MIDDLEBURY | COLLEGE | EAST INDIAN STUDIES | COURSE ON REPRESENTATIVE | MEN'; p. 2: blank; pp. 3–144: "Journal XXXVI. 1845"; p. 145: 'JOURNAL | PHILOSOPHY, ELOQUENCE | EVERETT'S INAUGURATION AT | HARVARD | POETRY HAFIZ | HUMILIATION OF THE NORTH | INTERCHANGE OF PORTRAITS | WITH CARLYLE | COLLEGE CLASS | POEMS PUBLISHED'; p. 146: blank; pp. 147–236: "Journal XXXVII. 1846"; p. 237: 'JOURNAL | STUDIES | A NEW QUARTERLY | NANTUCKET | PERSIAN AND NORSE READING | GARDEN AND ORCHARD | YANKEE FACULTY | CONCORD WALKS | ENGLAND | MEETING CARLYLE AGAIN | LECTURES TO WORKINGMEN | IN THE BLACK COUN-

TRY'; p. 238: blank; pp. 239–371: "Journal XXXVIII. 1847"; p. 372: blank; p. 373: 'JOURNAL | NORTHERN ENGLAND | SCOTLAND | EDINBORO' WITS | ENGLISHMEN | AUTHORS AND SAVANTS | CARLYLE, OWEN, TENNYSON | CLOUGH, PATMORE, MILNES | PARIS IN REVOLUTION | LONDON LECTURES AND SOCIETY | RETURN | CONCORD WALKS'; p. 374: blank; pp. 375–565: "Journal XXXIX. 1848"; p. 566: printer's imprint, the same as in A 52.I.1.a; pp. 567–568: blank.

Typography and paper: The same as in A 52.I.1.a. Running heads: rectos: pp. vii–xix: 'CONTENTS'; pp. 5–143, 149–235, 241–371, 377–565: the same as in A 52.I.1.a; versos: pp. vi–xviii: 'CONTENTS'; pp. 4–144, 148–236, 240–370, 376–564: the same as in A 52.I.1.a.

Publication: On the copyright page is '*Published November 1912*'. According to the publisher's records, published 29 November 1912. Listed in *Publishers' Weekly*, 82 (7 December 1912), 2015. Copyright, 29 November 1912; renewed, 26 June 1940. Deposit copy: DLC (2 December 1912). Same pricing schedule as for A 52.I.1.a.

Printing: The same printer's imprint as in A 52.I.1.a.

Locations: CtY, DLC, MB, MBAt, MH, MHi, NN (dust jacket), RPB, TxU, VtU.

Note: 1,215 copies of all printings in this format sold by 1923.

A 52.VII.1.b
First edition, second printing (1912)

The same as A 52.VII.1.a, except the page size is $7^{15}/_{16}''$ × 5″.

Publication: 200 copies advertised for sale. Price, $2.00.

Locations: CtY, RPB, VtMiM.

A 52.VII.1.c
First edition, third printing (1912)

Boston and New York: Houghton, Mifflin Company, The Riverside Press, 1912.

The same as A 52.VII.1.a, except: p. 566: '[gothic] The Riverside Press | PRINTED BY H. O. HOUGHTON & CO. | CAMBRIDGE, MASS. | U.S.A.'.

Locations: JM, ViU.

Note: Copies of later printings of this volume have 'ALL RIGHTS RESERVED IN-CLUDING THE RIGHT TO REPRODUCE | THIS BOOK OR PARTS THEREOF IN ANY FORM' on the copyright page.

A 52.VII.1.d
First edition, fourth printing for English sale (1912)

London: Constable & Co., Limited; Boston and New York: Houghton Mifflin Company, 1912.

The same as A 52.VII.1.a, except: pp. a–b (the Houghton Mifflin advertisements) are blank; the title leaf verso has 'COPYRIGHT, 1912, BY EDWARD WALDO EMERSON | ALL RIGHTS RESERVED'.

Publication: Reviewed in *Athenæum*, no. 4454 (8 March 1913), 276. Deposit copies: BL (26 February 1913), BC (21 July 1914), BE (21 July 1914), BO (24 July 1914). Price, 6s.

Locations: BC, BE, BL, BO (partial dust jacket).

A 52.VII.1.e
First edition, fifth (large paper) printing (1912)

Two issues have been noted:

A 52.VII.1.e₁
First issue

The title page is the same as in A 52.I.1.d₁, except '1845–1848' is substituted for '1820–1824' and '1912' for '1909'.

Contents: pp. a–d: the same as in A 52.I.1.d₁; pp. i–ii: the same as in A 52.I.1.d₁, except p. i has 'VII'; inserted leaf, the same as in A 52.VII.1.a; p. iii: title page; p. iv: copyright page, the same as in A 52.I.1.d₁, except '1912'; pp. v–565: the same as in A 52.VII.1.a; pp. 566–568: blank.

Printing: The Riverside Press, Cambridge.

Locations: JM, MB, TxU, VtMiM.

A 52.VII.1.e₂
Second issue

The same as vol. I (*Large Paper Edition*, A 52.I.1.d₂).

Location: JM.

VOLUME VIII

A 52.VIII.1.a
First edition, first printing (1912)

The title page is the same as in A 52.I.1.a, except '1849–1885' is substituted for '1820–1824' and '1912' for '1909'.

[a–b] [i–v] vi–xxiii [xxiv–xxvi] [1–3] 4–82 [83–85] 86–158 [159–161] 162–267 [268–271] 272–356 [357–359] 360–437 [438–441] 442–511 [512–515] 516–588 [589–592]

[1⁶ 2–39⁸]   Inserted leaves of coated paper, with a painting of Margaret Fuller Ossoli and a photograph of Charles King Newcomb printed on the rectos, are positioned after pp. 116, 396.

Contents: p. a: blank; p. b: Houghton Mifflin advertisements for Emerson's writings; p. i: half title, the same as in A 52.I.1.a, except 'VIII'; p. ii: blank; inserted leaf with portrait and facsimile signature of Ellery Channing printed on verso, followed by protective tissue; p. iii: title page; p. iv: copyright page, the same as in A 52.I.1.a, except '1912' and new publication date; pp. v–xxiii: 'CONTENTS'; p. xxiv: blank; p. xxv: 'ILLUSTRA-TIONS'; p. xxvi: blank; p. 1: 'JOURNAL | HOME | LECTURES | TOWN AND COUNTRY CLUB | READING | PERSIAN POETRY | PREPARING NEW BOOK | CONCORD WALKS'; p. 2: blank; pp. 3–82: "Journal XL. 1849"; p. 83: 'JOURNAL | LECTURES NEAR AND FAR | PARLIAMENT ON THE TIMES | TOWN AND COUNTRY CLUB | WEBSTER'S FALL | DEATH OF | MARGARET FULLER OSSOLI | HIGHER LAW'; p. 84: blank; pp. 85–158: "Journal XLI. 1850"; p. 159: 'JOURNAL | LECTURES ON FATE, | POWER, CULTURE, ILLUSIONS | THE SEVENTH OF MARCH | WEBSTER'S FALL | SLAVERY AT THE DOOR | HUMILIATION | THE WOMAN'S CONVENTION'; p. 160: blank; pp. 161–267: "Journal XLII. 1851"; p. 268: blank; p. 269: 'JOURNAL | CON-DUCT OF LIFE COURSE | SPEECH TO ST. GEORGE'S SOCIETY | MONTREAL | KOS-SUTH VISITS CONCORD | DELIA BACON | WALKS AND TALKS WITH CHAN- | NING |

GLIMPSES OF THOREAU | WASHINGTON'S PORTRAIT | WINTHROP AT COMMENCE-
MENT | WRITING ON ENGLAND | WEBSTER'S DISAPPOINTMENT AND | DEATH'; p.
270: blank; pp. 271–356: "Journal XLIII. 1852"; p. 357: 'JOURNAL | WESTERN LEC-
TURES | ARTHUR HUGH CLOUGH | NEW YORK | LENOX AND CAPE COD | HORATIO
GREENOUGH'S DEATH | NOTES ON ENGLISH | AND FRENCH | MADAM EMERSON'S
DEATH'; p. 358: blank; pp. 359–437: "Journal XLIV. 1853"; p. 438: blank; p. 439:
'JOURNAL | LECTURES FAR AND NEAR | SEVENTH OF MARCH | ADDRESS ON
FUGITIVE SLAVE LAW | NEOPLATONISTS | ENGLAND, HER WRITERS, JUDGES | AND
STATESMEN | WILLIAMSTOWN COLLEGE | ADDRESS | KANSAS-NEBRASKA BILL'; p.
440: blank; pp. 441–511: "Journal XLV. 1854"; p. 512: blank; p. 513: 'JOURNAL | A
LONG LECTURE SEASON | VERSES | THOUGHTS ON SCIENCE, NATURE | AND
POETRY | FINISHING ENGLISH TRAITS | LECTURE ON WOMAN | AMHERST AD-
DRESS | SLEEPY HOLLOW | THE FAR WEST AGAIN'; p. 514: blank; pp. 515–588:
"Journal XLVI. 1855"; p. 589: blank; p. 590: printer's imprint, the same as in A 52.I.1.a;
pp. 591–592: blank.

Typography and paper: The same as in A 52.I.1.a. Running heads: rectos: pp. vii–
xxiii: 'CONTENTS'; pp. 5–81, 87–157, 163–267, 273–355, 361–437, 443–511, 517–
587: the same as in A 52.I.1.a; versos: pp. vi–xxii: 'CONTENTS'; pp. 4–82, 86–158,
162–266, 272–356, 360–436, 442–510, 516–588: the same as in A 52.I.1.a.

Publication: On the copyright page is '*Published November 1912*'. According to the
publisher's records, published 29 November 1912. Listed in *Publishers' Weekly,* 82 (7
December 1912), 2015. Copyright, 29 November 1912; renewed, 26 June 1940. Deposit copy: DLC (2 December 1912). Same pricing schedule as for A 52.I.1.a.

Printing: The same printer's imprint as in A 52.I.1.a.

Locations: CU, CtY, DLC, InU, JM, MB, MBAt, MH, MHi, NN, RPB, TxU, ViU, VtU.

Note one: 1,212 copies of all printings in this format sold by 1923.

Note two: Copies of later printings of this volume have 'ALL RIGHTS RESERVED
INCLUDING THE RIGHT TO REPRODUCE | THIS BOOK OR PARTS THEREOF IN ANY
FORM' on the copyright page, and '*Published November 1912*' is not present on the
copyright page.

A 52.VIII.1.b
First edition, second printing (1912)

The same as A 52.VIII.1.a, except the page size is 7¹⁵/₁₆″ × 5″.

Publication: 200 copies advertised for sale. Price, $2.00.

Locations: CtY, RPB, TxU, VtMiM.

A 52.VIII.1.c
First edition, third printing for English sale (1912)

London: Constable & Co., Limited; Boston and New York: Houghton Mifflin Company,
1912.

The same as A 52.VIII.1.a, except: pp. a–b (the Houghton Mifflin advertisements) are
blank; the title leaf verso has 'COPYRIGHT, 1912, BY EDWARD WALDO EMERSON |
ALL RIGHTS RESERVED'.

Publication: Reviewed in *Athenæum,* no. 4454 (8 March 1913), 276. Deposit copies:
BL (26 February 1913), BC (21 July 1914), BE (21 July 1914), BO (24 July 1914).

Locations: BC, BE, BL, BO (partial dust jacket).

A 52.VIII.1.d
First edition, fourth (large paper) printing (1912)

Two issues have been noted:

A 52.VIII.1.d₁
First issue

The title page is the same as in A52.I.1.d₁, except '1849–1855' is substituted for '1820–1824' and '1912' for '1909'.

Contents: pp. a–d: the same as in A52.I.1.d₁; pp. i–ii: the same as in A52.I.1.d₁, except p. i has 'VIII'; inserted leaf, the same as in A52.VIII.1.a; p. iii: title page; p. iv: copyright page, the same as in A52.I.1.d₁, except '1912'; pp. v–588: the same as in A52.VIII.1.a; pp. 589–590: blank.

Printing: The Riverside Press, Cambridge.

Locations: JM, MB, TxU, VtMiM.

A 52.VIII.1.d₂
Second issue

The same as vol. I (*Large Paper Edition*, A52.I.1.d₂).

Location: JM.

VOLUME IX

A 52.IX.1.a
First edition, first printing (1913)

Two issues have been noted:

A 52. IX.1.a₁
First issue

The title page is the same as in A52.I.1.a, except '1856–1863' is substituted for '1820–1824' and '1913' for '1909'.

[i–v] vi–xxii [xxiii–xxiv] [1–3] 4–71 [72–75] 76–140 [141–143] 144–164 [165–167] 168–255 [256–259] 260–289 [290–293] 294–350 [351–353] 354–474 [475–477] 478–581 [582–584]

[1–38⁸] Inserted leaves of coated paper, with photographs of "A Virgil Lesson" with Emerson and his children and of Ellen Tucker Emerson printed on the rectos, are positioned after pp. 126, 426.

Contents: p. i: half title, the same as in A52.I.1.a, except '1820–1876' and 'IX'; p. ii: blank; inserted leaf with photograph of Lidian Emerson printed on verso, followed by protective tissue; p. iii: title page; p. iv: copyright page, the same as in A52.I.1.a, except '1913' and new publication date; pp. v–xxii: 'CONTENTS'; p. xxiii: 'ILLUSTRA-TIONS'; p. xxiv: blank; p. 1: 'JOURNAL | WESTERN EXPERIENCES AND | ACQUAIN-TANCE | CLASSIC AND ROMANTIC | CONSIDERATIONS BY THE WAY | WALKS WITH THOREAU | THE SUMNER OUTRAGE | KANSAS MEETINGS | VISIT TO CAPE ANN | BRAHMA | TALK WITH A MEMBER OF | CONGRESS'; p. 2: blank; pp. 3–71: "Journal XLVII. 1856"; p. 72: blank; p. 73: 'JOURNAL | THE WEST | AGASSIZ | JOHN BROWN

AND KANSAS | WALKS WITH THOREAU | SATURDAY CLUB | VERSIFYING | THE QUINCYS | FARADAY | THE ATLANTIC MONTHLY | HARD TIMES'; p. 74: blank; pp. 75–140: "Journal XLVIII. 1857"; p. 141: 'JOURNAL | THOREAU | HAFIZ | MASSACHU-SETTS POLITICS | FRENCH METAPHYSICIANS | RAREY | ROWSE | THE ADIRONDAC CAMP | STILLMAN AND LOWELL'; p. 142: blank; pp. 143–164: "Journal XLIX. 1858"; p. 165: 'JOURNAL | BOSTON | LECTURE COURSE | THE BURNS CENTENARY | THE SPRAIN AND ITS RESULTS | DR. HOLMES'S BIRTHDAY | CELEBRATION AT CHELMS-FORD | SUNDAY DISCOURSES TO | PARKER FRATERNITY | JOHN BROWN'S RAID AND | EXECUTION'; p. 166: blank; pp. 167–255: "Journal L. 1859"; p. 256: blank; p. 257: 'JOURNAL | WINTER LECTURING IN | CANADA AND THE WEST | CULTURE, POLITICS | PHILLIPS AND CASSIUS M. CLAY | THEODORE PARKER DIES | ESTA-BROOK FARM | THE DANGEROUS SPEAKER | HENRY JAMES | MEMORABILIA OF PHILOSPHY | THE ELECTION'; p. 258: blank; pp. 259–289: "Journal LI. 1860"; p. 290: blank; p. 291: 'JOURNAL | IN THEODORE PARKER'S PULPIT | RIOT AT THE ANTI-SLAVERY | MEETING | CONCORD SCHOOLS | THE WAR CLOUD | LIFE AND LITERA-TURE COURSE | IN BOSTON | ADDRESSES | AT TUFTS' COLLEGE AND | YAR-MOUTH'; p. 292: blank; pp. 293–350: "Journal LII. 1861"; p. 351: 'JOURNAL | WASH-INGTON VISIT | PLEA FOR EMANCIPATION | PRESIDENT LINCOLN | THE CABINET. SUMNER | SPRING WALKS. THE TITMOUSE | THOREAU'S LAST DAYS AND | DEATH | HIS JOURNALS | WARTIME HOPES AND FEARS | EMANCIPATION AGAIN | THE PROCLAMATION | AMERICAN NATIONALITY'; p. 352: blank; pp. 353–474: "Journal LIII. 1862"; p. 475: 'JOURNAL | THE WAR | NEGRO SOLDIERS | VISIT TO WEST POINT | DARTMOUTH AND WATERVILLE | ADDRESSES | CONFUCIUS | SAADI | PRESIDENT LINCOLN | CONCORD TOWN MEETING | JUDGE HOAR | BOSTON'; p. 476: blank; pp. 477–581: "Journal LIV. 1863"; p. 582: printer's imprint, the same as in A 52.I.1.a; pp. 583–584: blank.

Typography and paper: The same as in A 52.I.1.a. Running heads: rectos: pp. vii–xxi: 'CONTENTS'; pp. 5–71, 77–139, 145–163, 169–255, 261–289, 295–349, 355–473, 479–581: the same as in A 52.I.1.a; versos: pp. vi–xxii: 'CONTENTS'; pp. 4–70, 76–140, 144–164, 168–254, 260–288, 294–350, 354–474, 478–580: the same as in A 52.I.1.a.

Publication: On the copyright page is '*Published November 1913*'. According to the publisher's records, published 22 November 1913. Copyright, 22 November 1913; renewed, 17 September 1941. Deposit copy: DLC (24 November 1913). Same pricing schedule as for A 52.I.1.a.

Printing: The same printer's imprint as in A 52.I.1.a.

Locations: CtY, DLC, MB, MBAt, MH, MHi, NN (dust jacket), TxU, ViU, VtU.

Note: 1,171 copies of all printings in this format sold by 1923.

A 52.IX.1.a₂
Second (English) issue

London: Constable & Co., Limited; Boston and New York: Houghton Mifflin Company, 1913.

The same as A 52.IX.1.a₁, except the title leaf is a cancel, with 'COPYRIGHT, 1913, BY EDWARD WALDO EMERSON | ALL RIGHTS RESERVED' on the verso.

Publication: Deposit copies: BL (26 June 1914), BC (3 July 1914), BE (3 July 1914), BO (24 July 1914). Price, 6s.

Locations: BC, BE, BL, BO (partial dust jacket).

A 52.IX.1.b
First edition, second printing (1913)

The same as A 52.XI.1.a₁, except the page size is $7^{15}/_{16}'' \times 5''$; front flyleaf.

Publication: 200 copies advertised for sale. Price, $2.00.

Locations: CtY, RPB, VtMiM.

A 52.IX.1.c
First edition, third (large paper) printing (1913)

Two issues have been noted:

A 52.IX.1.c₁
First issue

The title page is the same as in A 52.I.1.d₁, except '1856–1863' is substituted for '1820–1824' and '1913' for '1909'.

Contents: pp. a–d: the same as in A 52.I.1.d₁; pp. i–ii: the same as in A 52.I.1.d₁, except p. i has '1820–1876' and 'IX'; inserted leaf, the same as in A 52.IX.1.a₁; p. iii: title page; p. iv: copyright page, the same as in A 52.I.1.d₁, except '1913'; pp. v–581: the same as in A 52.IX.1.a₁; pp. 582–584: blank.

Printing: The Riverside Press, Cambridge.

Locations: JM, MB, TxU, VtMiM.

A 52.IX.1.c₂
Second issue

The same as vol. I (*Large Paper Edition*, A 52.I.1.d₂).

Location: JM.

VOLUME X

A 52.X.1.a
First edition, first printing (1914)

Two issues have been noted:

A 52.X.1.a₁
First issue

The title page is the same as in A 52.I.1.a, except '1864–1876' is substituted for '1820–1824' and '1914' for '1909'.

[a–b] [i–v] vi–xxii [xxiii–xxiv] [1–3] 4–88 [89–91] 92–126 [127–129] 130–177 [178–181] 182–224 [225–227] 228–272 [273–275] 276–306 [307–309] 310–344 [345–347] 348–373 [374–377] 378–401 [402–405] 406–425 [426–429] 430–438 [439–441] 442–445 [446–449] 450–476 [477–479] 480–546 [547–550]

[1–36⁸] Inserted leaves of coated paper, with a photograph of William Hathaway Forbes and portraits of Sarah Alden Ripley and George Partridge Bradford printed on the rectos, are positioned after pp. 160, 208, 254.

Contents: p. a: blank; p. b: Houghton Mifflin advertisements for Emerson's writings; p. i: half title, the same as in A 52.IX.1.a, except 'X'; p. ii: blank; inserted leaf with photograph of Carlyle and Ralph Emerson Forbes printed on verso, followed by protective tissue; p. iii: title page; p. iv: blank; pp. v–xxii: 'CONTENTS'; p. xxiii: 'ILLUSTRATIONS'; p. xxiv: blank; p. 1: 'JOURNAL | BEECHER. CHAPIN | AMERICAN WRITERS | CONCORD PUBLIC SCHOOLS | ENGLAND'S ATTITUDE | SATURDAY CLUB | SHAKSPEARE'S BIRTHDAY | CELEBRATION | COLLEGE CURRICULUM | MATHEMATICS | HAWTHORNE'S DEATH AND | BURIAL | INSPIRATION. OLD AGE. | AGASSIZ. FORBES. BRYANT'; p. 2: blank; pp. 3–88: "Journal LV. 1864"; p. 89: 'JOURNAL | LECTURING AFAR | END OF THE WAR | LINCOLN | DUTIES OF THE HOUR | UNIVERSITY CULTURE | WILLIAMSTOWN ADDRESS | INTELLECT. MANNERS | DR. JACKSON | STAR-GAZING | CASS AND TRACY | CARLYLE'; p. 90: blank; pp. 91–126: "Journal LVI. 1865"; p. 127: 'JOURNAL | TASKS. SENSE. MANNERS | CRITICISM. LOVE | LAWS OF MIND | POLARITY. READING'S TEMPTA- | TION | WAR CLARIFIES | HEGEL | AMERICA'S MORAL BIAS | THE CAMP ON MONADNOC | ATLANTIC CABLE | VISIT TO AGASSIZ | HINDOO THEOLOGY | UNIVERSE OF THOUGHT | ANALYZED SOUND'; p. 128: blank; pp. 129–177: "Journal LVII. 1866"; p. 178: blank; p. 179: 'JOURNAL | THE WEST | MORAL LAW. THE NEWNESS | NATIONALITY | MARY MOODY EMERSON | PROGRESS OF CULTURE | MRS. RIPLEY'S DEATH | QUOTATION AND ORIGINALITY | THE PREACHER | FALSE POSITION OF ENGLISH | AUTHORS | THE FREEZING MISSISSIPPI'; p. 180: blank; pp. 181–224: "Journal LVIII. 1867"; p. 225: 'JOURNAL | BEAUTY | FREE TRADE. SUFFRAGE. PEACE | A WORLD RELIGION | UNITY AND EVOLUTION | TENNYSON. WILLIAM MORRIS | CALVIN AND BUDDHA | THE FORTUNE-TELLER | HEGEL AND METAPHYSICIANS | VISIT TO NEWPORT | MIDDLEBURY | VERMONT MOUNTAINS | HARVARD UNIVERSITY | LOWELL'; p. 226: blank; pp. 227–272: "Journal LIX. 1868"; p. 273: 'JOURNAL | CELTIC BARDS | AND MORTE D'ARTHUR | TONE IN POETRY | FRIENDS | RICHARD HUNT | READINGS TO CLASS | COLLEGE MARKING | JUDGE HOAR | CHARLES SUMNER | HESIOD. HUMBOLDT. AGASSIZ | POETRY. GOOD WRITING'; p. 274: blank; pp. 275–306: "Journal LX. 1869"; p. 307: 'JOURNAL | MEMORY. DREAMS | THOREAU. ALVAH CROCKER | SAMPSON REED | METAPHYSICIANS | PLUTARCH. HIS MORALS | NANTASKET BEACH | MARY MOODY EMERSON | MOUNT WASHINGTON. THE | NOTCH | IMAGINATION. CHIVALRY | HARVARD MEMORIAL HALL | FOREIGN CULTURE | THE PILGRIMS'; p. 308: blank; pp. 309–344: "Journal LXI. 1870"; p. 345: 'JOURNAL | MUSEUM OF FINE ARTS | UNIVERSITY LECTURES | ORGANIC CHEMISTRY | MILL, PUSEY, FROUDE | JOHN MURRAY FORBES | THE CALIFORNIA EXCURSION | SPLENDORS OF THE AGE | CHANNING. BRET HARTE | POETRY IN SCIENCE | GEOFFREY SAINT-HILAIRE | SYMPATHY WITH BOYS | CULTURE IN ENGLAND AND | HERE | BOYHOOD'; p. 346: blank; pp. 347–373: "Journal LXII. 1871"; p. 374: blank; p. 375: 'JOURNAL | BALTIMORE AND WASHINGTON | BOSTON READINGS | CHILDHOOD'S MEMORIES | PARALLEL IN LITERATURE | OLD SUMMER STREET | AMHERST | BURNING OF THE HOME | FRIENDS TO THE RESCUE | FAILING HEALTH | ENGLAND. FRANCE. ITALY'; p. 376: blank; pp. 377–401: "Journal LXIII. 1872"; p. 402: blank; p. 403: 'JOURNAL | THE NILE | ROME, FLORENCE, PARIS | THREE WEEKS OF LONDON | OXFORD | RETURN HOME'; p. 404: blank; pp. 405–425: "Journal LXIV. 1873"; p. 426: blank; p. 427: 'JOURNAL | DEATH OF SUMNER | ABEL ADAMS | FRANCIS C. LOWELL | CANDIDACY FOR LORD RECTOR- | SHIP OF GLASGOW UNIVERSITY | PARNASSUS'; p. 428: blank; pp. 429–438: "JOURNAL LXV. 1874"; p. 439: 'JOURNAL | CABOT THE HELPER | MEETING OF OLD SCHOOLMATES | THE MINUTE MAN | LIFE AND THE CHILD | CARLYLE'S BIRTHDAY'; p. 440: blank; pp. 441–445: "Journal LXVI. 1875"; p. 446: blank; p. 447: 'JOURNAL | CARLYLE MEDAL | UNIVERSITY OF VIRGINIA | LATIN SCHOOL CENTENARY | ALLINGHAM'S POEM'; p. 448: blank; pp. 449–476: "Journal LXVII. 1876"; p. 477: 'INDEX'; p. 478: blank; pp. 479–546: index; p. 547: blank; p. 548: printer's imprint, the same as in A 52.I.1.a; pp. 549–550: blank.

Typography and paper: The same as in A 52.I.1.a. Running heads: rectos: pp. vii–xxi: 'CONTENTS'; pp. 5–87, 93–125, 131–177, 183–223, 229–271, 277–305, 311–343, 349–373, 379–401, 407–425, 431–437, 443–445, 451–475: the same as in A 52.I.1.a; pp. 481–545: 'INDEX'; versos: pp. vi–xxii: 'CONTENTS'; pp. 4–88, 92–126, 130–176, 182–224, 228–272, 276–306, 310–344, 348–372, 378–400, 406–424, 430–438, 442–444, 450–476: the same as in A 52.I.1.a; pp. 480–546: 'INDEX'.

Publication: According to the publisher's records, published 28 March 1914. Listed in *Publishers' Weekly,* 85 (11 April 1914), 1262. Copyright, 28 March 1914; renewed, 18 November 1941. Same pricing schedule as for A 52.I.1.a.

Printing: The same printer's imprint as in A 52.I.1.a.

Locations: CtY, RPB.

Note: 1,135 copies of all printings in this format sold by 1923.

A 52.X.1.a₂
Second (English) issue

London: Constable & Co., Limited; Boston and New York: Houghton Mifflin and Company, 1914.

The same as A 52.X.1.a₁, except: the leaf containing pp. a–b (the Houghton Mifflin advertisements) has been cancelled; the title leaf is a cancel, with 'COPYRIGHT, 1914, BY EDWARD WALDO EMERSON | ALL RIGHTS RESERVED' on the verso.

Publication: Deposit copies: BL (26 June 1914), BC (3 July 1914), BE (3 July 1914), BO (24 July 1914). Price, 6s.

Locations: BC, BE, BL, BO (partial dust jacket).

Note: Because the distinguishing mark between the first and third printings is on the title leaf verso, which has here been cancelled, this is presumed to be an issue of the first printing on the basis of the previous volume's publication history.

A 52.X.1.b
First edition, second printing (1914)

The same as A 52.X.1.a₁, except the page size is $7^{15}/_{16}''$ × 5''; front flyleaf.

Publication: 200 copies advertised for sale. Price, $2.00.

Locations: CtY, RPB, VtMiM.

Note: The binding cloth on all located copies has faded, in varying degrees, to dark gray blue.

A 52.X.1.c
First edition, third printing (1914)

Title page the same as in A 52.X.1.a₁. Same as A 52.X.1.a₁, except: p. iv: 'COPYRIGHT, 1914, BY EDWARD WALDO EMERSON | ALL RIGHTS RESERVED | *Published March 1914*'.

Publication: Presumably published soon after A 52.X.1.a, in March 1914. Deposit copy: DLC (30 March 1914).

Locations: CtY, DLC, InU, JM, MB, MBAt, MH, MWA, NN (dust jacket), ViU, VtU.

A 52.X.1.d
First edition, fourth (large paper) printing (1914)

Two issues have been noted:

A 52.X.1.d$_1$
First issue

The title page is the same as in A 52.I.1.d$_1$, except '1864–1876' is substituted for '1820–1824' and '1914' for '1909'.

Contents: pp. a–d: the same as in A 52.I.1.d$_1$; pp. i–ii: the same as in A 52.IX.1.c$_1$, except p. i has 'X'; inserted leaf, the same as in A 52.X.1.a$_1$, p. iii: title page; p. iv: copyright page, the same as in A 52.I.1.d$_1$, except '1914'; pp. v–546: the same as in A 52.X.1.a$_1$, pp. 547–548: blank.

Printing: The Riverside Press, Cambridge.

Locations: JM, MB, TxU, VtMiM.

A 52.X.1.d$_2$
Second issue

The same as vol. I (*Large Paper Edition*, A 52.I.1.d$_2$).

Location: JM.

A 52.2.a
Second edition, presumed first printing (1926)

The Heart of Emerson's Journals. Boston and New York: Houghton Mifflin, 1926.

357 pp. Edited by Bliss Perry. Selections. 'THREE HUNDRED COPIES OF THIS FIRST EDITION ARE BOUND WITH UNCUT EDGES' in red cloth with a paper label on the spine. Copyright, 27 August 1926. *Location:* JM.

A 52.2.b$_1$
Second edition, presumed second printing, American issue (1926)

The same title page as the first printing. Dust jacket. Price, $3.00. Also noted with "Book-of-the-Month Club Selection" stamped on spine. *Locations:* JM (both).

A 52.2.b$_2$
English issue

London: Constable, 1927.

The title leaf is a cancel. Listed as published "to-day," in *Times Literary Supplement*, 20 January 1927, p. 37. Published January 1927. Price, 7s. 6d. *Locations:* BL (17 January 1927), BE (21 January 1927), KMK.

A 52.2.c
Boston and New York: Houghton Mifflin, [1937].

Location: JM.

A 52.2.d
New York: Dover, [1958].

Facsimile reprinting. Wrappers. Price, $1.85. *Locations:* DLC (31 October 1958), JM.

Note: Copies of the Dover paperback were bound in cloth and sold at $3.75 by Peter Smith of Gloucester, Mass., in 1960.

A 52.3
The Journals of Ralph Waldo Emerson. New York: Modern Library, [1960].

463 pp. Dust jacket. Edited with an introduction by Robert N. Linscott. Selections. *The Modern Library,* ML192. Copyright, 14 June 1960. Price, $1.95. *Location:* JM.

A 53 RECORDS OF A LIFELONG FRIENDSHIP

A 53
First edition, only printing (1910)

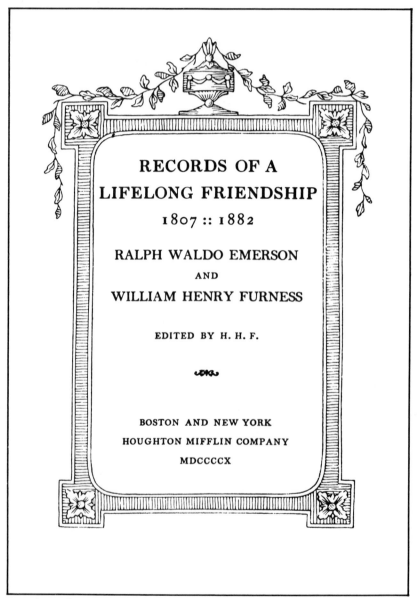

RECORDS OF A
LIFELONG FRIENDSHIP
1807 :: 1882

RALPH WALDO EMERSON

AND

WILLIAM HENRY FURNESS

EDITED BY H. H. F.

BOSTON AND NEW YORK
HOUGHTON MIFFLIN COMPANY
MDCCCCX

A 53: 9^{1}/₈″ × 6^{9}/₁₆″

[a–b] [i–v] vi–xvii [xviii] [xix–xx] [1] 2–3 [4] 5 [6] 7–8 [9] 10–12 [13] 14–17 [18] 19 [20] 21 [22] 23 [24–25] 26–29 [30] 31–32 [33] 34 [35–36] 37 [38–40] 41 [42] 43 [44] 45 [46] 47–49 [50] 51 [52–54] 55–59 [60] 61–62 [63] 64 [65] 66 [67–68] 69 [70] 71 [72–73] 74 [75] 76 [77] 78 [79] 80 [81] 82 [83] 84–87 [88] 89 [90] 91 [92] 93 [94–95] 96 [97] 98 [99–100] 101–102 [103–106] 107 [108–111] 112 [113] 114 [115–116] 117–118 [119] 120 [121] 122 [123] 124 [125] 126 [127–128] 129 [130] 131 [132–133] 134 [135] 136 [137] 138 [139] 140 [141] 142 [143] 144 [145] 146 [147–149] 150 [151–152] 153 [154–155] 156 [157] 158 [159] 160 [161] 162–163 [164–165] 166 [167] 168 [169–177] 178–185 [186–189] 190–195 [196–198]

[1^6 2–27^4]

Contents: pp. a–b: blank; p. i: 'RECORDS | OF | A LIFELONG FRIENDSHIP | 1807–1882'; p. ii: blank; inserted leaf with portrait of Emerson printed on recto, with protective tissue; p. iii: title page; p. iv: copyright page and statement of limitation; pp. v–xvii: 'INTRODUCTION', signed '*H* [orace]. *H*[oward]. *F*[urness]. | *September,* 1910.'; p. xviii: blank; p. xix: 'LETTERS'; p. xx: blank; pp. 1–12: text of letters; inserted leaf with portrait of Furness printed on verso, with protective tissue; pp. 13–102: text of letters; inserted leaf with 14-line description of letter printed overleaf printed on recto, and facsimile of Furness's letter containing a drawing of Thoreau printed on verso; pp. 103–148: text of letters; inserted leaf with picture of Samuel Bradford printed on verso, with protective tissue with '*Samuel Bradford*' printed on recto: pp. 149–164: text of letters; inserted leaf with photograph of Emerson, Furness, and Bradford printed on verso, with protective tissue; pp. 165–166: text of letter; inserted leaf with photograph of Bradford, Emerson, and Furness printed on recto, with protective tissue; pp. 167–174: text of letters; p. 175: 'APPENDIX'; p. 176: blank; pp. 177–185: "Fortus" [inserted double leaves after pp. 178 and 184 with facsimiles of "Fortus" manuscript on pp. 1–3 of the first and pp. 2–3 of the second]; p. 186: blank; p. 187: 'CONTRIBUTIONS | TO | 'THE GIFT' AND 'THE DIADEM' | BY | R. W. EMERSON'; p. 188: blank; pp. 189–195: 'INDEX'; p. 196: printer's imprint; pp. 197–198: blank.

Typography and paper: 5¹⁵⁄₁₆″ × 3⅞″; laid paper with 1¼″ vertical chain marks, watermarked with lyre-and-wreath design; 27 lines per page. No running heads.

Binding: Medium brown T cloth (rib). Front and back covers: blindstamped triple-rule frame with fleur-de-lis in corners and 4⅞″ oval ornament in center; spine: blind-stamped rules with goldstamped 'RECORDS OF | A LIFELONG | FRIENDSHIP | [leaf design] | 1910'. Light brown laid endpapers. Top edges trimmed; bottom and side edges untrimmed. Sold in a black paper-covered box.

Publication: 800 copies printed 11 November 1910. Listed in *Publishers' Weekly,* 78 (10 December 1910), 2325. According to the publisher's records, published 26 November 1910. Copyright, 7 December 1910; renewed, 1 December 1938. Deposit copies: DLC (12 December 1910), BL (26 January 1911). Inscribed copy: TxU (from H. H. Furness, 10 December 1910). According to the statement of limitation, limited to 780 numbered copies (p. [iv]), of which 750 were for sale (circular; see *Note three* below). Price, $5.00.

Locations: BL, CU, CtY, InU, JM, MB, MBAt, MH, NN (box), NjP, RPB, TxU (box), ViU (box), VtMiM.

Note one: Designed by Bruce Rogers.

Note two: In gathering [1], the following leaves are conjugate: 1_1 and 1_6, 1_2 and 1_3, 1_4 and 1_5.

Note three: 5,000 copies of a four-page circular printed 26 October 1910. *Location:* CtY.

Note four: 5,000 copies of an order blank printed 31 October 1910. *Location:* CtY.

A 54.1.a
First edition, first printing (1912)

UNCOLLECTED WRITINGS

ESSAYS, ADDRESSES, POEMS, REVIEWS AND LETTERS

BY

RALPH WALDO EMERSON

Now First Published in Book Form

THE LAMB PUBLISHING COMPANY
NEW YORK

A 54.1.a: $8^{1}/4'' \times 5^{1}/2''$

[a–d] [i–ii] iii–v [vi] vii–viii [1–2] 3–27 [28–30] 31–133 [134–136] 137–182 [183–184] 185–189 [190–192] 193–208 [209–212]

[1–14⁸]

Contents: pp. a–d: blank; inserted leaf with photograph of Emerson's library printed on verso: p. i: title page; p. ii: copyright page; pp. iii–v: 'INTRODUCTION'; p. vi: blank; pp. vii–viii: contents; p. 1: 'ESSAYS AND ADDRESSES'; p. 2: blank; pp. 3–8: "Nature"; pp. 9–10: "Amos Bronson Alcott"; pp. 11–14: "Right Hand of Fellowship at Ordination of Henry Bradford Goodwin, 1830"; pp. 15–17: "Address at Japanese Banquet, Aug. 2, 1872"; pp. 18–19: "Address at the James Anthony Froude Dinner at Delemonico's, New York, October 15, 1872"; pp. 20–22: "Speech at the Bryant Festival at 'The Century,' November 5, 1864"; pp. 23–25: "Arthur Hugh Clough"; pp. 26–27: "Carlyle's French Revolution"; p. 28: blank; p. 29: 'PAPERS FROM THE DIAL'; p. 30: blank; pp. 31–35: "The Editors to the Readers"; pp. 36–51: "Thoughts on Art"; pp. 52–59: "The Senses and the Soul"; pp. 60–64: "Transcendentalism"; pp. 65–70: "Veeshnoo Sarma"; pp. 71–76: "Fourierism and the Socialists"; pp. 77–83: "Intelligences"; pp. 84–112: "English Reformers"; pp. 113–114: "The Death of Dr. Channing"; pp. 115–122: "Tantalus"; pp. 123–133: "Ethical Scriptures"; p. 134: blank; p. 135: 'BOOK REVIEWS FROM THE DIAL'; p. 136: blank; pp. 137–182: book reviews; p. 183: 'POEMS'; p. 184: blank; pp. 185–189: poems; p. 190: blank; p. 191: 'LETTERS'; p. 192: blank; pp. 193–208: texts of letters; pp. 209–212: blank.

Selections: "Nature" †; "Amos Bronson Alcott" †; "Right Hand of Fellowship" †; "Address at Japanese Banquet" †; "Address at the James Anthony Froude Dinner" †; "Speech at the Bryant Festival" †; "Arthur Hugh Clough" †; "Carlyle's French Revolution" †; "The Editiors to the Reader" †; "Thoughts on Art" †; "The Senses and the Soul" †; "Transcendentalism" †; "Veeshnoo Sarma" †; "Fourierism and the Socialists" †; "Intelligence" [reprints E 57–63] †; "English Reformers" †; "The Death of Dr. Channing" †; "Tantalus" †; "Ethical Scriptures. Chaldæan Oracles" †; "New Poetry" †; "Two Years Before the Mast" †; "Social Destiny of Man" §; "Michael Angelo" §; "The Worship of the Soul" §; "Jones Very's Essays and Poems" †; "The Ideal Man" §; "The Zincali" †; "Ancient Spanish Ballads" †; "Tecumseh" †; "Tennyson's Poems" §; "Letter to Rev. Wm. E. Channing" †; "Confessions of St. Augustine" †; "The Bible in Spain" †; "Paracelsus" §; "Antislavery Poems" †; "Wm. Lloyd Garrison's Sonnets and Poems" †; "America" †; "Wm. E. Channing's Poems" †; "To Correspondents" †; "The Huguenots in France and America" §; "The Spanish Student" §; "The Dream of a Day" §; "My Thoughts" †; "The Phoenix" †; "Faith" †; "The Poet" ["Hoard knowledge in thy coffers"] †; "Word and Deed" †; "To Himself" †; "Letter to Chandler Robbins" †; "Letter on William Emerson" †; "Letter to Samuel Gridley Howe" †; "Two Letters to Henry Ware, Jr." †; "Letter to the Second Church and Society, March, 1829" †; "Letter to the Second Church and Society, December, 1832" †; "Letter of Protest" †; "Letter to Walt. Whitman" †.

Typography and paper: 6³/₈″ (6¹/₁₆″) × 3³/₄″; wove paper; 36 lines per page. Running heads: rectos: p. v: 'INTRODUCTION'; pp. 5–7, 13, 17–21, 25–27, 33–63, 67–69, 73–75, 79–111, 117–121, 125–133: titles of selections; pp. 139–181: 'REVIEWS OF BOOKS'; pp. 187–189: 'POEMS'; p. 199: 'HENRY WARE, Jr.'; pp. 201–205: 'THE SECOND CHURCH'; p. 207: 'LETTER OF PROTEST'; versos: p. iv: 'INTRODUCTION'; p. viii: 'CONTENTS'; pp. 4–16, 22–24, 32–34, 38–50, 54–58, 62–82, 86–132: titles of selections; pp. 138–182: 'REVIEWS OF BOOKS'; pp. 186–188: 'POEMS'; p. 196: 'SAM-UEL GRIDLEY HOWE'; p. 198: 'HENRY WARE, Jʀ.'; p. 204: 'THE SECOND CHURCH'.

Binding: Medium green T cloth (rib). Front cover: blindstamped double-rule frame with goldstamped 'R. Waldo Emerson' facsimile signature in center; back cover: blank; spine: goldstamped '[rule] | [rule] | UNCOLLECTED | WRITINGS | EMERSON | NEW YORK | [rule] | [rule]'. White endpapers. All edges trimmed. Top edges gilded.

Publication: Copyright, 22 November 1912. Deposit copy: DLC (2 December 1912). MB copy received 6 December 1912. MBAt copy received 12 December 1912. Inscribed copy: JM (25 December 1912). Price, $1.50.

Locations: BL, CU, DLC, InU, JM, MB, MBAt, NNC, NjP, RPB, TxU, ViU, VtMiM, VtU.

Note one: Possibly edited by Charles C. Bigelow.

Note two: Some items are definitely not by Emerson: "Social Destiny of Man" and "The Worship of the Soul" are by George Ripley; "Michael Angelo," "Tennyson's Poems," and "Paracelsus" are by Margaret Fuller; "The Ideal Man" is by Elizabeth Palmer Peabody (see Joel Myerson, "An Annotated List of Contributions to the Boston *Dial,*" *Studies in Bibliography,* 26 [1973], 133–166).

Note three: "Address at Japanese Banquet" is reprinted from the 10 August 1872 *Commonwealth* (Boston); "Address at the James Anthony Froude Dinner" from the 16 October 1872 *New York Daily Tribune.*

LATER PRINTING WITHIN THE FIRST EDITION

A 54.1.b
Port Washington, N.Y., and London: Kennikat, [1971].

Facsimile reprinting. Price, $9.00. *Locations:* DLC (5 December 1970), JM.

A 55 UNCOLLECTED LECTURES

A 55.1.a
First edition, first printing (1932)

UNCOLLECTED

LECTURES

By

RALPH WALDO EMERSON

Reports of Lectures on

AMERICAN LIFE *and* NATURAL RELIGION

Reprinted from

THE COMMONWEALTH

EDITED BY CLARENCE GOHDES

NEW YORK

WILLIAM EDWIN RUDGE

1932

A 55.1.a: 8³/₄″ × 5¹⁵/₁₆″

```
┌─────────────────────────────────────────────────────────────┐
│                   COPYRIGHT 1932 BY                           │
│          THE PRINTING HOUSE OF WILLIAM EDWIN RUDGE            │
│                     INCORPORATED                              │
│                                                               │
│             WILLIAM EDWIN RUDGE, PUBLISHER                    │
│               475 FIFTH AVENUE, NEW YORK                     │
│                                                               │
│                PRINTED IN THE UNITED STATES                  │
└─────────────────────────────────────────────────────────────┘
```

[i–v] vi–viii [ix–x] [1–3] 4–16 [17] 18–22 [23] 24–29 [30–31] 32–38 [39] 40–42 [43] 44–46 [47] 48–60 [61–62]

[1–6⁶]

Contents: p. i: '*Uncollected* | *Lectures*'; p. ii: blank; p. iii: title page; p. iv: copyright page; pp. v–viii: 'NOTE'; p. ix: contents; p. x: blank; p. 1: '*UNCOLLECTED* | *LECTURES*'; p. 2: blank; pp. 3–16: "Public and Private Education"; pp. 17–22: "Social Aims"; pp. 23–29: "Resources"; p. 30: blank; pp. 31–38: "Table-Talk"; pp. 39–42: "Books"; pp. 43–46: "Character"; pp. 47–60: "Natural Religion"; p. 61: colophon and statement of limitation; p. 62: blank.

Lectures: "Public and Private Education" #; "Social Aims" #; "Resources" #; "Table-Talk" #; "Books" #; "Character" #; "Natural Religion" #.

Typography and paper: 6⁵/₁₆" (6") × 3¹¹/₁₆"; wove paper watermarked '100% [script capitals] BR RAG | VALLEY | 1928'; 29 lines per page. Running heads: rectos: pp. 5–15, 19–21, 25–29, 33–37, 41, 45, 49–59: titles of lectures; versos: pp. 4–28, 32–60: 'Uncollected Lectures'.

Binding: Deep red B cloth (linen). Front and back covers: blank; spine: white paper label with '[triangle-and-line rule] | [triangle-and-line rule] | [triangle-and-line rule] | Un- | collected | Lectures | of | Emerson | [triangle-and-line rule] | [triangle-and-line rule] | [triangle-and-line rule] | [triangle-and-line rule]'. White endpapers. All edges trimmed. Top edges gilded.

Dust jacket: Light pink laid paper with 1⁵/₁₆" vertical chain marks. Front cover: same as the title page, except: no publisher's logo; back cover: blank; spine: same as the paper label on the binding with '[publisher's logo] | William | Edwin | Rudge' at bottom; front flap: 'THREE | DOLLARS' at bottom; back flap: blank.

Publication: Copyright, 2 May 1932. Deposit copy: DLC (25 May 1932). According to the statement of limitation: "Printed . . . in April 1932   1100 copies for sale in America" (p. [61]). Price, $3.00.

Locations: CU, DLC, InU, JM (dust jacket), MB, MBAt, MCo, MH, NN, NNC, NjP, TxU (dust jacket), ViU, VtMiM.

Note one: The first six lectures are from the "American Life" series, and are reprinted from the 3, 10, 17, 24, and 31 December 1864, and 7 January 1865 *Commonwealth* (Boston); the last lecture is reprinted from the 8 May 1869 *Commonwealth* (Boston).

Note two: Altered versions of some of these lectures appeared in Emerson's published writings: "Social Aims" in *Letters and Social Aims* (A 34); "Resources" in both "Resources" and "Inspiration" in *Letters and Social Aims;* and "Character" in the April 1866 *North American Review* (E 168) and *Lectures and Biographical Sketches* (A 41).

UNCOLLECTED

LECTURES

By

RALPH WALDO EMERSON

Reports of Lectures on

AMERICAN LIFE and NATURAL RELIGION

Reprinted from

THE COMMONWEALTH

EDITED BY CLARENCE GOHDES

NEW YORK

WILLIAM EDWIN RUDGE

1932

Un-
collected
Lectures
of
Emerson

William
Edwin
Rudge

LATER PRINTINGS WITHIN THE FIRST EDITION

A 55.1.b
[Folcroft, Penn.: Folcroft Library Editions, 1971].

Facsimile reprinting. Price $10.00. *Location:* CaOWtU.

A 55.1.c
[Folcroft, Penn.]: Folcroft Library Editions, 1974.

Facsimile reprinting. Limited to 100 copies. *Location:* DLC (24 June 1974).

A 55.1.d
[Norwood, Penn.]: Norwood Editions, 1976.

Facsimile reprinting. Limited to 100 copies. Price, $10.00. *Location:* DLC (22 April 1976).

A 56 EMERSON-CLOUGH LETTERS

A 56.1.a
First edition, first printing (1934)

Emerson-Clough
Letters

EDITED BY

HOWARD F. LOWRY

AND

RALPH LESLIE RUSK

Cleveland
THE ROWFANT CLUB
1934

A 56.1.a: $9^{3}/_{16}''$ × $5^{3}/_{4}''$

[a–b] [i–iv] v–ix [x] [1–68]

[1–10⁴]

Contents: pp. a–b: blank; p. i: '*EMERSON-CLOUGH | LETTERS*'; p. ii: blank; p. iii: title page; p. iv: 'COPYRIGHT 1934, BY HOWARD F. LOWRY'; pp. v–ix: 'INTRODUCTION', signed by the editors; p. x: blank; pp. 1–53: text of letters; p. 54: blank; pp. 55–65: 'NOTES'; p. 66: colophon and statement of limitation; pp. 67–68: blank.

Typography and paper: 6³/₈″ × 3⁵/₈″; laid paper with 1¹/₈″ vertical chain marks, watermarked '[script] *B F K* [script] *Rives* LIAMPRE FRANCE'; various lines per page. No running heads.

Binding. Green, black, gray, and white; or orange, white, black, and gray swirled nonpareil marbled B cloth (linen) (see illustration). Front cover: white label at top with '[band of stylized leaves] | [rule] | EMERSON-CLOUGH | LETTERS | [rule] | [band of stylized leaves]' within double-rule rectangular frame; back cover: blank; spine: white label with '[stylized leaf] | [rule] | [rule] | [printed vertically, from bottom to top] EMERSON-CLOUGH LETTERS | [rule] | [rule] | [stylized leaf]'. Laid paper flyleaves. White laid endpapers. All edges trimmed.

EMERSON-CLOUGH
LETTERS

EMERSON-CLOUGH LETTERS

Publication: Copyright, 26 February 1934. Deposit copy: DLC (5 March 1934). According to the statement of limitation: "One hundred sixty-five copies of this book have been printed . . . This is Number . . . " (p. [66]). For private distribution to members of the Rowfant Club.

Printing: The Lakeside Press, Chicago.

Locations: Green &c.: DLC, NjP; orange &c.: CSt, CtY, JM, MCo, MH, NN, NNC, RPB, ViU.

Note: All of Emerson's letters were reprinted in *The Correspondence of Arthur Hugh Clough,* ed. Frederick L. Mulhauser (Oxford: Clarendon Press, 1957).

LATER PRINTINGS WITHIN THE FIRST EDITION

A 56.1.b
[Hamden, Conn.]: Archon Books, 1968.

Facsimile reprinting. Price, $3.50. *Location:* MB.

A 56.1.c
[Folcroft, Penn.: Folcroft Library Editions, 1968].

Facsimile reprinting. *Location:* JM.

A 56.1.d
Darby, Penn.: Darby Books, [1969].

Facsimile reprinting. *Location:* CaOOCC.

A 56.1.e
[Folcroft, Penn.]: Folcroft Library Editions, 1977.

Facsimile reprinting. Price, $15.00. *Location:* ScU.

A 56.1.f
[Norwood, Penn.]: Norwood Editions, 1977.

Facsimile reprinting. *Location:* NmU.

A 57
First edition, only printing (1934)

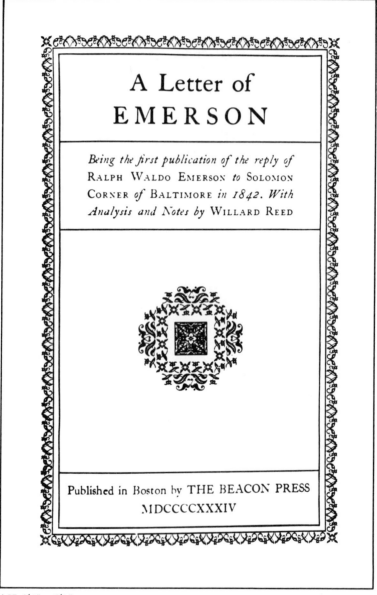

A 57: 9¹/₄″ × 6¹/₄″

[1–6] 7–8 [9–12] 13–15 [16] 17–19 [20] 21–33 [34–36]

[1–3⁴ 4⁶]

Contents: p. 1: '*A LETTER OF EMERSON* '; p. 2: blank; inserted leaf with picture of Emerson printed on verso; p. 3: title page; p. 4. copyright page; p. 5: contents; p. 6: blank; pp. 7–8: '*INTRODUCTORY NOTE*', signed 'WILLARD REED | Cambridge, July, 1934'; pp. 9–12: facsimile of Emerson's letter; pp. 13–15: text of Corner's May 1842 letter to Emerson; p. 16: blank; inserted leaf with picture of Corner printed on recto; pp. 17–19: text of Emerson's letter; p. 20: blank; pp. 21–24: text of Corner's 19 July 1842 letter to Emerson; pp. 25–26: '*BIOGRAPHICAL NOTE ON SOLOMON CORNER*'; pp. 27–30: '*PHILOSOPHICAL NOTE*'; pp. 31–33. '*ANALYSIS OF EMERSON'S LETTER*'; pp. 34–36: blank.

Typography and paper: 6¹¹/₁₆″ × 4″; wove paper; 31 lines per page. No running heads.

Binding: Medium gray paper-covered boards. Front cover: reddish brown double-rule frame within reddish brown ornate rectangular frame with 'A LETTER | of | EMER-SON' in the center; back cover: blank; spine: from top to bottom: 'A LETTER OF EMERSON'. Cream endpapers. Top edges trimmed.

Dust jacket: Reddish pink laid paper with 1¹¹/₁₆″ vertical chain marks. Front cover: '*A Letter of | Emerson*' | [drawing of Emerson's head within circular frame] | *With Analysis and Notes | By* Willard Reed'; back cover: 32-line blurb for book within double-rule frame; spine: from top to bottom: '*A Letter of Emerson*'; front and back flaps: blank.

Publication: Copyright, 30 November 1934. Deposit copies: DLC (7 December 1934), BL (2 January 1935). MB copy received 10 December 1934. Price, $1.00.

Locations: BL, CtY, DLC, JM (dust jacket), MB, MH, NN, RPB, ViU.

A Letter of Emerson

With Analysis and Notes
By Willard Reed

A Letter of Emerson

A Letter of Emerson

The first publication of the reply of Ralph Waldo Emerson to Solomon Corner of Baltimore in 1842

With Analysis and Notes by WILLARD REED

THE fundamentals of Ralph Waldo Emerson's philosophy—indeed the fundamentals of all philosophy—Reality, and Man's Apprehension of Reality, form the theme of this profound letter, written in 1842 during the period characterized by Professor Bliss Perry as that of Emerson's very best writing.

The letter was a response evoked by an appeal from Solomon Corner, a young merchant of Baltimore, who, inspired by the courage of desperation, wrote the great philosopher for advice, hardly daring to hope that he would receive the favor of a reply. Emerson answered with a masterful letter, compact and orderly, summing up his whole philosophy. The ideas expressed make it a letter for all time, and it is especially timely today when persons and nations are groping for stable foundations of thought. The clear delineation of such foundations is here encompassed in a few pages. The letter is strikingly in tune with the utterances of the most able minds of our time.

Here is matter for careful reading and for pondering. This eloquent and stirring challenge to reflection will stand as a noteworthy addition to the literature of spiritual discipline and will contribute much to a fuller understanding of Emerson.

This handsome gift edition is illustrated and contains a facsimile of Emerson's letter. There is also included Solomon Corner's request for guidance, as well as notes and a foreword by his grandson, Willard Reed, who prepared the correspondence for publication.

36 pages. $1.00.

THE BEACON PRESS, Inc.
25 Beacon Street   Boston, Mass.

A 58.1.a
First edition, first printing (1938)

Young Emerson

Speaks

Unpublished Discourses on Many Subjects

By RALPH WALDO EMERSON

Edited by

Arthur Cushman McGiffert, Jr.

HOUGHTON MIFFLIN COMPANY · BOSTON

The Riverside Press Cambridge

1938

A 58.1.a: 8^{1}/$_{8}$″ × 5^{7}/$_{16}$″

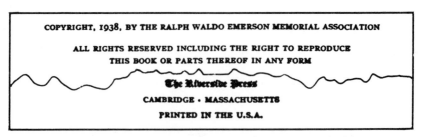

[i–iv] v–vi [vii–x] xi–xxxix [xl] [xli–xlii] 1–11 [12] 13–20 [21] 22–29 [30] 31–37 [38] 39–44 [45] 46–52 [53] 54–58 [59] 60–65 [66] 67–73 [74] 75–80 [81] 82–88 [89] 90– 97 [98] 99–103 [104] 105–110 [111] 112–118 [119] 120–125 [126] 127–136 [137] 138–143 [144] 145–149 [150] 151–161 [162] 163–168 [169] 170–178 [179] 180–189 [190] 191–201 [202] 203–211 [212–214] 215–258 [259–260] 261 [262] 263–270 [271–272] 273–275 [276–278]

[1–20⁸]

[1–20^8]

Contents: p. i: '*Young Emerson | Speaks*'; p. ii: blank; p. iii: title page; p. iv: copyright page; pp. v–vii: 'PREFACE', signed 'ARTHUR CUSHMAN MCGIFFERT, JR. | *December,*1937'; p. viii: blank; p. ix: contents; p. x: blank; pp. xi–xl: "Introduction"; p. xli: '*Young Emerson | Speaks*'; p. xlii: blank; pp. 1–212: texts of sermons; p. 213: 'Notes'; p. 214: blank; pp. 215–259: notes; p. 260: blank; pp. 261–262: "The Preaching Record"; pp. 263–271: "A List of the Sermons"; p. 272: blank; pp. 273–276: "Index"; pp. 277–278: blank.

Sermons: "Pray Without Ceasing" #; "On Showing Piety at Home" #; "The Christian Minister: Part I" #; "The Christian Minister: Part II" #; "Summer" #; "Trifles" #; "A Feast of Remembrance" #; "Conversation" #; "The Ministry: A Year's Retrospect" #; "The Individual and the State" #; "Religious Liberalism and Rigidity" #; "The Authority of Jesus" #; "Self-Culture" #; "Trust Yourself" #; "How Old Art Thou?" #; "Miracles" #; "Self and Others" #; "Consolation for the Mourner" #; "Hymn Books" #; "The Choice of Theisms" #; "Find Your Calling" #; "Astronomy" #; "The Genuine Man" #; "Religion and Society" #; "The Miracle of Our Being" #.

Typography and paper: 6⁹/₁₆″ (6¹/₄″) × 4¹/₈″; wove paper; 35 lines per page. Running heads: rectos: p. vii: '*PREFACE*'; pp. xiii–xxxix: '*INTRODUCTION*'; pp. 3–11, 15–29, 33–37, 41–65, 69–73, 77–97, 101–103, 107–125, 129–143, 147–149, 153–161, 165–189, 193–201, 205–211: titles of sermons; pp. 217–259: '*NOTES*'; pp. 265–271: '*A LIST OF THE SERMONS*'; p. 275: '*INDEX*'; versos: p. vi: '*PREFACE*'; pp. xii–xl: '*INTRODUCTION*'; pp. 2–20, 24–44, 48–52, 56–58, 62–80, 84–88, 92–110, 114–118, 122–136, 140–168, 172–178, 182–212: '*YOUNG EMERSON SPEAKS*'; pp. 216–258: '*NOTES*'; p. 260: '*THE PREACHING RECORD*'; pp. 264–270: '*A LIST OF THE SER- MONS*'; pp. 274–276: '*INDEX.*'

Binding: Slightly reddish brown V cloth (smooth). Front cover: all within a blue rec- tangular background: goldstamped frame enclosing goldstamped '*Young Emerson | Speaks* | UNPUBLISHED DISCOURSES ON MANY SUBJECTS'; back cover: blank; spine: all within a blue rectangular background: goldstamped '[rule] | *Young* | *Emerson* | *Speaks* | MCGIFFERT | [rule]'. White endpapers. All edges trimmed.

Dust jacket: Front cover: over a design of four concentric white rectangles on a light blue background: 'Edited by ARTHUR CUSHMAN MCGIFFERT, JR. | [drawing of Emer- son's head] | YOUNG | EMERSON | SPEAKS' and below, printed on a white band, 'Unpublished Discourses on Many Subjects by Ralph Waldo Emerson'; back cover: publisher's advertisements for six books; spine: white parallel vertical lines on a light

$3.60

YOUNG EMERSON
SPEAKS

Unpublished Discourses on Many
Subjects by

Ralph Waldo Emerson

Edited by Arthur Cushman McGiffert

This important Emerson first edition contains twenty-five sermons which throw vivid light upon the life and thought of the young man during critical and formative years.

Emerson's place in modern American thought and culture assumes new significance in the light of the discourses. They have been printed in chronological order, so that the growth of Emerson's powers and interests may be observed.

Edited by ARTHUR CUSHMAN McGIFFERT

Young Emerson Speaks

YOUNG EMERSON SPEAKS

Unpublished Discourses on Many Subjects by Ralph Waldo Emerson

HOUGHTON MIFFLIN CO.

Books about Books

BOOKS AND BATTLES *by Irene and Allen Cleaton*

An informal, entertaining record of the literary twenties which does for American literature what 'Only Yesterday' did for the whole American scene. Illustrated.

PORTRAITS FROM LIFE *by Ford Madox Ford*

Memories and criticism of Galsworthy, Conrad, Hardy, Swinburne, James, Lawrence, Crane, Wells, Dreiser, Turgenev, and Hudson. Illustrated.

THE GREAT POETS and the Meaning of Life *by Charles Allen Dinsmore*

A popular study of Homer and Aeschylus, Lucretius and Virgil, Dante, Shakespeare, and the Bible.

A BOOK HUNTER'S HOLIDAY *by A. S. W. Rosenbach*

A world-famous book collector describes his adventures with books and manuscripts. Illustrated.

PORTRAITS AND SELF-PORTRAITS *by Georges Schreiber*

Forty of the leading writers of today self-described, with forty full-page drawings by the author. Illustrated.

ESSAYS IN APPRECIATION *by John Livingston Lowes*

Essays on the King James version of the Bible, Chaucer, Bunyan, Hardy, Meredith, and Amy Lowell.

THE WORKS OF THOREAU

Selected and edited by
Henry Seidel Canby

Never has Thoreau's reputation stood higher than it does today. As Dr. Canby says, 'One feels inclined to prophesy that he is the most durable of American writers.'

This new edition is an omnibus of Thoreau's best in one volume. It is not a limited edition, but an organized reprint of all the important material in the best of the famous Journals, hitherto buried in fourteen volumes of an expensive twenty-volume set.

The arrangement is designed for easy reading and easy reference. The stimulating introduction and short biography are followed by essays from the Journals, the 'Week,' and 'Walden,' the Poems, 'Ktaadn' from 'The Maine Woods,' 'Cape Cod,' essays on nature, on friendship and religion, the famous 'Civil Disobedience,' and finally the great addresses on slavery. There is also a selected bibliography; also twelve illustrations from photographs by Henry B. Kane.

Dust jacket for A 58.1.a

blue background, with 'McGiffert | Young | Emerson | Speaks | HOUGHTON | MIFFLIN CO.'; front flap: blurb for *Young Emerson Speaks;* back flap: blurb for *The Works of Thoreau,* ed. Canby.

Publication: 2,000 copies printed. Copyright, 5 April 1938. Published 15 February 1938. Deposit copies: DLC (13 April 1938), BL (3 January 1940). MB copy received 5 April 1938. MBAt copy received 12 April 1938. Inscribed copy: ViU (19 April 1938). Price, $3.00.

Locations: BL, DLC (dust jacket), InU, JM (dust jacket), MB (dust jacket), MBAt (dust jacket), MH-AH, NN, NNC (dust jacket), TxU, ViU (dust jacket), VtMiM.

A 58.1.b
First edition, second printing [1968]

Port Washington, N.Y.: Kennikat, [1968].

Facsimile reprinting. Price, $9.00. *Location:* ScU.

A 59 THE LETTERS OF RALPH WALDO EMERSON

A 59.1.a
First edition, first printing (1939)

THE LETTERS OF

RALPH WALDO

EMERSON

IN SIX VOLUMES

EDITED BY

RALPH L. RUSK

PROFESSOR OF ENGLISH IN
COLUMBIA UNIVERSITY

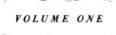

VOLUME ONE

NEW YORK : MORNINGSIDE HEIGHTS

COLUMBIA UNIVERSITY PRESS

1939

A 59.1.a: 9⁵/₁₆″ × 6¹/₈″; interior lines in the lettering of Emerson's name and the braces around the volume numbers are in red

I: [a–b] [i–v] vi–viii [ix] x [xi] xii–lxiv [lxv] lxvi [1–4] 5–8 [9] 10–12 [13] 14–31 [32] 33–53 [54] 55–74 [75] 76–88 [89] 90–98 [99] 100–105 [106] 107–126 [127] 128–139 [140] 141–157 [158] 159–165 [166] 167–183 [184] 185–223 [224] 225–257 [258] 259–290 [291] 292–315 [316] 317–343 [344] 345–361 [362] 363–403 [404] 405–429 [430] 431–458 [459–460]

I: [1–33^8]

Contents: I: pp. a–b: blank; p. i: 'THE LETTERS OF | RALPH WALDO EMERSON'; p. ii: blank; two-leaf insert [unpaginated, printed as follows: p. 1: '*Facsimile Pages of Letter to William Emerson | November 10, 1814*'; pp. 2–3: facsimile; p. 4: blank]; p. iii: title page; p. iv: copyright page; pp. v–viii: 'Preface', dated '*April, 1938*'; pp. ix–x: contents for all six volumes; pp. xi–lxiv: 'Introduction'; pp. lxv–lxvi: 'Explanatory Note'; p. 1: 'THE LETTERS OF | RALPH WALDO EMERSON | 1813–1835'; p. 2: blank; pp. 3–458: text of letters; pp. 459–460: blank.

II: [i–vi] [1–3] 4–52 [53] 54–105 [106] 107–177 [178] 179–247 [248] 249–375 [376] 377–471 [472–474]

II: [1–30^8]

Contents: II: pp. i–ii: blank; p. iii: set half title, the same as in vol. I; p. iv: blank; inserted leaf with facsimile of letter printed on verso; p. v: title page, the same as in vol. I, except '*VOLUME TWO*'; p. vi: copyright page; p. 1: volume half title, the same as in vol. I, except '1836–1841'; p. 2: blank; pp. 3–471: text of letters; pp. 472–474: blank.

III: [i–vi] [1–3] 4–109 [110] 111–232 [233] 234–275 [276] 277–321 [322] 323–367 [368] 369–462 [463–466]

III: [1–28^8 29^4 30^8]

Contents: III: pp. i–ii: blank; p. iii: set half title, the same as in vol. I; p. iv: blank; inserted leaf with facsimile of letter printed on verso; p. v: title page, the same as in vol. I, except '*VOLUME THREE*'; p. vi: copyright page; p. 1: volume half title, the same as in vol. I, except '1842–1847'; p. 2: blank; pp. 3–462: text of letters; pp. 463–466: blank.

IV: [i–vi] [1–3] 4–126 [127] 128–173 [174] 175–240 [241] 242–270 [271] 272–340 [341] 342–412 [413] 414–481 [482] 483–541 [542–546]

IV: [1–2^8 3^4 4–35^8]

Contents: IV: pp. i–ii: blank; p. iii: set half title, the same as in vol. I; p. iv: blank; inserted leaf with facsimile of letter printed on verso; p. v: title page, the same as in vol.

I, except 'VOLUME FOUR'; p. vi: copyright page; p. 1: volume half title, the same as in vol. I, except '1848–1855'; p. 2: blank; pp. 3–541: text of letters; pp. 542–546: blank.

V: [i–vi] [1–3] 4–50 [51] 52–93 [94] 95–129 [130] 131–186 [187] 188–235 [236] 237–261 [262] 263–301 [302] 303–345 [346] 347–399 [400] 401–444 [445] 446–486 [487] 488–546 [547–550]

V: [1–34⁸ 35⁶]

Contents: V: pp. i–ii: blank; p. iii: set half title, the same as in vol. I; p. iv: blank; inserted leaf with facsimile of letter printed on verso; p. v: title page, the same as in vol. I, except: 'VOLUME FIVE'; p. vi: copyright page; p. 1: volume half title, the same as in vol. I, except '1856–1867'; p. 2: blank; pp. 3–546: text of letters; pp. 547–550: blank.

VI: [i–vi] [1–3] 4–51 [52] 53–95 [96] 97–141 [142] 143–192 [193] 194–232 [233] 234–253 [254] 255–269 [270] 271–288 [289] 290–300 [301] 302–308 [309] 310–315 [316] 317–321 [322] 323–324 [325–329] 330–332 [333] 334–338 [339] 340–343 [344–347] 348–633 [634–638]

VI: [1–8⁸ 9¹⁰ 10–40⁸]

Contents: VI: pp. i–ii: blank; p. iii: set half title, the same as in vol. I; p. iv: blank; inserted leaf with facsimile of letter printed on verso; p. v: title page, the same as in vol. I, except 'VOLUME SIX'; p. vi: copyright page; p. 1: volume half title, the same as in vol, I, except '1868–1881'; p. 2: blank; pp. 3–325: text of letters; p. 326: blank; p. 327: 'APPENDICES'; p. 328: blank; pp. 329–332: 'APPENDIX I | Two Early Poems'; pp. 333–338: 'APPENDIX II | Undated Prose Fragments'; pp. 339–343: 'APPENDIX III | Letters and Packets'; p. 344: blank; p. 345: 'INDEX'; p. 346: blank; pp. 347–633: index; pp. 634–638: blank.

Typography and paper: 7¼″ (7″) × 4⁵/₁₆″; laid paper with vertical chain marks ¹³/₁₆″ apart; 39 lines per page (though most pages have various numbers of lines). Running heads: vol. I: rectos: p. vii: 'PREFACE'; pp. xiii–lxiii: 'INTRODUCTION'; pp. 5–7, 11, 15–73, 77–87, 91–97, 101–125, 129–289, 293–457: dates of letters; versos: pp. vi–viii: 'PREFACE'; p. x: 'CONTENTS'; pp. xii–lxiv: 'INTRODUCTION'; p. lxvi: 'EXPLANATORY NOTE'; pp. 6–30, 34–52, 56–104, 108–138, 142–156, 160–182, 186–222, 226–256, 260–314, 318–342, 346–360, 364–402, 406–428, 432–458: dates of letters; vol. II: rectos: pp. 5–51, 55–471: dates of letters; versos: pp. 4–104, 108–176, 180–246, 250–374, 376–470: dates of letters; vol. III: rectos: pp. 5–231, 235–461: dates of letters; versos: pp. 4–108, 112–274, 278–320, 324–366, 370–462: dates of letters; vol. IV: rectos: pp. 5–125, 129–239, 243–269, 273–339, 343–411, 415–541: dates of letters; versos: pp. 4–172, 176–480, 484–540: dates of letters; vol. V: rectos: pp. 5–49, 53–185, 189–443, 447–485, 489–545: dates of letters; versos: pp. 4–92, 96–128, 132–234, 238–260, 264–300, 304–344, 348–398, 402–546: dates of letters; vol. VI: rectos: pp. 5–191, 195–231, 235–287, 291–299, 303–307, 311–323: dates of letters; p. 331: 'TWO EARLY POEMS'; pp. 335–337: 'UNDATED PROSE FRAGMENTS'; pp. 341–343: 'LETTERS AND PACKETS'; pp. 349–633: 'INDEX'; versos: pp. 4–50, 54–94, 98–140, 144–252, 256–268, 272–314, 318–320, 324: dates of letters; pp. 330–332: 'TWO EARLY POEMS'; pp. 334–338: 'UNDATED PROSE FRAGMENTS'; pp. 340–342: 'LETTERS AND PACKETS'; pp. 348–632: 'INDEX'.

Binding: Medium reddish orange buckram. Front cover: goldstamped 'R. W. E.' facsimile signature; back cover: blank; spine: goldstamped '[rule] | [five lines on black background] THE LETTERS OF | RALPH WALDO | EMERSON | [rule] | *RALPH L. RUSK* | VOL. I [–VI] | [rule] | 1813–1835 [–1868–1881] | COLUMBIA'. Cream endpapers. All edges trimmed. Top edges gilded or stained dark orange.

Box: Black paper covered cardboard box with paper label at top with '[orange] THE LETTERS OF | [two lines in orange and black ornate lettering, the same as on the title page] RALPH WALDO | EMERSON | [two lines in orange] *IN SIX VOLUMES* | *EDITED BY* | RALPH L. RUSK'.

Publication: Copyright, 8 May 1939. Deposit copies: DLC (9 May 1939), BL (18 May 1939). MBAt copy received 18 May 1939. MCo copy received May 1939. Prices: prepublication, $25.00; publication, $30.00.

Locations: BL, CSt, DLC, JM (box), MB, MBAt, MCo, MH-AH, ScU, ViU.

Note one: Two states have been noted for vol. II; in the headnote to the first letter (p. 3):

   1st state: TO WILLIAM NEWELL, CONCORD? JANUARY c. 24? 1836

   2d state: TO ELIZABETH HOAR, CONCORD? JANUARY 1, 1836[1]

Locations: 1st state: BL, DLC, MB, MBAt, MCo, MH-AH, ScU, ViU; 2d state: CSt, JM. In addition, copies (with the correct reading) have been noted with an erratum slip inserted before p. 3 (CSt, JM).

Note two: A four-page prospectus was printed. *Location:* NNC.

A 59.1.b
First edition, second printing [1966]

The same as the first printing, except: the title page is in black only; the title page imprint is undated and reads 'NEW YORK AND LONDON | COLUMBIA UNIVERSITY PRESS'; the title page verso reads 'Second printing 1966'; the collation is different; printed on wove paper. Also, there is a "Note to the Second Printing" [by Eleanor M. Tilton], stating that "the few original misprints and errors of fact have been corrected" (I, viii). *Location:* JM.

Note: Revisions are on I, 13, 19, 237, 289, 296, 328, 329; II, 3, 123, 293, 385, 419; III, 250, 283, 371, 408; IV, 28, 195; V, 177, 307, 333, 353, 389, 516; VI, 169, 228, 325, 352, 365, 366, 415, 416, 417, 423, 444, 445, 524, 559, 564, 567, 596, 617.

A 60 R. W. EMERSON TO ELIZABETH HOAR

A 60
First edition, only printing [1942]

R. W. EMERSON

TO

ELIZABETH HOAR

A 60: 7^1/$_2$″ × 5^1/$_{16}$″

[1–12]

[a]⁶

Contents: pp. 1–2: blank; p. 3: 'R. W. EMERSON | TO | ELIZABETH HOAR'; p. 4: blank; pp. 5–7: text of Emerson's 3 August 1859 letter; p. 8: blank; p. 9: colophon and description of manuscript; pp. 10–12: blank.

Typography and paper: 4³/₁₆″ × 2¹¹/₁₆″; wove paper, watermarked 'Strathmore Bond | Rag Content U.S.A.'; 35 lines per page. No running heads.

Binding: Cover title; yellow green stiff wrappers (8¹/₂″ × 5¹/₂″). Front recto: 'R. W. EMERSON | TO | ELIZABETH HOAR'; front verso and back recto and verso: blank. Unstitched sheets loosely laid in. All edges trimmed.

Publication: According to statement of limitation in colophon: "Thirty copies printed by Edwin B. Hill on his private press at Ysleta, Texas, September, 1942" (p. [9]).

Locations: JM, MH, NNC, PSt, VtMiM.

A61 THOREAU'S PENCILS

A61
First edition, only printing [1944]

THOREAU'S PENCILS

An Unpublished Letter from
Ralph Waldo Emerson
to Caroline Sturgis
19 May 1844

A61: Cover title, 9″ × 6″

[1–8]

[1]⁴

Contents: p. 1: 'Introductory Note.'; pp. 2–4: blank; p. 5: text of Emerson's 19 May 1844 letter; pp. 6–7: blank; p. 8: extract from Caroline Sturgis's reply to Emerson of 22 May 1844, colophon, and statement of limitation.

Typography and paper: 5³/₈ × 3¹⁵/₁₆″; laid paper with 1¹/₁₆″ vertical chain marks; 21 lines per page. No running heads.

Binding: Cover title; very light yellowish brown stiff laid paper wrappers in french fold, with 1¹/₁₆″ vertical chain marks. Front recto: 'THOREAU'S PENCILS | *An Unpublished Letter from* | *Ralph Waldo Emerson* | *to Caroline Sturgis* | *19 May 1844*'; front verso and back recto: blank; back verso: 'Houghton Library Brochure Number Four'. Text, in French fold, is stitched to wrapper with brown thread. Top edges uncut; side and bottom edges partially trimmed.

Publication: According to the statement of limitation: "Seventy-five copies have been printed by hand on Laverstroke mould-paper from Caslon Old Face type. This copy is Number   Cambridge, Massachusetts   6 January 1944' (p. [8]).

Locations: DLC, JM, MH, NjP, RPB.

Note one: The numbers were written in with pencils manufactured by Thoreau.

Note two: *Harvard Library Brochure Number Four.*

A 62 [LETTER TO MARY MOODY EMERSON]

A 62.1.a
First edition, presumed first printing [1948]

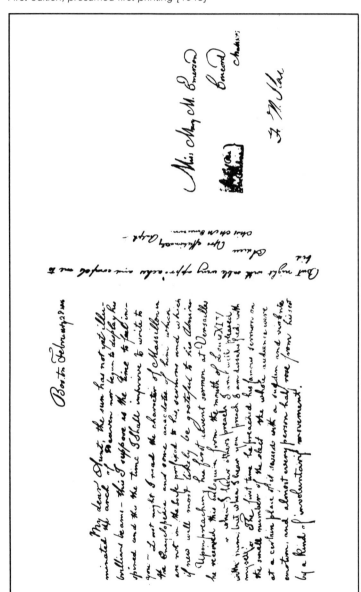

A 62: Broadside, 12⁹/₁₆″ × 6½″

Broadside, printed in linecut on recto only.

Typography and paper: Wove paper. No running head.

Publication: Not for sale. Distributed to visitors at the Old Manse, Concord, Mass.

Locations: MCo, PSt.

Note one: The manuscript letter was discovered in 1948 and probably published that same year.

Note two: The text of the letter was edited and printed in a four-page undated pamphlet distributed to visitors at the Old Manse (JM).

Note three: Kenneth Walter Cameron facsimiles and edits the letter in "Emerson's Early Use of the Encyclopaedia Brittanica," *Emerson Society Quarterly*, no. 3 (2nd Quarter 1956), 7–8.

A 62.1.b

First edition, presumed second printing [1948]

The same as the first printing, except: printed in halftone, the side of the broadside containing the facsimile being glossy paper; page size is $12^5/_8'' \times 6^9/_{16}''$.

Location: JM.

A 63 INDIAN SUPERSTITION

A 63
First edition, only printing (1954)

Indian Superstition

BY RALPH WALDO EMERSON

EDITED WITH

A Dissertation on Emerson's Orientalism at Harvard by

KENNETH WALTER CAMERON

◆

The Friends of the Dartmouth Library

HANOVER, NEW HAMPSHIRE, 1954

A 63: 9″ × 5⁵/₁₆″

Copyright 1954 by Kenneth Walter Cameron

This is Volume One of a bibliographical series
issued under the auspices of the Friends of the
Dartmouth Library, Hanover, New Hampshire

Edition Limited to 450 Copies

✦

PRINTED IN THE UNITED STATES OF AMERICA
BY CAYUGA PRESS, INC., ITHACA, NEW YORK

[1–6] 7–9 [10–12] 13–47 [48] 49–86 [87–88]

[1–4^8 5^4 6^8]

Contents: p. 1: 'Indian Superstition'; p. 2: blank; inserted leaf with facsimile of manuscript page printed on recto; p. 3: title page; p. 4: copyright page; p. 5: 'To CARL
FERDINAND STRAUCH | who best knows Emerson's poetry'; p. 6: blank; pp. 7–8:
'Foreword', signed 'K[enneth]. W[alter]. C[ameron]. | *Trinity College* | *Hartford, Connec-
ticut* | May, 1953'; p. 9: contents; p. 10: blank; p. 11: 'Indian Superstition'; p. 12: blank;
pp. 13–47: "Young Emerson's Orientalism at Harvard"; p. 48: blank; pp. 49–54: text of
"Indian Superstition"; pp. 55–63: "Commentary on 'Indian Superstition'"; pp. 64–66:
"Appendix A. Notes on Massachusetts Orientalism"; pp. 67–69: "Appendix B. Oriental
Themes and Climate in Harvard Commencement and Exhibition Parts (1800–1834)";
pp. 70–72: "Appendix C. Emerson's Reading for His Poem"; pp. 73–86: "Index"; pp.
87–88: blank.

Typography and paper: $6^{11}/_{16}"$ × 4"; wove paper; 34 lines per page. No running
heads.

Binding: Medium bluish green B cloth (linen). Front cover: silverstamped 'INDIAN
SUPERSTITION'; back cover: blank; spine: silverstamped vertically from top to bottom
'[ornamental band] INDIAN SUPERSTITION [ornamental band]'. White endpapers. All
edges trimmed.

Dust jacket: Unprinted glassine.

Publication: Copyright, 5 February 1954. Deposit copy: DLC (5 February 1954).
According to the statement of limitation: "Edition limited to 450 copies" (p. [4]).

Locations: BL, CU, DLC, InU, JM, MB, MCo, MH, MWA, MWiW-C, NjP, TxU, VtMiM.

A 64 MR. EMERSON WRITES A LETTER ABOUT WALDEN

A 64.1.a
First edition, only printing (1954)

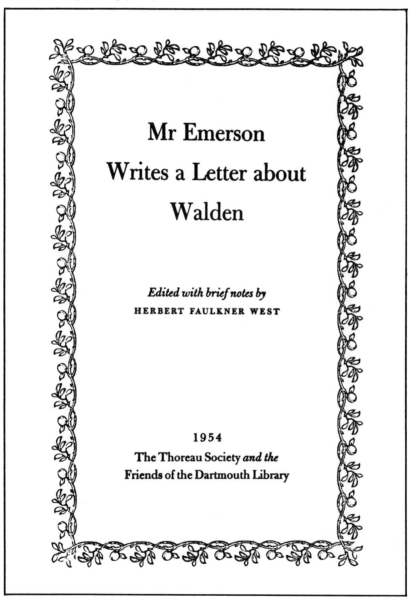

Mr Emerson
Writes a Letter about
Walden

Edited with brief notes by
HERBERT FAULKNER WEST

1954
The Thoreau Society *and the*
Friends of the Dartmouth Library

A 64: 8^{15}/$_{16}$″ × 5^{15}/$_{16}$″

DEDICATED

in the year of our Lord 1954

to the memory of two great

and gallant individualists

RALPH WALDO EMERSON

HENRY DAVID THOREAU

PRINTED BY THE STINEHOUR PRESS : LUNENBURG : VERMONT

Two issues have been noted:

A 64.1.a₁
First issue

[1–20]

[a]¹⁰

Contents: pp. 1–2: blank; p. 3: title page; p. 4: dedication page and printer's imprint; p. 5: 'Editor's Note', signed 'HERBERT F. WEST'; p. 6: 'Ralph Waldo Emerson's letter is reproduced here | in facsimile by offset lithography by The Meriden | Gravure Company, Meriden, Connecticut.'; pp. 7–14: facsimile of letter; pp. 15–16: printed text of letter; pp. 17–19: commentary on letter; p. 20: blank.

Typography and paper: 6⅝″ × 4″; wove paper; 37 lines per page. No running heads.

Binding: Brownish orange stiff wrappers. Front recto: 'Mr Emerson | Writes a Letter about | Walden | [woodcut of three apples and a glass of water]'; front verso and back recto and verso: blank. All edges trimmed.

Locations: BL, JM, MB, MCo, MH.

A 64.1.a₂
Second issue

The same as the first issue, except: p. 1: 'Thoreau Society Booklet number 9'.

Location: ViU.

Note one: *Thoreau Society Booklet*, no. 9.

Note two: Presumably those copies with the *Thoreau Society Booklet* information were distributed to members of the Society, and those copies without this information were distributed to the Friends of the Dartmouth College Library.

Mr Emerson
Writes a Letter about
Walden

A 65 DANTE'S *VITA NUOVA*

A 65.1
First edition, only printing (1957)

Dante's *Vita Nuova*

Translated by
Ralph Waldo Emerson

Edited by
J. Chesley Mathews

The Ralph Waldo Emerson
Memorial Association
1957

A 65.1: 10⁵/₁₆″ × 7″

[a–b] i–viii [ix–xii] 1–46

[1]^30

Contents: p. a: title page; p. b: copyright page; pp. i–viii: "Introduction"; pp. ix–xii: facsimiles of manuscript pages; pp. 1–46: text.

Typography and paper: $7^7/8''$ ($7^5/8''$) × $4^7/8''$; wove paper; 39 lines per page. Running heads: rectos: pp. iii–vii: '*Introduction*'; pp. 3–45: '*Dante's* Vita Nuova'; versos: pp. ii–viii: '*Introduction*'; pp. 2–46: '*Dante's* Vita Nuova'.

Binding: Light blue stiff wrappers with dark blue printing. Front recto: the same as the title page; front verso and back recto and verso: blank. All edges trimmed.

Publication: December 1957. Apparently sold only at the Emerson House, Concord, Mass.

Location: JM.

Note: Reprinted from the plates of the spring and autumn 1957 *Harvard Library Bulletin* (see E 291–292). Preceded by an offprint from the *Bulletin,* not for sale. The offprint contains the two parts stapled together in a stiff wrapper, reading 'Emerson's Translation of Dante's | *Vita Nuova* | BY | J. CHESLEY MATHEWS | OFFPRINT FROM | HARVARD LIBRARY BULLETIN | VOLUME XI, NUMBERS 2 AND 3 | SPRING AND AUTUMN 1957' (Collection of J. Chesley Mathews). The separately reprinted pamphlet described as A 65.1 adds a title page and repaginates the text.

A 65.2.a
Second edition, first printing (1960)

Dante's *Vita Nuova*

Translated by
Ralph Waldo Emerson

Edited and annotated by
J. Chesley Mathews

University of North Carolina
Studies in Comparative Literature
Chapel Hill, 1960

A 65.2.a: $10^{1}/_{8}''$ × $6^{3}/_{4}''$

[a–b] [i–iv] v–xiii [xiv] 1–46 [47–49] 50–62 [63] 64–145 [146–148]

$[1-9^8 \ 10^{10}]$

Contents: p. a: blank; p. b: partial list of books in *Studies in Comparative Literature Series;* p. i: title page; p. ii: copyright page; p. iii: contents; p. iv: blank; pp. v–xiii: "Introduction"; p. xiv: blank; double leaf inserted with facsimiles of the manuscript on all four pages; pp. 1–46: text; pp. 47–48: blank; pp. 49–62: "Notes for the Introduction"; pp. 63–145: "Notes for the Translation"; pp. 146–148: blank.

Typography and paper: $7^{3}/_{4}''$ ($7^{3}/_{8}''$) × $4^{7}/_{8}''$; wove paper, watermarked 'WARREN'S | OLDE STYLE'; 39 lines per page. Running heads: rectos: pp. vii–xiii: '*Introduction*'; pp. 3–45: '*Dante's* Vita Nuova'; pp. 51–61: 'NOTES FOR THE INTRODUCTION'; pp. 65–145: 'NOTES FOR THE TRANSLATION'; versos: pp. vi–xii: '*Introduction*'; pp. 2–46: '*Dante's* Vita Nuova'; pp. 50–62: 'NOTES FOR THE INTRODUCTION'; pp. 64–144: 'NOTES FOR THE TRANSLATION'.

Binding: Medium green V cloth (smooth). Front cover: goldstamped 'Emerson's Translation of the | Vita Nuova | [rule] | Edited and Annotated by | J. Chesley Mathews'; back cover: blank; spine: goldstamped from top to bottom 'EMERSON'S TRANSLA-TION OF THE VITA NUOVA'. White endpapers. All edges trimmed.

Publication: Deposit copy: DLC (8 March 1960). Price, $7.00.

Locations: DLC, JM, LNHT, NcU, NjP, ViU.

Note one: *University of North Carolina Studies in Comparative Literature,* vol. 26.

Note two: The introduction and text are unchanged, but the annotations are greatly expanded and are placed at the end of the book.

A 65.2.b
Second edition, second printing [1966]

New York: Johnson Reprint Corporation; London: Johnson Reprint Company Limited, [1966].

Facsimile reprinting. Price, $8.00. *Location:* JM.

A 66 THE EARLY LECTURES OF RALPH WALDO EMERSON

VOLUME I

A 66.I.1.a
First edition, first printing (1959)

THE EARLY LECTURES OF

Ralph Waldo Emerson

VOLUME I

1 8 3 3 - 1 8 3 6

Edited by

Stephen E. Whicher and Robert E. Spiller

HARVARD UNIVERSITY PRESS

Cambridge, Massachusetts

1 9 5 9

A 66.I.1.a: $9^3/_{16}$″ × $6^1/_{16}$″; Emerson's name is in blue [i–iv] v–vii [viii] ix–x [xi–xii] xiii–xxvii [xxviii–xxx] 1–83 [84–86] 87–90 [91–92] 93–201 [202–204] 205–385 [386–388] 389–391 [392] 393–545 [546]

[1^8 $2-18^{16}$ 19^8] An eight-leaf gathering of coated paper, with photographs of manuscript pages, is inserted after p. 386.

Contents: p. i: '*THE EARLY LECTURES OF* | Ralph Waldo Emerson | VOLUME I | 1833–1836'; p. ii: blank; p. iii: title page; p. iv: copyright page; pp. v–vii: '*Preface*'; p. viii: blank; pp. ix–x: '*CONTENTS*'; p. xi: '*INTRODUCTION*'; p. xii: blank; pp. xiii–xxvii: '*Introduction*'; p. xxviii: blank; p. xxix: 'I | *SCIENCE*'; p. xxx: blank; pp. 1–4: introduction to the "Science" series; pp. 5–26: "The Uses of Natural History"; pp. 27–49: "On the Relation of Man to the Globe"; pp. 50–68: "Water"; pp. 69–83: "The Naturalist"; p. 84: blank; p. 85: 'II | *ITALY*'; p. 86: blank; pp. 87–88: introduction to "Italy" series; pp. 89–90: "Italy"; p. 91: 'III | *BIOGRAPHY*'; p. 92: blank; pp. 93–96: introduction to the "Biography" series; p. 97: "[Introduction]"; pp. 98–117: "Michel Angelo Buonaroti"; pp. 118–143: "Martin Luther"; pp. 144–163: "John Milton"; pp. 164–182: "George Fox"; pp. 183–201: "Edmund Burke"; p. 202: blank; p. 203: 'IV | *ENGLISH LITERATURE*'; p. 204: blank; pp. 205–208: introduction to the "English Literature" series; pp. 209–216: "On the Best Mode of Inspiring a Correct Taste in English Literature"; pp. 217–232: "English Literature: Introductory"; pp. 233–252: "Permanent Traits of the English National Genius"; pp. 253–268: "The Age of Fable"; pp. 269–286: "Chaucer"; pp. 287–304: "Shakspear [First Lecture]"; pp. 305–319: "Shakspear [Second Lecture]"; pp. 320–336: "Lord Bacon"; pp. 337–355: "Ben Jonson, Herrick, Herbert, Wotton"; pp. 356–370: "Ethical Writers"; pp. 371–385: "Modern Aspects of Letters"; p. 386: blank; p. 387: '*Bibliography* | *Textual Notes* | *Index*'; p. 388: blank; pp. 389–391: '*Bibliography of Principal Sources*'; p. 392: blank; pp. 393–536: '*Textual Notes and Variant Passages*'; pp. 537–545: '*Index*'; p. 546: blank.

Lectures: All are first appearances of these texts, although Emerson may have published different versions elsewhere (see index): "The Use of Natural History," "On the Relation of Man to the Globe," "Water," "The Naturalist," "Italy," "Michel Angelo Buonaroti," "Martin Luther," "John Milton," "George Fox," "Edmund Burke," "On the Best Mode of Inspiring a Correct Taste in English Literature," "English Literature: Introductory," "Permanent Traits of the English National Genius," "The Age of Fable,"

"Chaucer," "Shakspear [First Lecture]," "Shakspear [Second Lecture]," "Lord Bacon," "Ben Jonson, Herrick, Herbert, Wotton," "Ethical Writers," "Modern Aspects of Letters."

Typography and paper: 7″ (6³/₄″) × 4⁵/₁₆″; wove paper, with 'WARREN'S | OLDE STYLE' watermark; 37 lines per page. Running heads: rectos: p. vii: *'PREFACE'*; pp. xv–xxvii: *'INTRODUCTION'*; pp. 3, 7–25, 29–67, 71–83, 95, 99–181, 185–201, 207, 211–215, 219–231, 235–251, 255–267, 271–285, 289–303, 307–335, 339–369, 373–385: titles of lecture series; p. 391: *'BIBLIOGRAPHY'*; pp. 395–535: titles of lectures; pp. 539–545: *'INDEX'*; versos: p. vi: *'PREFACE'*; p. x: *'CONTENTS'*; pp. xiv–xxvi: *'INTRODUCTION'*; pp. 2–48, 52–82, 88–90, 94–96, 100–116, 120–142, 146–162, 166–200, 206–318, 322–354, 358–384: titles of lectures; p. 390: *'BIBLIOGRA-PHY'*; pp. 394–536: *'TEXTUAL NOTES AND VARIANT PASSAGES'*; pp. 538–544: *'IN-DEX'*.

Binding: Light greenish blue very coarse hair-vein paper covered boards with dark purplish blue buckram shelfback. Front and back covers: blank; spine: goldstamped *'THE | EARLY | LECTURES | OF* | Ralph | Waldo | Emerson | [leaf design] | [leaf design] | 1833–1836 | Whicher | [rule] | Spiller | HARVARD | UNIVERSITY | PRESS'. Deep yellow endpapers. All edges trimmed.

Dust jacket: Front cover: on very yellow background '[white] *THE EARLY LECTURES OF* | Ralph Waldo Emerson | [two lines in white] VOLUME I | 1833–1836 | [portrait of Emerson within a double-rule frame] | EDITED BY | Stephen E. Whicher ,and Robert E. Spiller'; back cover: blurbs for three Harvard University Press books by Perry Miller on white background; spine: on very yellow background the same lettering as on the binding, except the first four lines are in white; front flap: description of volume; back flap: description of volume continued and information on editors.

Publication: 2,000 copies printed. Copyright, 13 November 1959. Published 26 October 1959. Price, $12.50. Deposit copy: DLC (19 November 1959).

Locations: DLC, JM (dust jacket), ScU.

A 66.I.1.b
First edition, second printing (1961)

Title page is the same as in A 66.I.1.a, except: '1961' is substituted for '1959'; copyright page has *'Second printing'*. *Location:* InU.

A 66.I.1.c
First edition, third printing (1966)

Title page is the same as in A 66.I.1.a, except: '1966' is substituted for '1959' and all printing is black; copyright page has *'Third printing'*. *Location:* InU.

VOLUME II

A 66.II.1
First edition, only printing (1964)

Title page is the same as in A 66.I.1.a, except: 'II | 1836–1838 | *Edited by* | Stephen E. Whicher   Robert E. Spiller | Wallace E. Williams | [publisher's logo] | THE BELKNAP PRESS | OF HARVARD UNIVERSITY PRESS | *Cambridge, Massachusetts* | 1964'. Emerson's name and publisher's logo are in blue.

THE EARLY LECTURES OF
Ralph Waldo Emerson

VOLUME I
1833-1836

EDITED BY

Stephen E. Whicher and Robert E. Spiller

The Early Lectures of Ralph Waldo Emerson

Volume I 1833-1836

Whicher
Spiller

HARVARD UNIVERSITY PRESS

THE TRANSCENDENTALISTS
An Anthology
Edited by Perry Miller

THE NEW ENGLAND MIND
The Seventeenth Century
By Perry Miller

THE NEW ENGLAND MIND
From Colony to Province
By Perry Miller

HARVARD UNIVERSITY PRESS · CAMBRIDGE 38, MASS.

(continued from front flap)

HARVARD UNIVERSITY PRESS
Cambridge 38, Massachusetts

Dust jacket for A 66.I.1.a

[i–iv] v–viii [ix–x] xi–xx [xxi–xxii] 1–188 [189–190] 191–204 [205–206] 207–364 [365–366] 367–494 [495–498]

[1⁸ 2–11¹⁶ 12²⁰ 13–16¹⁶ 17⁸] A four-leaf gathering of coated paper, with an engraving of the Masonic Temple and photographs of manuscript pages, is inserted after p. 266.

Contents: p. i: half title, the same as in A 66.I.1.a, except 'II | 1836–1838'; p. ii: blank; p. iii: title page; p. iv: copyright page; pp. v–vi: '*Preface*'; pp. vii–viii: '*CONTENTS*'; p. ix: '*INTRODUCTION*'; p. x: blank; pp. xi–xx: '*Introduction*'; p. xxi: 'I | *THE PHILOSOPHY* | *OF HISTORY* | [six lines, reproducing a newspaper notice for the series]'; p. xxii: blank; pp. 1–6: introduction to "The Philosophy of History" series; pp. 7–21: "Introductory"; pp. 22–40: "Humanity of Science"; pp. 41–54: "Art"; pp. 55–68: "Literature"; pp. 69–82: "Politics"; pp. 83–97: "Religion"; pp. 98–112: "Society"; pp. 113–128: "Trades and Professions"; pp. 129–142: "Manners"; pp. 143–156: "Ethics"; pp. 157–172: "The Present Age"; pp. 173–188: "The Individual"; p. 189: 'II | *ADDRESS ON EDUCATION* | [23 lines, reproducing a newspaper notice for the lecture]'; p. 190: blank; pp. 191–193: introduction to the lecture; pp. 194–204: "Address on Education"; p. 205: 'III | *HUMAN CULTURE* | [eight lines, reproducing a newspaper notice of the series]'; p. 206: blank; pp. 207–212: introduction to the "Human Culture" series; pp. 213–229: "Introductory"; pp. 230–245: "Doctrine of the Hands"; pp. 246–261: "The Head"; pp. 262–277: "The Eye and Ear"; pp. 278–294: "The Heart"; pp. 295–309: "Being and Seeming"; pp. 310–326: "Prudence"; pp. 327–339: "Heroism"; pp. 340–356: "Holiness"; pp. 357–364: "General Views"; p. 365: '*Bibliography* | *Textual Notes* | *Index*'; p. 366: blank; pp. 367–368: '*Bibliography of Principal Sources*'; pp. 369–482: '*Textual Notes and Variant Passages*'; pp. 483–494: '*Index*'; pp. 495–498: blank.

Lectures: All are first appearances of these texts, although Emerson may have published different versions elsewhere (see index): "Introductory" lecture to "The Philosophy of History" series, "Humanity of Science," "Art," "Literature," "Politics," "Religion," "Society," "Trades and Professions," "Manners," "Ethics," "The Present Age," "The Individual," "Address on Education," "Introductory" to "Human Culture" series, "Doctrine of the Hands," "The Head," "The Eye and Ear," "The Heart," "Being and Seeming," "Prudence," "Heroism," "Holiness," "General Views."

Typography and paper: The same as in A 66.I.1.a. Running heads: rectos: pp. xiii–xix: '*INTRODUCTION*'; pp. 3–5, 9–39, 43–53, 57–67, 71–81, 85–111, 115–127, 131–141, 145–155, 159–171, 175–187, 193–203, 209–211, 215–293, 297–325, 329–355, 359–363: titles of lecture series; pp. 371–481: titles of lectures; pp. 485–493: '*INDEX*'; versos: p. vi: '*PREFACE*'; p. viii: '*CONTENTS*'; pp. xii–xx: '*INTRODUCTION*'; pp. 2–20, 24–96, 100–188, 192, 196–204, 208–228, 232–244, 248–260, 264–276, 280–308, 312–338, 342–364: titles of lectures; p. 368: '*BIBLIOGRAPHY*'; pp. 370–482: '*TEXTUAL NOTES AND VARIANT PASSAGES*'; pp. 484–494: '*INDEX*'.

Binding: The same as for A 66.I.1.a, except: spine has '[leaf design] II [leaf design] | 1836–1838 | Whicher | [rule] | Spiller | [rule] | Williams'.

Dust jacket: The same as for A 66.I.1.a, except: front cover: medium grayish blue background and 'II | 1836–1838 | [engraving of Masonic Temple, Boston, within a double-rule frame] | EDITED BY | Stephen E. Whicher   Robert E. Spiller | Wallace E. Williams'; back cover: blurbs for vols. I–V of *JMN;* spine: medium grayish blue background with the same lettering as on the spine, with the first four lines in white; front flap: description of volume and information on editors; back flap: blurbs for A 66.I.1.a.

Publication: 2,000 copies printed. Published 21 December 1964. Copyright, 14 December 1964. Deposit copy: DLC (17 December 1964). Price, $12.50.

Locations: DLC, JM (dust jacket), ScU.

VOLUME III

A 66.III.1
First edition, only printing (1972)

Title page is the same as in A 66.I.a, except 'III | 1838–1842 | *Edited by* | Robert E. Spiller and Wallace E. Williams'; '1972' is substituted for '1959'.

[i–iv] v–vi [vii] viii [ix–x] xi–xxiv [xxv–xxvi] 1–171 [172–174] 175–315 [316–318] 319–331 [332–334] 335–345 [346] 347–382 [383–384] 385–525 [526] 527–590

[$1–18^{16}$ 19^4 20^{16}] A four-leaf gathering of coated paper, with a map of central Concord and photographs of manuscript pages, is inserted after p. 326.

Contents: p. i: half title, the same as in A 66.I.1.a, except '*The Early Lectures of*' and 'III | 1838–1842'; p. ii: blank; p. iii: title page; p. iv: copyright page; pp. v–vi: '*Preface*'; pp. vii–viii: '*Contents*'; p. ix: '*INTRODUCTION* '; p. x: blank; pp. xi–xxiv: '*Introduction*'; p. xxv: 'I | *HUMAN LIFE* | [nine lines, reproducing a newspaper notice of the series]'; p. xxvi: blank; pp. 1–4: introduction to "Human Life" series; pp. 5–22: "Doctrine of the Soul"; pp. 23–33: "Home"; pp. 34–50: "The School"; pp. 51–67: "Love"; pp. 68–84: "Genius"; pp. 85–102: "The Protest"; pp. 103–120: "Tragedy"; pp. 121–137: "Comedy"; pp. 138–150: "Duty"; pp. 151–171: "Demonology"; p. 172: blank; p. 173: 'II | *THE PRESENT AGE* | [nine lines, reproducing a newspaper notice of the series]'; p. 174: blank; pp. 175–184: introduction to "The Present Age" series; pp. 185–201: "Introductory"; pp. 202–223: "Literature [First Lecture]"; pp. 224–237: "Literature [Second Lecture]"; pp. 238–247: "Politics"; pp. 248–255: "Private Life"; pp. 256–270: "Reforms"; pp. 271–285: "Religion"; pp. 286–301: "Education"; pp. 302–315: "Tendencies"; p. 316: blank; p. 317: 'III | *ADDRESS TO THE PEOPLE* | *OF EAST LEXINGTON*'; p. 318: blank; pp. 319–326: introduction to the address; pp. 327–331: "Address to the People of East Lexington"; p. 332: blank; p. 333: 'IV | *THE TIMES* | [10 lines, reproducing a newspaper notice of the series]'; p. 334: blank; pp. 335–345: introduction to "The Times" series; p. 346: blank; pp. 347–365: "The Poet"; pp. 366–382: "Prospects"; p. 383: '*Bibliography* | *Textual Notes* | *Index*'; p. 384: blank; pp. 385–386: '*Bibliography and Principal Sources*'; pp. 387–525: '*Textual Notes and Variant Passages*'; p. 526: blank; pp. 527–590: '*Index*'.

Lectures: All are first appearances of these texts, although Emerson may have published different versions elsewhere (see index): "Doctrine of the Soul," "Home," "The School," "Love," "Genius," "The Protest," "Tragedy," "Comedy," "Duty," "Demonology," "Introductory" to "The Present Age" series, "Literature [First Lecture]," "Literature [Second Lecture]," "Politics," "Private Life," "Reforms," "Religion," "Education," "Tendencies," "Address to the People of East Lexington," "The Poet," "Prospects."

Typography and paper: The same as in A 66.I.1.a, except: oval Harvard University Press seal watermark. Running heads: rectos: pp. xiii–xxiii: '*INTRODUCTION*'; pp. 3, 7–21, 25–49, 53–83, 87–101, 105–119, 123–149, 153–171, 177–183, 187–269, 273–315, 321–325, 329–331, 337–345, 349–381: titles of lecture series; pp. 389–525: titles of lectures; pp. 529–589: '*INDEX*'; versos: p. vi: '*PREFACE*'; p. viii: '*CONTENTS*'; pp. xii–xxiv: '*INTRODUCTION*'; pp. 2–32, 36–66, 70–136, 140–170, 176–200, 204–222, 226–236, 240–246, 250–254, 258–284, 288–300, 304–314, 320–330, 336–344, 348–364, 368–382: titles of lectures; p. 386: '*BIBLIOGRAPHY*'; pp. 388–524: '*TEXTUAL NOTES AND VARIANT PASSAGES*'; pp. 528–590: '*INDEX*'.

Binding: The same as for A 66.I.1.a, except: spine has '[leaf design] III [leaf design] | 1838–1842 | Spiller | [rule] | Williams | BELKNAP | PRESS | HARVARD'.

Dust jacket: The same as for A 66.I.1.a, except: front cover: deep red background and 'III | 1838–1842 | [map of central Concord within a double-rule frame] | EDITED BY | Robert E. Spiller and Wallace E. Williams'; back cover: blurbs for A 66.II.1.a; spine: deep red background and the same lettering as on the spine, with the first four lines in white; front flap: description of volume and information on editors; back flap: blurbs for A 66.I.1.a.

Publication: 2,500 copies printed. Published 26 May 1972. Copyright, 31 March 1972. Price, $20.00. Deposit copy: DLC (6 April 1972).

Locations: DLC, JM (dust jacket), ScU.

A 67 THE JOURNALS AND MISCELLANEOUS NOTEBOOKS OF RALPH WALDO EMERSON

VOLUME I

A 67.I.1.a
First edition, first printing (1960)

The Journals and
Miscellaneous Notebooks

of

RALPH WALDO EMERSON

EDITED BY

WILLIAM H. GILMAN   ALFRED R. FERGUSON
GEORGE P. CLARK   MERRELL R. DAVIS

THE BELKNAP PRESS
OF HARVARD UNIVERSITY PRESS
Cambridge, Massachusetts
1 9 6 0

A 67.I.1.a: $9^{3}/_{16}''$ × $6^{1}/_{8}''$

[i–vi] vii–xi [xii] xiii–xliii [xliv] xlv–l [1–2] 3–158 [159–160] 161–399 [400–402] 403–417 [418] 419–430

[1^8 $2–15^{16}$ 16^8]   A six-leaf gathering of coated paper, with photographs of manuscript pages, is inserted after p. 158.

Contents: p. i: 'The Journals and | Miscellaneous Notebooks | of | RALPH WALDO EMERSON | VOLUME I | 1819–1822'; p. ii: blank; inserted leaf of coated paper, with photograph of Emerson's manuscript journals and miscellaneous notebooks printed on verso; p. iii: title page; p. iv: copyright page; p. v: *"This edition | of his grandfather's journals | is dedicated to | EDWARD WALDO FORBES'*; p. vi: blank; pp. vii–viii: *'Preface'*; pp. ix–x: contents; p. xi: *'Illustrations'*; p. xii: blank; pp. xiii–xliii: *'Introduction'*; pp. xlv–l: *'Foreword to Volume I'*; p. 1: 'PART ONE | The Journals'; p. 2: blank; pp. 3–32: "Wide World 1"; pp. 33–58: "Wide World 2"; pp. 59–90: "Wide World 3"; pp. 91–113: "Wide World 4"; pp. 114–158: "Wide World 6"; p. 159: 'PART TWO | Miscellaneous Notebooks'; p. 160: blank; pp. 161–205: "College Theme Book"; pp. 206–248: "No. XVII"; pp. 249–357: "No. XVIII"; pp. 358–394: "The Universe"; pp. 395–399: "Catalogue of Books Read"; p. 400: blank; p. 401: *'Editorial Title List | Alphabetical Title List | Textual Notes | Index '*; p. 402: blank; pp. 403–412: "Editorial Title List"; pp. 413–415: "Alphabetical Title List with Houghton Number"; pp. 416–417: "Textual Notes"; p. 418: blank; pp. 419–430: "Index".

Typography and paper: $6^7/8''$ ($6^{11}/_{16}''$) × $4^5/_{16}''$; wove paper; 37 lines per page. Running heads: rectos: pp. xv–xxxiii: 'EMERSON IN HIS JOURNALS'; p. xxxv: 'THE MANUSCRIPTS'; pp. xxxvii–xli: 'THE EDITORIAL METHOD'; p. xliii: 'THE SOURCE OF THE TEXT'; p. xlvii: 'CHRONOLOGY'; p. xlix: 'SYMBOLS AND ABBREVIATIONS'; pp. 5–31, 33–57, 61–89, 93–157: dates and titles of journal volumes; pp. 163–247, 251–393, 397–399: dates and titles of notebook volumes; pp. 405–411: 'EDITORIAL TITLE LIST'; p. 415: 'ALPHABETICAL TITLE LIST'; p. 417: 'TEXTUAL NOTES'; pp. 421–429: 'INDEX'; versos: p. viii: 'PREFACE'; p. x: 'CONTENTS'; pp. xiv–xlii: 'INTRODUCTION'; pp. xlvi–l: 'FOREWORD TO VOLUME I'; pp. 4–112, 116–158: 'JOURNALS OF RALPH WALDO EMERSON' and abbreviations for journal volumes; pp. 162–204, 208–356, 360–398: 'NOTEBOOKS OF RALPH WALDO EMERSON' and abbreviations for notebook volumes; pp. 404–412: 'EDITORIAL TITLE LIST'; p. 414: 'ALPHABETICAL TITLE LIST'; pp. 420–430: 'INDEX'.

Binding: Light green B cloth (linen) with dark green buckram shelfback. Front and back covers: blank; spine: goldstamped 'The | Journals | of | RALPH | WALDO |

EMERSON | GILMAN | FERGUSON | CLARK | DAVIS | I | 1819–1822 | [publisher's logo] | BELKNAP | PRESS | HARVARD'. Light green endpapers. All edges trimmed.

Dust jacket: Front cover: '[five lines on gray yellow green background] [two lines in gray purplish blue] *The Journals | and Miscellaneous Notebooks of* | [three lines in white] RALPH | WALDO | EMERSON | [three lines in white on gray purplish blue background] *Edited by* | WILLIAM H. GILMAN; ALFRED R. FERGUSON | GEORGE P. CLARK; MERRELL R. DAVIS'; back cover: blurb for *Early Lectures*, vol. I, in gray purplish blue lettering on white background; spine: '[11 lines on gray yellow green background] [three lines in gray purplish blue] *The | Journals | of* | [four lines in white] RALPH | WALDO | EMER- | SON | [four lines in gray purplish blue] GILMAN | FERGU- SON | CLARK | DAVIS | [six lines in white on gray purplish blue background] VOLUME | I | 1819–1822 | *Belknap | Press* | HARVARD'; front flap: description of volume; back flap: description of volume continued and information on the editors.

Publication: Published 30 September 1960. Copyright, 26 September 1960. Deposit copies: DLC (30 September 1960), BL (16 January 1961). Price, $10.00.

Locations: BL, DLC, ScU, VtU (dust jacket).

Note: For an earlier, incomplete edition, see A 52.

A 67.I.1.b
First edition, second printing [1968]

The same as A 67.I.1.a, except: the title page is undated; the title leaf verso has 'Second printing, 1968'; the collation is different; the advertisements on the dust jacket have been changed, and "*Second Printing*" is on the front flap. Also, a "Note to the Second Printing," listing the page numbers on which changes have been made, is on p. viii. *Location:* JM (dust jacket).

VOLUME II

A 67.II.1
First edition, only printing (1961)

Title page is the same as in A 67.I.1.a, except 'II | 1822–1826 | EDITED BY | WILLIAM H. GILMAN   ALFRED R. FERGUSON | MERRELL R. DAVIS'; '1961' is substituted for '1960'.

[i–iv] v–xvi [1–2] 3–351 [352–354] 355–420 [421–422] 423–425 [426] 427–438 [439–440]

[1^8 2–14^{16} 15^{12}] A two-leaf gathering of coated paper, with photographs of manuscript pages, is inserted after p. 352.

Contents: p. i: '*The Journals and | Miscellaneous Notebooks | of* | RALPH WALDO EMERSON | [leaf design] GENERAL EDITORS [leaf design] | WILLIAM H. GILMAN   ALFRED R. FERGUSON | MERRELL R. DAVIS | MERTON M. SEALTS, JR.   HARRISON HAYFORD'; p. ii: blank; p. iii: title page; p. iv: copyright page; pp. v– vi: '*Preface*'; pp. vii–viii: '*Merrell Rees Davis*'; p. ix: 'Contents'; p. x: '*Illustrations*'; pp. xi–xvi: '*Foreword to Volume II*'; p. 1: 'PART ONE | *The Journals*'; p. 2: blank; pp. 3–39: "Wide World 7"; pp. 40–73: "Wide World 8"; pp. 74–103: "Wide World 9"; pp. 104– 143: "Wide World 10"; pp. 144–176: "Wide World 11"; pp. 177–186: "Walk to the Connecticut"; pp. 187–213: "Wide World 12"; pp. 214–271: "Wide World XIII"; pp. 272–351: "No. XV"; p. 352: blank; p. 353; 'PART TWO | *Miscellaneous Notebooks*'; p.

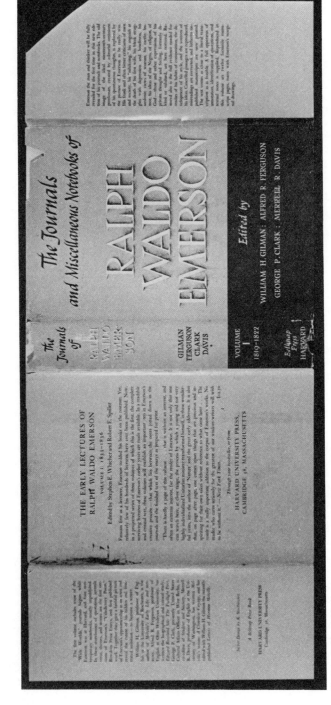

Dust jacket for A 67.1.1.a

354: blank; pp. 355–395: "No. XVIII[A]"; pp. 396–412: "No. XVI"; pp. 413–420: "No. II"; p. 421: *'Textual Notes | Index'*; p. 422: blank; pp. 423–425: *'Textual Notes'*; p. 426: blank; pp. 427–438: *'Index'*; pp. 439–440: blank.

Typography and paper: The same as in A 67.I.1.a. Running heads: rectos: p. xiii: 'THE EARLY JOURNALS: 1822–1826'; p. xv: 'SYMBOLS AND ABBREVIATIONS'; pp. 5–175, 179–185, 189–351: dates and titles of journal volumes; pp. 357–411, 415–419: dates and titles of notebook volumes; p. 425: 'TEXTUAL NOTES'; pp. 429–437: 'INDEX'; versos: p. vi: 'PREFACE'; p. viii: 'MERRELL REES DAVIS'; pp. xii–xvi: 'FORE-WORD TO VOLUME II'; pp. 4–38, 42–72, 76–102, 106–142, 146–212, 216–270, 274–350: 'JOURNALS OF RALPH WALDO EMERSON' and abbreviations for journal volumes; pp. 356–394, 398–420: 'NOTEBOOKS OF RALPH WALDO EMERSON' and abbreviations for notebook volumes; p. 424: 'TEXTUAL NOTES'; pp. 428–438: 'INDEX'.

Binding: The same as for A 67.I.1.a, except: spine has 'GILMAN | FERGUSON | DAVIS | II | 1822–1826'.

Dust jacket: The same as for A 67.I.1.a, except: very deep green replaces gray purplish blue; front cover: *'Edited by* | WILLIAM H. GILMAN; ALFRED R. FERGUSON | MERRELL R. DAVIS | MERTON M. SEALTS; HARRISON HAYFORD' at bottom; spine: 'GILMAN | FERGUSON | DAVIS | SEALTS | HAYFORD' and 'II | 1822–1826'; front flap: description of volume and information on the editors; back flap: blurb for A 67.I.1.a.

Publication: Copyright, 11 September 1961. Deposit copies: DLC (13 September 1961), BL (16 January 1962). Price, $10.00.

Locations   BL, DLC, JM (dust jacket), ScU, VtU.

VOLUME III

A 67.III.1
First edition, only printing (1963)

Title page is the same as in A 67.I.1.a, except 'III | 1826–1832 | EDITED BY WILLIAM H. GILMAN   ALFRED R. FERGUSON'; '1963' is substituted for '1960'.

[i–iv] v–xvii [xviii] [1–2] 3–329 [330–332] 333–375 [376] 377–379 [380] 381–398

[1⁸ 2–13¹⁶ 14⁸]   A two-leaf gathering of coated paper, with photographs of manuscript pages, is inserted after p. 238.

Contents: p. i: half title, the same as in A 67.II.1; p. ii: blank; p. iii: title page; p. iv: copyright page; pp. v–vi: *'Preface'*; p. vii: *'Contents'*; p. viii: *'Illustrations'*; pp. ix–xvii: *'Foreword to Volume III'*; p. xviii: blank; p. 1: 'PART ONE | *The Journals'*; p. 2: blank; pp. 3–41: "Journal 1826"; pp. 42–112: "Journal 1826–1828"; pp. 113–118: "Memo St. Augustine"; pp. 119–158: "Sermons and Journal"; pp. 159–162: "Meredith Village"; pp. 163–202: "Blotting Book Y"; pp. 203–263: "Blotting Book Psi"; pp. 264–329: "Blotting Book III"; p. 330: blank; p. 331: 'PART TWO | *Miscellaneous Notebooks'*; p. 332: blank; pp. 333–337: "Blue Book"; pp. 338–348: "Pocket Diary 1"; pp. 349–358: "Genealogy"; pp. 359–375: "Blotting Book IV"; p. 376: blank; pp. 377–378: *'Textual Notes'*; p. 379: *'Addenda'*; p. 380: blank; pp. 381–398: *'Index'*.

Typography and paper: The same as in A 67.I.1.a, except: oval Harvard University Press seal watermark. Running heads: rectos: pp. xi–xiii: 'THE JOURNALS FROM 1826 TO 1832'; p. xv: 'CHRONOLOGY'; p. xvii: 'SYMBOLS AND ABBREVIATIONS'; pp. 5–111, 115–117, 121–157, 161–201, 205–329: dates and titles of journal volumes; pp. 335–347, 351–357, 361–375: dates and titles of notebook volumes; pp. 383–397:

'INDEX'; versos: p. vi: 'PREFACE'; pp. x–xvi: 'FOREWORD TO VOLUME III'; pp. 4–40, 44–262, 266–328: 'JOURNALS OF RALPH WALDO EMERSON' and abbreviations for journal volumes; pp. 334–336, 340–374: 'NOTEBOOKS OF RALPH WALDO EMERSON' and abbreviations for notebook volumes; p. 378: 'TEXTUAL NOTES'; pp. 382–398: 'INDEX'.

Binding: The same as for A 67.I.1.a, except: spine has "GILMAN | FERGUSON | III | 1826–1832'.

Dust jacket: The same as for A 67.II.1, except: dark red replaces very deep green; back cover: blurbs for A 67.I.1.a and A 67.II.1; spine: 'GILMAN | FERGUSON' and 'III | 1826–1832'; front flap: description of volume and information on editors; back flap: blurbs for *One First Love*.

Publication: Copyright, 9 October 1963. Deposit copies: DLC (15 October 1963), BL (6 January 1964). Price, $10.00.

Locations: BL, DLC, JM (dust jacket), ScU, VtU.

VOLUME IV

A 67.IV.1
First edition, only printing (1964)

Title page is the same as in A67.I.1.a, except 'IV | 1832–1834 | EDITED BY | ALFRED R. FERGUSON'; '1964' is substituted for '1960'.

[i–iv] v–xxi [xxii] [1–2] 3–391 [392–394] 395–438 [439–440] 441–474

[1⁸ 2–15¹⁶ 16–17⁸] A two-leaf gathering of coated paper, with photographs of manuscript pages, is inserted after p. 298.

Contents: p. i: half title, the same as in A 67.II.1; p. ii: blank; p. iii: title page; p. iv: copyright page; pp. v–vi: '*Preface*'; p. vii: '*Contents*'; p. viii: '*Illustrations*'; pp. ix–xxi: '*Foreword to Volume IV*'; p. xxii: blank; p. 1: 'PART ONE | *The Journals*'; p. 2: blank; pp. 3–101: "Q"; pp. 102–133: "Sicily"; pp. 134–162: "Italy"; pp. 163–208: "Italy and France"; pp. 209–235: "Scotland and England"; pp. 236–248: "Sea 1833"; pp. 249–387: "A"; pp. 388–391: "Maine"; p. 392: blank; p. 393: 'PART TWO | *Miscellaneous Notebooks*'; p. 394: blank; pp. 395–419: "France and England"; pp. 420–426: "Pocket Diary 2"; pp. 427–438: "Composition"; p. 439: '*Appendix* | *Textual Notes* | *Index*'; p. 440: blank; pp. 441–444: '*Appendix*'; pp. 445–446: 'Textual Notes'; pp. 447–474: '*Index*'.

Typography and paper: The same as in A 67.III.1. Running heads: rectos: pp. xi–xv: 'THE JOURNALS FROM 1832 THROUGH 1834'; pp. xvii–xix: 'CHRONOLOGY'; p. xxi: 'SYMBOLS AND ABBREVIATIONS'; pp. 5–161, 165–207, 211–247, 251–391: dates and titles of journal volumes; pp. 397–425, 429–437: dates and titles of notebook volumes; p. 443: 'APPENDIX'; pp. 449–473: 'INDEX'; versos: p. vi: 'PREFACE'; pp. x–xx: 'FOREWORD TO VOLUME IV'; pp. 4–100, 104–132, 136–234, 238–386, 390: 'JOURNALS OF RALPH WALDO EMERSON' and abbreviations for journal volumes; pp. 396–418, 424–438: 'NOTEBOOKS OF RALPH WALDO EMERSON' and abbreviations for notebook volumes; pp. 442–444: 'APPENDIX'; p. 446: 'TEXTUAL NOTES'; pp. 448–474: 'INDEX'.

Binding: The same as for A 67.I.1.a, except: spine has 'FERGUSON | IV | 1832–1834'.

Dust jacket: The same as for A 67.III.1, except: deep violet replaces dark red; spine: 'FERGUSON' and 'IV | 1832–1834'; front flap: description of volume and information on editor; back flap: blurbs for A 67.III.1.

Publication: Copyright, 9 July 1964. Deposit copies: DLC (20 July 1964), BL (26 October 1964). Price, $12.50.

Locations: BL, DLC, JM (dust jacket), ScU, VtU.

VOLUME V

A 67.V.1
First edition, only printing (1965)

Title page is the same as in A 67.I.1.a, except 'V | 1835–1838 | EDITED BY | MERTON M. SEALTS, JR.'; '1965' is substituted for '1960'.

[a–b] [i–iv] v–xx [1–2] 3–509 [510] 511 [512] 513–542 [543–546]

[1^8 2–15^{16} 16^{12} 17–18^{16} 19^8] A two-leaf gathering of coated paper, with photographs of manuscript pages, is inserted after p. 330.

Contents: pp. a–b: blank; p. i: half title, the same as in A 67.II.1; p. ii: blank; p. iii: title page; p. iv: copyright page; pp. v–vi: '*Preface*'; p. vii: '*Contents*'; p. viii: '*Illustrations*'; pp. ix–xx: '*Foreword to Volume V*'; p. 1: '*The Journals*'; p. 2: blank; pp. 3–268: "B"; pp. 269–276: "RO Mind"; pp. 277–509: "C"; p. 510: blank; p. 511: '*Textual Notes*'; p. 512: blank; pp. 513–542: '*Index*'; pp. 543–546: blank.

Typography and paper: The same as in A 67.III.1. Running heads: rectos: pp. xi–xv: 'THE JOURNALS FROM 1835 TO 1838'; p. xvii: 'CHRONOLOGY'; p. xix: 'SYMBOLS AND ABBREVIATIONS'; pp. 5–267, 271–275, 279–509: dates and titles of journal volumes; pp. 515–541: 'INDEX'; versos: p. vi: 'PREFACE'; pp. x–xviii: 'FOREWORD TO VOLUME V'; pp. 4–508: 'JOURNALS OF RALPH WALDO EMERSON' and abbreviations for journal volumes; pp. 514–542: 'INDEX'.

Binding: The same as for A 67.I.1.a, except: spine has 'SEALTS | V | 1835–1838'.

Dust jacket: The same as for A 67.IV.1, except: dark blue replaces dark violet; back cover: blurbs for A 67.I–IV; spine: 'SEALTS' and 'V | 1835–1838'; front flap: description of volume and information on editor; back flap: description of *Early Lectures,* vol. II.

Publication: Copyright, 24 June 1965. Deposit copies: DLC (28 June 1965), BL (3 December 1965). Price, $12.50.

Locations: BL, DLC, JM (dust jacket), ScU, VtU.

VOLUME VI

A 67.VI.1
First edition, only printing (1966)

Title page is the same as in A 67.I.1.a, except 'VI | 1824–1838 | EDITED BY | RALPH H. ORTH'; '1966' is substituted for '1960'.

[a–b] [i–iv] v [vi] vii–xxii [1–2] 3–399 [400] 401 [402] 403–422 [423–424]

[1^8 2–14^{16} 15^8] A two-leaf gathering of coated paper, with photographs of manuscript pages, is inserted after p. 218.

Contents: pp. a–b: blank; p. i: half title, the same as in A 67.II.1; p. ii: blank; p. iii: title page; p. iv: copyright page; p. v: *'Preface'*; p. vi: blank; p. vii: *'Contents'*; p. viii: *'Illustrations'*; pp. ix–xxii: *'Foreword to Volume VI'*; p.1: *'Miscellaneous Notebooks'*; p. 2: blank; pp. 3–10: "Collectanea"; pp. 11–57: "Blotting Book I"; pp. 58–101: "Blotting Book II"; pp. 102–114: "Blotting Book IV[A]"; pp. 115–234: "Encyclopedia"; pp. 235–254: "Notebook 1833"; pp. 255–286: "Charles C. Emerson"; pp. 287–316: "Z"; pp. 317–399: "T"; p. 400: blank; p. 401: *'Textual Notes'*; p. 402: blank; pp. 403–422: *'Index'*; pp. 423–424: blank.

Typography and paper: The same as in A 67.III.1. Running heads: rectos: pp. xi–xvii: 'THE NOTEBOOKS FROM 1824 TO 1838'; p. xix: 'CHRONOLOGY'; p. xxi: 'SYMBOLS AND ABBREVIATIONS'; pp. 5–9, 13–113, 117–233, 237–253, 257–285, 289–315, 319–399: dates and titles of notebook volumes; pp. 405–421: 'INDEX'; versos: pp. x–xxii: 'FOREWORD TO VOLUME VI'; pp. 4–56, 60–100, 104–398: 'NOTEBOOKS OF RALPH WALDO EMERSON' and abbreviations for notebook volumes; pp. 404–422: 'INDEX'.

Binding: The same as for A 67.I.1.a, except: spine has 'ORTH | VI | 1824–1838'.

Dust jacket: The same as for A 67.V.1, except: medium olive replaces dark blue; spine: 'ORTH' and 'VI | 1824–1838'; front flap: description of volume and information on editor; back flap: blurbs for A 67.V.1.

Publication: Copyright, 31 October 1966. Deposit copies: DLC (9 November 1966), BL (30 January 1967). Price, $12.00.

Locations: BL, DLC, JM (dust jacket), ScU, VtU.

VOLUME VII

A 67.VII.1
First edition, only printing (1969)

Title page is the same as in A 67.I.1.a, except 'VII | 1838–1842 | EDITED BY | A. W. PLUMSTEAD HARRISON HAYFORD'; '1969' is substituted for '1960'.

[i–iv] v–xxiii [xxiv] [1–2] 3–547 [548] 549–575 [576]

[1^8 2–15^{16} 16^{12} 17–19^{16} 20^8]   A two-leaf gathering of coated paper, with photographs of manuscript pages, is inserted after p. 312.

Contents: p. i: half title, the same as in A 67.II.1, except 'WILLIAM H. GILMAN   *Chief Editor* | ALFRED R. FERGUSON   *Senior Editor* | HARRISON HAYFORD   RALPH H. ORTH | J. E. PARSONS   A. W. PLUMSTEAD | *Editors'*; p. ii: blank; p. iii: title page; p. iv: copyright page; pp. v–vi: *'Preface'*; p. vii: *'Contents'*; p. viii: *'Illustrations'*; pp. ix–xxiii: *'Foreword to Volume VII'*; p. xxiv: blank; p. 1: *'The Journals'*; p. 2: blank; pp. 3–262: "D"; pp. 263–484: "E"; pp. 485–547: "F 2"; p. 548: blank; pp. 549–550: *'Textual Notes'*; pp. 551–575: *'Index'*; p. 576: blank.

Typography and paper: The same as in A 67.III.1. Running heads: rectos: pp. xi–xvii: 'THE JOURNALS FROM 1838 TO 1842'; p. xix: 'CHRONOLOGY'; pp. xxi–xxiii: 'SYMBOLS AND ABBREVIATIONS'; pp. 5–261, 265–483, 487–547: dates and titles of journal volumes; pp. 553–575: 'INDEX'; versos: p. vi: 'PREFACE'; pp. x–xxii: 'FOREWORD TO VOLUME VII'; pp. 4–546: 'JOURNALS OF RALPH WALDO EMERSON' and abbreviations for journal volumes; p. 550: 'TEXTUAL NOTES'; pp. 552–574: 'INDEX'.

Binding: The same as for A 67.I.1.a, except: spine has 'PLUMSTEAD | HAYFORD | VII | 1838–1842'.

Dust jacket: The same as for A 67.VI.1, except: deep brown replaces medium olive; front cover: 'WILLIAM H. GILMAN CHIEF EDITOR | ALFRED R. FERGUSON SENIOR EDITOR | HARRISON HAYFORD RALPH H. ORTH | J. E. PARSONS A. W. PLUM-STEAD | EDITORS'; back cover: blurbs for A 67.I–VI; spine: 'PLUMSTEAD | AND | HAYFORD' and 'VII | 1838–1842'; front flap: description of volume; back flap: description of volume continued and information on editors.

Publication: Copyright, 28 August 1969. Deposit copies: DLC (2 September 1969), BL (2 March 1970). Price, $15.00.

Locations: BL, DLC, JM (dust jacket), ScU, VtU.

VOLUME VIII

A 67.VIII.1
First edition, only printing (1970)

Title page is the same as in A 67.I.1.a, except 'VIII | 1841–1843 | EDITED BY | WILLIAM H. GILMAN J. E. PARSONS'; '1970' is substituted for '1960'.

[i–iv] v–xxiii [xxiv] [1–2] 3–479 [480–482] 483–576 [577–578] 579–587 [588] 589–618 [619–620]

[1–18^{16} 19^{18} 20^{16}] A four-leaf gathering of coated paper, with photographs of manuscript pages, is inserted after p. 328.

Contents: p. i: half title, the same as in A 67.VII.1; p. ii: blank; p. iii: title page; p. iv: copyright page; pp. v–vi: *'Preface'*; p. vii: *'Contents'*; p. viii: *'Illustrations'*; pp. ix–xxiii: *'Foreword to Volume VIII'*; p. xxiv: blank; p. 1: 'PART ONE | The Journals'; p. 2: blank; pp. 3–77 "Journal G"; pp. 78–145: "Journal H"; pp. 146–197: "Journal J"; pp. 198–247: "Journal K"; pp. 248–308: "Journal N"; pp. 309–348: "Journal Z[A]"; pp. 349–441: "Journal R"; pp. 442–479: "Books Small"; p. 480: blank; p. 481: 'PART TWO | *Miscellaneous Notebooks'*; p. 482: blank; pp. 483–517: "Dialling"; pp. 518–533: "Trees [A]"; pp. 534–549: "Trees [A] [Sequence II]"; pp. 550–576: "Books Small [Sequence II]"; p. 577: *'Appendix | Textual Notes | Index'*; p. 578: blank; pp. 579–584: *'Appendix'*; pp. 585–587: *'Textual Notes'*; p. 588: blank; pp. 589–618: *'Index'*; pp. 619–620: blank.

Typography and paper: The same as in A 67.III.1, except 'WARREN'S | OLDE STYLE' watermark. Running heads: rectos: pp. xi–xvii: 'THE JOURNALS FROM 1841 TO 1843'; p. xix: 'CHRONOLOGY'; pp. xxi–xxiii: 'SYMBOLS AND ABBREVIATIONS'; pp. 5–307, 311–347, 351–479: dates and titles of journal volumes; pp. 485–575: dates and titles of notebook volumes; pp. 581–583: 'APPENDIX'; p. 587: 'TEXTUAL NOTES'; pp. 591–617: 'INDEX'; versos: p. vi: 'PREFACE'; pp. x–xxii: 'FOREWORD TO VOLUME VIII'; pp. 4–76, 80–144, 148–196, 200–246, 250–440, 444–478: 'JOURNALS OF RALPH WALDO EMERSON' and abbreviations for journal volumes; pp. 484–516, 520–532, 536–548, 552–576: 'NOTEBOOKS OF RALPH WALDO EMERSON' and abbreviations for notebook volumes; pp. 580–584: 'APPENDIX'; p. 586: 'TEXTUAL NOTES'; pp. 590–618: 'INDEX'.

Binding: The same as for A 67.I.1.a, except: spine has 'GILMAN | PARSONS | VIII | 1841–1843'.

Dust jacket: The same as for A 67.VII.1, except: deep orange replaces deep brown; front cover: *'Chief Editor'*, *'Senior Editor'*, and *'Editors'*; back cover: blurbs for A 67.I–VII; spine: 'GILMAN | AND | PARSONS' and 'VIII | 1841–1843'; front flap: description of volume; back flap: description of volume continued and information on editors.

Publication: Copyright, 18 December 1970. Deposit copies: DLC (19 January 1971), BL (9 July 1971). Price, $18.50.

Locations: BL, DLC, JM (dust jacket), ScU, VtU.

VOLUME IX

A 67.IX.1
First edition, only printing (1971)

Title page is the same as in A 67.I.1.a, except 'IX | 1843–1847 | EDITED BY | RALPH H. ORTH   ALFRED R. FERGUSON'; '1971' is substituted for '1960'.

[i–iv] v–xxiii [xxiv] [1–2] 3–126 [126a–126b] 127–170 [170a–170b] 171–448 [448a–448b] 449–462 [462a–462b] 463–470 [471–472] 473–500 [501–504]

[1–8¹⁶ 9¹² 10–17¹⁶]

Contents: p. i: half title, the same as in A 67.VII.1; p. ii: blank; p. iii: title page; p. iv: copyright page; pp. v–vi: '*Preface*'; p. vii: '*Contents*'; p. viii: '*Illustrations*'; pp. ix–xxiii: '*Foreword to Volume IX*'; p. xxiv: blank; p. 1: '*The Journals*'; p. 2: blank; pp. 3–92: "U"; pp. 93–126: "V"; p. 126a: photograph of manuscript page; p. 126b: blank; pp. 127–170: text continues; p. 170a: photograph of manuscript page; p. 170b: blank; pp. 171–181: text continues; pp. 182–255: "W"; pp. 256–354: "Y"; pp. 355–448: "O"; p. 448a: photograph of manuscript page; p. 448b: blank; pp. 449–462: text continues; p. 462a: photograph of manuscript page; p. 462b: blank; pp. 463–470: text continues; p. 471: '*Textual Notes | Index*'; p. 472: blank; pp. 473–474: '*Textual Notes*'; pp. 475–500: '*Index*'; pp. 501–504: blank.

Typography and paper: The same as in A 67.VIII.1. Running heads: rectos: pp. xi–xvii: 'THE JOURNALS FROM 1843 TO 1847'; p. xix: 'CHRONOLOGY'; pp. xxi–xxiii: 'SYMBOLS AND ABBREVIATIONS'; pp. 5–91, 95–353, 357–469: dates and titles of journal volumes; pp. 477–499: 'INDEX'; versos: p. vi: 'PREFACE'; pp. x–xxii: 'FOREWORD TO VOLUME IX'; pp. 4–180, 184–254, 258–470: 'JOURNALS OF RALPH WALDO EMERSON' and abbreviations for journal volumes; p. 474: 'TEXTUAL NOTES'; pp. 476–500: 'INDEX'.

Binding: The same as for A 67.I.1.a, except: spine has 'ORTH | FERGUSON | IX | 1843–1847'.

Dust jacket: The same as for A 67.VIII.1, except: very green replaces deep orange; back cover: list of previously published volumes in the edition; spine: 'ORTH | AND | FERGUSON' and 'IX | 1843–1847'; front flap: description of volume; back flap: description of volume continued and information on editors.

Publication: Copyright, 30 December 1971. Price, $17.00.

Locations: JM (dust jacket), ScU, VtU.

Note one: Leaves containing illustrations, here designated pp. 126a–126b, 170a–170b, 448a–448b, and 462a–462b, are on the same paper as the text, unnumbered, and not accounted for in the volume's pagination sequence.

Note two: An unknown number of dust jackets were printed with Ferguson's academic affiliation incorrectly given as Ohio Wesleyan University, rather than the correct Ohio State University, and were destroyed. *Location:* Collection of Ralph H. Orth.

VOLUME X

A 67.X.1
First edition, only printing (1973)

Title page is the same as in A 67.I.1.a, except 'X | 1847–1848 | EDITED BY | MERTON M. SEALTS, JR.'; '1973' is substituted for '1960'.

[i–iv] v [vi] vii–xxix [xxx] [1–2] 3–362 [363–364] 365–568 [569–570] 571–615 [616–618]

[1–17¹⁶ 18²⁰ 19–20¹⁶] A two-leaf gathering on the same paper as the text, with photographs of manuscript pages, is inserted after p. 226.

Contents: p. i: half title, the same as in A 67.VII.1; p. ii: blank; p. iii: title page; p. iv: copyright page; p. v: '*Preface*'; p. vi: blank; p. vii: '*Contents*'; p. viii: '*Illustrations*'; pp. ix–xxix: '*Foreword to Volume X*'; p. xxx: blank; p. 1: 'PART ONE | *The Journals*'; p. 2: blank; pp. 3–57: "AB"; pp. 58–123: "CD"; pp. 124–199: "GH"; pp. 200–207: "Sea-Notes"; pp. 208–287: "London"; pp. 288–362: "LM"; p. 363: 'PART TWO | *Miscellaneous Notebooks*'; p. 364: blank; pp. 365–404: "JK"; pp. 405–406: "Pocket Diary 1"; pp. 407–445: "England and Paris"; pp. 446–457: "Pocket Diary 3"; pp. 458–467: "Xenien"; pp. 468–488: "Platoniana"; pp. 489–493: "Warren Lot"; pp. 494–568: "ED"; p. 569: '*Textual Notes | Index*'; p. 570: blank; pp. 571–572: '*Textual Notes*'; pp. 573–615: '*Index*'; pp. 616–618: blank.

Typography and paper: The same as in A 67.VIII.1. Running heads: rectos: pp. xi–xxv: 'THE JOURNALS FROM 1847 TO 1848'; p. xxvii: 'CHRONOLOGY'; pp. xxix: 'SYMBOLS AND ABBREVIATIONS'; pp. 5–361: dates and titles of journal volumes; pp. 367–403, 407–487, 491–567: dates and titles of notebook volumes; pp. 575–615: 'INDEX'; versos: pp. x–xxviii: 'FOREWORD TO VOLUME X'; pp. 4–56, 60–122, 126–198, 202–206, 210–286, 290–362: 'JOURNALS OF RALPH WALDO EMERSON' and abbreviations for journal volumes; pp. 366–444, 448–456, 460–466, 470–492, 496–568: 'NOTEBOOKS OF RALPH WALDO EMERSON' and abbreviations for notebook volumes; p. 572: 'TEXTUAL NOTES'; pp. 574–614: 'INDEX'.

Binding: The same as for A 67.I.1.a, except: two-piece buckram casing; spine has 'SEALTS | X | 1847–1848'.

Dust jacket: The same as for A 67.IX.1, except: standard greenish blue replaces very green; back cover: list of previously published volumes in the edition; spine: 'SEALTS' and 'X | 1847–1848'; front flap: description of volume; back flap: description of volume continued and information on editor.

Publication: Copyright, 21 September 1973. Deposit copy: DLC (16 October 1973). Price, $25.00.

Locations: DLC, JM (dust jacket), ScU, VtU.

VOLUME XI

A 67.XI.1
First edition, only printing (1975)

Title page is the same as in A 67.I.1.a, except 'XI | 1848–1851 | EDITED BY | A. W. PLUMSTEAD WILLIAM H. GILMAN | RUTH H. BENNETT | ASSOCIATE EDITOR' and 'Massachusetts | and London, England | 1975'.

[i–iv] v–xxv [xxvi] [1–2] 3–390 [390a–390h] 391–452 [453–454] 455–540 [541–542] 543–545 [546] 547–586 [587–590]

$[1–17^{16}\ 18^8\ 19–20^{16}]$

Contents: p. i: half title, the same as in A 67.VII.1; p. ii: blank; p. iii: title page; p. iv: copyright page; pp. v–vi: '*Preface*'; pp. vii–viii: '*Alfred Riggs Ferguson*'; p. ix: '*Contents*'; p. x: '*Illustrations*'; pp. xi–xxv: '*Foreword to Volume XI*'; p. xxvi: blank; p. 1: 'PART ONE | *The Journals*'; p. 2: blank; pp. 3–86: "S"; pp. 87–182: "TU"; pp. 183–278: "AZ"; pp. 279–365: "BO"; pp. 366–390: "CO"; pp. 390a–390h: photographs of manuscript pages; pp. 391–452: text continues; p. 453: 'PART TWO | *Miscellaneous Notebooks*'; p. 454: blank; pp. 455–509: "Margaret Fuller Ossoli"; pp. 510–540: "Journal at the West"; p. 541: '*Appendix* | *Textual Notes* | *Index*'; p. 542: blank; pp. 543–545: '*Appendix*'; p. 546: blank; pp. 547–548: '*Textual Notes*'; pp. 549–586: '*Index*'; pp. 587–590: blank.

Typography and paper: The same as in A 67.I.1.a. Running heads: rectos: pp. xiii–xix: 'THE JOURNALS FROM 1848 TO 1851'; p. xxi: 'CHRONOLOGY'; pp. xxiii–xxv: 'SYMBOLS AND ABBREVIATIONS'; pp. 5–85, 89–181, 185–277, 281–451: dates and titles of journal volumes; pp. 457–539: dates and titles of notebook volumes; p. 545: 'APPENDIX'; pp. 551–585: 'INDEX'; versos: p. vi: 'PREFACE'; p. viii: 'ALFRED RIGGS FERGUSON'; pp. xii–xxiv: 'FOREWORD TO VOLUME XI'; pp. 4–364, 368–452: 'JOURNALS OF RALPH WALDO EMERSON' and abbreviations for journal volumes; pp. 456–508, 512–540: 'NOTEBOOKS OF RALPH WALDO EMERSON' and abbreviations for notebook volumes; p. 544: 'APPENDIX'; p. 548: 'TEXTUAL NOTES'; pp. 550–586: 'INDEX'.

Binding: The same as for A 67.X.1, except: spine has 'PLUMSTEAD | GILMAN | XI | 1848–1851'.

Dust jacket: The same as for A 67.X.1, except: very red replaces standard greenish blue; back cover: list of previously published volumes in the edition; spine: 'PLUMSTEAD | AND | GILMAN' and 'XI | 1848–1851'; front flap: description of volume; back flap: description of volume continued and information on editors.

Publication: Copyright, 29 December 1975. Deposit copies: DLC (17 March 1976), BL (12 April 1976). Price, $35.00.

Locations: BL, DLC, JM (dust jacket), ScU, VtU.

Note: Leaves containing illustrations, here designated pp. 390a–390h, are on the same paper as the text, unnumbered, and not accounted for in the volume's pagination sequence.

VOLUME XII

A 67.XII.1
First edition, only printing (1976)

Title page is the same as in A 67.I.1.a, except 'XII | 1835–1862 | EDITED BY | LINDA ALLARDT'; '1976' is substituted for '1960'.

[i–iv] v–xlviii [1–2] 3–176 [176a–176f] 177–614 [615–616] 617–621 [622] 623–657 [658]

$[1–21^{16}\ 22^4\ 23^{16}]$

Contents: p. i: half title, the same as in A 67.VII.1, except: '. . . *Senior Editor* | LINDA ALLARDT   HARRISON HAYFORD | RALPH H. ORTH   J. E. PARSONS | A. W. PLUM-

STEAD | *Editors*'; p. ii: blank; p. iii: title page; p. iv: copyright page; pp. v–vi: '*Preface*'; pp. vii–viii: '*William Henry Gilman*'; p. ix: '*Contents*'; p. x: '*Illustrations*'; pp. xi–xlviii: '*Foreword to Volume XII*'; p. 1: '*Miscellaneous Notebooks*'; p. 2: blank; pp. 3–32: "L Concord"; pp. 33–55: "L Literature"; pp. 56–74: "Man"; pp. 75–176: "F No. 1"; pp. 176a–176f: photographs of manuscript pages; p. 177: text continues; pp. 178–268: "Delta"; pp. 269–419: "Phi"; pp. 420–517: "Psi"; pp. 518–580: "Index Minor"; pp. 581–614: "BO Conduct"; p. 615: '*Appendixes | Textual Notes | Index*'; p. 616: blank; pp. 617–619: '*Appendix I*'; pp. 620–621: '*Appendix II*'; p. 622: blank; pp. 623–624: '*Textual Notes*'; pp. 625–657: '*Index*'; p. 658: blank.

Typography and paper: The same as in A 67.I.1.a. Running heads: rectos: pp. xiii–xliii: 'THE LECTURE NOTEBOOKS FROM 1835 TO 1862'; p. xlv: 'CHRONOLOGY'; p. xlvii: 'SYMBOLS AND ABBREVIATIONS'; pp. 5–31, 35–73, 77–267, 271–579, 583–613: titles of notebook volumes; p. 619: 'APPENDIX I'; p. 621: 'APPENDIX II'; pp. 627–657: 'INDEX'; versos: p. vi: 'PREFACE'; p. viii: 'WILLIAM HENRY GILMAN'; pp. xii–xlviii: 'FOREWORD TO VOLUME XII'; pp. 4–54, 58–176, 180–418, 422–516, 520–614: 'NOTEBOOKS OF RALPH WALDO EMERSON' and abbreviations for notebook volumes; p. 618: 'APPENDIX I'; p. 624: 'TEXTUAL NOTES'; pp. 625–656: 'INDEX'.

Binding: The same as for A 67.X.1, except: spine has 'ALLARDT | XII | 1835–1862'.

Dust jacket: The same as for A 67.XI.1, except: very orange replaces very red; front cover: ' . . . *Senior Editor* | LINDA ALLARDT   HARRISON HAYFORD | RALPH H. ORTH   J. E. PARSONS | A. W. PLUMSTEAD | *Editors*'; back cover: list of previously published volumes in the edition; spine: 'ALLARDT' and 'XII | 1835–1862'; front flap: description of volume; back flap: description of volume continued and information on editor.

Publication: Copyright, 12 October 1976. Deposit copies: DLC (3 November 1976), BL (22 December 1976). Price, $37.50.

Locations: BL, DLC, JM (dust jacket), ScU, VtU.

Note: Leaves containing illustrations, here designated pp. 176a–176f, are on the same paper as the text, unnumbered, and not accounted for in the volume's pagination sequence.

VOLUME XIII

A 67.XIII.1
First edition, only printing (1977)

Title page is the same as in A 67.I.1.a, except 'XIII | 1852–1855 | EDITED BY | RALPH H. ORTH   ALFRED R. FERGUSON' and 'Massachusetts | and | London, England | 1977'.

[i–iv] v–xxi [xxii] [1–2] 3–469 [470–472] 473–515 [516–518] 519–521 [522] 523–555 [556–562]

[1–17^{16} 18^4 19^{16}]   A two-leaf gathering on the same paper as the text, with photographs of manuscript pages, is inserted after p. 266.

Contents: p. i: half title, the same as in A 67.VII.1; p. ii: blank; p. iii: title page; p. iv: copyright page; pp. v–vi: '*Preface*'; p. vii: '*Contents*'; p. viii: '*Illustrations*'; pp. ix–xxi: '*Foreword to Volume XIII*'; p. xxii: blank; p. 1: 'PART ONE | *The Journals*'; p. 2: blank; pp. 3–57: "DO"; pp. 58–128: "GO"; pp. 129–206: "VS"; pp. 207–289: "HO"; pp. 290–378: "IO"; pp. 379–469: "NO"; p. 470: blank; p. 471: 'PART TWO | *Miscellaneous*

Notebooks'; p. 472: blank; pp. 473–482: "Pocket Diary 4"; pp. 483–501: "Pocket Diary 5"; pp. 502–515: "Pocket Diary 6"; p. 516: blank; p. 517: '*Appendix | Textual Notes | Index*'; p. 518: blank; pp. 519–521: '*Appendix*'; p. 522: blank; pp. 523–524: '*Textual Notes*'; pp. 525–555: '*Index*'; pp. 556–562: blank.

Typography and paper: The same as in A 67.I.1.a. Running heads: rectos: pp. xi–xv: 'THE JOURNALS FROM 1852 TO 1855'; p. xvii: 'CHRONOLOGY'; pp. xix–xxi: 'SYMBOLS AND ABBREVIATIONS'; pp. 5–127, 131–205, 209–377, 381–469: dates and titles of journal volumes; pp. 475–481, 485–515: dates and titles of notebook volumes; p. 521: 'APPENDIX'; pp. 527–555: 'INDEX'; versos: p. vi: 'PREFACE'; pp. x–xx: 'FOREWORD TO VOLUME XIII'; pp. 4–56, 60–288, 292–468: 'JOURNALS OF RALPH WALDO EMERSON' and abbreviations for journal volumes; pp. 474–500, 504–514: 'NOTEBOOKS OF RALPH WALDO EMERSON' and abbreviations for notebook volumes; p. 520: 'APPENDIX'; p. 524: 'TEXTUAL NOTES'; pp. 526–554: 'INDEX'.

Binding: The same as for A 67.X.1, except: spine has 'ORTH | FERGUSON | XIII | 1852–1855'.

Dust jacket: The same as for A 67.XII.1, except: standard yellow green replaces very orange; back cover: list of previously published volumes in the edition; spine: 'ORTH | AND | FERGUSON' and 'XIII | 1852–1855'; front flap: description of volume; back flap: description of volume continued and information on editors.

Publication: Copyright, 4 March 1977. Deposit copies: DLC (6 April 1977), BL (15 June 1977). Price, $35.00.

Locations: BL, DLC, JM (dust jacket), ScU, VtU.

VOLUME XIV

A 67.XIV.1
First edition, only printing (1978)

Title page is the same as in A 67.I.1.a, except: all in black; 'XIV | 1854–1861 | EDITED BY | SUSAN SUTTON SMITH   HARRISON HAYFORD'; '1978' is substituted for '1960'.

[i–iv] v–xxvi [1–2] 3–369 [370] [370a–370f] [371–372] 373–482 [483–484] 485–523 [524–528]

[1–16¹⁶ 17⁸ 18¹⁶]

Contents: p. i: half title, the same as in A 67.I.1.a, except 'RALPH H. ORTH   *Chief Editor* | LINDA ALLARDT   HARRISON HAYFORD | J. E. PARSONS   SUSAN SUTTON SMITH | *Editors*'; p. ii: blank; p. iii: title page; p. iv: copyright page; pp. v–vi: '*Preface*'; p. vii: '*Contents*'; p. viii: '*Illustrations*'; pp. ix–xxvi: '*Foreword to Volume XIV*'; p. 1: 'PART ONE | *The Journals*'; p. 2: blank; pp. 3–39: "RO"; pp. 40–118: "SO"; pp. 119–207: "VO"; pp. 208–290: "AC"; pp. 291–369: "CL"; p. 370: blank; pp. 370a–370f: photographs of manuscript pages; p. 371: 'PART TWO | *Miscellaneous Notebooks*'; p. 372: blank; pp. 373–430: "WO Liberty"; pp. 431–445: "Pocket Diary 7"; pp. 446–455: "Pocket Diary 8"; pp. 456–464: "Pocket Diary 9"; pp. 465–473: "Pocket Diary 11"; pp. 474–482: "Pocket Diary 12"; p. 483: '*Appendix | Textual Notes | Index*'; p. 484: blank; pp. 485–488: '*Appendix*'; pp. 489–490: '*Textual Notes*'; pp. 491–523: '*Index*'; pp. 524–528: blank.

Typography and paper: The same as in A 67.I.1.a. Running heads: rectos: pp. xi–xxi: 'THE JOURNALS FROM 1854 TO 1861'; p. xxiii: 'CHRONOLOGY'; p. xxv: 'SYMBOLS AND ABBREVIATIONS'; pp. 5–117, 121–289, 293–369: dates and titles of journal volumes; pp. 375–429, 433–463, 467–481: dates and titles of notebook volumes; p. 487: 'APPENDIX'; pp. 493–523: 'INDEX'; versos: p. vi: 'PREFACE'; pp. x–xxvi: 'FORE-WORD TO VOLUME XIV'; pp. 4–38, 42–206, 210–368: 'JOURNALS OF RALPH WALDO EMERSON' and abbreviations of journal volumes; pp. 374–444, 448–454, 458–472, 476–482: 'NOTEBOOKS OF RALPH WALDO EMERSON' and abbreviations for notebook volumes; pp. 486–488: 'APPENDIX'; p. 490: 'TEXTUAL NOTES'; pp. 492–522: 'INDEX'.

Binding:　The same as for A 67.X.1, except: spine has 'SMITH | HAYFORD | XIV | 1854–1861'.

Dust jacket:　The same as for A 67.XIII.1, except: deep reddish purple replaces standard yellow green; front cover: 'RALPH H. ORTH Chief Editor | LINDA ALLARDT HARRISON HAYFORD | J. E. PARSONS SUSAN SUTTON SMITH | Editors'; back cover: list of previously published volumes in the edition; spine: 'SMITH | AND | HAYFORD' and 'XIV | 1854–1861'; front flap: description of volume; back flap: description of volume continued and information on editors.

Publication:　Published 15 May 1978. Deposit copies: DLC (12 April 1978), BL (1 August 1978). Price, $37.50.

Locations:　BL, DLC, JM (dust jacket), ScU, VtU.

Note:　Leaves containing illustrations, here designated pp. 370a–370f, are on the same paper as the text, unnumbered, and not accounted for in the volume's pagination sequence.

A 68 THE CORRESPONDENCE OF EMERSON AND CARLYLE

A 68.1.a
First edition, first printing (1964)

THE CORRESPONDENCE OF

Emerson AND *Carlyle*

EDITED BY

Joseph Slater

COLUMBIA UNIVERSITY PRESS

NEW YORK AND LONDON 1964

A 68.1.a: 9¼" × 6⅛"

[a–b] [i–v] vi–viii [ix–x] [1–3] 4–15 [16] 17–29 [30] 31–43 [44] 45–52 I–VIII [53] 54–63 [64] 65–72 [73] 74–94 [95–97] 98–111 [112] 113–141 [142] 143–155 [156] 157–175 [176] 177–209 [210] 211–255 [256] 257–281 [282] 283–288 [289] 290–315 [316] 317–335 [336] 337–355 [356] 357–373 [374] 375–387 [388] 389–411 [412] 413–437 [438] 439–448 [449] 450–458 [459] 460–466 [467] 468–474 [475] 476–484 [485] 486–496 [497] 498–502 [503] 504–507 [508] 509–518 [519–520] 521–525 [526] 527–528 [529] 530–532 [533] 534 [535] 536–538 [539] 540–542 [543] 544–545 [546] 547–550 [551] 552–553 [554] 555–556 [557] 558–576 [577] 578–584 [585] 586–589 [590–591] 592–601 [602–603] 604–622 [623–628]

$[1–2^{16}\,3^4\,4–21^{16}]$ Gathering [3] is on coated paper

Contents: pp. a–b: blank; p. i: 'THE CORRESPONDENCE OF | EMERSON AND CARLYLE'; p. ii: blank; p. iii: title page; p. iv: copyright page; pp. v–viii: 'PREFACE' dated '*June, 1964*'; p. ix: contents; p. x: blank; pp. 1–52: "Introduction"; pp. I–VIII: photographs of Emerson and Carlyle; pp. 53–94: "Introduction"; p. 95: 'THE CORRESPONDENCE'; p. 96: blank; pp. 97–590: text of letters; pp. 591–601: "Bibliography"; p. 602: blank; pp. 603–622: "Index"; pp. 623–628: blank.

Typography and paper: 7¼″ (6¹³/₁₆″) × 4⅜″; wove paper; 38 lines per page. Running heads: rectos: p. vii: 'PREFACE'; pp. 5–15: 'PRELUDE: 1827–1833'; pp. 17–29: 'BIBLIOPOLY: 1835–1847'; pp. 31–43: 'INTERLUDE: 1847–1848'; pp. 45–51: 'SILENCES: 1848–1872'; pp. 55–63: 'POSTLUDE: 1872–1882'; pp. 65–71: 'THE FIRST EDITION'; pp. 75–93: 'THE ART OF THE LETTERS'; pp. 99–287, 291–447, 451–457, 461–465, 469–473, 477–483, 487–495, 499–501, 505–517, 521–527, 531, 537, 541, 545–549, 553–555, 559–575, 579–583, 587–589: dates of letters; pp. 593–601: 'BIBLIOGRAPHY'; pp. 605–621: 'INDEX'; versos: pp. vi–viii: 'PREFACE'; pp. 4–14: 'PRELUDE: 1827–1833'; pp. 18–28: 'BIBLIOPOLY: 1835–1847'; pp. 32–42: 'INTERLUDE: 1847–1848'; pp. 46–52: 'SILENCES: 1848–1872'; pp. 54–62: 'POSTLUDE: 1872–1882'; pp. 66–72: 'THE FIRST EDITION'; pp. 74–94: 'THE ART OF THE LETTERS'; pp. 98–110, 114–140, 144–154, 158–174, 178–208, 212–254, 258–280, 284–314, 318–334, 338–354, 358–372, 376–386, 390–410, 414–436, 440–506, 510–518, 522–524, 528–544, 548–552, 556–588: dates of letters; pp. 592–600: 'BIBLIOGRAPHY'; pp. 604–622: 'INDEX'.

Binding: Medium reddish orange buckram. Front and back covers: blank; spine: goldstamped '[swirling double lines] | [rule] | [next six lines on black background] THE | CORRESPONDENCE OF | EMERSON | AND | CARLYLE | SLATER | [rule] | [swirling double lines] | COLUMBIA'. White endpapers. All edges trimmed. Top edges stained reddish brown.

Dust jacket: Front cover: on reddish brown background with gray geometrical patterns: 'THE | CORRESPONDENCE | OF | [yellow] EMERSON | AND | [yellow] CARLYLE | [oval photographs of Emerson and Carlyle] | [next two lines in white] EDITED BY | JOSEPH SLATER'; back cover: 12-line blurb for Emerson's *Letters* and 13-line blurb for

Ralph L. Rusk, *The Life of Ralph Waldo Emerson,* on white background; spine: on reddish brown background with gray geometrical patterns: '[white] SLATER | [next two lines printed vertically from top to bottom] THE CORRESPONDENCE OF | [yellow] EMERSON [each letter on separate line] AND [yellow] CARLYLE | [next two lines in white] [crown publisher's logo] COLUMBIA'; front flap: white background with '[41-line description of book] | *(Continued on back flap)* | [next two lines within single-rule frame] JACKET BY | [script] T&R'; back flap: on white background '*(Continued from front flap)* | [55-line description of book and three-line biography of editor]'.

Publication: Copyright, 23 November 1964. Deposit copy: BL (13 January 1965). Price, $10.00.

Locations: BL, JM (dust jacket), ScU, ViU, VtU.

Note: For earlier, incomplete editions, see A 39 and A 43.

A 68.1.b
First edition, second printing [1965]

The same as the first printing, except: the title page is undated; the title leaf verso states "*First printing 1964 | Second printing 1965*"; the advertisements on the dust jacket have been changed; the collation is different. *Location:* JM (dust jacket).

THE
CORRESPONDENCE OF
EMERSON
AND
CARLYLE

EDITED BY
JOSEPH SLATER

THE CORRESPONDENCE OF
EMERSON AND CARLYLE

THE
CORRESPONDENCE OF
EMERSON
AND
CARLYLE
Edited by Joseph Slater

On May 14, 1834, Ralph Waldo Emerson wrote to Thomas Carlyle: "There are some purposes we nourish...this is the first time in design of writing you an Epistle." Carlyle replied on August 12. Thus began a correspondence, which was to continue for thirty-eight years, between two of the nineteenth century's major literary figures.

The two men had met in August, 1833, when Emerson had paid a one-day visit to Carlyle and his wife at Craigenputtock farm. Those twenty-four hours had served to establish a friendship that would be continued chiefly by the letters which are collected here.

This new edition of the Emerson-Carlyle correspondence, prepared by Joseph Slater, is based, wherever possible, on the manuscripts. In a few cases in which these are no longer available the versions appearing in Charles Eliot Norton's edition of 1883 have been used.

Back and forth across the Atlantic went the mail packets, bearing ideas, literary and philosophical, reactions to politics and work, enthusiasm for Carlyle's work led him to superintend the American sales of The French Revolution—a friendly labor of love to occupy much time and thought. His pride in the literature of his own country prompted him to send Carlyle

(Continued on back flap)

THE LETTERS OF RALPH WALDO EMERSON

Edited by Ralph L. Rusk

Here is the first attempt ever made at a comprehensive collection of the letters of Emerson. In six volumes there are contained 2,313 letters of Emerson which have never before been published; also, there are 271 which previously have been only partly published and are now given more fully or completely. The letters throw new light on almost every aspect of Emerson's life and work and give a picture of the whole man, not merely of the Transcendental mystic. Many contain the germs of ideas that later became the themes of essays and addresses; others give new details of Emerson's life as teacher and minister, of his travels in Europe, Africa, and America, and of his reading.

6 vols. $35.00

THE LIFE OF RALPH WALDO EMERSON

by Ralph L. Rusk

"Immeasurable pieces of fresh evidence, a judiciously balanced interpretation, and a readable style make Mr. Rusk's book the definitive biography of Emerson if one shares the biographer's dream of recreating an entire man, much as a novelist or dramatist of insight and imagination creates a character. Mr. Rusk has by no means neglected Emerson's ideas, but he is more interested in the man as a personality, sketched against his time and place and in relation to the many other leading personalities he met on his travels. ... This is certainly superior to any biography yet written of an American author."

—American Historical Review

$10.00

Columbia University Press
New York and London

B. Collected Editions

All collected works of Emerson's writings through 1980, including those published, advertised, or sold as "Emerson's Writings" by Fields, Osgood and its successors (James R. Osgood; Houghton, Osgood; Houghton, Mifflin). Also other contemporary editions which cumulate Emerson's works to date, and posthumous editions which include the bulk of Emerson's published writings. All works printed from the same plates are grouped together in chronological order. Plate groups follow in the order of the first appearance of the first work in each group unless otherwise indicated.

PEDIGREE OF PRIMARY COLLECTED EDITIONS

Printed from the "Little Classic Edition" plates

B 3   "Little Classic Edition" (1876–1893)
B 4   "Fireside Edition" (1879)

Printed from the Riverside Edition plates

B 7   *Riverside Edition (trade)* (1883–1893)
B 8   *Riverside Edition (American large paper)* (1883–1893)
B 9   *Riverside Edition (English large paper)* (1883)
B 10   *Riverside Edition (Copyright)* (1883–1893)
B 11   *Standard Library Edition* [1894]
B 12   "Sovereign Edition" (1903)
B 13   *Fireside Edition* (1909)
B 14   "Jefferson Press Edition" [ca. 1912]
B 15   *University Edition* [ca. 1912]
B 16   "Waverley" *Riverside Edition* [n.d.]

Printed from the Centenary Edition plates

B 18   *Centenary Edition (trade)* (1903–1904)
B 19   *Autograph Centenary Edition* (1903–1904)
B 20   *Concord Edition* (1903–1904)
B 21   *Centenary Edition (English)* [1903–1909]
B 22   *Riverside Pocket Edition* [1914]
B 23   *Emerson's Complete Works* (1921)
B 24   *Current Opinion Edition* (1923)
B 25   *Harvard Edition* (1929)
B 26   *Medallion Edition* (1929)
B 27   "AMS Press" *Centenary Edition* [1968]

Printed from the "John D. Morris Edition" plates

B 29   "John D. Morris Edition" [1906]
B 30   *Works* (C. T. Brainard) [n.d.]
B 31   *Works* (Caxton Society) [n.d.]
B 32   *Works* (National Library Co.) [n.d.]
B 33   *Works* (Nottingham Society) [n.d.]

Printed from the New National Edition plates

B 35   *New National Edition* [1914]
B 36   *Works* (Tudor) [1942]

B 37   *Works* (Charles C. Bigelow) [n.d.]
B 38   *Works* (Bigelow, Brown) [n.d.]
B 39   *Works* (Bigelow, Smith) [n.d.]
B 40   *Writings* (Brentano's) [n.d.]
B 41   *Works* (Harper and Brothers) [n.d.]
B 42   *Works* (Jefferson Press) [n.d.]
B 43   *Works* (Library Society) [n.d.]
B 44   *Works* (Three Sirens) [n.d.]

B 1 COMPLETE WORKS
1866–1883

The Complete Works of Ralph Waldo Emerson Comprising His Essays, Lectures, Poems, and Orations, 2 vols. London: Bell & Daldy, 1866. Vol. III added in 1883 under George Bell and Sons imprint. Title changed in 1879 to *The Works . . . .*

Half title reads 'EMERSON'S WORKS.'. Later printings in *Bohn's Standard Library.* Printed from sterotype plates by William Clowes and Sons, London. Early binding is dark yellow green C cloth (sand). Later bindings of dark yellow green C cloth (sand), or horizontal T cloth (rib), or dark reddish brown H cloth (fine diaper) noted. Bell & Daldy imprint at base of spine replaced in reprint bindings with George Bell and Sons imprint, then Bohn's Libraries imprint. Bell & Daldy title page imprint replaced in 1876 and subsequent reprintings with George Bell and Sons imprint. Copies have been noted with mixed title page and binding imprints. Original price, 3s. 6d per volume.

1. *Essays, Representative Men, Poems,* vol. I (1866)

494 pp. Listed in *Athenæum,* no. 2017 (23 June 1866), 833. *Locations:* BL (10 September 1866), MH-AH.

Reprinted 1868, 1870, 1873, 1876, 1879, 1882, 1883, 1884, 1886, 1889, 1897.

2. *English Traits, Nature; Addresses, and Lectures, The Conduct of Life,* vol. II (1866)

448 pp. Listed in *Athenæum,* no. 2022 (28 July 1866), 113. *Locations:* BL (10 September 1866), MB.

Reprinted 1868, 1870, 1873, 1876, 1881, 1882, 1883, 1888.

3. *Society and Solitude, Letters and Social Aims, Miscellaneous Papers, May-Day, Additional Poems,* vol. III (1883)

First collected appearance of "Milton and His Works," "Walter Savage Landor," "Carlyle's Past and Present," "Tantalus," "Henry D. Thoreau," "Plutarch," "Parnassus," and "The Sovereignty of Ethics."

485 pp. Listed in *Athenæum,* no. 2908 (21 July 1883), 79; as published between 16 and 31 July 1883, in *Publishers' Circular and Booksellers' Record,* 46 (1 August 1883), 656. *Locations:* BO (6 May 1884), CaOTTC. Price, 3s. 6d. New price for the set, 5s.

Reprinted 1884, 1886.

Note: First collected edition of Emerson's works.

B 2 PROSE WORKS
1870–1879

The Prose Works of Ralph Waldo Emerson, 2 vols. Boston: Fields, Osgood, 1870. Vol. III added in 1879 under Houghton, Osgood imprint.

No works half title. Printed from sterotype plates by Welch, Bigelow, Cambridge, Mass. Primary bindings, dark reddish brown or dark green P cloth (pebbled). Later bindings of dark green C cloth (sand), dark reddish orange C cloth (sand), dark reddish orange or grayish purple FL cloth (dotted line), or dark reddish orange TB cloth (net). Fields, Osgood logo at base of spine replaced in reprint bindings with James R.

Osgood logo, then Houghton, Osgood logo, then Houghton, Mifflin logo. Copies have been noted with mixed title page and binding imprints. Original prices: cloth, $5.00 a set; half calf, $9.00; morocco, $12.00. Royalty, 50¢ a set.

1. *Miscellanies [Nature; Addresses, and Lectures] and Essays [First and Second Series]*, vol. I (1870)

566 pp. Electrotyped 28 September 1869. Advertised for autumn 1869, in *Atlantic,* 25 (October 1869), wrappers. Emerson wrote in his journal that a copy had been sent to Carlyle on 19 October ("Journal New York," p. 194 [MH]; see *CEC,* p. 558n.). Advertised as "Published This Day," in *Boston Daily Advertiser,* 27 October 1869, p. 1. Listed in *American Literary Gazette and Publishers' Circular,* 14 (15 October 1869), 68. Noted in *American Bibliopolist,* 1 (December 1869), 383. Listed as an importation at 24s., in *Publishers' Circular and Booksellers' Record,* 33 (1 February 1870), 80. Deposited for copyright: title, 13 October 1869; book, 26 October 1869. *Locations:* DLC (26 October 1869), JM.

2,000 copies printed October 1869; 280 copies, April–May 1872, 14 December 1872; 480 copies, June 1873; 280 copies, August–September 1874, November 1874, February–March 1875; 500 copies, August–September 1875; 280 copies, August 1876, August–October 1876, 12 October 1878, 26 November 1878, 5 January 1880; 270 copies, 8 December 1880, 15 February 1882, 16 September 1882.

2. *Representative Men, English Traits, The Conduct of Life,* vol. II (1870)

491 pp. For publication information, see under vol. I, above. *Location:* JM.

2,000 copies printed October 1869; 280 copies, April–May 1872, 14 December 1872; 480 copies, June 1873; 280 copies, August–September 1874, November 1874, February–March 1875; 500 copies, August–September 1875; 280 copies, August 1876, August–October 1876, 12 October 1877, 26 November 1878, 5 January 1880; 270 copies, 8 December 1880, 15 February 1882, 11 September 1882.

3. *Society and Solitude, Letters and Social Aims, Fortune of the Republic,* vol. III (1879)

407 pp. Advertised for fall 1879 publication, in *Publishers' Weekly,* 16 (6 September 1879), 238; for autumn 1879, in *Atlantic,* 44 (October 1879), wrappers. Listed in *Publishers' Weekly,* 16 (20 December 1879), 848. Copyright, 28 May 1884. Price, $2.50. New price for the set, $7.50. *Location:* JM.

500 copies printed 18 September 1879, 26 April 1880; 270 copies, 5 May 1882, 21 September 1882.

Note one: Copies have been noted with the following title page dates: 1870, 1872, 1873, 1875, 1876, 1878, 1879, 1880, 1882, 1883.

Note two: Emerson's contract, dated 9 April 1869, called for Fields, Osgood to pay for and retain the plates, and Emerson to retain copyright and receive 50¢ a set after the first 300 sets.

Note three: By 15 January 1884, 16 sets of *Prose Works* were still in stock.

Note four: The plates of *Prose Works* were ordered destroyed 15 May 1889.

Primary collected editions bindings: B 1 (later binding); B 2; B 4 (later binding); B 7; B 8 (the same for B9); B 10; B 3 (first binding); B 6; B 3 (second binding); B 11; B 18 (the same for B20); B 19; B 13

B 3 "LITTLE CLASSIC EDITION"
1876–1893

"Little Classic Edition," 9 vols. Boston: James R. Osgood, 1876. Vol. [I], *Miscellanies,* retitled *Nature, Addresses, and Lectures* in 1883. Vol. [IX], *Selected Poems,* replaced with *Poems* in 1884 under Houghton Mifflin imprint. Vols. [X] and [XI] added in 1884 under Houghton, Mifflin imprint. Vol. [XII] added in 1893 under Houghton, Mifflin imprint.

Listed in the *Costbooks* and advertised as the "Little Classic Edition," but not so identified in the works. No works half title. Printed from stereotype plates by H. O. Houghton, The Riverside Press, Cambridge, Mass. Title page printed in red and black. Early bindings (1876–1884?) dark yellow green, dark purple, dark reddish orange, or medium red brown S cloth (diagonal rib). All edges tinted red (see illustration for B 3 binding). James R. Osgood imprint at base of spine and on title page replaced in reprintings with Houghton, Osgood imprint, then Houghton, Mifflin imprint. Copies have been noted with mixed title page and binding imprints. Later binding (1884? on) medium blue V cloth (smooth). Title page completely reset and printed in black only. Top edges gilded (see illustration for B 3 binding). Original prices: cloth, $1.50 per volume and $13.50 a set; half calf and half morocco, $24.50; tree calf, $31.50. English importation sold for 70s. a set.

1. *Miscellanies,* vol. [I] (1876); retitled *Nature, Addresses, and Lectures* (1883)

2. *Essays: First Series,* vol. [II] (1876)

3. *Essays: Second Series,* vol. [III] (1876)

4. *Representative Men,* vol. [IV] (1876)

5. *English Traits,* vol. [V] (1876)

6. *The Conduct of Life,* vol. [VI] (1876)

7. *Society and Solitude,* vol. [VII] (1876)

8. *Letters and Social Aims,* vol. [VIII] (1876)

9. *Selected Poems,* vol. [IX] (1876); replaced by *Poems* (1884)

10. *Lectures and Biographical Sketches,* vol. [X] (1884)

11. *Miscellanies,* vol. [XI] (1884)

12. *Natural History of Intellect,* vol. [XII] (1893)

Note one: Emerson's contract, dated 1 January 1876, called for him to receive a flat annual fee of $1,500 for all his books, including those in the "Little Classic Edition," rather than a per copy royalty. This contract was extended with Houghton, Osgood on 1 January 1878, and with Houghton, Mifflin on 1 May 1880.

Note two: On 7 June 1886, Edward Waldo Emerson gave Houghton, Mifflin permission to reduce the per volume price from $1.50 to $1.25.

Note three: Publisher's records indicate that 125 sets of "Little Classic Edition" sheets were bound in flexible leather and sold between 1903 and 1908. *Location:* JM (vol. [VIII] only).

Note four: The "Little Classic Edition" was in print as late as 1923.

B 4 "FIRESIDE EDITION"
1879

"Fireside Edition," 5 vols. Boston: Houghton, Osgood, 1879.

Listed in the *Costbooks* and advertised as the "Fireside Edition," but not so identified in the works. No works half title. Printed from the plates of the "Little Classic Edition" combined (vols. I–IV) in two-volumes-in-one format. Printed from stereotype plates by Welch, Bigelow, The University Press, Cambridge, Mass. Primary binding dark olive brown S cloth (diagonal rib). Houghton, Osgood imprint at base of spine and on title page replaced in reprintings with Houghton, Mifflin imprint. Copies of Houghton, Osgood sheets have been noted in Houghton, Mifflin bindings. Original prices: cloth, $10.00 a set; half calf, $20.00; tree calf, $25.00. English importation sold for 50s. a set. Sold only in sets.

1. *Essays, First and Second Series,* vol. I (1879)

Advertised for autumn 1879, in *Atlantic,* 44 (October 1879), wrappers.

2. *Representative Men, Society and Solitude,* vol. II (1879)

3. *English Traits, The Conduct of Life,* vol. III (1879)

4. *Letters and Social Aims, [Selected] Poems,* vol. IV (1879)

5. *Miscellanies [Nature; Addresses, and Lectures],* vol. V (1879)

Note: By 15 January 1884, 11 sets of the "Fireside Edition" were still in stock.

B 5 WORKS
1883

Works of Ralph Waldo Emerson. London and New York: George Routledge and Sons, 1883.

634 pp., double columns. Also in *Books for the People* (BL). Price, 3s. 6d. *Location:* BL (9 April 1883).

Contents: Essays: First Series; Essays: Second Series; Representative Men; Society and Solitude; English Traits; The Conduct of Life; Letters and Social Aims; Poems; Miscellanies [Nature; Addresses, and Lectures].

3,000 copies printed 30 January 1883; 2,000 copies, 4 September 1883; 1,000 copies, 1 April 1885; 2,000 copies, 22 January 1886; 4,000 copies, 1 January 1888; 3,000 copies, 2 July 1888, 4 April 1889, 16 July 1890; 2,300 copies, 7 January 1892; 2,000 copies, 28 July 1893; 2,100 copies, 22 January 1895; 2,000 copies, 11 January 1897, 26 October 1898, 1 November 1899; 2,040 copies, 27 February 1891; 3,000 copies, 10 April 1902; 1905. Copies have been noted with the following title page dates: 1884, 1888, 1889, 1897, 1900, 1901, 1905, [n.d.].

B 6 WORKS
1883–1884

The Works of Ralph Waldo Emerson, 6 vols. London: Macmillan and Co., 1883. Later printings have dual New York: Macmillan Co. imprint.

Half title reads 'THE WORKS | OF | RALPH WALDO EMERSON | VOL. I. [II.–VI.]'. Printed by R. & R. Clark, Edinburgh. Bound only in deep red V cloth (smooth). Advertised as included in "Eversley Series." Original price, 5s. per volume.

1. *Miscellanies [Nature; Addresses, and Lectures],* vol. I (1884)

2. *Essays [First and Second Series],* vol. II (1883)

3. *Poems,* vol. III (1883)

4. *English Traits, Representative Men,* vol. IV (1883)

5. *The Conduct of Life, Society and Solitude,* vol. V (1883)

6. *Letters and Social Aims,* vol. VI (1883)

Note: The publication of vol. I was delayed pending the receipt of John Morley's introduction (*Publishers' Circular and Booksellers' Record,* 46 [2 April 1883], 280].

B 7 RIVERSIDE EDITION (TRADE)
1883–1893

Riverside Edition, 11 vols. Boston and New York: Houghton, Mifflin, 1883–1884. Vol. XII added in 1893 under Houghton, Mifflin imprint.

Half title reads '[gothic] Riverside Edition | [rule] | [TITLE] | BEING VOLUME I. [II.–XII.] | OF | EMERSON'S COMPLETE WORKS | [leaf design]'. Printed from stereotype plates by H. O. Houghton, The Riverside Press, Cambridge, Mass. Primary binding medium blue H cloth (fine diaper). Top edges gilded. Original prices: cloth, $1.75 per volume and $19.25 a set; half calf, $33.00; tree calf, $35.00; half levant, $44.00.

1. *Nature, Addresses, and Lectures,* vol. I (1883)

2. *Essays: First Series,* vol. II (1883)

3. *Essays: Second Series,* vol. III (1883)

4. *Representative Men,* vol. IV (1883)

5. *English Traits,* vol. V (1883)

6. *The Conduct of Life,* vol. VI (1883)

7. *Society and Solitude,* vol. VII (1883)

8. *Letters and Social Aims,* vol. VIII (1883)

9. *Poems,* vol. IX (1884)

10. *Lectures and Biographical Sketches,* vol. X (1884)

11. *Miscellanies,* vol. XI (1884)

12. *Natural History of Intellect,* vol. XII (1893)

Note one: 1,680 copies of a 4-page prospectus were printed 4 August 1883. *Not seen.*

Note two: 200 salesmen's dummies were printed 25 June 1886. *Not seen.*

Note three: A contract of 15 March 1883 called for the Emerson heirs to receive a 20% royalty.

Note four: Also combined with Edward Waldo Emerson, *Emerson in Concord* (D 140), James Elliot Cabot, *A Memoir of Ralph Waldo Emerson* (D 138), and the Carlyle-Emerson *Correspondence* (A 39) as a 16-volume (before 1893) and a 17-volume (1893 on) set. The 16-volume set sold at $48.00 in half calf and $56.00 in half calf with gilded tops; the 17-volume set sold at $59.25 in half calf with gilded tops. Apparently no copies of the additional volumes were bound in *Riverside Edition* bindings.

Note five: On 11 June 1903, Houghton, Mifflin wrote to Edward Waldo Emerson in a successful attempt to raise the number of copies printed for each volume in the *Riverside Edition* from 150 to 250, since it was cheaper to print in larger numbers.

Note six: The *Riverside Edition* was apparently last advertised for sale in 1908, although it remained in print until 1913.

B8 RIVERSIDE EDITION (AMERICAN LARGE PAPER) 1883–1893

Riverside Edition (large paper), 11 vols. Cambridge: The Riverside Press, 1883–1884. Vol. XII added in 1893 under Riverside Press imprint. Published by Houghton, Mifflin.

Listed in the *Costbooks* as the "De Luxe Edition," but not so advertised or identified in the works. Works half title the same as the *Riverside Edition,* trade printing. Printed from the *Riverside Edition* plates in large paper format. Printed on laid paper. Title page printed in red and black. Bound only in gray-white paper covered boards, with blackstamping on spine. Pages untrimmed. Same volume order and arrangement as the *Riverside Edition,* trade printing. Limited to 500 numbered copies; limitation notice at foot of copyright page. Advertised as "nearly all of which are subscribed for," in *Atlantic,* 52 (November 1883), wrappers; vols. I–XI did sell out within a year of publication. Price, $4.00 per volume.

Note one: 5,000 copies of a circular printed 22 May 1883. *Not seen.*

Note two: 50 copies of a prospectus printed 11 July 1883. *Not seen.*

Note three: Sold with brown paper dust jackets imprinted the same as the spine and unprinted glassine dust jackets, each volume boxed. *Location:* Emerson House, Concord.

Note four: The *Costbooks* show "Book Labels" for 525 each of 11 volumes printed 11 July 1883, but no copies have been located with paper labels on spine.

B 9 RIVERSIDE EDITION (ENGLISH LARGE PAPER)
1883

Riverside Edition (English large paper), 11 vols. London: Kegan Paul, Trench, MDCCCLXXXIII.

Works half title the same as the *Riverside Edition,* trade printing. Printed from the *Riverside Edition* plates in large paper format. Printed on laid paper. Title page printed in red and black. Same binding as the *Riverside Edition,* American large paper printing. Pages untrimmed. Same volume order and arrangement as the *Riverside Edition,* trade printing. Title page leaf (verso is blank) is a cancel, tipped to the stub of the cancelled American title leaf. Leaf with statement of limitation (see illustration) is tipped to the leaf following the title leaf. Limited to 25 numbered copies, signed by H. O. Houghton & Co., for sale to English subscribers.

Note one: The English title pages were electrotyped by Houghton, Mifflin on 14 September 1883.

Note two: There is no record in the *Costbooks* for printing 25 copies for English sale; therefore, this may be an issue of 25 sets from the American printing of 500.

TWENTY-FIVE COPIES OF THIS VOLUME, ALL OF WHICH ARE NUMBERED AND SIGNED, WERE PRINTED ON LARGE PAPER (FOR SUBSCRIBERS IN ENGLAND) IN THE MONTH OF JULY, 1883.

This is No. / 4.

H. O. Houghton + Co

Statement of limitation for B 9

B 10 RIVERSIDE EDITION (COPYRIGHT)
1883–1893

Riverside Edition (Copyright), 11 vols. London and New York: George Routledge and Sons, 1883–1884. Vol. XII added in 1893 under George Routledge and Sons imprint.

Designated as the *Riverside Edition* on the front cover, and as the *Riverside Edition (Copyright)* on the title page. Works half title the same as the *Riverside Edition,* trade printing. Printed from the *Riverside Edition* plates. Printed from stereotype plates by William Clowes and Sons, London. Primary binding dark greenish blue S cloth (diagonal fine rib). Later bindings lack *Riverside Edition* stamping on front cover. Also noted with undated title page in very red B cloth (linen) (JM). Same volume order and arrangement as the *Riverside Edition,* trade printing. The works half title may not be present in later printings. Price, 3s. 6d per volume.

Note one: A four-page subscription form has been noted (BO).

Note two: The *Costbooks* record charges for resetting the title page with the Routledge imprint for the first six volumes on 1 September 1883. The *Riverside Edition (Copyright)* was printed from duplicate plates Houghton, Mifflin had sent to England. Charges for the duplicate plates were made to Routledge as follows: vols. I–V, 24 July 1883; vols. VI–VII, 22 August 1883; vol. VIII, 14 September 1883; vol. IX, 19 November 1883; vol. X, 9 November 1883; vol. XI, 15 November 1883.

Note three: On 31 May 1883, H. O. Houghton wrote Routledge, acting on behalf of the Emerson heirs and Houghton, Mifflin, agreeing to terms for reprinting the *Riverside Edition.* On 1 January 1884, a memorandum between Routledge and the Emersons, agreeing to give Routledge "all our Copyright" in the eleven volumes of the *Riverside Edition* and the "further right to purchase at reasonable prices any further volume or volumes" for £150, was signed by Edward Waldo Emerson, Ellen Tucker Emerson, and Edith Emerson Forbes (Routledge Archives).

B 11 STANDARD LIBRARY EDITION
[1894]

Standard Library Edition, 14 vols. Boston and New York: Houghton, Mifflin, [1894].

Half title reads '[gothic] Standard Library Edition | [rule] | THE WORKS OF | RALPH WALDO EMERSON | WITH A GENERAL INDEX AND A MEMOIR | BY JAMES ELLIOT CABOT | *WITH STEEL PORTRAITS AND ETCHINGS* | IN FOURTEEN VOLUMES | VOLUME I. [II.–XIV.] | [leaf design]'. Printed from the *Riverside Edition* plates. Primary binding medium reddish brown H cloth (fine diaper), with leather label on spine. Reprinted (1898?) on laid paper and bound in medium yellow green T cloth (rib), with goldstamped oval portrait of the Emerson house in Concord on the front cover (JM). Top edges gilded in both formats. Same volume order and arrangement as the *Riverside Edition,* trade printing, with the addition of Cabot's *A Memoir of Ralph Waldo Emerson* (D 138) as vols. XIII–XIV. Sold only by subscription. Original prices: cloth, $28.00 a set; half crushed levant, $56.00.

Note one: 250 copies of a prospectus printed 28 August 1894; 300 copies on 10 April 1895. *Not seen.*

Note two: 2,000 copies of an eight-page circular printed 10 October 1894; 1,000 copies on 31 August 1895. *Not seen.*

Note three: The *Costbooks* have numerous entries for dust jackets, possibly of plain paper with an aperture at top of spine for title to show through; no jackets have been located.

Note four: A contract of 1 June 1894 called for sales by subscription only and a 20% royalty.

Note five: Numerous reprintings with undated title pages. Approximately 4,800 sets of the *Standard Library Edition* were sold between 1894 and 31 March 1906, when it was apparently allowed to go out of print.

B 12 "SOVEREIGN EDITION"
1903

"Sovereign Edition," 4 vols. London: George Routledge & Sons, 1903.

Half title reads 'EMERSON'S | WORKS: VOL. I. [II.–IV.]'. Listed in the publisher's records as the "Sovereign Edition," but not so identified in the works. Printed by William Clowes and Sons, London. Printed from the *Riverside Edition (Copyright)* plates, combined in twelve-volumes-in-four format. Primary binding half leather with gray-green CM cloth (patterned sand).

1. *Nature, Addresses, and Lectures, Essays: First Series, Essays: Second Series*, vol. I (1903)

2. *Representative Men, English Traits, The Conduct of Life*, vol. II (1903)

3. *Society and Solitude, Letters and Social Aims, Poems*, vol. III (1903)

4. *Lectures and Biographical Sketches, Miscellanies, Natural History of Intellect*, vol. IV (1903)

B 13 FIRESIDE EDITION
1909

Fireside Edition, 12 vols. Boston and New York: [Houghton Mifflin], MDCCCCIX.

Designated as the *Fireside Edition* on the title page and the spine. No works half title. Printed from the *Riverside Edition* plates. Primary binding is medium brown coarse B cloth (linen), with paper label on spine. Top edges gilded. Same volume order and arrangement as the *Riverside Edition*, trade printing.

Note one: The *Costbooks* have numerous entries for dust jackets of Quaker drab paper, possibly with an aperture at top of spine for title to show through; no jackets have been located.

Note two: Approximately 650 copies in cloth and 450 copies in half leather were sold by 1923. Another 552 copies were probably sold to an agent.

B 14 "JEFFERSON PRESS EDITION"
[ca. 1912]

"Jefferson Press Edition," 6 vols. Boston and New York: The Jefferson Press, [ca. 1912].

Known as the "Jefferson Press Edition," but not so identified in the works. No works half title. Printed from the *Riverside Edition* plates by arrangement with Houghton Mifflin. Combined in two-volumes-in-one format, rearranging the order of the volumes. Possibly limited to 145 copies, printed by Houghton Mifflin. Volumes are unnumbered; order below is arbitrary.

1. *Nature, Addresses, and Lectures, Representative Men*, vol. [I] [n.d.]

2. *Essays: First and Second Series*, vol. [II] [n.d.]

3. *English Traits, The Conduct of Life*, vol. [III] [n.d.]

4. *Society and Solitude, Letters and Social Aims*, vol. [IV] [n.d.]

5. *Poems, Lectures and Biographical Sketches*, vol. [V] [n.d.]

6. *Miscellanies, Natural History of Intellect*, vol. [VI] [n.d.]

B 15 UNIVERSITY EDITION
[ca. 1912]

University Edition, 12 vols. New York: Sully and Kleinteich, [ca. 1912].

Designated as the *University Edition* on the title page. No works half title. Printed from the *Riverside Edition* plates. Same volume order and arrangement as the *Riverside Edition*, trade printing. Prices: cloth, $18.00 a set; three-quarter leather, $30.00.

B 16 "WAVERLEY" RIVERSIDE EDITION
[n.d.]

"Waverley" *Riverside Edition*, 12 vols. London: Waverley Book Company, [n.d.].

Designated as the *Riverside Edition (Copyright)* on the title page, and as the *Riverside Edition* on the works half title. Printed from the *Riverside Edition (Copyright)* plates. Same volume order and arrangement as the *Riverside Edition*, trade printing.

B 17 COMPLETE PROSE WORKS
1889

The Complete Prose Works of Ralph Waldo Emerson. London, New York, Melbourne: Ward, Lock, 1889.

656 pp., double columns. Introduction by G.T. B[ettany]. *The Minerva Library of Famous Books*. Listed in *Bookseller*, no. 381 (7 August 1889), 783. Price, 2s. *Locations:* BL (4 September 1889), BE.

Contents: Essays: First Series; Essays: Second Series; Representative Men; English Traits; Miscellanies [Nature; Addresses, and Lectures]; Society and Solitude; Fortune of the Republic; The Conduct of Life; Letters and Social Aims.

Reprinted 1889 ("Second Edition" [N]), 1890 ("Third Edition" [CtW]), 1890 ("Fourth Edition" [N]), [n.d.] (JM). Also noted with undated London, New York, Melbourne: Ward, Lock, Bowden imprint ("Sixth Edition" [BRU]). Also noted with cancel title leaf and undated Glasgow: Grand Colosseum Warehouse imprint (JM).

B 18 CENTENARY EDITION (TRADE)
1903–1904

Centenary Edition, 12 vols. Boston and New York: Houghton, Mifflin, 1903–1904.

Half title reads '[gothic] Centenary Edition | THE COMPLETE WORKS OF | RALPH WALDO EMERSON | WITH | A BIOGRAPHICAL | INTRODUCTION AND NOTES | BY

EDWARD WALDO EMERSON AND | A GENERAL INDEX | VOL. | I. [II.–XII.]'. Printed from stereotype plates by H. O. Houghton, The Riverside Press, Cambridge, Mass. Printed on laid paper. Primary binding dark green T cloth (rib), with goldstamped 'R. Waldo Emerson' facsimile signature on front cover. Top edges gilded. Later printings have been noted with volume numbers stamped on spine. Original prices: cloth, $1.75 per volume and $21.00 a set; half calf, $39.00; half polished morocco, $42.00; half levant, $48.00.

1. *Nature, Addresses, and Lectures*, vol. I (1903)

2. *Essays: First Series*, vol. II (1903)

3. *Essays: Second Series*, vol. III (1903)

4. *Representative Men*, vol. IV (1903)

5. *English Traits*, vol. V (1903)

6. *The Conduct of Life*, vol. VI (1904)

7. *Society and Solitude*, vol. VII (1904)

8. *Letters and Social Aims*, vol. VIII (1904)

9. *Poems*, vol. IX (1904)

Contains new collected material; see A 18.16.

10. *Lectures and Biographical Sketches*, vol. X (1904)

11. *Miscellanies*, vol. XI (1904)

Contains new collected material; see A 40.3.

12. *Natural History of Intellect*, vol. XII (1904)

Contains new collected material; see A 44.3.

Note one: 35 salesmen's dummies printed 13 March 1903. *Not seen.*

Note two: 260 copies of a prospectus printed 18 March 1903. *Not seen.*

Note three: 1,500 copies of an eight-page circular printed 31 March 1903. *Not seen.*

Note four: 2,400 copies of a four-page circular printed 24 June 1903 and 17 July 1903. *Not seen.*

Note five: A contract was signed 9 March 1903, with the Emerson family receiving a 20% royalty and retaining the plates. The plates were sold to Houghton Mifflin on 1 July 1932.

Note six: The *Centenary Edition* was apparently in print through 1952.

Note seven: For further information on the *Centenary Edition*, see Joel Myerson, "Introduction" to the 1979 AMS reprint (B 27), I, [v–xliv].

B 19 AUTOGRAPH CENTENARY EDITION
1903–1904

Autograph Centenary Edition, 12 vols. Cambridge: The Riverside Press, 1903–1904. Published by Houghton, Mifflin.

Designated as the *Autograph Centenary Edition* in the statement of limitation and on the verso of the works half title. Half title reads '[red] THE COMPLETE WORKS OF | [red] RALPH WALDO EMERSON | WITH | A BIOGRAPHICAL | INTRODUCTION AND NOTES | BY EDWARD WALDO EMERSON AND | A GENERAL INDEX | VOLUME | I [II–XII]'. Printed from the *Centenary Edition* plates in large paper format. Printed on laid paper. Title page printed in red and black. Primary binding dark yellow brown coarse B cloth (linen), with paper label on spine. Pages rough trimmed. Same volume order and arrangement as the *Centenary Edition,* trade printing. Limited to 600 numbered copies, signed by the publisher; limitation notice on sheet inserted before works half title. A page of Emerson manuscript inserted after the works half title in vol. I. Prices: cloth, $72.00 a set; three-quarter levant, $150.00; full levant, price unknown.

Note one: 1,500 advertising cards printed 8 May 1903. *Not seen.*

Note two: 1,200 advertising cards on Danish Ledger paper printed 15 May 1903. *Not seen.*

Note three: 1,000 order blanks printed 19 May 1903. *Not seen.*

Note four: An eight-page advertising brochure has been noted (Collection of Raymond Borst).

Note five: The *Costbooks* have numerous entries for dust jackets, possibly of plain paper with an aperture at top of spine for title to show through; no jackets have been located.

Note six: According to the advertising brochure, "numbers from 1 to 200 will be reserved for customers ordering the three-quarters levant binding, or special bindings in full levant" (p. [7]).

Note seven: According to a 9 March 1903 contract, the Emerson family recieved a 12½% royalty.

B 20 CONCORD EDITION
1903–1904

Concord Edition, 12 vols. Boston and New York: Houghton, Mifflin, 1903–1904.

Designated as the "Subscription Centenary Edition" in the publisher's records, but not so advertised or identified in the works. Half title reads '[gothic] Concord Edition | THE COMPLETE WORKS OF | RALPH WALDO EMERSON | WITH A BIOGRAPHICAL INTRODUCTION AND NOTES BY | EDWARD WALDO EMERSON AND A GENERAL INDEX | ILLUSTRATED WITH PHOTOGRAVURES | VOLUME I [II–XII] | [leaf design]'. Printed from the *Centenary Edition* plates. Bound only in very deep red T cloth (rib), with same stamping as for the *Centenary Edition,* trade printing, bindings but without facsimile signature on front cover. Top edges gilded. Same volume order and arrangement as the *Centenary Edition,* trade printing.

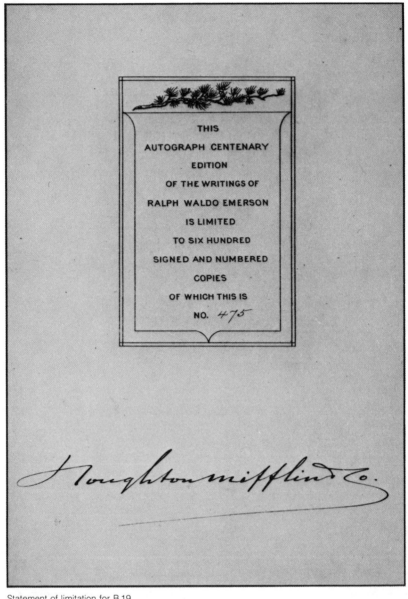

THIS
AUTOGRAPH CENTENARY
EDITION
OF THE WRITINGS OF
RALPH WALDO EMERSON
IS LIMITED
TO SIX HUNDRED
SIGNED AND NUMBERED
COPIES
OF WHICH THIS IS
NO. 475

Houghton Mifflin Co.

Statement of limitation for B 19

Note one: 5,000 copies of an eight-page circular printed 2 November 1903 and 21 August 1903. *Not seen.*

Note two: 5,000 copies of an order blank printed 27 August 1903; 3,000 copies on 25 March 1904. *Not seen.*

Note three: 500 copies of a prospectus printed 8 September 1903. *Not seen.*

Note four: The *Costbooks* have numerous entries for dust jackets of Straw laid paper, possibly with an aperture at top of spine for title to show through; no jackets have been located.

Note five: A salesman's dummy was offered for sale by Roger Butterfield, Special List 17, 1978.

Note six: According to a 9 March 1903 contract, the Emerson family received a 12½% royalty.

B 21 CENTENARY EDITION (ENGLISH)
    [1903–1909]

Centenary Edition (English), 12 vols. Vols. I–IX, London: A. P. Watt & Son; vols. X–XII, London: Archibald Constable & Company; Boston and New York: Houghton, Mifflin, [1903–1909].

Designated as the *Centenary Edition* on the works half title. Works half title the same as the *Centenary Edition,* trade printing. Sheets from the *Centenary Edition,* trade printing, with altered or cancel title leaves; see below. Binding information below. Same volume order and arrangement as the *Centenary Edition,* trade printing. Price, 6s. per volume.

1. *Nature, Addresses, and Lectures,* vol. I [1903]

Title page has label pasted over Houghton, Mifflin imprint, with 'A. P. WATT & SON | [gothic] Hastings House | NORFOLK STREET, STRAND | LONDON'. Binding is the same as for the *Centenary Edition,* trade printing, except the Houghton, Mifflin imprint is blotted out and goldstamped over it is 'A. P. WATT | AND SON'.

2. *Essays: First Series,* vol. II [1903]

Title page has the same label as in vol. I. Binding is the same for the *Centenary Edition,* trade printing, except: either goldstamped 'A. P. WATT & SON' at bottom, or Houghton, Mifflin imprint is blotted out and goldstamped over it is 'A. P. WATT & SON'.

3. *Essays: Second Series,* vol. III [1903]

Title page has the same label as in vol. I. Binding is the same as for the *Centenary Edition,* trade printing, except: either goldstamped 'A. P. WATT | AND SON' at bottom, or Houghton, Mifflin imprint is blotted out and goldstamped over it is 'A. P. WATT | AND SON'.

4. *Representative Men,* vol. IV [1903]

Title page has the same label as in vol. I. Binding is the same as for the *Centenary Edition,* trade printing (with Houghton, Mifflin imprint).

5. *English Traits,* vol. V [1903]

Title page has the same label as in vol. I. Binding is the same as for the *Centenary Edition,* trade printing (with Houghton, Mifflin imprint).

6. *The Conduct of Life*, vol. VI [1904]

Title page has the same label as in vol. I. Binding is the same as for the *Centenary Edition*, trade printing, except: goldstamped 'A. P. WATT & SON' at bottom.

7. *Society and Solitude*, vol. VII [1904]

Title page has the same label as in vol. I. Binding is the same as for vol. VI.

8. *Letters and Social Aims*, vol. VIII [1904]

Title page has the same label as in vol. I. Binding is the same as for vol. VI.

9. *Poems*, vol. IX [1904]

Title page has the same label as in vol. I. Binding is the same as for vol. VI.

10. *Lectures and Biographical Sketches*, vol. X [1909]

Title leaf is a cancel with London: Archibald Constable & Company; Boston and New York: Houghton, Mifflin, [n.d.]. Light brown coarse B cloth (linen), with paper label on spine.

11. *Miscellanies*, vol. XI [1909]

Title leaf is a cancel with the same imprint as in vol. X. Binding is the same as for vol. X.

12. *Natural History of Intellect*, vol. XII [1909]

Title leaf is a cancel with the same imprint as in vol. X. Binding is the same as for vol. X.

Note: It appears that Watt either failed or discontinued the *Centenary Edition* in 1904, and that Constable picked up the last three volumes in time to sell them with *Journals* (see A 52) and in similar bindings. Copies of vols. I–IX were deposited for copyright in 1903 and 1904; copies of vols. X–XII in 1909.

B 22 RIVERSIDE POCKET EDITION
1914

Riverside Pocket Edition, 12 vols. Boston and New York: Houghton Mifflin, [1914].

Half title reads '[gothic] Riverside Pocket Edition | [rule] | THE COMPLETE WORKS OF | RALPH WALDO EMERSON | IN TWELVE VOLUMES | VOLUME I [II–XII]'. Printed from the *Centenary Edition* plates. Title page printed in red and black. Primary binding greenish black leather over flexible boards. Top edges gilded. Same volume order and arrangement as the *Centenary Edition*, trade printing.

B 23 EMERSON'S COMPLETE WORKS
1921

Emerson's Complete Works, 6 vols. Boston and New York: Houghton Mifflin, 1921.

Designated in the publisher's records as the "Fireside Edition," but not so advertised or identified in the works. Title page lettering and vignette the same as in the *Fireside Edition*. Designated as *Emerson's Complete Works* on the spine. No works half title. Printed from the *Centenary Edition* plates, text only without the notes, combined in two-volumes-in-one format. Bound in medium green coarse B cloth (linen) or deep red T cloth (rib). The order of the volumes is taken from the spine stamping.

1. *Essays First and Second Series*, vol. I (1921)

2. *Nature, Addresses, and Lectures, and Letters and Social Aims*, vol. II (1921)

3. *Representative Men and Miscellanies*, vol. III (1921)

4. *English Traits and Lectures and Biographical Sketches*, vol. IV (1921)

5. *The Conduct of Life and Natural History of Intellect*, vol. V (1921)

6. *Society and Solitude and Poems*, vol. VI (1921)

Note: Approximately 430 sets of *Emerson's Complete Works* were sold by 1923. Another 208 sets were probably sold to an agent.

B 24 CURRENT OPINION EDITION
1923

Current Opinion Edition, 6 vols. New York: Wm. H. Wise, 1923.

Designated as the *Current Opinion Edition* on the works half title. Printed from the *Centenary Edition* plates, combined in two-volumes-in-one format. Possibly 10,000 copies printed by Houghton Mifflin for sale by Wise.

1. *Nature, Addresses, and Lectures; Essays: First Series*, vol. I (1923)

2. *Essays: Second Series; Representative Men*, vol. II (1923)

3. *English Traits; The Conduct of Life*, vol. III (1923)

4. *Society and Solitude; Letters and Social Aims*, vol. IV (1923)

5. *Poems; Lectures and Biographical Sketches*, vol. V (1923)

6. *Miscellanies; Natural History of Intellect*, vol. VI (1923)

B 25 HARVARD EDITION
1929

Harvard Edition, 6 vols. Boston and New York: Houghton Mifflin, 1929.

Designated as the *Harvard Edition* on the title page. No works half title. Printed from the *Centenary Edition* plates, text only without the notes, combined in two-volumes-in-one format. Bound only in deep red T cloth (rib). Order of volumes not stated in works, but same two-volumes-in-one combinations as *Emerson's Complete Works* and order of volumes is therefore considered to be the same. Price, $21.00 a set. Apparently in print through 1951.

B 26 MEDALLION EDITION
1929

Medallion Edition, 6 vols. New York: Wm. H. Wise, 1929.

Designated as the *Medallion Edition* on the works half title. Printed from the *Centenary Edition* plates, combined in two-volumes-in-one format. Same volume order and arrangement as the *Current Opinion Edition.*

B 27 "AMS PRESS" CENTENARY EDITION
[1968]

"AMS Press" *Centenary Edition,* 12 vols. [New York: AMS Press, 1968].

Designated as the *Centenary Edition* on the works half title, which also contains the AMS Press imprint. Facsimile reprinting of the *Centenary Edition,* trade printing. Price, $175.00. Reprinted 1979, with an "Introduction" by Joel Myerson. Same volume order and arrangement as the *Centenary Edition,* trade printing.

B 28 YORK LIBRARY EDITION
1904–1905

York Library Edition, 5 vols. London: George Bell and Sons, 1904–1905.

Designated as the *York Library Edition* on the works half title. Later printings designated *Bohn's Standard Library* or *Bohn's Popular Library* on the works half title. Edited by George Sampson. Original prices: cloth, 2s. per volume; leather, 3s. per volume. Distributed in the United States by Macmillan of New York at 80¢ in cloth and $1.25 in leather.

1. *Essays [First and Second Series], Representative Men,* vol. I (1904)

513 pp. Macmillan importation listed in *Publishers' Weekly,* 66 (8 October 1904), 852. *Location:* BL (23 June 1904).

Published June 1904; reprinted April 1906, April 1913, 1919.

2. *English Traits, The Conduct of Life, Nature,* vol. II (1904)

416 pp. Macmillan importation listed in *Publishers' Weekly,* 66 (8 October 1904), 852. *Locations:* BL (2 January 1905), MdBJ.

Published August 1904; reprinted April 1906, April 1913, 1924.

3. *Society and Solitude, Letters and Social Aims, Addresses,* vol. III (1904)

541 pp. Macmillan importation listed in *Publishers' Weekly,* 67 (18 March 1905), 852. *Locations:* BL (2 January 1905), MdBJ.

Published August 1904; reprinted April 1906, October 1913.

4. *Miscellaneous Pieces,* vol. IV (1905)

462 pp. Macmillan importation listed in *Publishers' Weekly,* 67 (18 March 1905), 852. *Locations:* BL (14 April 1905), MdBJ.

Published January 1905; reprinted April 1906, October 1913.

5. *Poems*, vol. V (1905)

281 pp. *Locations:* BL (22 December 1905), MiU.

Published July 1905; reprinted April 1906, March 1914.

> B 29   "JOHN D. MORRIS EDITION"
>   *[1906]*

The Works of Ralph Waldo Emerson, 6 vols. Philadelphia: John D. Morris, [1906].

Known as the "John D. Morris Edition." No works half title. Sets noted designated *Cambridge Edition de Luxe, Dial Edition DeLuxe,* and *Saadi Edition DeLuxe,* each limited to 1,000 numbered copies. Edition designation and statement of limitation on title leaf verso. Listed in *Publishers' Weekly,* 70 (21 July 1906), 80. Copyright, 13 February 1906. Published July 1906. *Locations:* DLC (13 February 1906), JM. Price: Persian morocco, $9.75 a set.

1. *Representative Men*, vol. I [1906], 267 pp.

2. *English Traits*, vol. II [1906], 304 pp.

3. *Nature, Addresses, and Lectures*, vol. III [1906], 368 pp.

4. *The Conduct of Life*, vol. IV [1906], 319 pp.

5. *Essays First and Second Series*, vol. V [1906], 461 pp.

6. *Poems*, vol. VI [1906], 244 pp.

Introduction by J. Ellis Burdick. Based on examination of reprintings from the "John D. Morris Edition" plates, copies may exist with an introduction by Henry Ketcham.

> B 30   WORKS
>   *[n.d.]*

The Works of Ralph Waldo Emerson, 6 vols. Boston and New York: C. T. Brainard, [n.d.].

Designated as the *Edition de Luxe,* limited to 1,000 numbered copies. Edition designation on title page and on title leaf verso; statement of limitation on title leaf verso. No works half title. Printed from the "John D. Morris Edition" plates.

1. *Essays First and Second Series*, vol. I [n.d.]

2. *Nature, Addresses, and Lectures*, vol. II [n.d.]

3. *Poems*, vol. III [n.d.]

Introduction by Henry Ketcham.

4. *Representative Men*, vol. IV [n.d.]

Also contains selections from Richard Garnett's *Life.*

5. *English Traits*, vol. V [n.d.]

6. *The Conduct of Life*, vol. VI [n.d.]

B 31 WORKS
[n.d.]

The Works of Ralph Waldo Emerson, 6 vols. New York: Caxton Society, [n.d.].

Designated as the *Edition de Luxe*, limited to 1,000 numbered copies. Edition designation and statement of limitation on title leaf verso. No works half title. Printed from the "John D. Morris Edition" plates, but with volume order and arrangement of the C. T. Brainard reprinting (see B 30).

B 32 WORKS
[n.d.]

The Works of Ralph Waldo Emerson, 6 vols. New York: National Library Co., [n.d.].

Designated as the *Edition de Luxe*, limited to 1,000 numbered copies. Edition designation on title page and title leaf verso; statement of limitation on title leaf verso. No works half title. Printed from the "John D. Morris Edition" plates, but with volume order and arrangement of the C. T. Brainard reprinting (see B 30).

B 33 WORKS
[n.d.]

The Works of Ralph Waldo Emerson, 6 vols. Philadelphia, New York, Chicago: Nottingham Society, [n.d.].

Designated as the *Edition de Luxe*, limited to 1,000 numbered copies. Edition designation and statement of limitation on title leaf verso. No works half title. Printed from the "John D. Morris Edition" plates, but with volume order and arrangement of the C. T. Brainard reprinting (see B 30).

B 34 EDINA EDITION
1906

Edina Edition. Edinburgh: W. P. Nimmo, Hay, & Mitchell, 1906.

Designated the *Edina Edition* on the title page. Two one-volume editions have been noted, priority undetermined.

1. 1042 pp., double columns. Advertised in various bindings at various prices. Edited with an introduction by J. P[ennells]. Published August 1906. Reprinted, edited with an introduction by A. C. Hearn, 1907, [n.d.]. *Locations:* BE (24 November 1906), CaNSHPL (1907), JM (n.d.).

2. 713 pp. Advertised in various bindings at various prices. Edited with an introduction by A. C. Hearn. Title page is undated. *Location* JM.

Contents: Edition 1: *Essays: First Series; Essays: Second Series; English Traits; Society and Solitude; The Conduct of Life; Letters and Social Aims; Representative Men; Miscellanies [Nature; Addresses, and Lectures]; Fortune of the Republic; Poems;* Edition 2: *Essays: First Series; Essays: Second Series; English Traits; Society and Solitude; The Conduct of Life; Letters and Social Aims.*

B 35 NEW NATIONAL EDITION
[1914]

New National Edition, 5 vols. New York: Hearst's International Library Co., [1914].

Introduction by Chester Noyes Greenough. Designated as the *New National Edition* on the title page and the spine. No works half title. Also reprinted without the *New National Edition* designation. Deposit copy: DLC (24 June 1914). Prices: cloth, $3.00 a set; flexible leather, $6.00 a set.

1. *Essays First and Second Series,* vol. I (1914), 423 pp.

2. *English Traits, Representative Men, Addresses,* vol. II (1914), 604 pp.

3. *The Conduct of Life, Society and Solitude, and Other Essays and Addresses,* vol. III (1914), 574 pp.

4. *Nature, Addresses, Papers from the Dial,* vol. IV (1914), 554 pp.

5. *Poems,* vol. V (1914), 326 pp.

Also contains Richard Garnett's *Life* and an index.

B 36 WORKS
[1942]

The Works of Ralph Waldo Emerson. New York: Tudor Publishing Company, [1942].

Works half title. Printed from the *New National Edition* plates, with contents abridged, in four-volumes-in-one format. Dust jacket. *Locations:* DLC (12 February 1943), JM. Price, $1.95.

B 37 WORKS
[n.d.]

The Works of Ralph Waldo Emerson, 5 vols. New York: Charles C. Bigelow, [n.d.].

No works half title. Printed from the *New National Edition* plates. Same volume order and arrangement as the *New National Edition.*

B 38 WORKS
[n.d.]

The Works of Ralph Waldo Emerson, 5 vols. New York: Bigelow, Brown, [n.d.].

No works half title. Printed from the *New National Edition* plates, except: vol. V has been noted in two formats: *Poems,* 322 pp. (no index); *Poems, Addresses,* 428 pp.

(JM; MoSU). Same volume order and arrangement as the *New National Edition*. Also noted with *Edition de Luxe* designation on title leaf verso. Prices: buckram, $20.00 a set; three-quarter leather, $28.75.

B 39 WORKS
[n.d.]

The Works of Ralph Waldo Emerson, 5 vols. New York: Bigelow, Smith, [n.d.].

No works half title. Printed from the *New National Edition* plates, except: no index to vol. V. Same volume order and arrangement as the *New National Edition*. Three-quarter leather.

B 40 WRITINGS
[n.d.]

The Writings of Ralph Waldo Emerson, 5 vols. New York: Brentano's, [n.d.].

No works half title. Printed from the *New National Edition* plates. Same volume order and arrangement as the *New National Edition,* except: no index to vol. V. Price, $20.00 a set.

B 41 WORKS
[n.d.]

The Works of Ralph Waldo Emerson, 5 vols. New York: Harper and Brothers, [n.d.].

No works half title. Printed from the *New National Edition* plates. Same volume order and arrangement as the *New National Edition,* except: no index to vol. V.

B 42 WORKS
[n.d.]

The Works of Ralph Waldo Emerson, 5 vols. Boston and New York: Jefferson Press, [n.d.].

Designated as the *Edition de Luxe* on the title leaf verso. No works half title. Printed from the *New National Edition* plates. Same volume order and arrangement as the *New National Edition,* except: no index to vol. V.

B 43 WORKS
[n.d.]

The Works of Ralph Waldo Emerson, 5 vols. [N.p.]: Library Society, [n.d.].

Designated as the *Edition de Luxe* on the title page. No works half title. Printed from the *New National Edition* plates. Same volume order and arrangement as the *New National Edition,* except: no index to vol. V.

       B 44 WORKS
       [n.d.]

Works, 3 vols. New York: Three Sirens Press, [n.d.].

Printed from the *New National Edition* plates, abridged, vols. I–III only.

1. *Essays First and Second Series*, vol. I [n.d.]

2. *English Traits, Representative Men, Addresses*, vol. II [n.d.]

3. *The Conduct of Life, Society and Solitude, and Other Essays and Addresses*, vol. III [n.d.]

       B 45 COMPLETE WRITINGS
       [1929]

The Complete Writings of Ralph Waldo Emerson, 2 vols. New York: Wm. H. Wise, [1929].

1435 pp., double columns (paged continously). No works half title. Also noted combined in two-volumes-in-one format. Published May 1929. Copyright, 21 May 1929. Price, $9.65 a set. *Location:* JM.

Contents: Nature; Addresses, and Lectures; Essays: First Series; Essays: Second Series; Representative Men; English Traits; The Conduct of Life; Society and Solitude; Letters and Social Aims; Poems; Lectures and Biographical Sketches; Miscellanies; Natural History of Intellect; "Papers from the Dial."

Reprinted June 1929 ("Second Edition"), November 1929 ("Third Edition"), August 1930 ("Fourth Edition"). *Locations:* JM (all).

       B 46 COLLECTED WORKS
       1971–

The Collected Works of Ralph Waldo Emerson, 2 vols. to date. Cambridge: The Belknap Press of Harvard University Press, 1971–.

Designated as the *Collected Works* on title page, works half title, and dust jacket.

1. *Nature, Addresses, and Lectures*, vol. 1 (1971), 333 pp.

2. *Essays: First Series*, vol. II (1979), 368 pp.

C. Miscellaneous Collections

All miscellaneous collections of Emerson's writings through 1980, arranged chronologically. Included are anthologies, birthday books, and topical studies.

C 1

Nature: An Essay. And Orations. London: William Smith, MDCCCXLIV.

47 pp., double columns. Cover title. *Smith's Standard Library.* Advertised in *Publishers' Circular and Booksellers' Record,* 6 (15 December 1843), 396; as "Just published," in *Athenæum,* no. 842 (16 December 1843), 1098; as "Nearly Ready," in *Athenæum,* no. 845 (6 January 1844), 2. Listed as published between 28 February and 15 March 1844, in *Publishers' Circular and Booksellers' Record,* 7 (15 March 1844), 82. Possibly 2,500 copies printed (see *JMN,* X, 427). Price, 1s. 6d. *Location:* ViU (lacks wrappers).

Contents: Nature, "The American Scholar," "Divinity School Address," "Literary Ethics," "Man the Reformer."

C 2.1.a

Nature: An Essay. To Which is Added, Orations, Lectures, and Addresses. London: Aylott and Jones, 1845.

175 pp. Cloth or wrappers. Listed in *Athenæum,* no. 907 (15 March 1845), 266; in *Literary Gazette,* no. 1469 (15 March 1845), 173. Price: cloth, 1s. 6d. *Locations:* JM (cloth), NNC (wrappers).

Contents: Nature, "The American Scholar," "Divinity School Address," "Literary Ethics," "The Method of Nature," "Man the Reformer," and "The Young American."

C 2.1.b–c

Nature: An Essay. To Which Are Added, Orations, Lectures, and Addresses. London: Henry G. Bohn, 1852.

Listed in *Athenæum,* no. 1289 (10 July 1852), 750. Price, 1s. Reprinted 1860. *Locations:* BL (9 March 1853), JM (1860).

C 2.1.d

London: Bell & Daldy, 1873.

Location: CaOTU.

C 3

Essays Lectures and Orations. London: William S. Orr, M DCCC XLVIII.

364 pp. Cloth or wrappers. Possibly published in late 1847 (see *L,* IV, 14). See also "Literary News," *Boston Daily Evening Transcript,* 8 January 1848, p. 2, in which a London correspondent writes that Orr has announced this title for sale. Price: wrappers, 3s. *Locations:* BL, CSt, CtY, JM, ViU (wrappers).

Contents: Essays: First Series, Nature, "Lectures on the Times," "The American Scholar," "Divinity School Address," "Man the Reformer," and "The Method of Nature."

569

C 4.1.a
Essays. London: William Tegg, 1848.

Wrappers. Advertised in *Literary Gazette*, no. 1658 (28 October 1848), 719. Price, 2s. *Not seen*.

C 4.1.b–c
Essays Orations and Lectures. London: William Tegg; Aylott & Jones; Glasgow: W. Collins; R. Griffin; Edinburgh: Thomas Nelson, MDCCCXLVIII.

175 pp. Listed in *Literary Gazette*, no. 1646 (5 August 1848), 526. Advertised in *Literary Gazette*, no. 1658 (28 October 1848), 719. Price, 3s. 6d. Reprinted 1852. Listed in *Literary Gazette*, no. 1823 (27 December 1851), 921. *Location:* CaSSU (1848).

Contents: Essays: First Series, Nature, "The American Scholar," "Divinity School Address," "Literary Ethics," "The Method of Nature," "Man the Reformer," "The Young American."

C 5.1.a–c
Orations and Lectures. London: William Tegg, 1848.

Wrappers. Advertised in *Literary Gazette*, no. 1658 (28 October 1848), 719. Price, 1s. 6d. *Not seen*. Also combined with *Essays* (C 4.1.a) in two-volumes-in-one format; see C 4.1.b–c.

C 6
Essays, Lectures and Orations. London: William S. Orr, MDCCCLI.

568 pp. Price, 3s. *Locations:* BL (30 June 1851), InU, NNC.

Contents: Essays: First Series, Essays: Second Series, Nature, Representative Men, "Lectures on the Times," "The American Scholar," "Divinity School Address," "Literary Ethics," "The Method of Nature," "Man the Reformer."

C 7
Essai sur la Nature. Paris: Librairie Internationale, 1865.

253 pp. Translated by Xavier Eyma. *Location:* MB.

C 8.1.a
Orations, Lectures and Essays. London: Charles Griffin, 1866.

284 pp. Listed as published between 1 and 16 January 1866, in *Publishers' Circular and Booksellers' Record*, 29 (17 January 1866), 5. Price, 2s. 6d. *Locations:* BC, BL (16 July 1866), KU.

C 8.1.b
London: James Blackwood, [1873].

'NEW EDITION'. Listed as published between 16 and 30 August 1873, in *Publishers' Circular and Booksellers' Record*, 36 (1 September 1873), 395. Price, 2s. *Location:* MH.

C 9.1.a$_1$–c
The Emerson Birthday-Book. Boston: Houghton, Mifflin, 1881.

398 pp. Cloth or leather. Advertised for 21 May 1881, in *Publishers' Weekly*, 19 (14 May 1881), 537. Listed in *Publishers' Weekly*, 19 (28 May 1881), 564. Advertised for 23 May

1881, in *Atlantic*, 47 (June 1881), wrappers. According to the publisher's records, published 21 May 1881. Prices: cloth, $1.00; flexible calf, morocco, or sealskin, $3.50. Reprinted 1882; with Boston and New York imprint, [n.d.]. *Locations:* JM (all).

Note one: Numerous reprintings with undated title pages. Approximately 47,000 copies were sold through 1923.

Note two: The plates of *The Emerson Birthday-Book* were ordered destroyed 14 October 1929.

C 9.1.a₂
English issue

London: Sampson Low, Marston, Searle & Rivington, 1881.

The title leaf is a cancel. Listed in *Athenæum*, no. 2811 (10 September 1881), 335. Price, 3s. 6d. *Location:* BL (3 September 1881).

Note: An importation by Trübner was listed in *Athenæum*, no. 2812 (17 September 1881), 367, almost certainly of the Houghton, Mifflin printing.

C 10
Uit Emerson's Laatste Essays. Haarlem: H. D. Tjeenk Willink, 1881.

181 pp. Wrappers. Translated by M. A. N. Rovers. *Location:* NNC.

C 11.1.a–b
Culture, Behavior, Beauty. Books, Art, Eloquence. Power, Wealth, Illusions. Boston: Houghton, Mifflin, 1882.

108 + 104 + 107 pp. Cloth or flexible leather. *Modern Classics*, no. 2. Advertised in *Atlantic*, 46 (November 1880), wrappers. Price, 75¢. Reprinted [n.d.]. *Location:* JM (both).

Note one: Printed from the plates of the *Vest-Pocket Series* (see A 26.29, A 31.15, A 26.36).

Note two: Numerous reprintings with undated title pages. Approximately 8,700 copies sold by 1898, when the title was apparently allowed to go out of print.

C 12.1.a–b
Nature. Love, Friendship, Domestic Life. Success, Greatness, Immortality. Boston: Houghton, Mifflin, 1882.

93 + 93 + 96 pp. *Modern Classics*, no. 3. Advertised in *Atlantic*, 46 (November 1880), wrappers. Price, 75¢. Reprinted [n.d.]. *Location:* JM (both).

Note one: Printed from the plates of the *Vest-Pocket Series* (see A 3.4, A 10.72, A 34.9).

Note two: Numerous reprintings with undated title pages. Approximately 8,700 copies sold by 1898, when the title was apparently allowed to go out of print.

C 13.1.a–b
Thoughts from Emerson. Edinburgh: William P. Nimmo, 1883.

128 pp. Miniature book. Listed in *Publishers' Circular and Booksellers' Record*, 13 August 1883. Reprinted [Edinburgh: Nimmo, Hay, & Mitchell; London: Simpkin, n.d.], 127 pp. ("Threnody," pp. 127–128, is omitted), in *The Miniature Series (Secular)*, no. 1. Prices: velvet calf, 1s; cloth, 6d. *Locations:* BL (11 September 1883), JM (both).

C 14.1.a–e
Essays   Representative Men   Society and Solitude. London: George Routledge and
Sons, 1886.

282 pp., double columns. Introduction by Henry Morley. *Morley's Universal Library,* no.
33. Price, 1s. Reprinted 1886 (*'Second Edition'*), 1887 (*'Third Edition'*), 1890 (*'Fourth
Edition'*), [n.d.]. *Locations:* BL (4 March 1886), JM (1886, 1890), CaQMM (1887), TxU
(n.d.).

C 15
Essay-Gems of Emerson. London and New York: George Routledge and Sons, 1886.

160 pp. Cloth or wrappers. Introduction by Hugh Reginald Haweis. *Routledge's World
Library,* no. 27. Published 1 September 1886. Prices: cloth, 6d; wrappers, 3s. *Locations:* BL (23 November 1886), N.

C 16
Nature and Other Addresses. New York: John B. Alden, 1886.

101 pp. Listed for 4 September 1886, in *Publishers' Weekly,* 31 (29 January 1887), 130.
Also advertised as included in "Brilliant Books." Price, 40¢. *Location:* JM.

C 17.1.a
Transcendentalism and Other Addresses. New York: John B. Alden, 1886.

103 pp. Listed in *Publishers' Weekly,* 30 (4 December 1886), 892. Price, 40¢. *Location:*
MH.

Note: "Transcendentalism" is not by Emerson. In *New England Reformers and Divinity College Address* (see C 17.1.b), which reprints the essay, the following disclaimer is
present: "The paper on Transcendentalism has been wrongly attributed to Emerson. Its
author is not known." For the first printing of this paper, see [Charles Mayo Ellis], *An
Essay on Transcendentalism* (Boston: Crocker and Ruggles, 1842).

C 17.1.b
New England Reformers and Divinity College Address. New York: John B. Alden, 1887.

Location: DAU.

C 18
Love, Friendship, Heroism, Character. London: Ward, Lock, 1886.

132 pp. Cloth or wrappers. Advertised as published between 2 and 16 August 1886, in
Publishers' Circular and Booksellers' Record, 49 (16 August 1886), 881. Advertised as
included in "Royal Library of Literary Treasures," no. 19, and "Ward and Lock's Popular
Library." Prices: cloth, 6d; wrappers, 3d. *Not seen.*

C 19.1.a
The Conduct of Life, Social Aims and Other Essays. London and New York: Ward,
Lock, [1887].

123 pp., double columns. Introduction by G. T. Bettany. *Popular Library of Literary
Treasures,* no. 23. Listed as published between 1 and 15 December 1886, in *Publishers' Circular and Booksellers' Record,* 49 (15 December 1886), 1657. *Location:* BC
(22 April 1887).

C 19.1.b
Essays. Representative Men, English Traits, The Conduct of Life, Miscellaneous Essays. London, New York, Melbourne: Ward, Lock, [n.d.].

Location: CaBVa.

C 20.1.a–b
Select Writings of Ralph Waldo Emerson. London: Walter Scott; Toronto: W. J. Gage, 1888.

351 pp. Introduction by Percival Chubb. *The Camelot Series.* Price, 1s. Reprinted with Scott imprint only in *The Scott Library,* no. 33 [n.d.]. *Locations:* BL (26 March 1888), JM (both).

C 20.1.c
London: Mudie's Select Library, [n.d.].

New Camelot Series. Location: UPB.

C 21.1.a–c
Selections from the Writings of Ralph Waldo Emerson. Boston and New York: Houghton, Mifflin, 1888.

Unpaged (55 leaves). Self-wrappers. Reprinted 1890, [n.d.]. *Locations:* RPB, JM (1890, n.d.).

C 22.1.a–e
The Fortune of the Republic and Other American Addresses. Boston and New York: Houghton, Mifflin, 1889.

109 pp. Wrappers. *Riverside Literature Series,* no. 42, April 1889. Listed in *Publishers' Weekly,* 35 (15 June 1889), 789. According to the publisher's records, published 5 June 1889. Price, 15¢. Reprinted 1890. Reprinted in 142 pp., with "The American Scholar" added 1897, 1906, 1920. *Locations:* DLC (29 March 1889), PSC (1890), KMK (1906), MB (1920).

Note: Numerous reprintings with undated title pages. Approximately 30,100 copies sold through 1898.

C 22.1.f–i
Poems and Essays. Boston, New York, Chicago: Houghton, Mifflin, [1897].

Combined with *Poems* in two-volumes-in-one format; see A 18.11.b–e.

C 23
Emerson Gems. Boston: Samuel E. Cassino, [1892].

Unpaged (4 leaves). Wrappers. Illustrated by William Goodrich Beal. *Location:* LNHT.

C 24.1.a
The American Scholar   Self-Reliance   Compensation. New York, Cincinnati, Chicago: American Book Company, 1893.

108 pp. *English Classics for Schools.* Listed in *Publishers' Weekly,* 44 (12 August 1893), 203. Copyright, 31 May 1893. Price, 20¢. *Location:* JM.

C 24.1.b–c
New York, Cincinnati, Chicago: American Book Company, [1911].

132 pp. Edited with notes by Orren Henry Smith. *Eclectic English Classics*. Copyright, 18 March 1911. Price, 20¢. Reprinted 1921. *Locations:* JM (both).

C 25.1.a–d
Emerson Year Book. New York: E. P. Dutton, 1893.

157 pp. Selected by A. R. C. Listed in *Publishers' Weekly*, 44 (14 October 1893), 556. Copyright, 11 May 1893. Price, $1.00. Reprinted 1894, 1902, 1903. *Locations:* JM (1893, 1902, 1903), CtY (1894).

C 25.1.e–f
[Folcroft, Penn.]: Folcroft Library Editions, 1976.

Facsimile reprinting. Reprinted 1977, limited to 100 copies. *Locations:* CU-I (1976), DLC (30 January 1978).

C 26.1
Select Essays and Poems. Boston, New York, Chicago: Allyn and Bacon, [1898].

120 pp. Edited by Eva March Tappan. *The Academy Classics*. Price, 30¢. *Location:* DLC (22 December 1898).

C 26.2
Essays and Poems. Boston [&c.]: Allyn and Bacon, [1926].

161 pp. *The Academy Classics*. Copyright, 16 January 1926. Price, 50¢. *Location:* UU.

C 27
The Superlative and Other Essays. Boston, New York, Chicago: Houghton, Mifflin, [1899].

108 pp. Wrappers. *Riverside Literature Series*, no. 130, 4 January 1899. According to the publisher's records, published 4 January 1899. Listed in *Publishers' Weekly*, 55 (4 March 1899), 369. Price, 15¢. *Location:* DLC (16 February 1899).

C 28
Emerson's Essays   Nature   The American Scholar   Friendship. Boston [&c.]: Educational Publishing Company, [1900].

185 pp. Cloth or wrappers. Edited with notes by M. A. Eaton. Also advertised as included in "Red Shield English Classics" and "Ten Cent Classics." Prices: cloth, 25¢; wrappers, 10¢. *Location:* JM.

C 29
Ralph Waldo Emerson. Taylorville, Ill.: C. M. Parker, 1900.

[411]–442 pp. Cover title. Pamphlet. Introduction by Thomas Arkle Clark. Price, 10¢. *Location:* JM.

C 30
Beautiful Thoughts from Ralph Waldo Emerson. New York: James Pott, MCMI.

369 pp. Cloth or leather. Edited by Margaret B. Shipp. Listed in *Publishers' Weekly*, 60 (31 August 1901), 348. Published 31 August 1901. Importation listed in *English Cata-*

logue for November 1901 at 4s. Prices: cloth, 75¢; leather, $1.00. *Location:* DLC (1 August 1901).

C 31.1.a–c
History   Self-Reliance   Nature   Spiritual Laws   The American Scholar. New York: Doubleday, Page, 1901.

180 pp. Edited by Bliss Perry. *Little Masterpieces.* Listed in *Publishers' Weekly,* 61 (5 April 1902), 871. Copyright, 9 December 1901. Price, 40¢. Reprinted 1902, 1913. *Locations:* DLC (9 December 1901), JM (1902), MB (1913).

C 31.2
History   Self-Reliance   Spiritual Laws   Heroism   The American Scholar   Friendship. London: Masterpiece Press, 1905.

181 pp. Edited by William Stead, Jr. *Little Masterpieces. Location:* BL (21 June 1905).

C 32
Earlier Essays. Rahway, N.J.: Mershon, 1902.

Wrappers. *Not seen.*

C 33
Every Day with Emerson. Buffalo, N.Y.: [White-Evans-Penfold], 1902.

Unpaged (47 leaves). Vellum wrappers. Compiled by Harriet A. Townsend. *Location:* MH.

C 34.1
Ralph Waldo Emerson. Chicago: Unity Office, [1902].

30 pp. Head title. Selected by William C. Gannett. *Unity Mission Tract,* no. 20. Price, 5¢. *Location:* NRU.

C 34.2
London: British & Foreign Unitarian Association, 1902.

34 pp. Wrappers. *Locations:* BL (9 January 1903), CoU.

C 34.3.a–i
Emerson. Boston: American Unitarian Association, [1925].

31 pp. Cover title. *Biographical Series,* no. 2; *AUA Tracts, AUA Series,* no. 332. Published May 1925. Numerous reprintings in both series; the latest located reprint is in the *AUA Tracts,* 9th printing, December 1937. *Locations:* JM (1925), MH-AH (1937).

C 35
Thoughts from Emerson. Boston: James H. Earle, [1902].

166 pp. Edited by Ann Bachelor. Copyright, 10 March 1903. Price, 75¢. *Locations:* DLC (10 March 1903), JM.

C 36.1.a–c
Addresses and Essays. [London]: Watts, 1903.

142 pp., double columns. Cloth or wrappers. Introduction by Stanton Coit. "Issued for the Rationalist Press Association, Limited." *R.P.A. Cheap Reprints,* no. 12. Prices: cloth,

1s.; wrappers, 6d. Reprinted 1907 (twice); latest located reprint states "Third Impression (completing 30,000 copies)." *Locations:* BL (3 October 1903), CaQMM (1907), RPB (1907, 3d).

C 37.1.a–b
Insist on Yourself   The Only Law of Success   Master-Thoughts from Emerson. London: St. Martin's, [1903].

45 pp. Cloth or wrappers. *Wisdom in Brief* series. Prices: cloth, 1s.; wrappers, 6d. Published October 1903. Reprinted October 1906. *Locations:* BL (4 November 1903), BC (23 August 1907).

C 38
Emerson's Thoughts   A Treasury of Wisdom. London: Gay & Bird, [1903].

95 pp. Also advertised as included in "Wisdom in Brief Series." Price, 2s. *Location:* BL (30 January 1904).

C 39.1.a
An "Emerson" Treasury. Manchester: Albert Broadbent; London: F. R. Henderson, 1903.

46 pp. Wrappers. Selected by Albert Broadbent. Introduction by Thomas Pole. *Location:* BC (8 February 1904).

C 39.1.b–c
An Emerson Treasury. Manchester: Albert Broadbent; London: F. R. Henderson; Philadelphia: The Broadbent Press, 1904.

Revised Edition. Wrappers. Prices, 3d or 10¢. Reprinted in 1905 ("Tenth Thousand") in wrappers in *The Broadbent Treasuries,* no. 9. *Locations:* BE (1904), BO (16 February 1905), JM (1905).

Note: Listed for 1910 as included in the "Treasury Series" by Thomas Y. Crowell of New York in *Cumulative Book Index* for 1912; no copies have been located.

C 40
Emerson's Essays. London [&c.]: Cassell, MCMIV.

192 pp. Introduction by C. Lewis Hind. *Cassell's National Library,* no. 17. Published March 1904. *Locations:* BC (6 May 1904), BE (6 May 1904).

Note: Listed as *Selected Essays* in cloth or wrappers as included in the "National Library" by Funk & Wagnalls of New York in *Cumulative Book Index* for 1928; no copies have been located.

C 41
Pointers from Life (From "Emerson's Thoughts"). London: Gay & Bird, St. Martin's, [1904].

53 pp. Wrappers. *Wisdom in Brief* series. Price, 1s. *Location:* BL (12 March 1904).

Note: Selections from *Emerson's Thoughts* (C 38).

C 42
Gems from Emerson. Boston: DeWolfe, Fiske, [1904].

Unpaged (18 leaves). Cloth over foam covered boards. *Coronal Series*. Listed in *Publishers' Weekly*, 66 (3 December 1904), 1501. Copyright, 23 July 1904. Published 3 December 1904. Price, 50¢. *Locations:* DLC (23 July 1904), JM.

C 43

Emerson New Thought Calendar. [Holyoke, Mass.: William E. Towne, 1904].

Copyright, 28 October 1904. *Not seen.*

C 44.1.a

An Emerson Treasury. London: Astolat, MDCCCCV.

96 pp. Edited by J. Pennells. *Locations:* BC (27 March 1905), JM.

C 44.1.b

London: H. Siegle. 1907.

Advertised as included in "Astolat Reprints." Published August 1907. *Not seen.*

C 44.1.c

London: Siegle, Hill, [1912].

Published 12 July 1912. Price, 1s. 6d. *Location:* BL (12 November 1912).

C 44.1.d

London: L. B. Hill, 1922.

Advertised as included in "Value of Friendship Series." Published 22 May 1922. Price, 1s. *Not seen.*

C 44.1.f

[Folcroft, Penn.]: Folcroft Library Editions, 1973.

Facsimile reprinting of C 44.1.a. Limited to 100 copies. *Location:* DLC (19 July 1973).

C 44.1.g

[Norwood, Penn.]: Norwood Editions, 1978.

Facsimile reprinting of C 44.1.a. Limited to 100 copies. Price, $12.50. *Location:* DLC (13 December 1977).

C 44.2.a

An Emerson Treasury. London: Siegle, Hill, [1909].

126 pp. Cloth or limp leather. Edited by J. Pennells. *The Queen's Library of Literary Treasures*. Published August 1909. Price, 3s. *Location:* BL (18 January 1910).

C 44.2.b

New York: H. M. Caldwell, 1911.

Advertised as included in "Hampton Classics." Price, $1.35. *Not seen.*

C 44.2.c

[Folcroft, Penn.]: Folcroft Library Editions, 1977.

Facsimile reprinting of C 44.2.a. *Location:* CLSU.

C 44.3
An Emerson Treasury. London: Siegle, Hill, [1911].

143 pp. Limp leather. Edited by J. Pennells. *Langham Booklets,* no. 64. Published 11 June 1911. Price, 1s. *Location:* BL (22 September 1911).

C 45
Selections from R. W. Emerson. London: Edward Arnold, [1905].

48 pp. Cloth or wrappers. *The Arnold Prose Books,* no. 24. Prices: cloth, 4d; wrappers, 2d. *Location:* BL (25 May 1905).

C 46.1.a
An Emerson Calendar. New York: Thomas Y. Crowell, [1905].

118 pp. Edited by Huntington Smith. Listed in *Publishers' Weekly,* 68 (21 October 1905), 1037. Also advertised as included in "Chiswick Series." Published 21 October 1905. Copyright, 29 June 1905. Price, 50¢. *Locations:* DLC (29 June 1905), JM.

C 46.1.b
London: George G. Harrap, [1906].

Cloth or leather. Boxed. *Locations:* BC (13 July 1906), MH.

C 46.1.c
Emerson Day by Day. London: George G. Harrap, [1910].

Designs by Margaret Tarrant. *The Poets Day by Day,* no. 1. Published September 1910. Price, 1s. *Locations:* BL (20 September 1910), JM.

C 46.1.d
Emerson Day by Day. New York: Thomas Y. Crowell, [1910].

Published December 1910. *Location:* JM.

Note: Also listed as *The Best of Emerson* in cloth or leather as included in the "Elite Series" by Crowell in *Cumulative Book Index;* no copies have been located.

C 46.1.e
An Emerson Calendar. [Folcroft, Penn.]: Folcroft Library Editions, 1974.

Facsimile reprinting of C 46.1.a. Limited to 100 copies. Price, $15.00. *Location:* DLC (8 April 1974).

C 46.1.f
An Emerson Calendar. [Norwood, Penn.]: Norwood Editions, 1976.

Facsimile reprinting of C 46.1.a. Limited to 100 copies. *Location:* DLC (19 July 1977).

C 46.1.g
Emerson Day by Day. [Folcroft, Penn.]: Folcroft Library Editions, 1977.

Facsimile reprinting of C 46.1.d. Limited to 100 copies. Price, $17.50. *Location:* DLC (30 August 1977).

C 47
Through the Year with Emerson. New York: Dodge, [1905].

119 pp. Cloth or self-wrappers. Edited by Edith E. Wood. Listed in *Publishers' Weekly*, 68 (16 September 1905), 562. Published 16 September 1905. Copyright, 8 August 1905. *Locations:* DLC (8 August 1905), JM.

C 48.1.a–j
Select Essays and Addresses. New York: Macmillan Company; London: Macmillan & Co., 1905.

275 pp. Introduction and notes by Eugene D. Holmes. *Macmillan's Pocket American and English Classics.* Published November 1905. Price, 25¢. Reprinted February 1907, June 1908, July 1909, 1912, 1920, 1921, 1922, 1924, 1925. *Location:* UPB (1907).

C 48.2
Essays. [New York]: Macmillan, [1930].

378 pp. Edited by Eugene D. Holmes. Revised by H. Y. Moffett. Illustrated by Homer W. Colby. Published May 1930. Copyright, 20 May 1930. *Location:* MH.

C 49
The Ralph Waldo Emerson Birthday Book. Edinburgh: W. P. Nimmo, Hay, & Mitchell, [1905].

Unpaged. Miniature book. Edited by J. Pennells. Also advertised as included in "Nimmo's Birthday Books," no. 22. Price, 1s. *Location:* BL (25 January 1906).

C 50
Open Your Eyes   Man's Wealth and Resources in Nature   Master-Thoughts from Emerson. London: St. Martin's, [1905].

70 pp. Wrappers. *Wisdom in Brief* series. Published December 1905. *Location:* BC (19 October 1906).

C 51.1.a–b
The Emerson Yearbook. [London]: Siegle, Hill, 1906.

187 pp. Miniature book. Edited by J. Pennells. *Langham Booklets.* Published October 1906. Price, 6d. Reprinted 1906. *Location:* BC (19 June 1907; reprint).

C 52
Leaves of Friendship from Ralph Waldo Emerson. London and Edinburgh: T. N. Foulis, [1906].

44 pp. Wrappers. *Leaves of Life Series,* no. 1. Published October 1906. *Location:* BE (18 February 1907).

C 53.1
Moments with Emerson. London: Chapman & Hall, [1906].

Unpaged (31 leaves). Miniature book. Leather. Published October 1906. Price, 1s. *Location:* BL (1 January 1907).

C 53.2
Emerson. London: Henry Frowde, [1909].

Unpaged (31 leaves). Miniature book. *The Moment Series. Location:* BC (4 February 1910).

C 54
The Pocket Emerson. London: Chatto & Windus, 1906.

272 pp. Cloth or leather. Dust jacket. Edited by Alfred H. Hyatt. Prices: cloth, 2s.; leather, 3s. *Locations:* BL (5 October 1906), CtW.

C 55
Thoughts from Emerson. Hampstead [England]: Sydney C. Mayle, The Priory Press, [1907].

36 pp. Wrappers. Edited by V. N. *Priory Press Booklets.* Published November 1907. Price, 3d. *Location:* BO (8 February 1908).

C 56
Emerson Birthday Book. New York: Dodge, [1906].

Unpaged (94 leaves). Advertised in various bindings at various prices. *Location:* JM.

Note: Also listed as *Emerson Year Book* by Dodge in 1912 in *Cumulative Book Index;* no copies have been located.

C 57.1.a–c
Essays and Addresses. Chicago: Scott, Foresman, [1906].

293 pp. Edited by Benjamin A. Heydrick. *The Lake English Classics.* Price, 35¢. Reprinted 1907, 1908. *Locations:* CU, DLC (20 February 1907), OrU (1908).

C 57.2
Chicago and New York: Scott, Foresman, [1919].

302 pp. *Revised Edition. The Lake English Classics.* Price, 52¢. *Location:* OU.

C 58
Stars of Thought. Portland, Maine: Thomas B. Mosher, MDCCCCVI.

79 pp. Advertised in various bindings at various prices. Selected by Thomas Coke Watkins. Also advertised as included in "Vest Pocket Series," no. 14. *Location:* JM.

C 59
Select Essays of Ralph Waldo Emerson. New York, Cincinnati, Chicago: American Book Company, [1907].

245 pp. Introduction and notes by Henry Van Dyke. *Gateway Series.* Published 11 May 1907. Copyright, 19 February 1907. Price, 35¢. *Location:* JM.

C 60.1.a
Compensation, Self-Reliance and Other Essays. Boston, New York, Chicago: Houghton Mifflin, [1907].

168 pp. Wrappers. Edited by Mary A. Jordan. *Riverside Literature Series,* no. 171. According to the publisher's records, published 28 September 1907. Copyright, 16 September 1907. Price, 15¢. *Location:* OkHi.

C 60.1.b
Essays. Boston, New York, Chicago: Houghton Mifflin, [1907].

Combined with *Manners, Friendship and Other Essays* (C 61) in two-volumes-in-one format in cloth. In combining C 60 and C 61, the notes from the first title were placed at the end of the volume. *Riverside Literature Series,* nos. 171–172. According to the publisher's records, published 28 September 1907. Price, 40¢. *Location:* JM.

C 61.1.a
Manners, Friendship and Other Essays. Boston [&c.]: Houghton Mifflin, [1907].

[133]–324 pp. Wrappers. Edited by Mary A. Jordan. *Riverside Literature Series,* no. 172. Copyright, 16 September 1907. Price, 15¢. *Location:* DLC (18 September 1907).

C 61.1.b
Essays. Boston, New York, Chicago: Houghton Mifflin, [1907].

Combined with *Compensation, Self-Reliance and Other Essays* (C 60.1.a) in two-volumes-in-one format; see C 60.1.b.

C 62.1.a–b
Essays and Other Writings. London [&c.]: Cassell, MCMVII.

425 pp. Cloth or flexible leather. *The People's Library.* Published November 1907. Price: cloth, 1s. 6d. Reprinted 1911. *Locations:* BL (4 December 1907), JM (1907), OCIW (1911).

Note: Listed as included in "People's Library" at 75¢ for 1928 by Funk & Wagnalls of New York in *Cumulative Book Index;* no copies have been located.

C 63
The Ideal Life Thoughts from Emerson. London: C. W. Daniel, [1907].

62 pp. Wrappers. *Little Books on Life,* no. 2. Published December 1907. *Location:* BC (18 March 1909).

C 64
Essays. New York: Charles E. Merrill, 1908.

336 pp. Edited by Edna H. L. Turpin. *Merrill's English Texts.* Published 4 January 1908. Copyright, 10 December 1907. Price, 30¢. *Location:* MoU.

C 65.1.a–i
English Traits Representative Men & Other Essays. London: J. M. Dent; New York: E. P. Dutton, [1908].

375 pp. Dust jacket. Advertised in various bindings at various prices. Introduction by Ernest Rhys. *Everyman's Library,* no. 279. Published (New York) 22 February 1908. Reprinted 1910, 1913, 1916, 1919, 1923, 1927, 1932, 1951. *Locations:* BL (24 February 1908), MH.

C 66
Golden Thoughts. Buffalo, N.Y.: Berger, [1908].

Unpaged (8 leaves). Copyright, 24 April 1908. *Not seen.*

C 67.1.a–f
The Conduct of Life Nature & Other Essays. London: J. M. Dent; New York: E. P. Dutton, [1908].

308 pp. Dust jacket. Advertised in various bindings at various prices. Introduction by Ernest Rhys. *Everyman's Library,* no. 322. Published: London, June 1908; New York, 19

September 1908. Prices: cloth, 35¢; leather, 70¢. Reprinted 1911, 1915, 1919, 1927, 1937. *Locations:* BL (4 June 1908), JM.

C 67.1.g–h
Nature, The Conduct of Life and Other Essays. London: J. M. Dent; New York: E. P. Dutton, [1963].

Dust jacket. Introduction by Sherman Paul. *Everyman's Library,* no. 322. Published (London) 2 May 1963. Prices: 10s. 6d; $1.95. Reprinted 1970. *Locations:* BL (16 April 1963), TxHR, JM (1970).

C 68
Worldly Wisdom from Emerson. Philadelphia: Henry Altemus, [1908].

95 pp. Edited by F. S. Bigelow. Also advertised as included in "Altemus' Worldly Wisdom Series" and "World's Wisdom Classics." Copyright, 7 August 1908. *Location:* DLC (16 October 1908).

C 69
Power   Success   and Greatness. New York: Century, 1908.

194 pp. Introduction by Richard Watson Gilder. Advertised as included in "Thumb-nail" series. Listed in *Publishers' Weekly,* 74 (10 October 1908), 988. Published 10 October 1908. Price, $1.00. *Location:* JM.

C 70.1.a–c
Emerson's Essays and Representative Men. London and Glasgow: Collins' Clear-Type Press, [1908].

541 pp. Cloth or leather. *Library of Classics.* Also titled *Essays and Representative Men.* Also advertised as included in "Illustrated Pocket Classics." Published October 1908. Prices: cloth, 1s.; leather, 2s. Reprinted February 1931, April 1934. *Locations:* MH (1908), JM (*Essays*).

C 71.1.a–b
Emerson. London: Arthur L. Humphreys, 1908.

303 pp. Cloth or wrappers. *The Royal Library, Belles Lettres Series.* Published October 1908. Price, 6s. Reprinted 1914. *Locations:* BC (22 January 1909), JM, NNF (1914).

C 72
The Pocket Emerson. London: George Routledge & Sons; New York: E. P. Dutton, [1908].

342 pp. Edited by W. T. S. Sonnenschein. *Wayfaring Books.* Published December 1908. Price, 2s. 6d. *Locations:* BL (13 January 1909), JM.

C 73.1.a
Great Thoughts from Emerson. London: George G. Harrap, [1908].

72 pp. Miniature book. Wrappers. *Sesame Booklets,* no. 8. *Location:* BC (10 December 1908).

C 73.1.b
Philadelphia: David McKay, [n.d.].

Advertised as included in "Sesame Booklets." Price, 75¢. *Not seen.*

C 74
Echoes from Emerson. London: Gay & Hancock, 1908.

48 pp. Limp leather. Introduction by R. Dimsdale Stocker. *Simple Truths* series. *Location:* BC (15 January 1909).

C 75.1
Nature Thoughts from Emerson. A Calendar for 1909. London: Ernest Nister; New York: E. P. Dutton, [1908].

Unpaged (12 leaves). *Location:* BL (24 December 1908).

C 75.2
Nature Thoughts from Emerson. A Calendar for 1910. London: Ernest Nister; New York: E. P. Dutton, [1909].

Unpaged (12 leaves). *Location:* JM.

C 76
Education An Essay and Other Selections. Boston, New York, Chicago: Houghton Mifflin, [1909].

76 pp. *Riverside Educational Monographs.* Published 17 April 1909. Copyright, 26 March 1909. Price, 35¢. *Location:* NcD.

C 77.1.a–c
Essays and English Traits. New York: P. F. Collier & Son, [1909].

493 pp. Advertised in various bindings at various prices. *The Harvard Classics,* vol. 5. Copyright, 14 July 1909. Price, $2.00. Reprinted 1937, 1961 (with Collier imprint). *Locations:* JM (1909), MShrew (1937), MH (1961).

C 78
Selected Essays of Ralph Waldo Emerson. London [&c.]: T. Nelson & Sons, [1909].

475 pp. Dust jacket. Introduction by J. B. Also advertised as included in "The Nelson Classics," no. 54. Also noted without places of publication on title page. *Locations:* BL (18 November 1909), JM (both).

C 79.1.a–b
The Wisdom of Ralph Waldo Emerson. New York: Brentano's, MCMIX.

163 pp. Introduction by William B. Parker. Also advertised as included in "Wisdom Series." Price, $1.00. Reprinted 1911. *Locations:* OkTU (1909), RNR (1911).

C 80
Emerson. London: G. Bell and Sons, 1910.

377 pp. Dust jacket. Edited by George Herbert Perris. *Masters of Literature.* Published May 1910. Price, 3s. 6d. *Locations:* BC (25 May 1910), JM.

C 81.1.a
Through the Year with Emerson. London: Simpkin, Marshall, Hamilton, Kent, [1910].

120 pp. Advertised in various bindings at various prices. *Through the Year with Great Authors* series. Published October 1910. *Locations:* BL (3 March 1911), PLT.

C 81.1.b
New York: H. M. Caldwell, 1911.

Advertised in calf at $1.35. *Not seen.*

C 82
Essays. New York and London: G. P. Putnam's Sons, [1910].

153 pp. Flexible leather. Boxed. *Ariel Booklets.* Published 31 October 1910. Price, 75¢. *Location:* JM.

C 83.1.a
Thoughts. London and Edinburgh: T. C. and E. J. Jack, [1910].

63 pp. Miniature book. Edited by Louey Chisholm. *The Ivory Booklets. Location:* BL (12 October 1910).

C 83.1.b
Philadelphia: George W. Jacobs, [1912].

Advertised as included in "Ivory Booklets." Price, 15¢. *Location:* AzTeS.

C 84
Thoughts of Friendship. New York: Dodge, 1910.

46 pp. Advertised in various bindings at various prices. Advertised as included in "Favorite Thoughts" series. *Location:* NN.

C 85
To Day. Buffalo, N.Y.: Hayes Lithographing Company, [1910].

Unpaged (6 leaves). *The Best Wishes Series. Location:* JM.

C 86
Leaves of Friendship. Buffalo, N.Y.: Hayes Lithographing Company, [1911].

Unpaged (11 leaves). Copyright, 25 March 1911. *Location:* GAE.

C 87
Essays (First, Second and Third Series). New York: Harper & Brothers; London: Ward, Lock, [1911].

416 pp. *The World Library.* Published (London) May 1911. Price, 1s. *Location:* JM.

C 88.1.a–c
Society & Solitude & other Essays. London: J. M. Dent & Sons; New York: E. P. Dutton, [1912].

307 pp. Dust jacket. Advertised in various bindings at various prices. *Everyman's Library,* no. 567. Published February 1912. Reprinted 1916, 1922. *Locations:* BC (29 February 1912), MH (1912), JM (1916), IaU (1922).

C 89.1.a
Representative Men   English Traits and Other Essays. London: Melbourne, Toronto: Ward, Lock, 1912.

383 pp. Dust jacket. Advertised in various bindings at various prices. *The World Library.* Published May 1912. *Location:* BC (10 September 1912).

C 89.1.b
New York: Harper & Brothers; London: Ward, Lock, [n.d.].

The World Library. Location: JM.

C 90
Emerson Book of Birthday Gems. Chicago: M. A. Donohue, [1912?].

Advertised in various bindings at various prices. *Not seen.*

C 91
Great Thoughts from Emerson. New York: Thomas Y. Crowell, [1912?].

32 pp. Advertised in various bindings at various prices. Also advertised as included in "Choice Treasury" and "Colonial" series. *Location:* JM.

C 92
Essays. London: George Bell and Sons, 1913.

410 pp. Edited by G. K. Chesterton. Advertised as included in "Bohn's Standard Library." Published October 1913. Price, 3s. 6d. *Not seen.*

C 93
Thoughts on Friendship. [N.p.]: Sealfield, 1913.

Advertised as included in "Buckeye Series." *Not seen.*

C 94
Essays First and Second Series   English Traits   Representative Men   Addresses. New York: Hearst's International Library, [1914].

423 + 604 pp. Introduction by Arthur Brisbane. *International Edition.* Price, $1.00. *Location:* JM.

Note: Printed from the plates of vols. I–II of the *New National Edition* (see B 35).

C 95
Emerson's Essays on Manners, Self-Reliance, Compensation, Nature, Friendship. New York and Chicago: Longmans, Green, 1915.

140 pp. Introduction and notes by Eunice J. Cleveland. *Longmans' English Classics.* Copyright, 23 September 1915. Price, 25¢. *Location:* MH.

C 96
Essays. Leipzig: Bernhard Tauchnitz, 1915.

285 pp. Advertised in various bindings at various prices. Edited by Edward Waldo Emerson. *Collection of British Authors,* no. 4510. *Location:* JM.

C 97
Essays and Representative Men. [N.p.]: Winston, 1915.

Advertised in half calf. Advertised as included in "Fine Arts Classics and Poets" series. Price, $2.00. *Not seen.*

C 98
Nature and Thought. Leipzig: Bernhard Tauchnitz, 1915.

285 pp. Wrappers. Edited by Edward Waldo Emerson. *Collection of British Authors*, vol. 4512. *Location:* JM.

C 99
The Social Message of Ralph Waldo Emerson. [Boston]: Unitarian Fellowship for Social Justice, 1915.

20 pp. Wrappers. Edited by Franklin Kent Gifford. *Location:* JM.

C 100
Nature. Two Essays. Leipzig: Bernhard Tauchnitz, 1916.

Advertised as included in "Pocket Library," no. 48. *Not seen.*

C 101
Emerson's Epigrams. London: George G. Harrap, [1917].

140 pp. Boards or leather. Edited by Eric Briton. *The Choice Books,* no. 20. Published April 1917. Prices: boards, 1s. 6d; leather, 3s. 6d. *Location:* BL (29 January 1917).

C 102.1
Emerson's Essays. New York, Chicago, Boston: Charles Scribner's Sons, [1920].

298 pp. Dust jacket. Introduction by Arthur Hobson Quinn. *The Modern Student's Library.* Copyright, 20 August 1920. Price, $1.00. *Location:* JM.

C 102.2
Emerson's Essays and Poems. New York, Chicago, Boston: Charles Scribner's Sons, [1926].

376 pp. *The Modern Student's Library. Location:* JM.

C 103
Character and Other Essays. New York: J. H. Sears, [1920?].

241 pp. Also advertised as included in "American Home Classics" and "Royal Blue Library." Price, 75¢. *Location:* JM.

C 104
Essays and Poems of Emerson. New York: Harcourt, Brace, 1921.

525 pp. Introduction by Stuart P. Sherman. Copyright, 8 December 1921. Price, $1.20. Reprinted [n.d.]. *Locations:* ScU, MeB (n.d.).

C 105
Timely Extracts from the Writings of Ralph Waldo Emerson. [Boston: Thomas Todd, 1921].

18 pp. Privately printed Christmas 1921. *Location:* JM.

C 106
Selected Essays. London: T. Nelson and Sons, [1923].

482 pp. Edited by Sir Henry Newbolt. Advertised as included in "Cheap Edition" series. Published February 1923. Price, 1s. 6d. *Not seen.*

C 107
Considerations. London and Toronto: J. M. Dent & Sons; New York: E. P. Dutton, 1923.

185 pp. Cloth or leather. *Bedside Library*. Prices: cloth, 2s. 6d, $1.00; leather, 3s. 6d, $1.60. *Location:* BL (19 November 1923).

C 108
Emerson's Five Essays. Tokyo: Kōbunsha, 1924.

78 pp. *Not seen*.

C 109
My Little Book of Emerson. Chicago [&c.]: P. F. Volland, [1924].

141 pp. Edited by Edwin Osgood Grover. *My Little Book* series. Price, $1.00. *Location:* RPB.

C 110
Emerson's Concept of Truth. Holyoke, Mass.: Elizabeth Towne, [1926].

28 pp. Wrappers. Edited by Henry Richardson Thayer. Copyright, 17 May 1926. Price, 25¢. *Location:* NNUT.

C 111
Selections from the Prose Works of Ralph Waldo Emerson. Boston [&c.]: Houghton Mifflin, [1926].

380 pp. Edited with an introduction and notes by Bliss Perry. *Riverside College Classics*. Copyright, 9 August 1926. Price, $1.00. *Location:* NcD.

C 112
Epigrams. New York: A. L. Chatterton, [1926?].

66 pp. *Location:* RPB.

C 113
Emerson's Epigrams. New York: Thomas Y. Crowell, [1928?]

Advertised in leather as included in "Choice Literary Masterpieces." Price, $2.00. *Not seen*.

C 114
Leaves of Friendship. New York: C. E. Graham, [1928?].

22 pp. Advertised as included in "Acalia Series." Price, 60¢. *Not seen*.

C 115
Emerson's Representative Men and Other Essays. Boston [&c.]: D. C. Heath, [1929].

280 pp. Edited by Ezra Kempton Maxfield and Jane Crowe Maxfield. *Golden Key Series*. Copyright, 19 October 1929. Price, 80¢. *Location:* JM.

C 116.1.a
The Works of Ralph Waldo Emerson. New York: Walter J. Black, [ca. 1930].

568 pp., double columns. *The Great International Series*. *Location:* JM.

C 116.1.b
Roslyn, N.Y.: Black's Readers Service, [ca. 1930].

Location: Md.

C 117
Philosograms of Emerson. Cleveland: Rex, [1930].

Unpaged (11 leaves). Edited by H. H. Emmons. Copyright, 13 March 1930. Price, 50¢. *Location:* JM.

C 118.1.a
Light of Emerson   A Complete Digest with Key-Word Concordance   The Cream of All He Wrote   Majestic, Inspiring, Thought-Provoking Paragraphs and Utterances of America's Greatest Literary Genius—the Most Quoted Man of Modern Times—Known as "The Sage of Concord". Cleveland: Rex, [1930].

337 pp. Dust jacket. Edited by H. H. Emmons. Copyright, 10 May 1930. Price, $2.40. *Location:* JM.

C 118.1.b
[Folcroft, Penn.]: Folcroft Library Editions, 1979.

Facsimile reprinting. Limited to 150 copies. *Location:* ScU.

C 119
My Progress Book on Emerson's Essays. Columbus, Ohio: American Education Press, [1930].

Not seen.

C 120
The Heart of Emerson's Essays. Boston and New York: Houghton Mifflin, 1933.

368 pp. Dust jacket. Introduction and notes by Bliss Perry. Copyright, 13 September 1933. Price, $3.00. *Location:* JM.

C 121
Ralph Waldo Emerson   Representative Selections. New York [&c.]: American Book Company, [1934].

456 pp. Introduction, bibliography, and notes by Frederic I. Carpenter. *American Writers Series.* Copyright, 27 March 1934. Price, $1.50. *Locations:* DLC (30 March 1934), JM.

C 122
A Candidate for Truth   Passages from Emerson. London: Watts & Co., [1938].

146 pp. Edited by Gerald Bullett. *The Thinker's Library,* no. 71. Published September 1938. Price, 1s. *Locations:* BL (6 September 1938), CaOLU.

C 123.1.a
The Gospel of Emerson. Reading, Mass.: Newton Dillaway, [1939].

78 pp. Cloth or wrappers. Edited by Newton Dillaway. Copyright, 2 October 1939. Prices: cloth, $1.50; wrappers, $1.00. *Location:* JM.

C 123.1.b
Reading, Mass.: Newton Dillaway, [1940].

82 pp. *Second Edition Revised.* Flexible leather. Copyright, 15 March 1940. *Location:* JM.

C 123.1.c–f
Wakefield, Mass.: Montrose, [1944].

Third Edition Revised. Reprinted 1944 (*Fourth Edition Revised*), in wrappers 1946 (*Fifth Edition Revised;* copyright, 14 June 1946), 1949 (*Sixth Edition Revised*). *Locations:* DLC (29 June 1944), MnU (1944, 4th), JM (1946, 1949), DLC (16 May 1949).

C 123.1.g
Boston: Beacon Press, [1949].

Seventh printing. Dust jacket. Price, $2.50. *Location:* JM.

C 123.1.h
Boston: Tudor Publications, [1949].

Eighth Edition. Unprinted glassine dust jacket. *Location:* JM.

C 123.2
Lee's Summit, Mo.: Unity, [1968?].

128 pp. *Twelfth Edition.* Wrappers. *Location:* NcWsW.

C 124
Three Essays. Camden [N.J.]: Haddon Craftsmen, MCMXXXIX.

90 pp. Boxed. Appreciation by Van Wyck Brooks. Limited to 1,100 copies. *Locations:* DLC (25 December 1939), JM.

C 125.1.a
Emerson's Theory of Poetry. Iowa City, Iowa: Midland House, 1939.

60 pp. Compiled by Charles Howell Foster. Introduction by Hubert H. Hoeltje. Price, $2.00. *Location:* DLC (23 February 1940).

C 125.1.b
New York: Haskell House, 1965.

Facsimile reprinting. *Location:* JM.

C 126
Selections from Ralph Waldo Emerson. [Washington, D.C.: National Educational Association, 1939?].

16 pp. Cover title. Edited by Joy Elmer Morgan. *Personal Growth Leaflet,* no. 26. Numerous reprintings; the latest located is the third printing, indicating that 51,250 copies had been printed. *Location:* BL.

C 127.1
The Living Thoughts of Emerson. New York and Toronto: Longmans, Green, 1940.

170 pp. Dust jacket. Presented by Edgar Lee Masters. *The Living Thoughts Library,* no. 16. Copyright, 13 March 1940. Price, $1.00. *Locations:* BL (26 March 1940), JM.

C 127.2.a–b
London [&c.]: Cassell, [1941].

153 pp. Dust jacket. *Living Thoughts Library,* no. 15. Price, 3s. 6d. Reprinted 1947. *Locations:* BL (6 March 1941), JM (both).

C 127.3
Greenwich, Conn.: Fawcett, [1958].

174 pp. Wrappers. *A Premier Book* d67. Published June 1958. Price, 50¢. *Location:* JM.

C 128.a
The Complete Essays and Other Writings of Ralph Waldo Emerson. New York: Modern Library, [1940].

930 pp. Dust jacket. Introduction by Brooks Atkinson. *Modern Library* 91. Copyright, 10 October 1940. Price, 95¢. Numerous undated reprintings. *Location:* JM.

C 128.b–d
The Selected Writings of Ralph Waldo Emerson. New York: Modern Library, [1950].

Cloth (with dust jacket) or wrappers. Foreword by Tremaine McDowell. Introduction by Brooks Atkinson. Cloth: *Modern Library* 91. Price, $1.25. Reprinted 1964, 1968 (not identified as a volume in the *Modern Library* series). Wrappers: *Modern Library College Editions* T14. Price, 65¢. Copyright, 24 August 1950. Numerous undated reprintings. *Locations:* JM (all).

C 129
Seven Essays. New York: Council of Books in Wartime, [ca. 1940].

192 pp. Wrappers. *Armed Services Editions* E-122. *Location:* TxU.

C 130.1.a
The Best of Ralph Waldo Emerson. Published for the Classics Club by Walter J. Black, [1941].

283 pp. Prices: cloth, 89¢; deluxe edition, $1.39. *Location:* JM.

C 130.1.b
New York, Toronto, London: D. Van Nostrand, [1949?].

Introduction by Gordon S. Haight. *A Classics Club College Edition.* Price, $1.25. Importation by Macmillan listed in the *English Catalogue* for 1950 at 10s. 6d. *Location:* JM.

C 131
Essays of Ralph Waldo Emerson. Garden City, N.Y.: Blue Ribbon Books, [1941].

603 pp. Cloth or leather. Prices: cloth, $1.00; leather, $1.98. *Location:* DLC (19 December 1941).

C 132
Emerson on the Wave of the Future. [Reading, Mass.: Newton Dillaway, 1941].

4 pp. *Location:* DLC (5 January 1942).

C 133.1.a
Essays of Ralph Waldo Emerson. New York: Book League of America, [1941].

478 pp. Foreword by V. H. C. *Location:* JM.

C 133.1.b
Garden City, N.Y.: Famous Classics Library, [1941].

Location: NbU.

C 133.1.c
New York: A. S. Barnes, [1941].

376 pp. Abridged. *Location:* JM.

C 133.1.d
Collected Works of Ralph Waldo Emerson. New York: Greystone, [n.d.].

478 pp. Dust jacket. *Masterworks Library. Location:* JM.

C 134.1
Select Essays. Mount Vernon, N.Y.: Peter Pauper, [1941].

108 pp. Decorated by Paul McPharlin. Price, $2.00. *Location:* MeBa.

C 134.2
Selected Essays. Mount Vernon, N.Y.: Peter Pauper, [1941].

122 pp. Limited to 1,450 copies. *Location:* JM.

C 135
The Essays of Ralph Waldo Emerson. [New York: A. S. Barnes, 1944].

557 pp. Boxed. Illustrations by John Steuart Curry. *The Illustrated Modern Library.* Price, $2.50. *Locations:* DLC (4 November 1944), JM.

C 136
Essays of Ralph Waldo Emerson. New York: Literary Classics, [1945].

396 pp. Foreword by Carl Van Doren. Notes by Burton Rascoe. Introduction by Robert Van Gelder. *Literary Classics Book Club. Location:* JM.

C 137.1.a–r
The Portable Emerson. New York: Viking, 1946.

664 pp. Dust jacket. Edited with introduction and notes by Mark Van Doren. *The Viking Portable Library,* no. 25. Published October 1946. Price, $2.00. Reprinted October 1956 (first printing in wrappers), 1959, 1960, January 1962, 1963, March 1965, October 1967, 1968, 1969 (twice), October 1970, 1971, October 1972, 1973, 1974, 1975, 1976. *Location:* JM.

C 137.1.s–v
[New York]: Penguin, [1977].

Wrappers. *The Viking Portable Library.* Price, $4.95. Reprinted 1978, 1979, 1980. *Location:* JM.

C 138
Emerson speaks. [Fairmount, Ind.]: Dorothy Lloyd Gilbert and Leonard S. Kenworthy, 1946.

8 pp. Head title. *Speaks Series. Location:* OrU.

C 139.1.a
Emerson   The Basic Writings of America's Sage. New York: Penguin, [1947].

183 pp. Wrappers. Edited by Eduard C. Lindeman. *Pelican Books* P15. Copyright, 26 March 1947. Published March 1947. *Locations:* DLC, JM.

C 139.1.b–d
[New York]: New American Library, [1949].

Wrappers. *Mentor Books* M15. Published July 1949. Price, 35¢. Reprinted July 1952, July 1953. *Locations:* JM (all).

C 139.2.a–m
Basic Selections from Emerson. [New York]: New American Library, [1954].

215 pp. Wrappers. Edited by Eduard C. Lindeman. *Mentor Book* M15. Published January 1954. Copyright, 4 January 1954. Price, 35¢. Reprinted: as *Mentor Book* MD102, February 1958, September 1959, November 1960; as *Mentor Book* MP433, June 1962, February 1963, [n.d.]; as *Mentor Book* MY106, [n.d.]; the latest located printing is the thirteenth. *Location:* JM.

C 140.1.a
Selected Essays. Chicago: Fountain, [1949].

328 pp. Illustrated by Walter S. Oschman. Advertised as included in "World's Greatest Literature" series. Copyright, 22 December 1949. Price, $4.00. *Location:* DLC.

C 140.1.b
Chicago: Peoples Book Club, [1949].

Location: JM.

C 141
Inspiring Thoughts of Emerson. Delhi, India: S. C. Dass, [1950].

96 pp. Compiled by S. C. Dass. *Location:* DLC (20 June 1950).

C 142.1.a–g
Selected Prose and Poetry. New York and Toronto: Rinehart, [1950].

485 pp. Wrappers. Introduction by Reginald L. Cook. *Rinehart Editions,* no. 30. Copyright, 30 June 1950. Price, 75¢. Reprinted June 1955 (4th), October 1956 (5th), April 1958 (7th). *Location:* Ct.

C 142.1.h–p
New York: Holt, Rinehart and Winston, [1960].

Wrappers. Published August 1960 (8th). Reprinted March 1965 (14th), March 1966 (15th), November 1966 (16th). *Location:* VtBra.

C 142.2.a
New York [&c.]: Holt, Rinehart and Winston, [1969].

568 pp. Wrappers. *Second Edition. Rinehart Editions,* no. 30. Copyright, 3 March 1969. Price, $1.75. *Location:* JM.

C 142.2.b
San Francisco: Rinehart Press, [1969].

Wrappers. *Second Edition. Rinehart Editions,* no. 30. *Location:* NcD.

C 143
Selected Essays. New York: Greystone, [1951].

159 pp. *Castle Books.* Illustrated by Lester Elliot. *Location:* IEIsP.

C 144.1.a–d
Essays and Poems. London and Glasgow: Collins, [1954].

510 pp. Cloth or leather. Selected by G. F. Maine. Introduction by DeLancey Ferguson. Published June 1954. Reprinted 1962, 1965, 1967. Importation by W. W. Norton in cloth or leather listed in *Books in Print* at $1.50 and $2.75. *Locations:* BL (22 June 1954), JM.

C 145.1.a
Five Essays on Man and Nature. New York: Appleton-Century-Crofts, [1954].

120 pp. Wrappers. Edited by Robert E. Spiller. *Crofts Classics.* Copyright, 15 September 1954. Price, 50¢. Numerous undated reprints. *Location:* JM.

C 145.1.b
Skokie, Ill.: AHM, [n.d.].

Wrappers. *Crofts Classics.* Numerous undated reprints; the latest located is the 11th. *Location:* JM.

C 146
The Power of Emerson's Wisdom. New York: Pageant, [1954].

180 pp. Edited by Hugh P. MacDonald. Price, $3.50. *Location:* DLC (6 August 1954).

C 147
We Thank Thee. Racine, Wisc.: Whitman, [1955].

Unpaged (8 leaves). Pictures by Elinore Blaisdell. *A Cozy-Corner Book.* Copyright, 18 August 1955. Price, 25¢. *Location:* DLC.

C 148.1.a–b
Selections from Ralph Waldo Emerson. Boston: Houghton Mifflin, 1957.

517 pp. Wrappers. Edited by Stephen E. Whicher. *Riverside Editions* A13. Copyright, 8 October 1957. Price, $1.15. Reprinted in cloth or wrappers, 1960. *Locations:* JM (both).

C 149.1.a–b
Emerson   A Modern Anthology. [New York: Dell, 1958].

384 pp. Wrappers. Edited by Alfred Kazin and Daniel Aaron. Cover drawing by Leonard Baskin. *Laurel Edition* LC116. Published September 1958. Price, 50¢. Reprinted November 1960. *Locations:* OKentU (1958), JM (1960).

C 149.1.c–f
Boston: Houghton Mifflin, [1959].

399 pp. Dust jacket. Price, $4.00. Reprinted 1959 (three times). *Locations:* DLC (1 December 1959), JM.

C 150
Emerson on Man & God. Mount Vernon, N.Y.: Peter Pauper, [1961].

61 pp. Dust jacket. Copyright, 1 March 1961. Price, $1.00. *Location:* JM.

C 151.1.a–c
Selected Essays, Lectures, and Poems of Ralph Waldo Emerson. New York: Washington Square, [1965].

396 pp. Wrappers. Edited with an introduction by Robert E. Spiller. Copyright, 15 January 1965. Published February 1965. Price, 60¢. Reprinted August 1967, January 1970. *Locations:* DLC (1965), JM (1967, 1970).

C 152
Wisdom of Emerson. Tucson, Arizona: Unity of Knowledge Publications, World University College, [1965].

149 pp. Mimeographed. Wrappers. Selected and introduced by Harry Lewis Custard and Edith Mary Custard. Copyright, 28 September 1965. Price, $3.00. *Location:* MB.

C 153.1.a–c
Selected Writings of Ralph Waldo Emerson. New York and Toronto: New American Library; London: New English Library, [1965].

479 pp. Wrappers. Edited with a foreword by William H. Gilman. *Signet Classic* CQ292. Published November 1965. Copyright 29 November 1965. Copies in the New English Library are composed of American sheets with the same wrapper as the New American Library, except it is imprinted with the English price. Prices: 95¢; 7s. 6d. Later undated reprintings as *Signet Classic* CW593; the latest located reprint is the 3rd. *Location:* JM (all).

C 154.1.a_{1-2}
An Emerson Reader. Bombay: Popular Prakashan, [1965].

288 pp. Dust jacket. Edited by Nissim Ezekiel. An American issue was created by the American distributor, Lawrence Verry of Mystic, Conn., pasting his label on the dust jacket, spine, title page, and copyright page. Price, $4.00. *Location:* JM (American).

C 155
Emerson on Education. New York: Teachers College, [1966].

277 pp. Cloth (dust jacket) or wrappers. Selected by Howard Mumford Jones. Preface by Lawrence A. Cremin. *Classics in Education,* no. 26. Copyright, 15 February 1966. Prices: cloth, $3.95; wrappers, $1.95. *Location:* JM.

C 156.1.a
Essays and Journals. Garden City, N.Y.: International Collectors Library, [1968].

671 pp. Edited with an introduction by Howard Mumford Jones. Copyright, 20 September 1968. *Location:* JM.

C 156.1.b
Garden City, N.Y.: Doubleday, 1968.

Price, $6.95. *Location:* NcD.

C 156.1.c
[N.p.]: The Programmed Classics, [n.d.].

The Programmed Classics. Location: JM.

C 157
Emerson. [Kansas City, Mo.]: Hallmark Editions, [1969].

61 pp. Dust jacket. Selected by Stanley Hendricks. Copyright, 1 August 1969. Price, $2.50. *Location:* JM.

C 158
Twelve Selections from Emerson. [Hornchurch, Essex (England): Printed at the Chestnut Leaf Private Press of Colin Smith, 1970].

12 pp. Miniature book. Wrappers. Selected by Colin Smith. Limited to 100 copies. *Location:* BL (8 January 1970).

C 159
America the Beautiful In the Words of Ralph Waldo Emerson. Waukesha, Wis.: Country Beautiful, [1970].

98 pp. Copyright, 30 October 1970. Price, $7.95. *Location:* JM.

C 160
Emerson's Essays on Nature. Tokyo: Hokuseido, 1970.

Edited by Norikane Tokahashi. *Not seen.*

C 161
The Sound of Trumpets. New York: Viking, [1971].

127 pp. Illustrated by James Daugherty. Copyright, 1 November 1971. Price, $6.95. *Location:* JM.

C 162
A friend is a person with whom I may be sincere. [N.p.]: Continental, 1972.

Unpaged. Copyright, 14 January 1973. *Not seen.*

C 163
Emerson: Three Famous Essays. Logan, Iowa: Perfection Form, [1974].

90 pp. Wrappers. *A Perfection Micro-Classic MC 869. Location:* JM.

C 164
Hitch Your Wagon to a Star. [San Francisco: Scriptorium St. Francis, 1975].

Unpaged (6 leaves). Cloth or wrappers. Calligraphy and illumination by Thomas Ingmire. Printed by the Double-H Press. Limited to 300 copies, 20 of which are hand-illuminated and bound in cloth. Price: wrappers, $3.50. *Location:* JM.

C 165
Essays. [N.p.]: Westvaco, [1978].

210 pp. Boxed. Foreword by John C. Callihan. *Location:* JM.

C 166
Emerson's Literary Criticism. Lincoln and London: University of Nebraska Press, 1979.

251 pp. Dust jacket. Edited by Eric W. Carlson. *Regents Critics Series.* Published 12 October 1979. Price, $21.50. *Location:* JM.

UNDATED EDITIONS

C 167
Emerson   A Conspectus. [Trivandrum, India: C. V. Krishna, n.d.].

549 pp. Foreword by Sir Evelyn Wrench. *Location:* NNC.

C 168
Emerson Year Book. Philadelphia: David McKay, [n.d.].

Price, 50¢. *Not seen.*

C 169
Gems from Emerson. [N.p.: n.p., n.d.].

6 pp., printed on rectos only. Stiff wrappers. Illustrated by L. P. Canby. *Location:* JM.

C 170
Gems from Emerson. Girard, Kansas: Haldeman-Julius, [n.d.].

32 pp. Wrappers. *Little Blue Book,* no. 179. *Location.* JM.

C 171
Gems from Emerson. Girard, Kansas: Haldeman-Julius, [n.d.].

52 pp. Wrappers. *Ten Cent Pocket Series,* no. 179. *Location:* K.

C 172
Haunts of Emerson. Boston: L. Prang, [n.d.].

Unpaged (9 leaves), printed on rectos only. Stiff wrappers. Illustrated by Louis K. Harlow. *Location:* MCo.

C 173
Leaves from Emerson's Nature. Cliftondale, Mass.: Coates Brothers, [n.d.].

Unpaged (14 leaves), printed on rectos only. Wrappers. Edited by I. M. P. *Location:* RPB.

C 174
Pearls of Wisdom from Ralph Waldo Emerson. San Francisco: Zoe Varney, [n.d.].

126 pp. Comments by Eugenia Rabbas. *Location:* JM.

C 175
Ralph Waldo Emerson. [Boston: American Unitarian Association, n.d.].

4 pp. Head title. *Great Leaders,* no. 6. *Location:* MH-AH.

C 176
Selections from Ralph Waldo Emerson. Philadelphia: Toyme, [n.d.].

Unpaged (8 leaves). Wrappers. *Location:* JM.

C 177
Words of Wisdom. London: Hills, [n.d.].

Unpaged (29 leaves). Miniature book. Limp leather. *Location:* JM.

D. First Book and Pamphlet Appearances

Titles in which material by Emerson appears for the first time in a book or pamphlet, arranged chronologically. All items are signed unless otherwise noted. Previously published items are so identified. The first printings only of these titles are described, but English editions, retitled reprintings, and selected reprintings are also noted.

D 1 THE OFFERING
1829

THE | OFFERING, | FOR | 1829. | [rule] | CAMBRIDGE: | PUBLISHED BY HILLIARD AND BROWN. | [rule] | 1829.

Edited by Andrews Norton.

"An Extract from Unpublished Travels in the East," pp. [8]–10. Unsigned.
  "William Rufus and the Jew," pp. [17]–18. Unsigned.
  "Fame," pp. [52]–53. Unsigned. See A 18.6.

Location: MH.

Note one: For a discussion of Emerson's authorship of these pieces, see Ralph Thompson, "Emerson and *The Offering for 1829*," *American Literature,* 6 (May 1934), 151–157.

Note two: "Fame" was reprinted in *Radical,* 9 (August 1871), 52.

D 2 SERMON AT THE ORDINATION OF HERSEY BRADFORD GOODWIN
1830

A | SERMON, | DELIVERED AT THE ORDINATION | OF | HERSEY BRADFORD GOOD-WIN, | AS COLLEAGUE PASTOR WITH | EZRA RIPLEY, D.D. | OF THE | CONGREGA-TIONAL CHURCH AND SOCIETY | IN CONCORD, MASS. FEB. 17, 1830. | [rule] | BY JAMES KENDALL, D.D. | Pastor of the First Church in Plymouth. | [rule] | PUBLISHED BY REQUEST OF THE SOCIETY. | CONCORD. | PUBLISHED AT THE GAZETTE OF-FICE. | M DCCC XXX.

Wrappers.

"Right Hand of Fellowship," pp. [29]–31. See A 54.

Location: JM.

D 3 SERMON AT THE ORDINATION OF CHANDLER ROBBINS
1833

[all within an ornamental frame outside of a single wavy-rule frame] ORDER OF SER-VICES | AT THE | ORDINATION OF MR CHANDLER ROBBINS, | AS PASTOR OF THE | SECOND CHURCH AND SOCIETY IN BOSTON, | Wednesday, December 4, 1833. | [rule] | [text in double columns, separated by a rule: 53 lines in col. 1, 49 lines in col. 2] | [below frames] I. R. BUTTS, SCHOOL STREET.

599

Broadside, printed on recto only.

Hymn ["We love the venerable house"], col. 1, ll. 4–53, col. 2, ll. 1–16. See A 18.4.

Location: MB.

Note: Reprinted in 'A | SERMON | DELIVERED | AT THE ORDINATION | OF | REV. CHANDLER ROBBINS, | OVER THE | SECOND CONGREGATIONAL CHURCH | IN | BOSTON, | DECEMBER 4, 1833. | [rule] | BY REV. HENRY WARE, JR. | [rule] | [rule] | BOSTON: | JAMES W. BURDITT. | 1833.' (wrappers) on p. 32 (JM).

D 4 DR. S. C. HEWETT, BONE-SETTER
1835

Persons into whose hands this Pamphlet may fall will, per- | haps, find it of service to preserve it for future reference. | [band] | [rule] | Dr. S. C. Hewett, | BONE-SETTER, | Successor to the late Dr. JOB SWEET, who died in Boston, about nine | years since. Dr. H. may be found at 297 Washington Street, | nearly opposite Avon Place, BOSTON, Mass. | [band] | [rule] | [45 lines of text, double-colums]

Head title.

Testimonial letter of 10 December 1832, p. 10.

Location: MBCo.

Note one: Facsimiled in Kenneth Walter Cameron, "Emerson Recommends Dr. Si-mon Hewett," *Emerson Society Quarterly,* no. 2 (1st Quarter 1956), pp. 10–12.

Note two: Reprinted in double columns, with Emerson's letter on the same page, with the following head title: *'Persons who receive this Pamphlet are requested to | read and preserve it for a reference.',* and with the text beginning "DR. S. C. HEWETT, Bonesetter, would respectfully inform the public, that his profession extends to general dis-eases of the limbs and joints." The latest letter included in this pamphlet is dated 19 January 1838. *Location:* MBAt.

D 5 SARTOR RESARTUS
1836

SARTOR RESARTUS. | IN THREE BOOKS. | [rule] | [two lines of verse in gothic] | [rule] | BOSTON: | JAMES MUNROE AND COMPANY. | [rule] | M DCCC XXXVI.

"Preface of the American Editors," dated 'BOSTON, MARCH, 1836.', pp. [iii]–v. Unsigned.

Location: JM.

Note: For further information on Emerson's involvement with Carlyle's book, see I 1.

D 6 TWO SERMONS ON THE DEATH OF EZRA RIPLEY
1841

[all within a triple-rule frame] TWO SERMONS | ON THE DEATH OF | REV. EZRA RIPLEY, D.D. | ONE PREACHED AT THE FUNERAL, | BY REV. BARZILLAI FROST, | OF CONCORD; | THE OTHER ON THE FOLLOWING SABBATH, | BY REV. CONVERS FRANCIS, D.D., | OF WATERTOWN. | [rule] | BOSTON: | JAMES MUNROE AND COM-PANY. | 1841.

Cover title.

Emerson's notice of Ezra Ripley, pp. [41]–43. *Reprint.* See E 34.

Location: JM.

D 7 GEMS FROM AMERICAN POETS
1842

[all within a single-rule frame with circles in corners] GEMS | FROM | AMERICAN POETS. | [rule] | [four lines of verse] | NEW-YORK: | D. APPLETON AND COMPANY, | 200 Broadway.

"Good-bye, Proud World!" pp. 109–110. *Reprint.* See E 14.

Location: MH.

Note one: Also noted with following addition to imprint: ' . . . Broadway. | and *Geo. S. Appleton,* 148 Chesnut-st. Philadelphia.' (JM).

Note two: New edition, with "The Problem" (*Reprint;* see E 18) on pp. 77–79 and "Good-B'ye, Proud World" on pp. 79–80: 'GEMS | FROM | THE AMERICAN POETS, | WITH | BRIEF BIOGRAPHICAL NOTICES, | BY | RUFUS W. GRISWOLD. | [rule] | PHILADELPHIA: | H. HOOKER, No. 178, CHESTNUT ST. | OPPOSITE MASONIC HALL. | STEREOTYPED BY C. W. MURRAY & CO. | [wavy rule] | 1844.' (JM).

Note three: New edition reprinted, with Emerson's poems on the same pages: '[all within a single-rule frame] GEMS | FROM | [ornate initial capitals] THE AMERICAN POETS | WITH | BRIEF BIOGRAPHICAL NOTICES, | BY | RUFUS W. GRISWOLD. | [rule] | [gothic] Philadelphia: | PORTER & COATES, | 822 Chestnut Street.' (RPB).

D 8 THE POETS AND POETRY OF AMERICA
1842

[all within a double-rule frame] THE | POETS AND POETRY | OF | AMERICA. | WITH AN HISTORICAL INTRODUCTION. | BY RUFUS W. GRISWOLD. | [four lines from Bryant] | [two lines from Hoffman] | PHILADELPHIA: | CAREY AND HART, CHESNUT STREET. | MDCCCXLII.

"Each in All," p. 237. *Reprint.* See E 12.
  "'Good-Bye, Proud World,'" pp. 237–238. *Reprint.* See E 14.
  "To the Humble-Bee," p. 238. *Reprint.* See E 13.
  "The Rhodora," p. 238. *Reprint.* See E 15.
  "The Snow-Storm," p. 238. *Reprint.* See E 24.

Location: JM.

Note: Emerson's account of Jones Very in his letter of 25 September 1841 to Griswold (see D 161) is used as the basis of the biographical sketch of Very on p. 392.

D 9 THE GIFT
1844

THE GIFT: | A CHRISTAMAS AND NEW YEAR'S | PRESENT. | MDCCCXLIV. | [rule] | PHILADELPHIA: | CAREY AND HART. | 1844.

"The Garden of Plants. A Leaf from a Journal," pp. [143]–147.

Location: JM.

Note: Reprinted by H. R. Steeves, "An Ungarnered Emerson Item," *Nation,* 100 (20 May 1915), 563–564.

D 10 CARLYLE'S CRITICAL AND MISCELLANEOUS ESSAYS
1845

CRITICAL | AND | MISCELLANEOUS | ESSAYS. | BY THOMAS CARLYLE, | AUTHOR OF THE HISTORY OF THE FRENCH REVOLUTION. | A NEW EDITION, | COMPLETE IN ONE VOLUME. | PHILADELPHIA: | CAREY & HART, 126 CHESNUT STREET. | 1845.

The Modern British Essayists, vol. V.

"Advertisement," letter of June 1845 to Carey & Hart, p. [3].

Location: MBAt.

D 11 THE GIFT
1845

THE GIFT: | A | CHRISTMAS, NEW YEAR, | AND | BIRTHDAY PRESENT. | MDCCCXLV. | [rule] | PHILADELPHIA: | CAREY AND HART. | 1845.

"The Poet's Apology," p. [77]. Reprinted as "The Apology"; see A 18.
  "Dirge," pp. [94]–95. See A 18.

Location: JM.

D 12 OUR PASTORS' OFFERING
1845

OUR PASTORS' OFFERING. | A | COMPILATION | FROM | THE WRITINGS OF THE PASTORS | OF THE | SECOND CHURCH. | FOR THE LADIES' FAIR | TO ASSIST IN FURNISHING THE NEW CHURCH EDIFICE. | BOSTON: | PRINTED BY GEORGE COOLIDGE, | No. 57 Washington Street. | MDCCCXLV.

Edited by Chandler Robbins.

Letter of 2 March 1845 to Robbins, p. [34].
  "The Last Farewell," pp. [34]–36. Signed. The author is Emerson's brother Edward.
  "Woodnotes," pp. [70]–76. *Reprint.* See E 22; A 18.
  "My Thoughts," pp. [107]–108. See A 54.

Location: JM.

D 13 ADDRESS OF THE COMMITTEE APPOINTED BY A PUBLIC MEETING
1846

ADDRESS | OF THE | COMMITTEE APPOINTED BY A PUBLIC MEETING, | HELD AT | Faneuil Hall, September 24, 1846, | FOR THE PURPOSE OF CONSIDERING THE RE-CENT CASE OF | KIDNAPPING FROM OUR SOIL, | AND OF TAKING MEASURES TO

PREVENT THE RECURRENCE OF | SIMILAR OUTRAGES. | [wavy rule] | WITH AN APPENDIX. | [wavy rule] | BOSTON: | WHITE & POTTER, PRINTERS, | Chronotype Office. | 1846.

Wrappers.

Letter of 23 September 1846 to Samuel Gridley Howe and Associates of the Committee of Citizens, p. 31.

Location: ScU.

Note one: Reprinted, with Emerson's letter on I, 182–183: 'LIFE AND CORRESPON- DENCE | OF | HENRY INGERSOLL BOWDITCH | BY HIS SON | VINCENT Y. BOW- DITCH | IN TWO VOLUMES | VOL. I [II] | [publisher's logo] | BOSTON AND NEW YORK | HOUGHTON, MIFFLIN AND COMPANY | [gothic] The Riverside Press, Cambridge | 1902' (ScU).

Note two: Reprinted in Francis B. Dedmond, "A Fugitive Emerson Letter," *American Transcendental Quarterly,* no. 41 (Winter 1979), 13–16.

D 14 CHARACTERISTICS OF MEN OF GENIUS
1846

CHARACTERISTICS | OF | MEN OF GENIUS; | A SERIES OF | [gothic] Biographical, Historical, and Critical | ESSAYS, | SELECTED, BY PERMISSION, | CHIEFLY FROM THE NORTH AMERICAN REVIEW. | [three lines of verse in gothic] | [gothic] Schiller. | [wavy rule] | VOL. I. [II.] | [wavy rule] | LONDON: | JOHN CHAPMAN, 121, NEWGATE STREET. | [rule] | M.DCCC.XLVI.

Edited by John Chapman.

"Milton," I, [193]–213. Unsigned. *Reprint.* See E 11; A 44.
  "Michael Angelo," II, [137]–156. Unsigned. *Reprint.* See E 6; A 44.

Location: JM.

Note: Reprinted, with Emerson's essays on the same pages: 'CHARACTER- ISTICS . . . VOL. I. [II.] | [wavy rule] | BOSTON: | OTIS, BROADERS, & CO., 120, WASHINGTON STREET. | LONDON: | CHAPMAN, BROTHERS, 121, NEWGATE STREET. | [rule] | M.DCCC.XLVII.' (JM).

D 15 THE DIADEM
1846

THE | DIADEM | FOR MDCCCXLVI. | A PRESENT FOR ALL SEASONS. | WITH | TEN ENGRAVINGS, | AFTER PICTURES BY | INMAN, LEUTZE, ETC. | [wavy rule] | PHILA- DELPHIA: | CAREY & HART, 126 CHESNUT STREET. | 1846.

"Loss and Gain," p. [9]. Signed. See A 18.
  "A Fable," p. [38]. Signed. See A 18.
  "The Fore-Runners," pp. 95–[96]. See A 18.

Location: MH.

D 16 MEMOIR OF HENRY WARE, JR.
1846

MEMOIR | OF THE | LIFE OF HENRY WARE, JR. | BY HIS BROTHER | JOHN WARE, M.D. | [rule] | BOSTON: | JAMES MUNROE AND COMPANY. | LONDON: | JOHN CHAPMAN, 121 NEWGATE STREET. | 1846.

Letters of 28 July 1838 and 8 October 1838 to Henry Ware, Jr., pp. 395–396, 398–399.

Location: JM.

Note: Reprinted in Cabot, *A Memoir of Ralph Waldo Emerson* (D 138), II, 690–691, 693–694.

D 17 THE DIADEM
1847

THE | DIADEM | FOR MDCCCXLVII. | A PRESENT FOR ALL SEASONS | WITH | TEN ENGRAVINGS | FROM PICTURES BY | LEUTZE, SULLY, GRAY, | ETC. ETC. ETC. | [rule] | PHILADELPHIA: | CAREY & HART, 126 CHESNUT STREET. | BOSTON: | HILL & BROADHEAD. | 1847.

"The World-Soul," pp. 76–78. See A 18.

Location: JM.

Note one: Also noted with Philadelphia imprint only (JM).

Note two: An earlier version of this poem was printed in Margaret Fuller, "Asylum for Discharged Female Convicts," *New-York Daily Tribune,* 19 June 1845, p. 1; reprinted in *New-York Weekly Tribune,* 28 June 1845, p. 6, and *Life Without and Life Within* (Boston: Brown, Taggard and Chase, 1860), pp. 283–286.

D 18 ÆSTHETIC PAPERS
1849

ÆSTHETIC PAPERS. | EDITED BY | ELIZABETH P. PEABODY. | [rule] | [ten lines of verse] | *Spenser.* | [rule] | BOSTON: | THE EDITOR, 13, WEST STREET. | NEW YORK: | G. P. PUTNAM, 155, BROADWAY. | 1849.

Wrappers.

"War," pp. 36–50. Unsigned but identified as Emerson's in the table of contents. See A 40.

Location: InU.

D 19 MEMOIR OF DAVID SCOTT
1850

[flourishes around first three and eighth lines] MEMOIR | OF | DAVID SCOTT, R.S.A. | CONTAINING | HIS JOURNAL IN ITALY, NOTES ON ART | AND OTHER PAPERS: | WITH SEVEN ILLUSTRATIONS. | BY WILLIAM B. SCOTT. | [rule] | [rule] | [engraving by

Scott of nude man and woman on hilltop] | ADAM & CHARLES BLACK, EDINBURGH. | MDCCCL.

Letter of [11? July? 1848] to David Scott, pp. 331–332.

Location: MHi.

D 20 THE LIBERTY BELL
1851

THE | [gothic] Liberty Bell. | BY | FRIENDS OF FREEDOM. | [four lines of verse] | BOSTON: | NATIONAL ANTI-SLAVERY BAZAAR. | MDCCCLI.

"Translations from the Persian of Hafiz," pp. 78–81. Contains "The Phoenix," "Faith," "The Poet" ["Hoard knowledge in thy coffers"], and "To Himself." See A 54.
    "Translation from the Persian of Nisami," pp. 156–157. Contains "Word and Deed." See A 54.

Location: MH.

D 21 KOSSUTH IN NEW ENGLAND
1852

KOSSUTH | IN | NEW ENGLAND: | A FULL ACCOUNT OF THE | HUNGARIAN GOVER- NOR'S VISIT TO MASSACHUSETTS; | WITH | HIS SPEECHES, | AND | THE AD- DRESSES THAT WERE MADE TO HIM, | CAREFULLY REVISED AND CORRECTED. | WITH AN APPENDIX. | BOSTON: | JOHN P. JEWETT & CO. | CLEVELAND, OHIO: | JEWETT, PROCTOR, AND WORTHINGTON. | 1852.

"Mr. Emerson's Address," pp. 222–224. See A 40.

Location: JM.

D 22 MEMORIAL OF JAMES FENIMORE COOPER
1852

[all but date in gothic] Memorial | of | James Fenimore Cooper | New York   G P Putnam | 1852

Letter of [13 December 1851] to Rufus W. Griswold and others, pp. 32–33.

Location: MH.

D 23 AUTOGRAPHS FOR FREEDOM
1854

AUTOGRAPHS | FOR FREEDOM. | EDITED BY JULIA GRIFFITHS. | [four lines of verse] | AUBURN: | ALDEN, BEARDSLEY & CO. | ROCHESTER: | WANZER, BEARDSLEY & CO. | [rule] | 1854.

"On Freedom," pp. [235]–236. Signed with facsimile signature. Reprinted as "Free- dom"; see A 28.

Location: JM.

Note: Reprinted, with Emerson's poem on the same pages: 'VOICES OF FREEDOM |
BY | HARRIET BEECHER STOWE, CHAS. F. ADAMS, THEODORE PARKER, | N. P.
WILLIS, HORACE GREELEY, R. W. EMERSON, | HENRY WARD BEECHER, AND
OTHERS, WITH | FAC-SIMILES OF THEIR SIGNATURES, | ETC., ETC. | EDITED BY |
JULIA GRIFFITHS | [maltese cross design] | NEW YORK | WORTHINGTON CO., 747
BROADWAY' (RPB).

D 24 REPORTS OF THE CONCORD SELECTMEN
1854

REPORTS | ——OF THE—— | SELECTMEN, | OVERSEERS OF THE POOR, | SUPERIN-
TENDENT OF PUBLIC GROUNDS, | —AND OF THE— | CHIEF ENGINEER OF FIRE
DEPARTMENT, | RELATIVE TO THE EXPENSES OF THE | [gothic] Town of Concord, |
FOR THE YEAR | 1853––54. | ALSO, | THE MARRIAGES, BIRTHS AND DEATHS | IN
CONCORD, IN 1853. | [rule] | CONCORD: | SILAS B. WILDE, PRINTER. | 1854.

Wrappers.

"Second Annual Report of the Town Library Committee," dated 4 March 1854, signed
by Emerson and others, pp. [16]–17.

Location: CtY.

D 25 REPORTS OF THE CONCORD SELECTMEN
1855

REPORTS | OF THE | SELECTMEN, | OVERSEERS OF THE POOR, | LIBRARY COMMIT-
TEE, | SUPERINTENDENT OF PUBLIC GROUNDS, | AND OF THE | CHIEF ENGINEER
OF FIRE DEPARTMENT, | RELATIVE TO THE EXPENSES OF THE | TOWN OF CON-
CORD, | FOR THE YEAR 1854, 55. | ALSO, | THE MARRIAGES, BIRTHS AND DEATHS |
IN CONCORD, IN 1854. | [rule] | B. TOLMAN, PRINTER. | 1855.

Wrappers.

"Third Annual Report of the Town Library Committee," dated 5 March 1855, signed by
Emerson and others, pp. [14]–15.

Location: CtY.

D 26 LEAVES OF GRASS
1856

[script] Leaves | *of* | Grass. | [wavy rule] | BROOKLYN, NEW YORK, | 1856.

By Walt Whitman.

Letter of 21 July 1855 to Whitman, pp. [345]–346. *Reprint.* See A 23.

Location: MWiW-C.

Note: Goldstamped at the bottom of the spine is the following extract from Emerson's
letter: 'I Greet you at the | beginning of a | Great Career | R. W. Emerson'.

D 27 REPORTS OF THE CONCORD SELECTMEN
1856

REPORTS | OF THE | SELECTMEN, | OVERSEERS OF THE POOR, | AND OTHER TOWN OFFICERS, | RELATIVE TO THE EXPENSES | OF THE | TOWN OF CONCORD, | FOR THE YEAR 1855, '56. | ALSO, | The Marriages, Births and Deaths in Town, in 1855. | [rule] | CONCORD: | BENJAMIN TOLMAN, PRINTER. | 1856.

Wrappers.

"Fourth Annual Report of the Town Library Committee," dated 3 March 1856, signed by Emerson and others, pp. 16–17.

Location: CtY.

D 28 REPORTS OF THE CONCORD SELECTMEN
1857

REPORTS OF THE | SELECTMEN, | AND OTHER OFFICERS, | OF THE | TOWN OF CONCORD, | FROM MARCH 3, 1856, TO MARCH 2, 1857. | [rule] | BENJAMIN TOLMAN, PRINTER. | 1857.

Wrappers.

"Fifth Annual Report of the Town Library Committee," dated 2 March 1857, signed by Emerson and others, pp. [15]–16.

Location: MCo.

D 29 THE NEW AMERICAN CYCLOPÆDIA
1858

THE NEW | AMERICAN CYCLOPÆDIA: | A | [gothic] Popular Dictionary | OF | GENERAL KNOWLEDGE. | EDITED BY | GEORGE RIPLEY AND CHARLES A. DANA. | VOLUME I. | A—ARAGUAY. | NEW YORK: | D. APPLETON AND COMPANY, | 346 & 348 BROADWAY. | LONDON: 16 LITTLE BRITAIN. | M.DCCC.LVIII.

"Alcott, Amos Bronson," pp. 301–302. Unsigned. See A 54.

Location: MWA.

D 30 REPORTS OF THE CONCORD SELECTMEN
1858

REPORTS | OF THE | SELECTMEN AND OTHER OFFICERS, | OF THE | TOWN OF CONCORD, | FROM MARCH 2, 1857, TO MARCH 1, 1858, | AND | The Marriages, Births, and Deaths in Town, in 1857. | ALSO, | THE REPORTS OF THE SCHOOL COMMITTEE, | AND THE | SUPERINTENDENT OF PUBLIC SCHOOLS, | FOR THE YEAR ENDING APRIL 1, 1858. | [rule] | 1858: | BENJAMIN TOLMAN, PRINTER, CONCORD.

Wrappers.

"Sixth Annual Report of the Town Library Committee," dated 1 March 1858, signed by Emerson and others, pp. [12]–13.

"Report of the Cemetery Committee," signed by Emerson and others, pp. [16]–17.

Location: CtY.

D 31 TRANSACTIONS OF THE MIDDLESEX AGRICULTURAL SOCIETY
1858

TRANSACTIONS | OF THE | MIDDLESEX | AGRICULTURAL SOCIETY, | FOR THE YEAR 1858. | [rule] | CONCORD: | BENJAMIN TOLMAN, PRINTER. | 1858.

Wrappers.

"Address," pp. [45]–52. Reprinted as "Farming"; see A 31.

Location: MHi.

Note: Printed as "corrected from the Report in the Boston Courier."

D 32 CELEBRATION OF THE BIRTH OF ROBERT BURNS
1859

CELEBRATION | OF THE | HUNDREDTH ANNIVERSARY | OF THE | [gothic] Birth of Robert Burns, | BY THE | BOSTON BURNS CLUB. | JANUARY 25th, 1859. | [rule] | BOSTON: | PRINTED BY H. W. DUTTON AND SON, | Transcript Building. | 1859.

Cloth or wrappers.

"Speech of Ralph Waldo Emerson," pp. 35–37. See G 114; A 40.

Location: JM.

D 33 CIRCULAR
1859

CIRCULAR. | [rule] | BOSTON, Nov. 2, 1859. | Dear Sir:— | [¶] You are invited and urged to contribute and obtain | contributors to aid in the defence of Capt. Brown and his | companions, on trial for their lives in Virginia. *Every moment is | precious,* and whatever is done must be done now. The following | gentlemen (with others who may be hereafter announced in the | papers) will act as a Committee to receive money and appropriate | it to this purpose *only*. | S. E. SEWALL, Esq., 46 Washington St., Boston. | S. G. HOWE, M.D., 22 Bromfield St., [i.e., Boston] | R. W. EMERSON, Esq., Concord, Mass. | Rev. T. W. HIGGINSON, Worcester, Mass.

Single leaf, printed on recto only.

Location: MB.

D 34 REPORTS OF THE CONCORD SELECTMEN
1859

REPORTS | OF THE | SELECTMEN AND OTHER OFFICERS | OF THE | TOWN OF CONCORD, | FROM MARCH 1, 1858, TO MARCH 7, 1859. | INCLUDING | The Marriages, Births and Deaths in Town, in 1858. | ALSO, | THE REPORT OF THE SCHOOL COMMITTEE | FOR THE YEAR ENDING APRIL 1, 1859. | [rule] | CONCORD: | BENJA-MIN TOLMAN, PRINTER. | 1859.

Wrappers.

"Seventh Annual Report of the Town Library Committee," dated 7 March 1859, signed by Emerson and others, p. 12.
   "Report of the Cemetery Committee," dated 7 March 1859, signed by Emerson and others, pp. 14–15.

Location: CtY.

D 35 ECHOES OF HARPER'S FERRY
1860

ECHOES | OF | HARPER'S FERRY. | [rule] | [four lines from "Concord Hymn"] | R. W. EMERSON. | [rule] | JAMES REDPATH. | [rule] | [circular picture of two Roman warriors with motto 'SIC SEMPER TYRANNIS!'] | BOSTON: | THAYER AND ELDRIDGE, | 114 AND 116 WASHINGTON ST. | 1860.

"Ralph Waldo Emerson," pp. 67–70. Signed with facsimile signature. See D 36; A 40.
   "Speech by Ralph Waldo Emerson," pp. 119–122. See A 40.

Location: JM.

D 36 THE JOHN BROWN INVASION
1860

THE | JOHN BROWN INVASION | AUTHENTIC HISTORY | OF THE | HARPER'S FERRY TRAGEDY | WITH FULL DETAILS OF THE | CAPTURE, TRIAL, AND EXECUTION OF THE INVADERS, | AND OF ALL THE INCIDENTS CONNECTED THEREWITH. | WITH A LITHOGRAPHIC PORTRAIT OF CAPT. JOHN BROWN, | FROM A PHOTOGRAPH BY WHIPPLE. | [one line Bible quotation] | [five lines of prose] | JOHN BROWN'S ADDRESS TO THE COURT. | BOSTON: | PUBLISHED BY JAMES CAMPBELL. | FOR SALE BY J. J. DYER & CO., A. WILLIAMS & CO., FEDERHEN & CO., | AND BY NEWSMEN AND PERIODI-CAL DEALERS THROUGHOUT THE FREE STATES. | 1860.

"Speech of Mr. Ralph Waldo Emerson," pp. 103–105. See D 35; A 40.

Location: MWA.

D 37 REPORTS OF THE CONCORD SELECTMEN
1860

REPORTS | OF THE | SELECTMEN AND OTHER OFFICERS | OF THE | TOWN OF CONCORD, | FROM MARCH 7, 1859, TO MARCH 5, 1860. | INCLUDING | The Mar-riages, Births and Deaths in Town, in 1859. | ALSO, | THE REPORT OF THE SCHOOL COMMITTEE | FOR THE YEAR ENDING APRIL 1, 1860. | [rule] | CONCORD: | BENJA-MIN TOLMAN, PRINTER. | 1860.

Wrappers.

"Eighth Annual Report of the Town Library Committee," dated 5 March 1860, signed by Emerson and others, p. 13.

"Report of the Cemetery Committee," dated 5 March 1860, signed by Emerson and others, pp. 15–16.

Location: CtY.

D 38 TRIBUTES TO THEODORE PARKER
1860

TRIBUTES | TO | THEODORE PARKER, | COMPRISING THE | EXERCISES AT THE MUSIC HALL, | ON SUNDAY, JUNE 17, 1860, | WITH THE | PROCEEDINGS | OF THE | NEW ENGLAND ANTI-SLAVERY CONVENTION, | AT THE MELODEON, MAY 31, | AND THE | RESOLUTIONS OF THE FRATERNITY AND THE TWENTY- | EIGHTH CONGRE-GATIONAL SOCIETY. | [rule] | BOSTON: | PUBLISHED BY THE FRATERNITY. | 1860.

Wrappers.

"Remarks by Ralph Waldo Emerson," pp. 14–19. See A 40.

Location: JM.

D 39 REPORTS OF THE CONCORD SELECTMEN
1861

REPORTS | OF THE | SELECTMEN AND OTHER OFFICERS | OF THE | TOWN OF CONCORD, | FROM MARCH 5, 1860, TO MARCH 4, 1861. | INCLUDING | The Marriages, Births and Deaths in Town in 1860. | ALSO, | THE REPORT OF THE SCHOOL COMMITTEE | FOR THE YEAR ENDING APRIL 1, 1861. | [rule] | CONCORD: | PRINTED BY BENJAMIN TOLMAN. | 1861.

Wrappers.

"Ninth Annual Report of the Town Library Committee," dated 4 March 1861, signed by Emerson and others, p. 12.

Location: MCo.

D 40 [COPYRIGHT PETITION]
1862

To the Hon. [dotted line] | DEAR SIR, | [43 lines of text] | NEW YORK, April 25, 1862. | [two columns of names, three names per column]

Single sheet, folded once to make four pages.

Petition regarding the copyright law, signed by Emerson and others.

Location: MH.

D 41 REPORTS OF THE CONCORD SELECTMEN
1862

REPORTS | OF THE | SELECTMEN, | AND OTHER OFFICERS, | OF THE | TOWN OF CONCORD, | [pasted label] FROM MARCH 4, 1861, TO MARCH 3, 1862, | INCLUDING

THE | MARRIAGES, BIRTHS, AND DEATHS, | IN THE TOWN IN 1861. | [rule] | CON-CORD: | PRINTED BY BENJAMIN TOLMAN. | 1862.

Wrappers.

"Tenth Annual Report of the Town Library Committee," dated 3 March 1862, signed by Emerson and others, pp. 12–13.

Location: CtY.

D 42 TENTH ANNUAL REPORT OF THE BOSTON PUBLIC LIBRARY
1862

City Document.—No. 85. | [rule] | [rule] | [ornate letters] CITY OF BOSTON. | [rule] | [rule] | [Boston city seal] | [rule] | [rule] | TENTH | ANNUAL REPORT | OF THE | TRUSTEES OF THE PUBLIC LIBRARY. | 1862. | [rule] | [rule] | *In Board of Aldermen,* November 17, 1862. | Laid on the table, and 800 copies ordered to be printed. | Attest: S. F. McCLEARY, *City Clerk.*

Wrappers.

Petition, dated January 1862, signed by Emerson and others, p. [46].

Location: DLC.

D 43 LIFE AND CORRESPONDENCE OF THEODORE PARKER
1863

LIFE AND CORRESPONDENCE | OF | THEODORE PARKER, | MINISTER OF THE TWENTY-EIGHTH CONGREGATIONAL SOCIETY, | BOSTON. | BY | JOHN WEISS. | IN TWO VOLUMES. | VOL. I. [II.] | LONDON: | LONGMAN, GREEN, LONGMAN, ROB-ERTS, AND GREEN. | 1863.

Letter of 19 March 1853 to Parker, II, 45.

Location: JM.

Note: American reprinting, with Emerson's letter on the same page: 'LIFE . . . VOL. I. [II.] | NEW YORK: | D. APPLETON & COMPANY, 443 & 445 BROADWAY | 1864.' (JM).

D 44 MESSAGE OF THE PRESIDENT OF THE UNITED STATES
1863

38TH CONGRESS, [brace extending to next line] HOUSE OF REPRESENTATIVES. [brace extending to next line] Ex. Doc. | *1st Session.* [to left of brace]   No. 1. [to right of brace] | [rule] | [rule] | MESSAGE | OF THE | PRESIDENT OF THE UNITED STATES, | AND | ACCOMPANYING DOCUMENTS, | TO THE | TWO HOUSES OF CONGRESS, | AT | THE COMMENCEMENT OF THE FIRST SESSION | OF | THE THIRTY-EIGHTH CONGRESS. | [rule] | WASHINGTON: | GOVERNMENT PRINTING OFFICE | 1863.

Cover title.

"Report of the Board of Visitors of the U.S. Military Academy at West Point for 1863," signed by Emerson and others, pp. 76–94.

Location: RPB.

D 45 PITMAN'S POPULAR LECTURER AND READER
1863

Pitman's | Popular Lecturer and Reader. | *Edited by* | Henry Pitman, | of Manchester. | [rule] | VOL. 8 NEW SERIES. 1863. | [rule] | LONDON: F. PITMAN Publisher

"American Hymn" ["Boston Hymn"], pp. 252–254. *Reprint.* See E 162; A 28.

Location: NN.

Note: A bound volume containing all the year's issues of *Pitman's Popular Lecturer and Reader;* see E 162.

D 46 REPORTS OF THE CONCORD SELECTMEN
1863

REPORTS | OF THE | SELECTMEN, | AND OTHER OFFICERS, | OF THE | TOWN OF CONCORD, | FROM MARCH 3, 1862, TO MARCH 1, 1863. | INCLUDING THE | MARRIAGES, BIRTHS, AND DEATHS, | IN THE TOWN IN 1862. | [rule] | CONCORD: | PRINTED BY BENJAMIN TOLMAN. | 1863.

Wrappers.

"Eleventh Annual Report of the Town Library Committee," dated 2 March 1863, signed by Emerson and others, pp. [41]–42.

Location: CtY.

D 47 CLOUD CRYSTALS
1864

CLOUD CRYSTALS; | A | SNOW-FLAKE ALBUM. | COLLECTED AND EDITED | BY A LADY. | [three lines of verse] | *Dante.* | NEW YORK: | D. APPLETON & COMPANY, | 443 & 445 BROADWAY. | LONDON: | 16 LITTLE BRITAIN. | 1864.

Edited by Mrs. Frances E. Chickering.

"The Snow Storm," pp. [50]–51. Unsigned but identified as Emerson's in the table of contents. *Reprint.* See E 24; A 18.
   "Extract" [from "Voluntaries"], p. [156]. Unsigned but identified as Emerson's in the table of contents. *Reprint.* See E 164; D 49; A 28.

Location: MH.

D 48 THE HIGH TIDE
1864

THE HIGH TIDE, | BY | JEAN INGELOW, | WITH | NOTICES OF HER POEMS. | [rule] | BOSTON: | ROBERTS BROTHERS, PUBLISHERS, | 143 Washington Street. | 1864.

Wrappers.

Six-line blurb, "Notices of Jean Ingelow's Poems," supplement, p. 3.

Location: MB.

D 49 MEMORIAL RGS
1864

[all within a single-rule frame] MEMORIAL | [ornamentally intertwined] RGS | *Cambridge* | UNIVERSITY PRESS | 1864

Letter of 10 September 1863 to [Francis George Shaw], p. 160.
  "Voluntaries," pp. 161–164. See E 164. A 28.

Location: TxU.

D 50 OVER-SONGS
1864

[all within a single-rule red frame with a floral design in each corner] [ornate purple and gold initial capitals] [gothic] Over=Songs | [purple and gold with green and purple leaf-and-vine design] L | [green] M DCCC LXIV

Printed by the University Press, Cambridge. Printed on rectos only. Probably limited to five copies.

"Lover's Petition," pp. 10–11. See A 28.

Location: MH.

D 51 REPORTS OF THE CONCORD SELECTMEN
1864

REPORTS | OF THE | SELECTMEN, | AND OTHER OFFICERS, | OF THE | TOWN OF CONCORD, | FROM MARCH 1, 1863, TO MARCH 1, 1864. | INCLUDING THE | MARRIAGES, BIRTHS AND DEATHS, | IN THE TOWN, IN 1863. | [rule] | CONCORD: | PRINTED BY BENJAMIN TOLMAN. | 1864.

Wrappers.

"Twelfth Annual Report of the Town Library Committee," dated 7 March 1864, signed by Emerson and others, pp. [23]–25.

Location: CtY.

D 52 STATEMENT OF R. MORRIS COPELAND
1864

STATEMENT | OF | R. MORRIS COPELAND, | [gothic] Asst. Adjutant-General and Major of Volunteers, | DISCHARGED FROM SERVICE | August 6, 1862. | [rule] | BOSTON: | PRINTED BY PRENTISS AND DELAND, | 40, Congress Street. | 1864.

Wrappers.

Petitions to Abraham Lincoln and Charles Sumner, dated late March 1863, signed by Emerson and others, pp. 38–39, 39–40.

Location: DLC.

D 53 ANNALS OF THE AMERICAN PULPIT
1865

ANNALS | OF THE | AMERICAN PULPIT; | OR | COMMEMORATIVE NOTICES | OF | DISTINGUISHED AMERICAN CLERGYMEN | OF THE | VARIOUS DENOMINATIONS, | FROM THE EARLY SETTLEMENT OF THE COUNTRY TO THE CLOSE OF THE YEAR | EIGHTEEN HUNDRED AND FIFTY-FIVE | WITH HISTORICAL INTRODUCTIONS. | BY WILLIAM B. SPRAGUE, D. D. | [rule] | VOLUME VIII. | [rule] | NEW YORK: | ROBERT CARTER & BROTHERS, | 530 BROADWAY. | 1865.

Vol. VIII is *Unitarian Congregational.*

Letter of 25 October 1848 to [William Buell Sprague], pp. 117–118.
  Letter of 5 October 1849 to [William Buell Sprague], pp. 244–245.

Location: MH-AH.

D 54 THE BRYANT FESTIVAL
1865

THE | BRYANT FESTIVAL | AT | "The Century," | November 5, M.DCCC.LXIV. | New York: | D. APPLETON AND COMPANY, | 443 & 445 Broadway. | M.DCCC.LXV.

"Mr. Ralph Waldo Emerson's Remarks," pp. 16–19. See A 54.

Location: ScU.

D 55 THE GULISTAN OR ROSE GARDEN
1865

THE | GULISTAN | OR ROSE GARDEN. | BY | MUSLE-HUDDEEN SHEIK SAADI, | OF SHIRAZ. | TRANSLATED FROM THE ORIGINAL BY | FRANCIS GLADWIN. | WITH AN ESSAY ON SAADI'S LIFE AND GENIUS, | By JAMES ROSS, | AND A PREFACE, | By R. W. EMERSON. | [publisher's logo] | BOSTON: | TICKNOR AND FIELDS. | 1865.

"Preface to the American Edition," signed 'Concord, February, 1864.', pp. [iii]–xv.

Location: JM.

D 56 THE LINCOLN MEMORIAL
1865

THE | LINCOLN MEMORIAL: | A RECORD | OF | THE LIFE, ASSASSINATION, | AND | OBSEQUIES | OF THE | MARTYRED PRESIDENT. | NEW YORK: | BUNCE & HUNTINGTON. | 540 BROADWAY. | 1865.

Edited by John Gilmary Shea. Table of contents on p. [5].

Emerson's address at Concord, pp. 146–150. *Reprint.* See E 167; A 40.

Location: MH.

Note one: Also noted with table of contents on pp. [5]–6 and title page reading' . . . PRESIDENT. | EDITED BY | JOHN GILMARY SHEA, LL. D., | EDITOR OF THE HISTORICAL MAGAZINE, ETC. | [rule] | NEW . . . ' (JM).

Note two: Also noted with table of contents on pp. [5]–6 and title page reading '. . . PRESIDENT. | EDITED BY | JOHN GILMARY SHEA, LL.D., | EDITOR OF THE HIS-TORICAL MAGAZINE, ETC. | [rule] | NEW YORK: | BUNCE AND HUNTINGTON. | CHI-CAGO: | S. M. KENNEDY, 194 CLARK STREET. | 1865.' (FU).

D 57 THE PRESIDENT'S WORDS
1865

THE | PRESIDENT'S WORDS: | [gothic] A Selection of Passages | FROM THE | SPEECHES, ADDRESSES, AND LETTERS | OF | ABRAHAM LINCOLN. | [rule] | "All goes well with us. Every thing seems quiet now." | A. Lincoln: Telegram, April 2. | [rule] | BOSTON: | WALKER, FULLER, AND COMPANY, | 245, Washington Street. | 1865.

Selection from Emerson's address at Concord on Lincoln's death, pp. vii–viii. *Reprint.* See E 167; D 56; A 40.

Location: JM.

D 58 REPORTS OF THE CONCORD SELECTMEN
1865

REPORTS | OF THE | SELECTMEN AND OTHER OFFICER, | OF THE | TOWN OF CONCORD, | FROM | MARCH 1, 1864, TO MARCH 1, 1865, | INCLUDING THE | MARRIAGES, BIRTHS AND DEATHS IN 1864. | ALSO, | The Report of the School Committee. | [rule] | CONCORD: | PRINTED BY BENJAMIN TOLMAN. | 1865.

Wrappers.

Appendix to Bronson Alcott's School Committee report, signed by Emerson and others, pp. 12–13.

Location: CtY.

Note: This year's Library Committee report is signed by only E. R. Hoar, the committee's chairman.

D 59 ALUMNI HALL
1866

ALUMNI HALL: | [gothic] An Appeal | TO | THE ALUMNI AND FRIENDS | OF | HAR-VARD COLLEGE. | [rule] | CAMBRIDGE: | PRESS OF JOHN WILSON AND SON. | 1866.

Wrappers.

Signed by Emerson and others as the "Committee of Fifty."

Location: NN.

D 60 NATIONAL TESTIMONIAL TO WILLIAM LLOYD GARRISON
1866

NATIONAL TESTIMONIAL TO WILLIAM LLOYD GARRISON. | [rule] | [30 lines of text]

Single sheet, folded once to make four pages.

Testimonial, dated 25 April 1866, signed by Emerson and others.

Location: MB.

D61 REPORTS OF THE CONCORD SELECTMEN
1866

REPORTS | OF THE | SELECTMEN AND OTHER OFFICERS | OF THE | TOWN OF CONCORD, | FROM | MARCH 1, 1865, TO MARCH 1, 1866, | INCLUDING THE | MARRIAGES, BIRTHS AND DEATHS IN 1865. | ALSO, | The Report of the School Committee. | [rule] | CONCORD: | PRINTED BY BENJAMIN TOLMAN | 1866.

Wrappers.

"Fourteenth Annual Report of the Town Library Committee," dated 5 March 1866, signed by Emerson and others, pp. [19]–20.
    "Annual Report of the School Committee of the Town of Concord, 1865–66," signed by Emerson and others, supplement, pp. [3]–15.

Location: CtY.

D62 REPORT ON THE PERMANENT MEMORIAL
1866

HARVARD COLLEGE | [rule] | REPORT ON THE PERMANENT MEMORIAL | [rule] | [20 lines of text]

Head title. Printed in Boston by John Wilson and Son.

Signed by Emerson and others.

Location: MH.

D63 GOOD COMPANY FOR EVERY DAY IN THE YEAR
1866

[gothic with ornate red initial capitals] Good Company | FOR EVERY DAY IN THE YEAR. | "Good company . . . . . . well approved in all." | SHAKESPEARE. | [publisher's logo] | [red] BOSTON: | TICKNOR AND FIELDS. | 1866.

Edited by James T. Fields.

"The Titmouse," pp. [284]–287. *Reprint.* See E159; A28.

Location: JM.

D64 A YANKEE IN CANADA
1866

A | YANKEE IN CANADA, | WITH | ANTI-SLAVERY AND REFORM | PAPERS. | BY | HENRY D. THOREAU, | AUTHOR OF "A WEEK ON THE CONCORD AND MERRIMACK RIVERS," | "WALDEN," "CAPE COD," ETC., ETC | [publisher's logo] | BOSTON: | TICK-NOR AND FIELDS. | 1866

"Prayers," pp. [117]–122. Unsigned; erroneously attributed to Thoreau. *Reprint.* See E 46; A 44.

Location: MH.

D 65 ANNUAL REPORTS OF THE CONCORD SELECTMEN
1867

ANNUAL REPORTS | OF THE | SELECTMEN AND OTHER OFFICERS | OF THE | TOWN OF CONCORD, | FROM | MARCH 1, 1866, TO MARCH 1; 1867, | INCLUDING THE | MARRIAGES, BIRTHS AND DEATHS IN 1866. | [rule] | CONCORD: | PRINTED BY BENJAMIN TOLMAN. | 1867.

Wrappers.

"Fifteenth Annual Report of the Town Library-Committee," dated 4 March 1867, signed by Emerson and others, pp. [24]–25.

Location: CtY.

D 66 THE ATLANTIC ALMANAC FOR 1868
1867

[all within a single-rule frame] [three lines of ornate letters over vine design] The | ATLANTIC ALMANAC | 1868 | EDITED BY | OLIVER WENDELL HOLMES AND DONALD G. MITCHELL. | [rule] | CONTENTS. | [40 lines of contents, some in double columns] | BOSTON: | TICKNOR AND FIELDS, | OFFICE OF THE ATLANTIC MONTHLY. | [below frame] [Entered according to act of Congress, in the year 1867, by TICKNOR AND FIELDS, in the Clerk's Office of the Discrict Court of the District of Massachusetts.]

Pictorial wrappers.

"Domestic Life," pp. 28–29. *Reprint.* See E 134; A 31.

Location: JM.

D 67 CEREMONIES AT THE DEDICATION OF THE SOLDIERS' MONUMENT
1867

CEREMONIES | AT | THE DEDICATION | OF THE | SOLDIERS' MONUMENT, | IN | CONCORD, MASS. | [ornate rule] | CONCORD: | PRINTED BY BENJAMIN TOLMAN. | 1867.

Glazed stiff wrappers.

"Address," pp. [27]–52. See A 30; A 40.

Location: JM.

D 68 FREE RELIGION
1867

FREE RELIGION. | [rule] | REPORT | OF ADDRESSES | AT A | MEETING HELD IN BOSTON, | MAY 30, 1867, | TO CONSIDER THE | CONDITIONS, WANTS, AND PROSPECTS | OF | FREE RELIGION IN AMERICA. | TOGETHER WITH | THE CONSTITUTION

OF THE FREE RELIGIOUS ASSOCIATION | THERE ORGANIZED. | BOSTON: | PUB-
LISHED BY ADAMS & CO. | No. 25 BROMFIELD STREET.

Wrappers.

"Remarks of Ralph Waldo Emerson," pp. 52–54. See G 76; A 40.

Location: MH.

D 69 ANNUAL REPORTS OF THE CONCORD SELECTMEN
1868

ANNUAL REPORTS | OF THE | SELECTMEN AND OTHER OFFICERS | OF THE | TOWN
OF CONCORD, | FROM | MARCH 1, 1867, TO MARCH 1, 1868, | INCLUDING THE |
MARRIAGES, BIRTHS AND DEATHS IN 1867. | [rule] | CONCORD: | PRINTED BY
BENJAMIN TOLMAN. | 1868.

Wrappers.

"Sixteenth Annual Report of the Town Library-Committee," dated 2 March 1868, signed
by Emerson and others, pp. 20–21.

Location: CtY.

D 70 A BRIEF MEMOIR OF REV. JOSEPH BANCROFT HILL
1868

A | BRIEF MEMOIR | OF | REV. JOSEPH BANCROFT HILL, | WHO DIED IN THE
SERVICE OF | U. S. CHRISTIAN COMMISSION, | AT | CHATTANOOGA, TENN., JUNE
16, 1864. | BY | REV. EDWIN R. HODGMAN. | BOSTON: | PRINTED BY A. MUDGE &
SON, 34 SCHOOL STREET. | 1868.

Letter to Hodgman, [19 March 1865], pp. 14–15.

Location: MWA.

D 71 INTERNATIONAL COPYRIGHT
1868

[gothic] International Copyright. | [rule] | MEETING | OF | AUTHORS AND PUB-
LISHERS, | AT THE | ROOMS OF THE NEW YORK HISTORICAL SOCIETY, | April 9,
1868 | AND | ORGANIZATION OF THE | [gothic] International Copyright Association. |
[rule] | NEW YORK: | INTERNATIONAL COPYRIGHT ASSOCIATION. | 661 BROAD-
WAY. | 1868.

Wrappers.

Petition, dated March 1868, signed by Emerson and others, pp. 42–46.

Location: CtY.

D 72 THE PUBLIC LEDGER BUILDING
1868

THE | PUBLIC LEDGER BUILDING, | PHILADELPHIA: | WITH AN | ACCOUNT OF THE

PROCEEDINGS | CONNECTED WITH ITS | OPENING JUNE 20, 1867. | PHILADEL-PHIA: | GEORGE W. CHILDS. | 1868.

Letter of 15 June 1867 to George W. Childs, p. 140.

Location: MH.

D73 RECEPTION AND ENTERTAINMENT OF THE CHINESE EMBASSY
1868

RECEPTION AND ENTERTAINMENT | OF THE | CHINESE EMBASSY, | BY THE | CITY OF BOSTON. | [ornate rendition of Boston city seal] | 1868. | BOSTON: | ALFRED MUDGE & SON, CITY PRINTERS, 34 SCHOOL STREET. | 1868.

Cloth or glazed stiff wrappers.

"Mr. Emerson's Speech," pp. 52–55. See A40.3.

Location: JM.

D74 ADDRESS ON THE ANNIVERSARY OF THE BIRTH OF ALEXANDER VON HUMBOLDT
1869

ADDRESS | DELIVERED ON | THE CENTENNIAL ANNIVERSARY | OF THE BIRTH OF | ALEXANDER VON HUMBOLDT, | UNDER THE AUSPICES OF THE | BOSTON SOCIETY OF NATURAL HISTORY, | BY | LOUIS AGASSIZ. | WITH AN ACCOUNT OF THE EVEN-ING RECEPTION. | BOSTON: | BOSTON SOCIETY OF NATURAL HISTORY. | 1869.

Wrappers.

Emerson's remarks, pp. 71–72. See A40.3.

Location: JM.

Note: For an argument that Emerson's remarks were not printed from manuscript but from someone else's notes, see Robert E. Spiller, "Emerson and Humboldt" (E310).

D75 ANNUAL REPORTS OF THE CONCORD SELECTMEN
1869

ANNUAL REPORTS | OF THE | SELECTMEN AND OTHER OFFICERS | OF THE | TOWN OF CONCORD, | FROM MARCH 1, 1868, TO MARCH 1, 1869, | INCLUDING THE | Marriages, Births and Deaths in 1868. | ALSO, THE | REPORT OF THE SCHOOL COMMITTEE. | [rule] | CONCORD: | PRINTED BY BENJAMIN TOLMAN. | 1869.

Wrappers.

"Seventeenth Annual Report of the Town Library-Committee," dated 1 March 1869, signed by Emerson and others, pp. 23–24.

Location: CtY.

D76 SECOND ANNUAL MEETING OF THE FREE RELIGIOUS ASSOCIATION
1869

[gothic] Free Religious Association. | [rule] | PROCEEDINGS | AT THE | SECOND

ANNUAL MEETING | OF THE | FREE RELIGIOUS ASSOCIATION, | HELD IN BOSTON, | MAY 27 AND 28, 1869. | [rule] | BOSTON: | ROBERTS BROTHERS. | 1869.

Wrappers.

"Address of Ralph Waldo Emerson," pp. 42–44. See G 76; A 40.

Location: MH.

D 77 ANNUAL REPORTS OF THE CONCORD SELECTMEN
1870

ANNUAL REPORTS | —OF THE— | SELECTMEN AND OTHER OFFICERS | —OF THE— | TOWN OF CONCORD, | FROM MARCH 1, 1869, TO MARCH 1, 1870, | INCLUDING THE | Marriages, Births and Deaths in 1869. | —ALSO, THE— | REPORT OF THE SCHOOL COMMITTEE. | [rule] | PRINTED BY TOLMAN & WHITE, | 221 WASHINGTON STREET, BOSTON. | 1870.

Wrappers.

"Annual Report of the Town Library Committee," dated 1 March 1870, signed by Emerson and others, pp. 27–28.

Location: CtY.

D 78 PLUTARCH'S MORALS
1870

PLUTARCH'S MORALS. | TRANSLATED FROM THE GREEK BY SEVERAL HANDS. | CORRECTED AND REVISED | BY | WILLIAM W. GOODWIN, PHD., | PROFESSOR OF GREEK LITERATURE IN HARVARD UNIVERSITY. | WITH | AN INTRODUCTION BY RALPH WALDO EMERSON. | VOL. I. | [Greek coin] | BOSTON: | LITTLE, BROWN, AND COMPANY. | 1870.

5 vols.

"Introduction," pp. [ix]–xxiv. Unsigned. See B 1; A 41.

Location: RNR.

Note: New edition, with Emerson's unsigned introduction on pp. [vii]–xxii: 'PLU-TARCH'S ESSAYS. | WITH | A PREFACE BY | THE REV. ANDREW P. PEABODY, D.D., | AND | AN INTRODUCTION BY | RALPH WALDO EMERSON, LL.D. | [Greek coin] | BOSTON: | LITTLE, BROWN, AND COMPANY. | 1881.' (DLC).

D 79 REPORTS TO THE BOARD OF OVERSEERS OF HARVARD UNIVER-SITY
1870

[gothic] Harvard University | [rule] | REPORTS | TO | THE BOARD OF OVERSEERS | OF THE | COMMITTEE ON REPORTS AND | RESOLUTIONS, | AND OF THE | COMMITTEE TO VISIT THE COLLEGE, | IN 1869–70. | [Harvard seal] | CAMBRIDGE: | PRESS OF JOHN WILSON AND SON. | 1870.

Cover title.

"Report," signed by Emerson and others, pp. 9–28.

Location: NNC.

D 80 ANNUAL REPORTS OF THE CONCORD TOWN OFFICERS
1871

ANNUAL REPORTS | OF THE | OFFICERS | OF THE | TOWN OF CONCORD, | FROM | MARCH 1, 1870, TO MARCH 1, 1871. | [rule] | TOLMAN & WHITE, PRINTERS, 221 WASHINGTON ST., BOSTON. | 1871.

Wrappers.

"Annual Report of the Town Library Committee," dated 1 March 1871, signed by Emerson and others, pp. 24–25.

Location: MCo.

D 81 NEW-ENGLAND SOCIETY CELEBRATION
1871

[all within an ornate oval frame with seals of six New England states; all but the first and last lines are curved] [gothic] Sixty-Fifth | [gothic] Anniversary Celebration | OF THE | [engraving of eagle] | NEW-ENGLAND SOCIETY | IN THE CITY OF NEW YORK | *AT* | [ornate letters] DELMONICO'S | [gothic] Dec. 22, 1870.

Wrappers.

"Speech of Mr. Emerson," pp. 30–33. See D 165.

Location: MH.

D 82 PROCEEDINGS OF THE MASSACHUSETTS HISTORICAL SOCIETY
1871

II. | PROCEEDINGS | OF THE | MASSACHUSETTS HISTORICAL SOCIETY, | FOR | MAY, JUNE, JULY, AND AUGUST, 1871. | [Society's seal]

Wrappers. Cover title.

Remarks on Walter Scott, pp. 145–147. See A 40.

Location: JM.

Note one: Reprinted from the same plates, with Emerson's remarks on pp. 6–8, in wrappers: 'TRIBUTE | TO | WALTER SCOTT, | ON THE | [gothic] One Hundredth Anniversary of his Birthday. | BY THE | MASSACHUSETTS HISTORICAL SOCIETY. | AUGUST 15, 1871. | [ornate rule] | BOSTON: | PRIVATELY REPRINTED FROM THE PROCEEDINGS OF THE SOCIETY. | 1872.' (JM).

Note two: Reprinted again from the same plates, with Emerson's remarks on pp. 145–147: 'PROCEEDINGS | OF THE | [gothic] Massachusetts Historical Society. | [rule] | 1871–1873. | [rule] | [gothic] Published at the Charge of the Peabody Fund. | [Society's logo] | BOSTON: | PUBLISHED BY THE SOCIETY. | M.DCCC.LXXIII.' (MHi).

D 83 THE UNITY OF ITALY
1871

THE | UNITY OF ITALY. | THE AMERICAN CELEBRATION OF THE UNITY OF ITALY, AT | THE ACADEMY OF MUSIC, NEW YORK, JAN. 12, 1871, | WITH THE ADDRESSES, LETTERS, AND | COMMENTS OF THE PRESS. | [two lines from Virgil] | NEW YORK: | G. P. PUTNAM & SONS, | ASSOCIATION BUILDING. | 1871.

Wrappers.

Letter of 11 January 1871, pp. 70–71.

Location: ScU.

D 84 THE WANDERER
1871

THE WANDERER. | A COLLOQUIAL POEM. | BY | WILLIAM ELLERY CHANNING. | [publisher's logo] | BOSTON: | JAMES R. OSGOOD AND COMPANY, | (LATE TICKNOR & FIELDS, AND FIELDS, OSGOOD, & CO.) | 1871.

"Preface," pp. v–viii.

Location: TxU.

D 85 ANNUAL REPORTS OF THE CONCORD TOWN OFFICERS
1872

ANNUAL REPORTS | OF THE | OFFICERS | OF THE | TOWN OF CONCORD | FROM | MARCH 1, 1871, TO MARCH 1, 1872, | BEING THE TWO HUNDRED AND THIRTY-SIXTH MUNICIPAL YEAR. | ALSO, | REPORT OF THE COMMITTEE | ON THE | WIDENING OF MAIN STREET. | [rule] | BOSTON: | TOLMAN & WHITE, PRINTERS, 221 WASHINGTON STREET. | 1872.

Wrappers.

"Annual Report of the Town Library Committee," dated 1 March 1872, signed by Emerson and others, pp. 40–41.

Location: MCo.

D 86 ANNUAL REPORTS OF THE CONCORD SELECTMEN
1873

ANNUAL REPORTS | OF THE | SELECTMEN AND OTHER OFFICERS | OF THE | TOWN OF CONCORD, | FROM | MARCH 1, 1872, TO MARCH 1, 1873, | BEING THE TWO HUNDRED AND THIRTY-SEVENTH MUNICIPAL YEAR. | ALSO, | THE REPORT OF THE | SCHOOL COMMITTEE. | [rule] | BOSTON: | TOLMAN & WHITE, PRINTERS, 221 WASHINGTON STREET. | 1873.

Wrappers.

"Annual Report of the Town Library Committee," dated 18 March 1873, signed by Emerson and others, pp. [30]–31.

Location: MCo.

D 87 DEDICATION OF THE CONCORD PUBLIC LIBRARY
1873

Dedication | OF THE | NEW BUILDING | FOR THE | Free Public Library | OF | CON-CORD, MASSACHUSETTS, | Wednesday, Oct. 1, 1873. | [rule] | [two lines about Julius Caesar] | [rule] | BOSTON: | TOLMAN & WHITE, PRINTERS, 221 WASHINGTON STREET. | 1873.

Wrappers.

"Address," pp. 37–45. See A 40.3.

Location: MCo.

Note: Reprinted 1874 (JM).

D 88 THOREAU: THE POET-NATURALIST
1873

THOREAU: THE POET-NATURALIST. | [gothic] With Memorial | Verses. | BY | WILLIAM ELLERY CHANNING. | [three lines of prose] | H.D.T. | BOSTON: | ROBERTS BROTHERS. | 1873.

Selections from Emerson's manuscript journals.

Location: JM.

Note: See D 169 for revised edition, with additional material.

D 89 ANNUAL REPORTS OF THE CONCORD SELECTMEN
1874

ANNUAL REPORTS | OF THE | SELECTMEN AND OTHER OFFICERS | OF THE | TOWN OF CONCORD, | FROM | MARCH 1, 1873, TO MARCH 1, 1874, | BEING THE TWO HUNDRED AND THIRTY-EIGHTH MUNICIPAL YEAR. | ALSO, | THE REPORT OF THE | SCHOOL COMMITTEE. | [rule] | BOSTON: | TOLMAN & WHITE, PRINTERS, 221 WASH-INGTON STREET. | 1874.

Wrappers.

"The Library. Report of the Town Committee," dated March 1874, signed by Emerson and others, pp. 44–54.

Location: MCo.

D 90 PROPHETIC VOICES CONCERNING AMERICA
1874

PROPHETIC VOICES | CONCERNING | AMERICA. | A MONOGRAPH. | BY | CHARLES SUMNER. | [eight lines of prose by John Bright] | [rule] | BOSTON: | LEE AND SHEP-ARD, PUBLISHERS. | NEW YORK: | LEE, SHEPARD, AND DILLINGHAM. | 1874.

"From Ralph Waldo Emerson" [testimonial], pp. 4–5 in terminal advertisements.

Location: JM.

D 91 QUIET HOURS
1874

QUIET HOURS. | [gothic] A Collection of Poems. | [five lines of verse] | J. G. WHITTIER. | BOSTON: | ROBERTS BROTHERS. | 1874.

Edited by Mary Wilder Tileston.

"The Rhodora," p. 19. *Reprint.* See E 15; A 18.
  "Each and All," pp. 33–35. *Reprint.* See E 12; A 18.
  "Days," p. 62. See E 131; A 28.
  "The Problem," pp. 66–68. *Reprint.* See E 18; A 18.
  "Dirge," pp. 157–159. *Reprint.* See D 11; A 18.

Location: TxU.

D 92 ANNUAL REPORTS OF THE CONCORD SELECTMEN
1875

ANNUAL REPORTS | OF THE | SELECTMEN AND OTHER OFFICERS | OF THE | TOWN OF CONCORD, | FROM | MARCH 1, 1874, TO MARCH 1, 1875, | BEING THE TWO HUN-DRED AND THIRTY-NINTH MUNICIPAL YEAR. | ALSO | THE REPORT OF THE SCHOOL COMMITTEE. | [rule] | BOSTON: | TOLMAN & WHITE, PRINTERS, 221 WA-SHINGTON STREET. | 1875.

Wrappers.

"The Library. Report of the Town Committee," dated 1 March 1875, signed by Emerson and others, pp. 39–43.

Location: MCo.

D 93 ATHENÆUM ADDRESSES
1875

[all within a single-rule frame] ATHENÆUM ADDRESSES | 1843–8, | AND REPORT OF | THE SOIRÉE OF 1875. | [REPRINTED FROM THE MANCHESTER CITY NEWS.] | [rule] | MANCHESTER: | PRINTED FOR THE DIRECTORS. | 1875.

Wrappers.

"Speech of Mr. Ralph Waldo Emerson, November 18, 1847," pp. [93]–97. For another version, see "Speech at Manchester," *English Traits* (A 24).

Location: MH.

D 94 CENTENNIAL ORATIONS ON THE AMERICAN REVOLUTION
1875

CENTENNIAL ORATIONS | COMMEMORATIVE OF | THE OPENING EVENTS | OF THE | AMERICAN REVOLUTION. | *WITH OTHER PROCEEDINGS.* | 1874—1875. | [New England Historic and Genealogical Society logo] | BOSTON: | 18 SOMERSET STREET. | 1875.

Cloth or wrappers. Limited to 250 copies.

Emerson's remarks, pp. 138–139. *Reprint.* See D 98; E 183.

Location: CtY.

D 95 INVITATION
1875

[ornate lettering curved across top] 1775—CONCORD FIGHT—1875. | [picture of minute-man] | [ornate lettering] APRIL 19TH 1775. | Wm. H. Brett & Co. Boston. | [remainder of text in script] To·············· | Sir············· | [six-line invitation to ceremonies] | E. R. Hoar. | R. W. Emerson. | George Heywood. [brace to the right of all three names with 'Committee of Invitation.' on the line with Emerson's name]

Single sheet, folded once to make four pages, printed on p. 1 only.

Location: JM.

D 96 TO THE ALUMNI
1875

TO THE ALUMNI. | [22 lines of text] | [10 lines of signatures]

Broadside, printed on recto only. An endorsement of James Elliot Cabot for the Harvard Board of Overseers, signed by Emerson and others.

Location: ViU.

D 97 MEMOIR OF ANNE JEAN LYMAN
1876

MEMOIR | OF THE | LIFE OF MRS. ANNE JEAN LYMAN. | [two lines from Luke] | [two lines from Galatians] | [gothic] Privately Printed. | CAMBRIDGE: | MASSACHUSETTS. | 1876.

Various letters.

Location: JM.

Note: All the letters appear in the following reprints: (1) 'RECOLLECTIONS OF MY MOTHER. | BY | SUSAN I. LESLEY. | [rule] | [two lines of verse] | [rule] | *PRINTED, NOT PUBLISHED.* | [rule] | BOSTON: | PRESS OF GEO. H. ELLIS, 141 FRANKLIN STREET. | 1886.'; (2) 'RECOLLECTIONS OF MY MOTHER. | BY | SUSAN I. LESLEY. | [rule] | [two lines of verse] | *THIRD EDITION* | [rule] | BOSTON: | PRESS OF GEO. H. ELLIS, 141 FRANKLIN STREET | 1889'; (3) 'RECOLLECTIONS OF MY | MOTHER | MRS. ANNE JEAN LYMAN | *OF NORTH-AMPTON* | BEING A PICTURE OF DOMESTIC AND | SOCIAL LIFE IN NEW ENGLAND IN | THE FIRST HALF OF THE NINE- | TEENTH CENTURY | BY | SUSAN I. LESLEY | [two lines of verse] | [publisher's logo] | BOSTON AND NEW YORK | HOUGHTON, MIFFLIN AND COMPANY | [gothic] The Riverside Press, Cambridge | 1899' (ScU [all]).

D 98 PROCEEDINGS AT THE CENTENNIAL CELEBRATION OF CONCORD FIGHT
1876

PROCEEDINGS | AT THE | CENTENNIAL CELEBRATION | OF | CONCORD FIGHT |

April 19, 1875. | ["Old North Bridge" device] | CONCORD, MASS. | PUBLISHED BY THE TOWN. | 1876.

"Address," pp. 79–81. *Reprint.* See D 94; E 183.

Location: JM.

D 99   TRANSCENDENTALISM IN NEW ENGLAND
         1876

TRANSCENDENTALISM | IN | NEW ENGLAND | *A HISTORY* | BY | OCTAVIUS BROOKS FROTHINGHAM | *Author of "Life of Theodore Parker," "Religion of Humanity," &c., &c.* | [publisher's logo] | NEW YORK | G. P. PUTNAM'S SONS | 182 FIFTH AVENUE | 1876

"Letter to the Second Church and Society," pp. 232–236. *Reprint.* See A 1; A 54.
  [Sermon on the Lord's Supper], pp. [363]–380. See A 40.

Location: JM.

D 100   THE ANCIENT AND HONORABLE ARTILLERY COMPANY OF MAS-
           SACHUSETTS
           1877

THE TWO HUNDRED AND THIRTY-EIGHTH | ANNUAL RECORD | OF THE | [gothic] Ancient and Honorable Artillery Co. | OF | MASSACHUSETTS. | 1875–76. | [rule] | SERMON BY REV. WILLIAM H. RYDER, | OF MALDEN. | [rule] BOSTON: | ALFRED MUDGE & SON, PRINTERS, | 34 SCHOOL STREET. | 1877.

Wrappers.

"Remarks by Ralph Waldo Emerson," p. 10.

Location: NNC.

D 101   ANNUAL REPORTS OF THE CONCORD SELECTMEN
           1877

ANNUAL REPORTS | OF THE | SELECTMEN AND OTHER OFFICERS | OF THE | TOWN OF CONCORD, | FROM | MARCH 1, 1876, TO MARCH 1, 1877. | Being the Two Hundred and Forty-first Municipal Year. | ALSO, | THE REPORT OF THE SCHOOL COMMITTEE. | [rule] | BOSTON: | TOLMAN & WHITE, PRINTERS, 383 WASHINGTON STREET. | 1877.

Wrappers.

"Report of the Library Committee," signed by Emerson as chairman, p. 34.

Location: MCo.

Note: No contribution by Emerson has been located in the 1876 *Annual Reports.*

D 102   BRYAN WALLER PROCTER
           1877

BRYAN WALLER PROCTER | (BARRY CORNWALL). | AN | AUTOBIOGRAPHICAL FRAGMENT | AND | BIOGRAPHICAL NOTES, | WITH | PERSONAL SKETCHES OF

CONTEMPORARIES, UNPUBLISHED | LYRICS, AND LETTERS OF LITERARY FRIENDS. | LONDON: GEORGE BELL AND SONS, YORK STREET, | COVENT GARDEN. | 1877.

Letter of 30 September 1847 to Bryan Waller Procter, pp. 294–295.

Location: MH.

D 103 PROCEEDINGS OF THE MASSACHUSETTS HISTORICAL SOCIETY
1877

II. | PROCEEDINGS | OF | THE | MASSACHUSETTS HISTORICAL SOCIETY, | DECEMBER, 1876, TO FEBRUARY, 1877, | (INCLUSIVE). | [Society's seal]

Wrappers.

Letter of 6 December 1875 to George E. Ellis, p. 191.

Location: MCo.

Note one: Reprinted from the same plates, with Emerson's letter on p. 12, in wrappers: 'MEMOIR | OF | CHARLES WENTWORTH UPHAM. | BY | GEORGE E. ELLIS. | REPRINTED FROM THE PROCEEDINGS OF THE MASSACHUSETTS | HISTORICAL SOCIETY, DECEMBER, 1876. | [ornate rule] | CAMBRIDGE: | PRESS OF JOHN WILSON AND SON. | 1877.' (NNC).

Note two: Reprinted again from the same plates, with Emerson's letter on p. 191 in "Memoir of Charles Wentworth Upham" (pp. 182–221): 'PROCEEDINGS | OF THE | [gothic] Massachusetts Historical Society | [rule] | 1876–1877. | [rule] | [gothic] Published at the Charge of the Peabody Fund. | [Society's seal] | BOSTON: | PUBLISHED BY THE SOCIETY. | M.DCCC.LXXVIII.' (MHi).

D 104 WORTHY WOMEN OF OUR FIRST CENTURY
1877

WORTHY WOMEN | OF | OUR FIRST CENTURY. | EDITED BY | MRS. O. J. WISTER | AND | MISS AGNES IRWIN. | [rule] | PHILADELPHIA: | J. B. LIPPINCOTT & CO. | 1877.

Emerson's obituary notice of Sarah Alden Ripley, pp. 223–225, in Elizabeth Hoar's section on "Mrs. Samuel Ripley," pp. 113–227. *Reprint.* See E 172; A 29.

Location: MH.

Note: Reprinted, with Emerson's notice on the same pages, in cloth or wrappers: 'MRS SAMUEL RIPLEY | [rule] | FROM | "WORTHY WOMEN OF OUR FIRST CENTURY" | [rule] | J B LIPPINCOTT & CO. | PHILADELPHIA | 1877' (MH).

D 105 ANNUAL REPORTS OF THE CONCORD SELECTMEN
1878

ANNUAL REPORTS | OF THE | SELECTMEN AND OTHER OFFICERS | OF THE | TOWN OF CONCORD, | FROM | MARCH 1, 1877, TO MARCH 1, 1878. | Being the Two Hundred and Forty-second Municipal Year. | ALSO, | THE REPORT OF THE SCHOOL COMMITTEE. | [rule] | BOSTON: | TOLMAN & WHITE, PRINTERS, 383 WASHINGTON STREET. | 1878.

Wrappers.

"Report of the Library Committee," signed by Emerson as chairman, pp. 33–34.

Location: MCo.

D 106 REMINISCENCES OF AN OLD TEACHER
1878

REMINISCENCES | OF AN | OLD TEACHER. | [rule] | BY George B. Emerson. | [rule] | BOSTON: | ALFRED MUDGE & SON, PRINTERS, 34 SCHOOL STREET | 1878.

Letter of 31 August 1872 to G. B. Emerson, p. 154.

Location: JM.

Note: A copy has been noted with p. 154 blank: NNC-T.

D 107 SCIENCE AND THEOLOGY AND THE SOVEREIGNTY OF ETHICS
1878

SCIENCE AND THEOLOGY: | ANCIENT AND MODERN. | BY | JAMES ANTHONY FROUDE, | AUTHOR OF "HISTORY OF ENGLAND," ETC. | AND | THE SOVEREIGNTY OF ETHICS. | BY | RALPH WALDO EMERSON. | [rule] | TORONTO: | ROSE-BELFORD PUBLISHING COMPANY. | [rule] | MDCCCLXXVIII.

"The Sovereignty of Ethics," pp. [42]–66. *Reprint.* See E 188; B 1; A 41.

Location: CaOTV.

Note: Reprinted from the same plates, with Emerson's essay on the same pages: 'SCIENCE [rule above and below next word] AND THEOLOGY | ANCIENT AND MOD-ERN. | BY | JAMES ANTHONY FROUDE. | *The English Historian,* | AND OTHER | RELIGIO-SCIENCE ESSAYS. | BY | EMERSON, LESLIE STEPHEN, HUXLEY, CANON FARAR, | EDISON, PLUMPTRE, COX AND MELLEN. | [rule] | [gothic] Toronto and Chicago: | ROSE-BELFORD PUBLISHING CO. | 1879.' (NcD).

D 108 BEDFORD SESQUI-CENTENNIAL CELEBRATION
1879

BEDFORD | SESQUI-CENTENNIAL CELEBRATION, | AUG. 27, 1879. | HISTORICAL DISCOURSE, | BY | JONATHAN F. STEARNS, D. D., | PASTOR OF THE FIRST PRESBY-TERIAN CHURCH, NEWARK, N. J. | ALSO, | [gothic] A Sketch of the Celebration. | [rule] | BOSTON: | ALFRED MUDGE & SON, PRINTERS, | 34 SCHOOL STREET. | 1879.

Wrappers.

Brief comment by Emerson, p. 79.

Location: MH.

D 109 THE HUNDRED GREATEST MEN
1879

THE | HUNDRED GREATEST MEN | PORTRAITS | OF THE | ONE HUNDRED GREAT-EST MEN OF HISTORY | *REPRODUCED FROM FINE AND RARE STEEL ENGRAVINGS*

| VOLUME I | [gothic] Poetry | POETS, DRAMATISTS, NOVELISTS | LONDON | SAMPSON LOW, MARSTON, SEARLE, AND RIVINGTON | CROWN BUILDINGS, 188 FLEET STREET | 1879 | (*All rights reserved.*)

Originally sold in a series of eight portfolios, which were then bound up and sold as a four-volume set.

"General Introduction to the Work," pp. [i]–iii. *Reprint*. See A 37.

Location: MH.

Note one: American edition, with Emerson's introduction on pp. [v]–vi: 'THE | HUNDRED GREATEST MEN | PORTRAITS | OF THE | ONE HUNDRED GREATEST MEN OF HISTORY | *REPRODUCED FROM FINE AND RARE STEEL ENGRAVINGS.* | WITH GENERAL INTRODUCTION BY RALPH WALDO EMERSON | AND TO | [eight lines listing other contributors of introductions to each section] | [gothic] New York | D. APPLETON AND COMPANY | 1885' (JM).

Note two: English reprinting of the second edition, with Emerson's introduction on the same pages: 'THE . . . *ENGRAVINGS.* | EDITED BY WALLACE WOOD, M. D. | WITH . . .', and after list of other contributors, 'NEW EDITION | [gothic] London | SAMPSON LOW, MARSTON, SEARLE, & RIVINGTON | CROWN BUILDINGS, 188, FLEET STREET | 1885 | [*All rights reserved*]' (IHi).

> D 110 PROCEEDINGS AT A RECEPTION IN HONOR OF O. B. FROTHINGHAM
> *1879*

PROCEEDINGS AT A RECEPTION | IN HONOR OF THE | REV. O. B. FROTHINGHAM | GIVEN BY THE | INDEPENDENT LIBERAL CHURCH | AT THE UNION LEAGUE THEATRE | TUESDAY EVENING, APRIL 22, 1879 | TOGETHER WITH THE REPORT OF THE FAREWELL SERMON | DELIVERED BY HIM AT MASONIC TEMPLE | APRIL 27, 1879 | [rule] | NEW YORK | G. P. PUTNAM'S SONS | 182 FIFTH AVENUE | 1879

Cover title.

Letter of 16 April [1879] to James Herbert Morse, p. 51. *Reprint*. See E 189.

Location: MH.

> D 111 TESTIMONIALS
> *1879*

TESTIMONIALS. | [rule] | PRIVATELY PRINTED—NOT PUBLISHED. | [rule] | BOSTON: | PRESS OF GEORGE H. ELLIS, 101 MILK STREET. | 1879.

Cover title.

Letter of 23 April 1867 to the Trustees of Cornell University in support of Francis Ellingwood Abbot, p. 32.

Location: MH.

Note: New edition, with Emerson's letter on p. 12: '[all within a double-rule frame] SCHOOL FOR BOYS. | [ornate rule] | REFERENCES. | [rule] | [twelve lines of names and addresses]'; cover title, pamphlet; the latest included letter is dated April 1881 (JM).

D 112 MEMORIAL BIOGRAPHIES
1880

MEMORIAL | BIOGRAPHIES | OF | THE NEW ENGLAND HISTORIC | GENEALOGICAL
SOCIETY | TOWNE MEMORIAL FUND | Volume I | 1845—1852 | BOSTON | PUBLISHED
BY THE SOCIETY | 18 Somerset Street | 1880

Letter to Haskins, p. 479, in [David Greene Haskins], "Ralph Haskins," pp. [465]–482.

Location: CtY.

D 113 SKETCHES AND REMINISCENCES OF THE RADICAL CLUB
1880

Sketches and Reminiscences | OF | THE RADICAL CLUB | OF | *CHESTNUT STREET,*
BOSTON. | EDITED BY | MRS. JOHN T. SARGENT. | [publisher's logo] | BOSTON: |
JAMES R. OSGOOD AND COMPANY. | 1880.

Edited by Mary E. Sargent.

"Religion," pp. [3]–6. See A 42.
  Letter of [4 November 1867] to John T. Sargent, pp. 21–22.
  Remarks, pp. 28, 41–42, 221, 236–237.
  "Boston," pp. 294–295. *Reprint.* See E 184; A 18.4.
  "The beggar begs by God's command," p. 398. See A 18.6.

Location: JM.

D 114 SOME INCIDENTS IN THE LIFE OF SAMUEL BRADFORD
1880

SOME INCIDENTS | IN THE LIFE OF | SAMUEL BRADFORD, SENIOR, | BY HIS SON. |
[rule] | ALSO, THE | AUTOBIOGRAPHY OR A BRIEF NARRATIVE | OF THE LIFE OF |
SAMUEL BRADFORD, JUNIOR, | TO JANUARY 1, 1879. | [rule] | PRINTED, NOT
PUBLISHED. | [rule] | PHILDELPHIA, 1880.

Letter of 11 March 1875 to Samuel Bradford, pp. 78–79.
  Letter "Lines Addressed to Samuel Bradford on the Death of his Sister, January 24,
1816," p. 40.

Location: MH.

D 115 PROCEEDINGS OF THE MASSACHUSETTS HISTORICAL SOCIETY
1881

PROCEEDINGS | OF THE | [gothic] Massachusetts Historical Society. | Vol. XVIII. |
[rule] | 1880–1881. | [rule] | [gothic] Published at the Charge of the Peabody Fund. |
[Society's seal] | BOSTON: | PUBLISHED BY THE SOCIETY. | M.DCCC.LXXXI.

Emerson's remarks on Carlyle, pp. 324–328. *Reprint.* See E 194; A 41.

Location: MHi.

D116 RALPH WALDO EMERSON
1881

RALPH WALDO EMERSON: | HIS LIFE, WRITINGS, AND PHILOSOPHY. | BY | GEORGE WILLIS COOKE. | [publisher's logo] | BOSTON: | JAMES R. OSGOOD AND COMPANY. | 1881.

Previously unpublished material from letters.

Location: JM.

D117 THOMAS CARLYLE
1881

THOMAS CARLYLE | BY | MONCURE D. CONWAY | *ILLUSTRATED* | NEW YORK | HARPER & BROTHERS, FRANKLIN SQUARE | 1881

Letters of [26 September 1864] to Thomas Carlyle and 30 August 1833 to Alexander Ireland, pp. 95–96, 220–223.

Location: JM.

D118 THE CENTENNIAL OF THE SOCIAL CIRCLE IN CONCORD
1882

THE | CENTENNIAL | OF THE | SOCIAL CIRCLE IN CONCORD | *March 21, 1882* | [two lines of verse] | *Chas. Morris's Farewell to the Beef Steak Club, London, 1831* | CAMBRIDGE | PRINTED AT THE RIVERSIDE PRESS | 1882

"Memoir of Rev. Ezra Ripley, D.D.," pp. 168–176. See E34; A41.

Location: JM.

D119 EMERSON AT HOME AND ABROAD
1882

EMERSON | AT HOME AND ABROAD | BY | MONCURE DANIEL CONWAY | AUTHOR OF "THE SACRED ANTHOLOGY," "THE WANDERING JEW," | "THOMAS CARLYLE," &C. | [publisher's logo] | BOSTON: | JAMES R. OSGOOD AND COMPANY. | 1882.

Previously unpublished material from letters.

Location: JM.

Note: English edition: 'EMERSON . . . OF | "THE . . . CARLYLE," ETC. ETC. | LONDON | TRÜBNER & CO., LUDGATE HILL | 1883 | [All rights reserved]' (MCo).

D120 GEORGE RIPLEY
1882

[gothic] American Men of Letters. | [rule] | GEORGE RIPLEY, | BY | OCTAVIUS BROOKS FROTHINGHAM. | [publisher's logo] | BOSTON | HOUGHTON, MIFFLIN AND

COMPANY | New York: 11 East Seventeenth Street | [gothic] The Riverside Press, Cambridge | 1882

Letter of [15 December 1840] to George Ripley, pp. 314–318.

Location: JM.

D 121 HENRY D. THOREAU
1882

[gothic] American Men of Letters. | [rule] | HENRY D. THOREAU. | BY | F. B. SANBORN. | [publisher's logo] | BOSTON: | HOUGHTON, MIFFLIN AND COMPANY | New York: 11 East Seventeenth Street | [gothic] The Riverside Press, Cambridge | 1882

Letters of [7 June 1841?] and [21] May 1843 to Thoreau, pp. 155, 135.

Location: JM.

D 122 IN MEMORIAM. RALPH WALDO EMERSON
1882

[gothic] In Memoriam. | [rule] | RALPH WALDO EMERSON: | RECOLLECTIONS OF HIS VISITS TO ENGLAND | IN | 1833, 1847–8, 1872–3, | AND | EXTRACTS FROM UNPUB-LISHED LETTERS. | BY | ALEXANDER IRELAND. | [three lines of verse] | [rule] | [nine lines of verse] | SAMUEL DANIEL (1562–1619). | LONDON: SIMPKIN, MARSHALL, & CO. | EDINBURGH: DAVID DOUGLAS. GLASGOW: DAVID M. MAIN. | MANCHESTER: J. E. CORNISH. | LIVERPOOL: J. CORNISH & SONS. BIRMINGHAM: CORNISH BROTHERS. | 1882.

Previously unpublished material from letters.

Location: JM.

D 123 RALPH WALDO EMERSON
1882

RALPH WALDO EMERSON | HIS | LIFE, GENIUS, AND WRITINGS | A BIOGRAPHICAL SKETCH | TO WHICH ARE ADDED | *PERSONAL RECOLLECTIONS OF HIS VISITS TO ENGLAND* | *EXTRACTS FROM UNPUBLISHED LETTERS* | *AND MISCELLANEOUS CHARACTERISTIC RECORDS* | BY | ALEXANDER IRELAND | [gothic] Second Edition, Largely Augmented | THREE AUTOTYPE PORTRAITS | LONDON: SIMPKIN, MAR-SHALL, & CO. | 1882 | ALL RIGHTS RESERVED

Previously unpublished material from letters.

Location: CU.

D 124 TO THE SUBSCRIBERS TO THE FUND FOR THE REBUILDING OF MR. EMERSON'S HOUSE
1882

TO THE SUBSCRIBERS TO THE FUND FOR THE REBUILDING OF MR. EMERSON'S HOUSE, AFTER THE | FIRE OF JULY 24, 1872: | [24-line letter] | LE BARON RUSSELL. | BOSTON, May 8, 1882.

Single sheet folded once to make four pages. Head title.

Letters of 16 August 1872 and 8 October 1872 to Russell, pp. [2]–[3].

Location: JM.

Note: Reprinted in Cabot, *A Memoir of Ralph Waldo Emerson* (D 138), II, 703–709.

D 125 AUTOBIOGRAPHY AND LETTERS OF ORVILLE DEWEY
1883

AUTOBIOGRAPHY | AND | LETTERS | OF | ORVILLE DEWEY, D.D. | [gothic] Edited by his Daughter, | MARY E. DEWEY. | [rule] | BOSTON: | ROBERTS BROTHERS. | 1883.

Letter of 23 May 1836 to Orville Dewey, pp. 156–158.

Location: JM.

D 126 CONCORD LECTURES ON PHILOSOPHY
1883

CONCORD LECTURES | ON | PHILOSOPHY | COMPRISING OUTLINES OF ALL THE LECTURES AT THE CONCORD | SUMMER SCHOOL OF PHILOSOPHY IN 1882 | WITH AN | HISTORICAL SKETCH | COLLECTED AND ARRANGED BY RAYMOND L. BRIDG-MAN | REVISED BY THE SEVERAL LECTURERS | APPROVED BY THE FACULTY | [rule] | CAMBRIDGE, MASS. | MOSES KING, PUBLISHER | HARVARD SQUARE.

Letters of [1851] and [ca. 30? October? 1852] to John Albee, pp. 66–68, in Albee, "Reminiscences and Eulogy," pp. 66–69. *Reprint.* See E 202.

Location: MCo.

D 127 POEMS BY JONES VERY
1883

POEMS BY JONES VERY | WITH | [gothic] An Introductory Memoir | BY | WILLIAM P. ANDREWS | [three lines of verse] | Gᴇᴏʀɢᴇ Hᴇʀʙᴇʀᴛ | [publisher's logo] | BOSTON | HOUGHTON, MIFFLIN AND COMPANY | New York: 11 East Seventeenth Street | [gothic] The Riverside Press, Cambridge | 1883

Previously unpublished material from letters in Andrews's "Memoir," pp. [3]–31.

Location: JM.

D 128 TRANSACTIONS OF THE WORDSWORTH SOCIETY
1883

[rule] | [rule] | TRANSACTIONS | OF | THE WORDSWORTH SOCIETY. | EDITED BY | THE HON. SECRETARY. | *No.* 5. | [rule] | [rule]

Cover title. Printed by the Edinburgh University Press.

Letter of [14] January 1854 to Henry Reed, p. [124].

Location: MH.

D 129 LIFE AND LETTERS OF BAYARD TAYLOR
1884

LIFE AND LETTERS OF | BAYARD TAYLOR | EDITED BY | MARIE HANSEN-TAYLOR | AND | HORACE E. SCUDDER | IN TWO VOLUMES | VOL. I. [II.] | [engraving of house and grounds] | BOSTON | HOUGHTON, MIFFLIN AND COMPANY | New York: 11 East Seventeenth Street | [gothic] The Riverside Press, Cambridge | 1884

Letter of 12 December 1870 to James T. Fields, II, 542–543.

Location: JM.

D 130 NATHANIEL HAWTHORNE AND HIS WIFE
1884

[red] NATHANIEL HAWTHORNE | AND HIS WIFE | [gothic] A Biography | BY | [red] JULIAN HAWTHORNE | VOL. I. [II.] | [I: sepia-tinted engraving of Salem Custom House] [II: sepia-tinted engraving of Hilda's tower] | [red] CAMBRIDGE | [gothic] Printed at the University Press | 1884

Limited to 350 copies in large paper format.

Letter of 22 December 1850 to Nathaniel Hawthorne, I, 381–382.

Location: ViU.

Note: Trade printing, with Emerson's letter on the same page: all in black 'NATHAN-IEL . . . [engravings] | BOSTON: | JAMES R. OSGOOD AND COMPANY | 1885' (MCo).

D 131 THE GENIUS AND CHARACTER OF EMERSON
1885

THE | GENIUS AND CHARACTER | OF | EMERSON | *LECTURES AT THE CONCORD SCHOOL* | *OF PHILOSOPHY* | EDITED BY | F. B. SANBORN | [publisher's logo] | BOSTON | JAMES R. OSGOOD AND COMPANY | 1885

Previously unpublished material from letters in [F. B. Sanborn], "Emerson and Alcott," pp. 36–67.

Location: JM.

D 132 LOUIS AGASSIZ
1885

LOUIS AGASSIZ | HIS LIFE AND CORRESPONDENCE | EDITED BY | ELIZABETH CARY AGASSIZ | IN TWO VOLUMES | VOL. I. [II.] | [I: engraving of well] [II: engraving of house] | BOSTON | HOUGHTON, MIFFLIN AND COMPANY | New York: 11 East Seventeenth Street | [gothic] The Riverside Press, Cambridge | 1885

Letter of 13 December 1864 to Agassiz, II, 620–622.

Location: ScU.

D 133 RALPH WALDO EMERSON
1885

[gothic] American Men of Letters. | [rule] | RALPH WALDO EMERSON. | BY | OLIVER WENDELL HOLMES. | [publisher's logo] | BOSTON: | HOUGHTON, MIFFLIN AND COMPANY. | New York: 11 East Seventeenth Street | [gothic] The Riverside Press, Cambridge. | 1885

Selections from Emerson's unpublished manuscripts and material from previously unpublished letters.

Location: MH.

D 134 LIFE OF HENRY WADSWORTH LONGFELLOW
1886

LIFE | OF | HENRY WADSWORTH LONGFELLOW | *WITH EXTRACTS FROM HIS JOUR-NALS AND* | *CORRESPONDENCE* | EDITED BY | SAMUEL LONGFELLOW | VOL. I. [II.] | [I: engraving of house] [II: engraving of porch steps] | BOSTON | TICKNOR AND COMPANY | 1886

Previously unpublished material from letters.

Location: MH.

Note one: Large paper printing, limited to 300 numbered copies, of which 25 were reserved for sale in England: 'LIFE | OF | [red] HENRY WADSWORTH LONGFELLOW | WITH ... BY | [red] SAMUEL LONGFELLOW | VOL. I. [II.] | [I: sepia-tinted engraving of house] [II: sepia-tinted engraving of porch steps] | BOSTON | [red gothic] Ticknor and Company | MDCCCLXXXVI' (ViU).

Note two: English issue of American sheets, trade printing, with cancel title leaf: 'LIFE ... [engravings] | LONDON | *KEGAN PAUL, TRENCH & CO.* | 1886 | [*All rights reserved*]' (JM).

D 135 RALPH WALDO EMERSON HIS MATERNAL ANCESTORS
1886

RALPH WALDO EMERSON | HIS MATERNAL ANCESTORS | WITH SOME REMINISCENCES OF HIM | BY | DAVID GREENE HASKINS, D.D. | [rule] | *Every man is a bundle of his ancestors* — EMERSON | [rule] | BOSTON | CUPPLES, UPHAM & COMPANY | [gothic] The Old Corner Bookstore | 1886

Wrappers. Printed from the type of the *Literary World*. Limited to 350 copies. Letters of 21 May 1880 and 18 June 1839 to David Greene Haskins, pp. 35, 51–53. *Reprint.* See E 212– 214.

Location: MCo.

Note one: New edition, with Emerson's letters on pp. 83–84 and 125–129, and with addition of "On the Death of Mr. John Haskins" (E 212), p. 27: 'RALPH ... ANCESTORS | WITH | [gothic] Some Reminiscences of Him | BY | DAVID GREENE HASKINS, D.D. | [rule] | *Every* man is a bundle of his ancestors | —EMERSON ... Bookstore | 1887' (JM).

Note two: Large paper printing with the same title page as the new edition, numbered (unknown number of copies) and signed by the publisher (JM).

D 136 FINAL MEMORIALS OF HENRY WADSWORTH LONGFELLOW
1887

FINAL MEMORIALS | OF | HENRY WADSWORTH LONGFELLOW | EDITED BY | SAMUEL LONGFELLOW | [oval drawing of man kneeling] | NON CLAMOR SED AMOR | BOSTON | TICKNOR AND COMPANY | 1887

Letters of 5 January 1849 and 10 October 1869 to Longfellow, pp. 29–30, 123–124.

Location: NjP.

Note one: Large paper printing, limited to 300 numbered copies, of which 15 were reserved for sale in England: 'FINAL . . . OF | [red] HENRY WADSWORTH LONGFELLOW | EDITED BY | [red] SAMUEL LONGFELLOW | [oval drawing of man kneeling] | NON . . . BOSTON | [red gothic] Ticknor and Company | MDCCCLXXXVII' (ViU).

Note two: English issue of American sheets, trade printing, with cancel title leaf: 'FINAL . . . AMOR | LONDON | *KEGAN PAUL, TRENCH & CO.* | 1887 | [*All rights reserved*]' (JM).

D 137 HISTORY OF WOMAN SUFFRAGE
1887

HISTORY | OF | Woman Suffrage. | EDITED BY | ELIZABETH CADY STANTON, | SUSAN B. ANTHONY, AND | MATILDA JOSLYN GAGE. | ILLUSTRATED WITH STEEL ENGRAVINGS. | *IN THREE VOLUMES.* | VOL. I. | 1848–1861. | [rule] | "GOVERNMENTS DERIVE THEIR JUST POWERS FROM THE CONSENT OF THE GOVERNED." | [rule] | SUSAN B. ANTHONY. | Rochester, N. Y.: Charles Mann. | London: 25 Henrietta Street, Covent Garden. | Paris: G. Fischbacher, 33 Rue de Seine. | 1887.

"The Call of the Convention" at Worcester, Mass., on 23–24 October 1850, printed (pp. 221–222), along with "Names of Persons who Signed the Call of 1850" (pp. 820–821), including Emerson's.

Location: ScU.

D 138 A MEMOIR OF RALPH WALDO EMERSON
1887

A MEMOIR | OF | RALPH WALDO EMERSON | BY | JAMES ELLIOT CABOT | IN TWO VOLUMES | VOL. I. [II.] | [publisher's logo] | BOSTON AND NEW YORK | HOUGHTON, MIFFLIN AND COMPANY | [gothic] The Riverside Press, Cambridge | 1887.

Selections from Emerson's unpublished letters, journals, and other manuscripts.

Location: JM.

Note one: An unknown number of copies, probably no more than 50, were printed and distributed prior to 25 May: title page has '[*ADVANCE COPY—CONFIDENTIAL*]' at top; slip tipped in before title page, printed on recto only: '*This advance copy of Mr. | Cabot's Memoir of Mr. | Emerson is sent to you in accordance with the author's | desire that, as a personal friend of Mr. Emerson, you* | *may have it on the latter's birthday, May* | *25; but as* | *the work will not be issued till September next, you are* | *respectfully and* | *earnestly requested to regard it as con-* | *fidential, until its formal publication, and* | *especially to* | *guard against its being reviewed in the press before that* | *time.* | *HOUGHTON, MIFFLIN & CO.'* (JM).

Note two: A large paper printing from the trade edition plates was done on 2 June 1888, limited to 500 numbered copies bound in gray-white paper covered boards; limitation notice on foot of copyright page; title page: 'A MEMOIR | OF | [red] RALPH WALDO EMERSON | BY | JAMES ELLIOT CABOT | IN TWO VOLUMES | VOL. I [II.] | [pine branch] | [red] CAMBRIDGE | [gothic] Printed at the Riverside Press | 1887' (JM).

Note three: English printing: 'A MEMOIR | OF | RALPH WALDO EMERSON | BY | JAMES ELLIOT CABOT | IN TWO VOLUMES | VOL. I. [II.] | [gothic] London | MACMIL-LAN AND CO. | AND NEW YORK | 1887' (JM).

Note four: Copies bound in half calf were added to specially-bound sets of the *Riverside Edition*, trade printing (see B 7, *Note four*).

Note five: Added as vols. XIII and XIV of the *Standard Library Edition* in 1894; see B 11.

D 139   DELIA BACON
1888

DELIA BACON | A BIOGRAPHICAL SKETCH | [six lines of verse] | [publisher's logo] | BOSTON AND NEW YORK | HOUGHTON, MIFFLIN AND COMPANY | [gothic] The Riverside Press, Cambridge | 1888

By Theodore Bacon.

Previously unpublished material from letters.

Location: JM.

D 140   MEMOIRS OF THE SOCIAL CIRCLE IN CONCORD, SECOND SERIES
1888

MEMOIRS | OF | MEMBERS OF THE SOCIAL CIRCLE | IN CONCORD | *SECOND SERIES* | FROM 1795 TO 1840 | [two lines of verse] | *Chas. Morris's Farewell to the Beef Steak Club, London, 1831.* | PRIVATELY PRINTED | [gothic] The Riverside Press, Cambridge | 1888

'MEMOIR | OF | RALPH WALDO EMERSON. | BY | EDWARD W. EMERSON.', supplement, pp. [1]–266. Previously unpublished material from letters and manuscripts.

Location: JM.

Note one: Reprinted from the same plates: 'EMERSON IN CONCORD | [gothic] A Memoir | WRITTEN FOR THE "SOCIAL CIRCLE" IN | CONCORD, MASSACHUSETTS | BY | EDWARD WALDO EMERSON | [publisher's logo] | BOSTON AND NEW YORK | HOUGHTON, MIFFLIN AND COMPANY | [gothic] The Riverside Press, Cambridge | 1889' (JM).

Note two: English reprinting: 'EMERSON . . . EMERSON | LONDON: | SAMPSON LOW, MARSTON, SEARLE, & RIVINGTON, | *Limited,* | [gothic] St. Dunstan's House | FETTER LANE, FLEET STREET, E.C. | 1889. | [*All rights reserved.*]' (JM).

Note three: Copies bound in half calf were added to specially-bound sets of the *Riverside Edition,* trade printing (see B 7, *Note four*).

D 141   RALPH WALDO EMERSON
1888

RALPH WALDO EMERSON | [gothic] Philosopher and Seer | *AN ESTIMATE OF* | HIS CHARACTER AND GENIUS | [gothic] In Prose and Verse | BY | A. BRONSON ALCOTT | *ILLUSTRATED* | BOSTON | CUPPLES & HURD, PUBLISHERS

Letter of 5 July 1865 to Mary Preston Stearns, pp. [v]–vi.

Location: JM.

Note: Emerson's letter does not appear in the 1865 first edition (Cambridge: privately printed) or in the first printing of this edition (Boston: A. Williams, 1882).

D 142   THE JEWELS OF PYTHIAN KNIGHTHOOD
1890

THE | JEWELS OF PYTHIAN | KNIGHTHOOD | [design] | BEING A CHOICE COLLEC-TION OF THE BEST WRITINGS, IN | PROSE AND POETRY, OF THE MOST PROMI-NENT KNIGHTS | IN THE LAND; INCLUDING A FEW SELECTED ADDRESSES OF | EXCEPTIONAL MERIT, SEVERAL OF WHICH WERE DELIV- | ERED UPON THE OCCA-SION OF THE CELEBRATION OF THE | SILVER ANNIVERSARY OF THE ORDER :: :: :: :: :: :: :: :: :: | EDITED BY | JOHN VAN VALKENBURG | PAST SUPREME CHAN-CELLOR | ⋯[gothic] Illustrated⋯ | CINCINNATI, O. | THE PETTIBONE MANUFACTUR-ING CO | FRATERNITY PUBLISHERS | 1890.

Letter of 26 February 1833 to William Emerson, pp. 296–297.

Location: TxEU.

Note: Even though presented as a first printing, the text is drawn from Cabot, *A Memoir of Ralph Waldo Emerson* (D 138).

D 143   LIFE OF RICHARD MONCKTON MILNES
1890

THE | Life, Letters, and Friendships | of | RICHARD MONCKTON MILNES, | *FIRST LORD HOUGHTON.* | BY | T. WEMYSS REID. | IN TWO VOLUMES. | VOL. I. [II.] | CASSELL & COMPANY, Limited; | *LONDON, PARIS, & MELBOURNE.* | [rule] | 1890. | [ALL RIGHTS RESERVED.]

Letters of 30 May 1840 and 4 October 1875 to Milnes, I, 241–242, II, 318.

Location: BL.

Note: American reprinting, with Emerson's letters on the same pages, in 1891: 'THE . . . REID. | INTRODUCTION BY | RICHARD HENRY STODDARD. | *IN TWO VOL-UMES.* | VOL. I. [II.] | NEW YORK: | CASSELL PUBLISHING COMPANY, | 104 & 106 Fourth Avenue.' (JM).

D 144 TALKS WITH RALPH WALDO EMERSON
1890

TALKS WITH | RALPH WALDO EMERSON | BY | CHARLES J. WOODBURY | NEW YORK | THE BAKER & TAYLOR CO.

Records of conversations with Emerson.

Location: JM.

Note: English edition: 'TALKS WITH | RALPH WALDO EMERSON | BY | CHARLES J. WOODBURY | LONDON | KEGAN PAUL, TRENCH, TRÜBNER & CO., LT.ᴰ | 1890' (JM).

D 145 AUTOBIOGRAPHY, DIARY AND CORRESPONDENCE
1891

JAMES FREEMAN CLARKE | AUTOBIOGRAPHY, DIARY AND | CORRESPONDENCE | EDITED BY | EDWARD EVERETT HALE | [publisher's logo] | BOSTON AND NEW YORK | HOUGHTON, MIFFLIN AND COMPANY | [gothic] The Riverside Press, Cambridge | 1891

Letters of 7 December 1838 and 27 February 1839 to Clarke, pp. 123, 126–128.

Location: JM.

D 146 AUTOBIOGRAPHICAL NOTES OF THE LIFE OF WILLIAM BELL SCOTT
1892

[red initial capital] AUTOBIOGRAPHICAL NOTES | OF THE LIFE OF | [red] WILLIAM BELL SCOTT | *H. R. S. A., LL. D.* | And Notices of his Artistic and Poetic | Circle of Friends | 1830 to 1882 | [red] EDITED BY W. MINTO | *Illustrated by Etchings by Himself* | *and Reproductions of Sketches by Himself and Friends* | [red] VOL. I [II] | [publisher's logo] | NEW YORK | [red] HARPER & BROTHERS, FRANKLIN SQUARE | 1892

Letter to W. B. Scott, [29 November 1847], I, 240.

Location: NN.

D 147 A. BRONSON ALCOTT
1893

A. BRONSON ALCOTT | HIS LIFE AND PHILOSOPHY | BY | F. B. SANBORN | AND | WILLIAM T. HARRIS | IN TWO VOLUMES | VOL. I. [II.] | BOSTON | ROBERTS BROTHERS | 1893

Selections from Emerson's previously unpublished letters and manuscripts: " . . . an important addition has been made through the kindness of Mr. Edward Waldo Emerson, from his father's papers, not hitherto published" (I, iii).

Location: JM.

D 148 MEMOIRS OF A REFORMER
1893

"REFORM *is the wisest and most natural* PREVENTIVE *of* | REVOLUTION."—*Emerson.* | [rule] | MEMOIRS | OF | A REFORMER. | (1832—1892.) | BY | ALEXANDER MILTON ROSS, | [eight lines of Ross's publications] | [two lines from Jesus] | TORONTO: | HUNTER, ROSE & COMPANY. | 1893.

Letters of [ca. 8? August? 1875] and [ca. 18 August 1879] to Alexander Milton Ross, p. 169.

Location: MH.

D 149 FAMILIAR LETTERS OF THOREAU
1894

FAMILIAR LETTERS OF | HENRY DAVID THOREAU | *EDITED, WITH AN INTRODUC-TION AND NOTES* | BY | F. B. SANBORN | [publisher's logo] | BOSTON AND NEW YORK | HOUGHTON, MIFFLIN AND COMPANY | [gothic] The Riverside Press, Cambridge | 1894

Various letters.

Location: MH.

Note one: Large paper printing, limited to 150 numbered copies: 'FAMILIAR LETTERS OF | [red] HENRY DAVID THOREAU . . . [publisher's logo] | [red] CAMBRIDGE | [gothic] Printed at the Riverside Press | 1894' (JM).

Note two: For an earlier edition, by Emerson, see F 6.

D 150 LIFE AND LETTERS OF JOHN GREENLEAF WHITTIER
1894

LIFE AND LETTERS | OF | JOHN GREENLEAF WHITTIER | BY | SAMUEL T. PICKARD | IN TWO VOLUMES | VOLUME I [II] | [publisher's logo] | BOSTON AND NEW YORK | HOUGHTON, MIFFLIN AND COMPANY | [gothic] The Riverside Press, Cambridge | 1894

Letter of [22 August 1873] to Whittier, II, 577.

Location: NjP.

Note: Large paper printing, limited to 400 numbered copies: 'LIFE AND LETTERS OF | [red] JOHN GREENLEAF WHITTIER . . . [II] | [sepia-tinted publisher's logo] | CAMBRIDGE | [red gothic] Printed at the Riverside Press | 1894' (JM).

D 151 MEMOIRS OF ANNE C. L. BOTTA
1894

MEMOIRS | OF | ANNE C. L. BOTTA | WRITTEN BY HER FRIENDS | WITH SELECTIONS FROM HER | CORRESPONDENCE AND FROM HER | WRITINGS IN PROSE AND POETRY | [two lines of verse] | *Dante* | NEW-YORK | J. SELWIN TAIT & SONS | PUBLISHERS | 31 EAST 17TH STREET | MDCCCXCIV

Edited by Vincenzo Botta.

Previously unpublished material from letters.

Location: MB.

D 152 AUTHORS AND FRIENDS
1896

[all within a single-rule frame] Authors and Friends | by | Annie Fields | [rule] | [rule] | BOSTON AND NEW YORK | HOUGHTON, MIFFLIN AND COMPANY | [gothic] The Riverside Press, Cambridge | 1896

Previously unpublished material from letters.

Location: JM.

D 153 THE BOOK-LOVER'S ALMANAC FOR 1897
1896

[all within an ornate frame with engravings of people reading or printing books in corners] [five lines in red] THE | BOOK-LOVER'S | ALMANAC | FOR | 1897 | [three lines within ornamental pedestal] DUPRAT & CO., | PUBLISHERS, | NEW YORK.

Limited to 400 numbered copies, of which 100 are on Japan paper.

"The Sabbath," pp. 22–23.
  "A Fragment," p. 23.

Location: MH.

Note: From the headnote to the selections: "We offer our readers two unpublished poems composed by Ralph Waldo Emerson when he was very young. . . . ["The Sabbath"] is said to have been written at the age of nine, when young Emerson was obliged for some fault to stop at home and keep his room while the rest of the family had gone to church."

D 154 WALT WHITMAN: THE MAN
1896

WALT WHITMAN | THE MAN | BY | THOMAS DONALDSON | "What about my hundred pages that I am getting out about | you?"—THOMAS DONALDSON. | "Go on, Tom, go on— and God be with you."—WALT WHITMAN. | *At a birthday dinner at his house at Camden, N.J.,* | *May* 31, 1891. | [rule] | *ILLUSTRATIONS AND FACSIMILES* | [rule] | NEW YORK | FRANCIS P. HARPER | 1896

Letter of 23 February 1863 to James Redpath, pp. 143–144.

Location: MH.

D 155 ALFRED LORD TENNYSON
1897

ALFRED LORD TENNYSON | A MEMOIR | BY HIS SON | [two lines of verse] | VOLUME I

[II] | [gothic] London | MACMILLAN AND CO., LIMITED | NEW YORK: THE MACMILLAN COMPANY | 1897 | [*All Rights reserved*]

By Hallam Tennyson.

Letter of 21 January 1872 to Alfred Tennyson, II, 111.

Location: CtY.

D 156   A CHAT ABOUT CELEBRITIES
1897

A | CHAT ABOUT CELEBRITIES | OR THE | STORY OF A BOOK | BY | CURTIS GUILD | AUTHOR OF "OVER THE OCEAN," "ABROAD AGAIN," "BRITONS | AND MUSCOVITES," "FROM SUNRISE TO SUNSET" ETC. | BOSTON | LEE AND SHEPARD, PUBLISHERS | 1897

Letter of 8 April 1864 to James T. Fields, signed by Emerson, James Russell Lowell, and Oliver Wendell Holmes, p. 255.

Location: NcD.

Note: The manuscript invitation is all in the hand of Emerson, who signed the names of Holmes and Lowell (NNC).

D 157   MEMORIES OF HAWTHORNE
1897

Memories of Hawthorne | By | Rose Hawthorne Lathrop | [publisher's logo] | BOSTON AND NEW YORK | HOUGHTON, MIFFLIN AND COMPANY | [gothic] The Riverside Press, Cambridge | 1897

Letter of [ca. 1843] to Sophia Peabody Hawthorne. p. 186.

Location: JM.

Note: Also reprinted are the letters first appearing in the 21 June 1885 *Boston Sunday Herald* (E 210).

D 158   EARLY LETTERS OF GEORGE WM. CURTIS TO JOHN S. DWIGHT
1898

[two lines in script] Early Letters | of | *George Wm. Curtis* | to | *John S. Dwight* | [two lines in script] Brook Farm and Concord | Edited by | *George Willis Cooke* | [publisher's logo] | NEW YORK AND LONDON | HARPER & BROTHERS PUBLISHERS | 1898

Letter of [9] June 1842 to Margaret Fuller, pp. 24–25.

Location: JM.

D 159   JOHN SULLIVAN DWIGHT
1898

JOHN SULLIVAN DWIGHT | Brook-Farmer, Editor, and Critic of Music | A BIOGRAPHY | By | GEORGE WILLIS COOKE | [publisher's logo] | BOSTON | SMALL, MAYNARD & COMPANY | 1898

Previously unpublished material from letters.

Location: JM.

D 160   ORESTES A. BROWNSON'S EARLY LIFE
1898

ORESTES A. BROWNSON'S | EARLY LIFE: | FROM 1803 TO 1844. | BY | HENRY F. BROWNSON. | [rule] | DETROIT, MICH. | H. F. BROWNSON, PUBLISHER. | 1898.

Letter of 15 November 1837 to O. A. Brownson, pp. 214–215.

Location: JM.

D 161   PASSAGES FROM THE CORRESPONDENCE OF RUFUS W. GRIS-WOLD
1898

PASSAGES | FROM THE CORRESPONDENCE | AND OTHER PAPERS | OF | RUFUS W. GRISWOLD. | *Noscitur a* Sociis. | [wreath design] | CAMBRIDGE, MASS., | W: M. GRISWOLD, | 1898.

Edited by W. M. Griswold.

Letter of 25 September 1841 to Rufus W. Griswold, pp. 98–99.

Location: MH.

D 162   LETTERS AND RECOLLECTIONS OF JOHN MURRAY FORBES
1899

LETTERS | AND RECOLLECTIONS | OF | JOHN MURRAY FORBES | EDITED BY HIS DAUGHTER | SARAH FORBES HUGHES | IN TWO VOLUMES | VOL. I. [II.] | [publisher's logo] | BOSTON AND NEW YORK | HOUGHTON, MIFFLIN AND COMPANY | [gothic] The Riverside Press, Cambridge | 1899

Previously unpublished material from letters.

Location: JM.

D 163   POEMS OF NATURE AND LIFE
1899

POEMS OF NATURE AND LIFE | BY | JOHN WITT RANDALL | EDITED BY FRANCIS ELLINGWOOD ABBOT | WITH AN INTRODUCTION ON THE RANDALL FAMILY | [one line of prose] | BOSTON | GEORGE H. ELLIS | 272 CONGRESS STREET | 1899

Letter of 11 September 1856 to John Witt Randall, p. 12.

Location: NN.

D 164 MEMOIRS AND CORRESPONDENCE OF COVENTRY PATMORE
1900

Memoirs | and Correspondence of | [red] Coventry Patmore | By | Basil Champneys | Vol. I [II] | [publisher's logo] | London | [red] George Bell and Sons | 1900

Letter of 5 October 1858 to Patmore, II, 382–383.

Location: NjP.

D 165 THE NEW ENGLAND SOCIETY ORATIONS
1901

THE | [red] NEW ENGLAND SOCIETY | [red] ORATIONS | ADDRESSES SERMONS AND POEMS DELIVERED BEFORE | THE NEW ENGLAND SOCIETY IN THE CITY OF NEW YORK | 1820–1885 | COLLECTED AND EDITED BY | [red] CEPHAS BRAINERD | AND | [red] EVELINE WARNER BRAINERD | PUBLISHED FOR THE SOCIETY | VOL- UME I [II] | [book and wreath device] | NEW YORK | [red gothic] The Century Co. | MCMI

"Oration" ["Boston"], II, 373–393. *Reprint.* See E 178.
    "Response," II, 394–396. *Reprint.* See D 81.

Location: JM.

Note: For another version of the oration, see "Boston," E 22 and *Natural History of Intellect* (A 44).

D 166 AN HISTORICAL AND BIOGRAPHICAL INTRODUCTION TO AC-
COMPANY *THE DIAL*
1902

An Historical and Biographical | Introduction to Accompany | The Dial | As Reprinted in Numbers for | The Rowfant Club | George Willis Cooke | In Two Volumes | Vol. I [II] | Cleveland | The Rowfant Club | 1902

Limited to 127 numbered copies; each volume is boxed.

Previously unpublished material from letters.

Location: JM.

D 167 MEDITATIONS OF AN AUTOGRAPH COLLECTOR
1902

[three lines in red] MEDITATIONS | OF AN | AUTOGRAPH COLLECTOR | *by* | ADRIAN H. JOLINE | *"The undevout autograph collector is mad"* | —Young, N. T. ix. | ILLUS- TRATED | [publisher's logo] | NEW YORK AND LONDON | HARPER & BROTHERS | PUBLISHERS 1902

Letter of 21 August 1865 to [Lewis] Cist, pp. 255–256.

Location: MB.

D 168 REMINISCENCES OF JOHN MURRAY FORBES
1902

REMINISCENCES | OF | JOHN MURRAY FORBES | EDITED BY HIS DAUGHTER | SARAH FORBES HUGHES | IN THREE VOLUMES | VOL. I. [II.] [III.] | BOSTON | GEORGE H. ELLIS, 272 CONGRESS STREET | 1902

Various letters to Mrs. J. M. Forbes, I, 42–43, III, 70–71.

Location: MHi.

D 169 THOREAU: THE POET-NATURALIST
1902

THOREAU | THE POET-NATURALIST | WITH MEMORIAL VERSES | BY WILLIAM ELLERY CHANNING | NEW EDITION, ENLARGED | EDITED BY F. B. SANBORN | [four lines of prose] | H. D. T. | CHARLES E. GOODSPEED | BOSTON: 1902

Previously unpublished manuscript material.

Location: JM.

Note one: Also printed on French handmade paper, limited to 250 numbered copies, and on Japan paper, limited to 25 numbered copies. Both limited printings have engravings by Sidney L. Smith.

Note two: For an earlier edition, see D 88.

D 170 UNITARIANISM IN AMERICA
1902

UNITARIANISM IN AMERICA | [gothic] A History of its Origin and Development | BY | GEORGE WILLIS COOKE | MEMBER OF THE AMERICAN HISTORICAL ASSOCIA-TION, AMERICAN ASSOCIATION | FOR THE ADVANCEMENT OF SCIENCE, AMERI-CAN ACADEMY OF | POLITICAL AND SOCIAL SCIENCE, ETC. | [leaf design] | BOS-TON | AMERICAN UNITARIAN ASSOCIATION | 1902

Letter of 9 October 1827 to Ezra Stiles Gannett, p. 151n.

Location: MH-AH.

Note: The letter is also printed in the 10 July 1902 *Christian Register* (E 235).

D 171 AUTOBIOGRAPHY OF SEVENTY YEARS
1903

AUTOBIOGRAPHY | OF SEVENTY YEARS | BY | GEORGE F. HOAR | WITH PORTRAITS | VOLUME I. [II.] | NEW YORK | CHARLES SCRIBNER'S SONS | 1903

Letter of 12 May [1836] to Mary Moody Emerson, I, 65–66.

Location: JM.

D 172 THE EMERSON CENTENARY
1903

THE CENTENARY | OF THE BIRTH OF | [gothic] Ralph Waldo Emerson | AS OB-
SERVED IN CONCORD MAY 25 1903 | UNDER THE DIRECTION OF | THE SOCIAL
CIRCLE IN CONCORD | [flower] | [four lines from "The Rhodora"] | [gothic] Printed at
The Riverside Press | FOR THE SOCIAL CIRCLE IN CONCORD | JUNE 1903

Cloth or wrappers.

Letter of [8 March 1835] to Lucia Russell, pp. 18–20.

Location: JM.

Note: Reprinted as "A Letter from Ralph Waldo Emerson," *Plymouth Journal and
Antiquarian Record,* 22 July 1925, p. 4.

D 173 A MEMOIR OF GEORGE PALMER PUTNAM
1903

[all within a single-rule frame] [four lines within a red single-rule frame] A Memoir of |
George Palmer Putnam | Together with a Record of the Publishing | House founded by
Him | [six lines within a red single-rule frame] By | George Haven Putnam | [rule] |
Privately Printed | [rule] | Volume I [II] | [three lines within a red single-rule frame] G. P.
PUTNAM'S SONS | New York and London | 1903

Letters of 9 April 1846 to Wiley and Putnam and 11 October 1852 to G. P. Putnam and
Company, I, 164–165, 292–293.

Location: JM.

Note: New edition, with Emerson's letters on pp. 102–103, 177: '[red] George Palmer
Putnam | *A Memoir* | *Together with a Record of the Earlier Years of the* | *Publishing
House Founded by Him* | By | [red] George Haven Putnam, Litt.D. | Author of "Books
and Their Makers," "The Censorship of the Church," | "Abraham Lincoln," etc. | [leaf
design] | [red] G. P. Putnam's Sons | New York and London | [gothic] The Knicker-
bocker Press | 1912' (JM).

D 174 MY OWN STORY
1903

MY OWN STORY | WITH RECOLLECTIONS OF | NOTED PERSONS | BY | JOHN
TOWNSEND TROWBRIDGE | ILLUSTRATED | Ne cede malis.—*Heraldic Motto.* | [pub-
lisher's logo] | BOSTON AND NEW YORK | HOUGHTON, MIFFLIN AND COMPANY |
[gothic] The Riverside Press, Cambridge | 1903

Letter of [1 June 1857] to F. H. Underwood[?], p. 245.

Location: JM.

D 175 THE PERSONALITY OF EMERSON
1903

THE PERSONALITY OF | EMERSON | BY F. B. SANBORN | [publisher's logo] | BOSTON
| CHARLES E. GOODSPEED | 1903

Letters of [27 February 1836] to Bronson Alcott and 13 November 1870 to F. B. Sanborn, pp. 58–59, 105–106 (and facsimiled between pp. 104 and 105).

Location: JM.

Note: Limited to 525 numbered copies, of which 500 are on French handmade paper and 25 on Japan paper.

D 176   A READER'S HISTORY OF AMERICAN LITERATURE
1903

A | READER'S HISTORY | OF | AMERICAN LITERATURE | BY | THOMAS WENTWORTH HIGGINSON | AND | HENRY WALCOTT BOYNTON | [publisher's logo] | BOSTON, NEW YORK AND CHICAGO | HOUGHTON, MIFFLIN AND COMPANY | [gothic] The Riverside Press, Cambridge

Facsimiles letter of 18 July 1864 to Thomas Wentworth Higginson, between pp. 174 and 175.

Location: JM.

D 177   AUTOBIOGRAPHY, MEMORIES AND EXPERIENCES
1904

AUTOBIOGRAPHY | MEMORIES AND EXPERIENCES | OF | MONCURE DANIEL CONWAY | IN TWO VOLUMES | VOL. I [II] | [publisher's logo] | BOSTON AND NEW YORK | HOUGHTON, MIFFLIN AND COMPANY | [gothic] The Riverside Press, Cambridge | 1904

Previously unpublished material from letters.

Location: JM.

D 178   THE LIFE AND PUBLIC SERVICES OF GEORGE LUTHER STEARNS
1907

THE LIFE | AND | PUBLIC SERVICES | OF | George Luther Stearns | BY | FRANK PRESTON STEARNS | [four lines of Stearns's publications] | [publisher's logo] | PHILADELPHIA & LONDON | J. B. LIPPINCOTT COMPANY | 1907

Letters of 28 May 1855 (erroneously dated 1852) to Mary Preston Stearns and [ca. 10? June? 1865] to George Luther Stearns, pp. 95, 347.

Location: InU.

D 179   MEMOIRS OF THE SOCIAL CIRCLE IN CONCORD, THIRD SERIES
1907

MEMOIRS | OF | MEMBERS OF THE SOCIAL CIRCLE | IN CONCORD | *THIRD SERIES* | FROM 1840 TO 1895 | [two lines of verse] | *Chas. Morris's Farewell to the Beef Steak Club, London, 1831.* | PRIVATELY PRINTED | [gothic]The Riverside Press, Cambridge | 1907

Letter to William Emerson, 20 December 1826, p. 18, in James B. Thayer, "Samuel Ripley," pp. [1]–24.

Location: JM.

D 180 A BIBLIOGRAPHY OF RALPH WALDO EMERSON
1908

A BIBLIOGRAPHY OF | RALPH WALDO EMERSON | COMPILED BY GEORGE WILLIS COOKE | [publisher's logo] | BOSTON AND NEW YORK | HOUGHTON, MIFFLIN AND COMPANY | MDCCCCVIII

Limited to 530 numbered copies. Boxed.

"Prospectus" for Carlyle's *Critical and Miscellaneous Essays,* pp. 153–154. *Reprint.* See A 9.

Location: JM.

D 181 THE LIFE AND LETTERS OF GEORGE BANCROFT
1908

THE LIFE AND LETTERS | OF | GEORGE BANCROFT | BY | M. A. DeWOLFE HOWE | *ILLUSTRATED* | Volume I [II] | NEW YORK | CHARLES SCRIBNER'S SONS | 1908

Letters of [ca. 10? May?] 1858 and 21 September 1872 to George Bancroft, II, 107, 261–262.

Location: JM.

D 182 PARK-STREET PAPERS
1908

[all within an ornate leaf-and-vine design surrounding a five-rule frame] Park-Street Papers | By Bliss Perry | [publisher's logo] | Boston and New York | Houghton Mifflin Company | 1908

Previously unpublished material from letters.

Location: JM.

D 183 FIFTY YEARS IN CAMP AND FIELD
1909

FIFTY YEARS | IN CAMP AND FIELD | DIARY OF MAJOR-GENERAL | ETHAN ALLEN HITCHCOCK, U. S. A. | EDITED BY | W. A. CROFFUT, Ph.D. | [leaf design] | G. P. PUTNAM'S SONS | NEW YORK AND LONDON | [gothic] The Knickerbocker Press | 1909

Letter of 20 November 1863 to Ethan Allen Hitchcock, p. 457.

Location: MH.

D 184 RECOLLECTIONS OF SEVENTY YEARS
1909

RECOLLECTIONS | OF SEVENTY YEARS | By F. B. SANBORN | OF CONCORD | IN
TWO VOLUMES | [rule] | VOLUME ONE [TWO] | [publisher's logo] | BOSTON | RICH-
ARD G. BADGER | THE GORHAM PRESS | 1909

Previously unpublished material from letters.

Location: JM.

Note: Also a so-called "large paper" printing, limited to 50 numbered copies: untrimmed sheets with an inserted slip before the title page with statement of limitation
(Thoreau Lyceum, Concord, Mass.).

D 185 DANIEL RICKETSON
1910

DANIEL RICKETSON | AUTOBIOGRAPHIC | AND | MISCELLANEOUS | *EDITED BY* |
HIS DAUGHTER AND SON | ANNA AND WALTON RICKETSON | *WITH ILLUSTRA-*
TIONS | [leaf-and-vine ornament] | NEW BEDFORD, MASS. | E. ANTHONY & SONS,
INC. | 1910

Letters of 21 November 1857 and 11 October 1869 to Daniel Ricketson, pp. 115, 117.

Location: RPB.

D 186 LIFE AND LETTERS OF EDMUND CLARENCE STEDMAN
1910

LIFE AND LETTERS | OF | EDMUND CLARENCE STEDMAN | BY | LAURA STEDMAN |
AND | GEORGE M. GOULD, M.D. | [publisher's logo] | VOLUME ONE [TWO] | NEW
YORK | MOFFAT, YARD AND COMPANY | 1910

Letter of 11 November 1873 to Stedman, II, 480–481.

Location: ScU

D 187 BOSTON DAYS
1911

BOSTON DAYS | [rule] | THE CITY OF BEAUTIFUL IDEALS | CONCORD, AND ITS
FAMOUS AUTHORS | THE GOLDEN AGE OF GENIUS | DAWN OF THE TWENTIETH
CENTURY | FIRST DECADE OF TWENTIETH CENTURY | [rule] | *By* LILIAN WHITING |
[four lines of Whiting's publications] | [two lines of verse] | [rule] | *BOSTON*·LITTLE,
BROWN | AND COMPANY····*MCMXI*

Previously unpublished material from letters.

Location: JM.

D 188 THE CONTRIBUTION OF EMERSON TO LITERATURE
1911

[gothic] The University of Chicago | FOUNDED BY JOHN D. ROCKEFELLER | [rule] | THE CONTRIBUTION OF | EMERSON TO LITERATURE | A DISSERTATION | SUBMIT-TED TO THE FACULTY | OF THE | GRADUATE SCHOOL OF ARTS AND LITERATURE | IN CANDIDACY FOR THE DEGREE OF | DOCTOR OF PHILOSOPHY | DEPARTMENT OF ENGLISH LITERATURE | [rule] | BY | DAVID LEE MAULSBY | A.B. (Tufts, 1887), A.M. (Tufts, 1892, Harv., 1898) | [rule] | TUFTS COLLEGE, MASS. | THE TUFTS COL-LEGE PRESS | 1911

Wrappers.

Letter of 17 June 1845 (erroneously dated June 1843) to Elizabeth Hoar, pp. 122–123.

Location: JM.

Note: Reprinted, with Emerson's letter on the same pages, in 1911: 'EMERSON | HIS CONTRIBUTION | TO LITERATURE | BY DAVID LEE MAULSBY | TUFTS COLLEGE, MASS. | THE TUFTS COLLEGE PRESS' (JM).

D 189 LETTERS TO WILLIAM ALLINGHAM
1911

LETTERS | TO | WILLIAM ALLINGHAM | EDITED BY | H. ALLINGHAM | AND | E. BAUMER WILLIAMS | *WITH ILLUSTRATIONS* | LONGMANS, GREEN AND CO. | 39 PATERNOSTER ROW, LONDON | NEW YORK, BOMBAY, AND CALCUTTA | 1911 | All rights reserved

Letters of 24 June 1848 and 14 July 1851 to William Allingham, pp. 44–46.

Location: ScU

D 190 JAMES HUTCHISON STIRLING
1912

[red] JAMES | [red] HUTCHISON STIRLING | HIS LIFE AND WORK | BY | [red] AMELIA HUTCHISON STIRLING, M.A. | JOINT-TRANSLATOR OF SPINOZA'S "ETHIC," | AU-THOR OF "TORCHBEARERS OF HISTORY," ETC. | WITH PREFACE BY THE RIGHT HON. | [red] VISCOUNT HALDANE OF CLOAN | [publisher's logo] | [red] T. FISHER UNWIN | LONDON: ADELPHIA TERRACE | LEIPSIC: INSELSTRASSE 20 | 1912

Various letters.

Location: MH.

D 191 LETTERS OF CHARLES ELIOT NORTON
1913

LETTERS OF | CHARLES ELIOT NORTON | WITH BIOGRAPHICAL COMMENT | BY | HIS DAUGHTER SARA NORTON | AND M. A. DEWOLFE HOWE | ILLUSTRATED |

VOLUME I [II] | [publisher's logo] | BOSTON AND NEW YORK | HOUGHTON MIFFLIN COMPANY | [gothic] The Riverside Press Cambridge | 1913

Letters of 23 February 1870 and 11 November 1873 to Charles Eliot Norton, I, 340–341, II, 137–138.

Location: JM.

D 192 RAMBLES IN AUTOGRAPH LAND
1913

RAMBLES IN | AUTOGRAPH LAND | BY | ADRIAN H. JOLINE | ILLUSTRATED WITH | MANY PORTRAITS | AND FACSIMILES | G. P. PUTNAM'S SONS | NEW YORK AND LONDON | [gothic] The Knickerbocker Press | MCMXIII

Letter of 2 October [1863?] to George William Curtis, pp. 281–282.

Location: MH.

D 193 JULIA WARD HOWE
1916

JULIA WARD HOWE | 1819–1910 | BY | LAURA E. RICHARDS | AND MAUD HOWE ELLIOTT | ASSISTED BY | FLORENCE HOWE HALL | *With Portraits and other* | *Illustrations* | [publisher's logo] | VOLUME I [II] | BOSTON AND NEW YORK | HOUGHTON MIFFLIN COMPANY | [gothic] The Riverside Press Cambridge | 1916

Letter of 30 December 1853 to Julia Ward Howe, I, 139–140.

Location: JM.

D 194 CORRESPONDENCE OF SIR ARTHUR HELPS
1917

CORRESPONDENCE OF | SIR ARTHUR HELPS | K.C.B., D.C.L. EDITED BY | HIS SON, E. A. HELPS | LONDON: JOHN LANE, THE BODLEY HEAD | NEW YORK: JOHN LANE COMPANY MCMXVII

Letter of 17 July 1855 to Arthur Helps, p. 177.

Location: MH.

D 195 THE LIFE AND LETTERS OF CHRISTOPHER PEARSE CRANCH
1917

THE LIFE AND LETTERS | OF | CHRISTOPHER PEARSE CRANCH | BY HIS DAUGHTER | LEONORA CRANCH SCOTT | *With Illustrations* | [publisher's logo] | BOSTON AND NEW YORK | HOUGHTON MIFFLIN COMPANY | [gothic] The Riverside Press Cambridge | 1917

Various letters.

Location: MB.

D 196 THE EARLY YEARS OF THE SATURDAY CLUB
       1918

[all within a double-rule frame] THE EARLY YEARS | *of the* | SATURDAY CLUB | 1855–1870 | [rule] | *By* EDWARD WALDO EMERSON | *WITH ILLUSTRATIONS* | [rule] | [publisher's logo] | [rule] | *BOSTON AND NEW YORK* | HOUGHTON MIFFLIN COMPANY | MDCCCCXVIII

Previously unpublished material from letters.

Location: JM.

D 197 MEMORIES OF A HOSTESS
       1922

MEMORIES OF A HOSTESS | A CHRONICLE OF | EMINENT FRIENDSHIPS | DRAWN CHIEFLY FROM THE DIARIES OF | MRS. JAMES T. FIELDS | BY | M. A. DEWOLFE HOWE | [two lines of verse] | [publisher's logo] | *WITH ILLUSTRATIONS* | THE ATLANTIC MONTHLY PRESS | BOSTON

Facsimiles letter of [ca. 1868?] to Annie Fields, p. 100.

Location: JM.

D 198 THE LIFE AND LETTERS OF JOHN MUIR
       1924

THE LIFE AND LETTERS OF | JOHN MUIR | BY | WILLIAM FREDERIC BADÈ | VOLUME I [II] | [publisher's logo] | BOSTON AND NEW YORK | HOUGHTON MIFFLIN COMPANY | [gothic] The Riverside Press Cambridge | 1924

Letter of 5 February 1872 to Muir, I, 259–260.

Location: NjP.

D 199 EDWARD EVERETT
       1925

EDWARD EVERETT | *Orator and Statesman* | BY | PAUL REVERE FROTHINGHAM | *With Illustrations* | [publisher's logo] | BOSTON AND NEW YORK | HOUGHTON MIFFLIN COMPANY | [gothic] The Riverside Press Cambridge | 1925

Letter of 24 November 1855 to Edward Everett, p. 369.

Location: JM.

D 200 A TROUTBECK LETTER-BOOK
       1925

[ornate letters] A Troutbeck Letter-book | (1861–1867) | BEING UNPUBLISHED LETTERS TO MYRON B. BENTON FROM | EMERSON, SOPHIA THOREAU, MONCURE CONWAY, | AND OTHERS | [rule] | *With an introduction by George Edward Woodberry* | [rule] | TROUTBECK LEAFLETS [leaf design] [leaf design] NUMBER NINE | [rule] | [leaf-and-vine design] |

AMENIA · NEW YORK | *Privately Printed at the Troutbeck Press* | CHRISTMAS, MDCCCCXXV

Wrappers. Limited to 200 copies.

Letter of 13 March 1865 to Myron B. Benton, p. 11.

Location: NNS.

D 201 MAY ALCOTT   A MEMOIR
1928

[all within a single-rule frame, surrounding a red zigzaglike frame, both surrounding a single-rule frame] MAY ALCOTT | [rule] | [red] *A Memoir* | [rule] | *By* CAROLINE TICKNOR | [rule] | [three lines between parallel vertical rules] WITH | ILLUSTRATIONS | [red publisher's logo] | [rule] | BOSTON · MCMXXVIII | [rule] | LITTLE, BROWN, | AND COMPANY

Letter of [3 January 1875] to May Alcott, pp. 118–119.

Location: JM.

D 202 WORD SHADOWS OF THE GREAT
1930

[ornamental rule] | WORD SHADOWS | OF THE GREAT | The Lure of Autograph Collecting | [ornamental rule] | *By* THOMAS F. MADIGAN | [publisher's logo] | WITH FORTY-ONE REPRODUCTIONS IN | HALF-TONE AND TWELVE IN LINE | [ornamental rule] | FREDERICK A. STOKES COMPANY | [flush left] NEW YORK [flush right] MCMXXX

Letter of 15 February 1842 to David Hatch Barlow, pp. 189–192.

Location: CtY.

D 203 THE PERIODICALS OF AMERICAN TRANSCENDENTALISM
1931

The Periodicals of American | Transcendentalism | BY | CLARENCE L. F. GOHDES | [publisher's logo] | DURHAM · NORTH CAROLINA | DUKE UNIVERSITY PRESS | 1931

["John Sterling"], pp. 255–256. *Reprint.* See E 118.
  "New Translation of Dante," p. 256. *Reprint.* See E 119.

Location: JM.

D 204 THE COLLECTION OF G. WHITNEY HOFF
1934

LETTRES | AUTOGRAPHES | COMPOSANT LA COLLECTION | DE MADAME | [red] G. WHITNEY HOFF | [oval heraldic design] | PARIS | [single vertical rule dividing the next three lines into two columns] [red] PIERRE CORNUAU   PIERRE LA BRELY | EXPERT PRÈS LE TRIBUNAL CIVIL   EXPERT PRÈS LES DOUANES FRANÇAISES | 22, RUE LAFFITTE, 22   17, RUE JEAN LECLAIRE, 17 | 1934 | [stamped] MADE IN FRANCE

Facsimiles letter of 14 April 1873 to William Allingham, facing p. 64.

Location: MH.

D 205 EMERSON'S VIEW OF FRANCE AND THE FRENCH
1935

[all within a double-rule frame containing scroll designs between the rules, surrounding a single-rule frame] FRANCO-AMERICAN PAMPHLET SERIES | NUMBER 5 | [rule] | *Emerson's View of* | *France and the* | *French* | *By Lestrois Parish* | [rule] | NEW YORK | 1935

Wrappers. Published by the American Society of the French Legion of Honor.

Selections from the manuscript of "France, or Urbanity," a lecture delivered in Concord in 1848 (pp. 6–12).

Location: DLC.

D 206 THE THOUGHT AND CHARACTER OF WILLIAM JAMES
1935

THE | THOUGHT AND CHARACTER OF | WILLIAM JAMES | *As revealed in unpub-lished correspondence and* | *notes, together with his published writings* | *By* RALPH BARTON PERRY | VOLUME I [II] | INHERITANCE AND VOCATION [PHILOSOPHY AND PSYCHOLOGY] | [publisher's logo] | *With Illustrations* | BOSTON | LITTLE, BROWN, AND COMPANY | 1935

Various letters to Henry James, Sr., vol. I.

Location: MCo.

D 207 LETTERS TO EMMA LAZARUS
1939

LETTERS TO | EMMA LAZARUS | IN THE COLUMBIA UNIVERSITY LIBRARY | EDITED BY | RALPH L. RUSK | PROFESSOR OF ENGLISH IN | COLUMBIA UNIVERSITY | [Columbia University seal] | NEW YORK: MORNINGSIDE HEIGHTS | COLUMBIA UNIVERSITY PRESS | 1939

Various letters, pp. [3]–16.

Location: JM.

D 208 RALPH WALDO EMERSON'S READING
1941

RALPH WALDO EMERSON'S | READING | *A Guide for Source-Hunters and Scholars* | *To the One Thousand Volumes Which* | *He Withdrew from Libraries* | Together With | SOME UNPUBLISHED LETTERS | and | A list of Emerson's contemporaries (1827–1850)—many | prominent in American Literature and in Transcenden- | talism—whose book borrowings are inscribed in the | charging records of the Boston Athenæum; | Also | Other Emerson Materials and an introduction describing | bibliographical resources in New England | *By* | Kenneth Walter Cameron | [leaf design] | THE THISTLE PRESS | RALEIGH, NORTH CAROLINA | 1941

Letters of 6 May 1856 to Charles Thomas Jackson[?] and 27 March 1838 to G. F. Simmons, H. G. O. Blake, and W. D. Wilson, pp. 129–130.

Location: MB.

D 209 JONES VERY: EMERSON'S "BRAVE SAINT"
1942

JONES VERY | *EMERSON'S "BRAVE SAINT"* | WILLIAM IRVING BARTLETT | [publisher's logo] | DUKE UNIVERSITY PRESS | DURHAM, NORTH CAROLINA | 1942

Letter of 18 November 1838 to Very, p. 59, and facsimiled between pp. 58 and 59.

Location: JM.

D 210 EMERSON THE ESSAYIST
1945

EMERSON THE | ESSAYIST | AN OUTLINE OF HIS PHILOSOPHICAL DEVELOPMENT | THROUGH 1836 | with | SPECIAL EMPHASIS ON THE SOURCES AND | INTERPRETA-TION OF *NATURE* | Also | Bibliographical Appendices of General and Special Interest | to Students of American Literature, Emphasizing Thoreau, | Emerson, the Boston Library Society and Selected Docu- | ments of New England Transcendentalism. | *By* | KENNETH WALTER CAMERON | VOLUME | I [II] | THE THISTLE PRESS | RALEIGH, NORTH CAROLINA | 1945

Various letters, II, 215, 217, 221, 222.

Location: MB.

D 211 MR. EMERSON LECTURES AT THE PEABODY INSTITUTE
1949

MR. EMERSON LECTURES | AT THE | PEABODY INSTITUTE | [leaf design] | THE PEABODY INSTITUTE LIBRARY | BALTIMORE, MARYLAND | 1949

Wrappers.

Letters of 10 June, 5 October, and 25 December 1871 to Nathaniel H. Morison, pp. 7–9.

Location: JM.

D 212 PERKINS FAMILY LETTERS
1949

CHARLES ELLIOTT PERKINS | *AND* | *EDITH FORBES PERKINS* | FAMILY LETTERS | *1861–1869* | *Edited by their Daughter* | EDITH PERKINS CUNNINGHAM | [pineapple design] | BOSTON | *Privately Printed* | 1949

Letter of 3 March 1867 to Ellen Emerson, pp. [303]–305. *Reprint.* See E 256.

Location: MH.

D 213 THIRTEEN AUTHOR COLLECTIONS OF THE NINETEENTH CEN-
TURY
1950

CARROLL A. WILSON | [red leaf-and-dot design] | *Thirteen Author Collections of the* |
Nineteenth Century | *AND* | *Five Centuries of Familiar Quotations* | *Edited by* | JEAN C.
S. WILSON | *and* | DAVID A. RANDALL | *Privately Printed for* | CHARLES SCRIBNER'S
SONS | New York : 1950

2 vols. Limited to 375 numbered copies, of which 350 were for sale. Boxed. Various
letters, vol. I.

Location: JM.

D 214 THE CORRESPONDENCE OF HENRY DAVID THOREAU
1958

The Correspondence of | HENRY DAVID THOREAU | *Edited by* WALTER HARDING
and CARL BODE | [publisher's logo] | WASHINGTON SQUARE | NEW YORK UNIVER-
SITY PRESS | 1958

Previously unpublished material from letters.

Location: JM.

D 215 THE TRANSCENDENTALISTS AND MINERVA
1958

THE TRANSCENDENTALISTS | AND MINERVA | CULTURAL BACKGROUNDS OF THE
AMERICAN | RENAISSANCE WITH FRESH DISCOVERIES | IN THE INTELLECTUAL
CLIMATE OF | EMERSON, ALCOTT AND THOREAU | *By* | KENNETH WALTER CAM-
ERON | IN THREE VOLUMES | VOLUME | I [II] [III] | TRANSCENDENTAL BOOKS |
HARTFORD 1 | 1958

Facsimiles document appointing Emerson administrator of the late Charles Emerson's
estate, signed by Emerson, I, 6–7.
  Facsimiles Emerson's manuscript will, dated 14 April 1876, III, 856–862.

Location: MB.

D 216 OVER THOREAU'S DESK
1965

OVER THOREAU'S DESK: | NEW CORRESPONDENCE | 1838–1861 | EDITED WITH
NOTES AND AN INDEX | *By* | KENNETH WALTER CAMERON | [drawing of sunrise] |
TRANSCENDENTAL BOOKS   DRAWER 1080   HARTFORD 1

Facsimiles letter of 2 May 1838 to Thoreau, p. 54.

Location: ScU.

D 217 THE AMERICAN WRITER IN ENGLAND
1969

THE AMERICAN | WRITER IN ENGLAND | *An Exhibition* | *Arranged in Honor of the* | *Sesquicentennial of the University of Virginia* | *With a Foreword by* | Gordon N. Ray | *and* | *an Introduction by* | C. Waller Barrett | The University Press of Virginia | Charlottesville

Letter of 31 July 1847 to Alexander Ireland, pp. 42, 44, and facsimiles manuscript of "Concord Hymn" (*Reprint;* See A 4), p. 43.

Location: JM.

D 218 STUDIES IN BIBLIOGRAPHY
1972

STUDIES | IN BIBLIOGRAPHY | Edited by | FREDSON BOWERS | L. A. BEAURLINE, *Associate Editor* | [university seal] | Volume Twenty-Five | *Published for* | The Bibliographical Society of the University of Virginia | By The University Press of Virginia, Charlottesville | 1972

Emerson's translation of Tacitus's eulogy to Agricola, pp. 215–216, in Wendell Glick, "Thoreau Rejects an Emerson Text," pp. 213–216.

Location: ScU.

D 219 BETWEEN CONCORD AND PLYMOUTH
1973

BETWEEN CONCORD AND PLYMOUTH | THE TRANSCENDENTALISTS | AND THE WATSONS | With the Hillside Collection | of Manuscripts | [quill pen, book, and writing paper design] | by | L. D. GELLER | M.A., F.P.S. | Director | The Pilgrim Society | THOREAU FOUNDATION INC. | THOREAU LYCEUM | Concord | PILGRIM SOCIETY | Plymouth | 1973

Limited to 1,500 copies.

Letters of 11 July 1837 to Mary Howland Russell and 6 July 1855 to Benjamin Marston Watson, pp. 19, 39.

Location: JM.

D 220 THE LETTERS OF JOHN GREENLEAF WHITTIER
1975

The Letters | of | John Greenleaf Whittier | [rule] | Edited by | John B. Pickard | Volume I [II] [III] | 1828–1845 [1846–1860] [1861–1892] | The Belknap Press of | Harvard University Press | Cambridge, Massachusetts | and | London, England | 1975

Letters of 8 April 1864 to Whittier, one of which is signed by Emerson, James Russell Lowell, and Oliver Wendell Holmes, III, 66.

Location: JM.

Note: The manuscript invitation is all in the hand of Emerson, who signed the names of Holmes and Lowell (MiMtpT).

D 221 THE AMERICAN RENAISSANCE IN NEW ENGLAND
1978

Dictionary of Literary Biography · Volume One | The American Renaissance | in New England | Edited by Joel Myerson | *University of South Carolina* | A Bruccoli Clark Book | Gale Research Company · Book Tower · Detroit, Michigan 48226 | 1978

Facsimiles letter of 10 November 1843 to Bailey E. Borden and manuscript page on "Originality and Quotation," pp. 50, 51, in Lawrence Buell, "Ralph Waldo Emerson," pp. 48–60.

Location: JM.

D 222 NINETEENTH CENTURY NEW ENGLAND AUTHORS COLLECTION
1978

Nineteenth Century | New England Authors | Collection | *Ralph Waldo Emerson Room* | MINNEAPOLIS PUBLIC LIBRARY | AND INFORMATION CENTER

Wrappers.

Letters of 19 November 1854 to Mr. Edmonds, 13 January 1865 to Mrs. S. G. Perkins (*Reprint;* See E 211), and 16 April 1879 to James Herbert Morse (*Reprint;* See E 189; D 110), pp. 2–3.

Location: JM.

D 223 STUDIES IN THE AMERICAN RENAISSANCE 1979
1979

[band] | [rule] | [rule] | STUDIES | IN THE | AMERICAN | RENAISSANCE | [rule] | [rule] | [band] | 1979 | [band] | [rule] | *Edited by* JOEL MYERSON | [rule] | [band] | BOSTON: | TWAYNE PUBLISHERS

Joel Myerson, "Emerson's 'Thoreau': A New Edition from Manuscript," pp. 17–92. Edited, with complete textual apparatus, from the printer's copy manuscript at the Henry E. Huntington Library.

Location: JM.

D 224 PETITION FOR A COPYRIGHT TREATY
N.D.

[nine lines of text] | [12 signatures] | PETITION OF AUTHORS AND PUBLISHERS FOR A COPYRIGHT TREATY, 1880 | [seven-line commentary]

Broadside, printed on recto only. *National Archives Facsimile* No. 15. Facsimiles manuscript petition, dated 12 August 1880, signed by Emerson and others.

Location: MCo.

E. First-Appearance Contributions to Magazines and Newspapers

First American and English publication in magazines and newspapers of material by Emerson through 1980, arranged chronologically. All items are signed unless otherwise indicated.

E 1
"Thoughts on the Religion of the Middle Ages." *Christian Disciple and Theological Review*, n.s. 4 (November–December 1822), [401]–408.

Signed "H. O. N." (an acronym from the final letters in Emerson's name).

E 2
"Collection of Psalms and Hymns." *Christian Examiner*, 10 (March 1831), 30–34.

Unsigned. Review of F. W. P. Greenwood, *A Collection of Psalms and Hymns for Christian Worship*.

Note: First attributed by Kenneth Walter Cameron, "An Early Prose Work of Emerson," *American Literature*, 22 (November 1950), 332–338; see also *JMN*, IX, 373n.

E 3
[Review of Lemuel Shattuck, *History of Concord*]. Yeoman's Gazette, 3 October 1835, p. 3.

Signed "E."

Note: See *L*, I, 456, for Emerson's authorship.

E 4
[Legal notice], *Yeoman's Gazette,* 20 August 1836, p. 3.

Announces that Emerson is the administrator of the late Charles Emerson's estate.

E 5
[Advertisement for "The Philosophy of History" lecture series]. *Boston Daily Advertiser,* 12 November 1836, p. 1.

Unsigned.

Note one: For a draft of this notice, see *JMN*, XII, 77.

Note two: This notice may have appeared in other Boston newspapers.

Note three: Emerson may have written other advertisements for his lectures but only this one and the one for the "Human Culture" series (E 8) can be attributed with certainty.

E 6
"Michael Angelo," *North American Review*, 44 (January 1837), 1–16.

Unsigned. Reprinted in *Characteristics of Men of Genius* (D 14), II, 137–156; *Natural History of Intellect* (A 44), pp. 115–142.

E 7

"To the Editor of the Courier," *Boston Courier*, 4 April 1837, p. 2.

Signed "R." Undated letter.

E 8

[Advertisement for "Human Culture" lecture series]. *Boston Daily Advertiser*, 8 November 1837, p. 4.

Unsigned.

Note: For a draft of this notice, see *JMN*, XII, 181.

E 9

[Review of Thomas Carlyle, *History of the French Revolution*]. Christian Examiner, 23 (January 1838), 386–387.

Unsigned. Reprinted in *Uncollected Writings* (A 54), pp. 26–27.

Note: See *L*, II, 108, and *JMN*, V, 431, for Emerson's authorship.

E 10

"Communication." *Daily National Intelligencer* [Washington], 14 May 1838, p. 2.

Letter of 23 April 1838 to President Van Buren. Reprinted in *Miscellanies* (A 40.3), pp. 89–96.

Note: Reprinted in *Yeoman's Gazette*, 19 May 1838; *Christian Register*, 2 June 1838, p. 1; *Old Colony Memorial*, 2 June 1838; as "Words Fitly Spoken," *Liberator*, 8 (22 June 1838), 98.

E 11

"Milton." *North American Review*, 47 (July 1838), 56–73.

Unsigned. Reprinted in *Characteristics of Men of Genius* (D 14), I, 193–213; as "Milton and His Works," *Works* (B 1), III, 291–305; *Natural History of Intellect* (A 44), pp. 145–174.

E 12

"Each and All." *Western Messenger*, 6 (February 1839), 229–230.

Reprinted in *Poems* (A 18.2), pp. 14–16.

E 13

"To the Humble-Bee." *Western Messenger*, 6 (February 1839), 239–241.

Reprinted as "The Humble-Bee," *Poems* (A 18.2), pp. 60–63.

E 14

"Good-bye, Proud World." *Western Messenger*, 6 (April 1839), 402.

Unsigned. Reprinted as "Good-Bye," *Poems* (A 18.2), pp. 57–58.

E 15

"The Rhodora: on being asked, Whence is the flower?" *Western Messenger*, 7 (July 1839), 166.

Unsigned. Reprinted in *Poems* (A 18.2), p. 59.

E 16
"The Editors to the Reader." *Dial*, 1 (July 1840), 1–4.

Unsigned. Reprinted in *Uncollected Writings* (A 54), pp. 31–35.

E 17
"To ****." *Dial*, 1 (July 1840), 84.

Unsigned. Reprinted as "To Eva," *Poems* (A 18.2), p. 147.

E 18
"The Problem." *Dial*, 1 (July 1840), 122–123.

Unsigned. Reprinted in *Poems* (A 18.2), pp. 17–20.

E 19
"Thoughts on Modern Literature." *Dial*, 1 (October 1840), 137–158.

Signed "E." Reprinted in *Natural History of Intellect* (A 44), pp. 177–201.

E 20
"Silence." *Dial*, 1 (October 1840), 158.

Unsigned. Reprinted as "Eros" ["They put their finger on their lip"], *Poems* (A 18.2), p. 150.

E 21
"New Poetry." *Dial*, 1 (October 1840), 220–232.

Signed "E." Reprinted in *Uncollected Writings* (A 54), pp. 137–152.

E 22
"Woodnotes [I.]." *Dial*, 1 (October 1840), 242–245.

Unsigned. Reprinted in *Our Pastors' Offering* (D 12), pp. 67–74; *Poems* (A 18.2), pp. 67–74.

E 23
[Review of Richard Henry Dana, Jr., *Two Years Before the Mast*]. *Dial*, 1 (October 1840), 264–265.

Unsigned. Reprinted in *Uncollected Writings* (A 54), p. 153.

E 24
"The Snow-Storm." *Dial*, 1 (January 1841), 339.

Unsigned. Reprinted in *Poems* (A 18.2), pp. 65–66.

E 25
"Suum Cuique" ["The rain has spoiled the farmer's day"]. *Dial*, 1 (January 1841), 347.

Unsigned. Reprinted in *Poems* (A 18.2), p. 128.

E 26
"The Sphinx." *Dial*, 1 (January 1841), 348–350.

Unsigned. Reprinted in *Poems* (A 18.2), pp. 7–13.

E 27
"Thoughts on Art." *Dial*, 1 (January 1841), 367–378.

Unsigned. Reprinted in "Art," *Society and Solitude* (A 31), pp. 33–51; *Uncollected Writings* (A 54), pp. 36–51.

E 28
"Man the Reformer." *Dial*, 1 (April 1841), 523–528.

Reprinted as *Man the Reformer* (A 12); in *Nature; Addresses, and Lectures* (A 21), pp. 219–248.

E 29
[Review of Jones Very, *Essays and Poems*]. *Dial*, 2 (July 1841), 130–131.

Unsigned. Reprinted in *Uncollected Writings* (A 54), pp. 160–162.

E 30
"Painting and Sculpture." *Dial*, 2 (October 1841), 205.

Unsigned. Reprinted in *Poems* (A 18.2), p. 208.

E 31
"Fate" ["That you are fair or wise is vain"]. *Dial*, 2 (October 1841), 205–206.

Unsigned. Reprinted in *Poems* (A 18.2), pp. 45–47; as "Destiny," *Poems* (A 18.6), pp. 32–33.

E 32
"Woodnotes. Number II." *Dial*, 2 (October 1841), 207–214.

Unsigned. Reprinted in *Poems* (A 18.2), pp. 75–93.

E 33
"Walter Savage Landor." *Dial*, 2 (October 1841), 262–271.

Signed "E." Reprinted in *Works* (B 1), III, 306–311; *Natural History of Intellect* (A 44), pp. 201–212.

E 34
"Ezra Ripley, D.D." *Concord Republican*, 1 October 1841.

Unsigned. Reprinted in *Two Sermons on the Death of Ezra Ripley* (D 6), pp. 41–43; in expanded form in *The Centennial of the Social Circle in Concord* (D 118), pp. 168–176; *Atlantic Monthly Magazine*, 52 (November 1883), 592–596; *Lectures and Biographical Sketches* (A 41), pp. 357–370.

E 35
"The Park." *Dial*, 2 (January 1842), 373.

Unsigned. Reprinted in *Poems* (A 18.2), pp. 131–132.

E 36
"Forbearance." *Dial*, 2 (January 1842), 373.

Unsigned. Reprinted in *Poems* (A 18.2), p. 130.

E 37
"Grace." *Dial*, 2 (January 1842), 373.

Unsigned. Reprinted in *Poems* (A 18.6), p. 299.

E 38
"The Senses and the Soul." *Dial*, 2 (January 1842), 374–379.

Unsigned. Reprinted in *The Senses and the Soul and Moral Sentiment in Religion* (A 42), pp. 13–20; *Uncollected Writings* (A 54), pp. 52–59.

E 39
"Transcendentalism." *Dial*, 2 (January 1842), 382–384.

Unsigned. Reprinted in *Uncollected Writings* (A 54), pp. 60–64.

E 40
"Obituary [of Hannah Joy]." *Christian Register*, 2 April 1842, p. 55.

Unsigned.

Note: See *L*, III, 42, for Emerson's authorship.

E 41
"Lectures on the Times [Introductory]." *Dial*, 3 (July 1842), 1–18.

Signed. Reprinted in *Nature; Addresses, and Lectures* (A 21), pp. 251–282.

E 42
[Preliminary note to Henry David Thoreau, "Natural History of Massachusetts"]. *Dial*, 3 (July 1842), 19.

Unsigned.

E 43
"Tact." *Dial*, 3 (July 1842), 72–73.

Unsigned. Reprinted in *Poems* (A 18.2), pp. 51–52.

E 44
"Holidays." *Dial*, 3 (July 1842), 73.

Unsigned. Reprinted in *Poems* (A 18.2), pp. 206–207.

E 45
"The Amulet." *Dial*, 3 (July 1842), 73–74.

Unsigned. Reprinted in *Poems* (A 18.2), p. 148.

E 46
"Prayers." *Dial*, 3 (July 1842), 77–81.

Unsigned. Reprinted as by Thoreau in Thoreau, *A Yankee in Canada* (D 64), pp. 117–122; in *Natural History of Intellect* (A 44), pp. 212–219.

E 47
"Veeshnoo Sarma." *Dial*, 3 (July 1842), 82–85.

Unsigned. Selected by Emerson. Reprinted in *Uncollected Writings* (A 54), pp. 65–70.

E 48
"Fourierism and the Socialists." *Dial,* 3 (July 1842), 86–96.

Unsigned. Reprinted in *Uncollected Writings* (A 54), pp. 71–76.

E 49
"Chardon Street and Bible Conventions." *Dial,* 3 (July 1842), 100–112.

Unsigned. Reprinted as "Chardon Street Convention" in *Lectures and Biographical Sketches* (A 41), pp. 351–354.

E 50
"Agriculture of Massachusetts." *Dial,* 3 (July 1842), 123–126.

Unsigned. Reprinted in *Natural History of Intellect* (A 44), pp. 219–224.

E 51
[Review of George Borrow, *The Zincali*]. *Dial,* 3 (July 1842), 127–128.

Unsigned. Reprinted in *Uncollected Writings* (A 54), pp. 163–165.

E 52
[Review of James Lockhart, *Ancient Spanish Ballads*]. *Dial,* 3 (July 1842), 128–129.

Unsigned. Reprinted in *Uncollected Writings* (A 54), pp. 165–166.

E 53
[Review of George H. Colton, *Tecumseh: A Poem*]. *Dial,* 3 (July 1842), 129.

Unsigned. Reprinted in *Uncollected Writings* (A 54), pp. 166–167.

E 54
[Review of *The Cambridge Miscellany of Mathematics, Physics, and Astronomy* for April 1842]. *Dial,* 3 (July 1842), 131.

Unsigned.

E 55
[Notice of Orestes A. Brownson, *A Letter to Rev. W. E. Channing*]. *Dial,* 3 (July 1842), 132.

Unsigned.

E 56
[Notice of the *London Phalanx* for June 1842]. *Dial,* 3 (July 1842), 132.

Unsigned.

E 57
"Exploring Expedition." *Dial,* 3 (July 1842), 132–133.

Unsigned. Reprinted in *Uncollected Writings* (A 54), pp. 77–78.

E 58
"Association of State Geologists." *Dial,* 3 (July 1842), 133.

Unsigned. Reprinted in *Uncollected Writings* (A 54), pp. 78–79.

E 59
"Harvard University." *Dial*, 3 (July 1842), 133–134.

Unsigned. Reprinted in *Uncollected Writings* (A 54), pp. 79–81.

E 60
[Wordsworth's new poems]. *Dial*, 3 (July 1842), 135.

Unsigned. Reprinted in *Uncollected Writings* (A 54), pp. 81–82.

E 61
[Tennyson]. *Dial*, 3 (July 1842), 135.

Unsigned. Reprinted in *Uncollected Writings* (A 54), p. 82.

E 62
[Henry Taylor, John Sterling, Thomas Carlyle]. *Dial*, 3 (July 1842), 135.

Unsigned. Reprinted in *Uncollected Writings* (A 54), p. 82.

E 63
"Berlin [Schelling's lecture]." *Dial*, 3 (July 1842), 136.

Unsigned. Reprinted in *Uncollected Writings* (A 54), pp. 82–83.

E 64
"New Jerusalem Church." *Dial*, 3 (July 1842), 136.

Unsigned.

E 65
"Lectures on the Times. Lecture II. The Conservative." *Dial*, 3 (October 1842), 181–197.

Reprinted in *Nature; Addresses, and Lectures* (A 21), pp. 285–315.

E 66
"English Reformers." *Dial*, 3 (October 1842), 227–247.

Unsigned. Reprinted in *Uncollected Writings* (A 54), pp. 84–112.

E 67
[Introductory note to Charles Lane, "James Pierrepont Greaves"]. *Dial*, 3 (October 1842), 247.

Signed "Editor of the Dial."

E 68
"Saadi." *Dial*, 3 (October 1842), 265–269.

Unsigned. Reprinted in *Poems* (A 18.2), pp. 197–205; *Atlantic Monthly Magazine*, 14 (July 1864), 33–37.

E 69
[Introductory note to Samuel Gray Ward, "The Gallery"]. *Dial*, 3 (October 1842), 269.

Unsigned.

E 70
[Papers from England]. *Dial,* 3 (October 1842), 278.

Unsigned.

E 71
[John A. Heraud's lectures]. *Dial,* 3 (October 1842), 279.

Unsigned.

E 72
[Charles Lane and Henry G. Wright]. *Dial,* 3 (October 1842), 279.

Unsigned.

E 73
[French journals]. *Dial,* 3 (October 1842), 279–280.

Unsigned.

E 74
"Berlin." *Dial,* 3 (October 1842), 280.

Unsigned. Selected by Emerson.

E 75
"Lectures on the Times. Lecture III. The Transcendentalist." *Dial,* 3 (January 1843), 297–313.

Reprinted in *Nature; Addresses, and Lectures* (A 21), pp. 319–348.

E 76
"To Eva at the South." *Dial,* 3 (January 1843), 327–328.

Unsigned. Reprinted as "To Ellen, at the South" in *Poems* (A 18.2), pp. 144–146.

E 77
[Death of William Ellery Channing]. *Dial,* 3 (January 1843), 387.

Unsigned. Reprinted in *Uncollected Writings* (A 54), pp. 113–114.

E 78
[Death of Baron Degerando]. *Dial,* 3 (January 1843), 387.

Unsigned.

E 79
[Introductory note to Charles Stearns Wheeler, "Letter from Germany"]. *Dial,* 3 (January 1843), 387.

Unsigned.

E 80
[Review of *Confessions of St. Augustine*]. *Dial,* 3 (January 1843), 414–415.

Unsigned. Reprinted in *Uncollected Writings* (A 54), pp. 174–176.

E 81
[English books]. *Dial,* 3 (January 1843), 416.

Unsigned.

E 82
"Goethe and Swedenborg." *Dial,* 3 (January 1843), 416.

Unsigned.

E 83
"Europe and European Books." *Dial,* 3 (April 1843), 511–521.

Unsigned. Reprinted in *Natural History of Intellect* (A 44), pp. 225–237.

E 84
[Review of George Borrow, *The Bible in Spain*]. *Dial,* 3 (April 1843), 534–535.

Unsigned. Reprinted in *Uncollected Writings* (A 54), p. 176.

E 85
[Introduction to a passage from Thomas Carlyle, *Past and Present*]. *Concord Freeman,* 28 April 1843, p. 1.

Signed "R.W.E."

E 86
"Ethnical Scriptures. Extracts from the Desatir." *Dial,* 4 (July 1843), 59–62.

Unsigned. Selected by Emerson.

E 87
"Abou Ben Adhem. By Leigh Hunt." *Dial,* 4 (July 1843), 62.

Unsigned.

E 88
"Gifts." *Dial,* 4 (July 1843), 93–95.

Unsigned. Reprinted in *Essays: Second Series* (A 16), pp. 173–180.

E 89
"Past and Present." *Dial,* 4 (July 1843), 96–102.

Unsigned. Review of Thomas Carlyle, *Past and Present*. Reprinted as "Carlyle's Past and Present," *Works* (B 1), III, 312–317; in *Natural History of Intellect* (A 44), pp. 237–248.

E 90
"To Rhea." *Dial,* 4 (July 1843), 104–106.

Unsigned. Reprinted in *Poems* (A 18.2), pp. 21–24.

E 91
[Introductory note to Samuel Gray Ward, "Notes on Art and Architecture"]. *Dial,* 4 (July 1843), 107.

Unsigned.

E 92
[Notice to Correspondents]. *Dial,* 4 (July 1843), 133.

Unsigned.

E 93
[Review of John Pierpont, *Anti-Slavery Poems*]. *Dial,* 4 (July 1843), 134.

Unsigned. Reprinted in *Uncollected Writings* (A 54), pp. 177–178.

E 94
[Review of William Lloyd Garrison, *Sonnets and Other Poems*]. *Dial,* 4 (July 1843), 134.

Unsigned. Reprinted in *Uncollected Writings* (A 54), p. 178.

E 95
[Review of Nathaniel W. Coffin, *America—an Ode*]. *Dial,* 4 (July 1843), 134.

Unsigned. Reprinted in *Uncollected Writings* (A 54), p. 178.

E 96
[Review of Ellery Channing, *Poems*]. *Dial,* 4 (July 1843), 135.

Unsigned. Reprinted in *Uncollected Writings* (A 54), p. 179.

E 97
[Review of Fredrika Bremer, *The H. Family* and *The President's Daughters*]. *Dial,* 4 (July 1843), 135.

Unsigned.

E 98
"To Correspondents." *Dial,* 4 (July 1843), 136.

Unsigned. Reprinted in *Uncollected Writings* (A 54), pp. 179–180.

E 99
"Mr. Channing's Poems." *United States Magazine, and Democratic Review,* 13 (September 1843), 309–314.

Unsigned.

Note: See *L,* III, 197, and *The Correspondence of Henry David Thoreau* (D 214), p. 138, for evidence of editorial tamperings with Emerson's manuscript.

E 100
"The Three Dimensions." *Dial,* 4 (October 1843), 226.

Unsigned.

E 101
"The Comic." *Dial,* 4 (October 1843), 247–256.

Unsigned. Reprinted in *Letters and Social Aims* (A 34), pp. 139–154.

E 102
"Ode to Beauty." *Dial,* 4 (October 1843), 257–259.

Unsigned. Reprinted in *Poems* (A 18.2), pp. 136–140.

E 103
"A Letter." *Dial*, 4 (October 1843), 262–270.

Unsigned. Reprinted in *Natural History of Intellect* (A 44), pp. 249–260.

E 104
[Notices of books]. *Dial*, 4 (October 1843), 272.

Unsigned.

E 105
"Tantalus." *Dial*, 4 (January 1844), 357–363.

Unsigned. Reprinted in "Nature," *Essays: Second Series* (A 16), pp. 199–211; *Works* (B 1), III, 318–323; as *Tantalus* (A 50); in *Uncollected Writings* (A 54), pp. 115–122.

E 106
[Introductory note to Henry David Thoreau, "Pindar"]. *Dial*, 4 (January 1844), 379.

Unsigned.

E 107
"Eros" ["The sense of the world is short"]. *Dial*, 4 (January 1844), 401.

Unsigned. Reprinted in *Poems* (A 18.2), p. 150.

E 108
"The Times,—A Fragment." *Dial*, 4 (January 1844), 405–406.

Unsigned. Reprinted as "Blight," *Poems* (A 18.2), pp. 223–226.

E 109
[Review of *Deutsche Schnellpost*]. *Dial*, 4 (January 1844), 408.

Unsigned.

E 110
"The Young American." *Dial*, 4 (April 1844), 484–507.

Unsigned but identified as Emerson's in the volume's table of contents. Reprinted as *The Young American* (A 15); in *Nature; Addresses, and Lectures* (A 21), pp. 351–383.

E 111
"The Tragic." *Dial*, 4 (April 1844), 515–521.

Unsigned. Reprinted in *Natural History of Intellect* (A 44), pp. 260–272.

E 112
"The Visit." *Dial*, 4 (April 1844), 528.

Unsigned. Reprinted in *Poems* (A 18.2), pp. 25–26.

E 113
"Ethnical Scriptures. Chaldæan Oracles." *Dial*, 4 (April 1844), 529–536.

Unsigned. Selected by Emerson. Reprinted in *Uncollected Writings* (A 54), pp. 123–133.

E 114
"Mr. Hoar's Expulsion from S. Carolina." *New-York Daily Tribune*, 20 December 1844, p. 2.

Signed "E." Letter of 17 December 1844 to [Ellery Channing].

E 115
[Letter]. *Liberator*, 16 (16 January 1846), 10.

Letter of 17 November 1845 to William J. Rotch.

E 116
"Carlyle's Letters and Speeches of Cromwell." *Boston Daily Advertiser*, 31 January 1846, p. 2.

Unsigned.

Note: See *L*, III, 326, for Emerson's authorship.

E 117
"To the Public—Editor's Address." *Massachusetts Quarterly Review*, 1 (December 1847), 1–7.

Unsigned. Reprinted in *Miscellanies* (A 40), pp. 325–334.

E 118
[Notice of John Sterling, *Essays and Tales*]. *Massachusetts Quarterly Review*, 1 (September 1848), 515–516.

Unsigned. Reprinted in Gohdes, *The Periodicals of American Transcendentalism* (D 203), pp. 255–256; Gohdes also assigns Emerson's authorship.

E 119
"New Translation of Dante." *Massachusetts Quarterly Review*, 1 (September 1848), 527.

Unsigned. Reprinted in Gohdes, *The Periodicals of American Transcendentalism* (D 203), p. 256; Gohdes also assigns Emerson's authorship.

E 120
[Review of Arthur Hugh Clough, *The Bothie of Toper-na-Fuosich*]. *Massachusetts Quarterly Review*, 2 (March 1849), 249–252.

Unsigned. Reprinted in *Uncollected Writings* (A 54), pp. 23–25.

E 121
[Letter]. *Liberator*, 19 (27 July 1849), 119.

Letter of 24 July 1849 to William Lloyd Garrison.

E 122
"Middlesex Co. A. S. Society." *Liberator*, 21 (18 April 1851), 64.

Letter of 18 March 1851 to [Mary Merrick Brooks?].

E 123
"Women's Rights Convention. First Day." *New-York Daily Tribune*, 17 October 1851, p. 7.

Letter of 7 October 1851 to Lucy Stone. Reprinted in *Liberator*, 21 (7 November 1851), 180.

E 124
"Ralph Waldo Emerson." *Una*, 3 (15 August 1855), 126.

Letter of 13 June 1855 to Paulina Wright Davis.

E 125
"Complimentary Fruit Festival of the New York Publishers' Association to Authors and Booksellers, at the Crystal Palace, September 27, 1855." *American Publishers' Circular and Literary Gazette*, 1 (29 September 1855), 75.

Letter of 19 September 1855 to the New York Book Publishers' Association.

E 126
"Leaves of Grass." *New-York Daily Tribune*, 10 October 1855, p. 7.

Letter of 21 July 1855 to Walt Whitman. Reprinted as a broadside (A 23); in Whitman, *Leaves of Grass* (D 26), pp. 345–346; *Uncollected Writings* (A 54), p. 208.

E 127
"Samuel Hoar." *Putnam's Monthly Magazine*, 8 (December 1856), 645–646.

Unsigned.

E 128
"Character of Samuel Hoar." *Monthly Religious Magazine*, 17 (January 1857), 6–9.

Signed "R. W. E." Extracts from "Samuel Hoar" (E 127) are printed on pp. 9–11.

E 129
"The Romany Girl." *Atlantic Monthly Magazine*, 1 (November 1857), 46–47.

Unsigned. Reprinted in *May-Day* (A 28), pp. 109–110; *Poems* (A 18.16), pp. 227–228.

E 130
"The Chartist's Complaint." *Atlantic Monthly Magazine*, 1 (November 1857), 47.

Unsigned. Reprinted in *May-Day* (A 28), pp. 112–113; *Poems* (A 18.6), p. 197.

E 131
"Days." *Atlantic Monthly Magazine*, 1 (November 1857), 47.

Unsigned. Reprinted in *Selected Poems* (A 18.4), p. 172.

E 132
"Brahma." *Atlantic Monthly Magazine*, 1 (November 1857), 48.

Unsigned. Reprinted in *May-Day* (A 28), pp. 65–66; *Poems* (A 18.6), pp. 170–171.

E 133
"Illusions." *Atlantic Monthly Magazine*, 1 (November 1857), 58–62.

Unsigned. Reprinted in *The Conduct of Life* (A 26), pp. 271–272; *Poems* (A 18.16), pp. 287–288.

E 134
"Solitude and Society." *Atlantic Monthly Magazine*, 1 (December 1857), 225–229.

Unsigned. Reprinted as "Domestic Life," *Dial* [Cincinnati], 1 (October 1860), 585–602; as "Society and Solitude," *Society and Solitude* (A 31), pp. 3–14.

E 135
"Two Rivers." *Atlantic Monthly Magazine*, 1 (January 1858), 311.

Unsigned. Reprinted in *May-Day* (A 28), pp. 134–135; *Poems* (A 18.6), p. 213.

E 136
"Books." *Atlantic Monthly Magazine*, 1 (January 1858), 343–353.

Unsigned. Reprinted in *Society and Solitude* (A 31), pp. 169–197.

E 137
"Persian Poetry." *Atlantic Monthly Magazine*, 1 (April 1858), 724–734.

Unsigned. Reprinted in *Letters and Social Aims* (A 34), pp. 211–238.

E 138
"Eloquence." *Atlantic Monthly Magazine*, 2 (September 1858), 385–397.

Unsigned. Reprinted in *Society and Solitude* (A 31), pp. 55–89.

E 139
"Waldeinsamkeit." *Atlantic Monthly Magazine*, 2 (October 1858), 550–551.

Unsigned. Reprinted in *May-Day* (A 28), pp. 136–139; *Poems* (A 18.6), pp. 214–215.

E 140
"The Sacred Dance. [From the Persian]." *Dial* [Cincinnati], 1 (January 1860), 37.

Unsigned. Reprinted as "Song of Seid Nimetollah of Kuhistan," *May-Day* (A 28), pp. 203–205; as "Seyd," *Poems* (A 18.16), pp. 304–305.

E 141
"Song of Nature." *Atlantic Monthly Magazine*, 5 (January 1860), 18–20.

Unsigned. Reprinted in *May-Day* (A 28), pp. 128–133; *Poems* (A 18.6), pp. 209–212.

E 142
"Cras, Heri, Hodie." *Dial* [Cincinnati], 1 (February 1860), 131.

Unsigned. Reprinted as "Heri, Cras, Hodie," *May-Day* (A 28), p. 188; *Poems* (A 18.6), p. 242.

E 143
"Climacteric." *Dial* [Cincinnati], 1 (February 1860), 131.

Unsigned. Reprinted in *May-Day* (A 28), p. 188; *Poems* (A 18.6), p. 242.

E 144
"Botanist." *Dial* [Cincinnati], 1 (February 1860), 131.

Unsigned. Reprinted in *May-Day* (A 28), p. 184; *Poems* (A 18.6), p. 239.

E 145
"Forester." *Dial* [Cincinnati], 1 (February 1860), 131.

Unsigned. Reprinted in *May-Day* (A 28), p. 184; *Poems* (A 18.6), p. 240.

E 146
"Gardener." *Dial* [Cincinnati], 1 (March 1860), 195.

Unsigned. Reprinted in *May-Day* (A 28), p. 184; *Poems* (A 18.6), p. 239.

E 147
"Northman." *Dial* [Cincinnati], 1 (March 1860), 195.

Unsigned. Reprinted in *May-Day* (A 28), p. 185; *Poems* (A 18.6), p. 240.

E 148
"From Alcuin." *Dial* [Cincinnati], 1 (March 1860), 195.

Unsigned. Reprinted in *May-Day* (A 28), p. 185; *Poems* (A 18.6), p. 240.

E 149
"Nature" ["Boon Nature yields each day a brag"]. *Dial* [Cincinnati], 1 (March 1860), 195.

Unsigned. Reprinted in *May-Day* (A 28), p. 186; *Poems* (A 18.6), p. 241.

E 150
"Natura in Minimus." *Dial* [Cincinnati], 1 (March 1860), 195.

Unsigned. Reprinted as "Nature in Leasts," *May-Day* (A 28), p. 191; *Poems* (A 18.6), p. 244.

E 151
"Orator." *Dial* [Cincinnati], 1 (March 1860), 195.

Unsigned. Reprinted in *May-Day* (A 28), p. 182; *Poems* (A 18.6), p. 238.

E 152
"Poet" ["To clothe the fiery thought"]. *Dial* [Cincinnati], 1 (March 1860), 195.

Unsigned. Reprinted in *May-Day* (A 28), p. 183; *Poems* (A 18.6), p. 239.

E 153
"Artist." *Dial* [Cincinnati], 1 (March 1860), 195.

Unsigned. Reprinted in *May-Day* (A 28), p. 183; *Poems* (A 18.6), p. 239.

E 154
"Culture." *Atlantic Monthly Magazine,* 6 (September 1860), 343–353.

Unsigned. Reprinted in *The Conduct of Life* (A 26), pp. 113–144.

E 155
"The Test. (Musa loquitur.)." *Atlantic Monthly Magazine,* 7 (January 1861), 85.

Unsigned. Reprinted in *May-Day* (A 28), p. 97; *Poems* (A 18.6), p. 189.

E 156
"Old Age." *Atlantic Monthly Magazine,* 9 (January 1862), 134–140.

Unsigned. Reprinted in *Society and Solitude* (A 31), pp. 281–300.

E 157
"American Civilization." *Atlantic Monthly Magazine,* 9 (April 1862), 502–511.

Unsigned. Reprinted in *Miscellanies* (A 40), pp. 277–290.

E 158
"Henry D. Thoreau." *Boston Daily Advertiser,* 8 May 1862, p. 2.

Signed. "E." Reprinted as *Henry D. Thoreau* (A 51).

Note: Not to be confused with "Thoreau" (E 160).

E 159
"The Titmouse." *Atlantic Monthly Magazine,* 9 (May 1862), 585–587.

Unsigned. Reprinted in *May-Day* (A 28), pp. 119–124; *Poems* (A 18.6), pp. 200–203.

E 160
"Thoreau." *Atlantic Monthly Magazine,* 10 (August 1862), 239–249.

Unsigned but identified as Emerson's in the volume's table of contents. Reprinted as "Biographical Sketch," Thoreau, *Excursions* (F 5), pp. 7–33; as "Henry D. Thoreau," *Works* (B 1), III, 324–339; as "Thoreau," *Lectures and Biographical Sketches* (A 41), pp. 419–452.

E 161
"The President's Proclamation." *Atlantic Monthly Magazine,* 10 (November 1862), 638–642.

Unsigned but identified as Emerson's in the volume's table of contents. Reprinted in *Commonwealth* [Boston], 15 November 1862, p. 1; as "The Emancipation Proclamation," *Miscellanies* (A 40), pp. 293–303.

E 162
"Boston Hymn. Read in Music Hall, January 1, 1863." *Dwight's Journal of Music,* 22 (24 January 1863), 337.

Reprinted from *Atlantic Monthly Magazine,* 11 (February 1863), 227–228. Reprinted in *New England Loyal Publication Society,* no. 108 (ca. August 1863), 1; as "American Hymn," *Pitman's Popular Lecturer and Reader,* n.s. no. 8 (August 1863), 252–254 (see also D 45); in *May-Day* (A 28), pp. 75–80; *Poems* (A 18.6), pp. 174–177.

Note: The February *Atlantic Monthly Magazine* was published in late January, making the 24 January reprint possible.

E 163
[Petition for aid in the enlistment of colored troops]. Unidentified newspaper, ca. 3 August 1863.

Petition of 3 August 1863, signed by Emerson and others. Reproduced in Kenneth Walter Cameron, "Emerson, Alcott, and Holmes Sign Petition to Raise 50,000 Colored Soldiers," *American Transcendental Quarterly,* no. 17 (Winter 1973), 34.

Note: The introduction to the article implies that the petition was a separately published document; no copies have been located.

E 164
"Voluntaries." *Atlantic Monthly Magazine,* 12 (October 1863), 504–506.

Unsigned but identified as Emerson's in the volume's table of contents. Partially reprinted in "A Voluntary" ["Freedom all winged expands"], *New England Loyal Publication Society,* no. 126 (10 October 1863), 1; "A Voluntary" ["In an age of fops and toys"], *New England Loyal Publication Society,* no. 134 (31 October 1863), 1; reprinted in *Memorial RGS* (D 49), pp. 161–164; *May-Day* (A 28), pp. 81–88; *Poems* (A 18.6), pp. 178–182.

E 165
"Sea-Shore." *Boatswain's Whistle,* no. 9 (18 October 1864), 65.

Reprinted in *May-Day* (A 28), pp. 125–127; *Poems* (A 18.6), pp. 207–209.

E 166
"Mr. Emerson's Lecture Postponed." *Worcester Daily Spy,* 10 February 1865, p. 2.

Letter of 9 February 1865 to D. A. Goddard.

E 167
"Abraham Lincoln. Remarks at the Funeral Services of the President, in Concord, April 19, 1865." *Commonwealth* [Boston], 29 April 1865, p. 1.

Reprinted in *Liberator,* 35 (5 May 1865), 70; *Littell's Living Age,* 3d ser., 29 (13 May 1865), 282–284; *The Lincoln Memorial* (D 56), pp. pp. 146–150; *Miscellanies* (A 40), pp. 307–315.

E 168
"Character." *North American Review,* 102 (April 1866), 356–373.

Unsigned. Reprinted in *Lectures and Biographical Sketches* (A 41), pp. 93–121.

E 169
"My Garden." *Atlantic Monthly Magazine,* 18 (December 1866), 665–666.

Unsigned but identified as Emerson's in the volume's table of contents. Reprinted in *May-Day* (A 28), pp. 114–118; *Poems* (A 18.6), pp. 197–200.

E 170
"Terminus." *Atlantic Monthly Magazine,* 19 (January 1867), 111–112.

Unsigned but identified as Emerson's in the volume's table of contents. Reprinted in *May-Day* (A 28), pp. 140–142; *Poems* (A 18.6), pp. 216–217.

E 171
"Mr. Ralph Waldo Emerson's Remarks at The Unitarian Church at Medford, on the Character of Mr. Geo. L. Stearns, Sunday, April 14, 1867." *Commonwealth* [Boston], 27 April 1867, p. 2.

Reprinted as *Remarks on the Character of George L. Stearns* (A 32); in *Lectures and Biographical Sketches* (A 41.1.u), pp. 465–473.

E 172
"Mrs. Sarah A. Ripley." *Boston Daily Advertiser*, 31 July 1867, p. 2.

"E." Reprinted as *Mrs. Sarah A. Ripley* (A 29).

E 173
"XXVI. From Ralph Waldo Emerson." *Boston Daily Advertiser Supplement*, 23 November 1867, p. 2.

Letter of 18 February 1867 to Louis Prang.

E 174
"Aspects of Culture." *Atlantic Monthly Magazine*, 21 (January 1868), 87–95.

Unsigned but identified as Emerson's in the volume's table of contents. Reprinted as "Progress of Culture," *Letters and Social Aims* (A 34), pp. 185–209.

E 175
"Quotation and Originality." *North American Review*, 106 (April 1868), 543–557.

Reprinted in *Letters and Social Aims* (A 34), pp. 157–181.

E 176
"To the Graduates of Harvard College." *Boston Daily Advertiser*, 21 December 1868, p. 1.

Undated letter, signed by Emerson and others.

E 177
"Woman Suffrage Convention at Newburyport." *Boston Daily Advertiser*, 29 July 1869, p. 1.

Letter of 21 July 1869. Reprinted as "Woman's Suffrage," *New York Times*, 30 July 1869, p. 4.

E 178
"The Pilgrim Fathers." *New-York Daily Tribune*, 24 December 1870, pp. 3, 7.

Reprinted as "Oration," *New England Society Orations* (D 165), II, 373–393.

E 179
[Letter]. *Boston Daily Advertiser*, 23 August 1872.

Letter of 29 July 1872 to J. C. Sanborn.

E 180
"Letter from Mr. Emerson." *University Independent* [Glasgow University], 2d ser., no. 3 (7 April 1874), 1.

Letter of 18 March 1874 to W. R. Herkless et al. Reprinted as "Mr. Emerson and the Glasgow University Rectorship," *Boston Daily Advertiser*, 21 April 1874, p. 2.

E 181
"An Unpublished Speech of Mr. Emerson's." *Boston Evening Transcript*, 29 April 1874, p. 6.

"Remarks of Mr. R. W. Emerson at a Meeting in Concord, to Consider the Outrage upon Mr. Sumner" (1856). Reprinted in *Miscellanies* (A 40), pp. 233–237.

E 182
"Ralph Waldo Emerson and the Glasgow University." *New York Times,* 14 February 1875, p. 5.

Letter of 5 January 1875 to James Hutchison Stirling.

E 183
[Speech]. *New York Herald,* "Revolutionary Extra Edition," 19 April 1875.

Remarks at Concord, 19 April 1875. Reprinted in "Proceedings at Centennial Commemorations, 1874–5," *New-England Historical and Genealogical Register,* 29 (October 1875), 443–501 (Emerson's remarks on pp. 468–469); *Centennial Orations on the American Revolution* (D 94), pp. 138–139; *Proceedings at the Centennial Celebration of the Concord Fight* (D 98), pp. 79–81.

E 184
"Boston." *Atlantic Monthly Magazine,* 37 (February 1876), 195–197.

Reprinted in *Selected Poems* (A 18.4), pp. 214–218.

E 185
"Remarks by R. W. Emerson at the Centennial Celebration of the Latin School." *Boston Daily Advertiser,* 9 November 1876.

Reprinted as [*Remarks at the Boston Latin School*] (A 35).

E 186
"Demonology." *North American Review,* 124 (March 1877), 179–190.

Reprinted in *Lectures and Biographical Sketches* (A 41), pp. 9–32.

E 187
"Perpetual Forces." *North American Review,* 125 (September 1877), 271–282.

Reprinted in *Lectures and Biographical Sketches* (A 41), pp. 71–89.

E 188
"The Sovereignty of Ethics." *North American Review,* 126 (May–June 1878), 404–420.

Reprinted in *Works* (B 1), III, 372–376; *Science and Theology and The Sovereignty of Ethics* (D 107), pp. 42–66; *Lectures and Biographical Sketches* (A 41), pp. 177–205.

E 189
"Letters Received." *New York Times,* 23 April 1879, p. 5.

Letter of 16 April 1879 to [James H. Morse]. Reprinted as "Personal," *Boston Daily Advertiser,* 24 April 1879, p. 1; in *Proceedings at a Reception in Honor of O. B. Frothingham* (D 110), p. 51; in *Nineteenth Century New England Authors Collection* (D 222), p. 3.

E 190
"The Preacher." *Unitarian Review,* 13 (January 1880), 1–13.

Reprinted as *The Preacher* (A 38); in *Lectures and Biographical Sketches* (A 41), pp. 209–228.

E 191
"Sartor Resartus." *Boston Daily Advertiser,* 22 March 1881, p. 2.

Letter of 19 February 1872.

E 192
"Mr. Emerson on Woman Suffrage." *Woman's Journal,* 12 (26 March 1881), 100.

Described as written in 1862 and printed from Emerson's manuscript. Reprinted as "Woman," *Miscellanies* (A 40), pp. 337–356.

E 193
"University Notes." *Harvard University Bulletin,* 2 (1 April 1881), 166.

Letter of 14 March 1870 to Charles W. Eliot.

E 194
"Impressions of Thomas Carlyle in 1848." *Scribner's Monthly,* 22 (May 1881), 89–92.

Reprinted without title in *Proceedings of the Massachusetts Historical Society* (D 115), pp. 324–328; in *Tributes to Longfellow and Emerson* (G 114), pp. 51–56; as "Carlyle," *Lectures and Biographical Sketches* (A 41), pp. 455–463.

E 195
Cooke, George Willis. "Words from Emerson." *The Sword and the Pen,* no. 6 (13 December 1881), 3.

Selections from unpublished writings.

E 196
"The Superlative," *Century Magazine,* 23 (February 1882), 534–537.

Reprinted in *Lectures and Biographical Sketches* (A 41), pp. 159–174.

E 197
[Higginson, Thomas Wentworth]. "Emerson." *Nation,* 34 (4 May 1882), 375–376.

Letter of [ca. 1843] to Higginson (p. 376). Reprinted in Higginson, "The Personality of Emerson" (E 244), p. 221.

E 198
[Conway, Moncure Daniel]. "Emerson to Carlyle." *New-York Daily Tribune,* 7 June 1882, p. 6.

Letter of 26 September 1864 to Carlyle. Reprinted as "Emerson in England," *Harper's Weekly Magazine,* 26 (10 June 1882), 358–359.

Note: Shorter extracts from and a summary of this letter were given in Conway, *Thomas Carlyle* (D 117).

E 199
"Emerson to Carlyle." *Athenæum,* no. 2852 (24 June 1882), 796.

Letter of 20 November 1834 to Carlyle.

E 200
"Emerson to Carlyle." *Athenæum*, no. 2854 (8 July 1882), 47–48.

Letter of 10 May 1838 to Carlyle. Reprinted as "Emerson's Picture of His Home," *New-York Daily Tribune*, 18 July 1882, p. 6.

E 201
"Emerson to Carlyle." *Athenæum*, no. 2856 (22 July 1882), 114–115.

Letters of 15 March 1839 and 18 March 1840 to Carlyle.

E 202
Albee, John. "Reminiscences of Emerson." *New-York Daily Tribune*, 23 July 1882, p. 4.

Letters of [1851] and [ca. 30? October? 1852] to Albee. Reprinted in *Concord Lectures in Philosophy* (D 126); Albee, *Remembrances of Emerson* (New York: Robert G. Cooke, 1901), pp. 14, 30–31, and rev. ed. (New York: Robert Grier Cooke, 1903), pp. 22–23 (1851 letter only).

E 203
"Letters." *New-York Daily Tribune*, 22 October 1882, p. 3.

Letters of 30 June 1840, 31 July 1841, and 12 March 1835 to Carlyle.

E 204
[Emerson]. *Index*, 14 (14 June 1883), 594.

Letter of 1856 [i.e., 2 December 1851] to "a lady" [Julia Dalton].

E 205
Withington, Mary S. "Early Letters of Emerson." *Century Magazine*, 26 (July 1883), 454–458.

E 206
"Mary Moody Emerson." *Atlantic Monthly Magazine*, 52 (December 1883), 733–745.

Reprinted in *Lectures and Biographical Sketches* (A 41), pp. 373–404.

E 207
"Historic Notes on Life and Letters in Massachusetts." *Atlantic Monthly Magazine*, 52 (October 1883), 529–543.

Reprinted as "Historic Notes of Life and Letters in New England," *Lectures and Biographical Sketches* (A 41), pp. 307–347.

E 208
"Emerson to Carlyle." *Athenæum*, no. 2937 (9 February 1884), 185.

Letter of 15 May 1839 to Carlyle.

E 209
[Fields, Annie]. "Glimpses of Emerson." *Harper's New Monthly Magazine*, 68 (February 1884), 457–467.

Various letters.

E 210
Lathrop, George Parsons. "Unpublished Letters from Ralph Waldo Emerson to Mrs. Nathaniel Hawthorne." *Boston Sunday Herald,* 21 June 1885, p. 7.

Reprinted as "Emerson to Mrs. Hawthorne," *New-York Daily Tribune,* 21 June 1885, p. 8; in Rose Hawthorne Lathrop, *Memories of Hawthorne* (D 157).

E 211
"An Emerson Letter." *Boston Herald,* 28 December 1885.

Letter of 13 January 1865 to [Mrs. S. G. Perkins]. Reprinted in *Nineteenth Century New England Authors Collection* (D 222), p. 2.

E 212
Haskins, David Greene. "The Maternal Ancestors of Ralph Waldo Emerson. I." *Literary World,* 17 (7 August 1886), 265–268.

"On the Death of Mr. John Haskins," p. 267. Reprinted in Haskins, *Ralph Waldo Emerson His Maternal Ancestors* (D 135), p. 27 (new edition).

E 213
Haskins, David Greene. "The Maternal Ancestors of Ralph Waldo Emerson. II." *Literary World,* 17 (21 August 1886), 281–284.

Letter of 21 May 1880 to Haskins, p. 283. Reprinted in Haskins, *Ralph Waldo Emerson His Maternal Ancestors* (D 135), p. 35.

E 214
Haskins, David Greene. "The Maternal Ancestors of Ralph Waldo Emerson. III." *Literary World,* 17 (4 September 1886), 297–299.

Letter of 18 June 1839 to Haskins, p. 298. Reprinted in Haskins, *Ralph Waldo Emerson His Maternal Ancestors* (D 135), pp. 51–53.

E 215
S., A. T. [Emerson]. *Lippincott's Magazine,* 38 (October 1886), 451–452.

Letter of 12 April 1838 to [Frederic Henry Hedge], p. 452.

E 216
Cabot, J. Elliot. "A Glimpse of Emerson's Boyhood." *Atlantic Monthly Magazine,* 59 (May 1887), 650–667.

Letters of 16 April 1813 to Mary Moody Emerson and 24 February 1815 to William Emerson, pp. 662–663, 666. Reprinted in Cabot, *A Memoir of Ralph Waldo Emerson* (D 138); in Edward Waldo Emerson, "Ralph Waldo Emerson" (E 245), pp. 92–94.

E 217
Flügel, Ewald. "Ein Brief Emerson's." *Anglia,* 12 (1889), 454–459.

Letter of 30 April 1843 to Charles Stearns Wheeler. Reprinted in Alexander Ireland, "Two Letters of Emerson," *Manchester Guardian* [England], 3 December 1889, p. 12; as "A Letter of Emerson's," *Boston Evening Transcript,* 14 December 1889, p. 11; as "One of Emerson's Letters," *New-York Daily Tribune,* 15 December 1889, p. 22; in Felix Flügel, "Passages from an Autograph Collection," *University of California Chronicle,* 28 (October 1926), 347–353, with a partial facsimile of the manuscript (facing p. 351).

E 218
Van Buren, Anson de Puy. "The Log Schoolhouse Era in Michigan." *Historical Collections* [Michigan Pioneer and Historical Society], 14 (1889), 283–402.

Letter of 25 July 1860 to B. W. Procter, p. 336. Reprinted in C. J. Wasung, "Emerson Comes to Detroit," *Michigan History Magazine,* 29 (January–March 1945), 59–72 (on p. 62n.).

E 219
"Ralph Waldo Emerson In Newcastle." *Newcastle Monthly Chronicle,* November 1889, 495–496.

Various letters to George Crawshay. *Not seen.*

E 220
Ireland, Alexander. "Two Letters of Emerson." *Manchester Guardian* [England], 3 December 1889, p. 12.

Letters of 30 April 1843 to Charles Stearns Wheeler (see E 217) and 29 June 1846 to [Daniel Jefferson].

E 221
Higginson, Thomas Wentworth. "Glimpses of Authors. IV.—The Transcendental Authors." *Brains,* 1 (1 December 1891), 103–106.

Letter of 16 May 1849 to Higginson, p. 104. Reprinted in Sanborn and Harris, *A. Bronson Alcott* (D 147), II, 462–463; T. W. Higginson, "Emerson as the Reformer" (E 243), pp. 9, 16.

E 222
"Boston." *Atlantic Monthly Magazine,* 69 (January 1892), 26–35.

Reprinted in *Natural History of Intellect* (A 44), pp. 85–111.

E 223
Sanborn, F. B. "The Emerson-Thoreau Correspondence." *Atlantic Monthly Magazine,* 69 (May 1892), 577–596.

Signed. Concluded in the June number. Reprinted in *The Correspondence of Henry David Thoreau* (D 214).

E 224
Sanborn, F. B. "The Emerson-Thoreau Correspondence." *Atlantic Monthly Magazine,* 69 (June 1892), 736–753.

Concluded from the May number. Reprinted in *The Correspondence of Henry David Thoreau* (D 214).

E 225
Stewart, George. "Unpublished Letters of Bryant and Emerson." *Independent,* 45 (3 August 1893), 1045.

Letter of 22 January 1877 to Stewart. Reprinted by [George Stewart, Jr.] in "The Contributors' Club," *Atlantic Monthly Magazine,* 91 (June 1903), 858–859.

E 226
"To Lowell, On His Fortieth Birthday." *Century Magazine,* 47 (November 1893), 3–4.

E 227
"Tyndall and Emerson." *Atlantic Monthly Magazine,* 73 (February 1894), 281.

Letter of 27 June 1870 to [Maria Ellen MacKaye].

Note: This is an entry in "The Contributors' Club" feature.

E 228
Barber, William. "Dr. Jackson's Discovery of Ether." *National Magazine,* 5 (October 1896), 46–58.

Undated letter to "Agassy" [Louis Agassiz] and partial facsimile of the manuscript, p. 52.

E 229
[Emerson, Edward Waldo]. "A Correspondence Between John Sterling and Ralph Waldo Emerson." *Atlantic Monthly Magazine,* 80 (July 1897), 14–35.

Reprinted as *A Correspondence Between John Sterling and Ralph Waldo Emerson* (A 46).

E 230
"Theodore Parker's Bettine. IV." *Boston Evening Transcript,* 12 July 1897, p. 6.

Various letters to [Rebecca Duncan].

E 231
Hale, Edward Everett. "James Russell Lowell and His Friends." *Outlook,* 59 (7 May 1898), 39–55.

Facsimiles letter of 13 December 1849 to Hale, p. 40. Reprinted in "Ralph Waldo Emerson," *Booklovers Magazine,* 1 (February 1903), 149–180 (in facsimile on pp. 155, 159).

E 232
Sutton, Henry S. "Emerson. Reminiscences of His Visits to Manchester." *Manchester City News,* 20 May 1899, p. 20.

Letter of 31 January [1848] to Sutton. Reprinted in Kenneth Walter Cameron, "Emerson, Thoreau, and the Poet Henry Sutton," *Emerson Society Quarterly,* no. 1 (4th Quarter 1955), 10–16.

E 233
Higginson, Thomas Wentworth. "Walks with Ellery Channing." *Atlantic Monthly Magazine,* 90 (July 1902), 27–34.

Unpublished journal material.

E 234
"Those Red-Eyed Men." *Atlantic Monthly Magazine,* 90 (July 1902), 139.

Letter of 26 May 1858.

Note: This is an entry in "The Contributors' Club" feature.

E 235
Cooke, George Willis. "Emerson as Missionary." *Christian Register,* 81 (10 July 1902), 808–809.

Letters of 29 July [1827] and 9 October 1827 to Ezra Stiles Gannett. Reprinted in Cooke, *Unitarianism in America* (D 170), p. 151n. (9 October 1827 letter only).

E 236
Cooke, George Willis. "Two Unpublished Letters by Ralph Waldo Emerson." *Poet-Lore,* 14 (October 1902), 104–108.

Letters of 5 October 1840 and 23 February 1842 to Eliza Thayer Clapp. Reprinted in Cooke, *An Historical and Biographical Introduction to Accompany* The Dial (D 166).

E 237
"Ralph Waldo Emerson." *Booklovers Magazine,* 1 (February 1903), 149–180.

Facsimiles manuscript letters of 13 December 1849 (pp. 155, 159), 28 December 1848 (pp. 159, 163, 166), and 17 March [1849] (pp. 166, 170, 174) to Edward Everett Hale, spaced throughout the articles in this special Emerson number.

E 238
Holls, Frederick William. "Correspondence Between Ralph Waldo Emerson and Herman Grimm." *Atlantic Monthly Magazine,* 91 (April 1903), 467–479.

Reprinted as *Correspondence Between Ralph Waldo Emerson and Herman Grimm* (A 49).

E 239
Conway, Moncure D. "The Ministry of Emerson." *Open Court,* 17 (May 1903), 257–264.

Letter of [4?] October 1838 to William Silsbee (pp. 260–261). Another version is in Conway, *Emerson at Home and Abroad* (D 119), pp. 209–211.

E 240
Sanborn, F. B. "Emerson and Contemporary Poets." *Critic,* 42 (May 1903), 413–416.

Letters of [3 October 1839], 27 October 1839, and [16 June 1840] to Samuel Gray Ward.

E 241
Sanford, Orlin M. "Ralph Waldo Emerson." *Pittsburgh Index,* no. 395 (2 May 1903), 8–11.

Various letters.

E 242
"Two Interesting Emerson Letters." *Book-Lover,* 4 (May–June 1903), 118.

Letter of 11 February [1875] to George W. Childs.

Note: The other letter is about Emerson.

E 243
Higginson, T. W. "Emerson as the Reformer." *Boston Daily Advertiser,* 23 May 1903, pp. 9, 16.

Letters of 16 May 1849 (E 221), pp. 9, 16, and 19 May 1849, p. 16, to Higginson.

E 244
Higginson, Thomas Wentworth. "The Personality of Emerson." *Outlook,* 74 (23 May 1903), 221–227.

Various letters. Partially reprinted from E 197.

E 245
Emerson, Edward W. "Ralph Waldo Emerson." *Bookman* [London], 24 (June 1903), 92–97.

Letter of 16 April 1813 to Mary Moody Emerson, pp. 92–94.

E 246
[Letter]. *Bookman* [New York], 17 (June 1903), 331.

Facsimiles letter of 5 March 1857 to Evert A. Duyckinck.

E 247
"Washington in Wartime." *Atlantic Monthly Magazine,* 94 (July 1904), 1–8.

E 248
"Three Corncord Letters." *Old Colony Naturalist,* Special Midsummer Number, 1904, 10–11.

Letter of 31 August 1859 to Benjamin Marston Watson (p. 10).

E 249
"Shakespeare." *Atlantic Monthly Magazine,* 94 (September 1904), 365–367.

Reprinted in *Miscellanies* (A 40.3), pp. 447–453.

E 250
"Country Life." *Atlantic Monthly Magazine,* 94 (November 1904), 594–604.

Reprinted in *Natural History of Intellect* (A 44.3), pp. 135–167.

E 251
Sanborn, F. B. "A Concord Note-Book. Sixth Paper. The Women of Concord—I." *Critic,* 48 (February 1906), 154–160.

Letter of 31 July 1829 to Mary Moody Emerson p. 159. Reprinted in Sanborn, *Recollections of Seventy Years* (D 184), II, 373–374.

E 252
Sanborn, F. B. "A Concord Note-Book. The Women of Concord—Margaret Fuller and Her Friends—II. Seventh Paper." *Critic,* 48 (March 1906), 251–257.

Letter of 23 July 1850 to Marcus Spring, pp. 254–255. Reprinted in Sanborn, *Recollections of Seventy Years* (D 184), II, 415–416.

E 253
"Father Taylor." *Atlantic Monthly Magazine,* 98 (August 1906), 177–181.

Edited by Edward Waldo Emerson.

Note: The first printing of this text; parts had been used previously in the lecture on "The Poet" (A 66.III) and in "Eloquence," *Letters and Social Aims* (A 34).

E 254
"Literary Notes and News." *Westminster Gazette,* 28 (7 August 1906), 3.

Letter of 3 May 1873 to Louise Mercer.

E 255
Ames, Joseph B. "Some Literary Autographs." *Critic*, 49 (September 1906), 232–241.

Letter of 30 September 1847 to Alexander Ireland, p. 235.

E 256
[Letter]. *Burlington Gazette* [Iowa], 9 November 1907.

Letter of 3 March 1867 to Ellen Emerson. *Not seen*. Partially reprinted in Thomas Hedge, "Charles Elliot Perkins," *Annals of Iowa*, 3d ser., 8 (April 1908), 372–373; reprinted in Hoeltje, "Ralph Waldo Emerson in Iowa" (E 258); Cunnnigham, *Family Letters* (D 212).

E 257
"Poem, Spoken Before the Phi Beta Kappa Society, August, 1834." *Phi Beta Kappa Key*, 1 (January 1913), 25–28.

Re-edited in Strauch, "Emerson's Phi Beta Kappa Poem" (E 283).

E 258
Hoeltje, Hubert H. "Ralph Waldo Emerson in Iowa." *Iowa Journal of History and Politics*, 25 (April 1927), 236–276.

Letters of 26 August 1856 to Austin Adams and 3 March 1867 to Ellen Emerson (E 256).

E 259
Williams, Stanley T. "Unpublished Letters of Emerson." *Journal of English and Germanic Philology*, 26 (October 1927), 475–484.

E 260
Dyson, Walter. "What Books to Read." *Howard University Studies in History*, no. 9 (November 1928), 1–14.

Reprinted from the 11 January 1872 *New York Tribune*.

E 261
Cutler, Dorothy B. "An Unpublished Letter of Emerson." *Yale University Library Gazette*, 4 (July 1929), 15–17.

Letter of 21 September 1869 to W. J. Linton, p. 17.

E 262
McDowell, Tremaine. "A Freshman Poem by Emerson." *PMLA*, 45 (March 1930), 326–329.

"Song written for the Supper of the Freshman Class, at the close of the College Year 1818," edited from Josiah Quincy's transcript.

E 263
Hoeltje, Hubert H. "Ralph Waldo Emerson in Minnesota." *Minnesota History*, 11 (June 1930), 145–159.

Letter of 5 June 1870 to J. Fletcher Williams.

E 264
Hicks, Granville. "Letters to William Francis Channing." *American Literature*, 2 (November 1930), 294–298.

Letter of 1 September 1853 to Channing, p. 296.

E 265
Morse, Stearns. "An Emerson Letter." *Harvard Alumni Bulletin,* 33 (15 January 1931), 480–482.

Letter of 25 July 1859 to George Field, p. 480.

E 266
F., C. A. "9 to 4:30." *Washington Daily News,* 9 May 1931, p. 3.

Letter of 10 January 1863 to Salmon P. Chase. Reprinted in Carlos Baker, "The Road to Concord: Another Milestone in the Whitman-Emerson Friendship," *Princeton University Library Chronicle,* 7 (April 1946), 108.

E 267
Hoeltje, Hubert H. "Emerson in Virginia." *New England Quarterly,* 5 (October 1932), 753–768.

Letter of 21 December 1875 to Walter S. Perry et al., p. 754.

E 268
Meeks, Leslie H. "The Lyceum in the Early West." *Indiana Magazine of History,* 29 (June 1933), 87–95.

Letter of 3 November 1859 to Joseph Gilbert, p. 90.

E 269
"An Emerson Letter." *Athenæum Bulletin* [Providence Athenæum], no. 4 (March 1934), 1–2.

Letter of 16 September 1856 to Cyrus A. Bartol, p. 1.

E 270
Roberts, Arthur J. "Emerson's Visits to Waterville College." *Colby Mercury,* 5 (1 April 1934), 41–45.

Letter of 9 November 1855, p. 45.

E 271
Silver, Rollo G. "Mr. Emerson Appeals to Boston." *American Book Collector,* 6 (May–June 1935), 209–219.

Reprinted anti-slavery lecture from 26 January 1855 *Boston Daily Evening Traveller.*

E 272
Allen, Adèle. "The Boltwood Home. Memories of Amherst Friends and Neighbors." *Amherst Graduates' Quarterly,* 26 (August 1937), 297–307.

Letter of 3 September 1821 to George Shepard, pp. 304–305.

E 273
"Three Letters of Ralph Waldo Emerson, Etc." *Chronicle,* no. 229 (June 1939), 41–43.

Letters of 24 December 1851 to J. R. Wills, pp. 42–43, and 25 January 1879 to H. D. Parker, p. 43.

E 274
Richmond, Mrs. Henry L. "Ralph Waldo Emerson in Florida." *Florida Historical Quarterly,* 18 (October 1939), 75–93.

Prints Emerson's manuscript journal kept while at St. Augustine during January–March 1827, including his poem of farewell to that city, pp. 84–93 (facsimile of the poem facing p. 75). Re-edited in *JMN*.

E 275
Simison, Barbara Damon. "The Letters of Ralph Waldo Emerson: Addenda." *Modern Language Notes,* 55 (June 1940), 425–427.

Letters of 12 March 1841 to an anonymous autograph collector and 14 April 1851 to Emily Drury.

E 276
Stearns, A. Warren. "Four Emerson Letters to Dr. Daniel Parker." *Tuftonian,* 1 (November 1940), 6–9.

E 277
Randel, William Peirce. "A Late Emerson Letter." *American Literature,* 12 (January 1941), 496–497.

Letter of 26 December 1877 to J. K. Hosmer.

E 278
Strauch, Carl F. "The Background for Emerson's 'Boston Hymn.'" *American Literature,* 14 (March 1942), 36–47.

Letters of 28 December 1862 and 10 December 1863 to Mrs. George L. Stearns, pp. 40, 41.

E 279
Strauch, Carl F. "Emerson at Lehigh." *Lehigh Alumni Bulletin,* 29 (April 1942), 15–16.

Letters of 18 October [1867] and [28 October 1867] to Benjamin Norton.

E 280
"The Warren Collection." *Bostonia,* 20 (March 1947), 12–13.

Facsimiles letter of 15 October [1875] to William F. Warren, p. 13.

E 281
Davis, N. C. "Emerson and Ohio. A New Emerson Letter." *Ohio State Archaeological and Historical Society Quarterly,* 58 (January 1949), 101–102.

Letter of 26 February 1852 to [Sarah Clark Vaughan?].

E 282
Eidson, John Olin. "Two Unpublished Letters of Emerson." *American Literature,* 21 (November 1949), 335–338.

Letters of 31 January 1854 to Francis Hall and 8 November 1869 to General Ambrose Burnside.

E 283
Strauch, Carl F. "Emerson's Phi Beta Kappa Poem." *New England Quarterly,* 23 (March 1950), 65–90.

First complete printing (from Emerson's manuscript) of "Poem, Spoken Before the Phi Beta Kappa Society, August, 1834" (see E 257).

E 284
Haviland, Thomas P. "Two Emerson Letters." *American Literature*, 23 (March 1951), 127–128.

Letters of 11 December 1858 and 29 January 1859 to the Auburndale, Massachusetts, Lyceum.

E 285
Cameron, Kenneth Walter. "A Sheaf of Emerson Letters." *American Literature*, 24 (January 1953), 476–480.

E 286
Fish, Howard M., Jr. "Five Emerson Letters." *Amercian Literature*, 27 (March 1955), 25–30.

E 287
Naylor, Louise Hastings. "Emerson and an Italian Carriage Driver in 1833." *Emerson Society Quarterly*, no. 1 (4th Quarter 1955), 3–4.

Facsimile, with transcription, of the driver's holograph agreement to carry Emerson and his companions, signed by Emerson and others.

E 288
Cameron, Kenneth Walter. "Some Emerson Letters—Ungathered and Migrant." *Emerson Society Quarterly*, no. 3 (2d Quarter 1956), 4–6.

Letter of 13 February 1877 to [James R. Osgood and Company] and text of an autograph document concerning copyright, dated 6 June 1852, signed by Emerson and others.

E 289
Strauch, Carl F. "Emerson's 'New England Capitalist.'" *Harvard Library Bulletin*, 10 (Spring 1956), 245–253.

First printing, from Emerson's manuscript, of a poem written about 1843.

E 290
McDermott, John Francis. "Emerson at St. Louis, 1852: Unpublished Letters and Telegrams." *Emerson Society Quarterly*, no. 6 (1st Quarter 1957), 7–9.

E 291
Mathews, J. Chesley. "Emerson's Translation of Dante's *Vita Nuova*." *Harvard Library Bulletin*, 11 (Spring 1957), 208–244.

Concluded in the autumn number. Reprinted as *Dante's* Vita Nuova (A 65).

E 292
Mathews, J. Chesley. "Emerson's Translation of Dante's *Vita Nuova*." *Harvard Library Bulletin*, 11 (Autumn 1957), 346–362.

Concluded from the spring number. Reprinted as *Dante's* Vita Nuova (A 65).

E 293
Strauch, Carl F. "The Importance of Emerson's Skeptical Mood." *Harvard Library Bulletin*, 11 (Winter 1957), 117–139.

First printing, from Emerson's manuscript, of "The Skeptic" (1842).

E 294
Cameron, Kenneth Walter. "A Garland of Emerson Letters." *Emerson Society Quarterly,*
no. 10 (1st Quarter 1958), 32–41.

E 295
Gronewald, Benjamin F. "Emerson at Middletown in Connecticut." *Emerson Society
Quarterly,* no. 11 (2d Quarter 1958), 55–56.

Letter of 10 June 1846 to Daniel Martindale, p. 56.

E 296
Rusk, Ralph L. "Emerson in Salem, 1849." *Essex Institute Historical Collections,* 94
(July 1958), 194–195.

Letter of 12 January 1849 to Nathaniel Hawthorne, p. 194.

E 297
Wright, Nathalia. "Ralph Waldo Emerson and Horatio Greenough." *Harvard Library
Bulletin,* 12 (Winter 1958), 91–116.

Various letters.

E 298
White, William. "Two Unpublished Emerson Letters." *American Literature,* 31 (November 1959), 334–336.

Letters of 14 April 1843 and 26 December 1875 to Elizabeth Palmer Peabody.

E 299
Hopkins, Vivian C. "Two Unpublished Emerson Letters." *New England Quarterly,* 33
(December 1960), 502–506.

Letters of 19 October 1855 to George Putnam and 10 December 1857 to Caroline Dall.

E 300
Freniere, Emil A. "Emerson and Parker Letters in the Jackson Papers." *Emerson Society Quarterly,* no. 22 (1st Quarter 1961), 46–48.

Letters of 29 March 1851 to Henry James, Sr., and 26 August 1856 to Charles Sumner.

E 301
Cameron, Kenneth Walter. "Emerson's Walden Woodlots and the Fitchburg Railroad."
Emerson Society Quarterly, no. 22 (1st Quarter 1961), 67–68.

Transcription of a deed of sale, dated 30 April 1849, co-signed by Emerson.

E 302
Cameron, Kenneth Walter. "A Bundle of Emerson Letters." *Emerson Society Quarterly,*
no. 22 (1st Quarter 1961), 95–97.

Letters of 20 April 1845 to John S. Dwight, [8 October 1845] to Thoreau, and 16 March
1860 to W. D. Ticknor.

E 303
Cameron, Kenneth Walter. "The First Appearance of Emerson's 'Boston Hymn.'" *Emerson Society Quarterly,* no. 22 (1st Quarter 1961), 97–101.

Letter of [23 December 1862] to John S. Dwight, p. 97.

E 304
White, William. "Thirty-Three Unpublished Letters of Ralph Waldo Emerson." *American Literature,* 33 (May 1961), 159–178.

E 305
Murphy, Walter H. "A Letter by Emerson." *American Literature,* 36 (March 1964), 64–65.

Letter of 17 May 1870 to J. R. Leeson.

E 306
Stevens, David M. "Emerson on the Saxon Race: A Manuscript Fragment." *Emerson Society Quarterly,* no. 47 (2d Quarter 1967), 103–105.

Transcription and facsimile reproduction of an undated manuscript fragment.

E 307
Lindquist, Vernon R. "Unpublished Emerson Letter Reveals a Bangor Friendship." *University of Maine Studies* [*A Handful of Spice: A Miscellany of Maine Literature and History,* ed. Richard S. Sprague], 2d ser., no. 88 (1968), 155–157.

Letter of 1 March 1847 to William Emerson (a Bangor merchant).

E 308
Strauch, Carl F. "Emerson Rejects Reed and Hails Thoreau." *Harvard Library Bulletin,* 16 (July 1968), 257–273.

First complete printing, from Emerson's manuscript, of "S[ampson]. R[eed]."

E 309
Cameron, Kenneth Walter. "Emerson Applies for Church Membership in 1865." *American Transcendental Quarterly,* no. 1 (1st Quarter 1969), 103.

Letter of 30 April 1865 to John Brown, Jr.

E 310
Spiller, Robert E. "Emerson and Humboldt." *American Literature,* 42 (January 1971), 546–548.

Letter of 28 September 1869 to Robert C. Waterston, pp. 547–548.

E 311
Cummins, Roger Wm. "Unpublished Emerson Letters to Louis Prang and Whittier." *American Literature,* 43 (May 1971), 257–259.

Letters of September 1868 to Prang and 10 April 1875 and 24 August 1876 [i.e., 1860] to Whittier.

E 312
Maxfield-Miller, Elizabeth. "Emerson and Elizabeth of Concord." *Harvard Library Bulletin,* 19 (July 1971), 290–306.

Prints a manuscript (not in Emerson's hand) containing comments on and a poem about Elizabeth Hoar, both culled from his journals, pp. 294–302.

E 313
Mignon, Charles W. "Emerson to Chapman: Four Letters About Publishing." *ESQ: A Journal of the American Renaissance,* 19 (4th Quarter 1973), 224–230.

E 314
White, William. "Emerson as Editor: A Letter to Benjamin F. Presbury." *American Notes & Queries,* 12 (December 1973), 59–61.

Letter of 12 November 1841.

E 315
Dedmond, Francis B. "'Croaking at booksellers': An Unpublished Emerson Letter." *American Literature,* 49 (November 1977), 414–417.

Letter of 3 May 1843 to C. P. Cranch.

E 316
Hirsh, John C. "Ralph Waldo Emerson, Mrs. Bancroft, and Lady Morgan in 1848." *Notes and Queries,* n.s. 25 (June 1978), 228–229.

Letter of 5 March 1848 to Mrs. George Bancroft.

F. Books Edited by Emerson

First American and English publication of books edited by Emerson, arranged chronologically.

F 1 CRITICAL AND MISCELLANEOUS ESSAYS
1838–1839

CRITICAL AND MISCELLANEOUS | ESSAYS, | BY | THOMAS CARLYLE. | VOLUME I. [II.] [III.] [IV.] | [rule] | BOSTON: | JAMES MUNROE AND COMPANY. | 1838 [1838] [1839] [1839].

Edited by Emerson, with the assistance of Henry S. McKean, Ellis Gray Loring, and Charles Stearns Wheeler (see *CEC*, pp. 21–24). "Advertisement," signed 'R.W.E.' and dated '*Concord, June* 24, 1838.', I, [iii]–IV. 1,000 copies printed by the Cambridge Press, Metcalf, Torry, and Ballou. Vols. I–II announced in *Christian Register*, 14 July 1838, p. 111; advertised in *Boston Daily Advertiser*, 10 July 1838, p. 3. Vols. III–IV announced in *Christian Register*, 29 June 1839, p. 103; advertised in *Boston Daily Advertiser*, 1 July 1839, p. 3. Price, $2.50 per volume. *Locations:* JM, MWA, NN.

Note: English issue of American sheets with cancel title leaf: 'CRITICAL AND MIS-CELLANEOUS | ESSAYS: | COLLECTED AND REPUBLISHED: | BY THOMAS CARLYLE. | [rule] | IN FOUR VOLUMES. | VOL. I. [II.] [III.] [IV.] | [rule] | LONDON: | JAMES FRASER, 215 REGENT STREET. | [rule] | M.DCCC.XXXIX.'. Carlyle purchased 260 bound copies from Munroe for sale in London (see *CEC*, p. 23). *Location:* TxCM.

F 2 ESSAYS AND POEMS
1839

ESSAYS AND POEMS: | BY | JONES VERY. | [rule] | [rule] | BOSTON: | CHARLES C. LITTLE AND JAMES BROWN. | [rule] | MDCCCXXXIX.

Edited by Emerson. On 9 July 1839, Emerson wrote Margaret Fuller "I am editing Very's little book" (*L*, II, 209). 500 copies printed 5 July 1839 by Dutton & Wentworth; 350 were bound and 150 left in sheets (Account Books [MH]). Advertised in *Christian Register*, 7 September 1839, p. 133. Price: cloth or boards, 75¢. *Locations:* JM, MH.

Note one: In an accounting to Very in April 1841, Emerson reported that 38 bound copies and 150 copies in sheets were still in stock (Account Books [MH]).

Note two: A facsimile reprinting has been noted: New York: Arno, 1972 (ScU).

F 3 PAST AND PRESENT
1843

PAST AND PRESENT. | BY | THOMAS CARLYLE. | [gothic] Ernst ist das leben. | SCHILLER. | [rule] | BOSTON: | CHARLES C. LITTLE AND JAMES BROWN. | MDCCCXLIII.

697

Edited by Emerson (see *CEC,* pp. 342–343). "Amercian Editor's Notice," signed and dated 'CONCORD, MASS. | MAY 1, 1843.', p. [iii]. 1,500 copies printed by Freeman and Bolles, Washington Street, Boston. On 26 May 1843, Emerson left a copy for sale with a local bookseller (Account Books [MH]). Price: boards, 75¢. *Locations:* CtY, JM, MWA, NN.

F4 MEMOIRS OF MARGARET FULLER OSSOLI
    1852

MEMOIRS | OF | MARGARET FULLER OSSOLI. | VOL. I. [II.] | four lines of verse] | BEN JONSON. | [seven lines of verse] | LEONARDO DA VINCI. | BOSTON: | PHILLIPS, SAMPSON AND COMPANY. | M DCCC LII.

Written and edited by Emerson, William Henry Channing, and James Freeman Clarke. Stereotyped by Hobart & Robbins, New England Type and Stereotype Foundry, Boston. Emerson contributed "IV. Visits to Concord," "V. Conversations in Boston," and (with Channing) "VIII. Europe," I, 199–316, 317–351, II, 169–330. *Locations:* JM, MH.

Note one: Channing's marked copy of the *Memoirs* (MiD) attributes sections IV and V to Emerson, and notes that section VIII was done "chiefly" by himself, especially pp. 267–330. Channing also wrote in his copy of the *Memoirs:* "The plan of the book,—the division into parts or chapters,—the selection of mottoes,—the filling up of the spaces between the extracts, the interweaving of the whole,—and indeed all parts of it, not specially referred to others, are the work of W.H.C." The editors' names did not appear on the title page until the 1860 printing.

Note two: There were five printings in 1852 and the following reprintings: Phillips, Sampson, 1857; Boston: Brown, Taggard and Chase; New York: Sheldon; Philadelphia: J. B. Lippincott; London: Sampson Low, Son, 1860, 1862; New York: Tribune Association, 1869; Boston: Roberts Brothers, 1874, 1875, 1881, 1884. *Locations:* JM, MNatM (1862).

Note three: English edition: 'MEMOIRS | OF | MARGARET FULLER OSSOLI. | IN THREE VOLUMES. | VOL. I. [II.] [III.] | [four lines of verse] | BEN JONSON. | [seven lines of verse] | LEONARDO DA VINCI. | LONDON: | RICHARD BENTLEY, NEW BURLINGTON STREET, | [gothic] Publisher in Ordinary to Her Majesty. | 1852.' (JM).

Note four: Portions of Emerson's section of the *Memoirs* are printed in 'SUMMER ON THE LAKES. | WITH AUTOBIOGRAPHY. | BY | MARGARET FULLER OSSOLI. | [gothic] And Memoir, | BY | RALPH WALDO EMERSON, W. H. CHANNING, | AND OTHERS. | LONDON: | WARD AND LOCK, FLEET STREET. | MDCCCLXI.' (JM).

Note five: German edition, abridged: '[all gothic except date] Margarethe Fuller-Ossoli. | [wavy rule] | Ein amerifanisches Frauenbild | von | Ernestine Castell. | [ornamental rule] | Berlin, 1866. | Verlag von Reinhold Schlingmann.' (BL).

Note six: A facsimile reprinting has been noted: New York: Burt Franklin, 1973 (ScU).

Note seven: For full bibliographical information, see Joel Myerson, *Margaret Fuller: A Descriptive Bibliography* (Pittsburgh: University of Pittsburgh Press, 1978).

F5 EXCURSIONS
    1863

EXCURSIONS. | BY | HENRY D. THOREAU. | AUTHOR OF "WALDEN," AND "A WEEK

ON THE CONCORD AND | MERRIMACK RIVERS." | [publisher's logo] | BOSTON: | TICKNOR AND FIELDS. | 1863.

Edited by Emerson. "Biographical Sketch," unsigned, pp. [7]–33. *Reprint.* See E 160. Stereotyped and 1,500 copies printed 10 October 1863 by H. O. Houghton, Cambridge, Mass. Advertised as "Field Notes" and as "In Press," in *Atlantic,* 12 (February 1863), advertisements. Announced as in press, in *American Literary Gazette and Publishers' Circular,* 1 (15 September 1863), 371, 377. Advertised for autumn publication, in *Atlantic,* 12 (October 1863), wrappers; in *Boston Daily Advertiser,* 14 October 1863. Price, $1.00. *Locations:* JM, MH, NN.

Note one: Numerous reprintings through 1894, when the contents of *Excursions* were completely rearranged to include other writings by Thoreau as part of publication in the *Riverside Edition* of Thoreau's writings.

Note two: For full bibliographical information, see Raymond R. Borst, *Henry David Thoreau: A Descriptive Bibliography* (Pittsburgh: University of Pittsburgh Press, 1982).

F 6 LETTERS TO VARIOUS PERSONS
  1865

LETTERS | TO VARIOUS PERSONS. | BY | HENRY D. THOREAU, | AUTHOR OF "A WEEK ON THE CONCORD AND MERRIMACK RIVERS," | "WALDEN," ETC., ETC. | [publisher's logo] | BOSTON: | TICKNOR AND FIELDS. | 1865.

Edited by Emerson. "Editor's Notice," signed and dated '12 May, 1865.', p. [iii]. 2,100 copies printed by Welch, Bigelow, & Co., University Press, Cambridge, Mass. Advertised in *Boston Evening Transcript,* 22 July 1865; in *American Literary Gazette and Publishers' Circular,* 5 (1 August 1865), 149. Copyright, 14 August 1865. Price, $1.50. *Locations:* JM, MH, NN.

Note one: Numerous reprintings through 1894, when a more complete edition was prepared by F. B. Sanborn (see D 149) for publication in the *Riverside Edition* of Thoreau's writings.

Note two: For full bibliographical information, see Borst, *Henry David Thoreau: A Descriptive Bibliography.*

F 7 PARNASSUS
  1875

PARNASSUS | EDITED BY | RALPH WALDO EMERSON | [two lines of verse from Gascoigne] | [publisher's logo] | BOSTON: | JAMES R. OSGOOD AND COMPANY, | (LATE TICKNOR, AND FIELDS, AND FIELDS, OSGOOD, AND CO.) | 1875.

534 pp. Two editions noted; see *Note one* below. Edited by Emerson, with the assistance of Ellen Emerson and Edith Emerson Forbes. "Preface," pp. iii–xi. Listed in the publisher's records as included in the "Holiday," "Household," and "Library" editions series. Electrotyped and printed by Rand, Avery & Co., Boston. Emerson's contract with Osgood, dated 1 November 1874, called for him to retain copyright and pay for and retain the plates. Advertised as "Ready Tomorrow," in *Boston Daily Advertiser,* 18 December 1874. Listed in *Publishers' Weekly,* 6 (26 December 1874), 692. Advertised "with numerous corrections and revisions," in *Publishers' Weekly,* 7 (30 January 1875), 98. Copyright, 14 December 1874. Inscribed copy: 1st ed., InU (21 December 1874).

Prices: cloth, $4.00; half calf, $7.50; morocco, $10.00. Royalty, 80¢ per copy after the first 200. *Locations:* InU (1st), JM (both), MH (both).

Note one: Two editions have been noted, easily distinguished as follows: First Edition: "Index of Authors" on pp. xxv–xlii; Second Edition: "Index of Authors" on pp. xxv–xxxiv. Textual changes are also present throughout the selections in the volumes. The second edition plates were used for all subsequent reprintings, including modern facsimile reprintings.

Note two: Emerson's contract was renewed with Houghton, Osgood on 24 August 1878, and with Houghton, Mifflin on 1 May 1880. A codicil to the 24 August 1878 contract called for Emerson's royalty to be 40¢ per copy on the new format of *Parnassus* retailing for $2.00.

Note three: The following reprints have been noted: James R. Osgood, 1876, 1878; Houghton, Osgood, 1880; Houghton, Mifflin, 1881, 1882, 1884, [n.d.]. *Locations:* JM, MiU (1878), MH (1881), Ia (1882).

Note four: Approximately 8,300 copies of *Parnassus*, in all formats, were sold between 1874 and 1923.

Note five: The following facsimile reprintings have been noted: New York: Garrett, 1969 (ICarbS); Freeport, N.Y.: Books for Libraries, [1970] (KyU); New York: MSS Information Corporation, [1972] (OCIJC).

G. Reprinted Material in Books and Pamphlets

Reprinted prose, poetry, and letters by Emerson in books and pamphlets through 1882, the year of Emerson's death, arranged chronologically. All material in this section has had prior book publication. All material is signed unless otherwise indicated.

G 1 THE BIBLICAL ASSISTANT AND BOOK OF PRACTICAL PIETY
    1841

THE | BIBLICAL ASSISTANT, | AND | BOOK OF PRACTICAL PIETY; | DESIGNED FOR THE USE OF YOUNG PERSONS, TEACHERS, AND | UPPER CLASSES IN SABBATH SCHOOLS. | EDITED BY THE REV. D. G. GOYDER, | GLASGOW. | LONDON:—J. S. HODSON, 112, FLEET STREET; | W. NEWBERY, CHENIES STREET, BEDFORD SQUARE; | MANCHESTER:—EDWARD BAYLIS; | LIVERPOOL:—TAYLOR & SONS; GLASGOW:—S. & A. GOYDER; | BOSTON, U. S.:—OTIS CLAPP. | MDCCCXLI.

"The Religious Philosophy of Nature," pp. [387]–429. Reprint of *Nature*. See A 3.

Location: PBa.

Note: Kenneth Walter Cameron feels that this book was issued in parts, and that the part containing *Nature* was released in December 1840, but he has been unable to locate a copy or reviews of it (see "Emerson's *Nature* and British Swedenborgianism (1840–1841)," *Emerson Society Quarterly*, no. 30 [1st Quarter 1963], p. 13).

G 2 READINGS IN AMERICAN POETRY
    1843

READINGS | IN | AMERICAN POETRY. | BY | RUFUS W. GRISWOLD, | EDITOR OF THE "POETS AND POETRY OF AMERICA," ETC. | [six lines of verse from "*American Prospects* —1763"] | [gothic] New-York: | JOHN C. RIKER, ANN STREET. | 1843.

"Good-Bye, Proud World," pp. 176–177. See E 14; A 18.

Location: MB.

Note: Reprinted with Emerson's poem on the same pages: 'READINGS | IN | AMERI-CAN POETRY. | [gothic] For the Use of Schools. | BY RUFUS W. GRISWOLD. | [six lines of verse] | *American Prospects* —1763. | [gothic] New-York: | JOHN C. RIKER, ANN STREET. | 1843.' (JM).

G 3 THE ILLUSTRATED BOOK OF CHRISTIAN BALLADS
    1844

[all within an ornate frame in ornate lettering] THE | ILLUSTRATED | BOOK OF | CHRIS-TIAN BALLADS | AND | [gothic] OTHER POEMS. | [lyre] | EDITED BY | REV. RUFUS W. GRISWOLD. | [ornate rule] | PHILADELPHIA: | LINDSAY & BLAKISTON, | CHESTNUT STREET.

"Good-bye, Proud World," p. 55. Unsigned but identified as Emerson's in the table of contents. See E 14; A 18.

703

Location: TxU.

G 4 ORACLES FROM THE POETS
1844

[all within a single-rule scalloped frame with an ornate design in each corner] ORA-CLES FROM THE POETS: | A FANCIFUL DIVERSION | FOR | THE DRAWING-ROOM. | BY | CAROLINE GILMAN. | [four lines of verse] | *Dryden's and Symmon's Virgil.* | [five lines from *Macbeth*] | NEW YORK & LONDON: | WILEY AND PUTNAM. | M.DCCC.XLIV.

"When the south wind in May days," p. 116. From "The Humble-Bee." See E 13; A 18.
   "Thou seest only what is fair," p. 230. From "The Humble-Bee." See E 13; A 18.

Location: MH.

G 5 THE POETRY OF FLOWERS
1844

[all within a single-rule frame] THE | POETRY OF FLOWERS. | [gothic] Original and Selected. | [four lines of verse from Pope] | EDITED BY | RUFUS W. GRISWOLD. | [rule] | [gothic] Philadelphia: | PUBLISHED BY JOHN LOCKEN, | *No.* 311 *Market Street.* | ·········· | 1844.

"The Rhodora," p. 62. See E 15; A 18.

Location: MB.

G 6 THE WAIF
1845

THE WAIF: | A | COLLECTION OF POEMS. | [wavy rule] | [four lines of verse] | THE FAERIE QUEEN. | [rule] | CAMBRIDGE: | PUBLISHED BY JOHN OWEN. | [wavy rule] | 1845.

Edited by Henry Wadsworth Longfellow. Cloth, boards, or wrappers.

"Each in All," pp. 73–75. Unsigned but identified as Emerson's in the table of contents. See E 12; A 18.

Location: JM.

G 7 A BOOK OF HYMNS FOR PUBLIC AND PRIVATE DEVOTION
1846

A BOOK | OF | HYMNS | FOR | PUBLIC AND PRIVATE DEVOTION. | [rule] | CAM-BRIDGE: | METCALF AND COMPANY, | PRINTERS TO THE UNIVERSITY. | 1846.

Compiled by Samuel Johnson and Samuel Longfellow.

"The House Our Fathers Built to God," Hymn No. 423. See D 3; A 18.4.

Location: MB.

G 8 THE PIONEER
1846

THE PIONEER: | OR | LEAVES FROM AN EDITOR'S PORTFOLIO. | [wavy rule] | By HENRY CLAPP, Jr. | [wavy rule] | [four lines of prose] | Emma C. Embury. | [rule] | LYNN: | PRINTED BY J. B. TOLMAN, 12 EXCHANGE-ST. | [rule] | 1846.

"Each in All," pp. 75–76. See E 12; A 18.
  "The Lover of Nature," pp. 139–140. From "Wood-Notes." See E 22; A 18.

Location: ScU.

G 9 POETRY FOR HOME AND SCHOOL
1846

POETRY | FOR | HOME AND SCHOOL. | FIRST AND SECOND PARTS. | [rule] | SE-LECTED BY THE AUTHOR OF "THEORY OF TEACHING," "EDWARD'S | FIRST LES-SONS IN GRAMMAR," "FIRST LESSONS IN GEOMETRY," | AND "OLYMPIC GAMES." | [rule] | SECOND EDITION. | BOSTON: | PUBLISHED BY S. G. SIMPKINS. | 1846.

Edited by Anna Cabot (Jackson) Lowell.

"The Forerunners," Part I, pp. 239–240. See D 15; A 18.

Location: RPB.

Note one: The first edition does not contain anything by Emerson.

Note two: Reprinted, with Emerson's poem on the same pages: 'GLEANINGS | FROM | THE POETS, | FOR | HOME AND SCHOOL. | SELECTED BY THE AUTHOR OF | "THEORY OF TEACHING,"—"ELEMENTS OF ASTRONOMY, | OR THE WORLD AS IT IS, AND AS IT | APPEARS,"—&c., &c. | A NEW EDITION—ENLARGED. | BOSTON: | CROSBY, NICHOLS, LEE, AND COMPANY, | 117 Washington Street. | 1860.' (ScU).

Note three: Reprinted again, with Emerson's poem on the same pages: 'GLEAN-INGS . . . THE AUTHOR OF | "THEORY OF TEACHING," "ELEMENTS OF ASTRONOMY, OR THE | WORLD AS IT IS, AND AS IT APPEARS," ETC., ETC. | A NEW EDITION, EN-LARGED. | BOSTON: | CROSBY AND NICHOLS, | 117 Washington Street. | 1862.' (DLC).

G 10 VOICES OF THE TRUE-HEARTED
1846

VOICES | OF | THE TRUE-HEARTED. | [two lines of verse] | Festus. | PHILADELPHIA: | FOR SALE BY J. MILLER M'KIM, NO. 31 NORTH FIFTH STREET, | MERRIHEW & THOMPSON, PRINTERS. | 1846.

"Heroism," pp. [113]–117. See A 10.

Location: TxU.

G 11 THE ESTRAY
1847

THE ESTRAY: | A | COLLECTION OF POEMS. | [wavy rule] | [five lines of verse] | JOHN MINSHEW. | [rule] | BOSTON: | WILLIAM D. TICKNOR & CO. | 1847.

Edited by Henry Wadsworth Longfellow. Cloth, boards, or wrappers.

"The Problem," pp. 54–57. Unsigned. See E 18; A 18.

Location: TxU.

G 12 THE PROSE WRITERS OF AMERICA
1847

[all within a double-rule frame] THE | PROSE WRITERS | OF | AMERICA. | WITH | A
SURVEY OF THE HISTORY, CONDITION, AND PROSPECTS OF | AMERICAN LITERA-
TURE. | BY | RUFUS WILMOT GRISWOLD. | ILLUSTRATED WITH PORTRAITS FROM
ORIGINAL PICTURES. | PHILADELPHIA: | CAREY AND HART. | 1847.

"Beauty. From Nature," p. 442. See A 3.
  "Poetry and Nature. From Literary Ethics," pp. 442–443. See A 8.
  "The Power of Love. From an Essay on Love," p. 443. See A 10.
  "Genius. From the Method of Nature," p. 443. See A 11.
  "The Compensation of Calamity. From an Essay on Compensation," p. 444. See A 10.
  "Travelling. From Essay on Self-Reliance," pp. 444–445. See A 10.
  "Stateliness and Courtesy. From an Essay on Manners," p. 445. See A 16.
  "Truth and Tenderness. From an Essay on Friendship," p. 446. See A 10.

Location: ScU.

G 13 THE SIBYL
1848

[all within a single-rule frame with floral designs in each corner] THE SIBYL, | OR, | [two
lines in ornate lettering] NEW | ORACLES FROM THE POETS. | BY | CAROLINE GIL-
MAN, | [three lines of Gilman's books] | [five lines from Mrs. Brooks] | [four lines from
Cowper] | NEW YORK: | WILEY AND PUTNAM, 161 BROADWAY. | [rule] | 1848.

Epigrams from Emerson, pp. [267], 272. From "The Apology" (A 18) and "Woodnotes"
(A 18).

Location: RPB.

G 14 THE GOLDEN PRESENT
1849

[all within a single-rule frame] THE | GOLDEN PRESENT, | A | GIFT | FOR | [ornate
lettering] ALL SEASONS. | EDITED BY | MRS. J. THAYER. | [rule] | NASHUA, N.H. |
PUBLISHED BY J. BUFFUM. | 1849.

"Beauty," pp. 33–34. From "Love." See A 10.
  "Love," pp. 36–39. See A 10.

Location: RPB.

Note: The following reprintings have been noted: Worcester: S. A. Howland, 1849;
Nashua, N.H.: J. Buffum, 1850; Worcester: S. A. Howland, 1851; Worcester: S. A.
Howland, 1852; Boston: J. Buffum, 1853; Boston: J. Buffum, [n.d.] (all RPB).

G 15 THE ROSEMARY
1849

THE | ROSEMARY, | A COLLECTION | OF | SACRED AND RELIGIOUS POETRY, | FROM THE | ENGLISH AND AMERICAN POETS, | WITH | ELEGANT ILLUSTRATIONS. | [wavy rule] | [two lines of verse] | Sʜᴀᴋsᴘᴇᴀʀᴇ. | [wavy rule] | PHILADELPHIA: | LINDSAY AND BLAKISTON.

"Good-bye, Proud World," pp. 90–91. See E 14; A 18.

Location: MB.

G 16 THE BOSTON BOOK
1850

THE | BOSTON BOOK. | BEING SPECIMENS OF | METROPOLITAN LITERATURE. | BOSTON: | TICKNOR, REED, AND FIELDS. | MDCCCL.

"Nature," pp. [210]–216. See A 16.
   "Concord Monument. On the Completion of the Monument at Concord, April, 1836," p. [333]. See A 4; A 18.4.

Location: JM.

G 17 THE LIVING AUTHORS OF AMERICA
1850

THE | LIVING AUTHORS | OF | AMERICA. | [wavy rule] | [gothic] First Series. | [wavy rule] | BY | THOMAS POWELL, | AUTHOR OF "THE LIVING AUTHORS OF ENGLAND," | &c., &c. | [rule] | NEW YORK: | STRINGER AND TOWNSEND, | 222 BROADWAY | [rule] | 1850.

Letters of [28 July 1838] and [8 October 1838] to Henry Ware, Jr., pp. 71–75. See D 16.

Location: JM.

G 18 THE PRESENT
1850

THE PRESENT, | OR A | GIFT FOR THE TIMES. | [rule] | EDITED BY F. A. MOORE. | [rule] | [two lines of verse] | MANCHESTER, N.H.: | ROBERT MOORE. | 1850.

Various selections under the titles "Conformity," "Philanthropy," "Independence," "Friends," and "Sincerity," pp. 12–13, 77–79, 106, 113–115, 173–175.

Location: DLC.

G 19 COMPARATIVE PSYCHOLOGY AND UNIVERSAL ANALOGY
1851

COMPARATIVE PSYCHOLOGY | AND | UNIVERSAL ANALOGY. | VOL. I. | VEGETABLE PORTRAITS OF CHARACTER, | COMPILED FROM VARIOUS SOURCES, WITH ORIGI-

NAL ADDITIONS. | [rule] | BY | M. EDGEWORTH LAZARUS, M.D. | [four lines of verse from Emerson] | [one line of prose] | ALPHONSE CONSTANT. | NEW YORK: | FOWLERS & WELLS, PUBLISHERS, | CLINTON HALL, 131 NASSAU STREET. | 1851.

Title page motto. From "The Informing Spirit." See A 10.5; A 18.16.
  "Prelude of Mottoes," p. [1]. From "Bacchus" and "Woodnotes." See A 18.

Location: MH.

G 20 MEMORY AND HOPE
1851

MEMORY AND HOPE. | BOSTON: | TICKNOR, REED, AND FIELDS. | M DCCC LI.

"Dirge," pp. 237–239. See A 18.

Location: MH.

G 21 GARDEN WALKS WITH THE POETS
1852

[all within a single-rule frame][all gothic except date] Garden Walks with the Poets. | By Mrs. C. Kirkland. | New-York: | G. P. Putnam & Company, 10 Park Place. | 1852.

"The Rhodora," p. [68]. See E 15; A 18.
  "The Snow-Storm," pp. [293]–294. See E 24; A 18.

Location: TxU.

G 22 THE STRING OF DIAMONDS
1852

[all within a single-rule frame] THE | STRING OF DIAMONDS, | GATHERED | FROM MANY MINES. | [rule] | BY A GEM FANCIER. | [rule] | HARTFORD: | WM. JAMES HAMERSLEY. | 1852.

"Each in All," pp. [66]–67. See E 12; A 18.

Location: TxU.

G 23 POETS OF ENGLAND AND AMERICA
1853

[all within a single-rule red frame surrounding a leaf-and-vine-design frame] [gothic] [red 'P'] Poets | OF | [red] ENGLAND AND AMERICA; | BEING | [gothic] Selections from the best Authors of both Countries, | DESIGNED AS | A COMPANION TO ALL LOVERS OF POETRY. | WITH | [red] AN INTRODUCTORY ESSAY. | [rule] | [three lines from Wordsworth] | [rule] | LONDON: | WHITTAKER & CO., AVE MARIA LANE. | LIVER-POOL: | EDWARD HOWELL, CHURCH STREET. | MDCCCLIII.

"The Snow Storm," pp. 14–15. See E 24; A 18.
  "Each and All," pp. 235–236. See E 12; A 18.

Location: DLC.

G 24 SELECTIONS IN POETRY
1853

SELECTIONS IN POETRY | FOR | EXERCISES AT SCHOOL AND AT HOME. | [rule] | [gothic] Edited by Epes Sargent. | WITH ILLUSTRATIONS BY BILLINGS AND OTHERS. | [rule] | [two lines of verse] | Sɪʀ Pʜɪʟɪᴘ Sɪᴅɴᴇʏ. | [oval picture of woman and landscape] | PHILADELPHIA: | THOMAS, COWPERTHWAIT & CO. | M DCCC LIII.

"The Humble-Bee," pp. 81–83. See E 13; A 18.
  "The Snow Storm," pp. 253–254. See E 24; A 18.

Location: JM.

G 25 BEAUTIFUL POETRY
1853–1856

[all within a single-rule frame] [ornate lettering] BEAUTIFUL POETRY. | A SELECTION | OF THE CHOICEST OF | THE PRESENT AND THE PAST. | [rule] | [rule] | VOL. I. [II.] [III.] [IV.] [V.] [VI.] | [gothic] London: | HORACE COX, 10, WELLINGTON STREET, STRAND.

"To the Humble Bee," I, 66–67. See E 13; A 18.
  "Nature's Pity for Human Pride," I, 474. From "Hamatreya." See A 18.
  "Mutation," I, 475. From "Woodnotes." See D 17; A 18.
  "The Haughty Beauty of Muses," I, 476. From "The World-Soul." See A 18.
  "The House," III, 91–92. See A 18.

Location: DLC.

G 26 THE AMERICAN CLASSICAL AUTHORS
1854

Two title pages are present in the book:

HANDBUCH | DER | NORDAMERICANISCHEN | NATIONAL-LITERATUR. | [rule] | SAMMLUNG VON MUNSTERSTÜCKEN | NEBST EINER | LITERAR-HISTORISCHEN ABHANDLUNG | UEBER DEN | ENTWICKLUNGSGANG DER ENGLISCHEN SPRACHE UND LITERATUR | IN NORD-AMERICA | VON | Pʀᴏꜰ. Dᴿ L. HERRIG, | [four lines of Herrig's books and positions] | [rule] | BRAUNSCHWEIG, | DRUCK UND VERLAG VON GEORGE WESTERMANN. | [rule] | 1854.

THE | AMERICAN CLASSICAL AUTHORS. | [rule] | SELECT SPECIMENS | OF THE | ANGLO-AMERICAN LITERATURE. | PRECEDED BY | AN INTRODUCTORY ESSAY | ON ITS ORIGIN AND PROGRESS | WITH | BIOGRAPHICAL AND CRITICAL SKETCHES | BY | L. HERRIG, | PH.D. | [four lines of Herrig's books and positions] | [rule] | BRUNSWICK: | PRINTED AND PUBLISHED BY GEORGE WESTERMANN. | [rule] | 1854.

"Shakespeare; or, the Poet," pp. 413–419. In English. See A 22.

Location: NNC.

G 27 OFF-HAND TAKINGS
1854

OFF-HAND TAKINGS; | OR, | CRAYON SKETCHES | OF THE | NOTICEABLE MEN OF OUR AGE. | BY | GEORGE W. BUNGAY | [gothic] Embellished with Twenty Portraits on Steel. | [rule] | NEW YORK: | DE WITT & DAVENPORT, PUBLISHERS, | 160 & 162 NASSAU STREET.

"Speech of Ralph Waldo Emerson" [on Kossuth], pp. 123–126. See D 21; A 40.

Location: JM.

G 28 THE WHITE VEIL
1854

[all within a single-rule frame] THE | WHITE VEIL: | A BRIDAL GIFT. | EDITED BY | MRS. SARAH JOSEPHA HALE, | AUTHOR OF "WOMAN'S RECORD," ETC., ETC. | [two lines from Genesis 2:18] | [gothic] Elegantly Illustrated. | PHILADELPHIA: | PUBLISHED BY E. H. BUTLER & CO. | 1854,

"The Maiden and the Wife," p. 270. From "Each and All." See E 12; A 18.

Location: MB.

Note: Emerson's poem appears only in the second edition, which is not identified as such. In the first edition, "The Love Marriage" appears on pp. 19–42; in the second edition, "A Marriage Sermon" appears on pp. 19–37.

G 29 CYCLOPÆDIA OF AMERICAN LITERATURE
1855

CYCLOPÆDIA | OF | AMERICAN LITERATURE; | EMBRACING | PERSONAL AND CRITICAL NOTICES OF AUTHORS, | AND SELECTIONS FROM THEIR WRITINGS. | FROM THE EARLIEST PERIOD TO THE PRESENT DAY; | WITH | PORTRAITS, AUTO-GRAPHS, AND OTHER ILLUSTRATIONS. | BY | EVERT A. DUYCKINCK AND GEORGE L. DUYCKINCK. | IN TWO VOLUMES. | VOL. I. [II.] | NEW YORK: | CHARLES SCRIBNER. | [rule] | 1855.

"The Problem," II, 366–367. See E 18; A 18.
  "Tact," II, 367. See E 43; A 18.
  "Good-Bye," II, 367. See E 14; A 18.
  "The Humble-Bee," II, 367–368. See E 13; A 18.
  "The Apology," II, 368. See A 18.
  "Beauty—From Nature," II, 368–369. See A 3.
  "Love—From the Essays," II, 369–371. See A 10.
  "Montaigne—From Representative Men," II, 371–372. See A 22.

Location: JM.

G 30 THE WIDE-AWAKE GIFT
1855

THE | [gothic] Wide-Awake Gift: | A | KNOW-NOTHING TOKEN | FOR | [ornate letters] 1855. | EDITED BY "ONE OF 'EM." | [gothic] "Put None but Americans on Guard to-night." | [rule] | NEW YORK: | J. C. DERBY, 119 NASSAU STREET. | BOSTON: | PHILLIPS, SAMPSON & CO. | CINCINNATI: | H. W. DERBY. | 1855.

Edited by William Cullen Bryant.

"The Bible," p. 39. From "The Problem." See E 18; A 18.

Location: JM.

Note: Reprinted, with Emerson's poem on the same page: 'THE | AMERICAN GIFT BOOK; | A | PERPETUAL SOUVENIR. | [rule] | NEW YORK: | J. C. DERBY, 119 NASSAU STREET. | CINCINNATI: | H. W. DERBY. | 1856.' (NcD).

G 31 LEAFLETS OF MEMORY
       1856

[gothic] LEAFLETS | OF | [ornate letters] MEMORY. | COMPILED BY | THE EDITOR OF THE "ORIENTAL ANNUAL" | [rule] | [eight lines of verse] | German of Anastasius Grun. | [rule] | [gothic] New York: | PUBLISHED BY LEAVITT & ALLEN, | 379 BROADWAY.

"Good Bye," pp. [162]–163. See E 14; A 18.

Location: DLC.

G 32 NAPOLEON
       1857

VIE ET CARACTÈRE | DE | NAPOLÉON BONAPARTE | PAR | W. E. Channing et R. W. Emerson, | TRADUIT DE L'ANGLAIS | par | François Van Meenen. | [four lines of verse] | Aug. Barbier. | [rule] | BRUXELLES, | IMPRIMERIE DE FRANÇOIS VAN MEENEN | RUE NEUVE DU PACHÉCO 34. | 1857

"Napoléon ou L'Homme du Monde," pp. [143]–178. See A 22.

Location: CtY.

G 33 THE HOUSEHOLD BOOK OF POETRY
       1858

[all within a single-rule frame] THE | HOUSEHOLD BOOK | OF POETRY. | COMPILED AND EDITED | BY | CHARLES A. DANA. | NEW YORK: | D. APPLETON AND COM-PANY, | 346 & 348 BROADWAY. | LONDON: | 16 LITTLE BRITAIN. | 1858.

"The Rhodora," p. 38. See E 15; A 18.
   "The Snow Storm," p. 116. See E 24; A 18.
   "Threnody," pp. 171–173. See A 18.
   "Good-bye," p. 659. See E 14; A 18.
   "Guy," p. 660. See A 18.
   "Each and All," p. 687. See E 12; A 18.
   "The Problem," p. 689. See E 18; A 18.

Location: MH.

G 34 THE POETS OF THE NINETEENTH CENTURY
1858

THE POETS | OF THE | NINETEENTH CENTURY. | SELECTED AND EDITED | BY THE | REV. ROBERT ARIS WILLMOTT, | INCUMBENT OF BEARWOOD. | WITH ENGLISH AND AMERICAN ADDITIONS, | ARRANGED BY | EVERT A. DUYCKINCK, | EDITOR OF THE CYCLOPEDIA OF AMERICAN LITERATURE. | ILLUSTRATED WITH ONE HUN-DRED AND THIRTY-TWO ENGRAVINGS, | DRAWN BY EMINENT ARTISTS. | NEW YORK: | HARPER & BROTHERS, PUBLISHERS, | FRANKLIN SQUARE. | 1858.

"The Humble-Bee," pp. 406–407. See E 13; A 18.

Location: MH.

G 35 A COMPENDIUM OF AMERICAN LITERATURE
1859

A | COMPENDIUM | OF | AMERICAN LITERATURE, | CHRONOLOGICALLY AR RANGED; | WITH | BIOGRAPHICAL SKETCHES OF THE AUTHORS, | AND | SELEC-TIONS FROM THEIR WORKS. | ON THE PLAN OF THE AUTHOR'S "COMPENDIUM OF ENGLISH LITERATURE," | AND | "ENGLISH LITERATURE OF THE NINETEENTH CEN-TURY." | BY | CHARLES D. CLEVELAND. | STEREOTYPED EDITION. | PHILDELPHIA: | E. C. & J. BIDDLE, No. 508 MINOR STREET, | (*Between Market and Chestnut, and Fifth and Sixth Sts.*) | BOSTON: PHILLIPS, SAMPSON & CO.; SHEPARD, CLARK & BROWN. | NEW YORK: A. O. MOORE & CO. . . . . CINCINNATI: BICKEY, MALLORY & CO. | CHICAGO: W. B. KEEN. | 1859.

Various selections under the titles "The Compensations of Calamity," "Travelling," "Self-Reliance," and "Good-Bye, Proud World," pp. 513–516.

Location: InU.

G 36 GEMS FROM THE POETS
1859

[ornate border] | [four lines gothic] [ornate initial capital] Gems | from the | [ornate capitals] POETS | Illustrated. | [rule] | ROGERS, HEMANS, EMERSON, &c. | [rule] | LONDON: | GROOMBRIDGE AND SONS.

Stiff wrappers. Cover title.

"The Snow Storm," pp. 23–24. See E 24; A 18.

Location: BL.

Note one: Sold in parts; Emerson's contribution is in Part C, deposited at BL 8 January 1859. Part G, the final part, was deposited at BL 9 February 1860.

Note two: The seven parts were collected with Emerson's poem on the same pages, with the following title page: 'GEMS | FROM THE POETS, | ILLUSTRATED. | THE DESIGNS BY | F. A. LYDON. | PRINTED IN COLOURS, FROM WOOD BLOCKS. | LONDON: | GROOMBRIDGE AND SONS, 5, PATERNOSTER-ROW. | M DCCC LX.' (BL).

G 37 LEAVES OF GRASS IMPRINTS
1860

[gothic] Leaves of Grass | IMPRINTS. | [rule] | [ornate lettering] American and Euro-
pean Criticisms | ON | "LEAVES OF GRASS." | [rule] | BOSTON: | THAYER AND
ELDRIDGE. | 1860.

Wrappers. Edited by Walt Whitman.

Letter of 21 July 1855 to Whitman, p. [2]. See A 23.

Location: ViU.

G 38 NIGHTINGALE VALLEY
1860

NIGHTINGALE VALLEY. | A COLLECTION, | INCLUDING A GREAT NUMBER | OF THE
CHOICEST LYRICS | AND | SHORT POEMS | IN | THE ENGLISH LANGUAGE. | EDITED
BY GIRALDUS. | [four lines of verse] | Ariosto, *Orl. Fur.* x. 113. | [rule] | LONDON: |
BELL AND DALDY, 186, FLEET STREET. | 1860.

"The Amulet," p. 13. See E 45; A 18.
  "Fable," p. 89. See D 15; A 18.
  "Goodbye," pp. 113–114. See E 14; A 18.
  "The Humble-Bee," pp. 132–133. See E 13; A 18.
  "Forbearance," p. 167. See E 36; A 18.
  "The House," pp. 226–227. See A 18.

Location: MH.

G 39 FAVORITE AUTHORS
1861

[red ornate initial capitals] [gothic] Favorite Authors. | [red] A COMPANION-BOOK | OF
| PROSE AND POETRY. | [red] My Books, my best companions. | Fletcher. | BOSTON: |
[red] TICKNOR AND FIELDS. | M DCCC LXI.

Edited by James. T. Fields.

"Threnody," pp. [240]–248. See A 18.

Location: MH.

G 40 FOLK SONGS
1861

[gothic with red initial capitals] FOLK SONGS | SELECTED AND EDITED BY | JOHN
WILLIAMSON PALMER, M.D. | ILLUSTRATED FROM ORIGINAL DESIGNS | [drawing of
people gathered together] | NEW YORK: | CHARLES SCRIBNER, 124 GRAND STREET.
| LONDON: SAMPSON LOW, SON AND COMPANY. | M DCCC LXI.

"The Rhodora," p. 124. See E 15; A 18.

Location: TxU.

G 41 THE LIFE AND LETTERS OF JOHN BROWN
1861

THE LIFE AND LETTERS | OF | [red gothic] Captain John Brown, | WHO WAS | EXE-CUTED AT CHARLESTOWN, VIRGINIA, DEC. 2, 1859, FOR AN ARMED | ATTACK UPON AMERICAN SLAVERY; | WITH NOTICES OF | [red] SOME OF HIS CONFEDER-ATES. | EDITED BY | RICHARD D. WEBB. | LONDON: | SMITH, ELDER, AND CO. 65, CORNHILL. | [rule] | MDCCCLXI.

"From a speech delivered at the Tremont Temple, Boston, at a meeting held Dec. 18th, 1860, to adopt measures of relief for the family of John Brown," pp. 441–442. See D 35–36; A 40.

Location: TxU.

G 42 JEWELS FROM THE QUARRY OF THE MIND
1862

[all within a double-rule frame with fleur-de-lis device in each corner, all in green] [green; printed as arc] JEWELS | [five lines in purple] FROM THE QUARRY OF THE MIND. | [ornate rule] | PEARLS | GATHERED FROM THE SHORES OF LIFE. | [ornate rule] | [green] BUDS AND BLOSSOMS | [rest of page in purple] THAT MAKE GLAD THE GARDEN OF THE HEART. | [ornate rule] | CHIMES | THAT RING OUT SWEET MELODIES, AND FIND AN ECHO IN | THE CHAMBERS OF THE SOUL. | [ornate rule] | EDITED BY | JAMES H. HEAD, | Author of "Home Pastimes, or Tableaux Vivants." | [ornate rule] | BOSTON: | CROSBY AND NICHOLS. | 1862.

"The Snow Storm," p. 43. See E 24; A 18.

Location: TxU.

G 43 SNOW-FLAKES
1863

[all within a single-rule frame with design in each corner] [ornate letters] SNOW-FLAKES: | A CHAPTER FROM THE | BOOK OF NATURE. | [one line of prose] | JOB XXXVIII.22. | [six lines of verse] | COWPER. | [publisher's logo] | PUBLISHED BY THE | AMERICAN TRACT SOCIETY, | No. 28, CORNHILL, BOSTON.

Edited by Israel Perkins Warren.

"The Snow-Storm," pp. 55–56. See E 24; A 18.

Location: MBAt.

G 44 AUTOGRAPH LEAVES OF OUR COUNTRY'S AUTHORS
1864

[in arc] AUTOGRAPH LEAVES OF OUR COUNTRY'S AUTHORS. | [picture of woman sitting on hill] | BALTIMORE, | CUSHINGS & BAILEY | 1864.

Edited by John Pendleton Kennedy and Alexander Bliss.

"Worship" [facsimiles Emerson's manuscript], pp. 132–133. See A 26; A 28.

Location: JM.

G 45 HYMNS OF THE SPIRIT
1864

HYMNS | OF THE SPIRIT. | [leaf design] | BOSTON: | TICKNOR AND FIELDS. | 1864.

Edited by Samuel Longfellow and Samuel Johnson.

"The House Our Fathers Built to God," pp. 149–150. Unsigned but identified as Emerson's in the index. See D 3; A 18.4.
   "The Soul's Prophecy," p. 466. Unsigned but identified as Emerson's in the index. Not by Emerson; see H 32.

Location: JM.

G 46 LYRICS OF LOYALTY
1864

LYRICS OF LOYALTY | ARRANGED AND EDITED BY | FRANK MOORE | [leaf design] | [engraving of child holding two snakes] | NEW YORK | GEORGE P. PUTNAM | 1864

The Red, White, and Blue Series, no. 1.

"Boston Hymn," pp. 253–256. See E 162; A 28.

Location: JM.

G 47 THE SCHOOL-GIRL'S GARLAND
1864

THE | SCHOOL-GIRL'S GARLAND. | *A SELECTION OF POETRY,* | IN FOUR PARTS. | BY | MRS. C. M. KIRKLAND. | [gothic] Second Series. | PARTS THIRD AND FOURTH. | NEW YORK: | CHARLES SCRIBNER, 124 GRAND STREET. | 1864.

"The Mountain and the Squirrel" ["A Fable"], p. 290. See D 15; A 18.

Location: NRU.

G 48 GOLDEN LEAVES FROM THE AMERICAN POETS
1865

GOLDEN LEAVES | FROM THE | AMERICAN POETS | COLLECTED BY | JOHN W. S. HOWS | [rule] | NEW YORK | BUNCE AND HUNTINGTON | M DCCC LXV

"The Poet," pp. 403–405. See D 20; A 54.
   "Each and All," pp. 405–407. See E 12; A 18.
   "To the Humble-Bee," pp. 407–409. See E 13; A 18.
   "Good-By, Proud World!" pp. 409–410. See E 14; A 18.

Location: JM.

G 49 LOOKING TOWARD SUNSET
1865

[red] LOOKING TOWARD SUNSET. | *From Sources Old and New, Original | and Se-lected.* | By L. MARIA CHILD. | [two lines of verse] | Jean Paul Richter. | [five lines of verse from Goethe] | [publisher's logo in red and black] | [red] BOSTON | TICKNOR AND FIELDS. | 1865.

"Over the winter glaciers," p. 278. From "The World-Soul." See D 17; A 18.

Location: JM.

G 50 PICTURES AND FLOWERS FOR CHILD-LOVERS
1865

PICTURES AND FLOWERS | FOR | CHILD-LOVERS. | [line of verse] | Jean Paul. | [four lines of verse] | R. Edmonstone. | BOSTON: | WALKER, FULLER, AND COMPANY, | 245 Washington Street. | 1865.

"Threnody," pp. 151–153. Unsigned but identified as Emerson's in the table of contents. See A 18.

Location: TxU.

G 51 ORATION ON LINCOLN
1865?

THE ADDRESS | OF | HENRY WARD BEECHER | ON | RAISING THE FLAG OF THE UNITED STATES | AT FORT SUMTER, April 14th, 1865. | ALSO, | RALPH WALDO EMER-SON'S | ORATION | At the Funeral of Mr. Lincoln. | [flags] | WILLIAM WESLEY, | QUEEN'S HEAD PASSAGE, PATERNOSTER ROW. | *Sold by all Booksellers.*

Wrappers.

"Mr. Emerson's Oration on the Death of Mr. Lincoln," pp. [12]–13. See E 167; D 56–57; A 40.

Location: OClWHi.

G 52 THE BOOK OF RUBIES
1866

[all within a red single-rule frame with leaf designs in each corner] THE | [red] BOOK OF RUBIES: | A COLLECTION OF THE MOST NOTABLE | [red gothic] Love-Poems | IN THE | [red] ENGLISH LANGUAGE. | NEW YORK: | CHARLES SCRIBNER & CO., | 124 GRAND STREET. | 1866.

Edited by Thomas Dunn English.

"To Eva," p. 244. See E 17; A 18.
    "The Amulet," p. 245. See E 45; A 18.

Location: DLC.

G 53 FESTIVAL OF SONG
1866

FESTIVAL OF SONG: | A SERIES OF | EVENINGS WITH THE POETS. | PREPARED BY THE | AUTHOR OF "SALAD FOR THE SOLITARY," | "MOSAICS," ETC. | WITH SEVENTY-THREE PICTURES, BY MEMBERS OF THE NATIONAL | ACADEMY OF DESIGN. | ENGRAVED BY ROBBETT AND HOOPER. | [rule] | [line of verse from Horace] | [rule] | NEW YORK: | BUNCE AND HUNTINGTON, PUBLISHERS. | M.DCCC.LXVI.

Edited by Frederick Saunders.

"Each and All," pp. 326–328. See E 12; A 18.
  "Rhodora," p. 328. See E 15; A 18.

Location: TxU.

G 54 THE FLOWER OF LIBERTY
1866

THE | [red ornate intial capital] FLOWER OF [blue orante initial capital] LIBERTY. | [gothic] Edited and Illustrated | BY JULIA A. M. FURBISH. | [drawing of angel] | BOS-TON: | BENJAMIN B. RUSSELL, 55 CORNHILL. | PORTLAND, ME.: BAILEY AND NOYES. | CHICAGO, ILL.: S. S. BOYDEN. | 1866.

"Voluntaries," p. 29. See E 164; D 47; D 49; A 28.

Location: TxU.

G 55 THE ORATORICAL YEAR BOOK FOR 1865
1866

THE | ORATORICAL YEAR BOOK | FOR 1865: | BEING A COLLECTION OF | THE BEST CONTEMPORARY SPEECHES | DELIVERED | IN PARLIAMENT, AT THE BAR, AND | ON THE PLATFORM. | ARRANGED AND EDITED BY | ALSAGER HAY HILL, LL.B., | OF THE INNER TEMPLE, BARRISTER-AT-LAW. | [rule] | [line from Horace] | [rule] | LON-DON: | FREDERICK WARNE AND CO., | BEDFORD STREET, COVENT GARDEN. | 1866.

"Mr. Ralph Waldo Emerson's Oration on the Death of Mr. Lincoln," pp. [463]–466. See E 167; D 56–57; A 40.

Location: IHi.

Note: Reprinted as 'ABRAHAM LINCOLN | By RALPH WALDO EMERSON | Privately Printed | NEW YORK | 1914'; 12 pp.; introduction by Frederick Hill Meserve; limited to 30 numbered copies, signed by Meserve (MH).

G 56 POETRY OF THE CIVIL WAR
1866

POETRY | LYRICAL, NARRATIVE, AND SATIRICAL | OF | THE CIVIL WAR | SELECTED AND EDITED | BY RICHARD GRANT WHITE | NEW YORK | THE AMERICAN NEWS COMPANY | 119 & 121 NASSAU STREET | 1866

"Boston Hymn," pp. 139–142. See E 162; D 45; A 28.

Location: NcU.

G 57 POPULAR READINGS IN PROSE AND VERSE
1866

POPULAR READINGS | IN | PROSE AND VERSE. | SELECTED AND EDITED BY | J. E. CARPENTER, | COMPILER OF "SONGS: SACRED AND DEVOTIONAL." | * * * | LONDON: | FREDERICK WARNE AND CO. | BEDFORD STREET, COVENT GARDEN. | 1866.

"Shakspeare," pp. 51–63. See A 22.

Location: RPB.

Note: Introduced as "Abridged for Reading."

G 58 THE LADY'S ALMANAC FOR 1868
1867

[all within a single-rule frame] No.   THE   15. | [next two lines curved, ornate letters] LADY'S ALMANAC | FOR THE YEAR | [circular engraving of women reading and painting, with floral design at bottom enclosing '1868.'] | [ornate letters] BOSTON. | ISSUED BY GEORGE COOLIDGE, 3 MILK ST. | *(Price fifty cents, mailed postpaid.)*

"May-Day," pp. [34]–35. See A 28.

Location: MB.

G 59 A THOUSAND AND ONE GEMS OF ENGLISH POETRY
1867

A | THOUSAND AND ONE GEMS OF | ENGLISH POETRY | SELECTED AND AR-RANGED | BY | CHARLES MACKAY, LL.D. | [wreath-and-lyre design] | *ILLUSTRATED BY J. E. MILLAIS, R.A., SIR JOHN GILBERT, R.A., | JOHN TENNIEL, BIRKET FOSTER, AND OTHERS* | LONDON | GEORGE ROUTLEDGE AND SONS | BROADWAY, LUDGATE HILL | NEW YORK: 9 LAFAYETTE PLACE

"Threnody," pp. 476–477. See A 18.
  "Good-Bye, Proud World," p. 477. See E 14; A 18.
  "The Apology," p. 477. See A 18.
  "Dirge," pp. 477–478. See A 18.
  "To Eva," p. 478. See E 17; A 18.

Location: ScU.

Note: New edition, with Emerson's poems on pp. 536–538: '[all within a single-rule frame] A | THOUSAND AND ONE GEMS | OF | ENGLISH POETRY. | SELECTED AND ARRANGED | BY CHARLES MACKAY, LL.D., | AUTHOR OF "EGERIA," "STUDIES FROM THE ANTIQUE," "A MAN'S HEART," ETC. | ILLUSTRATED BY | J. E. MILLAIS, JOHN GILBERT, AND BIRKET FOSTER. | LONDON: | GEORGE ROUTLEDGE AND SONS, | THE BROADWAY, LUDGATE. | NEW YORK: 416, BROOME STREET. | 1869.' (DLC).

G 60 THE LADY'S ALMANAC FOR 1869
1868

[all within a double-rule frame on red background] THE | [next two lines curved, with ornate letters] | LADY'S ALMANAC | FOR THE YEAR | [circular engraving of women reading and painting, with floral design at bottom enclosing '1869.'] | [ornate letters] BOSTON. | ISSUED BY GEORGE COOLIDGE, 3 MILK ST. | *(Price fifty cents, mailed postpaid.)*

"Domestic Life," pp. [104]–105. See E 134; D 66; A 31.

Location: MB.

G 61 THE CALIFORNIA SCRAP-BOOK
1869

THE | CALIFORNIA SCRAP-BOOK: | A REPOSITORY OF | Useful Information and Select Reading. | COMPRISING | CHOICE SELECTIONS OF PROSE AND POETRY, TALES AND ANECDOTES, | HISTORICAL, DESCRIPTIVE, HUMOROUS, AND SENTI-MENTAL | PIECES, MAINLY CULLED FROM THE VARIOUS | NEWSPAPERS AND PERI-ODICALS OF | THE PACIFIC COAST. | COMPILED BY | OSCAR T. SHUCK. | ILLUS-TRATED. | [six lines of prose] | RUFUS CHOATE. | SAN FRANCISCO: | H. H. BANCROFT & COMPANY. | NEW YORK: 113 WILLIAM STREET. | [rule] | 1869.

"A Philosopher on Love," pp. 308–309. From "Love." See A 10.

Location: MH.

G 62 BEETON'S GREAT BOOK OF POETRY
1870

[all within a single-rule frame] BEETON'S | GREAT BOOK OF POETRY: | FROM | CÆDMON AND KING ALFRED'S BOETHIUS | TO BROWNING AND TENNYSON. | ALSO, | A SEPARATE SELECTION OF AMERICAN POEMS. | CONTAINING NEARLY | *TWO THOUSAND OF THE BEST PIECES IN THE* | *ENGLISH LANGUAGE;* | WITH SKETCHES OF THE | HISTORY OF THE POETRY OF OUR COUNTRY, | AND | BIO-GRAPHICAL NOTICES OF THE POETS. | EDITED BY S. O. BEETON. | LONDON: | WARD, LOCK, & TYLER, WARWICK HOUSE, | PATERNOSTER ROW.

"Good-Bye, Proud World!" no. 1864. See E 14; A 18.
  "To the Humble-Bee," no. 1865. See E 13; A 18.
  "The Snow-Storm," no. 1866. See E 24; A 18.
  "The Problem," no. 1867. See E 18; A 18.
  "The Poet" ["To clothe the fiery Thought]," no. 1868. See E 152; A 28.
  "Dirge," no. 1869. See A 18.
  "The Mountain and the Squirrel" ["A Fable"], no. 1870. See D 15; A 18.

Location: CtY.

Note: Reprinted in two volumes, with Emerson's poems in vol. II: 'LONDON: | WARD, LOCK & TYLER, WARWICK HOUSE, | PATERNOSTER ROW. | [rule] | PHILADELPHIA: GEO. GEBBIE. | 1871.' (DLC).

G 63 A LIBRARY OF POETRY AND SONG
1870

[all within a single-rule red frame with boxed corners surrounding a single-rule frame] A LIBRARY | OF | [red ornate initial capitals] POETRY AND SONG | BEING | [gothic] Choice Selections from the Best Poets | WITH AN INTRODUCTION | BY | WILLIAM CULLEN BRYANT | [publisher's logo] | [red] NEW YORK | J. B. FORD AND COMPANY

Facsimiles five lines from Emerson's manuscript of "Worship," p. [xxii]. See A 26; A 28.
  "The Snow-Storm," p. 319. See E 24; A 18.
  "To the Humble-Bee," pp. 354–355. See E 13; A 18.
  "The Rhodora," p. 366. See E 15; A 18.
  "Boston Hymn," pp. 460–461. See E 162; D 45; A 28.
  "Letters," p. 614. See A 28.
  "Brahma," pp. 614–615. See E 132; A 28.
  "Quatrains and Fragments," p. 625. Contains "Northman" (E 147; A 28), "Poet" ("To clothe the fiery thought"; E 152; A 28), "Justice" (from "Voluntaries"; E 164; D 47; D 49; A 28), and "Heroism" (A 10.5; A 28).

Location: TxU.

G 64 HAMLET AND MONTAIGNE
1871

HAMLET, | ein Tendenzdrama Sheakspeare's | gegen | die skeptische und kosmopoli-tische | Weltanschauung des Michael de Montaigne, | [wavy rule] | Mit einem Anhange | über Leben und Lehre Montaigne's von R. W. Emerson. | Frei übersetzt und mit Anmer-kungen begleitet | von | G. F. Stedefeld, | Kreisgerichtsrath, | Mitglied der deustchen Dante- | und Sheakspearegesellschaft | [rule] | Berlin, | Gebrüder Paetel. | 1871.

"Montaigne, der Zweifler (Skeptiker,)" pp. 47–94. See A 22.

Location: MH.

G 65 OUR POETICAL FAVORITES
1871

OUR | POETICAL FAVORITES | A SELECTION FROM THE BEST MINOR POEMS | OF THE ENGLISH LANGUAGE | By ASAHEL C. KENDRICK | PROFESSOR IN THE UNIVERSITY OF ROCHESTER | [rule] | NEW YORK | SHELDON & COMPANY | 498 & 500 BROADWAY | 1871

"The Day's Ration," pp. 231–232. See A 18.

Location: NN.

Note one: New edition, with "Each and All" (E 12; A 18) on pp. 247–248: 'OUR | POETICAL FAVORITES | A SELECTION FROM THE BEST MINOR POEMS | OF THE EN-GLISH LANGUAGE | BY ASAHEL C. KENDRICK | PROFESSOR IN THE UNIVERSITY OF ROCHESTER | NEW AND ENLARGED EDITION | NEW YORK | SHELDON & COMPANY | 677 BROADWAY, AND 214 & 216 MERCER STREET | 1872' (TxU).

Note two: New edition, with "Each and All" on pp. 247–248 and "The Day's Ration" on pp. 261–262: 'OUR | POETICAL FAVORITES | A SELECTION FROM THE BEST MINOR

POEMS | OF THE ENGLISH LANGUAGE | FIRST SERIES | BY | ASAHEL C. KEN-
DRICK | PROFESSOR IN THE UNIVERSITY OF ROCHESTER | *NEW AND REVISED
EDITION* | [publisher's logo] | BOSTON | JAMES R. OSGOOD AND COMPANY | 1881'
(NjP).

G 66 WINTER POEMS
1871

WINTER POEMS | BY | FAVORITE AMERICAN POETS | *WITH ILLUSTRATIONS* | [pub-
lisher's logo] | BOSTON | FIELDS, OSGOOD, & CO. | 1871

"The Snow-Storm," pp. [48]–50. Unsigned but identified as Emerson's in the table of
contents. See E 24; A 18.

Location: TxU.

G 67 AMERICAN POEMS
1872

AMERICAN POEMS. | *SELECTED AND EDITED* | BY | WILLIAM MICHAEL ROSSETTI. |
[line of verse] | Whitman | [publisher's logo] | LONDON: | E. MOXON, SON, & CO.,
DOVER STREET, | AND | 1 AMEN CORNER, PATERNOSTER ROW.

"The Apology," pp. 58–59. See A 18.
  "The Humble Bee," pp. 59–61. See E 13; A 18.
  "Each and All," pp. 61–62. See E 12; A 18.
  "Dirge," pp. 63–64. See A 18.
  "The World Soul," pp. 64–67. See D 17; A 18.
  "Hamatreya," pp. 67–69. See A 18.
  "Wood-Notes, I.," pp. 69–73. See E 22; A 18.
  "Wood-Notes, II.," pp. 73–83. See E 32; A 18.
  "Astræa," pp. 83–84. See A 18.
  "Ode to Beauty," pp. 84–87. See E 102; A 18.
  "To Eva," pp. 87–88. See E 17; A 18.
  "Eros," p. 88. See E 107; A 18.
  "Hermione," pp. 88–90. See A 18.
  "Bacchus," pp. 90–92. See A 18.
  "Saadi," pp. 92–96. See E 68; A 18.
  "Blight," pp. 97–98. See E 108; A 18.
  "May-day," pp. 98–115. See A 28.
  "Boston Hymn," pp. 116–118. See E 162; D 45; A 28.
  "Una," pp. 118–119. See A 28.
  "Solution," pp. 119–121. See A 28.
  "Song of Nature," pp. 121–123. See E 141; A 28.
  "Two Rivers," p. 124. See E 135; A 28.
  "Terminus," pp. 124–125. See E 170; A 28.
  "The Past," p. 126. See A 28.
  "Compensation," pp. 126–127. See A 10.5; A 28.

Location: DLC.

G 68 CHILD LIFE
1872

CHILD LIFE: | A COLLECTION OF POEMS, | EDITED BY | JOHN GREENLEAF WHITTIER. | WITH ILLUSTRATIONS. | [picture of children] | BOSTON: | JAMES R. OSGOOD AND COMPANY, | LATE TICKNOR & FIELDS, AND FIELDS, OSGOOD & CO. | 1872.

"The Mountain and the Squirrel" ["A Fable"], pp. 250–251. See D 15; A 18.

Location: TxU.

G 69 ILLUSTRATED LIBRARY OF FAVORITE SONG
1873

ILLUSTRATED LIBRARY | OF | FAVORITE SONG. | BASED UPON FOLK SONGS, AND COMPRISING SONGS OF THE HEART, | SONGS OF HOME, SONGS OF LIFE, AND SONGS OF NATURE. | WITH AN INTRODUCTION, | AND EDITED BY | J. G. HOLLAND, | AUTHOR OF "BITTER SWEET," "KATHRINA," ETC., ETC. | ILLUSTRATED WITH ONE HUNDRED AND TWENTY-FIVE ENGRAVINGS, | AFTER DESIGNS BY CHURCH, JOHNSON, DARLEY, HOPPIN, NAST, HENNESSY, MORAN, GRISWOLD, ETC | AND WITH TWENTY AUTOGRAPHS IN FACSIMILE. | [rule] | Sold only by Subscription. | [rule] | [picture of people gathered together] | NEW YORK: | SCRIBNER, ARMSTRONG, AND COMPANY. | CHICAGO: HADLEY BROTHERS & KANE.

"To the Humblebee," pp. 425–428. See E 13; A 18.

Location: TxU.

G 70 A MANUAL OF AMERICAN LITERATURE
1873

A MANUAL | OF | AMERICAN LITERATURE. | DESIGNED FOR THE USE OF | SCHOOLS OF ADVANCED GRADES. | BY | N. K. ROYSE. | PRINCIPAL OF THE SIXTH DISTRICT PUBLIC SCHOOL, CINCINNATI, OHIO. | [rule] | PHILADELPHIA: | COWPERTHWAIT & COMPANY. | 1873.

"Beauty," pp. 347–350. See A 3.
  "Napoleon; or, The Man of the World," pp. 350–353. See A 22.

Location: ScU.

G 71 SONGS OF NATURE
1873

[gothic with ornate red initial capitals] Songs of Nature | SELECTED FROM MANY SOURCES, | WITH MANY ILLUSTRATIONS FROM ORIGINAL DESIGNS | BY | T. MORAN, MISS HALLOCK, CHURCH, FENN, PARSONS, | KENSETT, JOHNSON, BOLLES, ETC. | [picture of children and sheet music] | NEW YORK: | SCRIBNER, ARMSTRONG, AND COMPANY, | SUCCESSORS TO | CHARLES SCRIBNER AND COMPANY. | 1873.

Facsimiles five lines from Emerson's manuscript of "The Humble-Bee," facing title page. See E 13; A 18.

"The Rhodora," p. 40. See E 15; A 18.
"To the Humblebee," pp. 63–65. See E 13; A 18.

Location: TxU.

G 72 HALF HOURS WITH THE POETS
1874

[all within a red single-rule frame] HALF HOURS | [red] WITH THE POETS: | A COLLEC-TION OF | [red gothic] Choice Poems, | FROM | [red] CHAUCER TO TENNYSON. | [red gothic] Elegantly Illustrated. | [rule] | NEW YORK: | JAMES MILLER, PUBLISHER, | 647 BROADWAY. | 1874.

"To Eva," p. 233. See E 17; A 18.
"The Amulet," p. 234. See E 45; A 18.

Location: TxU.

G 73 HYMNS OF PRAISE AND PRAYER
1874

HYMNS | OF | PRAISE AND PRAYER. | COLLECTED AND EDITED BY | JAMES MARTI-NEAU, LL.D. | Vatum suspiria solatium Ecclesiæ. | LONDON: | LONGMANS, GREEN, READER AND DYER. | 1874.

"The Everlasting Word," Hymn 112. From "The Problem." See E 18; A 18.
"The Soul's Prophecy," Hymn 176. Not by Emerson; see H 32.
"The Father's House of God," Hymn 728. See D 3; A 18.4.

Location: PPPD.

G 74 LITTLE PEOPLE OF GOD
1874

LITTLE PEOPLE | OF GOD | AND | WHAT THE POETS HAVE SAID OF THEM | EDITED BY | MRS GEORGE L AUSTIN | [publisher's logo] | BOSTON | SHEPARD AND GILL | 1874

"From 'Threnody,'" pp. 115–118. See A 18.

Location: MB.

G 75 SEA AND SHORE
1874

SEA AND SHORE. | [gothic] A Collection of Poems. | [four lines of verse] | CHARLES KINGSLEY. | BOSTON: | ROBERTS BROTHERS. | 1874.

Edited by Harriet Preston and Martha L. Goddard.

"Sea-Shore," pp. 118–120. See E 165; A 28.

Location: TxU.

G 76 FREEDOM AND FELLOWSHIP IN RELIGION
1875

FREEDOM AND FELLOWSHIP | IN | RELIGION. | *A COLLECTION OF ESSAYS AND* | *AD-DRESSES* | EDITED BY A COMMITTEE | OF | [gothic] The Free Religious Association. | [publisher's logo] | BOSTON: | ROBERTS BROTHERS. | 1875.

"Religious Needs of the Age," pp. 361–363. See D 68; A 40.
  "Natural Religion Universal and Sympathetic," pp. 384–388. See D 76; A 40.

Location: JM.

G 77 LITTLE CLASSICS
1875

[all within a double-rule frame; outer frame is red] [gothic] Fourteenth Volume. | [rule] | [red] LITTLE CLASSICS. | EDITED BY | ROSSITER JOHNSON. | [red] POEMS LYRICAL. | [nine lines describing contents] | [red] BOSTON: | JAMES R. OSGOOD AND COM-PANY, | Late Ticknor & Fields, and Fields, Osgood, & Co. | 1875.

"The Problem," pp. [121]–123. See E 18; A 18.

Location: MB.

G 78 WIDE AWAKE PLEASURE BOOK
1875

[all within a single-rule frame] WIDE AWAKE | PLEASURE BOOK. | [engraving of child's head within circular frame] | *BOSTON:* | *D. Lothrop & Co., Publishers,* | *38 and 40 Cornhill.*

"The Mountain and the Squirrel" ["A Fable"], p. 95. See D 15; A 18.

Location: MB.

G 79 THE MOUNTAINS
1876

THE MOUNTAINS. | [gothic] A Collection of Poems. | [three lines of verse] | F. W. FABER. | BOSTON: | ROBERTS BROTHERS. | 1876.

"Monadnoc," pp. 69–70. See A 18.

Location: TxU.

G 80 POETRY FOR HOME AND SCHOOL
1876

POETRY | FOR | HOME AND SCHOOL | SELECTED AND ARRANGED BY | ANNA C. BRACKET AND IDA M. ELLIOT. | [four lines from Plato] | [rule] | NEW YORK | G. P. PUTNAM'S SONS, | 182 FIFTH AVENUE | 1876.

"The Mountain and the Squirrel" ["A Fable"], p. 18. See D 15; A 18.
   "The House," pp. 229–230. See A 18.
   "Each and All," pp. 273–274. See E 12; A 18.

Location: DLC.

Note: Reprinted, with Emerson's poems on the same pages: '[all within an ornate silver frame] THE | [red initial capitals] SILVER TREASURY | BEING THE HOLIDAY EDITION OF | POETRY FOR HOME AND SCHOOL | SELECTED AND ARRANGED BY | [red] ANNA C. BRACKETT AND IDA M. ELIOT | [rule] *ILLUSTRATED* | [rule] | NEW YORK & LONDON | G. P. PUTNAM'S SONS | [gothic] The Knickerbocker Press | 1889' (TxU).

      G 81 ROADSIDE POEMS
          1876

[all within a double-rule frame; outer frame is red] [red] ROADSIDE POEMS | FOR SUMMER TRAVELLERS. | EDITED BY | [red] LUCY LARCOM. | [publisher's logo] | BOSTON: | [red] JAMES R. OSGOOD AND COMPANY, | (Late Ticknor & Fields, and Fields, Osgood & Co.) | 1876.

"Forerunners," pp. 34–35. See D 15; A 18.
   "Waldeinsamkeit," pp. 91–93. See E 139; A 28.
   "From 'Monadnoc,'" pp. 124–131. See A 18.

Location: TxU.

      G 82 SONGS OF THREE CENTURIES
          1876

[all within a single-rule frame with ornate corners] SONGS | OF | THREE CENTURIES. | EDITED BY | JOHN GREENLEAF WHITTIER. | [publisher's logo] | BOSTON: | JAMES R. OSGOOD AND COMPANY, | LATE TICKNOR & FIELDS, AND FIELDS, OSGOOD, & CO. | 1876.

"The Apology," p. 199. See A 18.
   "To Eva," p. 199. See E 17; A 18.
   "Thine Eyes Still Shone," p. 200. See A 18.
   "Each and All," p. 200. See E 12; A 18.
   "The Problem," pp. 200–201. See E 18; A 18.
   "Boston Hymn," pp. 201–202. See E 162; D 145; A 28.
   "The Soul's Prophecy," p. 202. Not by Emerson; see H 32.

Location: ScU.

      G 83 TREASURY OF WISDOM, WIT AND HUMOR
          1876

TREASURY OF WISDOM, | WIT AND HUMOR, | ODD COMPARISONS AND PROVERBS. | COMPLIED AND ARRANGED | BY | ADAM WOOLÉVER. | [two lines from Shirley] | HARRISBURG: | PATRIOT PUBLISHING COMPANY. | 1876.

Various quotations from Emerson, pp. 125, 219, 255, 265, 266, 282, 300, 324, 353.

Location: RPB.

G 84 HILLSIDE AND SEASIDE IN POETRY
1877

HILLSIDE AND SEASIDE | *IN POETRY* | A COMPANION TO "ROADSIDE POEMS" | EDITED BY | LUCY LARCOM | [publisher's logo] | BOSTON | JAMES R. OSGOOD AND COMPANY | (Late Ticknor & Fields, and Fields, Osgood, & Co.) | 1877

"The Apology," pp. 21–22. See A 18.
　"From 'Hermione,'" pp. 50–51. See A 18.
　"Fable," pp. 87–88. See D 15; A 18.
　"Sea-Shore," pp. 174–175. See E 165; A 28.

Location:　MH.

G 85 NEW LIBRARY OF POETRY AND SONG
1877

[all within a single-rule frame with spikes at corners, surrounding a single-rule frame with a box at each corner] [three lines of ornate curved lettering against a leaf-and-vine design] A New | Library of Poetry | and Song | EDITED BY | WILLIAM CULLEN BRYANT | [gothic] Illustrated | *WITH STEEL PORTRAITS, WOOD ENGRAVINGS BY ENGLISH AND AMERICAN ARTISTS,* | *SILHOUETTE TITLES, MANUSCRIPT* FAC-SIMILES, | ETC., ETC. | [publisher's logo] | [gothic] New York | FORDS, HOWARD, & HULBERT

"Friendship," I, 59. See A 10.
　"Each and All," I, 365–366. See E 12; A 18.
　"The Snow-Storm," I, 402. See E 24; A 18.
　"The Rhodora," I, 424. See E 15; A 18.
　"To the Humblebee," I, 448. See E 13; A 18.
　"Hymn: Sung at the Completion of the Concord Monument," II, 533–534. See A 4; A 18.4.
　"Boston Hymn," II, 556–557. See E 162; D 145; A 28.
　"The Sea," II, 562–563. Reprinting of "The Sea-Shore." See E 165; A 28.
　"The Problem," II, 673. See E 18; A 18.
　"Good By," II, 719–720. See E 14; A 18.
　"Letters," II, 721. See A 28.
　"Brahma," II, 722. See E 132; A 28.
　"Quatrains and Fragments," II, 746. Contains "Northman" (E 147; A 28), "Poet" ("To clothe the fiery thought"; E 152; A 28), "Justice" (from "Voluntaries"; E 164; D 47; A 28), "Heroism" (A 10.5; A 28), "Borrowing. From the French" (A 28), and "Heri, Cras, Hodie" (E 142; A 28).

Location:　ScU.

G 86 POEMS OF THE LIFE BEYOND AND WITHIN
1877

POEMS | OF THE | LIFE BEYOND AND WITHIN. | VOICES FROM MANY LANDS AND CENTURIES, SAYING, | "MAN, THOU SHALT NEVER DIE." | EDITED AND COMPILED BY | GILES B. STEBBINS, | DETROIT, MICH. | [seven lines of verse] | LONGFELLOW. | BOSTON: | COLBY AND RICH, PUBLISHERS, | 9 MONTGOMERY PLACE | 1877.

"The Soul's Prophecy," pp. 153–154. Not by Emerson; see H 32.
  "Threnody. (Extract.)," pp. 155–156. See A 18.

Location: MH.

G 87 ASPIRATIONS OF THE WORLD
1878

ASPIRATIONS | OF | THE WORLD. | [gothic] A Chain of Opals. | *COLLECTED, WITH AN INTRODUCTION,* | BY L. MARIA CHILD, | AUTHOR OF "PROGRESS OF RELIGIOUS IDEAS," ETC. | [publisher's logo] | BOSTON: | ROBERTS BROTHERS. | 1878.

[Six lines from "The Problem"], p. [ii]. See E 18; A 18.

Location: RPB.

G 88 FAVORITE POEMS
1878

FAVORITE POEMS, | SELECTED FROM | ENGLISH AND AMERICAN AUTHORS. | [publisher's logo] | NEW YORK: | PUBLISHED BY T. Y. CROWELL, | NO. 744 BROADWAY. | 1878.

Edited by Joseph H. Head.

"The Snow Storm," p. 43. See E 24; A 18.
  "Each and All," pp. 384–386. See E 12; A 18.

Location: RPB.

G 89 THE FIRESIDE ENCYCLOPÆDIA OF POETRY
1878

[all within a single-rule frame] THE | FIRESIDE ENCYCLOPÆDIA | OF POETRY. | COMPRISING | THE BEST POEMS OF THE MOST FAMOUS WRITERS, | ENGLISH AND AMERICAN. | COMPILED AND EDITED | BY | HENRY T. COATES. | [publisher's logo] | PORTER & COATES, | PHILADELPHIA.

"To Eva," p. 217. See E 17; A 18.
  "The Rhodora," p. 457. See E 15; A 18.
  "The Humble-Bee," pp. 480–481. See E 13; A 18.
  "Good-Bye," p. 657. See E 14; A 18.
  "The Problem," pp. 663–664. See E 18; A 18.
  "Each and All," p. 707. See E 12; A 18.

Location: DLC.

G 90 LATTER-DAY LYRICS
1878

LATTER-DAY LYRICS | BEING | *Poems of Sentiment and Reflection* | *By Living Writers* | SELECTED AND ARRANGED WITH NOTES | BY W. DAVENPORT ADAMS | [publisher's logo] |

WITH A NOTE ON SOME FOREIGN FORMS OF VERSE | *BY AUSTIN DOBSON* | London | CHATTO & WINDUS, PICCADILLY

The Mayfair Library.

"The Apology," pp. [229]–230. See A 18.

Location: TxU.

G 91 POEMS OF PLACES: ASIA
1878

[all within a double-rule frame; outer frame is red with boxed corners] | [red] Poems of Places | EDITED BY | HENRY W. LONGFELLOW | [two lines of verse] | CRABBE. | [red] ASIA. | [red] PERSIA, INDIA, CHINESE EMPIRE, JAPAN. | [leaf design] | [red] BOSTON: | HOUGHTON, OSGOOD AND COMPANY. | [gothic] The Riverside Press, Cambridge. | [red] 1878.

"Brahma," pp. 50–51. See E 132; A 28.

Location: TxU.

G 92 POETRY OF AMERICA
1878

POETRY OF AMERICA | SELECTIONS FROM ONE HUNDRED AMERICAN POETS | FROM 1776 TO 1876. | *WITH AN INTRODUCTORY REVIEW OF COLONIAL* | *POETRY,* | AND SOME SPECIMENS OF | NEGRO MELODY. | [rule] | By W. J. LINTON | [rule] | LONDON: GEORGE BELL & SONS, YORK STREET, | COVENT GARDEN. | 1878.

"The Poet," pp. 48–50. See E 152; A 28.
  "To the Humble Bee," pp. 50–52. See E 13; A 18.
  "Boston Hymn," pp. 52–54. See E 162; D 45; A 28.
  "Song of Nature," pp. 55–57. See E 141; A 28.
  "Brahma," p. 57. See E 132; A 28.
  "Friendship," p. 58. See A 10.5; A 28.
  "To Eva," p. 58. See E 17; A 18.

Location: DLC.

G 93 AMERICAN POEMS
1879

AMERICAN POEMS | LONGFELLOW: WHITTIER: BRYANT: | HOLMES: LOWELL: EMERSON | *WITH BIOGRAPHICAL SKETCHES* | *AND NOTES* | [publisher's logo] | BOSTON | HOUGHTON, OSGOOD AND COMPANY | [gothic] The Riverside Press, Cambridge | 1879

Edited by Horace E. Scudder.

"The Adirondacs," pp. 419–430. See A 28.
  "The Titmouse," pp. 431–434. See E 159; A 28.
  "Monadnoc," pp. 435–449. See A 18.

Location: TxU.

G 94 ESSAYS FROM THE NORTH AMERICAN REVIEW
1879

ESSAYS | FROM THE | North American | Review. | EDITED BY | ALLEN THORNDIKE RICE. | NEW YORK: | D. APPLETON AND COMPANY, | 549 AND 551 BROADWAY. | 1879.

"John Milton," pp. [99]–122. Unsigned but identified as Emerson's in the table of contents. See E 11; D 14; A 44.

Location: MeBa.

G 95 POEMS OF PLACES: NEW ENGLAND (I)
1879

[all within a double-rule frame; outer frame is red with boxed corners] [red] Poems of Places | EDITED BY | HENRY W. LONGFELLOW | [two lines of verse] | CRABBE. | [red] AMERICA. | [red] NEW ENGLAND. | VOL. I. | [leaf design] | [red] BOSTON: | HOUGH-TON, OSGOOD AND COMPANY. | [gothic] The Riverside Press, Cambridge. | [red] 1879.

"The Snow-Storm," pp. 51–52. See E 24; A 18.
  "Boston," pp. 89–90. See E 184; D 113; A 18.4.
  "Musketaquid," pp. 164–166. See A 18.
  "Concord Fight," p. 167. Reprinting of "Concord Hymn." See A 4; A 18.4.
  "Dirge," pp. 172–174. See A 18.
  "Two Rivers," pp. 178–179. See E 135; A 28.

Location: MH.

G 96 POEMS OF PLACES: NEW ENGLAND (II)
1879

[all within a double-rule frame; outer frame is red with boxed corners] [red] Poems of Places | EDITED BY | HENRY W. LONGFELLOW | [two lines of verse] | CRABBE. | [red] AMERICA. | [red] NEW ENGLAND. | VOL. II. | [leaf design] | [red] BOSTON: | HOUGH-TON, OSGOOD AND COMPANY. | [gothic] The Riverside Press, Cambridge. | [red] 1879.

"Monadnoc," pp. 67–72. See A 18.

Location: MH.

G 97 AMERICAN PROSE
1880

AMERICAN PROSE | HAWTHORNE: IRVING: LONGFELLOW: | WHITTIER: HOLMES: LOWELL: | THOREAU: EMERSON | *WITH INTRODUCTIONS AND NOTES* | BY THE EDITOR OF "AMERICAN POEMS" | [publisher's logo] | BOSTON | HOUGHTON, OS-GOOD AND COMPANY | [gothic] The Riverside Press, Cambridge | 1880

Edited by Horace E. Scudder.

"Behavior," pp. [373]–397. See A 26.
  "Books," pp. 397–424. See E 136; A 31.

Location: MH.

G 98 THE BIRTHDAY BOOK OF AMERICAN POETS
1880

[all within a single-rule frame] THE | Birthday Book | OF | [gothic] American Poets. | EDITED BY | ALMIRA L. HAYWARD. | [publisher's logo] | BOSTON: | JAMES R. OS-GOOD AND COMPANY. | 1880.

Quotations from Emerson, pp. 2, 4, 14, 48, 54, 56, 71, 78, 88, 100, 122, 154, 172, 182, 234, 255.

Location: MH.

Note: Reprinted, with Emerson's quotations on the same pages: '[all within a single-rule frame] THE | ILLUSTRATED | Birthday Book | OF | [gothic] American Poets | EDITED BY | ALMIRA L. HAYWARD. | [flower] | BOSTON | JAMES R. OSGOOD AND COMPANY | 1882' (DLC).

G 99 BIRTHPLACE COMMEMORATIVE SERVICES . . . WILLIAM ELLERY
CHANNING
1880

BIRTHPLACE COMMEMORATIVE SERVICES | OF THE | 100th ANNIVERSARY OF THE BIRTH OF WILLIAM ELLERY CHANNING, | Newport, R. I., April 7th, 1880.

Cover title.

"Hymns for Congregational Singing at the Evening Service," No. II, p. [3]. See D 3; A 18.4.

Location: MWA.

G 100 THE FAMILY LIBRARY OF POETRY AND SONG
1880

Memorial Edition: | [rule] | [gothic] The Family Library | OF | Poetry and Song | BEING | [gothic] Choice Selections from the Best Poets, | ENGLISH, SCOTTISH, IRISH, AND AMERICAN; | *INCLUDING TRANSLATIONS FROM THE GERMAN, SPANISH, FRENCH, PORTUGUESE,* | *PERSIAN, LATIN, GREEK, &c.* | EDITED BY | WILLIAM CULLEN BRYANT. | [gothic] With an Introductory Treatise by the Editor | ON THE | "POETS AND POETRY OF THE ENGLISH LANGUAGE." | INCLUDING ALSO | A Biographical Memoir of Bryant, | By JAMES GRANT WILSON. | [rule] | [gothic] With Indexes | *Of Authors, and Titles of their Poems; of First Lines; and of Famous Lines and Phrases, rendering* | *the Work a Completely Classified* | DICTIONARY OF POETICAL QUOTATIONS. | [rule] | ILLUSTRATED | WITH A NEW STEEL PORTRAIT OF MR. BRYANT; FULL-PAGE EN-GRAVINGS ON WOOD, ILLUSTRATIVE | OF POEMS IN THE WORK; AND AUTO-GRAPHIC FAC-SIMILES OF THE HANDWRITING | OF CELEBRATED POETS. | [rule] | NEW YORK: | FORDS, HOWARD, AND HULBERT.

"Friendship," p. 112. See A 10.5; A 28.
  "From 'Good-By,'" p. 311. See E 14; A 18.
  "Each and All," pp. 405–406. See E 12; A 18.
  "The Snow-Storm," p. 439. See E 24; A 18.
  "The Rhodora," p. 461. See E 15; A 18.
  "To the Humblebee," p. 484. See E 13; A 18.
  "Hymn: Sung at the Completion of the Concord Monument, April 19, 1836," pp. 589–590. See A 4; A 18.4.
  "Boston Hymn," pp. 597–598. See E 162; D 45; A 28.
  "The Sea," pp. 610–611. Reprinting of "The Sea-Shore." See E 165; A 28.
  "The Problem," p. 735. See E 18; A 18.
  "Good By," p. 744. See E 14; A 18.
  "Brahma," p. 746. See E 132; A 28.
  "Letters," p. 746. See A 28.

Location: DLC.

G 101 MODERN AMERICAN LYRICS
1880

MODERN | AMERICAN LYRICS. | [rule] | EDITED | BY | KARL KNORTZ AND OTTO DICKMANN. | [publisher's logo] | LEIPZIG: | F. A. BROCKHAUS. | [rule] | 1880.

"The Apology," pp. 103–104. See A 18.
  "The Dirge," pp. 104–105. See A 18.
  "To Eva," pp. 105–106. See E 17; A 18.
  "The Amulet," p. 106. See E 45; A 18.
  "Thine Eyes Still Shined," p. 106. See A 18.
  "The Romany Girl," pp. 106–107. See E 129; A 28.

Location: CtY.

G 102 YOUNG FOLKS' BOOK OF POETRY
1880

YOUNG FOLKS' | BOOK OF POETRY | CONTAINING | A COLLECTION OF THE BEST SHORT AND EASY | POEMS FOR READING AND RECITATION | IN SCHOOLS AND FAMILIES | *SELECTED AND ARRANGED* | BY | LOOMIS J. CAMPBELL | [rule] | BOSTON | LEE AND SHEPARD, PUBLISHERS | NEW YORK | CHARLES T. DILLINGHAM | 1880

"The Mountain and the Squirrel" ["A Fable"], Part 2, pp. 99–100. See D 15; A 18.
  "George Nidiver," Part 3, pp. 96–98. Not by Emerson; see A 31.1.a.

Location: RPB.

G 103 HARPER'S CYCLOPÆDIA OF BRITISH AND AMERICAN POETRY
1881

HARPER'S CYCLOPÆDIA | OF | BRITISH AND AMERICAN | POETRY | EDITED BY | EPES SARGENT | NEW YORK | HARPER & BROTHERS, FRANKLIN SQUARE | 1881

"The Snow Storm," p. 592. See E 24; A 18.
  "Good-Bye, Proud World!" p. 592. See E 14; A 18.

"Sursum Corda," p. 592. See A 18.

"To the Humblebee," pp. 592–593. See E 13; A 18.

"The Soul's Prophecy," p. 593. Not by Emerson; see H 32.

"The Apology," p. 593. See A 18.

"Hymn. Sung at the Completion of the Concord Monument, April 19, 1836," p. 594. See A 4; A 18.4.

Location: DLC.

G 104 INDIAN SUMMER
1881

[off-center, to the right, against silver and gray floral background] [gothic and curved] Indian Summer | Autumn | Poems and Sketches | L. Clarkson | To American poets only | I am indebted for | these verses, and to | the woods of Maryland | for the studies. | New York | E. P. Dutton & Company | 713 Broadway | 1881 | [bottom right] Copyright, 1880, by E. P. DUTTON & CO.

"Dirge," p. 40. See A 18.

Location: MH.

G 105 THE CAMBRIDGE BOOK OF POETRY AND SONG
1882

THE | CAMBRIDGE BOOK | OF | POETRY AND SONG | SELECTED FROM | ENGLISH AND AMERICAN AUTHORS | BY | CHARLOTTE FISKE BATES | [three lines of Bates's publications] | NEW YORK | THOMAS Y. CROWELL & COMPANY | PUBLISHERS

"Ode," p. 213. Reprinting of "Concord Hymn." See A 4; A 18.4.

"The Problem," pp. 213–214. See E 18; A 18.

"The Rhodora," p. 214. See E 15; A 18.

"The Humble-Bee," pp. 214–215. See E 13; A 18.

"Concord Fight," p. 215. See A 4; A 18.4.

"Forbearance," p. 215. See E 36; A 18.

Location: ScU.

G 106 FÜNFZEHN ESSAYS
1882

[all gothic except the date] Fünfzehn Essays | von | Herman Grimm. | [rule] | Dritte Folge. | [rule] | [rule] | Berlin, | Ferd. Dümmlers Verlagsbuchhandlung | Harwitz and Grossmann. | 1882.

"Über Goethe und Shakespeare," pp. 245–269. See A 22.42.

Location: InU.

G 107 GOLDEN POEMS
1882

GOLDEN POEMS | [gothic] By British and American Authors. | EDITED BY | FRANCIS F. BROWNE. | [two lines of verse] | [rule] | [one line of verse] | [rule] | [four lines of verse] | CHICAGO: | JANSEN, McCLURG & COMPANY. | 1882.

"Hymn," pp. 202–203. Reprinting of "Concord Hymn." See A 4; A 18.4.
 "Responses," pp. 343–344. From "The Problem." See E 18; A 18.

Location: TxU.

G 108 THE PARENT-HEART IN SONG
1882

THE | Parent-Heart IN SONG. | COMPILED BY | LEVIETTA BARTLETT CONNER | [rule] | *WITH ILLUSTRATIONS.* | [rule] | CINCINNATI: | PETER G. THOMSON. | 1882.

"Threnody," pp. 283–291. See A 18.

Location: RPB.

G 109 POEMS OF AMERICAN PATRIOTISM
1882

POEMS | OF | AMERICAN PATRIOTISM | CHOSEN BY | J. BRANDER MATTHEWS | NEW-YORK | CHARLES SCRIBNER'S SONS | 1882

"Boston," pp. [1]–8. See E 184; A 18.4.

Location: MH.

G 110 POETS AND ETCHERS
1882

POETS AND ETCHERS | [rule] | [gothic] Poems by | T. B. ALDRICH W. C. BRYANT R. W. EMERSON J. R. LOWELL | H. W. LONGFELLOW J. G. WHITTIER | [gothic] Etchings by | A. F. BELLOWS SAMUEL COLMAN HENRY FARRER | R. SWAIN GIFFORD J. D. SMILLIE | [publisher's logo] | BOSTON | JAMES R. OSGOOD AND COMPANY | 1882

"The Snow-Storm," pp. [21]–22. Unsigned but identified as Emerson's in the table of contents. See E 24; A 18.
 "The Apology," pp. [23]–24. Unsigned but identified as Emerson's in the table of contents. See A 18.

Location: MB.

G 111 PURPLE AND GOLD
1882

[all within a purple single-rule frame with purple-and-gold leafy designs in each corner] [bird-and-leaf design] | [ornate purple and gold initial capitals with purple letters] Purple and Gold | *ARRANGED BY* | [purple with ornate gold initial capitals] Kate Sanborn | *ILLUSTRATED BY* | [purple with ornate gold initial capitals] Rosina Emmet | [two lines of verse] | BOSTON | [purple] JAMES R. OSGOOD AND COMPANY | 1882 | [below frame] copyright, 1881, By Kate Sanborn

"Aster," p. 19. From "The Apology." See A 18.

Location: TxU.

G 112 SELECTIONS FOR SCHOOL EXHIBITIONS
1882

And God saw everything that He had made, and behold it was | very good.—GEN. 1: 31. | SELECTIONS | —FOR— | [ornate lettering] School Exhibitions | AND PRIVATE READING, | *ILLUSTRATING AND ADVOCATING KINDNESS* | *TO ALL CREATURES.* | Nos. 1, 2, 3. | [rule] | [four lines of verse] | *—Cowper.* | [three lines of verse] | *—Mrs. Browning.* | [rule] | BOSTON: | WRIGHT & POTTER PRINTING COMPANY. | No. 18 POST OFFICE SQUARE, | 1882.

"A Fable," p. 21. See D 15; A 18.
  "Each and All," p. 112. See E 12; A 18.

Location: MH.

G 113 SUNSHINE IN THE SOUL
1882

[all within a red single-rule frame] SUNSHINE | IN THE SOUL. | [three lines gothic] Poems | Selected by the Editor of "Quiet Hours," | "Sursum Corda," etc. | *SECOND SERIES.* | [four lines of verse] | [rule] | BOSTON: | [gothic] Roberts Brothers. | 1882

Edited by Mary Wilder Tileston.

"From 'Woodnotes,'" p. 10. See A 18.
  "From 'Terminus,'" p. 143. See E 170; A 28.

Location: TxU.

G 114 TRIBUTES TO LONGFELLOW AND EMERSON
1882

TRIBUTES | TO | [red] LONGFELLOW AND EMERSON | BY | [gothic] The Massachusetts Historical Society. | *WITH PORTRAITS.* | [red] BOSTON: | A. WILLIAMS AND CO., | PUBLISHERS, | OLD CORNER BOOKSTORE, 283 WASHINGTON ST. | 1882.

"Impressions of Thomas Carlyle in 1848," pp. [51]–56. See E 194; A 41.
  "Speech Before the Boston Burns Club," pp. 56–59. See D 32; A 40.
  "Sir Walter Scott," pp. 59–62. See D 82; A 40.

Location: JM.

Note one: Trade printing sold in decorated cloth or paper covered boards printed the same as the title page (JM).

Note two: Also a large paper printing, bound in the same decorated cloth as the trade printing, limited to 25 numbered copies printed on Whatman paper (MBAt). A copy, numbered "29" and described as unbound in original wrappers, was offered for sale in Brentano's spring 1976 catalogue.

H. Material Attributed to Emerson

Arranged chronologically.

H1
[Letter to the Editor]. *Boston Courier*, 15 August 1838, p. 2.

Signed "W." Attributed to Emerson by Robert A McGill, "Emerson's Letter to the Editor," *Emerson Society Quarterly*, no. 6 (1st Quarter 1957), 5–6. An unlikely attribution.

H2
[Review of Charles Fourier, *Social Destiny of Man*]. *Dial*, 1 (October 1840), 265–266.

Unsigned. Reprinted in *Uncollected Writings* (A54), pp. 153–154. The author was George Ripley.

H3
[Review of John Edward Taylor, *Michael Angelo*]. *Dial*, 1 (January 1841), 401–402.

Unsigned. Reprinted in *Uncollected Writings* (A54), pp. 154–157. The author was probably Margaret Fuller.

H4
[Review of Samuel D. Robbins, *Worship of the Soul*]. *Dial*, 1 (January 1841), 402–404.

Unsigned. Reprinted in *Uncollected Writings* (A54), pp. 157–160. The author was probably George Ripley.

H5
"The Ideal Man." *Dial*, 2 (January 1842), 408.

Unsigned. Reprinted in *Uncollected Writings* (A54), p. 162. The author was probably Elizabeth Palmer Peabody.

H6
[Review of G. Oegger, *The True Messiah*]. *Dial*, 3 (July 1842), 131.

Unsigned.

H7
[Review of *Günderode*, trans. Margaret Fuller]. *Dial*, 3 (July 1842), 131.

Unsigned.

H8
[Review of Novalis, *Henry of Ofterdingen*]. *Dial*, 3 (July 1842), 132.

Unsigned.

H9
[Notice of Caroline Southey, *Chapters in Church Yards*]. *Dial*, 3 (July 1842), 132.

Unsigned.

H 10
"Poems [Tennyson's]." *Dial,* 3 (October 1842), 273–276.

Unsigned. Reprinted in *Uncollected Writings* (A 54), pp. 167–172. The author was Margaret Fuller.

H 11
[Review of Orestes A. Brownson, *A Letter to Rev. Wm. E. Channing*]. *Dial,* 3 (October 1842), 276–277.

Unsigned. Reprinted in *Uncollected Writings* (A 54), pp. 172–174.

H 12
[Review of *Letters of Schiller,* trans. J. L. Weisse]. *Dial,* 3 (January 1843), 411–413.

Unsigned.

H 13
[Review of *Fables of La Fontaine,* trans. Elizur Wright, Jr.]. *Dial,* 3 (January 1843), 413–414.

Unsigned.

H 14
[Notice of Cornelius Mathews, *The Career of Puffer Hopkins*]. *Dial,* 3 (January 1843), 415.

Unsigned.

H 15
[Notice of the *Lowell Offering* for December 1842]. *Dial,* 3 (January 1843), 416.

Unsigned.

H 16
"Friendship. From Chaucer's 'Romaunt of the Rose.'" *Dial,* 3 (April 1843), 529–531.

Unsigned. Possibly selected by Emerson.

H 17
[Review of E. L. Bulwer, *The Last of the Barons*]. *Dial,* 3 (April 1843), 532–533.

Unsigned.

H 18
[Review of Robert Browning, *Paracelsus*]. *Dial,* 3 (April 1843), 535.

Unsigned. Reprinted in *Uncollected Writings* (A 54), p. 177. Probably by Margaret Fuller.

H 19
"Ethnical Scriptures. Chinese Four Books." *Dial,* 4 (October 1843), 205–210.

Unsigned. Possibly selected by Emerson. For Thoreau's possible authorship, see *Early Essays and Miscellanies,* ed. Joseph J. Moldenhauer (Princeton: Princeton University Press, 1975), pp. 385–386.

H 20
[Review of *The Huguenots in France and America*]. *Dial,* 4 (October 1843), 270.

Unsigned. Reprinted in *Uncollected Writings* (A 54), p. 180.

H 21
[Review of Henry Wadsworth Longfellow, *The Spanish Student*]. *Dial,* 4 (October 1843), 270–271.

Unsigned. Reprinted in *Uncollected Writings* (A 54), pp. 180–181.

H 22
[Review of James Gates Percival, *The Dream of a Day*]. *Dial,* 4 (October 1843), 271–272.

Unsigned. Reprinted in *Uncollected Writings* (A 54), pp. 181–182.

H 23
"Ethnical Scriptures. Hermes Trismegistus." *Dial,* 4 (January 1844), 402–404.

Unsigned. Possibly selected by Emerson. For Thoreau's possible authorship, see *Early Essays and Miscellanies,* ed. Moldenhauer, p. 390.

H 24
[Review of *President Hopkins's Address*]. *Dial,* 4 (January 1844), 407.

Unsigned.

H 25
[Review of *Human Nature*]. *Dial,* 4 (April 1844), 540.

Unsigned.

H 26
Report upon Phonotypy. Cambridge: Metcalf and Company, 1847.

Report of "Mr. Emerson," pp. 3–15. *BAL* (III, 67) reports this is sometimes attributed to Ralph Waldo Emerson. The author is George B. Emerson.

H 27
The Lady's Token: or Gift of Friendship. Nashua, N.H.: J. Buffum, 1848.

Edited by Cotesworth Pinckney. "On the Death of a Brother, Who was Drowned at Sea," pp. 38–39. Unsigned but identified as by "Emerson" in the table of contents. No other evidence exists that this is by Ralph Waldo Emerson.

H 28
Hymns for the Church of Christ. Boston: Crosby, Nichols, 1853.

Edited by Frederic H. Hedge and Frederic D. Huntington. Hymn 652 ["The Future is Better than the Past"], p. 455. Unsigned but identified as Emerson's in the table of contents. The author is Eliza Thayer Clapp.

H 29
Eolopoesis. American Rejected Addresses. Now First Published. From the Original Manuscripts. New York: J. C. Derby; Boston: Phillips, Sampson, [1855].

Edited by Jacob Bigelow? "The Unseen," pp. 73–83. Signed "R. W. E." A verse satire of Emerson's style; definitely not by him.

H 30

Eminent Men and Popular Books. London and New York: Routledge, Warne, & Routledge, 1859.

Anonymous. *BAL* (III, 67) reports that this is sometimes attributed to Emerson. The probable author is Samuel Lucas, though Samuel Phillips is sometimes given as the author.

H 31

Stanzas: Written to be sung at the funeral of Henry D. Thoreau, of Concord, Massachusetts, Friday, May 9th, 1862. [N.p.: n.p., 1862].

Single leaf, folded to make four pages, printed on p. [3] only. Attributed to Emerson as *BAL* 5235. The author is Ellery Channing. See Louisa May Alcott to Sophia Ford, 11 May 1862 ("Mr. Channing wrote the Stanzas"), *A Sprig of Andromeda: A Letter from Louisa May Alcott on the Death of Henry David Thoreau,* ed. John L. Cooley (New York: Pierpont Morgan Library, 1962), p. 9, and Kenneth Walter Cameron, "Channing's Hymn at Thoreau's Funeral," *Emerson Society Quarterly,* no. 2 (1st Quarter 1956), 16–17. The poem is reprinted in facsimile, correctly attributed to Channing, in *Sophia Thoreau's Scrapbook,* ed. Walter Harding (Geneseo, N.Y.: Thoreau Society, 1964), p. 29.

H 32

Lyra Americana. New York: D. Appleton, 1865.

Edited by George T. Rider. "The Soul's Prophecy," pp. 156–157. Signed. The author is Eliza Thayer Clapp.

H 33

Free-Trade Tracts. New York: American Free Trade League, 1866–1867.

BAL (III, 67) states that "as a member of the league's council, Emerson may have contributed to these tracts." An examination of the 36 numbers published indicates that most of the material was reprinted, and the authors of original contributions are identified. No Emerson material seems to be here.

H 34

"Midsummer." *Commonwealth* [Boston], 17 August 1867.

Signed. The author was John T. Trowbridge (see *BAL,* III, 68). Reprinted as Emerson's in *Garnered Treasures from the Poets* (H 36).

H 35

An Illustrated Catalogue of the Paintings of Mr. Constant Mayer. [New York]: Leavitt, Strebeigh, [1869].

Poem, p. 8. Signed. The author is Richard Henry Stoddard (see *BAL,* III, 67).

H 36

Garnered Treasures from the Poets. Philadelphia: Friends' Book Association, 1878.

"Midsummer," pp. 185–187. Signed "Emerson." The author is John T. Trowbridge; see H 34.

H 37
Hymns for the Free Religious Association, June 2d, 1882. [Boston: n.p., 1882].

Broadside, printed on both sides. "The Soul's Prophecy," recto. Signed. The author is
Eliza Thayer Clapp.

H 38
"An Emerson Souvenir." *Boston Evening Transcript,* 15 October 1883, p. 1.

Letter of 30 January 1829 to the Second Church and Society. Signed. Reprinted in
New-York Daily Tribune, 15 October 1883, p. 5; *Uncollected Writings* (A 54), pp. 200–
201. Refuted as being the text of Emerson's letter in Francis H. Brown, "That Souvenir
of Emerson," *Boston Daily Advertiser,* 10 November 1883, p. 2, and *L,* I, 260–261n.

H 39
Transcendentalism. New York: John B. Alden, 1886.

5–56 pp. Wrappers. Advertised as included in the "Elzevir Library," no. 234. Printed
from the plates of *Transcendentalism and Other Addresses* (C 17.1.a). A reprint, attributed to Emerson, of [Charles Mayo Ellis], *An Essay on Transcendentalism* (Boston:
Crocker and Ruggles, 1842).

H 40
Borrowings. San Francisco: C. A. Murdock, 1889.

Compiled by the Ladies of the First Unitarian Church of Oakland, California. The "build
a better mouse-trap" saying, p. 38 (see illustration). Signed. For a discussion of Emerson's possible authorship, see Burton E. Stevenson, "The Mouse Trap," *Colophon,* part
19 (December 1934), item 7. This is most likely someone's recollection of a line from
one of Emerson's lectures; the saying does not appear in Emerson's published or
unpublished writings.

Note: An interesting association item, printed by Carroll A. Wilson at Christmas 1938
(single sheet, folded to make four pages, printed on pp. [1] and [4] only), reproduces
in facsimile a manuscript note in Emerson's hand, reading in part "Will Mr Munroe send
Mr E. an effective Rat Trap." *Location:* JM.

H 41
Sanborn, F. B. "A Concord Note-Book. Theodore Parker and R. W. Emerson." *Critic,* 49
(September 1906), 273–281.

"Lines" (also titled "Summer Scenes in New England"), p. 281. Reprinted in Sanborn,
Recollections of Seventy Years (D 184), II, 554. Printed from a copy in Parker's manuscript journal (now at MH-AH), where it is attributed to "Emerson" in Parker's hand. The
attribution to Ralph Waldo Emerson is almost certainly mistaken.

H 42
At the End of the Sunset Trail. Chicago: Harold Rossiter Music Company, [1924].

Words by "Ralph Waldo Emerson." Music by Ethwell "Eddie" Hanson. Sheet music.
Definitely not by Emerson.

Wrapper for H 40

The cord that binds too strictly snaps itself.

—*Tennyson.*

The human heart concerns us more than poring into microscopes, and is larger than can be measured by the pompous figures of the astronomer.

—*Emerson.*

There is never an instant's truce between virtue and vice.

—*Thoreau.*

Quotation is a good thing, there is a community of thought in it.

— *Dr. Johnson.*

In proportion as we love truth more, and victory less, we shall become anxious to know what it is that leads our opponents to think as they do.

—*Herbert Spencer.*

Even for the dead I will not bind
    My soul to grief — death cannot long divide :
For is it not as if the rose had climbed
    My garden wall, and blossomed on the other
        side ?

—*Alice Cary.*

If a man can write a better book, preach a better sermon, or make a better mouse-trap, than his neighbor, though he builds his house in the woods, the world will make a beaten path to his door.

—*Emerson.*

" Somewhere in the secret of every soul
    Is the hidden gleam of a perfect life."

I. Compiler's Notes

Lists references to possible publications by Emerson which have not been dealt with elsewhere in the bibliography, arranged chronologically.

I 1
Carlyle, Thomas. *Sartor Resartus*. Boston: James Munroe, 1836.

Although Emerson is commonly listed as the editor, there is no evidence to support this attribution. The book was compiled and seen through the press by Le Baron Russell and Charles Stearns Wheeler (see John Olin Eidson, *Charles Stearns Wheeler* [Athens: University of Georgia Press, 1951], pp. 29–30, and *CEC*, pp. 16–17). Many years later, Russell wrote Oliver Wendell Holmes that after he had obtained the names of subscribers to *Sartor*, "I wrote to Emerson, who up to this time had taken no part in the enterprise, asking him to write a preface" (Holmes, *Ralph Waldo Emerson* [D 133], p. 81, and see Russell's letter of 16 December 1835 at ViU; see also D 5).

I 2
Carlyle, Thomas. *The French Revolution: A History*. Boston: Charles C. Little and James Brown, 1838.

Emerson is listed as editor in an announcement in the *United States Magazine, and Democratic Review*, 1 (January 1838), advertisements. While Emerson did arrange for the first American edition of this title and wrote a Prospectus for it (see A 6), he in no way served as editor (see *CEC*, pp. 18–19).

I 3
Essays. London: H. G. Clarke, 1844.

Listed as *BAL* 5342 on the basis of an advertisement in *Publishers' Circular and Booksellers' Record*, 7 (15 October 1844), 309. Undoubtedly this advertisement was for the 1845 Clarke edition (see A 10.4.a).

I 4
Nature and Orations. London: John Chapman, 1844.

Advertised in *The Young American* (A 15). No copies have been located. Probably an advertisement for *Nature and Lectures on the Times* (A 13), which Chapman may have distributed.

I 5
Lecture on Napoleon. 1845.

Listed as "Published in the United States During the Month of January," in *Wiley & Putnam's Literary News-Letter*, 4 (February 1845), 294. Price, 25¢. No copies have been located.

I 6
Essays. London: T. Bosworth, 1847.

Listed on the basis of Bosworth's advertisement in *Athenæum*, no. 1047 (20 November 1847), 1204, and a listing in *Literary Gazette*, no. 1629 (8 April 1848), 254. Undoubtedly copies of the 1841 Fraser printing sold by Bosworth. Fraser was succeeded in business by G. W. Nickisson in late 1842; Nickisson was succeeded by Bosworth in early 1847 (*Publishers' Circular and Booksellers' Record,* 5 [1 October 1842], 285; *Athenæum,* no. 1030 [24 July 1847], 798). See A 10.2.a.

I 7
Essays. London: Trübner, 1849.

Listed in the *British Museum Catalogue.* The entry is in error: the shelfmark after this entry corresponds to the 1849 Clarke printing (see A 10.4.b).

I 8
Essays and Miscellaneous Works, 4 vols. London: Sampson Low, 1858.

Listed as an importation at 24s., in *Athenæum,* no. 1580 (6 February 1858), 178. Undoubtedly an importation of the Phillips, Sampson sheets (possibly in their casings) to be sold with the Sampson Low importation of *English Traits* (see *Note three* to A 24.1.a). The four volumes have to be *Miscellanies* [*Nature; Addresses, and Lectures*], *Essays: First Series, Essays: Second Series,* and *Representative Men.*

I 9
Gems from Rogers, Mrs. Hemans, Emerson, and Cowper. London: Groombridge and Sons, 1858.

Listed in "Publications of the Month," in *Bookseller,* no. 12 (24 December 1858), 600. Price, 2s. 6d. Undoubtedly a reference to *Gems From the Poets* (G 36).

I 10
Poetical Hand-Book for Scholars and Students. 1871.

Announced in *Printers' Circular and Stationers' and Booksellers' Gazette,* 6 (October 1871), 331. An early notice for what would become *Parnassus* (F 7).

I 11
Uncollected Writings, Essays, and Lectures. 2 vols. London: John Camden Hotten, 1872.

Advertised as "A New Book" for 1870–1871, in *Publishers' Circular and Booksellers' Record,* 33 (1 October 1870), 611; as "The Uncollected Writings, Essays, and Lectures of Ralph Waldo Emerson, Introductory Preface by Moncure D. Conway and Alexander Ireland," published "By arrangement with Mr. Emerson," in *Athenæum,* no. 2298 (11 November 1871), 612, and *Bookseller,* no. 66 (3 October 1871), 854. The *Publishers' and Stationers' Weekly Trade Circular* carried this announcement: "Emerson has gone back to Concord to revise his earlier essays for the 'authorized' edition to which the English publisher Hotten virtually compelled him to give his assent, by announcing his intention to publish at all events, allowing the author to supervise the work if he chose" (n.s. 1 [8 February 1872], 101). Advertised in *Publishers' Circular and Booksellers' Record,* 34 (17 October 1871), 674; in *Bookseller,* no. 78 (1 October 1872), 832. At Emerson's insistence, this collection was not published, even though type was set and proofs pulled for the introduction (a set of proofs is at MH). See *L,* VI, 124–125, 134, 179–181, and Dennis Welland, "John Camden Hotten and Emerson's Uncollected Essays," *The Yearbook of English Studies,* 6 (1976), 156–175, for further information.

I 12
Poetry and Criticism. Boston, 1874.

Announced as "a new volume of essays" for "as early as May next," in *Publishers' and Stationers' Weekly Trade Circular*, n.s. 1 (28 March 1872), 273. Advertised in *Atlantic*, 29 (April 1872), advertising supplement; for November 1872, in *Atlantic*, 30 (September, October, November 1872), advertising supplements. Announced as "postponed till next spring, owing to [Emerson's] departure for Europe. . . . will then be published simultaneously in Boston and London," in *Publishers' and Stationers' Weekly Trade Circular*, n.s. 2 (31 October 1872), 465. Listed as an importation at 10s., in *Publishers' Circular and Booksellers' Record*, 37 (2 October 1874), 668. These are in fact over-enthusiastic advertisements for what would be published in 1876 as *Letters and Social Aims*. "Poetry and Criticism" was Emerson's own working title for the book (see letter to James R. Osgood, 13 August 1875 [MiD]).

I 13
"Impressions of Egypt." 1877.

Announced as a contribution by Emerson "to the forthcoming number of the North American Review," in *Printers' Circular and Stationers' and Booksellers' Gazette*, 12 (March 1877), 5. No work by Emerson on this topic has been located.

I 14
Two Addresses; I. Religious Needs of the Age. II. Religion. London: Foulger, 1883.

Advertised in John Fiske, *Evolution and Religion* (London: J. C. Foulger, 1883), p. [13]. This title was not published, becoming instead *The Senses and the Soul and Moral Sentiment in Religion;* see *Note two* to A 42.

I 15
Friendship. New York: Dodge, [1902].

Listed in *Cumulative Book Index*. Publisher's advertisements indicate that this was in fact an anthology of sayings about friendship, for which selections by Emerson were included.

I 16
Nature. New York: A. L. Burt, [1902].

Listed in *American Catalog*. Actually a reference to *Nature, Addresses, and Lectures* (A 21.11.a).

I 17
Haunts of Emerson. [N.p.: n.p., 1923?].

A collection of drawings of Emerson's homes and environs without accompanying text.

I 18
My Friend. New York: Dodge, [1928].

Listed in *Cumulative Book Index*. No copies have been located.

I 19
Letters and Social Aims. Freeport, N.Y.: Books for Libraries Press, 1973.

Listed in *Books in Print* as a facsimile reprinting of the 1883 printing of the *Riverside Edition*, trade printing. There is no evidence that this title was published.

I 20
Essays.

Advertisements for "Essays" have been noted from various publishers: Bay View, [1902], Mershon [1902], Hills and Hafely [1912], Winston [1912], and Consolidated [1933]. No copies have been located. Without further information, it is impossible to determine the series (or collection) of Emerson's essays to which these advertisements refer.

I 21
[Various titles]. Philadelphia: Richard West, 1974.

Listings for *The Correspondence of Thomas Carlyle and Ralph Waldo Emerson, Letters to a Friend, Uncollected Lectures,* and *Works* (in five volumes) are in the 1974 *Books in Print.* The only title seen, *Correspondence* (ScU), is actually a rebound 1883 printing, without any designation that it is a Richard West publication; presumably, the other titles were sold in a similar format.

Appendix / Index

Appendix

Principal Works about Emerson

Albee, John. *Remembrances of Emerson*. New York: Robert G. Cooke, 1901. Rev. ed.: New York: Robert Grier Cooke, 1903.

Alcott, Amos Bronson. *Emerson*. Cambridge: Privately printed, 1865. Reprint: *Ralph Waldo Emerson: An Estimate of His Character and Genius in Prose and Verse*. Boston: A. Williams, 1882. Rev. ed.: *Ralph Waldo Emerson: Philosopher and Seer*. Boston: Cupples and Hurd, 1888.

Allen, Gay Wilson. *Waldo Emerson: A Biography*. New York: Viking Press, 1981.

Anderson, John Q. *The Liberating Gods: Emerson on Poets and Poetry*. Coral Gables, Fla.: University of Miami Press, 1971.

Benton, Joel. *Emerson as a Poet*. New York: H. L. Holbrook, 1883.

Berry, Edmund G. *Emerson's Plutarch*. Cambridge: Harvard University Press, 1961.

Bishop, Jonathan. *Emerson on the Soul*. Cambridge: Harvard University Press, 1964.

Brooks, Van Wyck. *Emerson and Others*. New York: E. P. Dutton, 1927.

———. *The Life of Emerson*. New York: E. P. Dutton, 1932.

Burkholder, Robert E., and Joel Myerson. *Ralph Waldo Emerson: An Annotated Secondary Bibliography*. Pittsburgh: University of Pittsburgh Press, 1983.

———, eds. *Critical Essays on Ralph Waldo Emerson*. Boston: G. K. Hall, 1983.

Cabot, James Elliot. *A Memoir of Ralph Waldo Emerson*. Boston: Houghton, Mifflin, 1887.

Cameron, Kenneth Walter. *A Commentary on Emerson's Early Lectures (1833–1836). With an Index-Concordance*. Hartford, Conn.: Transcendental Books, 1961.

———. *Emerson the Essayist*. Raleigh, N.C.: Thistle Press, 1945.

———. *Emerson's Workshop: An Analysis of His Reading in Periodicals Through 1836*. Hartford, Conn.: Transcendental Books, 1964.

———. *Ralph Waldo Emerson's Reading*. Raleigh, N.C.: Thistle Press, 1941. Rev. ed.: Hartford, Conn.: Transcendental Books, 1962.

Carpenter, Frederic Ives. *Emerson and Asia*. Cambridge: Harvard University Press, 1930.

———. *Emerson Handbook*. New York: Hendricks House, 1953.

Celieres, André. *The Prose Style of Emerson*. Paris: Pierre André, 1936.

Charvat, William. *Emerson's American Lecture Engagements: A Chronological List*. New York: New York Public Library, 1961.

Conway, Moncure D. *Emerson at Home and Abroad*. Boston: James R. Osgood, 1882.

Cooke, George Willis. *Ralph Waldo Emerson*. Boston: James R. Osgood, 1881.

Cowan, Michael H. *City of the West: Emerson, America, and Urban Metaphor*. New Haven: Yale University Press, 1967.

Crothers, Samuel McChord. *Emerson: How to Know Him*. Indianapolis: Bobbs-Merrill, 1921.

Duncan, Jeffrey L. *The Power and Form of Emerson's Thought*. Charlottesville: University Press of Virginia, 1973.

Emerson, Edward Waldo. *Emerson in Concord*. Boston: Houghton, Mifflin, 1889.

Emerson, Ellen Tucker. *The Life of Lidian Jackson Emerson*. Edited by Delores Bird Carpenter. Boston: Twayne, 1980.

Engel, Mary Miller. *I Remember the Emersons*. Los Angeles: Times-Mirror, 1941.

Firkins, O. W. *Ralph Waldo Emerson*. Boston: Houghton Mifflin, 1915.

Garnett, Richard. *Life of Ralph Waldo Emerson*. London: Walter Scott, 1888.

Gay, Robert M. *Emerson: A Study of the Poet as Seer*. Garden City, N.Y.: Doubleday, Doran, 1928.

Gray, Henry D. *Emerson: A Statement of New England Transcendentalism as Expressed in the Philosophy of Its Chief Exponent*. Stanford: Stanford University, 1917.

Gregg, Edith W., ed. *One First Love: The Letters of Ellen Louisa Tucker to Ralph Waldo Emerson*. Cambridge: Harvard University Press, 1962.

Harding, Walter. *Emerson's Library*. Charlottesville: University Press of Virginia, 1967.

Harris, Kenneth Marc. *Carlyle and Emerson: Their Long Debate*. Cambridge: Harvard University Press, 1978.

Harrison, John S. *The Teachers of Emerson*. New York: Sturgis and Walton, 1910.

Haskins, David Greene. *Ralph Waldo Emerson: His Maternal Ancestors*. Boston: Cupples, Upham, 1886.

Hill, J. Arthur. *Emerson and His Philosophy*. London: William Rider, 1919.

Hoeltje, Hubert H. *Sheltering Tree: A Story of the Friendship of Ralph Waldo Emerson and Amos Bronson Alcott*. Durham: Duke University Press, 1943.

Holmes, Oliver Wendell. *Ralph Waldo Emerson*. Boston: Houghton, Mifflin, 1884.

Hopkins, Vivian C. *Spires of Form: A Study of Emerson's Aesthetic Theory*. Cambridge: Harvard University Press, 1951.

Hubbell, George S. *A Concordance to the Poems of Ralph Waldo Emerson*. New York: H. W. Wilson, 1932.

Ireland, Alexander. *In Memoriam. Ralph Waldo Emerson*. London: Simpkin, Marshall, 1882. Rev. ed.: *Ralph Waldo Emerson: His Life, Genius, and Writings*. London: Simpkin, Marshall, 1882.

Irie, Yukio. *Emerson and Quakerism*. Tokyo: Kenkyusha, 1967.

Jugaku, Bunsho. *A Bibliography of Ralph Waldo Emerson in Japan from 1878 to 1935*. Kyoto: Sunward Press, 1947.

Konvitz, Milton R., ed. *The Recognition of Ralph Waldo Emerson*. Ann Arbor: University of Michigan Press, 1972.

———, and Stephen E. Whicher, eds. *Emerson: A Collection of Critical Essays*. Englewood Cliffs, N.J.: Prentice-Hall, 1962.

Levin, David, ed. *Emerson: Prophecy, Metamorphosis, Influence*. New York: Columbia University Press, 1975.

McQuiston, Raymer. *The Relation of Ralph Waldo Emerson to Public Affairs*. Lawrence, Kansas: The University, 1923.

Matthiessen, F. O. *American Renaissance: Art and Expression in the Age of Emerson and Whitman*. New York: Oxford University Press, 1941.

Maulsby, David Lee. *The Contribution of Emerson to Literature*. Tufts College, Mass.: Tufts College Press, 1911.

Metzger, Charles R. *Emerson and Greenough: Transcendental Pioneers of an American Aesthetic*. Berkeley: University of California Press, 1954.

Michaud, Régis. *Emerson: The Enraptured Yankee*. Translated by George Boas. New York: Harpers, 1930.

Miles, Josephine. *Ralph Waldo Emerson*. Minneapolis: University of Minnesota Press, 1964.

Myerson Joel. *The New England Transcendentalists and the Dial: A History of the Magazine and Its Contributors*. Rutherford, N.J.: Fairleigh Dickinson University Press, 1980.

———, ed. *Emerson Centenary Essays*. Carbondale: Southern Illinois University Press, 1982.

Nicoloff, Philip L. *Emerson on Race and History: An Examination of "English Traits."* New York: Columbia University Press, 1961.

Paul, Sherman. *Emerson's Angle of Vision: Man and Nature in the American Experience.* Cambridge: Harvard University Press, 1952.

Perry, Bliss. *Emerson Today.* Princeton: Princeton University Press, 1931.

Pommer, Henry F. *Emerson's First Marriage.* Carbondale: Southern Illinois University Press, 1967.

Porte, Joel. *Emerson and Thoreau: Transcendentalists in Conflict.* Middletown, Conn.: Wesleyan University Press, 1966.

————. *Representative Man: Ralph Waldo Emerson in His Time.* New York: Oxford University Press, 1979.

Porter, David. *Emerson and Literary Change.* Cambridge: Harvard University Press, 1978.

Reaver, J. Russell. *Emerson as Mythmaker.* Gainesville: University of Florida Press, 1954.

Rusk, Ralph L. *The Life of Ralph Waldo Emerson.* New York: Scribners, 1949.

Sanborn, F. B. *The Personality of Emerson.* Boston: Charles E. Goodspeed, 1903.

————. *Ralph Waldo Emerson.* Boston: Small, Maynard, 1901.

————, ed. *The Genius and Character of Emerson.* Boston: James R. Osgood, 1885.

Scheick, William J. *The Slender Human Word: Emerson's Artistry in Prose.* Knoxville: University of Tennessee Press, 1978.

Scudder, Townsend, III. *The Lonely Wayfaring Man: Emerson and Some Englishmen.* New York: Oxford University Press, 1936.

Sealts, Merton M., Jr., and Alfred R. Ferguson, eds. *Emerson's* Nature—*Origin, Growth, Meaning.* New York: Dodd, Mead, 1969. Rev. ed.: Carbondale: Southern Illinois University Press, 1979.

Searle, January [George Searle Phillips]. *Emerson: His Life and Writings.* London: Holyoake, 1855.

Simon, Julius. *Ralph Waldo Emerson in Deutschland (1851–1932).* Giessen: Junker und Dunnhaupt, 1937.

Snider, Denton J. *A Biography of Ralph Waldo Emerson.* St. Louis: William Harvey Miner, 1921.

Social Circle in Concord. *The Centenary of the Birth of Ralph Waldo Emerson.* Cambridge: The Riverside Press, 1903.

Sowder, William J. *Emerson's Impact on the British Isles and Canada.* Charlottesville: University Press of Virginia, 1966.

Staebler, Warren. *Ralph Waldo Emerson.* New York: Twayne, 1973.

Stoehr, Taylor. *Nay-Saying in Concord: Emerson, Alcott, and Thoreau.* Hamden, Conn.: Archon, 1979.

[Thayer, James Bradley]. *A Western Journey with Mr. Emerson.* Boston: Little, Brown, 1884.

Thurin, Erik Ingvar. *The Universal Autobiography of Ralph Waldo Emerson.* Lund: C. W. K. Gleerup, 1974.

Wagenknecht, Edward. *Ralph Waldo Emerson.* New York: Oxford University Press, 1974.

Waggoner, Hyatt H. *Emerson as Poet.* Princeton: Princeton University Press, 1974.

Wahr, Frederick B. *Emerson and Goethe.* Ann Arbor, Mich.: George Wahr, 1913.

Whicher, Stephen. *Freedom and Fate: An Inner Life of Ralph Waldo Emerson.* Philadelphia: University of Pennsylvania Press, 1953.

Woodberry, George E. *Ralph Waldo Emerson.* New York: Macmillan, 1907.

Woodbury, Charles J. *Talks with Ralph Waldo Emerson.* New York: Baker and Taylor, 1890.

Wynkoop, William M. *Three Children of the Universe: Emerson's Views of Shakespeare, Bacon, Milton.* The Hague: Mouton, 1966.

Yoder, R. A. *Emerson and the Orphic Poet in America.* Berkeley: University of California Press, 1978.

Young, Charles L. *Emerson's Montaigne.* New York: Macmillan, 1941.

Zink, Harriet R. *Emerson's Use of the Bible.* Lincoln: University of Nebraska Press, 1935.

Index

Pittsburgh Series in Bibliography